BUSINESS ACCOUNTING 1

BUSINESS ACCOUNTING 1

Eighth Edition

Frank Wood BSc (Econ), FCA
and
Alan Sangster BA, MSc, Cert TESOL, CA

FINANCIAL TIMES
PITMAN PUBLISHING

FINANCIAL TIMES
MANAGEMENT

LONDON • SAN FRANCISCO
KUALA LUMPUR • JOHANNESBURG

*Financial Times Management delivers the knowledge,
skills and understanding that enable students,
managers and organisations to achieve their ambitions,
whatever their needs, wherever they are.*

London Office:
128 Long Acre, London WC2E 9AN
Tel: +44 (0)171 447 2000
Fax: +44 (0)171 240 5771
Website: www.ftmanagement.com

A Division of Financial Times Professional Limited

Eighth edition published in Great Britain in 1999

ISBN 0 273 63742 8

British Library Cataloguing in Publication Data
A CIP catalogue record for this book can be obtained from the British Library.

10 9 8 7 6 5 4 3 2 1

Printed and bound in Great Britain by Clays Ltd, St Ives plc

The Publishers' policy is to use paper manufactured from sustainable forests.

Contents

Preface to the eighth edition

This textbook has been written so that a very thorough introduction to accounting is covered in two volumes. The split into two volumes is a recognition of the fact that many students will find all that they require contained in Volume 1. Volume 2 will then carry the studies of the remainder of the readers to a more advanced stage.

The textbook is ideal for anyone who wants to obtain a good grounding in financial accounting, for whatever purpose. In particular, it can be said to be very suitable for students who are starting to study the subject for the examinations of the following and other similar examining bodies:

Association of Accounting Technicians
Association of Chartered Certified Accountants
Chartered Institute of Management Accountants
Institute of Chartered Accountants
Institute of Chartered Secretaries and Administrators
Royal Society of Arts

and for examinations for:
General Certificate of Education 'A' Level
General Certificate of Secondary Education, and
Scottish Certificate of Education Higher Grade

The financial accounting requirements for National Vocational Qualifications are also fully covered.

As with the seventh edition, this book:
- provides clearly stated objectives at the start of each chapter;
- contains a list of new terms covered and a section headed '*Main points to remember*' towards the end of each chapter. These will help students to recall the new information learned by them;
- gives students the tools to use either horizontal or vertical style balance sheets from Chapter 1 onwards.

Some new questions have been included in Chapters 24, 26, 34, 43, 46 and 48; and four new chapters – 39, 40, 41 and 45 – have been added. One chapter on Accounting Theory has been removed and is now included in *Business Accounting 2*.

We would like to thank all those lecturers and teachers who gave us their advice as to the changes they would like to see incorporated in this edition. We are especially grateful to Michael Siaw Jun Choi and Muhammad Hanif Ghanghi for their insightful suggestions. There are many others too numerous to mention to whom we are indebted, and we trust that they will not be offended by our inability to list them all here.

We wish to acknowledge the permission to use past examination papers granted by the Edexcel Foundation, the Association of Chartered Certified Accountants, the Institute of Chartered Secretaries and Administrators, the Associated Examining Board, the Association of Accounting Technicians, the Midland Examining Group, the Southern Examining Group, the Scottish Qualifications Authority, and the Northern Examinations and Assessment Board.

We should point out that all answers to questions are the product of our own work and have not been supplied by any of the examining bodies.

Frank Wood and Alan Sangster

Available free to lecturers who adopt **Business Accounting**

Business Accounting Solutions Manual (8th edn)   (0 273 64147 6)

Fully-displayed answers to all questions with the suffix 'A' in the texts, together with overhead transparency masters, are available free of charge to lecturers who recommend *Business Accounting* Volumes 1 or 2 on their course.

Multiple Choice Question Test Software *Volume 1*   (0 273 62546 2)

Multiple Choice Question Test Software *Volume 2*   (0 273 62547 0)

Other books in the Frank Wood series:

Business Accounting Multiple Choice Question Book   (0 273 62545 4)

Business Accounting *Volume 2* **(8th edn)**   (0 273 63743 6)

Business Accounting: Irish Edition (2nd edn)   (0 273 60499 6)

Business Accounting: Irish Edition, Multiple Choice Question Book (0 273 60832 0)

Business Accounting: South African Edition   (0 273 62126 2)

Business Accounting: Hong Kong Edition *Volume 1*   (0 273 63847 5)

Business Accounting: Hong Kong Edition *Volume 2*   (0 273 63848 3)

Book-keeping and Accounts (4th edn)   (0 273 03770 6)

A-level Accounting (2nd edn)   (0 273 63161 6)

Business Accounting NVQ Level 2 Accounting *Student's Workbook* (0 273 60188 1)

Business Accounting NVQ Level 3 Accounting *Student's Workbook* (0 273 60446 5)

Transaction Accounting for NVQ Level 2   (0 273 61349 9)

FINANCIAL TIMES
PITMAN PUBLISHING

WEBSITE

A new feature of the Frank Wood range of accounting texts is a Website. This will support the many users of the books all over the world with valuable information and advice, including the teachers and lecturers who recommend Frank Wood's books and the many hundreds of thousands of students who learn about accounting from them.

The Website is contactable at **www.ftmanagement.com**

Main features are:

Welcome message from Frank Wood

Biographical information on Frank Wood and the history of his books
- information on Frank Wood's writing partners
- a list of current publications

Site map

Special area for students
- Which book? – matches your course to the books you require
- Updates on recent accounting standards
- Exam tips
- Tutorial support books
- Multiple-choice questions

Special password-protected area for lecturers
- Which book? feature – matches your course to the books and support material
- Updates on recent accounting standards
- Inspection copy ordering information
- On-line query service
- Additional questions and answers
- Case studies taken from *Financial Times*
- Overhead transparency masters
- *Solutions Manual*
- Order form
- Catalogue
- Links to other useful websites

Part 1

INTRODUCTION TO DOUBLE ENTRY

Introduction

This part is concerned with the basic principles underlying the double entry system of bookkeeping.

1

The accounting equation and the balance sheet

Objectives

After you have studied this chapter, you should:

- *know what accounting is*

- *be able to distinguish between bookkeeping and accounting*

- *know who are the main users of accounting information*

- *comprehend what is meant by assets, liabilities and capital*

- *understand the accounting equation*

- *be able to draw up balance sheets after different transactions have occurred*

- *know the difference between 'horizontal' and 'vertical' style balance sheets*

1.1 What is accounting?

People and businesses

Accounting is something that affects people in their personal lives just as much as it affects very large businesses. We all use accounting ideas when we plan what we are going to do with our money. We have to plan how much of it we will spend and how much we will save. We may write down a plan, known as a **budget**, or we may simply keep it in our minds.

Recording accounting data

However, when people normally talk about accounting it means the type used by businesses and other organisations. They cannot keep all the details in their minds so they have to keep records of it.

They will not only record cash received and paid out. They will also record goods bought and sold, items bought to use rather than to sell, and so on. This part of accounting is usually called the *recording of data*.

Classifying and summarising

When the data is being recorded it has to be sorted out so as to be most useful to the business. This is known as *classifying* and *summarising* data.

Following such classifications and summaries it will be possible to work out how much profit or loss has been made by the business during a particular period. It will also be possible to show what resources are owned by the business, and what is owed by it, on the closing date of the period.

Communicating information

From the data, someone skilled in accounting should be able to tell whether or not the business is performing well financially. They should be able to ascertain the strengths and weaknesses of the business.

Finally, they should be able to tell or *communicate* their results to the owners of the business, or to others allowed to receive this information.

Accounting is, therefore, concerned with:

- Recording of data.
- Classifying and summarising data.
- Communicating what has been learned from the data.

1.2 What is bookkeeping?

The part of accounting that is concerned with recording data is often known as **bookkeeping**. Until about one hundred years ago all accounting data was recorded in books, hence the term bookkeeping.

Nowadays, although books may be used, quite obviously a lot of accounting data is recorded by using computers.

1.3 A definition of accounting

It is probably too soon in the book to quote the definition of accounting that is most widely accepted. At this stage it could cause a lot of confusion for many students.

Putting it more simply than the usual definition we can say that, first of all, we have to record data. As we have said in 1.2, that is called bookkeeping. Accounting is concerned with the uses which accountants might make of the bookkeeping information given to them. This book will cover many such uses.

For those who cannot wait to see the generally accepted definition, see section 27.12 on p. 255.

1.4 Users of accounting information

The possible users can be:

- Owner(s) of the business. They want to be able to see whether or not the business is profitable. In addition they want to know what the financial resources of the business are.
- A prospective buyer. When the owner wants to sell their business the buyer will want to see such information.

- The bank. If the owner wants to borrow money for use in the business, then the bank will need such information.
- Tax inspectors. They need it to be able to calculate the taxes payable.
- A prospective partner. If the owner wants to share ownership with someone else, then the would-be partner will want such information.
- Investors, either existing ones or people wondering whether or not to invest their money in the business.

There could also be other users. One obvious fact is that without properly recorded accounting data a business would have many difficulties, as the needs of the users could not be served.

1.5 The accounting equation

The whole of financial accounting is based upon a very simple idea. This is called the *accounting equation*, which sounds complicated, but in fact is easy to understand.

It can be explained by saying that, if a firm is to be set up and start trading, then it needs resources. Let us assume that in the first place it is the owner of the business who has supplied all of the resources. This can be shown as:

> Resources in the business = Resources supplied by the owner

In accounting, terms are used to describe things. The amount of the resources supplied by the owner is called **capital**. The actual resources that are then in the business are called **assets**. This means that the accounting equation above, when the owner has supplied all of the resources, can be shown as:

> Assets = Capital

Usually, however, people other than the owner have supplied some of the assets. **Liabilities** is the name given to the amounts owing to these people for these assets. The equation has now changed to:

> Assets = Capital + Liabilities

It can be seen that the two sides of the equation will have the same totals. This is because we are dealing with the same thing from two different points of view. It is:

> Resources: what they are = Resources: who supplied them
> (Assets)   (Capital + Liabilities)

It is a fact that the totals of each side will always equal one another, and that this will always be true no matter how many transactions there may be. The actual assets, capital and liabilities may change, but the total of the assets will always equal the total of capital + liabilities.

Assets consist of property of all kinds, such as buildings, machinery, stocks of goods and motor vehicles. Also benefits such as debts owed by customers and the amount of money in the bank account are included.

Liabilities consist of money owing for goods supplied to the firm and for expenses. Also loans made to the firm are included.

Capital is often called the owner's **equity** or net worth.

1.6 The balance sheet and the effects of business transactions

The accounting equation is expressed in a financial position statement called the **balance sheet**. It is not the first accounting record to be made, but it is a convenient place to start to consider accounting.

The introduction of capital

On 1 May 19X7 B Blake started in business and deposited £5,000 into a bank account opened specially for the business. The balance sheet would appear:

B Blake
Balance Sheet as at 1 May 19X7

Assets	£		£
Cash at bank	5,000	Capital	5,000
	5,000		5,000

The purchase of an asset by cheque

On 3 May 19X7 Blake buys a building for £3,000 paying by cheque. The effect of this transaction is that the cash at the bank is decreased and a new asset, i.e. buildings, appears.

B Blake
Balance Sheet as at 3 May 19X7

Assets	£		£
Buildings	3,000	Capital	5,000
Cash at bank	2,000		
	5,000		5,000

The purchase of an asset and the incurring of a liability

On 6 May 19X7 Blake buys some goods for £500 from D Smith, and agrees to pay for them some time within the next two weeks. The effect of this is that a new asset, **stock of goods**, is acquired, and a liability for the goods is created. A person to whom money is owed for goods is known in accounting language as a **creditor**.

B Blake
Balance Sheet as at 6 May 19X7

Assets	£	Capital and liabilities	£
Buildings	3,000	Capital	5,000
Stock of goods	500	Creditor	500
Cash at bank	2,000		
	5,500		5,500

Sale of an asset on credit

On 10 May 19X7 goods which had cost £100 were sold to J Brown for the same amount, the money to be paid later. The effect is a reduction in the stock of goods and the creation of a new asset. A person who owes the firm money is known in accounting language as a **debtor**. The balance sheet now appears:

B Blake
Balance Sheet as at 10 May 19X7

Assets	£	Capital and liabilities	£
Buildings	3,000	Capital	5,000
Stock of goods	400	Creditor	500
Debtor	100		
Cash at bank	2,000		
	5,500		5,500

Sale of an asset for immediate payment

On 13 May 19X7 goods which had cost £50 were sold to D Daley for the same amount, Daley paying for them immediately by cheque. Here one asset, stock of goods, is reduced, while another asset, bank, is increased. The balance sheet now appears:

B Blake
Balance Sheet as at 13 May 19X7

Assets	£	Capital and liabilities	£
Buildings	3,000	Capital	5,000
Stock of goods	350	Creditor	500
Debtor	100		
Cash at bank	2,050		
	5,500		5,500

The payment of a liability

On 15 May 19X7 Blake pays a cheque for £200 to D Smith in part payment of the amount owing. The asset of bank is therefore reduced, and the liability of the creditor is also reduced. The balance sheet now appears:

B Blake
Balance Sheet as at 15 May 19X7

Assets	£	Capital and liabilities	£
Buildings	3,000	Capital	5,000
Stock of goods	350	Creditor	300
Debtor	100		
Cash at bank	1,850		
	5,300		5,300

Collection of an asset

J Brown, who owed Blake £100, makes a part payment of £75 by cheque on 31 May 19X7. The effect is to reduce one asset, debtor, and to increase another asset, bank. This results in a balance sheet as follows:

B Blake
Balance Sheet as at 31 May 19X7

Assets	£	Capital and liabilities	£
Buildings	3,000	Capital	5,000
Stock of goods	350	Creditor	300
Debtor	25		
Cash at bank	1,925		
	5,300		5,300

1.7 Equality of the accounting equation

It can be seen that every transaction has affected two items. Sometimes it has changed two assets by reducing one and increasing the other. Other times it has reacted differently. A summary of the effect of transactions upon assets, liabilities and capital is shown below.

	Example of transaction		Effect		
1	Buy goods on credit	↑	Increase asset (Stock of goods)	↑	Increase liability (Creditors)
2	Buy goods by cheque	↑	Increase asset (Stock of goods)	↓	Decrease asset (Bank)
3	Pay creditor by cheque	↓	Decrease asset (Bank)	↓	Decrease liability (Creditors)
4	Owner pays more capital into the bank	↑	Increase asset (Bank)	↑	Increase capital
5	Owner takes money out of the business bank account for his own use	↓	Decrease asset (Bank)	↓	Decrease capital
6	Owner pays creditor from private money outside the firm	↓	Decrease liability (Creditors)	↑	Increase capital

Each transaction has, therefore, maintained the same total for assets as that of capital + liabilities. This can be shown:

Number of transaction as above	Assets	Capital and Liabilities	Effect on balance sheet totals
1	+	+	Each side added to equally
2	+ –		A *plus* and a *minus* both on the assets side *cancelling out* each other
3	–	–	Each side has equal deductions
4	+	+	Each side has equal additions
5	–	–	Each side has equal deductions
6		– +	A plus and a minus both on the liabilities side cancelling out each other

1.8 Alternative form of balance sheet presentation

(*Some teachers and lecturers may prefer that students should not read this section at this stage in their studies.*)

Earlier in this chapter you have been shown balance sheets presented in the following manner:

B Blake
Balance Sheet as at ...

Assets	£	Capital and liabilities	£
Details of all assets	xxx	Capital	xxx
		Details of liabilities	xxx
	xxx		xxx

This is called a 'horizontal' or side-by-side form of presentation. There are no legal requirements saying that balance sheets have to be in a horizontal form. The author of this book is of the opinion that (to start with) accounting is easier to learn if the horizontal balance sheet is used to explain the basic system of accounting to students.

However, a large number of lecturers and teachers prefer to start their teaching of the subject using the 'vertical' form of balance sheet. It is simply a matter of preference, and this book will attempt to accommodate both methods.

The reason for the preference for the vertical method is that most modern businesses present their balance sheets in this way. In fact, once the basics of accounting have been mastered, this book will also adopt the vertical method of balance sheet presentation.

Let us now look at the balance sheet of B Blake as at 31 May 19X7, presented in the vertical style:

B Blake
Balance Sheet as at 31 May 19X7

	£	£
Fixed assets		
Buildings		3,000
Current assets		
Stock of goods	350	
Debtor	25	
Cash at bank	1,925	
	2,300	
Less Current liabilities		
Creditor	300	2,000
		5,000
Capital		5,000

You will have noticed the use of the terms 'fixed assets', 'current assets' and 'current liabilities'. Chapter 8 contains a full and proper examination of these terms. At this point we will simply say that:

- **Fixed assets**: are assets to be kept as such for a few years at least, e.g. buildings, machinery, fixtures, motor vehicles.
- **Current assets**: are assets which change from day to day, e.g. the value of stock in hand goes up and down as it is bought and sold. Similarly, the amount of money owing to us by debtors will change quickly, as we sell more to them on credit and they pay their debts. The amount of money in the bank will also change as we receive and pay out money.
- **Current liabilities**: are those liabilities which have to be paid within the near future, e.g. creditors for goods bought.

Horizontal balance sheets are in fact also shown with headings for 'fixed assets', 'current assets' and 'current liabilities'. We will leave a study of this aspect until Chapter 8, thus keeping explanations as simple as possible at this early stage.

New terms

Accounting (p. 3): The uses to which data recorded by bookkeeping can be put for various purposes.

Assets (p. 5): Resources owned by a business.

Balance sheet (p. 6): A statement showing the assets, capital and liabilities of a business.

Bookkeeping (p. 4): The recording of accounting data.

Budget (p. 3): A financial plan shown expressed in money.

Capital (p. 5): The total of resources supplied to a business by its owner.

Creditor (p. 6): A person to whom money is owed for goods or services.

Debtor (p. 7): A person who owes money to a business for goods or services supplied to him.

Equity (p. 5): Another name for the capital of the owner.

Horizontal balance sheets (p. 9): Where assets are shown on one side of a balance sheet and capital and liabilities on the other side.

Liabilities (p. 5): Total of money owed for assets supplied to a business.

Vertical balance sheets (p. 9): A form of presentation where the balance sheet items are shown listed under each other.

Main points to remember

1   Accounting is concerned with the recording and classifying and summarising of data, and then communicating what has been learned from it.

2   It may not only be the owner of a business who will need the accounting information; it may need to be shown to others, e.g. the bank or the Inspector of Taxes.

3   Accounting information can help the owner(s) of a business to plan for the future.

4   The accounting equation is: Assets = Capital + Liabilities.

5   The totals of each side of the balance sheet should always be equal to each other.

6   Every transaction affects two items in the balance sheet.

Note: Generally, the figures used for exhibits and for exercises have been kept down to relatively small amounts. This has been done deliberately to make the work of the user of this book that much easier. Constantly handling large figures does not add anything to the study of the principles of accounting, instead it simply wastes a lot of the student's time, and he/she will probably make far more errors if larger figures are used.

It could lead to the author being accused of not being 'realistic' with the figures given, but I believe that it is far more important to make learning easier for the student.

Review questions

Note: In all the review questions in this volume, questions with the letter A shown after the question number do not have answers shown at the back of the book. Answers to the others are shown on p. 584 onwards.

The author realises that students would like to have *all* the answers shown. However, teachers and lecturers would not then be able to test your knowledge with questions from this book, as you would already possess the answers. It is impossible to please everyone, and the compromise reached is that of putting a large number of review questions in the book.

This means that adequate use can be made by the student studying on his or her own, and by those studying under a lecturer or teacher.

Multiple-choice questions. There is a bank of such questions on p. 570. These are to be attempted later in the course.

1.1 You are to complete the gaps in the following table:

	Assets	Liabilities	Capital
	£	£	£
(a)	12,500	1,800	?
(b)	28,000	4,900	?
(c)	16,800	?	12,500
(d)	19,600	?	16,450
(e)	?	6,300	19,200
(f)	?	11,650	39,750

1.2A You are to complete the gaps in the following table:

	Assets	Liabilities	Capital
	£	£	£
(a)	55,000	16,900	?
(b)	?	17,200	34,400
(c)	36,100	?	28,500
(d)	119,500	15,400	?
(e)	88,000	?	62,000
(f)	?	49,000	110,000

1.3 Distinguish from the following list the items that are liabilities from those that are assets:

(a) Office machinery
(b) Loan from C Shirley
(c) Fixtures and fittings

(d) Motor vehicles
(e) We owe for goods
(f) Bank balance

1.4A Classify the following items into liabilities and assets:

(a) Motor vehicles
(b) Premises
(c) Creditors for goods
(d) Stock of goods
(e) Debtors

(f) Owing to bank
(g) Cash in hand
(h) Loan from D Jones
(i) Machinery

1.5 State which of the following are shown under the wrong classification for J White's business:

Assets	Liabilities
Loan from C Smith	Stock of goods
Cash in hand	Debtors
Machinery	Money owing to bank
Creditors	
Premises	
Motor vehicles	

1.6A Which of the following are shown under the wrong headings:

Assets	Liabilities
Cash at bank	Loan from J Graham
Fixtures	Machinery
Creditors	Motor vehicles
Building	
Stock of goods	
Debtors	
Capital	

1.7 A Smart sets up a new business. Before he actually sells anything, he has bought motor vehicle £2,000, premises £5,000, stock of goods £1,000. He did not pay in full for his stock of goods and still owes £400 in respect of them. He had borrowed £3,000 from D Bevan. After the events just described, and before trading starts, he has £100 cash in hand and £700 cash at bank. You are required to calculate the amount of his capital.

1.8A T Charles starts a business. Before he actually starts to sell anything, he has bought fixtures £2,000, motor vehicle £5,000 and a stock of goods £3,500. Although he has paid in full for the fixtures and the motor vehicle, he still owes £1,400 for some of the goods. J Preston had lent him £3,000. Charles, after the above, has £2,800 in the business bank account and £100 cash in hand. You are required to calculate his capital.

1.9 Draw up A Foster's balance sheet from the following as at 31 December 19X8:

	£
Capital	23,750
Debtors	4,950
Motor vehicles	5,700
Creditors	2,450
Fixtures	5,500
Stock of goods	8,800
Cash at bank	1,250

1.10A Draw up M Kelly's balance sheet as at 30 June 19X6 from the following items:

	£
Capital	15,000
Office machinery	9,000
Creditors	900
Stock of goods	1,550
Debtors	275
Cash at bank	5,075

1.11 Complete the columns to show the effects of the following transactions:

	Effect upon		
	Assets	Liabilities	Capital
(a) We pay a creditor £70 in cash.			
(b) Bought fixtures £200 paying by cheque.			
(c) Bought goods on credit £275.			
(d) The proprietor introduces another £500 cash into the firm.			
(e) J Walker lends the firm £200 in cash.			
(f) A debtor pays us £50 by cheque.			

	Effect upon		
	Assets	Liabilities	Capital

(g) We return goods costing £60 to a supplier whose bill
we had not paid.

(h) Bought additional shop premises paying £5,000 by cheque.

1.12A   Complete the columns to show the effects of the following transactions:

	Effect upon		
	Assets	Liabilities	Capital

(a) Bought a motor van on credit £500.
(b) Repaid by cash a loan owed to P Smith £1,000.
(c) Bought goods for £150 paying by cheque.
(d) The owner puts a further £5,000 cash into the business.
(e) A debtor returns to us £80 goods. We agree to make
an allowance for them.
(f) Bought goods on credit £220.
(g) The owner takes out £100 cash for his personal use.
(h) We pay a creditor £190 by cheque.

1.13   C Sangster has the following items in his balance sheet as on 30 April 19X8:

Capital £20,900; Creditors £1,600; Fixtures £3,500; Motor vehicle £4,200; Stock of goods £4,950;
Debtors £3,280; Cash at bank £6,450; Cash in hand £120.

During the first week of May 19X8:

(a) He bought extra stock of goods £770 on credit.
(b) One of the debtors paid him £280 in cash.
(c) He bought extra fixtures by cheque £1,000.

You are to draw up a balance sheet as on 7 May 19X8 after the above transactions have been
completed.

1.14A   F Dale has the following assets and liabilities as on 30 November 19X9:

Creditors £3,950; Equipment £11,500; Motor vehicle £6,290; Stock of goods £6,150; Debtors
£5,770; Cash at bank £7,280; Cash in hand £40.

The capital at that date is to be deduced by you.

During the first week of December 19X9, Dale:

(a) Bought extra equipment on credit for £1,380.
(b) Bought extra stock by cheque £570.
(c) Paid creditors by cheque £790.
(d) Debtors paid us £840 by cheque and £60 by cash.
(e) F Dale put in an extra £250 cash as capital.

You are to draw up a balance sheet as on 7 December 19X9 after the above transactions have
been completed.

2

The double entry system for assets, liabilities and capital

Objectives

After you have studied this chapter, you should:

- *understand what is meant by the double entry system*

- *see how the double entry system follows the rules of the basic accounting equation*

- *be able to enter transactions using the double entry system*

2.1 Nature of a transaction

In the last chapter we saw how various events had changed two items in the balance sheet. Events which do result in such changes are known as 'transactions'. This means that if the proprietor asks the price of some goods, but does not buy them, then there is no transaction. If he later asks the price of some other goods, and then buys them, then there would be a transaction, and two balance sheet items would then have to be altered.

2.2 The double entry system

We have seen that every transaction affects two items. If we want to show the effect of every transaction when we are doing our bookkeeping, we will have to show the effect of a transaction on each of the two items. For each transaction this means that a bookkeeping entry will have to be made to show an increase or decrease of that item, and another entry to show the increase or decrease of the other item. From this you will probably be able to see that the term **double entry system** of bookkeeping is a good one, as each entry is made twice (double entry).

It may be thought that drawing up a new balance sheet after each transaction would provide all the information required. However, a balance sheet does not give enough information about the business. It does not, for instance, tell who the debtors are and how much each one of them owes the firm, nor who the creditors are and the details of money owing to each of them.

Instead of constantly drawing up balance sheets after each transaction what we have instead is the 'double entry' system. The basis of this system is that the transactions which occur are entered in a set of **accounts**. An account is a place where all the information referring to a particular asset or liability, or to capital, is entered. Thus there will be an account where all the information concerning office machinery will be entered. Similarly there will be an account for buildings, where all the information concerned with buildings will be shown. This will be extended so that every asset, every liability and capital will have its own account for transactions in that item.

2.3 The accounts for double entry

Each account should be shown on a separate page. The double entry system divides each page into two halves. The left-hand side of each page is called the **debit** side, while the right-hand side is called the **credit** side. The title of each account is written across the top of the account at the centre.

You must not think that the words 'debit' and 'credit' in bookkeeping mean the same as the words 'debit' or 'credit' in normal language usage. If you do, you will become very confused.

This is a page of an accounts book:

Title of account written here	
Left-hand side of the page. This is the 'debit' side.	Right-hand side of the page. This is the 'credit' side.

If you have to make an entry of £10 on the debit side of the account, the instructions could say 'debit the account with £10' or 'the account needs debiting with £10'.

Chapter 1 showed that transactions increase or decrease assets, liabilities or capital. Double entry rules for accounts are:

Accounts	To record	Entry in the account
Assets	an increase a decrease	Debit Credit
Liabilities	an increase a decrease	Credit Debit
Capital	an increase a decrease	Credit Debit

Let us look once again at the accounting equation:

	Assets =	Liabilities and	Capital
To increase each item	Debit	Credit	Credit
To decrease each item	Credit	Debit	Debit

The double entry rules for liabilities and capital are the same, but they are the opposite of those for assets. This is because assets are on the opposite side of the equation and, therefore, follow opposite rules. Looking at the accounts the rules will appear as:

Any asset account		Any liability account		Capital account	
Increases	*Decreases*	*Decreases*	*Increases*	*Decreases*	*Increases*
+	−	−	+	−	+

We have not enough space in this book to put each account on a separate page, so we will have to list the accounts under each other. In a real firm at least one full page would be taken for each account.

2.4 Worked examples

The entry of a few transactions can now be attempted:

1 The proprietor starts the firm with £1,000 in cash on 1 August 19X8.

These are entered:

Effect	Action
1 Increases the *asset* of cash	Debit the cash account
2 Increases the capital	Credit the capital account

Cash

19X8		£	
Aug 1		1,000	

Capital

		19X8		£
		Aug 1		1,000

The date of the transaction has already been entered. Now there remains the description which is to be entered alongside the amount. This is completed by a cross-reference to the title of the other account in which the double entry is completed. The double entry to the item in the cash account is completed by an entry in the capital account; therefore the word 'Capital' will appear in the cash account. Similarly, the double entry to the item in the capital account is completed by an entry in the cash account; therefore the word 'Cash' will appear in the capital account.

The finally completed accounts are therefore:

Cash

19X8			£	
Aug 1	Capital		1,000	

Capital

		19X8		£
		Aug 1 Cash		1,000

2   A motor van is bought for £275 cash on 2 August 19X8.

Effect	Action
1 Increases the *asset* of motor van 2 Decreases the *asset* of cash	Debit the motor van account Credit the cash account

Motor van

19X8	£		
Aug 2 Cash	275		

Cash

		19X8	£
		Aug 2 Motor van	275

3   Fixtures bought on credit from Shop Fitters for £115 on 3 August 19X8.

Effect	Action
1 Increases the *asset* of fixtures 2 Increases the *liability* to Shop Fitters	Debit the fixtures account Credit the Shop Fitters account

Fixtures

19X8	£		
Aug 3 Shop Fitters	115		

Shop Fitters

		19X8	£
		Aug 3 Fixtures	115

4   Paid the amount owing in cash to Shop Fitters on 17 August 19X8.

Effect	Action
1 Decreases the *liability* to Shop Fitters 2 Decreases the *asset* of cash	Debit the Shop Fitters account Credit the cash account

Shop Fitters

19X8	£		
Aug 17 Cash	115		

Cash

		19X8	£
		Aug 17 Shop Fitters	115

5 Transactions to date.

Taking the transactions numbered **1** to **4** above, the records will now appear:

Cash

19X8	£	19X8	£
Aug 1 Capital	1,000	Aug 2 Motor van	275
		„ 17 Shop Fitters	115

Capital

		19X8	£
		Aug 1 Cash	1,000

Motor Van

19X8	£		
Aug 2 Cash	275		

Shop Fitters

19X8	£	19X8	£
Aug 17 Cash	115	Aug 3 Fixtures	115

Fixtures

19X8	£		
Aug 3 Shop Fitters	115		

Before you read further you are required to work through Review questions 2.1 and 2.2.

2.5 A further worked example

Now you have actually made some entries in accounts you are to go carefully through the following example. Make certain you can understand every entry.

Transactions	Effect	Action
19X8 May 1 Started an engineering business putting £1,000 into a business bank account.	↑ Increases *asset* of bank. ↑ Increases *capital* of owner.	Debit bank account. Credit capital account.
„ 3 Bought works machinery on credit from Unique Machines £275.	↑ Increases *asset* of machinery. ↑ Increases *liability* to Unique Machines.	Debit machinery account. Credit Unique Machines account.
„ 4 Withdrew £200 cash from the bank and placed it in the cash box.	↑ Increases *asset* of cash. ↓ Decreases *asset* of bank.	Debit cash account. Credit bank account.
„ 7 Bought a motor van paying in cash £180.	↑ Increases *asset* of motor van. ↓ Decreases *asset* of cash.	Debit motor van account. Credit cash account.
„ 10 Sold some of the machinery for £15 on credit to B Barnes.	↑ Increases *asset* of money owing from B Barnes. ↓ Decreases *asset* of machinery.	Debit B Barnes account. Credit machinery account.
„ 21 Returned some of the machinery, value £27, to Unique Machines.	↓ Decreases *liability* to Unique Machines. ↓ Decreases *asset* of machinery.	Debit Unique Machines. Credit machinery account.
„ 28 B Barnes pays the firm the amount owing, £15, by cheque.	↑ Increases *asset* of bank. ↓ Decreases *asset* of money owing by B Barnes.	Debit bank account. Credit B Barnes account.

Transactions	Effect	Action
May 30 Bought another motor van paying by cheque £420.	↑ Increases *asset* of motor vans. ↓ Decreases *asset* of Bank.	Debit motor van account. Credit bank account.
„ 31 Paid the amount of £248 to Unique Machines by cheque.	↓ Decreases *liability* to Unique Machines. ↓ Decreases *asset* of bank.	Debit Unique Machines. Credit bank acccount.

In account form this is shown:

Bank

19X8		£	19X8			£
May 1	Capital	1,000	May 4	Cash		200
„ 28	B Barnes	15	„ 30	Motor van		420
			„ 31	Unique Machines		248

Cash

19X8		£	19X8		£
May 4	Bank	200	May 7	Motor van	180

Capital

19X8		19X8		£
		May 1	Bank	1,000

Machinery

19X8		£	19X8		£
May 3	Unique Machines	275	May 10	B Barnes	15
			„ 21	Unique Machines	27

Motor Van

19X8		£	
May 7	Cash	180	
„ 30	Bank	420	

Unique Machines

19X8		£	19X8		£
May 21	Machines	27	May 3	Machinery	275
„ 31	Bank	248			

B Barnes

19X8	£	19X8	£
May 10 Machinery	15	May 28 Bank	15

2.6 Abbreviation of 'limited'

In this book when we come across transactions with limited companies the letters 'Ltd' are used as the abbreviation for 'Limited Company'. Thus we will know that, if we see the name of a firm as W Jones Ltd, then that firm will be a limited company. In our books the transactions with W Jones Ltd will be entered in the same way as for any other customer or supplier. It will be seen later that some limited companies use plc instead of Ltd.

New terms

Account (p. 16): Part of double entry records, containing details of transactions for a specific item.

Credit (p. 16): The right-hand side of the accounts in double entry.

Debit (p. 16): The left-hand side of the accounts in double entry.

Double entry bookkeeping (p. 15): A system where each transaction is entered twice, once on the debit side and once on the credit side.

Main points to remember

1 Double entry maintains the principle that every debit has a corresponding credit entry.

2 Each different kind of asset and liability has its own separate account, as does capital.

Review questions

2.1 Complete the following table:

	Account to be debited	Account to be credited
(a) Bought office machinery on credit from D Isaacs Ltd.		
(b) The proprietor paid a creditor, C Jones, from his private monies outside the firm.		
(c) A debtor, N Fox, paid us in cash.		
(d) Repaid part of loan from P Exeter by cheque.		
(e) Returned some of office machinery to D Isaacs Ltd.		
(f) A debtor, N Lyn, pays us by cheque.		
(g) Bought motor van by cash.		

2.2A Complete the following table showing which accounts are to be debited and which to be credited:

	Account to be debited	Account to be credited
(a) Bought motor lorry for cash.		
(b) Paid creditor, T Lake, by cheque.		
(c) Repaid P Logan's loan by cash.		
(d) Sold motor lorry for cash.		
(e) Bought office machinery on credit from Ultra Ltd.		
(f) A debtor, A Hill, pays us by cash.		
(g) A debtor, J Cross, pays us by cheque.		
(h) Proprietor puts a further amount into the business by cheque.		
(i) A loan of £200 in cash is received from L Lowe.		
(j) Paid a creditor, D Lord, by cash.		

2.3 Write up the asset and liability and capital accounts to record the following transactions in the records of G Powell.

19X7
July	1	Started business with £2,500 in the bank.
,,	2	Bought office furniture by cheque £150.
,,	3	Bought machinery £750 on credit from Planers Ltd.
,,	5	Bought a motor van paying by cheque £600.
,,	8	Sold some of the office furniture – not suitable for the firm – for £60 on credit to J Walker & Sons.
,,	15	Paid the amount owing to Planers Ltd £750 by cheque.
,,	23	Received the amount due from J Walker & Sons £60 in cash.
,,	31	Bought more machinery by cheque £280.

2.4 You are required to open the asset and liability and capital accounts and record the following transactions for June 19X8 in the records of C Williams.

19X8
June	1	Started business with £2,000 in cash.
,,	2	Paid £1,800 of the opening cash into a bank account for the business.
,,	5	Bought office furniture on credit from Betta-Built Ltd for £120.
,,	8	Bought a motor van paying by cheque £950.
,,	12	Bought works machinery from Evans & Sons on credit £560.
,,	18	Returned faulty office furniture costing £62 to Betta-Built Ltd.
,,	25	Sold some of the works machinery for £75 cash.
,,	26	Paid amount owing to Betta-Built Ltd £58 by cheque.
,,	28	Took £100 out of the bank and put it in the cash till.
,,	30	J Smith lent us £500 – giving us the money by cheque.

2.5A Write up the asset, capital and liability accounts in the books of C Walsh to record the following transactions:

19X9

June	1	Started business with £5,000 in the bank.
„	2	Bought motor van paying by cheque £1,200.
„	5	Bought office fixtures £400 on credit from Young Ltd.
„	8	Bought motor van on credit from Super Motors £800.
„	12	Took £100 out of the bank and put it into the cash till.
„	15	Bought office fixtures paying by cash £60.
„	19	Paid Super Motors a cheque for £800.
„	21	A loan of £1,000 cash is received from J Jarvis.
„	25	Paid £800 of the cash in hand into the bank account.
„	30	Bought more office fixtures paying by cheque £300.

2.6A Write up the accounts to record the following transactions:

19X7

March	1	Started with £1,000 cash.
„	2	Received a loan of £5,000 from M Chow by cheque, a bank account being opened and the cheque paid into it.
„	3	Bought machinery for cash £60.
„	5	Bought display equipment on credit from Betterview Machines £550.
„	8	Took £300 out of the bank and put it into the cash till.
„	15	Repaid part of Chow's loan by cheque £800.
„	17	Paid amount owing to Betterview Machines £550 by cheque.
„	24	Repaid part of Chow's loan by cash £100.
„	31	Bought additional machinery, this time on credit from D Smith for £500.

3

The asset of stock

Objectives

After you have studied this chapter, you should:

- *understand that different accounts are needed to record sales, purchases, returns inwards and returns outwards*

- *be able to record the transactions concerning the various dealings in stock using double entry methods*

- *be able to distinguish between the sales and purchases of goods from the sale and purchase of items which come under a different category*

- *realise why the double entry for cash and credit transactions differ from each other*

3.1 Stock movements

Goods are sometimes sold at the same price at which they are bought, but this is not usually the case. Normally they are sold above cost price, the difference being **profit**; sometimes, however, they are sold at less than cost price, the difference being **loss**.

If all sales were at cost price, it would be possible to have a stock account, the goods sold being shown as a decrease of an asset, i.e. on the credit side. The purchase of stock could be shown on the debit side as it would be an increase of an asset. The difference between the two sides would then represent the cost of the goods unsold at that date, if wastages and losses of stock are ignored. However, most sales are not at cost price, and therefore the sales figures include elements of profit or loss. Because of this, the difference between the two sides would not represent the stock of goods. Such a stock account would therefore serve no useful purpose.

The **Stock Account** is accordingly divided into several accounts, each one showing a movement of stock. These can be said to be:

1 **Increases in the stock.** This can be due to one of two causes:

    (*a*) The purchase of additional goods.

    (*b*) The return in to the firm of goods previously sold. The reasons for this are numerous. The goods may have been the wrong type, they may have been surplus to requirements, have been faulty and so on.

    To distinguish the two aspects of the increase of stocks of goods two accounts are opened. These are:

(*i*)   **Purchases Account** – in which purchases of goods are entered.

(*ii*)   **Returns Inwards Account** – in which goods being returned in to the firm are entered. The alternative name for this account is the **Sales Returns Account**.

2   **Decreases in the stock of goods.** This can be due to one of two causes if wastages and losses of stock are ignored:

(*a*)   The sale of goods.

(*b*)   Goods previously bought by the firm now being returned out of the firm to the supplier.

To distinguish the two aspects of the decrease of stocks of goods two accounts are opened. These are:

(*i*)   **Sales Account** – in which sales of goods are entered.

(*ii*)   **Returns Outwards Account** – in which goods being returned out to a supplier are entered. The alternative name for this is the **Purchases Returns Account**.

As stock is an asset, and these four accounts are all connected with this asset, the double entry rules are those used for assets. We shall now look at some entries in the following sections.

3.2 Purchase of stock on credit

1 August 19X8. Goods costing £165 are bought on credit from D Henry. First, the twofold effect of the transaction must be considered so that the bookkeeping entries can be worked out.

1   The asset of stock is increased. An increase in an asset needs a debit entry in an account. Here the account is a stock account showing the particular movement of stock; in this case it is the 'purchases' movement so that the account must be the purchases account.

2   An increase in a liability. This is the liability of the firm to D Henry because the goods bought have not yet been paid for. An increase in a liability needs a credit entry, so that to enter this part of the transaction a credit entry is made in D Henry's account.

Purchases

19X8	£		
Aug 1 D Henry	165		

D Henry

		19X8	£
		Aug 1 Purchases	165

3.3 Purchases of stock for cash

2 August 19X8. Goods costing £22 are bought, cash being paid for them immediately.

1   The asset of stock is increased, so a debit entry will be needed. The movement of stock is that of a purchase, so that it is the purchases account which needs debiting.

2   The asset of cash is decreased. To reduce an asset a credit entry is called for, and the asset is that of cash so that the cash account needs crediting.

Purchases

19X8			£	
Aug	2	Cash	22	

Cash

				19X8			£
				Aug	2	Purchases	22

3.4 Sales of stock on credit

3 August 19X8. Sold goods on credit for £250 to J Lee.

1 An asset account is increased. This is the account showing that J Lee is a debtor for the goods. The increase in the asset of debtors requires a debit and the debtor is J Lee, so that the account concerned is that of J Lee.
2 The asset of stock is decreased. For this a credit entry to reduce an asset is needed. The movement of stock is that of a 'sale' so the account credited is the sales account.

J Lee

19X8			£	
Aug	3	Sales	250	

Sales

				19X8			£
				Aug	3	J Lee	250

3.5 Sales of stock for cash

4 August 19X8. Goods are sold for £55, cash being received immediately upon sale.

1 The asset of cash is increased. This needs a debit in the cash account to show this.
2 The asset of stock is reduced. The reduction of an asset requires a credit and the movement of stock is represented by 'sales'. Thus the entry needed is a credit in the sales account.

Cash

19X8			£	
Aug	4	Sales	55	

Sales

				19X8			£
				Aug	4	Cash	55

3.6 Returns inwards

5 August 19X8. Goods which had been previously sold to F Lowe for £29 are now returned by him. This could be for various reasons such as:

- we have sent him goods of the wrong size, the wrong colour or the wrong model;
- the goods may have been damaged in transit;
- the goods are of poor quality;

and so on.

1 The asset of stock is increased by the goods returned. Thus a debit representing an increase of an asset is needed, and this time the movement of stock is that of **returns inwards**. The entry therefore required is a debit in the returns inwards account.
2 A decrease in an asset. The debt of F Lowe to the firm is now reduced, and to record this a credit is needed in F Lowe's account.

Returns Inwards

19X8		£		
Aug 5 F Lowe		29		

F Lowe

		19X8		£
		Aug 5 Returns inwards		29

An alternative name for a returns inwards account would be a **sales returns account**.

3.7 Returns outwards

6 August 19X8. Goods previously bought for £96 are returned by the firm to K Howe.

1 The liability of the firm to K Howe is decreased by value of the goods returned to him. The decrease in a liability needs a debit, this time in K Howe's account.
2 The asset of stock is decreased by the goods sent out. Thus a credit representing a reduction in an asset is needed, and the movement of stock is that of **returns outwards** so that the entry will be a credit in the returns outwards account.

K Howe

19X8		£		
Aug 6 Returns outwards		96		

Returns Outwards

		19X8		£
		Aug 6 K Howe		96

An alternative name for a returns outwards account would be a **purchases returns account**.

3.8 A worked example

19X9

May 1 Bought goods on credit £68 from D Small.
„ 2 Bought goods on credit £77 from A Lyon & Son.
„ 5 Sold goods on credit to D Hughes for £60.
„ 6 Sold goods on credit to M Spencer for £45.
„ 10 Returned goods £15 to D Small.
„ 12 Goods bought for cash £100.
„ 19 M Spencer returned £16 goods to us.
„ 21 Goods sold for cash £150.
„ 22 Paid cash to D Small £53.
„ 30 D Hughes paid the amount owing by him £60 in cash.
„ 31 Bought goods on credit £64 from A Lyon & Son.

Purchases

19X9		£	
May	1 D Small	68	
„	2 A Lyon & Son	77	
„	12 Cash	100	
„	31 A Lyon & Son	64	

Sales

	19X9		£
	May	5 D Hughes	60
	„	6 M Spencer	45
	„	21 Cash	150

Returns Outwards

	19X9		£
	May 10	D Small	15

Returns Inwards

19X9		£	
May 19	M Spencer	16	

D Small

19X9		£	19X9		£
May 10	Returns outwards	15	May	1 Purchases	68
„ 22	Cash	53			

A Lyon & Son

			19X9		£
			May	2 Purchases	77
			„	31 Purchases	64

D Hughes

19X9		£	19X9		£
May 5	Sales	60	May 30	Cash	60

M Spencer

19X9		£	19X9		£
May 6	Sales	45	May 19	Returns inwards	16

Cash

19X9		£	19X9		£
May 21	Sales	150	May 12	Purchases	100
„ 30	D Hughes	60	„ 22	D Small	53

3.9 Special meaning of 'sales' and 'purchases'

It must be emphasised that 'sales' and 'purchases' have a special meaning in accounting when compared to ordinary language usage.

'**Purchases**' in accounting means the *purchase of those goods which the firm buys with the prime intention of selling*. Obviously, sometimes the goods are altered, added to, or used in the manufacture of something else, but it is the element of resale that is important. To a firm that deals in typewriters, for instance, typewriters constitute purchases. If something else is bought, such as a motor van, such an item cannot be called purchases, even though in ordinary language it may be said that a motor van has been purchased. The prime intention of buying the motor van is for usage and not for resale.

Similarly, '**sales**' means the *sale of those goods in which the firm normally deals and which were bought with the prime intention of resale*. The word 'sales' must never be given to the disposal of other items.

If we did not keep to these meanings, it would result in the different kinds of stock accounts containing something other than goods sold or for resale.

3.10 Comparison of cash and credit transactions for purchases and sales

The difference between the records needed for cash and credit transactions can now be seen.

The complete set of entries for purchases of goods where they are paid for immediately by cash would be:

1 Debit the purchases account.
2 Credit the cash account.

On the other hand the complete set of entries for the purchase of goods on credit can be broken down into two stages. First, the purchase of the goods and second, the payment for them. The first part is:

1 Debit the purchases account.
2 Credit the supplier's account.

The second part is:

1 Debit the supplier's account.
2 Credit the cash account.

The difference can now be seen; with the cash purchase no record is kept of the supplier's account. This is because cash passes immediately and therefore there is no need to keep a check of indebtedness (money owing) to a supplier. On the other hand, in the credit purchase the records should show to whom money is owed until payment is made.

A study of cash sales and credit sales will reveal a similar difference.

Cash Sales	Credit Sales

Complete entry:
  Debit cash account
  Credit sales account
	First part:
	  Debit customer's account
	  Credit sales account
	Second part:
	  Debit cash account
	  Credit customer's account

New terms

Purchases (p. 26): Goods bought by the business for the purpose of selling them again.

Returns inwards (p. 26): Goods returned to the business by its customers.

Returns outwards (p. 26): Goods returned by the business to its suppliers.

Sales (p. 26): Goods sold by the business.

Main points to remember

1 Separate accounts are kept for each different type of movement of stock, i.e. sales account, purchases account, returns inwards account and returns outwards account.

2 Credit sales are entered on the debit side of the customer's personal account.

3 Credit purchases are entered on the credit side of the supplier's personal account.

4 Returns inwards are entered on the credit side of the customer's personal account.

5 Returns outwards are entered on the debit side of the supplier's personal account.

6 Cash sales require only two entries for the whole transaction. Credit sales require four entries for the whole transaction, being two entries for the sale and two entries for the receipt of money.

7 Cash purchases require only two entries for the whole transaction. Credit purchases require four entries for the whole transaction, being two entries for the purchase and two entries for the payment of money.

Review questions

3.1 Complete the following table showing which accounts are to be credited and which are to be debited:

	Account to be debited	Account to be credited
(a) Goods bought on credit from J Reid.		
(b) Goods sold on credit to B Perkins.		
(c) Motor vans bought on credit from H Thomas.		
(d) Goods sold, a cheque being received immediately.		
(e) Goods sold for cash.		
(f) Goods we returned to H Hardy.		
(g) Machinery sold for cash.		
(h) Goods returned to us by J Nelson.		
(i) Goods bought on credit from D Simpson.		
(j) Goods we returned to H Forbes.		

3.2A Complete the following table:

	Account to be debited	Account to be credited
(a) Goods bought on credit from T Morgan.		
(b) Goods returned to us by J Thomas.		
(c) Machinery returned to L Jones Ltd.		
(d) Goods bought for cash.		
(e) Motor van bought on credit from D Davies Ltd.		
(f) Goods returned by us to I Prince.		
(g) D Picton paid us his account by cheque.		
(h) Goods bought by cheque.		
(i) We paid creditor, B Henry, by cheque.		
(j) Goods sold on credit to J Mullings.		

3.3 You are to write up the following in the books:

19X8
July 1 Started business with £500 cash.
  ,, 3 Bought goods for cash £85.
  ,, 7 Bought goods on credit £116 from E Morgan.
  ,, 10 Sold goods for cash £42.
  ,, 14 Returned goods to E Morgan £28.
  ,, 18 Bought goods on credit £98 from A Moses.
  ,, 21 Returned goods to A Moses £19.
  ,, 24 Sold goods to A Knight £55 on credit.
  ,, 25 Paid E Morgan's account by cash £88.
  ,, 31 A Knight paid us his account in cash £55.

3.4A You are to enter the following in the accounts needed:

19X6
Aug 1 Started business with £1,000 cash.
,, 2 Paid £900 of the opening cash into the bank.
,, 4 Bought goods on credit £78 from S Holmes.
,, 5 Bought a motor van by cheque £500.
,, 7 Bought goods for cash £55.
,, 10 Sold goods on credit £98 to D Moore.
,, 12 Returned goods to S Holmes £18.
,, 19 Sold goods for cash £28.
,, 22 Bought fixtures on credit from Kingston Equipment Co £150.
,, 24 D Watson lent us £100 paying us the money by cheque.
,, 29 We paid S Holmes his account by cheque £60.
,, 31 We paid Kingston Equipment Co by cheque £150.

3.5 Enter up the following transactions in the records of E Sangster:

19X7
July 1 Started business with £10,000 in the bank.
,, 2 T Cooper lent us £400 in cash.
,, 3 Bought goods on credit from F Jones £840 and S Charles £3,600.
,, 4 Sold goods for cash £200.
,, 6 Took £250 of the cash and paid it into the bank.
,, 8 Sold goods on credit to C Moody £180.
,, 10 Sold goods on credit to J Newman £220.
,, 11 Bought goods on credit from F Jones £370.
,, 12 C Moody returned goods to us £40.
,, 14 Sold goods on credit to H Morgan £190 and J Peat £320.
,, 15 We returned goods to F Jones £140.
,, 17 Bought motor van on credit from Manchester Motors £2,600.
,, 18 Bought office furniture on credit from Faster Supplies Ltd £600.
,, 19 We returned goods to S Charles £110.
,, 20 Bought goods for cash £220.
,, 24 Goods sold for cash £70.
,, 25 Paid money owing to F Jones by cheque £1,070.
,, 26 Goods returned to us by H Morgan £30.
,, 27 Returned some of office furniture costing £160 to Faster Supplies Ltd.
,, 28 E Sangster put a further £500 into the business in the form of cash.
,, 29 Paid Manchester Motors £2,600 by cheque.
,, 31 Bought office furniture for cash £100.

3.6A Enter up the following transactions in the records:

19X9

May   1   Started business with £2,000 in the bank.

  ,,   2   Bought goods on credit from C Shaw £900.

  ,,   3   Bought goods on credit from F Hughes £250.

  ,,   5   Sold goods for cash £180.

  ,,   6   We returned goods to C Shaw £40.

  ,,   8   Bought goods on credit from F Hughes £190.

  ,,   10   Sold goods on credit to G Wood £390.

  ,,   12   Sold goods for cash £210.

  ,,   18   Took £300 of the cash and paid it into the bank.

  ,,   21   Bought machinery by cheque £550.

  ,,   22   Sold goods on credit to L Moore £220.

  ,,   23   G Wood returned goods to us £140.

  ,,   25   L Moore returned goods to us £10.

  ,,   28   We returned goods to F Hughes £30.

  ,,   29   We paid Shaw by cheque £860.

  ,,   31   Bought machinery on credit from D Lee £270.

4

The effect of profit or loss on capital and the double entry system for expenses and revenues

Objectives

After you have studied this chapter, you should:

- *understand the nature of profit and loss*

- *see how profits and losses affect capital*

- *appreciate the need for separate accounts for different types of expenses and revenues*

- *be able to enter expenses on the correct side of the expense accounts*

- *be able to enter revenues on the correct side of the revenue accounts*

- *recognise that drawings affect capital*

4.1 The nature of profit or loss

To an accountant **profit** means the amount by which **revenues** are greater than **expenses** for a set of transactions. The term revenues means the sales value of goods and services that have been supplied to customers. The term expenses means the value of all the assets that have been used up to obtain those revenues.

If, therefore, we had supplied goods and services valued for sale at £100,000 to customers, and the expenses incurred by us to be able to supply those goods and services amounted to £70,000, then the result would be a profit calculated:

		£
Revenues:	goods and services supplied to our customers for the sum of	100,000
Less Expenses:	value of all the assets used up to enable us to supply	
	the above goods and services	70,000
Profit is therefore:		30,000

On the other hand, it could also be possible that our expenses may exceed our revenues for a set of transactions. In this case the result is a loss. For instance a loss would be incurred given the following details:

		£
Expenses:	value of all the assets used up to supply goods and services to our customers	80,000
Less Revenues:	what we have charged to our customers in respect of all the goods and services supplied to them	60,000
Loss is therefore:		20,000

4.2 The effect of profit and loss on capital

We can now look at the effect of profit upon capital by the use of an example.
On 1 January the assets and liabilities of a firm are:

Assets: Fixtures £10,000, Stock £7,000, Cash at the bank £3,000.
Liabilities: Creditors £2,000.

The capital is found by the formula:

$$\text{Assets} - \text{Liabilities} = \text{Capital}$$

In this case, capital works out at £10,000 + £7,000 + £3,000 − £2,000 = £18,000.
During January the whole of the £7,000 stock is sold for £11,000 cash. On 31 January the assets and liabilities have become:

Assets: Fixtures £10,000, Stock nil, Cash at the bank £14,000.
Liabilities: Creditors £2,000.

The capital can be calculated:

Assets £10,000 + £14,000 − Liabilities £2,000 = £22,000

It can be seen that capital has increased from £18,000 to £22,000, a £4,000 increase because the £7,000 stock was sold for £11,000, a profit of £4,000. Profit, therefore, increases capital:

$$\text{Old capital} + \text{Profit} = \text{New capital}$$

£18,000 + £4,000 = £22,000

On the other hand, a loss would reduce the capital:

$$\text{Old capital} - \text{Loss} = \text{New capital}$$

4.3 Profit or loss and sales

Profit will be made when goods or services are sold at more than cost price, while the opposite will mean a **loss**.

4.4 Profit or loss and expenses

To alter the capital account it will be necessary to calculate profits or losses. How often this will be done will depend on the firm. Some only attempt to calculate their profits and losses once a year. Others do it at much more frequent intervals.

What it does mean is that accounts will be needed to collect together the expenses and revenues pending the calculation of profits for a period. All the expenses could be charged to one Expenses Account, but you would be able to understand the calculations better if full details of each type of expense are shown in profit and loss calculations. The same would apply to each type of revenue.

To serve this purpose a separate account is opened for each type of expense and for each type of revenue. For instance there may be accounts as follows:

Rent Account	Postages Account
Wages Account	Stationery Account
Salaries Account	Insurance Account
Telephone Account	Motor Expenses Account
Rent Receivable Account	General Expenses Account

It is purely a matter of choice in a firm as to the title of each expense or revenue account. For example, an account for postage stamps could be called 'Postage Stamps Account', 'Postages Account', 'Communication Expenses Account', and so on. Also different firms amalgamate expenses, some having a 'Rent and Telephone Account', others a 'Rent, Telephone and Insurance Account', etc. Infrequent or small items of expense are usually put into a 'Sundry Expenses Account' or a 'General Expenses Account'.

4.5 Debit or credit

We have to decide whether expense accounts are to be debited or credited with the amounts involved. Assets involve expenditure by the firm and are shown as debit entries. Expenses also involve expenditure by the firm and therefore should also be debit entries.

An alternative explanation may also be used for expenses. Every expense results in a decrease in an asset or an increase in a liability, and because of the accounting equation this means that the capital is reduced by each expense. The decrease of capital needs a debit entry and therefore expense accounts contain debit entries for expenses.

Revenue is the opposite of expenses and therefore appears on the opposite side to expenses, that is revenue accounts appear on the credit side of the books. Pending the periodical calculation of profit, therefore, revenue is collected together in appropriately named accounts, and until it is transferred to the profit calculations it will need to be shown as a credit.

Consider too that expenditure of money pays for expenses, which are used up in the short term, or assets, which are used up in the long term, both for the purpose of winning revenue. Both of these are shown on the debit side of the accounts, while the revenue which has been won is shown on the credit side of the accounts.

4.6 Effect of transactions

A few illustrations will demonstrate the double entry required.

1   The rent of £200 is paid in cash.
    Here the twofold effect is:

   (a) The total of the expenses of rent is increased. As expense entries are shown as debits, and the expense is rent, the action required is the debiting of the rent account.
   (b) The asset of cash is decreased. This means crediting the cash account to show the decrease of the asset.

   Summary: Debit the rent account with £200.
                  Credit the cash account with £200.

2   Motor expenses are paid by cheque £355.
    The twofold effect is:

   (a) The total of the motor expenses paid is increased. To increase an expenses account needs a debit, so the action required is to debit the motor expenses account.
   (b) The asset of money in the bank is decreased. This means crediting the bank account to show the decrease of the asset.

   Summary: Debit the motor expenses account with £355.
                  Credit the bank account with £355.

3   £60 cash is received for commission earned by the firm.

   (a) The asset of cash is increased. This needs a debit in the cash account to increase the asset.
   (b) The revenue of commissions received is increased. Revenue is shown by a credit entry, therefore to increase the revenue account in question the commissions received account is credited.

   Summary: Debit the cash account.
                  Credit the commissions received account.

It is now possible to study the effects of some more transactions showing the results in the form of a table:

	Increase	Action	Decrease	Action
June 1 Paid for postage stamps by cash £50	Expenses of postages	Debit postages account	Asset of cash	Credit cash account
„ 2 Paid for electricity by cheque £229	Expense of electricity	Debit electricity account	Asset of bank	Credit bank account
„ 3 Received rent in cash £138	Asset of cash Revenue of rent	Debit cash account Credit rent received account		
„ 4 Paid insurance by cheque £142	Expense of insurance	Debit insurance account	Asset of bank	Credit bank account

The above four examples can now be shown in account form:

Cash

	£			£
June 3 Rent received	138	June 1 Postages		50

Bank

			£
	June 2 Electricity		229
	„ 4 Insurance		142

Electricity

	£	
June 2 Bank	229	

Insurance

	£	
June 4 Bank	142	

Postages

	£	
June 1 Cash	50	

Rent Received

		£
	June 3 Cash	138

4.7 Drawings

Sometimes the owner will want to take cash out of the business for his private use. This is known as **drawings**. Any money taken out as drawings will reduce capital.

The capital account is a very important account. To help to stop it getting full of small details, each item of drawings is not entered in the capital account. Instead a drawings account is opened, and the debits are entered there.

The following example illustrates the entries for drawings.

25 August. Proprietor takes £50 cash out of the business for his own use.

Effect	Action
1 Capital is decreased by £50 2 Cash is decreased by £50	Debit the drawings account £50 Credit the cash account £50

Drawings

	£	
Aug 25 Cash	50	

Cash

		£
	Aug 25 Drawings	50

Sometimes goods also are taken for private use. These are also known as drawings. Entries for such transactions will be described later in the book.

New terms

Drawings (p. 39): Cash or goods taken out of a business by the owner for his private use.

Expenses (p. 35): Costs of operating the business.

Profit (p. 35): Result of selling goods for more than they cost.

Revenues (p. 35): Monetary value of goods and services supplied to the customers.

Main points to remember

1   Profit increases capital.

2   Losses reduce capital.

3   Every different type of expense will be shown in a separate account, specially named for that type of expense.

4   Expenses are shown as debit entries in the various expense accounts.

5   Revenues are shown as credit entries in the various revenue accounts.

Review questions

4.1   You are to enter the following transactions, completing the double entry in the books for the month of May 19X7.

19X7

May   1   Started business with £2,000 in the bank.
  „   2   Purchased goods £175 on credit from M Mills.
  „   3   Bought fixtures and fittings £150 paying by cheque.
  „   5   Sold goods for cash £275.
  „   6   Bought goods on credit £114 from S Waites.
  „ 10   Paid rent by cash £15.
  „ 12   Bought stationery £27, paying in cash.
  „ 18   Goods returned to M Mills £23.
  „ 21   Let off part of the premises receiving rent by cheque £5.
  „ 23   Sold goods on credit to U Henry for £77.
  „ 24   Bought a motor van paying by cheque £300.
  „ 30   Paid the month's wages by cash £117.
  „ 31   The proprietor took cash for himself £44.

4.2 Write up the following transactions in the books of L Thompson:

19X8

March 1 Started business with cash £1,500.
  „ 2 Bought goods on credit from A Hanson £296.
  „ 3 Paid rent by cash £28.
  „ 4 Paid £1,000 of the cash of the firm into a bank account.
  „ 5 Sold goods on credit to E Linton £54.
  „ 7 Bought stationery £15 paying by cheque.
  „ 11 Cash sales £49.
  „ 14 Goods returned by us to A Hanson £17.
  „ 17 Sold goods on credit to S Morgan £29.
  „ 20 Paid for repairs to the building by cash £18.
  „ 22 E Linton returned goods to us £14.
  „ 27 Paid Hanson by cheque £279.
  „ 28 Cash purchases £125.
  „ 29 Bought a motor van paying by cheque £395.
  „ 30 Paid motor expenses in cash £15.
  „ 31 Bought fixtures £120 on credit from A Webster.

4.3A Enter the following transactions in double entry:

July 1 Started business with £8,000 in the bank.
  „ 2 Bought stationery by cheque £30.
  „ 3 Bought goods on credit from I Walsh £900.
  „ 4 Sold goods for cash £180.
  „ 5 Paid insurance by cash £40.
  „ 7 Bought machinery on credit from H Morgan £500.
  „ 8 Paid for machinery expenses by cheque £50.
  „ 10 Sold goods on credit to D Small £320.
  „ 11 Returned goods to I Walsh £70.
  „ 14 Paid wages by cash £70.
  „ 17 Paid rent by cheque £100.
  „ 20 Received cheque £200 from D Small.
  „ 21 Paid H Morgan by cheque £500.
  „ 23 Bought stationery on credit from Express Ltd £80.
  „ 25 Sold goods on credit to N Thomas £230.
  „ 31 Paid Express Ltd by cheque £80.

4.4A Write up the following transactions in the records of D DaSilva:

Feb 1 Started business with £3,000 in the bank and £500 cash.
  „ 2 Bought goods on credit: T Small £250; C Todd £190; V Ryan £180.
  „ 3 Bought goods for cash £230.
  „ 4 Paid rent in cash £10.
  „ 5 Bought stationery paying by cheque £49.
  „ 6 Sold goods on credit: C Crooks £140; R Rogers £100; B Grant £240.
  „ 7 Paid wages in cash £80.
  „ 10 We returned goods to C Todd £60.
  „ 11 Paid rent in cash £10.
  „ 13 R Rogers returns goods to us £20.
  „ 15 Sold goods on credit to: J Burns £90; J Smart £130; N Thorn £170.
  „ 16 Paid rates by cheque £130.
  „ 18 Paid insurance in cash £40.

Feb 19 Paid rent by cheque £10.
„ 20 Bought motor van on credit from C White £600.
„ 21 Paid motor expenses in cash £6.
„ 23 Paid wages in cash £90.
„ 24 Received part of amount owing from B Grant by cheque £200.
„ 28 Received refund of rates £10 by cheque.
„ 28 Paid by cheque: T Small £250; C Todd £130; C White £600.

4.5 From the following statements which give the cumulative effects of individual transactions, you are required to state as fully as possible what transaction has taken place in each case. There is no need to copy out the table.

Transaction:		A	B	C	D	E	F	G	H	I
Assets	£000	£000	£000	£000	£000	£000	£000	£000	£000	£000
Land and buildings	450	450	450	450	575	575	275	275	275	275
Motor vehicles	95	100	100	100	100	100	100	100	100	100
Office equipment	48	48	48	48	48	48	48	48	48	48
Stock	110	110	110	110	110	110	110	110	110	93
Debtors	188	188	188	188	188	108	108	108	108	120
Bank	27	22	22	172	47	127	427	77	77	77
Cash	15	15	11	11	11	11	11	11	3	3
	933	933	929	1,079	1,079	1,079	1,079	729	721	716
Liabilities										
Capital	621	621	621	621	621	621	621	621	621	616
Loan from Lee	200	200	200	350	350	350	350	–	–	–
Creditors	112	112	108	108	108	108	108	108	100	100
	933	933	929	1,079	1,079	1,079	1,079	729	721	716

Note: the sign *£000* means that all the figures shown underneath it are in thousands of pounds, e.g. Office Equipment book value is £48,000. It saves constantly writing out 000 after each figure, and is done to save time and make comparison easier.

4.6A The following table shows the cumulative effects of a succession of separate transactions on the assets and liabilities of a business.

Transaction:		A	B	C	D	E	F	G	H	I
Assets	£000	£000	£000	£000	£000	£000	£000	£000	£000	£000
Land and buildings	500	500	535	535	535	535	535	535	535	535
Equipment	230	230	230	230	230	230	230	200	200	200
Stocks	113	140	140	120	120	120	120	120	119	119
Trade debtors	143	143	143	173	160	158	158	158	158	158
Prepaid expenses	27	27	27	27	27	27	27	27	27	27
Cash at bank	37	37	37	37	50	50	42	63	63	63
Cash on hand	9	9	9	9	9	9	9	9	9	3
	1,059	1,086	1,121	1,131	1,131	1,129	1,121	1,112	1,111	1,105
Liabilities										
Capital	730	730	730	740	740	738	733	724	723	717
Loan	120	120	155	155	155	155	155	155	155	155
Trade creditors	168	195	195	195	195	195	195	195	195	195
Accrued expenses	41	41	41	41	41	41	38	38	38	38
	1,059	1,086	1,121	1,131	1,131	1,129	1,121	1,112	1,111	1,105

Required:

Identify clearly and as fully as you can what transaction has taken place in each case. Give two possible explanations for transaction I. Do not copy out the table but use the reference letter for each transaction.

(*Association of Accounting Technicians*)

Authors' note: We have not yet come across the term 'accrued expenses'. It means the same as expenses owing, so in F obviously £3,000 was paid off expenses owing as well as another £5,000 being used for something else.

5

Balancing off accounts

Objectives

After you have studied this chapter, you should:

- *be able to balance off personal accounts for debtors and creditors*

- *be able to distinguish between a debit balance and a credit balance*

- *be able to show personal ledger accounts in a three-column style instead of as T accounts*

5.1 Accounts for debtors

Where debtors have paid their accounts

What you have been reading so far is the recording of transactions in the books by means of debit and credit entries. At the end of each period we will have to look at each account to see what is shown by the entries.

Probably the most obvious reason for this is to find out how much our customers owe us for goods we have sold to them. In most firms this is done at the end of each month. Let us look at the account of one of our customers, K Tandy, for transactions in August 19X6:

K Tandy

19X6		£	19X6		£
Aug 1	Sales	144	Aug 22	Bank	144
Aug 19	Sales	300	Aug 28	Bank	300

This shows that during the month we sold a total of £444 goods to Tandy, and have been paid a total of £444 by him. At the close of business at the end of August he therefore owes us nothing. His account can be closed off on 31 August 19X6 by inserting the totals on each side, as follows:

K Tandy

19X6		£	19X6		£
Aug 1	Sales	144	Aug 22	Bank	144
Aug 19	Sales	300	Aug 28	Bank	300
		444			444

Notice that totals in accounting are shown with a single line above them, and a double line underneath. Totals on accounts at the end of a period are always shown on a level with one another, as shown in the following completed account for C Lee.

C Lee

19X6		£	19X6		£
Aug 11	Sales	177	Aug 30	Bank	480
Aug 19	Sales	203			
Aug 22	Sales	100			
		480			480

In this account, C Lee also owed us nothing at the end of August 19X6, as he had paid us for all sales to him.

If an account contains only one entry on each side and they are equal, totals are unnecessary. For example:

K Wood

19X6		£	19X6		£
Aug 6	Sales	214	Aug 12	Bank	214

Where debtors still owe for goods

On the other hand, some of our customers will still owe us something at the end of the month. In these cases the totals of each side would not equal one another. Let us look at the account of D Knight for August 19X6:

D Knight

19X6		£	19X6		£
Aug 1	Sales	158	Aug 28	Bank	158
Aug 15	Sales	206			
Aug 30	Sales	118			

If you add the figures you will see that the debit side adds up to £482 and the credit side adds up to £158. You should be able to see what the difference of £324 (i.e. £482 − £158) represents. It consists of sales of £206 and £118 not paid for and therefore owing to us on 31 August 19X6.

In double entry we only enter figures as totals if the totals on both sides of the account agree. We do, however, want to close off the account for August, but showing that Knight owes us £324. If he owes £324 at close of business on 31 August 19X6, then he will still owe us that same figure when the business opens on 1 September 19X6. We show this by **balancing the account**. This is done in five stages:

1   Add up both sides to find out their totals. Do not write anything in the account at this stage.
2   Deduct the smaller total from the larger total to find the balance.
3   Now enter the balance on the side with the smallest total. This now means the totals will be equal.
4   Enter totals on a level with each other.
5   Now enter the balance on the line below the totals. The balance below the totals should be on the opposite side to the balance shown above the totals.

Against the balance above the totals, complete the date column by showing the last day of that period. Below the totals show the first day of the next period against the balance. The balance above the totals is described as balance *carried down*. The balance below the total is described as balance *brought down*.

Knight's account when 'balanced off' will appear as follows:

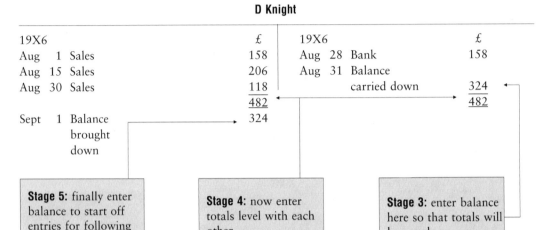

D Knight

19X6			£	19X6			£
Aug	1	Sales	158	Aug	28	Bank	158
Aug	15	Sales	206	Aug	31	Balance	
Aug	30	Sales	118			carried down	324
			482				482
Sept	1	Balance brought down	324				

Stage 5: finally enter balance to start off entries for following month.

Stage 4: now enter totals level with each other.

Stage 3: enter balance here so that totals will be equal.

Notes:

- In future we will abbreviate 'carried down' to c/d, and 'brought down' to b/d.
- The date given to balance c/d is the last day of the period which is finishing, and balance b/d is given the opening date of the next period.
- As the total of the debit side originally exceeded the total of the credit side, the balance is said to be a debit balance. This being a personal account (for a person), the person concerned is said to be a debtor – the accounting term for anyone who owes money to the firm. The use of the term debtor for a person whose account has a debit balance can again thus be seen.

If accounts contain only one entry it is unnecessary to enter the total. A double line ruled under the entry will mean that the entry is its own total. For example:

B Walters

19X6			£	19X6			£
Aug	18	Sales	51	Aug	31	Balance c/d	51
Sept	1	Balance b/d	51				

5.2 Accounts for creditors

Exactly the same principles will apply when the balances are carried down to the credit side. We can look at two accounts of our suppliers which are to be balanced off:

E Williams

19X6			£	19X6			£
Aug	21	Bank	100	Aug	2	Purchases	248
				Aug	18	Purchases	116

K Patterson

19X6		£	19X6		£
Aug 14	Returns outwards	20	Aug 8	Purchases	620
Aug 28	Bank	600	Aug 15	Purchases	200

We now add up the totals and find the balance, i.e. stages 1 and 2.

When balanced these will appear as:

E Williams

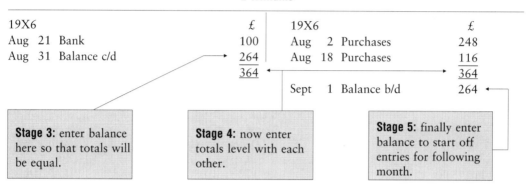

19X6		£	19X6		£
Aug 21	Bank	100	Aug 2	Purchases	248
Aug 31	Balance c/d	264	Aug 18	Purchases	116
		364			364
			Sept 1	Balance b/d	264

Stage 3: enter balance here so that totals will be equal.

Stage 4: now enter totals level with each other.

Stage 5: finally enter balance to start off entries for following month.

K Patterson

19X6		£	19X6		£
Aug 14	Returns outwards	20	Aug 8	Purchases	620
Aug 28	Bank	600	Aug 15	Purchases	200
Aug 31	Balance c/d	200			
		820			820
			Sept 1	Balance b/d	200

The type of accounts which have been demonstrated so far are often known as *T accounts*. This is because the accounts are in the shape of a T, as now illustrated.

Account title here – the top stroke of the T

This line divides the two sides and is the downstroke of the T.

Before you read further attempt Review questions 5.1 and 5.2 on p. 50.

5.3 Computers and accounts

Through the main part of this book the type of account used shows the left-hand side of the account as the debit side, and the right-hand side as the credit side. However, when most computers are used the style of the ledger account is different. It appears as three columns of figures, there being one column for debit entries, another column for credit entries, and the last column for the balance. If you have a current account at a bank your bank statements will normally be shown using this method.

The accounts used in this chapter will now be redrafted to show the ledger accounts drawn up in this way.

K Tandy

			Debit	Credit	Balance (and whether debit or credit)	
19X6			£	£	£	
Aug	1	Sales	144		144	Dr
Aug	19	Sales	300		444	Dr
Aug	22	Bank		144	300	Dr
Aug	28	Bank		300	0	

C Lee

			Debit	Credit	Balance	
19X6			£	£	£	
Aug	11	Sales	177		177	Dr
Aug	19	Sales	203		380	Dr
Aug	22	Sales	100		480	Dr
Aug	30	Bank		480	0	

K Wood

			Debit	Credit	Balance	
19X6			£	£	£	
Aug	6	Sales	214		214	Dr
Aug	12	Bank		214	0	

D Knight

			Debit	Credit	Balance	
19X6			£	£	£	
Aug	1	Sales	158		158	Dr
Aug	15	Sales	206		364	Dr
Aug	28	Cash		158	206	Dr
Aug	31	Sales	118		324	Dr

H Henry

			Debit	Credit	Balance	
19X6			£	£	£	
Aug	5	Sales	300		300	Dr
Aug	24	Returns		50	250	Dr
Aug	28	Sales	540		790	Dr
Aug	29	Bank		250	540	Dr

B Walters

19X6			Debit £	Credit £	Balance £	
Aug	18	Sales	51		51	Dr

E Williams

19X6			Debit £	Credit £	Balance £	
Aug	2	Purchases		248	248	Cr
Aug	18	Purchases		116	364	Cr
Aug	21	Bank	100		264	Cr

K Patterson

19X6			Debit £	Credit £	Balance £	
Aug	8	Purchases		620	620	Cr
Aug	14	Returns	20		600	Cr
Aug	15	Purchases		200	800	Cr
Aug	28	Bank	600		200	Cr

It will be noticed that the balance is calculated again after every entry. This can be done quite simply when using a computer because it is the machine which calculates the new balance.

However, when manual methods are being used it is often too much work to have to calculate a new balance after each entry. It also means that the greater the number of calculations the greater the possibility of errors. For these reasons it is usual for students to use two-sided accounts. However, it is important to note that there is no difference in principle; the final balances are the same using either method.

New terms

Balancing the account (p. 45): Finding and entering the difference between the two sides of an account on the lesser side, so as to equalise the two sides of an account.

Main points to remember

1 Debtors are disclosed by debit balances on customers' accounts.

2 Creditors are disclosed by credit balances on suppliers' accounts.

3 Both T accounts and three-column accounts will disclose the same balance, given identical information about transactions.

Review questions

5.1   Enter the following items in the necessary debtors accounts only; do *not* write up other accounts. Then balance down each personal account at the end of the month. (Keep your answer; it will be used as a basis for question 5.3.)

19X6
May   1   Sales on credit to H Harvey £690, N Morgan £153, J Lindo £420.
  „   4   Sales on credit to L Masters £418, H Harvey £66.
  „   10   Returns inwards from H Harvey £40, J Lindo £20.
  „   18   N Morgan paid us by cheque £153.
  „   20   J Lindo paid us £400 by cheque.
  „   24   H Harvey paid us £300 by cash.
  „   31   Sales on credit to L Masters £203.

5.2   Enter the following in the personal accounts only. Do *not* write up the other accounts. Then balance down each personal account at the end of the month. (Keep your answer, it will be used as the basis for question 5.4.)

19X8
June   1   Purchases on credit from J Young £458, L Williams £120, G Norman £708.
  „   3   Purchases on credit from L Williams £77, T Harris £880.
  „   10   We returned goods to G Norman £22, J Young £55.
  „   15   Purchases on credit from J Young £80.
  „   19   We paid T Harris by cheque £880.
  „   28   We paid J Young by cash £250.
  „   30   We returned goods to L Williams £17.

5.3   Redraft each of the accounts given in your answer to 5.1 in three-column ledger style accounts.

5.4   Redraft each of the accounts given in your answer to 5.2 in three-column ledger style accounts.

5.5   Enter the following in the personal accounts only. Do *not* write up the other accounts. Balance down each personal account at the end of the month. After completing this, state which of the balances represent debtors and those which are creditors.

19X8
Sept   1   Sales on credit to D Williams £458, J Moore £235, G Grant £98.
  „   2   Purchases on credit A White £77, H Samuels £231, P Owen £65.
  „   8   Sales on credit to J Moore £444, F Franklin £249.
  „   10   Purchases on credit from H Samuels £12, O Oliver £222.
  „   12   Returns inwards from G Grant £9, J Moore £26.
  „   17   We returned goods to H Samuels £24, O Oliver £12.
  „   20   We paid A White by cheque £77.
  „   24   D Williams paid us by cheque £300.
  „   26   We paid O Oliver by cash £210.
  „   28   D Williams paid us by cash £100.
  „   30   F Franklin pays us by cheque £249.

5.6A Enter the following, personal accounts only. Bring down balances at end of the month. After completing this state which of the balances represent debtors and those which are creditors.

19X7

May   1   Credit sales B Flynn £241, R Kelly £29, J Long £887, T Fryer £124.

„   2   Credit purchases from S Wood £148, T DuQuesnay £27, R Johnson £77, G Henriques £108.

„   8   Credit sales to R Kelly £74, J Long £132.

„   9   Credit purchases from T DuQuesnay £142, G Henriques £44.

„   10   Goods returned to us by J Long £17, T Fryer £44.

„   12   Cash paid to us by T Fryer £80.

„   15   We returned goods to S Wood £8, G Henriques £18.

„   19   We received cheques from J Long £500, B Flynn £241.

„   21   We sold goods on credit to B Flynn £44, R Kelly £280.

„   28   We paid by cheque the following: S Wood £140, G Henriques £50, R Johnson £60.

„   31   We returned goods to G Henriques £4.

5.7A Redraft each of the accounts given in your answer to 5.6A in three-column style accounts.

6

The trial balance

Objectives

After you have studied this chapter, you should:

- *understand why trial balance totals should equal one another*
- *be able to draw up a trial balance from a given set of accounts*
- *appreciate that some kinds of error can be made but the trial balance totals will still equal one another*

6.1 Total debit entries = Total credit entries

You have already seen that the method of bookkeeping in use is that of the double entry method. This means:

- for each debit entry there is a credit entry;
- for each credit entry there is a debit entry.

All the items recorded in all the accounts on the debit side should equal in *total* all the items recorded on the credit side of the books. We need to check that for each debit entry there is also a credit entry. To see if the two totals are equal, usually known as seeing if the two sides of the books 'balance', a **trial balance** may be drawn up at the end of a period.

A form of a trial balance could be drawn up by listing all the accounts and adding together all the debit entries, at the same time adding together all the credit entries. Using the worked exercise on pp. 29–30, such a trial balance would appear as shown on p. 53. Note that it could not be drawn up until after all the entries have been made. It will therefore be dated as on 31 May 19X9.

Trial Balance as on 31 May 19X9		
	Dr £	Cr £
Purchases	309	
Sales		255
Returns outwards		15
Returns inwards	16	
D Small	68	68
A Lyon & Son		141
D Hughes	60	60
M Spencer	45	16
Cash	<u>210</u>	<u>153</u>
	708	708

6.2 Total debit balances = Total credit balances

The method described in section 6.1 is not the accepted method of drawing up a trial balance, but it is the easiest to understand at first. In fact, a trial balance is a list of balances only, arranged according to whether they are debit balances or credit balances. If the trial balance above had been drawn up using the normal balances method it would appear as follows:

Trial Balance as on 31 May 19X9		
	Dr £	Cr £
Purchases	309	
Sales		255
Returns outwards		15
Returns inwards	16	
A Lyon & Son		141
M Spencer	29	
Cash	<u>57</u>	
	411	411

Here the two sides also 'balance'. The sums of £68 in D Small's account, £60 in D Hughes' account, £16 in M Spencer's account and £153 in the cash account have, however, been cancelled out from each side of these accounts by taking only the *balances* instead of *totals*. As equal amounts have been cancelled from each side, £297 in all, the new totals should still equal one another, as in fact they do at £411.

This form of trial balance is the easiest to extract when there are more than a few transactions during the period. Also, the balances are either used later when the profits are being calculated, or else appear in a balance sheet. Trial balances, therefore, are not just done to find errors.

6.3 Trial balances and errors

It may at first sight appear that the balancing of a trial balance proves that the books are correct. This, however, is quite wrong. It means that certain types of error have not been made, but there are several types of error that will not affect the balancing of a trial balance, such as omitting a transaction altogether. Examples of the errors which would be revealed, provided there are no compensating errors which cancel them out, are errors in additions, using one figure for the debit entry and another figure for the credit entry, entering only one aspect of a transaction, and so on. We shall consider these in greater detail in later chapters.

6.4 Multiple-choice self-test questions

A growing practice of examining boards is to set multiple-choice questions in accounting.

Multiple-choice questions certainly give an examiner the opportunity to cover large parts of the syllabus briefly but in detail. Students who omit to study areas of the syllabus will be caught out by an examiner's use of multiple-choice questions. No longer will it be possible to say that it is highly probable a certain topic will not be tested – the examiner can easily cover it with a multiple-choice question.

We have deliberately set blocks of multiple-choice questions at given places in this textbook, rather than a few at the end of each chapter. Such questions are relatively easy to answer a few minutes after reading the chapter. By asking the questions later your powers of recall and understanding are far better tested. It also gives you practice at answering a few questions in one block, as in an examination.

Each multiple-choice question has a 'stem' – this is a part which poses the problem, a 'key' which is the one correct answer – and a number of 'distractors', i.e. incorrect answers. The key plus the distractors are known as the 'options'.

If you do not know the answer, you should guess. You may be right by chance, or you may remember something subconsciously. In any event, unless the examiner warns otherwise, he will expect you to guess if you don't know the answer.

You should now attempt Set No 1, which contains 20 multiple-choice questions, on pp. 570–3.

New terms

Trial balance (p. 52): A list of account titles and their balances in the books, on a specific date, shown in debit and credit columns.

Main points to remember

1 Trial balances are one form of checking on the arithmetical accuracy of the books.

2 Errors can be made in the accounts which will not be shown up by the trial balance.

Review questions

6.1 You are to enter up the necessary amounts for the month of May from the following details, and then balance off the accounts and extract a trial balance as at 31 May 19X6.

19X6
May 1 Started firm with capital in cash of £250.
  „ 2 Bought goods on credit from the following persons: D Ellis £54; C Mendez £87; K Gibson £25; D Booth £76; L Lowe £64.
  „ 4 Sold goods on credit to: C Bailey £43; B Hughes £62; H Spencer £176.
  „ 6 Paid rent by cash £12.
  „ 9 Bailey paid us his account by cheque £43.
  „ 10 H Spencer paid us £150 by cheque.
  „ 12 We paid the following by cheque: K Gibson £25; D Ellis £54.
  „ 15 Paid carriage by cash £23.
  „ 18 Bought goods on credit from C Mendez £43; D Booth £110.
  „ 21 Sold goods on credit to B Hughes £67.
  „ 31 Paid rent by cheque £18.

6.2 Enter up the books from the following details for the month of March, and extract a trial balance as at 31 March 19X6.

19X6
March 1 Started business with £800 in the bank.
  „ 2 Bought goods on credit from the following persons: K Henriques £76; M Hyatt £27; T Braham £56.
  „ 5 Cash sales £87.
  „ 6 Paid wages in cash £14.
  „ 7 Sold goods on credit to: H Elliott £35; L Lane £42; J Carlton £72.
  „ 9 Bought goods for cash £46.
  „ 10 Bought goods on credit from: M Hyatt £57; T Braham £98.
  „ 12 Paid wages in cash £14.
  „ 13 Sold goods on credit to: L Lane £32; J Carlton £23.
  „ 15 Bought shop fixtures on credit from Betta Ltd £50.
  „ 17 Paid M Hyatt by cheque £84.
  „ 18 We returned goods to T Braham £20.
  „ 21 Paid Betta Ltd a cheque for £50.
  „ 24 J Carlton paid us his account by cheque £95.
  „ 27 We returned goods to K Henriques £24.
  „ 30 J King lent us £60 by cash.
  „ 31 Bought a motor van paying by cheque £400.

6.3A Record the following details for the month of November 19X7 and extract a trial balance as at 30 November:

19X7
Nov 1 Started with £5,000 in the bank.
 „   3 Bought goods on credit from: T Henriques £160; J Smith £230; W Rogers £400; P Boone £310.
 „   5 Cash sales £240.
 „   6 Paid rent by cheque £20.
 „   7 Paid rates by cheque £190.
 „ 11 Sold goods on credit to: L Matthews £48; K Allen £32; R Hall £1,170.
 „ 17 Paid wages by cash £40.
 „ 18 We returned goods to: T Henriques £14; P Boone £20.
 „ 19 Bought goods on credit from: P Boone £80; W Rogers £270; D Diaz £130.
 „ 20 Goods were returned to us by: K Allen £2; L Matthews £4.
 „ 21 Bought motor van on credit from U Z Motors £500.
 „ 23 We paid the following by cheque: T Henriques £146; J Smith £230; W Rogers £300.
 „ 25 Bought another motor van, paying by cheque immediately £700.
 „ 26 Received a loan of £400 cash from A Williams.
 „ 28 Received cheques from: L Matthews £44; K Allen £30.
 „ 30 Proprietor brings a further £300 into the business, by a payment into the business bank account.

6.4A Record the following for the month of January, balance off all the accounts, and then extract a trial balance as at 31 January 19X8:

19X8
Jan 1 Started business with £3,500 cash.
 „   2 Put £2,800 of the cash into a bank account.
 „   3 Bought goods for cash £150.
 „   4 Bought goods on credit from: L Coke £360; M Burton £490; T Hill £110; C Small £340.
 „   5 Bought stationery on credit from Swift Ltd £170.
 „   6 Sold goods on credit to: S Walters £90; T Binns £150; C Howard £190; P Peart £160.
 „   8 Paid rent by cheque £55.
 „ 10 Bought fixtures on credit from Matalon Ltd £480.
 „ 11 Paid salaries in cash £120.
 „ 14 Returned goods to: M Burton £40; T Hill £60.
 „ 15 Bought motor van by cheque £700.
 „ 16 Received loan from J Henry by cheque £600.
 „ 18 Goods returned to us by: S Walters £20; C Howard £40.
 „ 21 Cash sales £90.
 „ 24 Sold goods on credit to: T Binns £100; P Peart £340; J Smart £115.
 „ 26 We paid the following by cheque: M Burton £450; T Hill £50.
 „ 29 Received cheques from: J Smart £115; T Binns £250.
 „ 30 Received a further loan from J Henry by cash £200.
 „ 30 Received £500 cash from P Peart.

Part 2

THE FINAL ACCOUNTS OF SOLE TRADERS

Introduction

This part is concerned with the drawing up, from double entry records, of the final accounts of sole traders.

7

Trading and profit and loss accounts: an introduction

Objectives

After you have studied this chapter, you should:

- *understand the difference between gross profit and net profit*

- *be able to draw up a trading and profit and loss account from information given in a trial balance*

- *recognise that an adjustment is needed for the closing stock at the end of a period*

- *be able to enter up the capital account after the trading and profit and loss accounts have been drawn up*

- *be able to draw up trading and profit and loss accounts using both the horizontal and vertical methods*

7.1 Purpose of trading and profit and loss accounts

The main reason why people set up businesses is to make profits. Of course, if they are not successful they may well incur losses instead. The calculation of such profits and losses is probably the most important objective of the accounting function. The proprietor will want to know how the actual profits compare with the profits he had hoped to make. He may also want to know his profits for such diverse reasons as: to assist him to plan ahead, to help him to obtain a loan from a bank or from a private individual, to show to a prospective partner or to a person to whom he hopes to sell the business, or maybe he will need to know his profits for income tax purposes.

Chapter 4 dealt with the grouping of revenue and expenses prior to bringing them together to compute profit. In the case of a trader, meaning by this someone who is mainly concerned with buying and selling, the profits are calculated by drawing up a special account called a **Trading and Profit and Loss Account**. For a manufacturer it is also useful to prepare **Manufacturing Accounts** as well, but this will be dealt with in a later chapter.

7.2 Format for the trading and profit and loss account

One of the most important uses of the trading and profit and loss accounts is that of comparing the results obtained with the results expected. In a trading organisation a lot of attention is paid to how much profit is made, before deducting expenses, for every £100 of sales. So that this can easily be seen in the profit calculations, the account in which profit is calculated is split into two sections – one in which the **Gross Profit** is found, and the next section in which the **Net Profit** is calculated.

Gross Profit (calculated in the **trading account**)	This is the excess of sales over the cost of goods sold in the period.
Net Profit (calculated in the **profit and loss account**)	This is what is left of the gross profit after all other expenses have been deducted.

The gross profit, found by the use of the **Trading Account,** is the excess of sales over the cost of goods sold. The net profit, found when the **Profit and Loss Account** is prepared, consists of the gross profit plus any revenue other than that from sales, such as discounts received or commissions earned, less the total costs used up during the period. Where the cost of goods sold is greater than the sales the result would be a **Gross Loss,** but this is a relatively rare occurrence. Where the costs used up exceed the gross profit plus other revenue then the result is said to be a **Net Loss.** By taking the figure of sales less the cost of goods sold, it can be seen that the accounting custom is to calculate a trader's profits only when the goods have been disposed of and not before.

7.3 Horizontal and vertical trading and profit and loss accounts

In the next section, 7.4, we will look at trading and profit and loss accounts drawn up using the horizontal style. The left-hand side is the debit side, whilst the right-hand side is the credit side of these accounts. These accounts can therefore be seen as part of the double entry system, and students should be able to understand why each item is shown as a debit or a credit in them.

In section 7.6 we will see how the trading and profit and loss account can be shown using a vertical style.

7.4 Information needed

Before drawing up a trading and profit and loss account you should get out the trial balance. This contains nearly all the information needed. (Later on in this book you will see that certain adjustments have to be made, but we will ignore these at this stage.)

The trial balance of B Swift, Exhibit 7.1 drawn up as on 31 December 19X5 after the completion of his first year in business, can now be looked at.

Exhibit 7.1

B Swift Trial Balance as on 31 December 19X5		
	Dr	Cr
	£	£
Sales		3,850
Purchases	2,900	
Rent	240	
Lighting expenses	150	
General expenses	60	
Fixtures and fittings	500	
Debtors	680	
Creditors		910
Bank	1,510	
Cash	20	
Drawings	700	
Capital		2,000
	6,760	6,760

Usually some of the goods bought (purchases) have not been sold by the end of the accounting period. We have already seen that gross profit is calculated as follows:

> **Sales – Cost of Goods Sold = Gross Profit**

However, purchases only equal cost of goods sold if there is no stock at the end of a period. We can calculate cost of goods sold as follows:

What we bought in the period:	Purchases
Less Goods bought but not sold in the period:	Closing stock
	= Cost of goods sold

However, there is no record in the books of the value of the unsold stock on 31 December 19X5 for B Swift. The only way that Swift can find this figure is by stock-taking on 31 December 19X5 at the close of business. To do this he would have to make a list of all the unsold goods and then find out their value. The value he would normally place on them would be the cost price of the goods. Let us assume that this works out to be £300.

The cost of goods sold figure will be:

	£
Purchases	2,900
Less Closing stock	300
Cost of goods sold	2,600

Given the figure of sales £3,850, the gross profit can be calculated:

Sales – Cost of Goods Sold = Gross Profit
£3,850 – £2,600   = £1,250

This, however, is not performing the task by using double entry accounts. In double entry the following entries must be made.

The balance of the sales account is transferred to the trading account by:

1 Debiting the sales account (thus closing it).
2 Crediting the trading account.

The balance of the purchases account is transferred to the trading account by:

1 Debiting the trading account.
2 Crediting the purchases account (thus closing it).

There is as yet no entry for the closing stock in the double entry accounts. This is achieved as follows:

1 Debit a stock account with the value of the closing stock.
2 Credit the trading account (thus completing double entry).

It is now usual for the trading and profit and loss accounts to be shown under one combined heading, the trading account being the top section and the profit and loss account being the lower section of this combined account.

B Swift
Trading and Profit and Loss Account for the year ended 31 December 19X5

	£		£
Purchases	2,900	Sales	3,850
Gross profit c/d	1,250	Closing stock	300
	4,150		4,150
		Gross profit b/d	1,250

The balance shown on the trading account is shown as gross profit rather than being described as a balance. When found, the gross profit is carried down to the profit and loss section of the account. The accounts so far used appear as follows:

Sales

19X5		£	19X5		£
Dec	3 Trading	3,850	Dec 31	Balance b/d	3,850

Purchases

19X5		£	19X5		£
Dec 31	Balance b/d	2,900	Dec 31	Trading	2,900

Stock

19X5		£	
Dec 31	Trading	300	

The entry of the closing stock on the credit side of the trading and profit and loss account is in effect a deduction from the purchases on the debit side. In present-day accounting it is usual to find the closing stock actually shown as a deduction from the purchases on the debit side, and the figure then disclosed being described as 'cost of goods sold'. This is illustrated in Exhibit 7.2.

It must be remembered that we are concerned here with the very first year of trading, where there is no opening stock. In section 9.3 we will examine the accounting for stock in the later years of a business.

The profit and loss account can now be drawn up. Any revenue accounts, other than sales which have already been dealt with, would be transferred to the credit of the profit and loss account. Typical examples are commissions received and rent received. In the case of B Swift there are no such revenue accounts.

The costs used up in the year, in other words the expenses of the year, are transferred to the debit of the profit and loss account. It may also be thought, quite rightly so, that as the fixtures and fittings have been used during the year with the subsequent deterioration of the asset, that something should be charged for this use. The methods for doing this are left until Chapter 25.

The revised trading account with the addition of the profit and loss account will now appear as follows:

Exhibit 7.2

B Swift
Trading and Profit and Loss Account for the year ended 31 December 19X5

	£		£
Purchases	2,900	Sales	3,850
Less Closing stock	300		
Cost of goods sold	2,600		
Gross profit c/d	1,250		
	3,850		3,850
Rent	240	Gross profit b/d	1,250
Lighting expenses	150		
General expenses	60		
Net profit	800		
	1,250		1,250

The expense accounts closed off will now appear as:

Rent

19X5	£	19X5	£
Dec 31 Balance b/d	240	Dec 31 Profit and loss	240

Lighting Expenses

19X5	£	19X5	£
Dec 31 Balance b/d	150	Dec 31 Profit and loss	150

General Expenses

19X5	£	19X5	£
Dec 31 Balance b/d	60	Dec 31 Profit and loss	60

7.5 Effect on the capital account

Although the net profit has been calculated at £800, and is shown as a debit entry in the profit and loss account, no credit entry has yet been made. This now needs to be done. As net profit increases the capital of the proprietor the credit entry must be made in the capital account.

The trading and profit and loss accounts, and indeed all the revenue and expense accounts, can thus be seen to be devices whereby the capital account is saved from being concerned with unnecessary detail. Every sale of a good at a profit increases the capital of the proprietor as does each item of revenue such as rent received. On the other hand each sale of a good at a loss, or each item of expense, decreases the capital of the proprietor. Instead of altering the capital afresh after each transaction the respective items of profit and loss and of revenue and expense are collected together using suitably described accounts. Then the whole of the details are brought together in one set of accounts, the trading and profit and loss account, and the increase to the capital, i.e. the net profit, is determined. Alternatively, the decrease in the capital as represented by the net loss is ascertained.

The fact that a separate drawings account has been in use can now also be seen to have been in keeping with the policy of avoiding unnecessary detail in the capital account. There will thus be one figure for drawings which will be the total of the drawings for the whole of the period, and will be transferred to the debit of the capital account.

The capital account, showing these transfers, and the drawings account now closed are as follows:

Capital

19X5		£	19X5		£
Dec 31	Drawings	700	Jan 1	Cash	2,000
„ 31	Balance c/d	2,100	Dec 31	Net profit from Profit and loss	800
		2,800			2,800
			19X6		
			Jan 1	Balance b/d	2,100

Drawings

19X5		£	19X5		£
Dec 31	Balance b/d	700	Dec 31	Capital	700

7.6 The vertical style for trading and profit and loss accounts

We will now use in Exhibit 7.3 the vertical style for drawing up a trading and profit and loss account, using the information in Exhibit 7.2. It looks as follows:

Exhibit 7.3

B Swift
Trading and Profit and Loss Account for the year ended 31 December 19X5

	£	£
Sales		3,850
Less Cost of goods sold:		
Purchases	2,900	
Less Closing stock	300	2,600
Gross profit		1,250
Less Expenses		
Rent	240	
Lighting expenses	150	
General expenses	60	450
Net profit		800

You can see that the figures used are exactly the same with either the horizontal or vertical methods of display.

This is a more modern method of presentation. It would make more sense to someone who knew very little about accounting, as it does not show it in a debit/credit way.

However, showing the horizontal style first probably makes it easier to see how the double entry system is used to calculate profits.

7.7 The balances still in our books

It should be noticed that not all the items in the trial balance have been used in the trading and profit and loss account. The remaining balances are assets or liabilities or capital, they are not expenses or sales. These will be used up later when a balance sheet is drawn up, for as has been shown in Chapter 1, assets, liabilities and capital are shown in balance sheets.

In Exhibit 7.4, although it is not necessary to redraft the trial balance after the trading and profit and loss accounts have been prepared, it will be useful to do so in order to establish which balances still remain in the books. The first thing to notice is that the stock account, not originally in the trial balance, is in the redrafted trial balance, as the item was not created as a balance in the books until the trading account was prepared. These balances will be used by us when we start to look at the balance sheets.

Exhibit 7.4

B Swift
Trial Balance as on 31 December 19X5
(after Trading and Profit and Loss Accounts completed)

	Dr	Cr
	£	£
Fixtures and fittings	500	
Debtors	680	
Creditors		910
Stock	300	
Bank	1,510	
Cash	20	
Capital		2,100
	3,010	3,010

New terms

Gross loss (p. 60): Where the cost of goods sold exceeds the sales figure.

Gross profit (p. 60): Found by deducting cost of goods sold from the figure of sales.

Net loss (p. 60): Where the cost of goods sold plus expenses is greater than the revenue.

Net profit (p. 60): Gross profit less expenses.

Profit and loss account (p. 60): Account in which net profit is calculated.

Trading account (p. 60): Account in which gross profit is calculated.

Trading and profit and loss account (p. 59): Combined account in which both gross and net profits are calculated.

Main points to remember

1 Stocks of unsold goods need to be brought into the calculations in the trading account.

2 The net profit is added to capital by crediting it in the capital account.

3 Balances on accounts not closed off are carried forward to the following period.

4 Trading and profit and loss accounts can be drawn up using either a 'horizontal' or a 'vertical' style. The gross and net profits calculated are the same whichever method is used.

Review questions

7.1   From the following trial balance of B Webb, extracted after one year's trading, prepare a trading and profit and loss account for the year ended 31 December 19X6. A balance sheet is not required.

Trial Balance as on 31 December 19X6

	Dr £	Cr £
Sales		18,462
Purchases	14,629	
Salaries	2,150	
Motor expenses	520	
Rent	670	
Insurance	111	
General expenses	105	
Premises	1,500	
Motor vehicles	1,200	
Debtors	1,950	
Creditors		1,538
Cash at bank	1,654	
Cash in hand	40	
Drawings	895	
Capital		5,424
	25,424	25,424

Stock at 31 December 19X6 was £2,548.

(Keep your answer; it will be used later in question 8.1)

7.2 From the following trial balance of C Worth after his first year's trading, you are required to draw up a trading and profit and loss account for the year ended 30 June 19X8. A balance sheet is not required.

Trial Balance as on 30 June 19X8

	Dr	Cr
	£	£
Sales		28,794
Purchases	23,803	
Rent	854	
Lighting and heating expenses	422	
Salaries and wages	3,164	
Insurance	105	
Buildings	50,000	
Fixtures	1,000	
Debtors	3,166	
Sundry expenses	506	
Creditors		1,206
Cash at bank	3,847	
Drawings	2,400	
Motor vans	5,500	
Motor running expenses	1,133	
Capital		65,900
	95,900	95,900

Stock at 30 June 19X8 was £4,166.

(Keep your answer; it will be used later in question 8.2)

7.3A From the following trial balance of F Chaplin drawn up on conclusion of his first year in business, draw up a trading and profit and loss account for the year ended 31 December 19X8. A balance sheet is not required.

Trial Balance as on 31 December 19X8

	Dr	Cr
	£	£
General expenses	210	
Rent	400	
Motor expenses	735	
Salaries	3,560	
Insurance	392	
Purchases	18,385	
Sales		26,815
Motor vehicle	2,800	
Creditors		5,160
Debtors	4,090	
Premises	20,000	
Cash at bank	1,375	
Cash in hand	25	
Capital		24,347
Drawings	4,350	
	56,322	56,322

Stock at 31 December 19X8 was £4,960.

(Keep your answer; it will be used later in question 8.3A)

7.4A Extract a trading and profit and loss account for the year ended 30 June 19X8 for F Kidd. The trial balance as at 30 June 19X8 after his first year of trading was as follows:

	Dr	Cr
	£	£
Rent	1,560	
Insurance	305	
Lighting and heating expenses	516	
Motor expenses	1,960	
Salaries and wages	4,850	
Sales		35,600
Purchases	30,970	
Sundry expenses	806	
Motor vans	3,500	
Creditors		3,250
Debtors	6,810	
Fixtures	3,960	
Buildings	28,000	
Cash at bank	1,134	
Drawings	6,278	
Capital		51,799
	90,649	90,649

Stock at 30 June 19X8 was £9,960.

(Keep your answer; it will be used later in question 8.4A)

8

Balance sheets

Objectives

After you have studied this chapter, you should:

- *be able to draw up a balance sheet from information given in a trial balance*

- *understand that balance sheets are not part of the double entry system*

- *appreciate the need for showing balances under the headings 'fixed assets', 'current assets', 'current liabilities' and 'capital'*

- *be able to draw up balance sheets using both the horizontal and the vertical methods*

8.1 Contents of the balance sheet

You saw in Chapter 1 that balance sheets contain details of assets, liabilities and capital. These details have to be found in our records and then written out as a balance sheet.

It is easy to find these details. They consist of all the balances remaining in our records once the trading and profit and loss account for the period has been completed. All balances remaining have to be assets, capital or liabilities. All the other balances should have been closed off when the trading and profit and loss account was completed.

8.2 Drawing up a balance sheet (horizontal style)

Let us now look at Exhibit 8.1, the trial balance of B Swift (from Exhibit 7.4) as on 31 December 19X5 *after* the trading and profit and loss account had been prepared.

Exhibit 8.1

B Swift Trial Balance as on 31 December 19X5 (after Trading and Profit and Loss Account completed)		
	Dr £	*Cr* £
Fixtures and fittings	500	
Debtors	680	
Creditors		910
Stock	300	
Bank	1,510	
Cash	20	
Capital		2,100
	3,010	3,010

We can now draw up the balance sheet as at 31 December 19X5 using the horizontal style as in Exhibit 8.2 (the vertical style will be shown later in section 8.6). You saw examples of balance sheets in Chapter 1. We will not worry at this point whether or not this balance sheet is set out in good style.

As you saw in Chapter 1, assets are shown on the left-hand side, capital and liabilities on the right-hand side.

Exhibit 8.2

B Swift
Balance Sheet as at 31 December 19X5

Assets	£	*Capital and liabilities*	£
Fixtures and fittings	500	Capital	2,100
Stock	300	Creditors	910
Debtors	680		
Bank	1,510		
Cash	20		
	3,010		3,010

8.3 No double entry in balance sheets

It may seem very strange to you to learn that balance sheets are *not* part of the double entry system.

When we draw up accounts such as cash account, rent account, sales account, trading and profit and loss account and so on, then we are writing up part of the double entry system. We make entries on the debit sides and the credit sides of these accounts.

In drawing up a balance sheet we do not enter anything in the various accounts. We do not actually transfer the fixtures balance or the stock balance, or any of the others, to the balance sheet.

All we do is to *list* the asset, capital and liabilities balances so as to form a balance sheet. This means that none of these accounts have been closed off. *Nothing is entered in the accounts.*

When the next accounting period starts, these accounts are still open containing balances. As a result of business transactions, entries are then made in them to add to, or deduct from, the amounts shown in the accounts using normal double entry.

If you see the word 'account', you will know that it is part of the double entry system and will include debit and credit entries. If the word 'account' cannot be used, it is not part of double entry. For instance, the following items are not 'accounts', and are therefore *not* part of the double entry:

Trial balance: This is simply a proof of the equality of debit and credit balances in the accounts.

Balance sheet: A list of balances arranged according to whether they are assets, capital or liabilities, to depict the financial situation on a specific date.

8.4 Balance sheet layout

You would not expect to go into a department store and see goods for sale all mixed up and not laid out properly. You would expect that the goods would be displayed so that you could easily find them. Similarly, in balance sheets we do not want all the items shown in any order. We want them displayed so that useful information can easily be seen.

For people such as bank managers, accountants and investors who look at a lot of different balance sheets, we want to keep to one method so as to make a comparison of balance sheets easier. What you are going to look at now is a method for showing items in balance sheets.

Assets

Let us look at the assets side first. We are going to show the assets under two headings, **Fixed Assets** and **Current Assets**.

Assets are called fixed assets when they:

1   are of long life;
2   are to be used in the business; and
3   were not bought only for the purposes of resale.

Examples: buildings, machinery, motor vehicles, fixtures and fittings.

Fixed assets are listed starting with those the business will keep the longest, down to those which will not be kept so long. For instance:

Fixed Assets
1 Land and buildings
2 Fixtures and fittings
3 Machinery
4 Motor vehicles

Current assets are cash in hand, cash at bank, items held for resale at a profit or items that have a short life.

These are listed starting with the asset furthest away from being turned into cash, finishing with cash itself. For instance:

Current Assets
1 Stock
2 Debtors
3 Cash at bank
4 Cash in hand

The order with which most students would disagree is that stock has appeared before debtors. On first sight stock would appear to be more easily realisable than debtors. In fact, however, debtors could normally be more quickly turned into cash by factorising them, i.e. selling the rights to the amounts owing to a finance company for an agreed amount. On the other hand, to dispose of all the stock of a business is often a long and difficult task. Another advantage is that the method follows the order in which full realisation of the assets takes place. First, before any sale takes place there must be a stock of goods, which when sold on credit turns into debtors, and when payment is made by the debtors it turns into cash.

Capital and liabilities

The order on the other side of a horizontal style balance sheet is:

- Capital
- Long-term liabilities: for instance, loans which do not have to be repaid in the near future, this being taken to be the next twelve months.
- Current liabilities: items to be paid for in the near future.

In section 8.6 we will consider how capital and liabilities are shown in a vertical style balance sheet.

8.5 A properly drawn up balance sheet (horizontal style)

Exhibit 8.3 shows Exhibit 8.2 drawn up in better style. Also read the notes following the exhibit.

Exhibit 8.3

B Swift
Balance Sheet as at 31 December 19X5

Fixed assets	£	£	Capital	£	£
Furniture and					
fittings		500	Cash introduced	2,000	
			Add Net profit for		
			the year	800	
Current assets				2,800	
Stock	300				
Debtors	680		*Less* Drawings	700	
Bank	1,510				2,100
Cash	20		*Current liabilities*		
		2,510	Creditors		910
		3,010			3,010

Notes to Exhibit 8.3

(a) A total for capital and for each class of liabilities should be shown. An example of this is the £2,510 total of current assets. To do this the figures for each asset are listed, and only the total is shown in the end column.

(b) You do not have to write the word 'account' after each item.

(c) The owner will be most interested in his capital. To show only the final balance of £2,100 means that the owner will not know how it was calculated. So we show the full details of his capital account.

(d) Look at the date on the balance sheet. Now compare it with the dates put on the top of the trading and profit and loss account. The balance sheet is a position statement – it is shown as being at one point in time, i.e. as at 31 December 19X5. The trading and profit and loss account is different. It is for a period of time, in this case for a whole year.

8.6 Vertical style balance sheets

Exhibit 8.3 is now shown using the more modern vertical style:

B Swift
Balance Sheet as at 31 December 19X5

	£	£
Fixed assets		
Furniture and fittings		500
Current assets		
Stock	300	
Debtors	680	
Bank	1,510	
Cash	20	
	2,510	
Less Current liabilities		
Creditors	910	1,600
		2,100
Capital		
Cash introduced		2,000
Add Net profit for the year		800
		2,800
Less Drawings		700
		2,100

8.7 Examinations and vertical and horizontal style final accounts

Many examiners will prefer answers to be given using vertical style final accounts. However, questions are often asked in which the information given in the question uses horizontal style final accounts.

As examinations vary worldwide, it is best if students follow the advice given to them by their teacher or lecturer.

New terms

Current assets (p. 71): Assets consisting of cash, goods for resale or items having a short life.

Current liabilities (p. 72): Liabilities to be paid for in the near future, which is taken to be one year.

Fixed assets (p. 71): Assets bought which have a long life and are to be used in the business.

Long-term liabilities (p. 72): Liabilities that do not have to be paid within the next twelve months.

Main points to remember

1 All balances remaining on a trial balance after the trading and profit and loss account for a period has been drawn up are displayed in a balance sheet dated the last day of the period.

2 The balance sheet is *not* part of double entry.

3 Capital is shown before liabilities in a horizontal balance sheet.

4 Both horizontal and vertical style balance sheets show the same information, but presented in different ways.

Review questions

8.1 Complete question 7.1 by drawing up a balance sheet as at 31 December 19X6.

8.2 Complete question 7.2 by drawing up a balance sheet as at 30 June 19X8.

8.3A Complete question 7.3A by drawing up a balance sheet as at 31 December 19X8.

8.4A Complete question 7.4A by drawing up a balance sheet as at 30 June 19X8.

9

Trading and profit and loss accounts and balance sheets: further considerations

Objectives

After you have studied this chapter, you should:

- *be able to record returns inwards and returns outwards in the final accounts*

- *understand that carriage inwards on goods is treated to be part of the cost of the goods*

- *realise that carriage outwards is an expense to be entered in the profit and loss account*

- *be able to adjust the final accounts properly for both the opening and closing stocks of the period*

- *appreciate that costs of putting goods into a saleable condition should be charged to the trading account in a merchandising firm*

9.1 Returns inwards and returns outwards

In Chapter 3 the idea of different accounts for different movements of stock was introduced. There were accordingly sales, purchases, returns inwards and returns outwards accounts. In our first look at the preparation of a trading account in Chapter 7, returns inwards and returns outwards were omitted. This was done deliberately so that the first sight of trading and profit and loss accounts would not be a difficult one.

However, a large number of firms will return goods to their suppliers (returns outwards), and will have goods returned to them by their customers (returns inwards). When the gross profit is calculated these returns will have to come into the calculations. Suppose that in Exhibit 7.1, the trial balance of B Swift, the balances showing stock movements had instead been as follows:

B Swift Trial Balance as on 31 December 19X5	Dr	Cr
	£	£
Sales		4,000
Purchases	3,120	
Returns inwards	150	
Returns outwards		220

Looking at Exhibit 7.1 it can be seen that originally the example used was of Sales £3,850 and Purchases £2,900. If it had been as now shown instead, the Trading Account can be shown as it would have been for the year, and what gross profit would have been.

Comparing the two instances, they do in fact amount to the same thing as far as gross profit is concerned. Sales were £3,850 in the original example. In the new example returns inwards should be deducted to get the correct figure for goods sold to customers and *kept* by them, i.e. £4,000 – £150 = £3,850. Purchases were £2,900; in the new example returns outwards should be deducted to get the correct figure of purchases *kept* by Swift. The gross profit will remain at £1,250 as per Exhibit 7.1.

The trading account will appear as in Exhibit 9.1 in horizontal style, and as Exhibit 9.2 using the vertical style.

Exhibit 9.1 *Horizontal style*

Trading and Profit and Loss Account for the year ended 31 December 19X5

	£	£		£	£
Purchases	3,120		Sales	4,000	
Less Returns outwards	220	2,900	*Less* Returns inwards	150	3,850
Less Closing stock		300			
Cost of goods sold		2,600			
Gross profit c/d		1,250			
		3,850			3,850

The term used for Sales less Returns Inwards is often called 'Turnover'. In the illustration in Exhibit 9.1 it is £3,850.

Exhibit 9.2 *Vertical style*

Trading and Profit and Loss Account for the year ended 31 December 19X5

	£	£
Sales	4,000	
Less Returns inwards	150	3,850
Less Cost of goods sold:		
Purchases	3,120	
Less Returns outwards	220	
	2,900	
Less Closing stock	300	2,600
Gross profit		1,250

9.2 Carriage

Carriage (cost of transport of goods) into a firm is called **carriage inwards**. Carriage of goods out of a firm to its customers is called **carriage outwards**.

When goods are bought the cost of carriage inwards may either be included as part of the price, or else the firm may have to pay separately for it. Suppose the firm was buying exactly the same goods. One supplier might sell them for £100, and he would deliver the goods and not send you a bill for carriage. Another supplier might sell the goods for £95, but you would have to pay £5 to a haulage firm for carriage inwards, i.e. a total cost of £100.

To keep cost of buying goods being shown on the same basis, carriage inwards is always added to the purchases in the trading account.

Carriage outwards to customers is not part of our firm's expenses in buying goods, and is always entered in the profit and loss account.

Suppose that in the illustration shown in this chapter, the goods had been bought for the same total figure of £3,120, but in fact £2,920 was the figure for purchases and £200 for carriage inwards. The trial balance and trading accounts using both horizontal and vertical styles appear as Exhibit 9.3.

Exhibit 9.3

	Dr	Cr
Trial Balance as at 31 December 19X5		
	£	£
Sales		4,000
Purchases	2,920	
Returns inwards	150	
Returns outwards		220
Carriage inwards	200	

Horizontal style

Trading and Profit and Loss Account for the year ended 31 December 19X5

	£	£		£	£
Purchases	2,920		Sales	4,000	
Less Returns outwards	220	2,700	*Less* Returns inwards	150	3,850
Carriage inwards		200			
		2,900			
Less Closing stock		300			
Cost of goods sold		2,600			
Gross profit c/d		1,250			
		3,850			3,850
			Gross profit b/d		1,250

Vertical style

Trading and Profit and Loss Account for the year ended 31 December 19X5

	£	£
Sales	4,000	
Less Returns inwards	150	3,850
Less Cost of goods sold:		
Purchases	2,920	
Less Returns outwards	220	
	2,700	
Carriage inwards	200	
	2,900	
Less Closing stock	300	2,600
Gross profit		1,250

It can be seen that Exhibits 7.1, 9.1 and 9.3 have been concerned with the same overall amount of goods bought and sold by the firm, at the same overall prices. Therefore, in each case the same gross profit of £1,250 is shown.

Before you proceed further, attempt Exercises 9.1 and 9.2A.

9.3 The second year of a business

At the end of his second year of trading, on 31 December 19X6, B Swift extracts another trial balance.

Exhibit 9.4

B Swift
Trial Balance as at 31 December 19X6

	Dr	Cr
	£	£
Sales		6,700
Purchases	4,260	
Lighting and heating expenses	190	
Rent	240	
Wages: shop assistant	520	
General expenses	70	
Carriage outwards	110	
Buildings	2,000	
Fixtures and fittings	750	
Debtors	1,200	
Creditors		900
Bank	120	
Cash	40	
Drawings	900	
Capital		3,100
Stock (at 31 December 19X5)	300	
	10,700	10,700

Adjustments needed for stock

Previously we have done the accounts for new businesses only. They started without stock and therefore had closing stock only, as we were doing the first trading and profit and loss account.

When we prepare the trading and profit and loss account for the second year we can now see the difference. Looking at Exhibits 8.1 (p. 70) and 9.4 for B Swift we can see the stock figures needed for the trading accounts:

Trading Account for period ————————→	Year to 31 December 19X5	Year to 31 December 19X6
Opening stock 1.1.19X5	None	
Closing stock 31.12.19X5	£300	
Opening stock 1.1. 19X6		£300
Closing stock 31.12.19X6		£550 (see note below)

This means that calculations for the first year of trading, to 31 December 19X5, had only one stock figure included in them. This was the closing stock. For the second year of trading, to 31 December 19X6, both opening and closing stock figures will be in the calculations.

The stock shown in the trial balance, Exhibit 9.4, is that brought forward from the previous year on 31 December 19X5; it is, therefore, the opening stock of 19X6. The closing stock at 31 December 19X6 can only be found by stock-taking. Assume it amounts at cost to be £550.

Let us first of all calculate the cost of goods sold for 19X6:

	£
Stock of goods at start of year	300
Add Purchases	4,260
Total goods available for sale	4,560
Less What remains at the end of the year:	
i.e. stock of goods at close	550
Therefore cost of goods that have been sold	4,010

We can look at a diagram to illustrate this – *see* Exhibit 9.5.

Exhibit 9.5

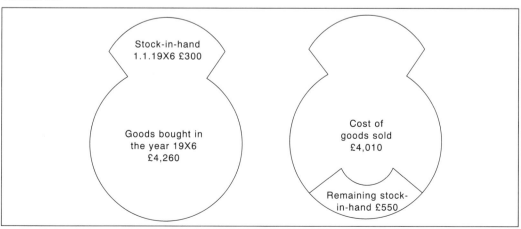

The sales were £6,700, so Sales £6,700 – Cost of Goods Sold £4,010 = Gross Profit £2,690.

Now the trading and profit and loss accounts can be drawn up in the horizontal style using double entry – *see* Exhibit 9.6. They are shown in the vertical style in Exhibit 9.8.

Exhibit 9.6 *Horizontal style*

B Swift
Trading and Profit and Loss Account for the year ended 31 December 19X6

	£		£
Opening stock	300	Sales	6,700
Add Purchases	4,260		
	4,560		
Less Closing stock	550		
Cost of goods sold	4,010		
Gross profit c/d	2,690		
	6,700		6,700
Wages	520	Gross profit b/d	2,690
Lighting and heating expenses	190		
Rent	240		
General expenses	70		
Carriage outwards	110		
Net profit	1,560		
	2,690		2,690

The balances now remaining in the books, including the new balance on the stock account, are now drawn up in the form of a horizontal style balance sheet – *see* Exhibit 9.7.

Exhibit 9.7 *Horizontal style*

B Swift
Balance Sheet as at 31 December 19X6

Fixed assets	£	£	*Capital*	£	£
Buildings		2,000	Balance 1 Jan 19X6	3,100	
Fixtures and fittings		750	Add net profit for year	1,560	
		2,750		4,660	
			Less Drawings	900	
Current assets					3,760
Stock	550		*Current liabilities*		
Debtors	1,200		Creditors		900
Bank	120				
Cash	40				
		1,910			
		4,660			4,660

Exhibits 9.8 and 9.9 show the same items using the vertical style.

Stock account

It is perhaps helpful if the stock account covering both years can now be seen:

Stock

19X5	£	19X6	£
Dec 31 Trading A/c	300	Jan 1 Trading A/c	300
19X5			
Dec 31 Trading A/c	550		

Exhibit 9.8 *Vertical style*

B Swift
Trading and Profit and Loss Account for the year ended 31 December 19X6

	£	£
Sales		6,700
Less Cost of goods sold:		
Opening stock	300	
Add Purchases	4,260	
	4,560	
Less Closing stock	550	4,010
Gross profit		2,690
Less Expenses:		
Wages	520	
Lighting and heating expenses	190	
Rent	240	
General expenses	70	
Carriage outwards	110	1,130
Net profit		1,560

Exhibit 9.9 *Vertical style*

B Swift
Balance Sheet as at 31 December 19X6

	£	£
Fixed assets		
Buildings	2,000	
Fixtures and fittings	750	2,750
Current assets		
Stock	550	
Debtors	1,200	
Bank	120	
Cash	40	
	1,910	
Less Current liabilities		
Creditors	900	1,010
		3,760
Financed by:		
Capital: Balance at 1 January 19X6	3,100	
Add Net profit for the year	1,560	
	4,660	
Less Drawings	900	3,760

Final accounts

The term **Final Accounts** is often used to mean collectively the trading and profit and loss account and the balance sheet. The term can be misleading as the balance sheet is not an account.

Other expenses in the trading account

The costs of putting goods into a saleable condition should be charged in the trading account. In the case of a trader these are relatively few. An instance could be a trader who sells clocks packed in boxes. If he bought the clocks from one source, and the boxes from another source, both of these items would be charged in the trading account as purchases. In addition, if a person's wages are paid to pack the clocks, then such wages would be charged in the trading account. The wages of shop assistants who sold the clocks would be charged in the profit and loss account. The wages of the person packing the clocks would be the only wages in this instance concerned with 'putting the goods into a saleable condition'.

For goods imported from abroad it is usual to find that the costs of import duty, marine insurance and freight, etc., are also treated as part of the cost of goods sold and are therefore debited to the trading account.

9.4 Review questions: the best approach

Before you attempt the review questions at the end of this chapter, you should read Appendix 1 on page 560.

New terms

Carriage inwards (p. 77): Cost of transport of goods into a business.

Carriage outwards (p. 77): Cost of transport of goods out to the customers of a business.

Final accounts (p. 82): Term that includes the trading and profit and loss accounts and balance sheet.

Main points to remember

1 Carriage inwards is shown as an expense item in the trading account.

2 Carriage outwards is shown as an expense in the profit and loss account.

3 In the second and later years of a business, both opening and closing stocks are brought into the trading account.

4 It is normal practice to show cost of goods sold as a separate figure in the trading account.

5 Expense items concerned with getting the goods into a saleable condition are charged in the trading account.

6 Returns inwards should be deducted from sales in the trading account.

7 Returns outwards should be deducted from purchases in the trading account.

8 For goods imported from abroad, the costs of import duty, insurance and freight are treated as part of the cost of goods sold.

Review questions

9.1   From the following details draw up the trading account of T Clarke for the year ended 31 December 19X7, which was his first year in business:

	£
Carriage inwards	670
Returns outwards	495
Returns inwards	890
Sales	38,742
Purchases	33,333
Stocks of goods: 31 December 19X7	7,489

9.2A   The following details for the year ended 31 March 19X8 are available. Draw up the trading account of K Taylor for that year.

	£
Stocks: 31 March 19X8	18,504
Returns inwards	1,372
Returns outwards	2,896
Purchases	53,397
Carriage inwards	1,122
Sales	54,600

9.3   From the following trial balance of R Graham draw up a trading and profit and loss account for the year ended 30 September 19X9, and a balance sheet as at that date.

	Dr	Cr
	£	£
Stock 1 October 19X8	2,368	
Carriage outwards	200	
Carriage inwards	310	
Returns inwards	205	
Returns outwards		322
Purchases	11,874	
Sales		18,600
Salaries and wages	3,862	
Rent	304	
Insurance	78	
Motor expenses	664	
Office expenses	216	
Lighting and heating expenses	166	
General expenses	314	
Premises	5,000	
Motor vehicles	1,800	
Fixtures and fittings	350	
Debtors	3,896	
Creditors		1,731
Cash at bank	482	
Drawings	1,200	
Capital		12,636
	33,289	33,289

Stock at 30 September 19X9 was £2,946.

9.4   The following trial balance was extracted from the books of B Jackson on 30 April 19X7. From it, and the note re stock, prepare his trading and profit and loss account for the year ended 30 April 19X7, and a balance sheet as at that date.

	Dr	Cr
	£	£
Sales		18,600
Purchases	11,556	
Stock 1 May 19X6	3,776	
Carriage outwards	326	
Carriage inwards	234	
Returns inwards	440	
Returns outwards		355
Salaries and wages	2,447	
Motor expenses	664	
Rent	576	
Sundry expenses	1,202	
Motor vehicles	2,400	
Fixtures and fittings	600	
Debtors	4,577	
Creditors		3,045
Cash at bank	3,876	
Cash in hand	120	
Drawings	2,050	
Capital		12,844
	34,844	34,844

Stock at 30 April 19X7 was £4,998.

9.5A   The following is the trial balance of J Smailes as at 31 March 19X9. Draw up a set of final accounts for the year ended 31 March 19X9.

	Dr	Cr
	£	£
Stock 1 April 19X8	18,160	
Sales		92,340
Purchases	69,185	
Carriage inwards	420	
Carriage outwards	1,570	
Returns outwards		640
Wages and salaries	10,240	
Rent and rates	3,015	
Communication expenses	624	
Commissions payable	216	
Insurance	405	
Sundry expenses	318	
Buildings	20,000	
Debtors	14,320	
Creditors		8,160
Fixtures	2,850	
Cash at bank	2,970	
Cash in hand	115	
Drawings	7,620	
Capital		50,888
	152,028	152,028

Stock at 31 March 19X9 was £22,390.

9.6A L Stokes drew up the following trial balance as at 30 September 19X8. You are to draft the trading and profit and loss account for the year to 30 September 19X8 and a balance sheet as at that date.

	Dr	Cr
	£	£
Capital		30,955
Drawings	8,420	
Cash at bank	3,115	
Cash in hand	295	
Debtors	12,300	
Creditors		9,370
Stock 30 September 19X7	23,910	
Motor van	4,100	
Office equipment	6,250	
Sales		130,900
Purchases	92,100	
Returns inwards	550	
Carriage inwards	215	
Returns outwards		307
Carriage outwards	309	
Motor expenses	1,630	
Rent	2,970	
Telephone charges	405	
Wages and salaries	12,810	
Insurance	492	
Office expenses	1,377	
Sundry expenses	284	
	171,532	171,532

Stock at 30 September 19X8 was £27,475.

10

Accounting concepts

Objectives

After you have studied this chapter, you should:

- *appreciate the assumptions which are made when recording accounting data*

- *realise one set of accounts is used for several different purposes*

- *understand what is meant by objectivity and subjectivity*

- *know the basic concepts of accounting*

- *see that the further overriding concepts of materiality, prudence, consistency and substance over form affect the recording and adjustment of data*

- *know that there are Statements of Standard Accounting Practice and also Financial Reporting Standards*

10.1 Introduction

What you have been reading about so far has been concerned with the recording of transactions in the books. Such recording has been based on certain assumptions. Quite deliberately these assumptions were not discussed in detail at the time. This is because it is much easier to look at them with a greater understanding *after* basic double entry has been covered. These assumptions are known as the concepts of *accounting*.

The trading and profit and loss accounts and balance sheets shown in the previous chapters were drawn up for the owner of the business. As shown later in the book, businesses are often owned by more than just one person and these accounting statements are for the use of all the owners.

An owner of a business may not be the only person to see his final accounts. He may have to show them to his bank manager if he wants to borrow money. The Inspector of Taxes will want to see them for the calculation of taxes. He may also need them to show to someone when he sells his business. Similarly, a new partner or investor would want to see them.

10.2 One set of final accounts for all purposes

If it had always been the custom to draft different kinds of final accounts for different purposes, so that one type was given to a banker, another type to someone wishing to buy the business, etc., then accounting would be different than it is today. However, copies of the same set of final accounts are given to all the different people.

This means that the banker, the prospective buyer of the business, the owner and the other people all see the same trading and profit and loss account and balance sheet. This is not an ideal situation as the interests of each party are different and each party needs different kinds of information from that wanted by the others. For instance, the bank manager would really like to know how much the assets would sell for if the firm ceased trading. He could then see what the possibility would be of the bank obtaining repayment of its loan. Other people would also like to see the information in the way that is most useful to them. Yet normally only one sort of final accounts is available for these different people.

This means that trading and profit and loss accounts have to be used for different needs, and to be of any use, the different parties have to agree to the way in which they are drawn up.

Assume that you are in a class of students and that you have the problem of valuing your assets, which consist of 10 textbooks. The first value you decide is that of how much you could sell them for. Your own guess is £30, but the other members of the class may give figures from £15 to £50.

Suppose that you now decide to put a value on their use to you. You may well think that the use of these books will enable you to pass your examinations and so you will get a good job. Another person may have the opposite idea concerning the use of the books. The use value placed on the books by others in the class will be quite different.

Finally you decide to value them by reference to cost. You take out of your pocket the bills for the books, which show that you paid a total of £60 for the books. If the rest of the class do not think that you have altered the bills, then they also can all agree that the value expressed as cost is £60. As this is the only value that you can all agree to, then each of you decides to use the idea of showing the value of the asset of books at the cost price.

10.3 Objectivity and subjectivity

The use of a method which all can agree to, instead of everyone using their own different method, is said to be **objective**. To use cost for the value of an asset is therefore a way to be objective.

When you are **subjective**, it means that you want to use your own method, even though no one else may agree to it.

The desire to provide the same set of accounts for many different parties, and thus to provide a measure that gains their consensus of opinion, means that objectivity is sought in financial accounting. If you are able to understand this desire for objectivity, then many of the apparent contradictions can be understood because it is often at the heart of the financial accounting methods in use at the present time.

Financial accounting seeks objectivity, and of course it must have rules which lay down the way in which the activities of the business are recorded. These rules have long been known as 'accounting concepts'. A group of these have become known as 'fundamental accounting concepts' (also referred to as 'accounting principles') and have been enforced through their incorporation in accounting standards issued on behalf of the accountancy bodies and, more recently, by their inclusion in Schedule 4 of the Companies Act 1985.

10.4 Accounting Standards and Financial Reporting Standards

At one time there used to be quite wide differences in the ways that accountants calculated profits. In the late 1960s a number of cases led to a widespread outcry against the lack of uniformity in accounting.

To reduce the possibility of very large variations in reported profits under different methods, the accounting bodies formed an Accounting Standards Committee. This committee over a period of about 20 years issued 25 Statements of Standard Accounting Practice, abbreviated as SSAPs. Accountants and auditors were expected to comply with the SSAPs. If they were not complied with, then the audit report had to give the reasons why the SSAP had been ignored.

The use of the SSAPs did not mean that two identical businesses would show exactly the same profits year by year. It did, however, considerably reduce the possibilities of very large variations in such profit reporting.

In 1990 the accountancy bodies replaced the ASC with the Accounting Standards Board (ASB). It took over the 22 SSAPs that were still in use. These continue to be known as SSAPs. Standards developed by the ASB are called Financial Reporting Standards, abbreviated as FRSs. At the time of writing, 13 FRSs have been issued. The ASB may issue pronouncements other than FRSs, announcing as each one appears, what authority, scope and application it will have.

In November 1997, the ASB issued a third category of standard – the Financial Reporting Standard for Smaller Entities (FRSSE). SSAPs and FRSs had generally been developed with the larger company in mind. The FRSSE was the ASB's response to the view that smaller companies should not have to apply all the cumbersome rules contained in the SSAPs and FRSs. It is, in effect, a collection of some of the rules from virtually all the other accounting standards. Small companies can choose whether to apply it or, as seems unlikely, continue to apply all the other accounting standards.

In this volume of the book the SSAPs, FRSs, and the FRSSE will only be mentioned when it is essential. Volume 2 will examine them in greater detail.

10.5 Accounting Standards and the legal framework

Accounting standards are drafted so that they comply with the laws of the United Kingdom and the Republic of Ireland. They also fit in with European Union Directives. This is all to ensure that there is no conflict between the law and accounting standards. Anyone preparing financial statements for publication must observe the rules laid down in the accounting standards.

10.6 Underlying accounting concepts

A number of accounting concepts have been applied ever since financial accounts were first produced for external reporting purposes. These have become second nature to accountants and are not generally reinforced, other than through custom and practice.

The historical cost concept

The need for this has already been described. It means that assets are normally shown at cost price, and that this is the basis for valuation of the asset.

The money measurement concept

Accounting information has traditionally been concerned only with those facts covered by (*a*) and (*b*) which follow:

(*a*) it can be measured in money, and

(b) most people will agree to the money value of the transaction.

This means that accounting can never tell you everything about a business. For example, accounting does not show the following:

(c) whether the firm has good or bad managers,
(d) that there are serious problems with the workforce,
(e) that a rival product is about to take away many of our best customers,
(f) that the government is about to pass a law which will cost us a lot of extra expense in future.

The reason that (c) to (f) or similar items are not recorded is that it would be impossible to work out a money value for them which most people would agree to.

Some people think that accounting tells you everything you want to know. The above shows that this is not true.

The business entity concept

This concept implies that the affairs of a business are to be treated as being quite separate from the non-business activities of its owner(s).

The items recorded in the books of the business are therefore restricted to the transactions of the business. No matter what activities the proprietor(s) get up to outside the business, they are completely disregarded in the books kept by the business.

The only time that the personal resources of the proprietor(s) affect the accounting records of a business is when they introduce new capital into the business, or take drawings out of it.

The dual aspect concept

This states that there are two aspects of accounting, one represented by the assets of the business and the other by the claims against them. The concept states that these two aspects are always equal to each other. In other words:

$$\text{Assets = Capital + Liabilities}$$

Double entry is the name given to the method of recording the transactions for the **dual aspect concept**.

The time interval concept

One of the underlying principles of accounting is that final accounts are prepared at regular intervals of one year. For internal management purposes they may be prepared far more frequently, possibly on a monthly basis or even more frequently.

10.7 Fundamental accounting concepts

These comprise a set of concepts considered so important that they have been enforced through accounting standards and/or through the Companies Act. Five have been enforced through the Companies Act 1985, and a sixth through an accounting standard, FRS 5 (*Reporting the substance of transactions*).

The five enforced through the Companies Act are:

1. Going concern

This is one of the fundamental accounting concepts. It implies that the business will continue to operate for the foreseeable future. It means that it is considered sensible to keep to the use of the cost concept when arriving at the valuations of assets.

Suppose, however, that a business is drawing up its final accounts at 31 December 19X8. Normally, using the cost concept, the assets would be shown at a total value of £100,000. It is known, however, that the business will be forced to close down in February 19X9, only two months later, and the assets are expected to be sold for only £15,000.

In this case it would not make sense to keep to the going concern concept, and so we can reject the cost concept for asset valuation purposes in cases such as this. In the balance sheet at 31 December 19X8 the assets will therefore be shown at the figure of £15,000. Such a case is the exception rather than the rule.

Examples where the going concern assumption should not be made are:

- if the business is going to close down in the near future;
- where shortage of cash makes it almost certain that the business will have to cease trading;
- where a large part of the business will almost certainly have to be closed down because of a shortage of cash.

2. Consistency

Even if we do everything already listed under concepts, there will still be quite a few different ways in which items could be recorded. This is because there can be different interpretations as to the exact meaning of the concept.

Each firm should try to choose the methods which give the most reliable picture of the business.

This cannot be done if one method is used in one year and another method in the next year and so on. Constantly changing the methods would lead to misleading profits being calculated from the accounting records. Therefore the convention of consistency is used. This convention says that when a firm has once fixed a method for the accounting treatment of an item, it will enter all similar items that follow in exactly the same way.

However, it does not mean that the firm has to follow the method until the firm closes down. A firm can change the method used, but such a change is not made without a lot of consideration. When such a change occurs and the profits calculated in that year are affected by a material amount, then either in the profit and loss account itself or in one of the reports with it, the effect of the change should be stated.

3. Prudence

Very often an accountant has to use his judgement to decide which figure he will take for an item. Suppose a debt has been owing for quite a long time, and no one knows whether it will ever be paid. Should the accountant be an optimist in thinking that it will be paid, or should he be more pessimistic?

It is the accountant's duty to see that people get the proper facts about a business. He should make certain that assets are not valued too highly. Similarly, liabilities should not be shown at values too low. Otherwise, people might inadvisedly lend money to a firm, which they would not do if they had the proper facts.

The accountant should always be on the side of safety, and this is known as prudence. The prudence concept means that normally he will take the figure which will understate rather than overstate the profit. Thus, he should choose the figure which will cause the capital of the firm to be shown at a lower amount rather than at a higher one. He will also normally make sure that all losses are recorded in the books, but profits should not be anticipated by recording them before they should be.

The recognition of profits at an appropriate time has long been recognised as being in need of guidelines and these have long been enshrined in what is known as the 'realisation concept'. This is not so much a separate concept. Rather, it is a part of the broader concept of prudence.

The realisation concept holds to the view that profit can only be taken into account when realisation has occurred. Several criteria have to be observed for realisation to have taken place:

- goods or services are provided for the buyer;
- the buyer accepts liability to pay for the goods or services;
- the monetary value of the goods or services has been established;
- the buyer will be in a situation to be able to pay for the goods or services.

Notice that it is not the time:

- when the order is received, or
- when the customer pays for the goods.

This can mean that profit is brought into account in one period, and then it is found to have been incorrectly taken as profit when the goods are returned in a later period because of some deficiency. Also the services can turn out to be subject to an allowance being given in a later period owing to poor performance. If the allowances or returns can be reasonably estimated an adjustment may be made to the calculated profit in the period when they passed to the customer.

As you will see if you take your studies to a more advantaged stage, there are times other than on completion of a sale when profit may be recognised. These could include profits on long-term contracts spanning several years, such as the building of a very large bridge. In this case profit might be calculated for each year of the contract, even though the bridge is not finished at that date.

4. The accruals concept

The **accruals concept** says net profit is the difference between revenues and expenses, i.e.

$$\text{Revenues} - \text{Expenses} = \text{Net Profit}$$

Determining the expenses used up to obtain the revenues is referred to as *matching* expenses against revenues. The key to the application of the concept is that all income and charges relating to the financial period to which the accounts relate should be taken into account without regard to the date of receipt or payment.

This concept is particularly misunderstood by people who have not studied accounting. To many of them, actual payment of an item in a period is taken as being matched against the revenue of the period when the net profit is calculated. The fact that expenses consist of the assets used up in a particular period in obtaining the revenues of that period, and that cash paid in a period and expenses of a period are usually different, as you will see later, comes as a surprise to a great number of them.

5. Separate determination

In determining the aggregate amount of each asset or liability, the amount of each individual asset or liability should be determined separately from all other assets and liabilities. For example, if you have three machines, the amount at which machinery is shown in the balance sheet should be the sum of the values calculated individually for each of the three machines. Only when individual values have been derived should a total be calculated.

This concept is, perhaps, best described in relation to potential gains and potential losses. If a business is being sued by a customer for £10,000 and there is a high probability that the business will lose the case, the prudence concept requires the £10,000 to be included as a liability in the financial statements. The same business may, itself, be suing a supplier for £6,000 and may have a high probability of winning the case. It might be tempting to offset the two claims, leaving a net liability of £4,000 to appear in the financial statements. Yet, this would be contrary to the prudence concept which would not allow the probable £6,000 gain to be realised until it was definitely going to be received. The separate determination concept prohibits the netting-off of potential liabilities and potential gains. As a result, only the probable £10,000 expense would be recognised in the financial statements.

The remaining fundamental accounting concept was established by the release of FRS 5:

Substance over form

It can happen that the legal form of a transaction can differ from its real substance. Where this happens accounting should show the transaction in accordance with its real substance, which is basically how the transaction affects the economic situation of the firm. This means that accounting in this instance will not reflect the exact legal position concerning that transaction.

You have not yet come across the best and easiest illustration of this concept. Later in your studies you may have to learn about accounting for fixed assets being bought on hire-purchase. We will take a car as an example.

- From a legal point of view the car does not belong to the firm until all the hire-purchase instalments have been paid, and an option has been taken up whereby you take over legal possession of the car.
- From an economic point of view you have used the car for business purposes, just as any other car owned by the business which was paid for immediately has been used. In this case the business will show the car being bought on hire-purchase in its accounts and balance sheet as though it were legally owned by the business, but also showing separately the amount still owed for it.

In this way, therefore, the substance of the transaction has taken precedence over the legal form of the transaction.

10.8 Materiality

The accounting concepts already discussed have become accepted in the business world, their assimilation having taken place over many years. However, there is one overriding rule applied to anything that appears in a financial accounting statement – it should be material. That is, it should be of interest to the stakeholders, those people who make use of financial accounting statements. It need not be material to every stakeholder, but it must be material to a stakeholder before it merits inclusion.

Accounting does not serve a useful purpose if the effort of recording a transaction in a certain way is not worthwhile. Thus, if a box of paper-clips was bought it would be used up over a period of time, and this cost is used up every time someone uses a paper-clip.

It is possible to record this as an expense every time it happens, but obviously the price of a box of paper-clips is so little that it is not worth recording it in this fashion. The box of paper-clips is not a material item, and therefore would be charged as an expense in the period it was bought, irrespective of the fact that it could last for more than one accounting period. **In other words do not waste your time in the elaborate recording of trivial items.**

Similarly, the purchase of a cheap metal ashtray would also be charged as an expense in the period it was bought because it is not a material item, even though it may in fact last for twenty years. A motor lorry would, however, be deemed to be a material item, and so, as will be seen in Chapter 25 on depreciation, an attempt is made to charge each period with the cost consumed in each period of its use.

Firms fix all sorts of arbitrary rules to determine what is material and what is not. There is no law that lays down what these should be – the decision as to what is material and what is not is dependent upon judgement. A firm may well decide that all items under £100 should be treated as expenses in the period in which they were bought even though they may well be in use in the firm for the following ten years. Another firm, especially a large one, may fix the limit at £1,000. Different limits may be set for different types of item.

It can be seen that the size and the type of firm will affect the decisions as to which items are material. With individuals, an amount of £1,000 may well be more than you, as a student, possess. For a multi-millionaire, what is a material item and what is not will almost certainly not be comparable. Just as individuals vary, then, so do firms. Some firms have a great deal of machinery and may well treat all items of machinery costing less than £1,000 as not being material, whereas another firm which makes about the same amount of profits, but has very little machinery, may well treat a £600 machine as being a material item as they have fixed their limit at £250.

10.9 The assumption of the stability of currency

One does not have to be very old to remember that a few years ago many goods could be bought with less money than today. If one listens to one's parents or grandparents then many stories will be heard of how little this item or the other could be bought for x years ago. The currencies of the countries of the world are not stable in terms of what each unit of currency can buy over the years.

Accounting, however, uses the historic cost concept, this stating that the asset is normally shown at its cost price. This means that accounting statements will be distorted because assets will be bought at different points in time at the price then ruling, and the figures totalled up to show the value of the assets in cost terms. For instance, suppose that you had bought a building 20 years ago for £20,000. You now decide to buy an identical additional building, but the price has now risen to £40,000. You buy it, and the buildings account now shows buildings at a figure of £60,000. One building is measured cost-wise in terms of the currency of 20 years ago, while the other is taken at today's currency value. The figure of a total of £60,000 is historically correct, but, other than that, the total figure cannot be said to be particularly valid for any other use.

This means that to make a correct assessment of accounting statements one must bear in mind the distorting effects of changing price levels upon the accounting entries as recorded. There are techniques of adjusting accounts so as to try and eliminate these distortions, but they fall outside the scope of this book and are dealt with in *Business Accounting 2*.

10.10 SSAP 2

This SSAP was the first accounting standard to cover the disclosure of accounting policies which include accounting concepts. It dealt with four of the fundamental accounting concepts, going concern, accruals, consistency, and prudence. Various matters dealt with in the standard have not yet been examined, and are covered in later chapters. A fuller discussion of the standard is left until 48.11.

10.11 Accounting concepts in action

This is too early a stage in your studies to be able to appreciate more fully how the concepts work in practice. It is far better left towards the end of this book, and therefore we consider it in section 48.12.

New terms

Accruals concept (p. 91): The concept that profit is the difference between revenue and expenses.

Business entity concept (p. 89): Assumption that only transactions that affect the firm, and not the owner's private transactions, will be recorded.

Consistency (p. 90): Keeping to the same method of recording transactions.

Cost concept (p. 88): Assets are normally shown at cost price.

Dual aspect concept (p. 89): The concept of dealing with both aspects of a transaction.

Going concern concept (p. 90): Assumption that a business is to continue for a long time.

Materiality (p. 92): Recording something in a special way only if the amount is not a small one.

Money measurement concept (p. 88): The concept that accounting is concerned only with facts measurable in money, and for which measurements can obtain general agreement.

Objectivity (p. 87): Using a method that everyone can agree to.

Prudence (p. 90): Ensuring that profit is not shown as being too high, or that assets are shown at too high a value.

Realisation concept (p. 91): The concept of profit as being earned at a particular point.

Separate determination concept (p. 91): The amount of each asset or liability should be determined separately.

Subjectivity (p. 87): Using a method that other people may not agree to, derived from one's own personal preferences.

Substance over form (p. 92): Where real substance takes precedence over legal form.

Time interval concept (p. 89): Final accounts are prepared at regular intervals.

Main points to remember

1 Normally one set of accounts has to serve many purposes.

2 The need for general agreement has given rise to the concepts and conventions that govern accounting records.

3 An assumption is made that monetary measures remain stable, i.e. that normally accounts are not adjusted for inflation or deflation.

4 The terms 'prudence' and 'conservatism' mean exactly the same thing.

Part 3

BOOKS OF ORIGINAL ENTRY

Introduction

This part is concerned with the books and journals into which transactions are first entered, together with chapters on VAT and on employees' pay, and an introduction to the use of computers in accounting.

11

Books of original entry and ledgers

Objectives

After you have studied this chapter, you should:

- *know the need for books of original entry*

- *understand what each book is used for*

- *appreciate how the books of original entry are used alongside the ledgers*

- *be able to list accounts as either personal or impersonal accounts*

- *be able to enter up a private or nominal ledger*

- *see the accountant's job as being that of a communicator of information*

11.1 The growth of the firm

While the firm is very small, all the double entry accounts can be kept in one book, which we would call the ledger. As the firm grows it would be impossible just to use one book, as the large number of pages needed for a lot of transactions would mean that the book would be too big to handle. Also, suppose we have several bookkeepers. They could not all do their work properly if there were only one ledger.

The answer to this problem is for us to use more books. When we do this we put similar types of transactions together and have a book for that type. In each book we will not mix together transactions which are different from one another.

11.2 Books of original entry

These are books in which we record transactions first of all. We have a separate book for each different kind of transaction. The nature of the transaction affects which book it is entered into. Sales will be entered in one book, purchases in another book, cash in another book, and so on. We enter the transactions in these books giving the following details:

- date: the transactions should be shown in date order;
- details column completed;
- folio column for cross-referencing purposes;
- money column completed.

11.3 Types of books of original entry

These are:

- **Sales Journal** – for credit sales.
- **Purchases Journal** – for credit purchases.
- **Returns Inwards Journal** – for returns inwards.
- **Returns Outwards Journal** – for returns outwards.
- **Cash Book** – for receipts and payments of cash and cheques.
- **General Journal** – for other items.

11.4 Using more than one ledger

Although we have now made lists of transactions in the books of original entry, we still have more work to do. We have got to show the effect of the transactions by putting them into double entry accounts. Instead of keeping all the double entry accounts in one ledger, we have several ledgers. This again makes it easier to divide the work between different bookkeepers.

11.5 Types of ledgers

The different types of ledgers are:

- **Sales Ledger**. This is kept just for customers' personal accounts.
- **Purchases Ledger**. This is kept just for suppliers' personal accounts.
- **General Ledger**. This contains the remaining double entry accounts such as expenses, fixed assets, capital etc.

11.6 Diagram of books used

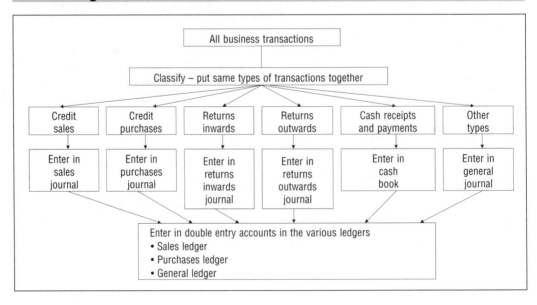

11.7 Description of books used

In the next few chapters we will look at the books used in more detail, except for the general journal which will be dealt with at a later stage.

11.8 Types of accounts

Some people describe all accounts as **personal** accounts or as **impersonal** accounts.

- **Personal Accounts** – these are for debtors and creditors.
- **Impersonal Accounts** – divided between real accounts and nominal accounts.
- **Real Accounts** – accounts in which property is recorded. Examples are buildings, machinery, fixtures and stock.
- **Nominal Accounts** – accounts in which expenses, income and capital are recorded.

A diagram may enable you to understand it better:

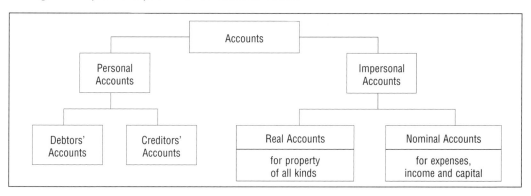

11.9 Nominal and private ledgers

The ledger in which the impersonal accounts are kept is known as the **nominal** (or general) **ledger**. Very often, to ensure privacy for the proprietor(s), the capital and drawing accounts and similar accounts are kept in a **private ledger**. By doing this office staff cannot see details of items which the proprietors want to keep secret.

11.10 The accountant as a communicator

Quite often the impression is given that all that the accountant does is to produce figures, arranged in various ways. Naturally, such forms of computation do take up quite a lot of the accountant's time, but what then takes up the rest of the accountant's time is exactly how these figures are communicated to other people.

First of all, the accountant can obviously arrange the figures in such a way as to present the information in as meaningful a way as possible. Suppose for instance that the figures produced are to be given to several people, all of whom are very knowledgeable about accounting. The accountant could, in such an instance, present the figures in a normal accounting way, knowing full well that the recipients of the information will understand it.

On the other hand, the accounting figures may well be needed by people who have absolutely no knowledge at all of accounting. In such a case a normal accounting statement would be no use to them at all; they would not understand it. In this case the accountant might set out the figures in a completely different way to try to make it easy for them to grasp. For instance, instead of preparing a normal trading and profit and loss account, the accountant might show the information as follows:

	£	£
In the year ended 31 December 19X9 you sold goods for		50,000
Now how much had those goods cost you to buy?		
At the start of the year you had stock costing	6,000	
+ You bought some more goods in the year costing	28,000	
So altogether you had goods available to sell of	34,000	
− At the end of the year you had stock of goods unsold of	3,000	
So the goods you had sold in the year had cost you	31,000	
Let us deduct this from what you had sold the goods for		31,000
This means that you had made a profit on buying and selling goods, before any other expenses had been paid, amounting to		19,000

(We call this sort of profit the *gross* **profit**)

But you suffered other expenses such as wages, rent, lighting and so on, and during the year the amount of these expenses, not including anything taken for yourself, amounted to		9,000
So, in this year your sales value exceeded all the costs involved in running the business, so that the sales could be made, by		£10,000

(We call this sort of profit the *net* **profit**)

An accountant is failing to perform appropriately and effectively if the figures are not arranged so as to make them meaningful to the recipient. The accountant's job is not just to produce figures for the accountant's own consumption, it is to communicate the results to other people.

Very often, the accountant will have to talk to people to explain the figures, or send a letter or write a report concerning them. The accountant will also have to talk or write to people to find out exactly what sort of accounting information is needed by them or explain to them what sort of information could be provided. If accounting examinations contain only computational type questions, they will not test the ability of the candidate to communicate in any way other than writing down accounting figures, and so will not examine other important aspects of the job. In recent years much more attention has been paid by examining boards to these other aspects of an accountant's work.

New terms

Books of original entry (p. 97): Books where the first entry of a transaction is made.

Cash book (p. 98): Books of original entry for cash and bank receipts and payments.

General journal (p. 98): Book of original entry for all items other than those for cash or goods.

General ledger (p. 98): Ledger for all accounts other than those for customers and suppliers.

Impersonal accounts (p. 99): All accounts other than debtors' and creditors' accounts.

Nominal accounts (p. 99): Accounts in which expenses, revenue and capital are recorded.

Nominal ledger (p. 100): Another name for the general ledger.

Personal accounts (p. 99): Accounts for both creditors and debtors.

Private ledger (p. 99): Ledger for capital and drawings accounts.

Purchases journal (p. 98): Book of original entry for credit purchases.

New terms continued

Purchases ledger (p. 98): A ledger for suppliers' personal accounts.

Real accounts (p. 99): Accounts in which property of all kinds is recorded.

Returns inwards journal (p. 98): Book of original entry for goods returned by customers.

Returns outwards journal (p. 98): Book of original entry for goods returned to suppliers.

Sales journal (p. 98): Book of original entry for credit sales.

Sales ledger (p. 98): A ledger for customers' personal accounts.

Main points to remember

1   Transactions are classified and listed in the appropriate book of original entry.

2   The books of original entry are used as a basis for posting the transactions to the double entry accounts in the various ledgers.

12

The banking system

Objectives

After you have studied this chapter, you should:

- *know the difference between current accounts and deposit accounts*
- *be able to make out cheques*
- *understand the effect of various kinds of crossing on cheques*
- *be able to endorse a cheque over to someone else*
- *be able to fill in bank paying-in slips*
- *realise the timing differences between entries in a cash book and those on a bank statement*

12.1 Introduction

We will be looking at payments into and out of bank accounts in Chapter 13. You therefore need to know some details about bank accounts.

12.2 Types of account

There are two main types of bank account:

Current accounts

Used for regular payments into and out of a bank account. A **cheque book** will be given by the bank to the holder of the account. The cheque book will be used to make payments to people to whom the account holder owes money.

So that the account holder can pay money into his/her current account, the holder will be given a paying-in book.

Deposit accounts

Such a bank account is for putting money into the bank and not taking it out quickly.

Usually interest is given by the bank on money kept in deposit accounts. Current accounts do not usually earn interest.

12.3 Cheques

1 When the bank has agreed to let you open a current account it will ask you for a signature. This allows them to prove that your cheques are in fact signed by you, and have not been forged. You will then be issued with a cheque book.

2 You can then use the cheques to make payments out of the account. Normally you must make sure that you have more money in the account than the amount paid out. If you wish to pay out more money than you have banked, you will have to see the bank manager. You will then discuss the reasons for this with him, and if he agrees he will give his permission for you to 'overdraw' your account. This is known as a **bank overdraft**.

3 The person filling in the cheque and using it for payment is known as the **drawer**. The person to whom the cheque is paid is known as the **payee**.

We can now look at Exhibit 12.1, which is a blank cheque form before it is filled in.

Exhibit 12.1

```
                                                          09-07-99
   ————— 19—     Cheshire Bank Ltd.  ————— 19—

   PAYEE —————    Stockport Branch
                  324 Low Road, Stockport, Cheshire SK6 8AP
   _____
                  PAY —————————————————— OR ORDER
   _____
                  ——————————————————     ┌──────────┐
   _____                        │ £        │
                                         └──────────┘
   ┌──────────┐    ——————————————————     J WOODSTOCK
   │ £        │
   └──────────┘
     914234       914234 09-07-99': 058899
```

. This part is
: the counterfoil

On the face of the cheque are various sets of numbers. These are:

914234   Every cheque printed for the Cheshire Bank for your account will be given a different number, so that individual items can be traced.

09-07-99   Each branch of every bank in the United Kingdom has a different number given to it. Thus this branch has a 'code' number 09-07-99.

058899   Each account with the bank is given a different number. This particular number is kept only for the account of J Woodstock at the Stockport branch.

When we fill in the cheque we copy the details on the counterfoil which we then detach and keep for our records.

We can now look at the completion of a cheque. Let us assume that we are paying seventy-two pounds and eighty-five pence to K Marsh on 22 May 19X5. Exhibit 12.2 shows the completed cheque.

Exhibit 12.2

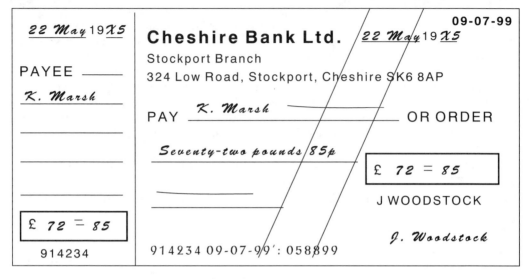

In Exhibit 12.2:

The drawer is: J Woodstock
The payee is: K Marsh

The two parallel lines across the face of the cheque are drawn as a safeguard. If we had not done this, the cheque would have been an 'uncrossed cheque'. If someone had stolen a signed uncrossed cheque, the thief could have gone to the Stockport branch of the Cheshire Bank and obtained cash in exchange for the cheque. When the cheque is crossed it *must* be paid into a bank account.

12.4 Cheque crossings

Cheques can be further safeguarded by using a specific crossing, i.e. writing a form of instruction within the crossing on the cheques as shown in Exhibit 12.3.

Exhibit 12.3

These are specific instructions to the banks about the use of the cheque. The use of 'A/c payee only' means the cheques should be paid only into the account of the payee named. If cheques are lost or stolen the drawer must advise their bank immediately and confirm by letter. These cheques will be 'stopped', i.e. payment will not be made on these cheques, provided they act swiftly. The safest crossing is that of 'A/c payee only. Not negotiable'. If the cheque is lost or stolen it will be of no use to the thief or finder. This is because it is impossible for this cheque to be paid into any bank account other than that of the named payee. Cheques are now often printed with the 'Account payee' crossing on them.

12.5 Cheque endorsements

Cheques with the above crossings can only be paid into the bank account of the payee. However, if the crossing does not forbid it, a cheque received by someone can be 'endorsed' over to someone else. The person then receiving the cheque could bank it. This means that if A Smith receives a cheque from J Wilson, he can 'endorse' the cheque and hand it to P Jones as payment of money owing to Jones.

To endorse the cheque Smith would write the words 'Pay P Jones or order' on the reverse side of the cheque and then sign underneath it. Jones would then usually bank the cheque, but he could endorse it over to someone else by adding yet another endorsement and signing it.

A cheque which has been paid to someone, and has passed through their bank account or been endorsed over by that person to someone else, would be legal proof of the fact that payment had been made.

12.6 Paying-in slips

When we want to pay money into our current accounts, either cash or cheques, or both, we use a **paying-in slip**. One of these is shown as Exhibit 12.4.

Exhibit 12.4

Face of paying-in slip

Date *22 May* 19*X5* Cashier's stamp and initials	Date *22 May* 19*X5* Cashier's stamp and initials	bank giro credit Destination Branch Code number		pounds	pence
			£5 notes and over	*20*	
		09 - 07 - 99	£1 coins	*3*	
			50p coins		*50*
		Bank *Cheshire Bank*	Other silver		*30*
		Branch *Stockport*	Bronze coins		*12*
A/c *J WOODSTOCK*			Total cash	*23*	*92*
			Cheques, PO's etc.	*249*	*59*
Cash *23 - 92*		Account Name (Block letters) & A/c. No	(see over)		
Cheques *249 - 59* PO's etc		*J. WOODSTOCK 058899*		*273*	*51*
£ *273 - 51*	Paid in by *J Woodstock*	Details for advice to recipient			

Counterfoil retained by Woodstock	Paying-in slip and cash and cheques handed in to bank

Reverse side of paying-in slip

Details of Cheques, PO's etc					
for cheques please specify Drawer's name and	Bank Code Number as shown in top right corner				
E. KANE & SON	*02-58-76*	*184*	*15*	*184*	*15*
J. GALE	*05-77-85*	*65*	*44*	*65*	*44*
In view of the risk of loss in course of clearing, customers are advised to keep an independent record of the drawers of cheques.	Total carried over £	*249*	*59*	*249*	*59*

Reverse of counterfoil

J Woodstock has banked the following items:

Four	£5 notes	
Three	£1 coins	
One	50p coin	
Other silver	30p	
Bronze coins	12p	
Cheques received from:		Code numbers:
E Kane & Son	£184.15	02-58-76
J Gale	£ 65.44	05-77-85

12.7 Cheque clearings

We will now look at how cheques paid from one person's bank account pass into another person's bank account.

Let us look at the progress of the cheque in Exhibit 12.2. We will assume that the Post Office is being very efficient and delivering all letters the following day after being posted.

19X5

May 22   Woodstock, in Stockport, sends the cheque to K Marsh, who lives in Leeds. Woodstock enters the payment in his cash book.

May 23   Cheque received by Marsh. He banks it the same day in his bank account at Barclays Bank in Leeds. Marsh shows the cheque in his cash book as being received and banked on 23 May.

May 24   Barclays in London receive it. They exchange it with the Head Office of the Cheshire Bank in London.
The Cheshire Bank send the cheque to their Stockport branch.

May 25   The Stockport branch of the Cheshire Bank examine the cheque. If there is nothing wrong with it, the cheque can now be debited by the bank to J Woodstock's account.

In Chapter 29 we will be examining bank reconciliation statements. What we have looked at –

19X5

May 22   This is the day on which Woodstock has made the entry in his cash book.

May 25   This is the day when the bank makes an entry in Woodstock's account in respect of the cheque.

– will become an important part of your understanding such statements.

New terms

Bank overdraft (p. 103): When we have paid more out of our bank account than we have paid into it.

Cheque book (p. 102): Book containing forms (cheques) used to pay money out of a current account.

Current account (p. 102): Bank account used for regular payments in and out of the bank.

Deposit account (p. 102): Bank account for money to be kept in for a long time. Interest is given on money deposited.

Drawer (p. 103): The person making out a cheque and using it for payment.

Endorsement (p. 105): A means by which someone may pass the right to collect money due on a cheque.

Payee (p. 103): The person to whom a cheque is paid.

Paying-in slip (p. 106): Form used for paying money into a bank account.

Main points to remember

1 A current account will be accompanied by the use of a cheque book, while a deposit account will not.

2 Crossings on cheques indicate that they must be banked before cash can be collected for them.

3 Special crossings on cheques act as instructions to the banker, and are usually used to ensure that the cheque cannot be used by anyone other than its rightful owner.

4 Cheque endorsements are to enable a rightful owner of the cheque to give it to someone else.

5 Cheque clearing is the way in which a cheque goes through the banking system and is credited to its rightful owner and charged against the drawer's bank account.

13

Cash books

Objectives

After you have studied this chapter, you should:

- *be able to enter up and balance off cash books*

- *be able to use folio columns for cross-referencing purposes*

- *be able to complete entries for discounts allowed and discounts received*

13.1 Introduction

The cash book consists of the cash account and the bank account put together in one book. We used to show these two accounts on different pages of the ledger. Now it is easier to put the two sets of account columns together. This means that we can record all money received and paid out on a particular date on the same page.

In the cash book the debit column for cash is put next to the debit column for bank. The credit column for cash is put next to the credit column for bank.

13.2 Drawing up a cash book

We can now look at a cash account and a bank account in Exhibit 13.1 as they would appear if they had been kept separately. Then in Exhibit 13.2 they are shown as if the transactions had instead been kept in a cash book.

The bank column contains details of the payments made by cheque and of the money received and paid into the bank account. The bank will have a copy of the account in its own books.

The bank will send a copy of the account in its books to the firm, this copy usually being known as the **bank statement**. When the firm receives the bank statement, it will check it against the bank column in its own cash book to ensure that there are no errors.

Exhibit 13.1

Cash

19X8		£	19X8		£
Aug	2 T Moore	33	Aug	8 Rent	20
„	5 K Charles	25	„	12 C Potts	19
„	15 F Hughes	37	„	28 Wages	25
„	30 H Howe	18	„	31 Balance c/d	49
		113			113
Sept	1 Balance b/d	49			

Bank

19X8		£	19X8		£
Aug	1 Capital	1,000	Aug	7 Rates	105
„	3 W P Ltd	244	„	12 F Small Ltd	95
„	16 K Noone	408	„	26 K French	268
„	30 H Sanders	20	„	31 Balance c/d	1,204
		1,672			1,672
Sept	1 Balance b/d	1,204			

Exhibit 13.2

Cash Book

		Cash	Bank			Cash	Bank
		£	£			£	£
19X8				19X8			
Aug	1 Capital		1,000	Aug	7 Rates		105
„	2 T Moore	33		„	8 Rent	20	
„	3 W P Ltd		244	„	12 C Potts	19	
„	5 K Charles	25		„	12 F Small Ltd		95
„	15 F Hughes	37		„	26 K French		268
„	16 K Noone		408	„	28 Wages	25	
„	30 H Sanders		20	„	31 Balance c/d	49	1,204
„	30 H Howe	18					
		113	1,672			113	1,672
Sept	1 Balances b/d	49	1,204				

13.3 Cash paid into the bank

In Exhibit 13.2, the payments into the bank have been cheques received by the firm which have been banked immediately. We must now consider cash being paid into the bank.

1 Let us look at the position when a customer pays his account in cash, and later a part of this cash is paid into the bank. The receipt of the cash is debited to the cash column on the date received, the credit entry being in the customer's personal account. The cash banked has the following effect needing action as shown:

Effect	Action
1 Asset of cash is decreased	Credit the asset account, i.e the cash account which is represented by the cash column in the cash book.
2 Asset of bank is increased	Debit the asset account, i.e. the bank account which is represented by the bank column in the cash book.

A cash receipt of £100 from M Davies on 1 August 19X8, later followed by the banking on 3 August of £80 of this amount, would appear in the cash book as follows:

Cash Book						
	Cash	Bank			Cash	Bank
19X8	£	£	19X8		£	£
Aug 1 M Davies	100		Aug 3 Bank		80	
„ 3 Cash		80				

The details column shows entries against each item stating the name of the account in which the completion of double entry has taken place. Against the cash payment of £80 appears the word 'bank', meaning that the debit £80 is to be found in the bank column, and the opposite applies.

2 Where the whole of the cash received is banked immediately the receipt can be treated in exactly the same manner as a cheque received, i.e. it can be entered directly in the bank column.

3 If the firm requires cash it may withdraw cash from the bank. This is done by making out a cheque to pay itself a certain amount in cash. The bank will give cash in exchange for the cheque over the counter.

The twofold effect and the action required may be shown:

Effect	Action
1 Asset of bank is decreased	Credit the asset account, i.e the bank column in the cash book.
2 Asset of cash is increased	Debit the asset account, i.e. the cash column in the cash book.

A withdrawal of £75 cash on 1 June 19X8 from the bank would appear in the cash book thus:

Cash Book						
	Cash	Bank			Cash	Bank
19X8	£	£	19X8		£	£
June 1 Bank	75		June 1 Cash			75

Both the debit and credit entries for this item are in the same book. When this happens it is known as a **contra** item.

13.4 The use of folio columns

As you have already seen, the details column in an account contains the name of the other account in which double entry has been completed. Anyone looking through the books would therefore be able to find where the other half of the double entry was.

However, when many books are being used, just to mention the name of the other account would not be enough information to find the other account quickly. More information is needed, and this is given by using **folio columns**.

In each account and in each book being used, a folio column is added, always shown on the left of the money columns. In this column the name of the other book, in abbreviated form, and the number of the page in the other book where double entry is completed is stated against each and every entry in the books.

An entry of receipt of cash from C Kelly whose account was on page 45 of the sales ledger, and the cash recorded on page 37 of the cash book, would use the folio column thus:

In the cash book. In the folio column would appear SL 45.
In the sales ledger. In the folio column would appear CB 37.

By this method full cross-reference would be given. Each of the contra items, being shown on the same page of the cash book, would use the letter 'C' in the folio column.

The act of using one book as a means of entering the transaction to the other account, so as to complete double entry, is known as '**posting**' the items.

13.5 Advantages of folio columns

These are:

- As described in 13.4 it speeds up reference to the other book where double entry for the item is completed.
- The folio column is filled in when double entry has been completed. If it has not been filled in, double entry will not have been made.

Looking through the folio columns to ensure they have all been filled in will help us to detect such errors.

13.6 Example of a cash book with folio columns

The following transactions are written up in the form of a cash book. The folio columns are filled in as though double entry had been completed to other accounts.

19X8			£
Sept	1	Proprietor puts capital into a bank account for the business.	940
„	2	Received cheque from M Boon.	115
„	4	Cash sales.	102
„	6	Paid rent by cash.	35
„	7	Banked £50 of the cash held by the firm.	50
„	15	Cash sales paid direct into the bank.	40
„	23	Paid cheque to S Wills.	277
„	29	Withdrew cash from bank for business use.	120
„	30	Paid wages in cash.	118

Cash Book								(page 1)
	Folio	*Cash*	*Bank*			*Folio*	*Cash*	*Bank*
19X8		£	£	19X8			£	£
Sept 1 Capital	GL1		940	Sept 6 Rent		GL65	35	
„ 2 M Boon	SL98		115	„ 7 Bank		C	50	
„ 4 Sales	GL87	102		„ 23 S Wills		PL23		277
„ 7 Cash	C		50	„ 29 Cash		C		120
„ 15 Sales	GL87		40	„ 30 Wages		GL39	118	
„ 29 Bank	C	120		„ 30 Balances		c/d	19	748
		222	1,145				222	1,145
Oct 1 Balances	b/d	19	748					

The abbreviations used in the folio column are as follows:
GL = General Ledger: SL = Sales Ledger: C = Contra: PL = Purchases Ledger.

13.7 Cash discounts

It is better if customers pay their accounts quickly. A firm may accept a smaller sum in full settlement if payment is made within a certain period of time. The amount of the reduction of the sum to be paid is known as a *cash discount*. The term 'cash discount' thus refers to the allowance given for quick payment. It is still called cash discount, even if the account is paid by cheque.

The rate of cash discount is usually stated as a percentage. Full details of the percentage allowed, and the period within which payment is to be made, are quoted on all sales documents by the selling company. A typical period during which discount may be allowed is one month from the date of the original transaction.

13.8 Discounts allowed and discounts received

A firm may have two types of cash discounts in its books. These are:

1 **Discounts allowed.** Cash discounts allowed by a firm to its customers when they pay their accounts quickly.
2 **Discounts received.** Received by a firm from its suppliers when it pays their accounts quickly.

We can now see the effect of discounts by looking at two examples.

Example 1

W Clarke owed us £100. He pays on 2 September 19X8 by cash within the time limit laid down, and the firm allows him 5 per cent cash discount. So he will pay £100 – £5 = £95 in full settlement of his account.

Effect	Action
1 Of cash: Cash is increased by £95. Asset of debtors is decreased by £95.	Debit cash account, i.e. enter £95 in debit column of cash book. Credit W Clarke £95.
2 Of discounts: Asset of debtors is decreased by £5. (After the cash was paid the balance of £5 still appeared. As the account has been paid this asset must now be cancelled.) Expenses of discounts allowed increased by £5.	Credit W Clarke £5. Debit discounts allowed account £5.

Example 2

The firm owed S Small £400. It pays him on 3 September 19X8 by cheque within the time limit laid down by him and he allows 2½ per cent cash discount. Thus the firm will pay £400 – £10 = £390 in full settlement of the account.

Effect	Action
1 Of cheque: Asset of bank is reduced by £390. Liability of creditors is reduced by £390.	Credit bank, i.e. enter in credit bank column £390. Debit S Small's account £390.
2 Of discounts: Liability of creditors is reduced by £10. (After the cheque was paid the balance of £10 remained. As the account has been paid the liability must now be cancelled.) Revenues of discounts received increased by £10.	Debit S Small's account £10. Credit discounts received account £10.

The accounts in the firm's books would appear:

Cash Book							(page 32)
	Folio	*Cash*	*Bank*		*Folio*	*Cash*	*Bank*
19X8		£	£	19X8		£	£
Sept 2 W Clarke	SL12	95		Sept 3 S Small	PL75		390

Discounts Received		(General Ledger *page 18*)
	Folio	£
19X8		
Sept 2 S Small	PL75	10

Discounts Allowed   (General Ledger *page 17*)

		Folio	£	
19X8				
Sept	2 W Clarke	SL12	5	

W Clarke   (Sales Ledger *page 12*)

		Folio	£			Folio	£
19X8				19X8			
Sept	1 Balance	b/d	100	Sept	2 Cash	CB32	95
				„	2 Discount	GL17	5
			100				100

S Small   (Purchases Ledger *page 75*)

		Folio	£			Folio	£
19X8				19X8			
Sept	3 Bank	CB32	390	Sept	1 Balance	b/d	400
„	3 Discount	GL18	10				
			400				400

It is the accounting custom to enter the word 'Discount' in the personal accounts, not stating whether it is a discount received or a discount allowed.

13.9 Discounts columns in cash book

The discounts allowed account and the discounts received account are in the general ledger along with all the other revenue and expense accounts. It has already been stated that every effort should be made to avoid too much reference to the general ledger.

In the case of discounts this is done by adding an extra column on each side of the cash book in which the amounts of discounts are entered. Discounts received are entered in the discounts column on the credit side of the cash book, and discounts allowed in the discounts column on the debit side of the cash book.

The cash book, if completed for the two examples so far dealt with, would appear:

		Folio	Discount	Cash	Bank		Folio	Discount	Cash	Bank
			£	£	£			£	£	£
19X8						19X8				
Sept 2	W Clarke	SL12	5	95		Sept 3 S Small	PL75	10		390

Cash Book (page 32)

There is no alteration to the method of showing discounts in the personal accounts.

To make entries in the discounts accounts

Total of discounts column on receipts side of cash book } Enter on debit side of discounts allowed account

Total of discounts column on payments side of cash book } Enter on credit side of discounts received account

13.10 A worked example

		£
19X8		
May 1	Balances brought down from April:	
	Cash balance	29
	Bank balance	654
	Debtors accounts:	
	B King	120
	N Campbell	280
	D Shand	40
	Creditors accounts:	
	U Barrow	60
	A Allen	440
	R Long	100
,, 2	B King pays us by cheque, having deducted 2½ per cent cash discount £3.	117
,, 8	We pay R Long his account by cheque, deducting 5 per cent cash discount £5.	95
,, 11	We withdrew £100 cash from the bank for business use.	100
,, 16	N Campbell pays us his account by cheque, deducting 2½ per cent discount £7.	273
,, 25	We paid wages in cash.	92
,, 28	D Shand pays us in cash after having deducted 5 per cent cash discount.	38
,, 29	We pay U Barrow by cheque less 5 per cent cash discount £3.	57
,, 30	We pay A Allen by cheque less 2½ per cent cash discount £11.	429

We have included folio numbers to make the example more realistic.

Cash Book										(page 64)
	Folio	Discount	Cash	Bank		Folio	Discount	Cash	Bank
19X8		£	£	£	19X8		£	£	£
May 1 Balance	b/d		29	654	May 8 R Long	PL58	5		95
,, 2 B King	SL13	3		117	,, 11 Cash	C			100
,, 11 Bank	C		100		,, 25 Wages	GL77		92	
,, 16 N Campbell	SL84	7		273	,, 29 U Barrow	PL15	3		57
,, 28 D Shand	SL91	2	38		,, 30 A Allen	PL98	11		429
					,, 31 Balances	c/d		75	363
		12	167	1,044			19	167	1,044
Jun 1 Balances	b/d		75	363					

Sales Ledger
B King (page 13)

19X8		*Folio*	£	19X8		*Folio*	£
May 1	Balance	b/d	120	May 2	Bank	CB64	117
				May 2	Discount	CB64	3
			120				120

N Campbell (page 84)

19X8		*Folio*	£	19X8		*Folio*	£
May 1	Balance	b/d	280	May 16	Bank	CB64	273
				May 16	Discount	CB64	7
			280				280

D Shand (page 91)

19X8		*Folio*	£	19X8		*Folio*	£
May 1	Balance	b/d	40	May 28	Cash	CB64	38
				May 28	Discount	CB64	2
			40				40

Purchases Ledger
U Barrow (page 15)

19X8		*Folio*	£	19X8		*Folio*	£
May 29	Bank	CB64	57	May 1	Balance	b/d	60
May 29	Discount	CB64	3				
			60				60

R Long (page 58)

19X8		*Folio*	£	19X8		*Folio*	£
May 8	Bank	CB64	95	May 1	Balance	b/d	100
May 8	Discount	CB64	5				
			100				100

A Allen (page 98)

19X8		*Folio*	£	19X8		*Folio*	£
May 30	Bank	CB64	429	May 1	Balance	b/d	440
May 30	Discount	CB64	11				
			440				440

General Ledger
Wages (page 77)

19X8		*Folio*	£
May 25	Cash	CB64	92

Discounts Received   *(page 88)*

		19X8	*Folio*	£
		May 31 Total for		
		the month	CB64	19

Discounts Allowed   *(page 89)*

19X8	*Folio*	£	
May 31 Total for the month	CB64	12	

Is the above method of entering discounts correct?
   You can easily check. See the following:

Discounts in Ledger Accounts	Debits		Credits	
		£		
Discounts Received	U Barrow	3	Discounts	
	R Long	5	received	
	A Allen	11	account	£19
		19		
				£
Discounts Allowed	Discounts		B King	3
	allowed		N Campbell	7
	account	£12	D Shand	2
				12

You can see that proper double entry has been carried out. Equal amounts, in total, have been entered on each side of the accounts.

13.11 Bank overdrafts

A firm may borrow money from a bank by means of a bank overdraft. This means that the firm is allowed to pay more out of the bank account, by paying out cheques, than the total amount which is placed in the account.
   Up to this point the bank balances have all been money at the bank, so they have all been assets, i.e. debit balances. When the account is overdrawn the firm owes money to the bank, so the account is a liability and the balance becomes a credit one.
   Taking the cash book last shown, suppose that the amount payable to A Allen was £1,429 instead of £429. Thus the amount in the bank account, £1,044, is exceeded by the amount withdrawn. We will take the discount for Allen as being £11. The cash book would appear as follows:

Cash Book *(page 64)*

19X8		Discount £	Cash £	Bank £	19X8		Discount £	Cash £	Bank £
May 1	Balances b/d		29	654	May 8	R Long	5		95
„ 2	B King	3		117	„ 11	Cash			100
„ 11	Bank		100		„ 25	Wages		92	
„ 16	N Campbell	7		273	„ 29	U Barrow	3		57
„ 28	D Shand	2	38		„ 30	A Allen	11		1,429
„ 31	Balance c/d			637	„ 31	Balance c/d		75	
		12	167	1,681			19	167	1,681
Jun 1	Balance b/d		75		Jun 1	Balance b/d			637

On a balance sheet a bank overdraft will be shown as an item included under the heading current liabilities.

13.12 Bank cash books

In the United Kingdom, except for very small organisations, three-column cash books will not usually be found. All receipts, whether of cash or cheques, will be banked daily. A petty cash book will be used for payments of cash. This means that there will not be a need for cash columns in the cash book itself. This is described on p. 161.

This would certainly not be true in many other countries in the world, especially where banking systems are not as developed or as efficient as in the UK. Three-column cash books will be much more widely used in these countries.

New terms

Bank statement (p. 109): Copy of our current account given to us by our bank.

Contra (p. 111): A contra, for cash book items, is where both the debit and the credit entries are shown in the cash book.

Discounts allowed (p. 113): A reduction given to customers who pay their accounts within the time allowed.

Discounts received (p. 113): A reduction given to us by a supplier when we pay their account before the time allowed has elapsed.

Folio columns (p. 112): Columns used for entering reference numbers.

Posting (p. 112): The act of using one book as a means of entering the transactions to another account.

Main points to remember

1 A cash book consists of a cash account and a bank account put together into one book.

2 Cash discounts are given to encourage people to pay their accounts within a stated time limit.

3 'Cash discount' is the name given for discount for quick payment even though in fact the payment may be made by cheque.

4 The discounts columns in the cash book make it easier to enter up the books. They act as a collection point for discounts allowed and discounts received, for which double entry is completed when the totals are transferred to the discounts accounts in the general ledger, usually at the end of the month.

Multiple-choice questions

Now attempt Set No 2 of multiple choice questions – *see* pp. 573–6.

Review questions

13.1 Write up a two-column cash book from the following details, and balance off as at the end of the month:

19X8
May   1   Started business with capital in cash £100.
  „   2   Paid rent by cash £10.
  „   3   F Lake lent us £500, paid by cheque.
  „   4   We paid B McKenzie by cheque £65.
  „   5   Cash sales £98.
  „   7   N Miller paid us by cheque £62.
  „   9   We paid B Burton in cash £22.
  „   11 Cash sales paid direct into the bank £53.
  „   15 G Moores paid us in cash £65.
  „   16 We took £50 out of the cash till and paid it into the bank account.
  „   19 We repaid F Lake £100 by cheque.
  „   22 Cash sales paid direct into the bank £66.
  „   26 Paid motor expenses by cheque £12.
  „   30 Withdrew £100 cash from the bank for business use.
  „   31 Paid wages in cash £97.

13.2A Write up a two-column cash book from the following:

19X9
Nov 1 Balance brought forward from last month: Cash £105; Bank £2,164.
„   2 Cash sales £605.
„   3 Took £500 out of the cash till and paid it into the bank.
„   4 J Matthews paid us by cheque £217.
„   5 We paid for postage stamps in cash £60.
„   6 Bought office equipment by cheque £189.
„   7 We paid J Lucas by cheque £50.
„   9 Received rates refund by cheque £72.
„ 11 Withdrew £250 from the bank for business use.
„ 12 Paid wages in cash £239.
„ 14 Paid motor expenses by cheque £57.
„ 16 L Levy lent us £200 in cash.
„ 20 R Norman paid us by cheque £112.
„ 28 We paid general expenses in cash £22.
„ 30 Paid insurance by cheque £74.

13.3 A three-column cash book is to be written up from the following details, balanced off, and the relevant discount accounts in the general ledger shown.

19X8
Mar 1 Balances brought forward: Cash £230; Bank £4,756.
„   2 The following paid their accounts by cheque, in each case deducting 5 per cent cash discounts: R Burton £140; E Taylor £220; R Harris £300.
„   4 Paid rent by cheque £120.
„   6 J Cotton lent us £1,000 paying by cheque.
„   8 We paid the following accounts by cheque in each case deducting a 2½ per cent cash discount: N Black £360; P Towers £480; C Rowse £800.
„ 10 Paid motor expenses in cash £44.
„ 12 H Hankins pays his account of £77, by cheque £74, deducting £3 cash discount.
„ 15 Paid wages in cash £160.
„ 18 The following paid their accounts by cheque, in each case deducting 5 per cent cash discount: C Winston £260; R Wilson & Son £340; H Winter £460.
„ 21 Cash withdrawn from the bank £350 for business use.
„ 24 Cash Drawings £120.
„ 25 Paid T Briers his account of £140, by cash £133, having deducted £7 cash discount.
„ 29 Bought fixtures paying by cheque £650.
„ 31 Received commission by cheque £88.

13.4A Enter the following in three-column cash book. Balance off the cash book at the end of the month and show the discount accounts in the general ledger.

19X8

June   1   Balances brought forward: Cash £97; Bank £2,186.
  „   2   The following paid us by cheque in each case deducting a 5 per cent cash discount: R Harris £1,000; C White £280; P Peers £180; O Hardy £600.
  „   3   Cash sales paid direct into the bank £134.
  „   5   Paid rent by cash £88.
  „   6   We paid the following accounts by cheque, in each case deducting 2½ per cent cash discount: J Charlton £400; H Sobers £640; D Shallcross £200.
  „   8   Withdrew cash from the bank for business use £250.
  „   10   Cash sales £206.
  „   12   D Deeds paid us their account of £89 by cheque less £2 cash discount.
  „   14   Paid wages by cash £250.
  „   16   We paid the following accounts by cheque: L Lucas £117 less cash discount £6; D Fisher £206 less cash discount £8.
  „   20   Bought fixtures by cheque £8,000.
  „   24   Bought motor lorry paying by cheque £7,166.
  „   29   Received £169 cheque from D Steel.
  „   30   Cash sales £116.
  „   30   Bought stationery paying by cash £60.

14

The sales journal and the sales ledger

Objectives

After you have studied this chapter, you should:

- *be able to draw up a sales invoice*

- *be able to enter up a sales journal and post to the sales ledger*

- *understand how trade discounts differ from cash discounts*

- *appreciate the need for credit control*

14.1 Introduction

In Chapter 11 we saw that the ledger had been split up into a set of journals and ledgers. This chapter explains about sales journals and sales ledgers.

14.2 Cash sales

When goods are paid for immediately by cash there is no need to enter such sales in the sales journal. In such cases we do not need to know the names and addresses of customers and what has been sold to them.

14.3 Credit sales

In many businesses most of the sales will be made on credit rather than for immediate cash. In fact, the sales of some businesses will consist entirely of credit sales.

For each credit sale the selling firm will send a document to the buyer showing full details of the goods sold and the prices of the goods. This document is known as an **invoice**, and to the seller it is known as a **sales invoice**. The seller will keep one or more copies of each sales invoice for his own use. Exhibit 14.1 is an example of an invoice.

Exhibit 14.1

Your Purchase Order 10/A/980		J Blake
	INVOICE No 16554	7 Over Warehouse
		Leicester LE1 2AP
		1 September 19X9

To: D Poole & Co
    45 Charles Street
    Manchester M1 5ZN

	Per unit	Total
	£	£
21 cases McBrand Pears	20	420
5 cartons Kay's Flour	4	20
6 cases Joy's Vinegar	20	120
		560

Terms 1¼% cash discount
if paid within one month

You must not think that all invoices will look exactly like the one chosen as Exhibit 14.1. Each business will have its own design. All invoices will be numbered, and they will contain the names and addresses both of the supplier and of the customer. In this case the supplier is J Blake and the customer is D Poole.

14.4 Copies of sales invoices

As soon as the sales invoices for the goods being sent have been made out, they are sent to the customer. The firm will keep copies of all these sales invoices. These copies will have been made at the same time as the original.

14.5 Entering into the sales journal

From the copy of the sales invoice the seller enters up his sales journal. This book is merely a list, showing the following:

- Date
- Name of customer
- Invoice number
- Folio column
- Final amount of invoice

There is no need to show details of the goods sold in the sales journal. This can be found by looking at copy invoices.

We can now look at Exhibit 14.2, which is a sales journal, starting with the record of the sales invoice already shown in Exhibit 14.1. Let us assume that the entries are on page 26 of the journal.

Exhibit 14.2

Sales Journal				(page 26)
		Invoice No	*Folio*	*Amount*
19X9				£
Sept 1	D Poole	16554		560
„ 8	T Cockburn	16555		1,640
„ 28	C Carter	16556		220
„ 30	D Stevens & Co	16557		1,100
				3,520

14.6 Posting credit sales to the sales ledger

Instead of having one ledger for all accounts, we now have a separate sales ledger for credit sale transactions. This was described in Chapter 11.

1 The credit sales are now posted, one by one, to the debit side of each customer's account in the sales ledger.

2 At the end of each period the total of the credit sales is posted to the credit of the sales account in the general ledger. This is now illustrated in Exhibit 14.3.

Exhibit 14.3 Posting credit sales

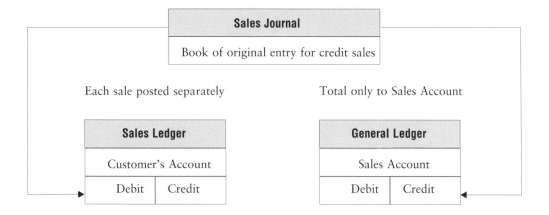

14.7 An example of posting credit sales

The sales journal in Exhibit 14.2 is now shown again. This time posting is made to the sales ledger and the general ledger. Notice the completion of the folio columns with the reference numbers.

Sales Journal			(page 26)
	Invoice No	Folio	Amount £
19X9			
Sept 1 D Poole	16554	SL 12	560
„ 8 T Cockburn	16555	SL 39	1,640
„ 28 C Carter	16556	SL 125	220
„ 30 D Stevens & Co	16557	SL 249	1,100
Transferred to Sales Account		GL 44	3,520

Sales Ledger

D Poole *(page 12)*

19X9	Folio	£	
Sept 1 Sales	SJ 26	560	

T Cockburn *(page 39)*

19X9	Folio	£	
Sept 8 Sales	SJ 26	1,640	

C Carter *(page 125)*

19X9	Folio	£	
Sept 28 Sales	SJ 26	220	

D Stevens & Co *(page 249)*

19X9	Folio	£	
Sept 30 Sales	SJ 26	1,100	

General Ledger

Sales *(page 44)*

	19X9	Folio	£
	Sept 30 Credit sales for the month	SJ 26	3,520

Alternative names for the sales journal are sales book and sales day book.

Before you continue you should attempt Review question 14.1.

14.8 Trade discounts

Suppose you are the proprietor of a business. You are selling to three different kinds of customer:

1 Traders who buy a lot of goods from you.
2 Traders who buy only a few items from you.
3 Direct to the general public.

The traders themselves have to sell the goods to the general public in their own areas. They have to make a profit to help finance their businesses, so they will want to pay you less than retail price.

The traders **1** who buy in large quantities will not want to pay as much as traders **2** who buy in small quantities. You want to attract such large customers, and so you are happy to sell to traders **1** at a lower price.

This means that your selling prices are at three levels: **1** to traders buying large quantities, **2** to traders buying small quantities, and **3** to the general public.

So that your staff do not need three different price lists, **1**, **2** and **3**, all goods are shown at the same price. However, a reduction (discount), called a **trade discount**, is given to traders **1** and **2**. Exhibit 14.4 is an example.

Exhibit 14.4

You are selling a make of food mixing machine. The basic price is £200. Trader group **1** is given 25 per cent trade discount, trader group **2** is given 20 per cent, and the general public get no trade discount. The price paid by each type of customer would be:

		Trader 1 £		Trader 2 £	General Public £
Basic price		200		200	200
Less Trade discount	(25%)	50	(20%)	40	nil
Price to be paid by customer		150		160	200

Exhibit 14.5 is an invoice for goods sold to D Poole. It is for the same items as were shown in Exhibit 14.1, but this time the seller is R Grant and he uses trade discounts to get to the price paid by his customers.

Exhibit 14.5

Your Purchase Order 11/A/G80	**INVOICE No 30756**	R Grant Higher Side Preston PR1 2NL 2 September 19X9 Tel (01703) 33122 Fax (01703) 22331
To: D Poole & Co 45 Charles Street Manchester M1 5ZN		

	Per unit £	Total £
21 cases McBrand Pears	25	525
5 cartons Kay's Flour	5	25
6 cases Joy's Vinegar	25	150
		700
Less 20% trade discount		140
		560

By comparing Exhibits 14.1 and 14.5 you can see that the prices paid by D Poole were the same. It is simply the method of calculating the price that is different.

14.9 No double entry for trade discounts

As trade discount is simply a way of calculating sales prices, no entry for trade discount should be made in the double entry records nor in the sales journal. The recording of Exhibit 14.5 in R Grant's sales journal and D Poole's personal account will appear:

Sales Journal				(page 87)
		Invoice No	*Folio*	*Amount* £
19X9 Sept 2	D Poole	30756	SL 32	560

Sales Ledger

D Poole   *(page 32)*

19X9		*Folio*	£	
Sept 2 Sales		SJ 87	560	

To compare with cash discounts:

- Trade discounts: not shown in double entry accounts.
- Cash discounts: are shown in double entry accounts.

14.10 Manufacturer's recommended retail price

Looking at an item displayed in a shop window, you will frequently see something like the following:

Automatic Washer:	Manufacturer's Recommended Retail Price	£500
	less discount of 20 per cent	£100
	You pay only	£400

Very often the manufacturer's recommended retail price is a figure above what the manufacturer would expect the public to pay for its product. Probably, in the case shown, the manufacturer would have expected the public to pay around £400 for its product.

The inflated figure used for the 'manufacturer's recommended retail price' is simply a sales gimmick. Most people like to feel they are getting a bargain. The salesmen know that someone usually would prefer to get '20 per cent discount' and pay £400, rather than the price simply be shown as £400 with no mention of a discount.

14.11 Credit control

Any organisation which sells goods on credit should keep a close check to ensure that debtors pay their accounts on time. If this is not done properly, the amount of debtors can grow to an amount that will make the business short of cash. The following procedures should be carried out:

1   For each debtor a limit should be set. They should then not be allowed to owe more than this limit. The amount of the limit will depend on the circumstances. Such

things as the size of the customer's firm and the amount of business done with it, as well as its past record of payments, will help in choosing the limit figure.

2   As soon as the payment date has been reached it should be seen whether payment has been made or not. Failure to pay on time may mean you refusing to supply any more goods unless payment is made quickly.

3   Where payment is not forthcoming, after investigation it may be necessary to take legal action to sue the customer for the debt. This will depend on the circumstances.

4   It is important that the customer is aware of what will happen if he does not pay his account by the correct date.

New terms

Sales invoice (p. 123): A document showing details of goods sold and the prices of those goods.

Trade discount (p. 126): A reduction given to a customer when calculating the selling prices of goods.

Main points to remember

1   Cash sales are not entered in the sales journal.

2   The sales journal is a list recording all credit sales for each period.

3   The sales journal is used for posting credit sales to the sales ledger.

4   The total of the sales journal for the period is posted to the credit of the sales account.

5   No entry is made for trade discounts in the double entry accounts.

6   All firms should have an adequate system of credit control over their debtors.

Review questions

14.1   You are to enter up the sales journal from the following details. Post the items to the relevant accounts in the sales ledger and then show the transfer to the sales account in the general ledger.

19X6

Mar	1	Credit sales to J Gordon	£187
„	3	Credit sales to G Abrahams	£166
„	6	Credit sales to V White	£12
„	10	Credit sales to J Gordon	£55
„	17	Credit sales to F Williams	£289
„	19	Credit sales to U Richards	£66
„	27	Credit sales to V Wood	£28
„	31	Credit sales to L Simes	£78

14.2A Enter up the sales journal from the following, then post the items to the relevant accounts in the sales ledger. Then show the transfer to the sales account in the general ledger.

19X8

Mar	1	Credit sales to J Johnson	£305
„	3	Credit sales to T Royes	£164
„	5	Credit sales to B Howe	£45
„	7	Credit sales to M Lee	£100
„	16	Credit sales to J Jakes	£308
„	23	Credit sales to A Vinden	£212
„	30	Credit sales to J Samuels	£1,296

14.3 F Benjamin of 10 Lower Street, Plymouth, is selling the following items, the recommended retail prices as shown: white tape £10 per roll, green baize at £4 per metre, blue cotton at £6 per sheet, black silk at £20 per dress length. He makes the following sales:

19X7

May 1 To F Gray, 3 Keswick Road, Portsmouth: 3 rolls white tape, 5 sheets blue cotton, 1 dress length black silk. Less 25 per cent trade discount.

„ 4 To A Gray, 1 Shilton Road, Preston: 6 rolls white tape, 30 metres green baize. Less 33⅓ per cent trade discount.

„ 8 To E Hines, 1 High Road, Malton: 1 dress length black silk. No trade discount.

„ 20 To M Allen, 1 Knott Road, Southport: 10 rolls white tape, 6 sheets blue cotton, 3 dress lengths black silk, 11 metres green baize. Less 25 per cent trade discount.

„ 31 To B Cooper, 1 Tops Lane, St Andrews: 12 rolls white tape, 14 sheets blue cotton, 9 metres green baize. Less 33⅓ per cent trade discount.

You are to (a) draw up a sales invoice for each of the above sales, (b) enter them up in the sales journal and post to the personal accounts, and (c) transfer the total to the sales account in the general ledger.

14.4A J Fisher, White House, Bolton, is selling the following items, the retail prices as shown: plastic tubing at £1 per metre, polythene sheeting at £2 per length, vinyl padding at £5 per box, foam rubber at £3 per sheet. He makes the following sales:

19X9

June 1 To A Portsmouth, 5 Rockley Road, Worthing: 22 metres plastic tubing, 6 sheets foam rubber, 4 boxes vinyl padding. Less 25 per cent trade discount.

„ 5 To B Butler, 1 Wembley Road, Colwyn Bay: 50 lengths polythene sheeting, 8 boxes vinyl padding, 20 sheets foam rubber. Less 20 per cent trade discount.

„ 11 To A Gate, 1 Bristol Road, Hastings: 4 metres plastic tubing, 33 lengths of polythene sheeting, 30 sheets foam rubber. Less 25 per cent trade discount.

„ 21 To L Mackeson, 5 Maine Road, Bath: 29 metres plastic tubing. No trade discount is given.

„ 30 To M Alison, Daley Road, Box Hill: 32 metres plastic tubing, 24 lengths polythene sheeting, 20 boxes vinyl padding. Less 33⅓ per cent trade discount.

Required:
(a) Draw up a sales invoice for each of the above sales, (b) enter them up in the sales journal and post to the personal accounts, and (c) transfer the total to the sales account in the general ledger.

15

The purchases journal and the purchases ledger

Objectives

After you have studied this chapter, you should:

- *be able to enter purchases invoices into the purchases journal*
- *be able to post the purchases journal to the purchases ledger*

15.1 Purchases invoices

An invoice is a **purchases invoice** when it is entered in the books of the firm purchasing the goods. The same invoice, in the books of the seller, would be a sales invoice. For example for Exhibit 14.1 which is an invoice:

1 In the books of D Poole: it is a purchases invoice;
2 In the books of J Blake: it is a sales invoice.

15.2 Entering into the purchases journal

From the purchases invoices for goods bought on credit, the purchaser enters the details in his purchases journal. This book is merely a list, showing the following:

- date
- name of supplier
- the reference number of the invoice
- folio column
- final amount of invoice

There is no need to show details of the goods bought in the purchases journal. This can be found by looking at the invoices themselves. Exhibit 15.1 is an example of a purchases journal.

Exhibit 15.1

Purchases Journal				(page 49)
		Invoice No	*Folio*	*Amount*
19X9				£
Sept 2	R Simpson	9/101		670
„ 8	B Hamilton	9/102		1,380
„ 19	C Brown	9/103		120
„ 30	K Gabriel	9/104		510
				2,680

15.3 Posting credit purchases to the purchases ledger

We now have a separate purchases ledger. The double entry is as follows:

1 The credit purchases are posted one by one, to the credit of each supplier's account in the purchases ledger.
2 At the end of each period the total of the credit purchases is posted to the debit of the purchases account in the general ledger. This is now illustrated in Exhibit 15.2.

Exhibit 15.2 Posting credit purchases

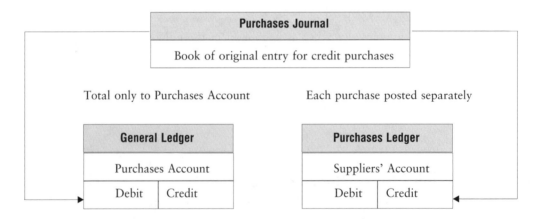

15.4 An example of posting credit purchases

The purchases journal in Exhibit 15.1 is now shown again. This time posting is made to the purchases ledger and the general ledger. Notice the completion of the folio columns.

Purchases Journal   *(page 49)*

		Invoice No	Folio	Amount
19X9				£
Sept 2	R Simpson	9/101	PL 16	670
„ 8	B Hamilton	9/102	PL 29	1,380
„ 19	C Brown	9/103	PL 55	120
„ 30	K Gabriel	9/104	PL 89	510
Transferred to Purchases Account			GL 63	2,680

Purchases Ledger

R Simpson   *(page 16)*

		19X9		Folio	£
		Sept 2	Purchases	PJ 49	670

B Hamilton   *(page 29)*

		19X9		Folio	£
		Sept 8	Purchases	PJ 49	1,380

C Brown   *(page 55)*

		19X9		Folio	£
		Sept 19	Purchases	PJ 49	120

K Gabriel   *(page 89)*

		19X9		Folio	£
		Sept 30	Purchases	PJ 49	510

General Ledger

Purchases   *(page 63)*

19X9		Folio	£
Sept 30 Credit purchases		PJ 49	2,680
for the month			

The purchases journal is often known also as the **purchases book** or as the **purchases day book**.

New terms

Purchases invoice (p. 131): A document received by a purchaser showing details of goods bought and their prices.

Main points to remember

1 Cash purchases are not entered in the purchases journal.

2 The purchases journal is a list of all credit purchases.

3 The purchases journal is used to post the items to the double entry personal accounts in the purchases ledger.

4 The total of credit purchases for the period is posted to the debit of the purchases account.

Review questions

15.1 B Mann has the following purchases for the month of May 19X8:

19X8

May 1 From K King: 4 radios at £30 each, 3 music centres at £160 each. Less 25 per cent trade discount.

„ 3 From A Bell: 2 washing machines at £200 each, 5 vacuum cleaners at £60 each, 2 dishwashers at £150 each. Less 20 per cent trade discount.

„ 15 From J Kelly: 1 music centre at £300 each, 2 washing machines at £250 each. Less 25 per cent trade discount.

„ 20 From B Powell: 6 radios at £70 each. Less 33⅓ per cent trade discount.

„ 30 From B Lewis: 4 dishwashers at £200 each. Less 20 per cent trade discount.

Required:
(a) Enter up the purchases journal for the month.
(b) Post the transactions to the suppliers' accounts.
(c) Transfer the total to the purchases account.

15.2A A Rowland has the following purchases for the month of June 19X9:

19X9

June 2 From C Lee: 2 sets golf clubs at £250 each, 5 footballs at £20 each. Less 25 per cent trade discount.

„ 11 From M Elliott: 6 cricket bats at £20 each, 6 ice skates at £30 each, 4 rugby balls at £25 each. Less 25 per cent trade discount.

„ 18 From B Wood: 6 sets golf trophies at £100 each, 4 sets golf clubs at £300. Less 33⅓ per cent trade discount.

„ 25 From B Parkinson: 5 cricket bats at £40 each. Less 25 per cent trade discount.

„ 30 From N Francis: 8 goal posts at £70 each. Less 25 per cent trade discount.

Required:
(a) Enter up the purchases journal for the month.
(b) Post the items to the suppliers' accounts.
(c) Transfer the total to the purchases account.

15.3 C Phillips, a sole trader, has the following purchases and sales for March 19X9:

Mar 1 Bought from Smith Stores: silk £40, cotton £80. All less 25 per cent trade discount.
„ 8 Sold to Grantley: linen goods £28, woollen items £44. No trade discount.
„ 15 Sold to A Henry: silk £36, linen £144, cotton goods £120. All less 20 per cent trade discount.
„ 23 Bought from C Kelly: cotton £88, linen £52. All less 25 per cent trade discount.
„ 24 Sold to D Sangster: linen goods £42, cotton £48. Less 10 per cent trade discount.
„ 31 Bought from J Hamilton: linen goods £270. Less 33⅓ per cent trade discount.

Required:
(*a*) Prepare the purchases and sales journals of C Phillips from the above.
(*b*) Post the items to the personal accounts.
(*c*) Post the totals of the journals to the sales and purchases accounts.

15.4A A Henriques has the following purchases and sales for May 19X6:

19X6
May 1 Sold to M Marshall: brass goods £24, bronze items £36. Less 25 per cent trade discount.
„ 7 Sold to R Richards: tin goods £70, lead items £230. Less 33⅓ per cent trade discount.
„ 9 Bought from C Clarke: tin goods £400. Less 40 per cent trade discount.
„ 16 Bought from A Charles: copper goods £320. Less 50 per cent trade discount.
„ 23 Sold to T Young: tin goods £50, brass items £70, lead figures £80. All less 20 per cent trade discount.
„ 31 Bought from M Nelson: brass figures £100. Less 50 per cent trade discount.

Required:
(*a*) Write up sales and purchases journals.
(*b*) Post the items to the personal accounts.
(*c*) Post the totals of the journals to the sales and purchases accounts.

16

The returns journals

Objectives

After you have studied this chapter, you should:

- *be able to enter up the returns inwards and returns outwards journals from source documents*

- *be able to post the journal entries to the sales and purchases ledgers*

- *be able to make out statements*

- *be able to enter up the accounts for credit card transactions*

- *understand the need for internal checks*

- *know what use may be made of factoring*

16.1 Returns inwards and credit notes

Sometimes we will agree to customers returning goods to us. This might be for reasons such as the following:

- Goods were of the wrong type
- They were the wrong colour
- Goods were faulty
- Customer had bought more than he needed

We might ask the customers to return the goods. Sometimes they may agree to keep the goods if an allowance is made to reduce the price of the goods.

In each of these cases a document known as a **credit note** will be sent to the customer, showing the amount of the allowance given by us for the return of the faulty goods. It is called a credit note because the customer's account will be credited with the amount of the allowance, to show the reduction in the amount he owes. Exhibit 16.1 shows an example of a credit note.

Exhibit 16.1

```
                                                    R Grant
                                                    Higher Side
   To: D Poole & Co                                 Preston PR1 2NL
       45 Charles Street                            8 September 19X9
       Manchester M1 5ZN

                        CREDIT NOTE No 9/37
```

	Per Unit	Total
	£	£
2 cases McBrand Pears	25	50
Less 20% trade discount		10
		40

To stop them being mistaken for invoices, credit notes are sometimes printed in red.

16.2 Returns inwards journal

The credit notes are listed in a returns inwards journal. This is then used for posting the items, as follows:

1 Sales ledger. Credit the amount of credit notes, one by one, to the accounts of the customers in the sales ledger.
2 General ledger. At the end of the period the total of the returns inwards journal is posted to the debit of the returns inwards account.

16.3 Example of a returns inwards journal

An example of a returns inwards journal showing the items posted to the sales ledger and the general ledger is now shown:

Returns Inwards Journal			(page 10)
	Note No	*Folio*	*Amount*
19X9			£
Sept 2 D Poole	9/37	SL 12	40
„ 17 A Brewster	9/38	SL 58	120
„ 19 C Vickers	9/39	SL 99	290
„ 29 M Nelson	9/40	SL 112	160
Transferred to Returns Inwards Account		GL 114	610

Sales Ledger

D Poole *(page 12)*

	19X9	*Folio*	*£*
	Sept 2 Returns inwards	RI 10	40

A Brewster *(page 58)*

	19X9	*Folio*	*£*
	Sept 17 Returns inwards	RI 10	120

C Vickers *(page 99)*

	19X9	*Folio*	*£*
	Sept 19 Returns inwards	RI 10	290

M Nelson *(page 112)*

	19X9	*Folio*	*£*
	Sept 29 Returns inwards	RI 10	160

General Ledger

Returns Inwards *(page 114)*

19X9	*Folio*	*£*	
Sept 30 Returns for the month	RI 10	610	

Alternative names in use for the returns inwards journal are **returns inwards book** or **sales returns book**, the latter name arising from the fact that it is the goods sold which are returned at a later date.

16.4 Returns outwards and debit notes

If the supplier agrees, goods bought previously may be returned. When this happens a **debit note** is sent to the supplier giving details of the goods and the reason for their return.

The credit note received from the supplier will simply be evidence of the supplier's agreement, and the amounts involved.

Also, an allowance might be given by the supplier for any faults in the goods. Here also, a debit note should be sent to the supplier. Exhibit 16.2 shows an example of a debit note.

Exhibit 16.2

```
                                                    R Grant
                                                    Higher Side
   To: B Hamilton                                   Preston PR1 2NL
        20 Fourth Street                             11 September 19X9
        Kidderminster KD2 4PP

                        DEBIT NOTE No 9/34
```

	Per Unit	Total
	£	£
4 cases Lot's salt	60	240
Less 25% Trade Discount		60
		180

16.5 Returns outwards journal

The debit notes are listed in a returns outwards journal. This is then used for posting the items, as follows:

1 Purchases ledger. Debit the amounts of debit notes, one by one, to the accounts of the suppliers in the purchases ledger.
2 General ledger. At the end of the period, the total of the returns outwards journal is posted to the credit of the returns outwards account.

16.6 Example of a returns outwards journal

An example of a returns outwards journal, showing the items posted to the purchases ledger and the general ledger, is now shown:

Returns Outwards Journal			*(page 7)*
	Note No	*Folio*	*Amount*
19X9			£
Sept 11 B Hamilton	9/34	PL 29	180
„ 16 B Rose	9/35	PL 46	100
„ 28 C Blake	9/36	PL 55	30
„ 30 S Saunders	9/37	PL 87	360
Transferred to Returns Outwards Account		GL 116	670

Purchases Ledger

B Hamilton   *(page 29)*

19X9		Folio	£	
Sept 11 Returns outwards		RO 7	180	

B Rose   *(page 46)*

19X9		Folio	£	
Sept 16 Returns outwards		RO 7	100	

C Blake   *(page 55)*

19X9		Folio	£	
Sept 28 Returns outwards		RO 7	30	

S Saunders   *(page 87)*

19X9		Folio	£	
Sept 30 Returns outwards		RO 7	360	

General Ledger

Returns outwards   *(page 116)*

		19X9		Folio	£
		Sept 30 Returns for the month		RO 7	670

Alternative names in use for the returns outwards journal are **returns outwards book** or **purchases returns book,** the latter name arising from the fact that it is the goods purchased which are returned at a later date.

16.7 Double entry and returns

Exhibit 16.3 shows how double entry is made for both returns inwards and returns outwards.

Exhibit 16.3 Posting returns inwards and returns outwards

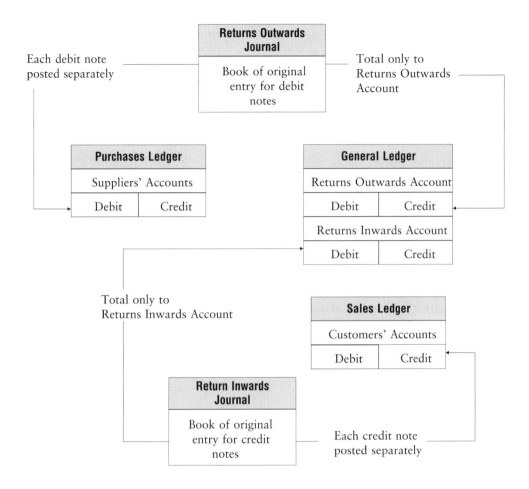

16.8 Statements

At the end of each month a **statement** should be sent to each debtor who owes money on the last day of each month. It is really a copy of the debtor's account in our books. It should show:

1 amount owing at start of month;
2 amount of each sales invoice sent to the debtor during the month;
3 credit notes sent to the debtor in the month;
4 cash and cheques received from the debtor during the month;
5 finally, the amount due from the debtor at the end of the month.

Debtors will use this to see if the account in their accounting records agrees with their account in our records. If in our books they are shown as owing £798, then, depending on items in transit between us, their books should show us as a creditor for £798. The statement also acts as a reminder to the debtors that they owe us money, and will show the date by which they should make payment.

An example of a statement is shown in Exhibit 16.4.

Exhibit 16.4

STATEMENT OF ACCOUNT

R GRANT
Higher Side
Preston PR1 2NL
Tel (0703) 33122
Fax (0703) 22331

Accounts Dept
D Poole & Co
45 Charles Street
Manchester M1 5ZN

Date	Details	Debit	Credit	Balance
19X9		£	£	£
Sept 1	Balance b/d			880
Sept 2	Invoice 30756	560		1,440
Sept 8	Returns 9/37		40	1,400
Sept 25	Bank		880	520
Sept 30	Balance owing c/d			520

All accounts due and payable within 1 month

16.9 Sales and purchases via credit cards

Various banks, building societies and other financial organisations issue credit cards to their customers. Examples are Visa and Access. The holder of the credit card purchases items or services without giving cash or cheques, but simply signs a special voucher used by the store or selling organisation. Later on, usually several weeks later, the credit card holder pays the organisation for which he holds the card, e.g. Visa, for all of his previous month's outgoings.

The sellers of the goods or services then present the vouchers to the credit card company and the total of the vouchers less commission is paid to them by that credit card company.

In effect the sales are 'cash sales' for as far as the purchaser is concerned he has seen goods (or obtained services) and has received them, and in his eyes he has paid for them by using his credit card. Such sales are very rarely sales to anyone other than the general public, as compared with professionals in a specific trade.

Once the customer has departed with his goods, or had the necessary services, he does not become a debtor needing an entry for him in a sales ledger. All the selling company is then interested in, from a recording point of view, is collecting the money from the credit card company.

The double entry needed is:

Sale of items via credit cards:
Dr: Credit card company
Cr: Cash sales

Receipt of money from credit card company:
Dr: Bank
Cr: Credit card company

Commission charged by credit card company:
Dr: Selling expenses
Cr: Credit card company

16.10 Internal check

When sales invoices are being made out they should be scrutinised very carefully. A system is usually set up so that each stage of the preparation of the invoice is checked by someone other than the person whose job it is to send out the invoice. If this were not done then it would be possible for someone inside a firm to send out an invoice, as an instance, at a price less than the true price. Any difference could then be split between that person and the outside firm. If an invoice should have been sent to Ivor Twister & Co for £2,000, but the invoice clerk made it out deliberately for £200, then, if there was no cross-check, the difference of £1,800 could be split between the invoice clerk and Ivor Twister & Co.

Similarly, outside firms could send invoices for goods which were never received by the firm. This might be in collaboration with an employee within the firm, but there are firms sending false invoices which rely on the firms receiving them being inefficient and paying for items never received. There have been firms sending invoices for such items as advertisements which have never been published. The cashier of the firm receiving the invoice, if the firm is an inefficient one, might possibly think that someone in the firm had authorised the advertisements and would pay the bill.

Besides these there are, of course, genuine errors, and these should also be detected. A system is, therefore, set up whereby the invoices have to be subject to scrutiny, at each stage, by someone other than the person who sends out the invoices or is responsible for paying them. Incoming invoices will be stamped with a rubber stamp, with spaces for each stage of the check.

The spaces in the stamp will be filled in by the people responsible for making the checks. For instance:

- Person certifying that the goods were actually received.
- Person certifying that the goods were ordered.
- Person certifying that the prices and calculations on the invoice are correct, and in accordance with the order originally placed and agreed.
- Person certifying that the goods are in good condition and suitable for the purpose for which ordered.

Naturally in a small firm, simply because the office staff might be quite small, this cross-check may be in the hands of only one person other than the person who will pay the invoice. A similar sort of check will be made in respect of sales invoices being sent out.

16.11 Factoring

One of the problems that face many businesses is the time taken by debtors to pay their accounts. Few businesses have so much cash available to them that they do not mind how long the debtor takes to pay. It is a rather surprising fact that a lot of businesses which become bankrupt do so, not because the business is not making profits, but instead because the business has run out of cash funds. Once that happens, the confidence factor in business evaporates, and the business then finds that very few people will supply it with goods, and it also cannot pay its employees. Closure of the firm then happens fairly quickly in many cases.

In the case of debtors, the cash problem may be alleviated by using the services of a financial intermediary called a **factor**.

Factoring is a financial service designed to improve the cash flow of healthy, growing companies, enabling them to make better use of management time and the money tied up in trade credit to customers.

In essence, factors provide their clients with three closely integrated services covering sales accounting and collection, credit management which can include protection against bad debts, and the availability of finance against sales invoices.

16.12 E&OE

On some invoices and other documents you will see 'E&OE' printed at the bottom of the invoice. This abbreviation stands for 'Errors and Omissions Excepted'. Basically, this is a warning that there may possibly be errors or omissions which could mean that the figures shown could be incorrect, and that the recipient should check carefully the figures before taking any action concerning them.

New terms

Credit note (p. 136): A document sent to a customer showing allowance given by a supplier in respect of unsatisfactory goods.

Debit note (p. 138): A document sent to a supplier showing allowance to be given for unsatisfactory goods.

Statement (p. 141): A copy of a customer's personal account taken from the supplier's books.

Main points to remember

1   Goods returned to us by our customers are all entered in a returns inwards journal.

2   The returns inwards journal is used to post each item to the credit of the account of the customer concerned in the sales ledger.

3   The total of the returns inwards journal is debited at the end of the period to the returns inwards account in the general ledger.

4   Goods returned by us to our suppliers are all entered in a returns outwards journal.

5   The returns outwards journal is used to debit the account of each supplier concerned in the purchases ledger.

6   The total of the returns outwards journal is credited at the end of the period to the returns outwards account in the general ledger.

Review questions

16.1 You are to enter up the purchases journal and the returns outwards journal from the following details, then to post the items to the relevant accounts in the purchases ledger and to show the transfers to the general ledger at the end of the month.

19X7

May 1 Credit purchase from H Lloyd £119.
„ 4 Credit purchases from the following: D Scott £98; A Simpson £114; A Williams £25; S Wood £56.
„ 7 Goods returned by us to the following: H Lloyd £16; D Scott £14.
„ 10 Credit purchase from A Simpson £59.
„ 18 Credit purchases from the following: M White £89; J Wong £67; H Miller £196; H Lewis £119.
„ 25 Goods returned by us to the following: J Wong £5; A Simpson £11.
„ 31 Credit purchases from: A Williams £56; C Cooper £98.

16.2A Enter up the sales journal and the returns inwards journal from the following details. Then post to the customer's accounts and show the transfers to the general ledger.

19X8

June 1 Credit sales to: A Simes £188; P Tulloch £60; J Flynn £77; B Lopez £88.
„ 6 Credit sales to: M Howells £114; S Thompson £118; J Flynn £66.
„ 10 Goods returned to us by: A Simes £12; B Lopez £17.
„ 20 Credit sales to M Barrow £970.
„ 24 Goods returned to us by S Thompson £5.
„ 30 Credit sales to M Parkin £91.

16.3 You are to enter up the sales, purchases and the returns inwards and returns outwards journals from the following details, then to post the items to the relevant accounts in the sales and purchase ledgers. The total of the journals are then to be transferred to the accounts in the general ledger.

19X9

May 1 Credit sales: T Thompson £56; L Rodriguez £148; K Barton £145.
„ 3 Credit purchases: P Potter £144; H Harris £25; B Spencer £76.
„ 7 Credit sales: K Kelly £89; N Mendes £78; N Lee £257.
„ 9 Credit purchases: B Perkins £24; H Harris £58; H Miles £123.
„ 11 Goods returned by us to: P Potter £12; B Spencer £22.
„ 14 Goods returned to us by: T Thompson £5; K Barton £11; K Kelly £14.
„ 17 Credit purchases: H Harris £54; B Perkins £65: L Nixon £75.
„ 20 Goods returned by us to B Spencer £14.
„ 24 Credit sales: K Mohammed £57; K Kelly £65; O Green £112.
„ 28 Goods returned to us by N Mendes £24.
„ 31 Credit sales: N Lee £55.

16.4A You are to enter the following items in the books, post to personal accounts, and show transfers to the general ledger.

19X9

July	1	Credit purchases from: K Hill £380; M Norman £500; N Senior £106.
,,	3	Credit sales to: E Rigby £510; E Phillips £246; F Thompson £356.
,,	5	Credit purchases from: R Morton £200; J Cook £180; D Edwards £410; C Davies £66.
,,	8	Credit sales to: A Green £307; H George £250; J Ferguson £185.
,,	12	Returns outwards to: M Norman £30; N Senior £16.
,,	14	Returns inwards from: E Phillips £18; F Thompson £22.
,,	20	Credit sales to: E Phillips £188; F Powell £310; E Lee £420.
,,	24	Credit purchases from: C Ferguson £550; K Ennevor £900.
,,	31	Returns inwards from: E Phillips £27; E Rigby £30.
,,	31	Returns outwards to: J Cook £13; C Davies £11.

17

The journal

Objectives

After you have studied this chapter, you should:

- *be able to enter up the journal*

- *be able to post from the journal to the ledgers*

- *be able to complete opening entries for a set of books*

- *understand the accounting cycle*

17.1 Main books of original entry

We have seen in earlier chapters that most transactions are entered in one of the following special books of original entry:

- Cash book
- Sales journal
- Purchases journal
- Returns inwards journal
- Returns outwards journal

These books have grouped together similar things, e.g. all credit sales are in the sales journal. To trace any of them would be relatively easy, as we know exactly which book would contain the item.

17.2 The journal: the other book of original entry

The other items which do not pass through the above books are much less common, and sometimes much more complicated. It would be easy for a bookkeeper to forget the details of these transactions.

If the bookkeeper left the firm it could be impossible to understand such bookkeeping entries.

What is needed is a form of diary to record such transactions, before the entries are made in the double entry accounts. This book is called **the journal**. It will contain the following, for each transaction.

- The date.
- The name of account(s) to be debited and the amount(s).
- The name of the account(s) to be credited and the amount(s).
- A description and explanation of the transaction (this is called a '**narrative**').

- A reference number for the source documents giving proof of the transaction.

The use of the journal makes fraud by bookkeepers more difficult. It also reduces the risk of entering the item once only instead of having double entry. Despite these advantages there are many firms which do not have such a book.

17.3 Typical uses of the journal

Some of the main uses of the journal are listed below. It must not be thought that this list is a fully detailed one.

- The purchase and sale of fixed assets on credit.
- The correction of errors.
- Writing off bad debts.
- Opening entries. These are the entries needed to open a new set of books.
- Other items.

The layout of the journal can be shown:

The Journal

Date	Details	Folio	Dr	Cr
	The name of the account to be debited.			
	The name of the account to be credited.			
	The narrative.			

You can see that we put on the first line the account to be debited. The second line gives the account to be credited. We do not write the name of the account to be credited directly under the name of the account to be debited. This makes it easier to see which is the debit and which is the credit.

We should remember that the journal is not a double entry account. It is a form of diary, and entering an item in the journal is not the same as recording an item in an account. Once the journal entry is made, the entry in the double entry accounts can then be made.

Note for students

The vertical lines have been included above in order to illustrate how the paper within the journal may be printed. You may find it useful to rule your paper according to this layout when attempting examples and questions on this topic.

17.4 Journal entries in examination questions

If you were to ask examiners what type of bookkeeping and accounting questions are always answered badly by a lot of students they would certainly include 'questions involving journal entries'. This is not because they are difficult, but a lot of students seem to suffer some sort of mental block when doing such questions. The authors, who have been examiners for a large number of accounting bodies around the world, believe that this occurs because students fail to view the journal as a document containing instructions, three per transaction:

        (1) the account(s) to be debited,
        (2) the account(s) to be credited, and

(3) a description of the transaction.

To help you avoid this sort of problem with journal entries, we will first of all show what the entries are in the accounts, and then write up the journal for these entries. We will now look at a few examples, including folio numbers in them.

Purchase and sale on credit of fixed assets

1 A machine is bought on credit from Toolmakers Ltd for £550 on 1 July 19X8.

The transaction involves the acquisition of an asset matched by a new liability. From what you have learned in earlier chapters, you will know that the acquisition of an asset is represented by a debit entry in the asset account. You will also know that a new liability is recorded by crediting a liability account. The double entries would be:

				Machinery		Folio GL1
19X8			£			
July 1	Toolmakers Ltd	PL55	550			

		Toolmakers Ltd			Folio PL55
		19X8		£	
		July 1	Machinery	GL1	550

Now what we have to do is to record those entries in the journal. Remember, the journal is simply a kind of diary, not in account form but in ordinary written form. It says which account has been debited, which account has been credited, and then gives the narrative which simply describes the nature of the transaction. For the transaction above the journal entry will appear as follows:

Date	Details	Folio	Dr	Cr
19X8			£	£
July 1	Machinery	GL 1	550	
	Toolmakers Ltd	PL55		550
	Purchase of milling machine on credit, Capital Purchases invoice No 7/159			

2 Sale of stationery no longer required for £300 on credit to K Lamb on 2 July 19X8.

Here again it is not difficult to work out what entries are needed in the double-entry accounts. They are as follows:

				K Lamb		Folio SL79
19X8			£			
July 2	Stationery	PL55	300			

		Stationery			Folio GL51
		19X8		£	
		July 2	Machinery	GL1	300

The journal entry will appear as follows:

Date	Details	Folio	Dr	Cr
19X8			£	£
July 2	K Lamb	SL79	300	
	Motor vehicles disposal	GL51		300
	Sales of stationery no longer required,			
	See letter ref. KL3X8			

Bad debts

A debt of £78 owing to us from H Mander is written off as a bad debt on 31 August 19X8.

As the debt is now of no value we have to stop showing it as an asset. This means that we will credit H Mander to cancel it out of his account. A bad debt is an expense, and so we will debit it to a Bad Debts Account. The double entry for this is shown as:

	Bad Debts			Folio GL16
19X8			£	
Aug 31	H Mander	SL99	78	

		H Mander		Folio SL99
		19X8		£
		Aug 31 Bad debts	GL16	78

The journal entry is:

Date	Details	Folio	Dr	Cr
19X8			£	£
Aug 31	Bad debts	GL16	78	
	H Mander	SL99		78
	Debt written off as bad. See letter in file HM2X8			

Correction of errors

These are explained in detail in Chapters 31 and 32.

Opening entries

J Brew, after being in business for some years without keeping proper records, now decides to keep a double entry set of books. On 1 July 19X9 he establishes that his assets and liabilities are as follows:

Assets: Motor Van £840, Fixtures £700, Stock £390,
Debtors – B Young £95, D Blake £45, Bank £80, Cash £20.
Liabilities: Creditors – M Quinn £129, C Walters £41.

The Assets therefore total £840 + £700 + £390 + £95 + £45 + £80 + £20 = £2,170; and the Liabilities total £129 + £41 = £170.

The Capital consists of Assets – Liabilities, £2,170 – £170 = £2,000.

We must start the writing up of the books on 1 July 19X9. To do this we:

1   Open asset accounts, one for each asset. Each opening asset is shown as a debit balance.
2   Open liability accounts, one for each liability. Each opening liability is shown as a credit balance.
3   Open an account for the capital. Show it as a credit balance.

The journal records what you are doing, and why.
   Exhibit 17.1 shows:

• The journal
• The opening entries in the double entry accounts

Exhibit 17.1

The Journal   *(page 5)*

Date	Details	Folio	Dr	Cr
19X9			£	£
July 1	Motor van	GL1	840	
	Fixtures	GL2	700	
	Stock	GL3	390	
	Debtors – B Young	SL1	95	
	D Blake	SL2	45	
	Bank	CB1	80	
	Cash	CB1	20	
	Creditors – M Quinn	PL1		129
	C Walters	PL2		41
	Capital	GL4		2,000
	Assets and liabilities at this date entered to open the books.		2,170	2,170

General Ledger
Motor Van   *(page 1)*

19X9		Folio	£	
July 1 Balance		J 5	840	

Fixtures   *(page 2)*

19X9		Folio	£	
July 1 Balance		J 5	700	

Stock   *(page 3)*

19X9		Folio	£	
July 1 Balance		J 5	390	

Capital   *(page 4)*

		19X9		Folio	£
		July 1 Balance		J 5	2,000

Sales Ledger

B Young   *(page 1)*

19X9		Folio	£	
July 1 Balance		J 5	95	

D Blake   *(page 2)*

19X9		Folio	£	
July 1 Balance		J 5	45	

Purchases Ledger

M Quinn   *(page 1)*

	19X9		Folio	£
	July 1 Balance		J 5	129

C Walters   *(page 2)*

	19X9		Folio	£
	July 1 Balance		J 5	41

Cash Book

	Cash	*Bank*	*(page 1)*

19X9		Folio	£	£
July 1 Balances		J 5	20	80

Once these opening balances have been recorded in the books the day-to-day transactions can be entered in the normal manner. The need for opening entries will not occur very often. They will not be needed each year as the balances from last year will have been brought forward. At the elementary level of examinations in bookkeeping, questions are often asked which entail opening a set of books and recording the day-by-day entries for the ensuing period.

Other items

These can be of many kinds and it is impossible to write out a complete list. Several examples are now shown:

1 K Young, a debtor, owed £2,000 on 1 July. He was unable to pay his account in cash, but offers a motor car in full settlement of the debt. The offer is accepted on 5 July 19X9.

   The personal account has now been settled and needs to be credited with the £2,000. On the other hand, the firm now has an extra asset, a motor car, resulting in the motor car account needing to be debited with the £2,000 value that has been placed upon the new car.

   The double entry recorded in the ledgers is:

K Young   SL333

19X9			£	19X9			£
July 1	Balance	b/d	2,000	July 5	Motor car	GL171	2,000

Motor Car   GL171

19X9			£				
July 5	K Young	SL333	2,000				

The journal entry is:

Date	Details	Folio	Dr	Cr
19X9			£	£
July 5	Motor car	GL171	2,000	
	K Young	SL333		2,000
	Accepted motor car in full settlement of debt			
	per letter dated 5/7/19X9			

2   T Jones is a creditor. On 10 July 19X9 his business is taken over by A Lee to whom the debt now is to be paid.

   Here it is just one creditor being exchanged for another one. The action needed is to cancel the amount owing to T Jones by debiting his account, and to show it owing to Lee by opening an account for Lee and crediting it.

   The entry in the ledger accounts is:

T Jones   SL92

19X9			£	19X9			£
July 10	A Lee	SL244	150	July 1	Balance	b/d	150

A Lee   SL244

				19X9			£
				July 10	T Jones	SL92	150

The journal entry is:

Date	Details	Folio	Dr	Cr
19X9			£	£
July 10	T Jones	SL 92	150	
	A Lee	SL 244		150
	Transfer of indebtedness as per letter ref G/1335			

3   We had not yet paid for an office typewriter we bought on credit for £310 when it was discovered to be faulty. On 12 July 19X9 we returned it to the supplier, RS Ltd. An allowance of £310 was offered by the supplier and accepted. As a result, we no longer owe the supplier anything for the typewriter.

   The double entry in the ledger accounts is:

RS Ltd						PL124
19X9			£	19X9		£
July 12	Office machinery	GL288	310	July 1 Balance	b/d	310

Office Machinery						GL288
				19X9		£
				July 12 RS Ltd	PL124	310

The journal entry is:

Date	Details	Folio	Dr	Cr
19X9			£	£
July 12	RS Ltd	PL124	310	
	Office machinery	GL288		310
	Faulty typewriter returned to supplier.			
	Full allowance given. See letter 10/7/19X9.			

17.5 Examination guidance

Later on in your studies, especially in *Business Accounting 2*, you may find that some of the journal entries become rather more complicated than those you have seen so far. The best plan for nearly all students is to follow this advice:

(1) On your examination answer paper write a heading 'Workings'. Then, show the double entry accounts under that heading.

(2) Now put a heading 'Answer', and show the answer in the form of the journal, as shown in this chapter.

If you are so good at the subject that you can manage without showing the workings, leave them out.

If the question asks for journal entries you must *not* fall into the trap of just showing the double entry accounts, as you could get no marks at all even though your double entry records are correct. The examiner wants to see the journal entries, and you must show that as your answer.

17.6 The basic accounting cycle

Now that we have covered all aspects of bookkeeping entries, we can show the whole cycle in the form of the diagram in Exhibit 17.2.

Exhibit 17.2: The accounting cycle for a profit-making organisation

Source documents

Where original information is
to be found

- Sales and purchases invoices
- Debit and credit notes for returns
- Bank paying-in slips and cheque counterfoils
- Receipts for cash paid out and received
- Correspondence containing other financial
  information

Original entry

What happens to it

Classified and then entered in books of prime entry:

- Sales and purchases journals
- Returns inwards and outwards journals
- Cash books*
- The journal

Double entry accounts

Double entry

How the dual aspect of each
transaction is recorded

General ledger	*Sales ledger*	*Purchases ledger*	*Cash Books**
Real and nominal accounts	Debtors' accounts	Creditors' accounts	Cash book and petty cash book

(*Note*: Cash books fulfil both the roles of books
of prime entry and double entry accounts)

Check arithmetic

Checking the arithmetical
accuracy of double entry
accounts

Trial balance

Profit or Loss

Calculation of profit or loss for
the accounting period

Trading and profit and loss account

Closing financial position

Financial statement showing
liabilities, assets and capital at the
end of the accounting period

Balance sheet

New term

Narrative (p. 148): A description and explanation of the transaction recorded in the journal.

Main points to remember

1   The journal is the collection place for items that do not pass fully through the other main books of original entry.

2   Opening entries are made on opening a set of books using double entry.

3   The main parts of the accounting cycle are as follows:

   (*a*)   Collect source documents.

   (*b*)   Enter transactions in books of prime entry.

   (*c*)   Post to ledgers.

   (*d*)   Extract trial balance.

   (*e*)   Prepare trading and profit and loss accounts.

   (*f*)   Draw up balance sheet.

Review questions

17.1   You are to open the books of K Mullings, a trader, via the journal to record the assets and liabilities, and are then to record the daily transactions for the month of May. A trial balance is to be extracted as on 31 May 19X9.

19X9
May   1   *Assets:* Premises £2,000; Motor van £450; Fixtures £600; Stock £1,289. Debtors: N Hardy £40; M Nelson £180. Cash at bank £1,254; Cash in hand £45.
        Liabilities: Creditors: B Blake £60; V Reagan £200.
May   1   Paid rent by cheque £15.
  „   2   Goods bought on credit from: B Blake £20; C Harris £56; H Gordon £38; N Lee £69.
  „   3   Goods sold on credit to: K O'Connor £56; M Benjamin £78; L Staines £98; N Duffy £48; B Green £118; M Nelson £40.
  „   4   Paid for motor expenses in cash £13.
  „   7   Cash drawings by proprietor £20.
  „   9   Goods sold on credit to: M Benjamin £22; L Pearson £67.
  „   11   Goods returned to Mullings by: K O'Connor £16; L Staines £18.
  „   14   Bought another motor van on credit from Better Motors Ltd £300.
  „   16   The following paid Mullings their accounts by cheque less 5 per cent cash discount: N Hardy; M Nelson; K O'Connor; L Staines.
  „   19   Goods returned by Mullings to N Lee £9.
  „   22   Goods bought on credit from: J Johnson £89; T Best £72.
  „   24   The following accounts were settled by Mullings by cheque less 5 per cent cash discount: B Blake; V Reagan; N Lee.
  „   27   Salaries paid by cheque £56.
  „   30   Paid rates by cheque £66.
  „   31   Paid Better Motors Ltd a cheque for £300.

17.2 You are to show the journal entries necessary to record the following items:

(*a*) 19X8 May 1 Bought a motor vehicle on credit from Kingston Garage for £6,790.
(*b*) 19X8 May 3 A debt of £34 owing from H Newman was written off as a bad debt.
(*c*) 19X8 May 8 Office furniture bought by us for £490 was returned to the supplier Unique Offices, as it was unsuitable. Full allowance will be given us.
(*d*) 19X8 May 12 We are owed £150 by W Charles. He is declared bankrupt and we received £39 in full settlement of the debt.
(*e*) 19X8 May 14 We take £45 goods out of the business stock without paying for them.
(*f*) 19X8 May 28 Some time ago we paid an insurance bill thinking that it was all in respect of the business. We now discover that £76 of the amount paid was in fact insurance of our private house.
(*g*) 19X8 May 28 Bought machinery £980 on credit from Systems Accelerated.

17.3A Show the journal entries necessary to record the following items:

19X7
Apr   1   Bought fixtures on credit from J Harper £1,809.
 „   4   We take £500 goods out of the business stock without paying for them.
 „   9   £28 of the goods taken by us on 4 April is returned back into stock by us. We do not take any money for the return of the goods.
 „   12   K Lamb owes us £500. He is unable to pay his debt. We agree to take some office equipment from him at the value and so cancel the debt.
 „   18   Some of the fixtures bought from J Harper, £65 worth, are found to be unsuitable and are returned to him for full allowance.
 „   24   A debt owing to us by J Brown of £68 is written off as a bad debt.
 „   30   Office equipment bought on credit from Super Offices for £2,190.

18

The analytical petty cash book and the imprest system

Objectives

After you have studied this chapter, you should:

- *be able to write up a petty cash book*
- *be able to post the petty cash items to ledger accounts*
- *understand the imprest system*

18.1 Division of the cash book

With the growth of the firm it has been seen that it becomes necessary to have several books instead of just one ledger.

These ideas can be extended to the cash book. It is obvious that in almost any firm there will be many small cash payments to be made. It would be an advantage if the records of these payments could be kept separate from the main cash book. Where a separate book is kept it is known as a **petty cash book**.

The advantages of such an action can be summarised:

- The task of handling and recording the small cash payments could be given by the cashier to a junior member of staff. This person would then be known as the petty cashier. The cashier, who is a higher paid member of staff, would be saved from routine work.
- If small cash payments were entered into the main cash book, these items would then need posting one by one to the ledgers. If travelling expenses were paid to staff on a daily basis, this could mean over 250 postings to the staff travelling expenses account during the year, i.e. 5 days per week × 50 working weeks per year. However, if a special form of petty cash book is kept, it would only be the monthly totals for each period that need posting to the general ledger. If this were done, only 12 entries would be needed in the staff travelling expenses account instead of over 250.

When a petty cashier makes a payment to someone, then that person will have to fill in a voucher showing exactly what the payment was for. They usually have to attach bills, e.g. for petrol, to the petty cash voucher. They would sign the voucher to certify that their expenses had been received from the petty cashier.

18.2 The imprest system

The **imprest system** is where the cashier gives the petty cashier enough cash to meet his needs for the following period. At the end of the period the cashier finds out the amounts spent by the petty cashier, and gives him an amount equal to that spent. The petty cashier will produce the petty cash vouchers as evidence of the amount spent. The petty cash in hand should then be equal to the *original* amount with which the period was started. Exhibit 18.1 shows an example of this method.

Exhibit 18.1

		£
Period 1	The cashier gives the petty cashier	100
	The petty cashier pays out in the period	78
	Petty cash now in hand	22
	The cashier now gives the petty cashier the amount spent	78
	Petty cash in hand at the end of period 1	100
Period 2	The petty cashier pays out in the period	84
	Petty cash now in hand	16
	The cashier now gives the petty cashier the amount spent	84
	Petty cash in hand end of period 2	100

It may be necessary to increase the fixed sum, often called the cash 'float', to be held at the start of each period. In the above case, if we had wanted to increase the 'float' at the end of the second period to £120, then the cashier would have given the petty cashier an extra £20, i.e. £84 + £20 = £104.

18.3 Illustration of an analytical petty cash book

An analytical petty cash book is often used. One of these is shown as Exhibit 18.2. This is for an elementary school.

The receipts column is the debit side of the petty cash book. On giving £300 to the petty cashier on 1 September the credit entry is made in the cash book while the debit entry is made in the petty cash book. A similar entry is made on 30 September for the £244 paid by the headteacher to the petty cashier. This amount covers all expenses paid by the petty cashier. On the credit side:

1   Enter date and details of each payment. Put amount in the total column.
2   Put the amount in the column for the type of cxpense.
3   At the end of each period, add up the totals column.
4   Now add up each of the expense columns. The total of 3 should equal the total of all the expense columns. In Exhibit 18.2 this is £244.
5   Then balance off the petty cash book, carrying down the petty cash in hand balance to the next period.

To complete the double entry for petty cash expenses paid:

1   Total of each expense column is debited to the expense account in the general ledger.
2   Enter folio number of each general ledger page under each of the expense columns in the petty cash book.
3   The last column in the petty cash book is a ledger column. In this column items paid out of petty cash which need posting to a ledger other than the general ledger are shown. This would happen if a purchases ledger account was settled out of petty cash.

The double entry for all the items in Exhibit 18.2 appears as Exhibit 18.3.

19X8			£
Sept	1	The headteacher gives £300 as float to the petty cashier	
		Payments out of petty cash during September:	
,,	2	Petrol: School bus	16
,,	3	J Green – travelling expenses of staff	23
,,	3	Postages	12
,,	4	D Davies – travelling expenses of staff	32
,,	7	Cleaning expenses	11
,,	9	Petrol: School bus	21
,,	12	K Jones – travelling expenses of staff	13
,,	14	Petrol: School bus	23
,,	15	L Black – travelling expenses of staff	5
,,	16	Cleaning expenses	11
,,	18	Petrol: School bus	22
,,	20	Postages	12
,,	22	Cleaning expenses	11
,,	24	G Wood – travelling expenses of staff	7
,,	27	Settlement of C Brown's account in the Purchases Ledger	13
,,	29	Postages	12
,,	30	The headteacher reimburses the petty cashier the amount spent in the month.	

Exhibit 18.2

PETTY CASH BOOK *(page 31)*

Receipts	Folio	Date		Details	Voucher No	Total	Motor Expenses	Staff Travelling Expenses	Postages	Cleaning	Ledger Folio	Ledger Accounts
£						£	£	£	£	£		£
300	CB 19	Sept	1	Cash								
		,,	2	Petrol	1	16	16					
		,,	3	J Green	2	23		23				
		,,	3	Postages	3	12			12			
		,,	4	D Davies	4	32		32				
		,,	7	Cleaning	5	11				11		
		,,	9	Petrol	6	21	21					
		,,	12	K Jones	7	13		13				
		,,	14	Petrol	8	23	23					
		,,	15	L Black	9	5		5				
		,,	16	Cleaning	10	11				11		
		,,	18	Petrol	11	22	22					
		,,	20	Postages	12	12			12			
		,,	22	Cleaning	13	11				11		
		,,	24	G Wood	14	7		7				
		,,	27	C Brown	15	13					PL 18	13
		,,	29	Postages	16	12			12			
						244	82	80	36	33		13
							GL 17	GL 29	GL 44	GL 64		
244	CB 22	,,	30	Cash								
		,,	30	Balance	c/d	300						
544						544						
300		Oct	1	Balance	b/d							

Exhibit 18.3

			Cash Book (Bank Column only)		*(page 19)*
			19X8		£
			Sept 1 Petty cash PCB 31		300
			„ 30 Petty cash PCB 31		244

General Ledger

School Bus Expenses   *(page 17)*

19X8		*Folio*	£	
Sept 30 Petty cash		PCB 31	82	

Staff Travelling Expenses   *(page 29)*

19X8		*Folio*	£	
Sept 30 Petty cash		PCB 31	80	

Postages   *(page 44)*

19X8		*Folio*	£	
Sept 30 Petty cash		PCB 31	36	

Cleaning   *(page 64)*

19X8		*Folio*	£	
Sept 30 Petty cash		PCB 31	33	

Purchases Ledger

C Brown   *(page 18)*

19X8		Folio	£	19X8			£
Sept 30 Petty cash		PCB 31	13	Sept 1 Balance	b/d		13

18.4 Bank cash book

In an organisation with both a cash book and a petty cash book, the cash book is often known as a bank cash book. This means that *all* cash payments are entered in the petty cash book, and the bank cash book will contain *only* bank columns and discount columns. In this type of organisation any cash sales will be paid directly into the bank.

In such a cash book, as in fact could happen in an ordinary cash book, an extra column could be added. In this would be shown the details of the cheques banked, just the total of the banking being shown in the total column.

Exhibit 18.4 shows the receipts side of the bank cash book. The totals of the banking made on the three days were £192, £381 and £1,218. The details column shows what the bankings are made up of.

Exhibit 18.4

Bank Cash Book (Receipts side)

Date	Details	Discount	Items	Total Banked
19X9		£	£	£
May 14	G Archer	5	95	
„ 14	P Watts	3	57	
„ 14	C King		40	192
„ 20	K Dooley	6	114	
„ 20	Cash Sales		55	
„ 20	R Jones		60	
„ 20	P Mackie	8	152	381
„ 31	J Young		19	
„ 31	T Broome	50	950	
„ 31	Cash Sales		116	
„ 31	H Tiller	7	133	1,218

New terms

Imprest system (p. 159): A system where a refund is made of the total paid out in a period.

Petty cash book (p. 158): A cash book for small payments.

Main points to remember

1 The petty cash book saves (*a*) the main cash book and (*b*) the ledger accounts from containing a lot of trivial detail.

2 The use of the petty cash book enables the chief cashier or a senior member of staff to delegate this type of work to a much junior member of staff.

3 The chief cashier should periodically check the work performed by the petty cashier.

4 All payments made by the petty cashier should have petty cash vouchers as evidence of proof of expense.

Review questions

18.1 The following is a summary of the petty cash transactions of Jockfield Ltd for May 19X8.

May 1 Received from Cashier £300 as petty cash float

			£
„	2	Postages	18
„	3	Travelling	12
„	4	Cleaning	15
„	7	Petrol for delivery van	22
„	8	Travelling	25
„	9	Stationery	17
„	11	Cleaning	18
„	14	Postage	5

May	15	Travelling	8
„	18	Stationery	9
„	18	Cleaning	23
„	20	Postage	13
„	24	Delivery van 5,000 mile service	43
„	26	Petrol	18
„	27	Cleaning	21
„	29	Postage	5
„	30	Petrol	14

You are required to:

(a) Rule up a suitable petty cash book with analysis columns for expenditure on cleaning, motor expenses, postage, stationery, travelling.

(b) Enter the month's transactions.

(c) Enter the receipt of the amount necessary to restore the imprest and carry down the balance for the commencement of the following month.

(d) State how the double entry for the expenditure is completed.

(*Association of Accounting Technicians*)

18.2

(a) Why do some businesses keep a petty cash book as well as a cash book?

(b) Kathryn Rochford keeps her petty cash book on the imprest system, the imprest being £25. For the month of April 19X9 her petty cash transactions were as follows:

			£
Apr	1	Petty cash balance	1.13
„	2	Petty cashier presented vouchers to cashier and obtained cash to restore the imprest	23.87
„	4	Bought postage stamps	8.50
„	9	Paid to Courtney Bishop, a creditor	2.35
„	11	Paid bus fares	1.72
„	17	Bought envelopes	0.70
„	23	Received cash for personal telephone call	0.68
„	26	Bought petrol	10.00

(i)   Enter the above transactions in the petty cash book and balance the petty cash book at 30 April, bringing down the balance on 1 May.

(ii) On 1 May Kathryn Rochford received an amount of cash from the cashier to restore the imprest. Enter this transaction in the petty cash book.

(c) Open the ledger accounts to complete the double entry for the following:

(i)   The petty cash analysis columns headed *Postage and Stationery* and *Travelling Expenses*;

(ii) The transactions dated 9 and 23 April 19X9.

(*Northern Examinations and Assessment Board: GCSE*)

18.3A Rule up a petty cash book with analysis columns for office expenses, motor expenses, cleaning expenses, and casual labour. The cash float is £350 and the amount spent is reimbursed on 30 June.

19X7			£
June	1	H Sangster – casual labour	13
,,	2	Letterheadings	22
,,	2	Unique Motors – motor repairs	30
,,	3	Cleaning materials	6
,,	6	Envelopes	14
,,	8	Petrol	8
,,	11	J Higgins – casual labour	15
,,	12	Mrs Body – cleaner	7
,,	12	Paper-clips	2
,,	14	Petrol	11
,,	16	Typewriter repairs	1
,,	16	Petrol	9
,,	21	Motor taxation	50
,,	22	T Sweet – casual labour	21
,,	23	Mrs Body – cleaner	10
,,	24	P Dennis – casual labour	19
,,	25	Copy paper	7
,,	26	Flat Cars – motor repairs	21
,,	29	Petrol	12
,,	30	J Young – casual labour	16

19

Value added tax

Objectives

After you have studied this chapter, you should be able to:

- *enter up VAT in all the necessary books and accounts*

- *distinguish between taxable firms and other firms*

- *make out sales invoices including charges for VAT*

- *fill in a value added tax return form*

19.1 Introduction

Value Added Tax is a tax charged on the supply of most goods and services in the United Kingdom. Some goods and services are not taxable, for example postal services. In addition some persons and firms are exempted – these are dealt with later. Value Added Tax is usually abbreviated as VAT and is dealt with by the government's Customs and Excise department.

19.2 Rate of value added tax

The standard rate of VAT is decided by Parliament. It has been changed from time to time. At the time of writing it is 17.5 per cent. There is also currently a reduced rate of 8% on domestic fuel and power and one of 5% on the installation of some energy-saving materials, and a zero rate. In this book most of the examples shown will be at the rate of 10 per cent. This is simply because it is easy to calculate. Most examining bodies have set VAT questions assuming a rate of 10 per cent to make the calculations easier for examination candidates.

19.3 Taxable firms

Imagine that Firm A takes raw materials it has grown and sells some to the general public and some to traders.

1 **Sale to the general public**

   Firm A sells goods to Jones for £100 + VAT.

		£	
The sales invoice is for:	Price	100	
	+ VAT 10%	10	= Total price £110

   Firm A will then pay the £10 it has collected to the Customs and Excise.

2   **Sale to another trader, who then sells to the general public**
    Firm A sells goods to Firm B for £100 + VAT.

	£	
The sales invoice is for: Price	100	
+ VAT 10%	10	= Total price £110

Firm B alters the goods in some way, and then sells them to a member of the general public for £140 + VAT.

	£	
The sales invoice is for: Price	140	
+ VAT 10%	14	= Total price £154

In this case Firm A will pay the Customs and Excise £10 for VAT collected. Firm B will pay the Customs and Excise a cheque for £4, being the amount collected £14 less the VAT paid to A £10 = £4.

In the above cases you can see that the full amount of VAT has fallen on the person who finally buys the goods. Firms A and B have merely acted as collectors of the tax.

The value of goods sold by us or of services supplied by us is known as our **outputs**. Thus VAT on such items may be called **output tax**. The value of goods bought by us or of services supplied to us is known as **inputs**. The VAT on these items is, therefore, **input tax**.

19.4 Exempted firms

Some firms do not have to add VAT on to the price at which they sell their products or services. Some firms will not get a refund of the VAT they have themselves paid on goods and services bought by them. The types of firms exempted can be listed under two headings:

1   **Nature of business.** Various types of business do not have to add VAT to charges for goods or services. A bank for instance does not have to add VAT on to its bank charges.
2   **Small firms.** If small firms do register for VAT then they will have to keep full VAT records in addition to charging out VAT. To save very small businesses the costs and effort of keeping such records the government, therefore, allows them not to register unless they want to, provided that their turnover is below a certain amount (currently £50,000). They can also deregister if their turnover falls below a certain level (currently £48,000).

19.5 Zero rated firms

This special category of firm:

1   does not have to add VAT on to the selling price of products, and
2   can obtain a refund of all VAT paid on the purchase of goods or services.

If, therefore, £100,000 of goods are sold by the firm, nothing has to be added for VAT but, if £8,000 VAT had been paid by it on goods or services bought, then the firm would be able to claim a full refund of the £8,000 paid.

It is **2** above which distinguishes it from an exempted firm. A zero rated firm is, therefore, in a better position than an exempted firm. Examples of zero rated firms are firms selling food.

19.6 Partly exempt traders

Some traders will find that they are selling some goods which are exempt and some which are zero rated and others which are standard rated. These traders will have to apportion their turnover accordingly, and follow the rules already described for each separate part of their turnover.

19.7 Different methods of accounting for VAT

We can see from what has been said already that the accounting needed will vary between:

1   **Firms which can recover VAT paid.** All firms except exempted firms do not suffer VAT as an expense. They either:

- get a refund of whatever VAT they have paid, as in the case of a zero rated firm; or

- collect VAT from their customers, deduct the VAT paid on goods and services bought by the firm, and simply remit the balance owing to the Customs and Excise.

2   **Firms which cannot recover VAT paid.** This applies to all firms which are treated as exempted firms and, therefore, suffer the tax because they cannot get it refunded.

The following discussion of the accounting entries needed will, therefore, distinguish between these two types of firm: those which do not suffer VAT as an expense, and those to which VAT is an expense.

19.8 Firms which can recover VAT paid

1 Taxable firms

Value added tax and sales invoices

A taxable firm will have to add VAT to the value of the sales invoices. It must be pointed out that this is based on the amount of the invoice *after* any trade discount has been deducted. Exhibit 19.1 is an invoice drawn up from the following details:

On 2 March 19X8, W Frank & Co, Hayburn Road, Stockport, sold the following goods to R Bainbridge Ltd, 267 Star Road, Colchester. Bainbridge's order No was A/4/559, for the following items:

  200 Rolls T56 Black Tape at £6 per 10 rolls
  600 Sheets R64 Polythene at £10 per 100 sheets
  7,000 Blank Perspex B49 Markers at £20 per 1,000

All of these goods are subject to VAT at the rate of 10 per cent. A trade discount of 25 per cent is given by Frank & Co. The sales invoice is numbered 8851.

Exhibit 19.1

```
                              W Frank & Co
                              Hayburn Road
                            Stockport SK2 5DB

                          INVOICE No 8851              Date: 2 March 19X8
      To:  R Bainbridge
           267 Star Road
           Colchester CO1 1BT                         Your order no A/4/559
```

		£
200 Rolls T56 Black Tape @ £6 per 10 rolls		120
600 Sheets R64 Polythene @ £10 per 100 sheets		60
7,000 Blank Perspex B49 Markers @ £20 per 1,000		140
		320
Less Trade Discount 25%		80
		240
Add VAT 10%		24
		264

The sales book will normally have an extra column for the VAT contents of the sales invoice. This is needed to make it easier to account for VAT. The entry of several sales invoices in the sales book and in the ledger accounts can now be examined:

W Frank & Co sold the following goods during the month of March 19X8:

		Total of invoice, after trade discount deducted but before VAT added	VAT 10%
19X8		£	£
March 2	R Bainbridge Ltd (*see* Exhibit 19.1)	240	24
„ 10	S Lange & Son	300	30
„ 17	K Bishop	160	16
„ 31	R Andrews	100	10

Sales Book					*(page 58)*
	Invoice No	Folio	Net	VAT	Gross
19X8			£	£	£
March 2 R Bainbridge Ltd	8851	SL 77	240	24	264
„ 10 S Lange & Son	8852	SL 119	300	30	330
„ 17 K Bishop	8853	SL 185	160	16	176
„ 31 R Andrews	8854	SL 221	100	10	110
Transferred to general ledger			800	80	880
			GL 76	GL 90	

Now that the sales book has been written up, the next task is to enter the amounts of the invoices in the individual customers' accounts in the sales ledger. These are simply charged with the full amounts of the invoices including VAT.

As an instance of this K Bishop will be shown as owing £176. When he pays his account he will pay £176. It will then be the responsibility of W Frank & Co to ensure that the figure of £16 VAT in respect of this item is included in the total cheque payable to the Customs and Excise.

Sales Ledger

R Bainbridge Ltd (page 77)

19X8		Folio	£	
Mar 2 Sales		SB 58	264	

S Lange & Son (page 119)

19X8		Folio	£	
Mar 10 Sales		SB 58	330	

K Bishop (page 185)

19X8		Folio	£	
Mar 17 Sales		SB 58	176	

R Andrews (page 221)

19X8		Folio	£	
Mar 31 Sales		SB 58	110	

In total, therefore, the personal accounts have been debited with £880, this being the total of the amounts which the customers will have to pay. The actual sales of the firm are not £880; the amount which is actually sales is £800, the other £80 being simply the VAT that W Frank & Co are collecting on behalf of the government. The double entry is made in the general ledger:

1   Credit the sales account with the sales content only, i.e. £800.
2   Credit the Value Added Tax account with the VAT content only, i.e. £80.

These are shown as

General Ledger

Sales (page 76)

		19X8		Folio	£
		Mar 31 Credit sales		SB 58	800

Value Added Tax (page 90)

		19X8		Folio	£
		Mar 31 Sales book: VAT		SB 58	80

Value added tax and purchases

In the case of a taxable firm, the firm will have to add VAT to its sales invoices, but it will *also* be able to get a refund of the VAT which it pays on its purchases.

Instead of paying VAT to the Customs and Excise, and then claiming a refund of the VAT on purchases, the firm can set off the amount paid as VAT on purchases against the amount payable as VAT on sales. This means that only the difference has to be paid to the Customs and Excise. It is shown as:

		£
(a)	VAT collected on sales invoices	xxx
(b)	*Less* VAT already paid on purchases	xxx
(c)	Net amount to be paid to the Customs and Excise	xxx

In certain fairly rare circumstances (a) may be less than (b). If that were the case, then it would be the Customs and Excise that would refund the difference (c) to the firm. Such a settlement between the firm and the Customs and Excise will take place at least every three months.

The recording of purchases in the purchases book and purchases ledger follows a similar method to that of sales, but with the personal accounts being credited instead of debited. We can now look at the records of purchases for the same firm whose sales have been dealt with, W Frank & Co. The firm made the following purchases for March 19X8:

			Total of invoice, after trade discount deducted but before VAT added	VAT 10%
			£	£
19X8				
Mar	1	E Lyal Ltd (*see* Exhibit 19.2)	180	18
„	11	P Portsmouth & Co	120	12
„	24	J Davidson	40	4
„	29	B Cofie & Son Ltd	70	7

Before looking at the recording of these in the purchases records, compare the first entry for E Lyal Ltd with Exhibit 19.2 to ensure that the correct amounts have been shown.

Date: 1/3/19X8 Your order no BB/667 To: W Frank & Co Hayburn Road Stockport	E Lyal Ltd College Avenue St Albans Hertfordshire ST2 4JA **INVOICE No K453/A** Terms: Strictly net 30 days

	£
50 metres of BYC plastic 1 metre wide × £3 per metre	150
1,200 metal tags 500 mm × 10p each	120
	270
Less Trade discount at 33⅓%	90
	180
Add VAT 10%	18
	198

Exhibit 19.2

The purchases book can now be entered up.

Purchases Book				*(page 38)*
	Folio	*Net*	*VAT*	*Gross*
19X8		£	£	£
March 1 E Lyal Ltd	PL 15	180	18	198
„ 11 P Portsmouth	PL 70	120	12	132
„ 24 J Davidson	PL 114	40	4	44
„ 29 B Cofie Ltd	PL 166	70	7	77
Transferred to general ledger		410	41	451
		GL 54	GL 90	

These are entered in the purchases ledger. Once again there is no need for the VAT to be shown as separate amounts in the accounts of the suppliers.

Purchases Ledger

E Lyal Ltd   *(page 15)*

			19X8	*Folio*	£
			Mar 1 Purchases	PB 38	198

P Portsmouth   *(page 70)*

			19X8	*Folio*	£
			Mar 11 Purchases	PB 38	132

J Davidson   *(page 114)*

			19X8	*Folio*	£
			Mar 24 Purchases	PB 38	44

B Cofie Ltd   *(page 166)*

			19X8	*Folio*	£
			Mar 29 Purchases	PB 38	77

The personal accounts have been credited with a total of £451, this being the total of the amounts which W Frank & Co will have to pay to them.

The actual cost of purchases is not, however, £451. You can see that the correct amount is £410. The other £41 is the VAT which the various firms are collecting for the Customs and Excise. This amount is also the figure for VAT which is reclaimable from the Customs and Excise by W Frank & Co. The debit entry in the purchases account is, therefore, £410, as this is the actual cost of the goods to the firm. The other £41 is entered on the debit side of the VAT account.

Notice that there is already a credit of £80 in the VAT account in respect of the VAT added to Sales.

General Ledger

Purchases *(page 54)*

19X8		*Folio*	£	
Mar 31 Credit purchases		PB 38	410	

Value Added Tax *(page 90)*

19X8		*Folio*	£	19X8		*Folio*	£
Mar 31 Purchases Book:		PB 38	41	Mar 31 Sales Book:		SB 58	80
„ 31 Balance c/d			39				
			80				80
				Apr 1 Balance b/d			39

In the final accounts of W Frank & Co, the following entries would be made:

Trading Account for the month ended 31 March 19X8:
Debited with £410 as a transfer from the Purchases account
Credited with £800 as a transfer from the Sales account

Balance Sheet as at 31 March 19X8:
Balance of £39 (credit) on the VAT account would be shown as a current liability, as it represents the amount owing to the Customs and Excise for VAT.

2 Zero rated firms

These firms:

1 Do not have to add VAT on to their sales invoices, as their rate of VAT is zero or nil.
2 Can, however, reclaim from the Customs and Excise any VAT paid on goods or services bought.

Accordingly, because of **1** no VAT is entered in the Sales Book. VAT on sales does not exist. Because of **2** the Purchases Book and Purchases Ledger will appear exactly in the same manner as for taxable firms, as already shown in the case of W Frank & Co.

The VAT account will only have debits in it, being the VAT on Purchases. Any balance on this account will be shown in the balance sheet as a debtor.

19.9 VAT and cash discounts

Where a cash discount is offered for speedy payment, VAT is calculated on an amount represented by the value of the invoice less such a discount. Even if the cash discount is lost because of late payment, the VAT will not change.

Exhibit 19.3 shows an example of such a sales invoice, assuming a cash discount offered of 2.5 per cent and the VAT rate at 10 per cent.

Exhibit 19.3

Date: 1.3.19X8
Your Order No: TS/778
 	
To: R Noble
       Belsize Road
       Edgeley
       Stockport
	ATC Ltd
	18 High Street
	London WC2 E9AN
	
	INVOICE No ZT48910

	£
80 paper dispensers @ 20 each	1,600
Less Trade discount at 25%	400
	1,200
Add VAT 10%	117*
	1,317
Terms: Cash discount 2.5% if paid within 30 days	

* *Note*: The VAT has been calculated on the net price £1,200 less cash discount 2.5 per cent, i.e. £30 = £1,170 × 10% = £117.

19.10 Firms which cannot get refunds of VAT paid

As these firms do not add VAT on to the value of their sales invoices there is obviously no entry for VAT in the Sales Book or the Sales Ledger. They do not get a refund of VAT on purchases. This means that there will not be a VAT account. All that will happen is that VAT paid is included as part of the cost of the goods bought.

A purchase of goods for £120 + VAT £12 from D Oswald Ltd will appear as:

Purchases Book

	£
19X8	
May 16 D Oswald Ltd	132

Purchases Ledger
D Oswald Ltd

		£
	19X8	
	May 16 Purchases	132

General Ledger
Purchases

	£		£
19X8		19X8	
May 31 Credit purchases for		May 31 Transfer to Trading	
the month	132	Account	132

Trading Account for the month ended 31 May 19X8 (extract)

	£
Purchases	132

19.11 VAT included in gross amount

You will often know only the gross amount of an item. This figure will in fact be made up of the net amount plus VAT. To find the amount of VAT which has been added to the net amount, a formula capable of being used with any rate of VAT can be used. It is:

$$\frac{\% \text{ rate of VAT}}{100 + \% \text{ rate of VAT}} \times \text{Gross Amount} = \text{VAT}$$

Suppose that the gross amount of sales was £1,650 and the rate of VAT was 10 per cent. Find the amount of VAT and the net amount before VAT was added. Using the formula:

$$\frac{10}{100 + 10} \times £1,650 = \frac{10}{110} \times £1,650 = £150$$

Therefore the net amount was £1,500, which with VAT £150 added, becomes £1,650 gross.

Given a rate of 17.5 per cent VAT, to find the amount of VAT in a gross price of £705, the calculation is:

$$\frac{17.5}{100 + 17.5} \times £705 = \frac{7}{47} \times £705 = £105$$

19.12 VAT on items other than sales and purchases

VAT is not just paid on purchases. It is also payable on many items of expense and on the purchase of fixed assets.

Firms which *can* get refunds of VAT paid will not include VAT as part of the cost of the expense or fixed asset. Firms which *cannot* get refunds of VAT paid will include the VAT cost as part of the expense or fixed asset. For example, two firms buying similar items would treat the following items as shown:

	Firm which can reclaim VAT		*Firm which cannot reclaim VAT*	
Buys Machinery	Debit Machinery	£200	Debit Machinery	£220
£200 + VAT £20	Debit VAT Account	£20		
Buys Stationery	Debit Stationery	£150	Debit Stationery	£165
£150 + VAT £15	Debit VAT Account	£15		

19.13 Relief from VAT on bad debts

It is possible to claim relief on any debt which is more than six months old and has been written off in the accounts. Should the debt later be paid, the VAT refunded will then have to be paid back to the Customs and Excise.

19.14 Purchase of cars

Normally the VAT paid on a car bought for a business is not reclaimable.

19.15 VAT owing

VAT owing by or to the firm can be included with debtors or creditors, as the case may be. There is no need to show the amount(s) owing as separate items.

19.16 Columnar day books and VAT

The use of columns for VAT in both sales and purchases analysis books is shown on pp. 184–5.

19.17 Value added tax return forms

At the end of each VAT accounting period a form VAT 100 has to be filled in and sent to the Customs and Excise. The most important part of the form is concerned with columns 1 to 9 which are shown in Exhibit 19.4. For illustration we have assumed a VAT rate of 10 per cent.

The contents of the columns on form VAT 100 are now explained:

1 We have added £8,750 VAT on to our sales invoices for the period.
2 This column would show the VAT due (but not paid) on all goods and related services acquired in this period from other EC member states. In this case there were no such transactions.
3 Total of columns 1 and 2.
4 We have made purchases and incurred expenses during the period on which we have been charged £6,250 VAT.
5 As we have collected £8,750 VAT from our customers, but only suffered £6,250 on all purchases and expenses, we therefore owe the Customs and Excise £2,500, i.e. £8,750 – £6,250.
6 Our total value of sales for the period was £97,500.
7 Our total value of purchases and expenses was £71,900, but some of these expenses were not subject to a charge for VAT.
8 Of the sales included under 6 £10,000 of it was to other countries within the European Community. VAT was not charged on these sales.
9 Of the total purchases under 7 £1,450 was from other countries within the European Community.

Only columns **1**, **3**, **4** and **5** actually refer to accounting for VAT. The other columns are for statistical purposes so that the UK government can assess the performance of the economy and similar matters.

Exhibit 19.4

£

		£
VAT due in this period on **sales** and other outputs	1	8,750
VAT due in this period on **acquisitions** from other **EC Member States**	2	–
Total VAT due **(the sum of boxes 1 and 2)**	3	8,750
VAT reclaimed in this period on **purchases** and other inputs (including acquisitions from the EC)	4	6,250
Net VAT to be paid to Customs or reclaimed by you (difference between boxes 3 and 4)	5	2,500
Total value of **sales** and all other outputs excluding any VAT, **Include your box 8 figure**	6	97,500
Total value of **purchases** and all other inputs excluding any VAT. **Include your box 9 figure**	7	71,900
Total value of all supplies of goods and related services, excluding any VAT, to other **EC Member States**	8	10,000
Total value of all **acquisitions** of goods and related services, excluding any VAT, from other **EC Member States**	9	1,450

19.18 VAT on goods taken for private use

If a trader takes some goods out of his own business stock for his own private use, then he should be charged with any VAT due on these goods.

For instance, suppose that Smith, a furniture dealer, takes a table and chairs out of stock for permanent use in his own home. The cost to the business has been Cost price + Value added tax. Therefore the proprietor's drawings should be charged with both the cost price of the goods plus VAT.

The double entry needed, assuming goods taken of £1,000 + VAT 10 per cent, would therefore be:

Drawings:	Debit	£1,100
Purchases:	Credit	£1,000
VAT account:	Credit	£100

There can be complicating circumstances, outside the scope of this book, which might influence the amount of VAT to be charged on such drawings.

New terms

Exempted firms (p. 166): Firms which do *not* have to add VAT to the price of goods and services supplied to them, but which *cannot* obtain a refund of VAT paid on goods and services received by them.

Inputs (p. 166): Value of goods and services *received* by our firm from others.

Input tax (p. 166): VAT added on to the price of inputs received.

Outputs (p. 166): Value of goods and services *supplied* by our firm to others.

Output tax (p. 166): VAT added on to the prices of outputs by our firm.

Value added tax (p. 167): A tax charged on the supply of most goods and services.

Zero rated firms (p. 166): Firms which do not have to add VAT to goods and services supplied by them to others, but which also receive a *refund* of VAT on goods and services received by them.

Main points to remember

1 Very small firms with a low turnover (at the time of writing it is £46,000, but it changes frequently) do *not* have to register for VAT. They can, however, do so if they wish.

2 The VAT account should show the balance owing to, or by, the Customs and Excise department of HM Government.

3 If a firm cannot get a refund of VAT on its costs, then the VAT will form part of the cost transferred to the trading and profit and loss accounts, or be shown as a fixed asset in the balance sheet.

4 In a firm which charges VAT on sales invoices sent out, the VAT itself is not regarded as part of the sales figure in the trading account.

5 VAT is calculated on the sales value less any cash discount offered.

Review questions

19.1 On 1 May 19X7, D Wilson Ltd, 1 Hawk Green Road, Stockport, sold the following goods on credit to G Christie & Son, The Golf Shop, Hole-in-One Lane, Marple, Cheshire:

Order No A/496
3 sets 'Boy Michael' golf clubs at £270 per set.
150 Watson golf balls at £8 per 10 balls.
4 Faldo golf bags at £30 per bag.

Trade discount is given at the rate of $33\frac{1}{3}$%.
All goods are subject to VAT at 10%.

(*a*) Prepare the sales invoice to be sent to G Christie & Son. The invoice number will be 10586.
(*b*) Show the entries in the Personal Ledgers of D Wilson Ltd and G Christie & Son.

19.2A On 1 March 19X6, C Black, Curzon Road, Stockport, sold the following goods on credit to J Booth, 89 Andrew Lane, Stockport SK1 1AA, Order No 1697:

20,000 Coils Sealing Tape	@ £4.40 per 1,000 coils
40,000 Sheets Bank A5	@ £4.50 per 1,000 sheets
24,000 Sheets Bank A4	@ £4.25 per 1,000 sheets

      All goods are subject to VAT at 10%.

(*a*) Prepare the sales invoice to be sent to J Booth.
(*b*) Show the entries in the Personal Ledgers of J Booth, and C Black.

19.3 The following sales have been made by S Thompson Ltd during the month of June 19X9. All the figures are shown net after deducting trade discount, but before adding VAT at the rate of 10 per cent.

19X9

August 1	to M Sinclair & Co	£150
„ 8	to M Brown & Associates	£260
„ 19	to A Axton Ltd	£80
„ 31	to T Christie	£30

You are required to enter up the Sales Book, Sales Ledger and General Ledger in respect of the above items for the month.

19.4 The following sales and purchases were made by R Colman Ltd during the month of May 19X6.

		Net	*VAT added*
19X6		£	£
May 1	Sold goods on credit to B Davies & Co	150	15
„ 4	Sold goods on credit to C Grant Ltd	220	22
„ 10	Bought goods on credit from:		
	G Cooper & Son	400	40
	J Wayne Ltd	190	19
„ 14	Bought goods on credit from B Lugosi	50	5
„ 16	Sold goods on credit to C Grant Ltd	140	14
„ 23	Bought goods on credit from S Hayward	60	6
„ 31	Sold goods on credit to B Karloff	80	8

Enter up the Sales and Purchases Books, Sales and Purchases Ledgers and the General Ledger for the month of May 19X6. Carry the balance down on the VAT account.

19.5A The credit sales and purchases for the month of December 19X7 in respect of C Dennis & Son Ltd were:

			Net, after trade discount	VAT 10%
19X7			£	£
Dec	1	Sales to M Morris	140	14
„	4	Sales to G Ford Ltd	290	29
„	5	Purchases from P Hillman & Son	70	7
„	8	Purchases from J Lancia	110	11
„	14	Sales to R Volvo Ltd	180	18
„	18	Purchases from T Leyland & Co	160	16
„	28	Sales to G Ford Ltd	100	10
„	30	Purchases from J Lancia	90	9

Write up all of the relevant books and ledger accounts for the month.

19.6 Louise Baldwin commenced business as a wholesaler on 1 March 19X9.

Her sales on credit during March 19X9 were:

March 9	Neville's Electrical
	4 electronic typewriters list price £180 each, less 20% trade discount
March 17	Maltby plc
	20 computer printers list price £200 each, less 25% trade discount
March 29	Neville's Electrical
	Assorted software list price £460, less 20% trade discount

All transactions are subject to Value Added Tax at 10%.

(a) Rule up a sales day book and head the main columns as follows.

Date	Name and Details	List price less trade discount £–p	VAT £–p	Total £–p

Enter the above information in the sales day book, totalling and ruling off at the end of March 19X9.

(b) Make the necessary postings from the sales day book to the personal and nominal accounts in the ledger.

(c) Prepare a trial balance at 31 March 19X9.

(Edexcel Foundation, London Examinations: GCSE)

19.7A Mudgee Ltd issued the following invoices to customers in respect of credit sales made during the last week of May 19X7. The amounts stated are all net of Value Added Tax. All sales made by Mudgee Ltd are subject to VAT at 15%.

Invoice No	Date	Customer	Amount
			£
3045	25 May	Laira Brand	1,060.00
3046	27 May	Brown Bros	2,200.00
3047	28 May	Penfold's	170.00
3048	29 May	T Tyrrell	460.00
3049	30 May	Laira Brand	1,450.00
			£5,340.00

On 29 May Laira Brand returned half the goods (in value) purchased on 25 May. An allowance was made the same day to this customer for the appropriate amount.

On 1 May 19X7 Laira Brand owed Mudgee Ltd £2,100.47. Other than the purchases detailed above Laira Brand made credit purchases (including VAT) of £680.23 from Mudgee Ltd on 15 May. On 21 May Mudgee Ltd received a cheque for £2,500 from Laira Brand.

Required:
(a) Show how the above transactions would be recorded in Mudgee Ltd's Sales Book for the week ended 30 May 19X7.
(b) Describe how the information in the Sales Book would be incorporated into Mudgee Ltd's double entry system.
(c) Reconstruct the personal account of Laira Brand as it would appear in Mudgee Ltd's ledger for May 19X7.

(*Association of Accounting Technicians*)

20

Columnar day books

Objectives

After you have studied this chapter, you should be able to:

- *decide which basis is to be used for the selection of analysis columns for columnar day books*

- *write up analysis books for sales, purchases or for any other aspect of an organisation*

20.1 Purchases analysis books

Some firms use only one book to record all items obtained on credit. This will include purchases, stationery, fixed assets, motor expenses and so on. All credit invoices for any expense will be entered in this book.

However, all of the various types of items are not simply lumped together, as the firm needs to know how much was for purchases, how much for stationery, how much for motor expenses, etc., so that the relevant expense accounts can have the correct amount of expenses entered in them. This is achieved by having a set of analysis columns in the book; all of the items are entered in a total column, but then they are analysed as between the different sorts of expenses, etc.

Exhibit 20.1 shows such a purchases analysis book, or 'columnar purchases day book', drawn up for a month from the following list of items obtained on credit:

19X9				£
May	1	Bought goods from D Watson Ltd on credit		296
,,	3	Bought goods on credit from W Donachie & Son		76
,,	5	Motor van repaired, received invoice from Barnes Motors Ltd		112
,,	6	Bought stationery from J Corrigan		65
,,	8	Bought goods on credit from C Bell Ltd		212
,,	14	Motor lorry serviced, received invoice from Barnes Motors Ltd		39
,,	23	Bought stationery on credit from A Hartford & Co		35
,,	26	Bought goods on credit from M Doyle Ltd		243
,,	30	Received invoice for carriage inwards on goods from G Owen		58

Exhibit 20.1

Columnar Purchases Day Book   (page 105)

Date	Name of firm	PL Folio	Total	Purchases	Stationery	Motor expenses	Carriage inwards
19X9			£	£	£	£	£
May 1	D Watson Ltd	129	296	296			
„ 3	W Donachie & Son	27	76	76			
„ 5	Barnes Motors Ltd	55	112			112	
„ 6	J Corrigan & Co	88	65		65		
„ 8	C Bell Ltd	99	212	212			
„ 14	Barnes Motors Ltd	55	39			39	
„ 23	A Hartford & Co	298	35		35		
„ 26	M Doyle Ltd	187	243	243			
„ 30	G Owen	222	58				58
			1,136	827	100	151	58
				GL 77	GL 97	GL 156	GL 198

Exhibit 20.1 shows that the figure for each item is entered in the Total column, and is then also entered in the column for the particular type of expense. At the end of the month the arithmetical accuracy of the additions can be checked by comparing the total of the Total column with the sum of totals of all of the other columns.

It can be seen that the total of purchases for the month of May was £827 and therefore this can be debited to the Purchases Account in the General Ledger; similarly the total of stationery bought on credit in the month can be debited to the Stationery Account in the General Ledger and so on. The folio number of the page to which the relevant total has been debited is shown immediately under the total figure for each column, e.g. under the column for purchases is GL 77, meaning that the item has been entered in the General Ledger page 77.

Note for students

The vertical lines have been included above in order to illustrate how the paper within the purchases analysis book may be printed. You may find it useful to rule your paper according to this layout when attempting examples and questions on this topic. If you do, remember that the number of columns will vary according to the circumstances.

The entries can now be shown:

General Ledger

Purchases Account   (page 77)

		£
19X9		
May 31 Purchases analysis 105		827

Stationery   (page 97)

		£
19X9		
May 31 Purchases analysis 105		100

Motor Expenses   (page 156)

		£
19X9		
May 31 Purchases analysis 105		151

Carriage Inwards (page 198)

19X9	£	
May 31 Purchases analysis 105	58	

The individual accounts of the creditors, whether they be for goods or for expenses such as stationery or motor expenses, can be kept together in a single Purchases Ledger. There is no need for the Purchases Ledger simply to have accounts only for creditors for purchases. Perhaps there is a slight misuse of the name Purchases Ledger where this happens, but it is common practice amongst a lot of firms. Many firms will give it the more correct title of Bought Ledger.

To carry through the double entry involved with Exhibit 20.1 the Purchases Ledger is now shown.

Purchases Ledger

W Donachie & Son (page 27)

	19X9			£
	May 3 Purchases	PB 105		76

Barnes Motors Ltd (page 55)

	19X9			£
	May 5 Purchases	PB 105		112
	„ 14 „	PB 105		39

J Corrigan & Co (page 88)

	19X9			£
	May 6 Purchases	PB 105		65

C Bell Ltd (page 99)

	19X9			£
	May 8 Purchases	PB 105		212

D Watson Ltd (page 129)

	19X9			£
	May 1 Purchases	PB 105		296

M Doyle Ltd (page 187)

	19X9			£
	May 26 Purchases	PB 105		243

G Owen (page 222)

	19X9			£
	May 20 Purchases	PB 105		58

A Hartford & Co (page 298)

	19X9			£
	May 13 Purchases	PB 105		35

If the business were split up into departments or sections, instead of having one

Purchases column it would be possible to have one column for *each* of the departments. By this means the total purchases for each department for the accounting period could be ascertained.

20.2 Sales analysis books

Where, instead of knowing only the total of sales for the accounting period, it would be preferable to know the sales for each section or department of the business, a sales analysis book could be kept. For a firm selling sports goods, household goods and electrical items, it might appear as in Exhibit 20.2.

Exhibit 20.2

Columnar Sales Day Book

Date	Name of firm	SL Folio	Total	Sports Dept	Household Dept	Electrical Dept
19X9			£	£	£	£
May 1	N Coward Ltd	87	190		190	
„ 5	L Oliver	76	200	200		
„ 8	R Colman & Co	157	300	102		198
„ 16	Aubrey Smith Ltd	209	480			480
„ 27	H Marshall	123	220	110	45	65
„ 31	W Pratt	66	1,800		800	1,000
			3,190	412	1,035	1,743

Note for students

The vertical lines have been included above in order to illustrate how the paper within the sales day book may be printed. You may find it useful to rule your paper according to this layout when attempting examples and questions on this topic. If you do, remember that the number of columns will vary according to the circumstances.

20.3 Sales analysis books and VAT

If a firm was zero rated then it would not have to add VAT on to the value of its sales invoices. This could have been the case in Exhibit 20.2 where there is no mention of VAT. Suppose instead that the same firm had not been zero rated, then it might have had to add VAT.

All that would be wanted is an extra column for VAT. In Exhibit 20.3 that follows, the debtors would be charged up with gross amounts, e.g. N Coward Ltd with £209. The VAT account would be credited with £319 being the total of the VAT column. The sales account would be credited with the sales figures of £412; £1,035; and £1,743. (Assumed VAT rate of 10 per cent.)

Exhibit 20.3

Columnar Sales Day Book

Date	Name of firm	SL Folio	Total	VAT	Sports Dept	Household Dept	Electrical Dept
19X9			£	£	£	£	£
May 1	N Coward Ltd	87	209	19		190	
„ 5	L Oliver	76	220	20	200		
„ 8	R Colman & Co	157	330	30	102		198
„ 16	Aubrey Smith Ltd	209	528	48			480
„ 27	H Marshall	123	242	22	110	45	65
„ 31	W Pratt	66	1,980	180		800	1,000
			3,509	319	412	1,035	1,743

Similarly, a purchases analysis book could have a VAT column included. In this case the total of the VAT column would be debited to the VAT account. The total of the purchases column would be debited to the purchases account with the total of each expense column debited to the various expense accounts. Remember that VAT is not payable on some items, e.g. rent, electricity.

20.4 Advantages of analysis books

The advantages of analysis books are that we are provided with exactly the information we need, at the time when we want it. Different firms have different needs, and therefore analyse their books in different ways.

Analysis books will enable us to do such things as:

1 Calculate the profit or loss made by each part of a business.
2 Draw up control accounts for the sales and purchases ledgers (*see* Chapter 30).
3 Keep a check on the sales of each type of goods.
4 Keep a check on goods sold in the United Kingdom and those sold overseas.
5 Find the purchases of each type of goods.

20.5 Books as collection points

We can see that the various sales and purchases day books, and the ones for returns, are simply collection points for the data to be entered in the accounts of the double entry system. There is nothing by law that says that, for instance, a sales day book has to be written up. What we could do is to look at the sales invoices and enter the debits in the customers' personal accounts from them. Then we could keep all the sales invoices together in a file. At the end of the month we could add up the amounts of the sales invoices, and then enter that total to the credit of the sales account in the general ledger.

New term

Analysis book (p. 182): A book where there is a total column, and further columns where each item is analysed under appropriate headings.

Main point to remember

1   Analysis books, often referred to as 'columnar day books', are used in order to show the value of each of the various types of items bought and sold so that the relevant accounts may have the correct amount entered into them. While, there is strictly speaking no need for them to be used if entries are made directly into the ledger accounts from the source documents, it is considered good practice to do so, particularly when the accounting records are not computerised.

Review questions

20.1   C Taylor, a wholesale dealer in electrical goods, has three departments: (a) Hi Fi, (b) TV, and (c) Sundries. The following is a summary of Taylor's sales invoices during the period 1 to 7 February 19X7:

	Customer	Invoice No	Depart-ment	List price less trade discount	VAT	Total invoice price
				£	£	£
Feb 1	P Small	586	TV	2,600	260	2,860
„ 2	L Goode	587	Hi Fi	1,800	180	1,980
„ 3	R Daye	588	TV	1,600	160	1,760
„ 5	B May	589	Sundries	320	Nil	320
„ 7	L Goode	590	TV	900	90	990
„ 7	P Small	591	Hi Fi	3,400	340	3,740

(a)   Record the above transactions in a columnar book of original entry and post to the general ledger in columnar form.

(b)   Write up the personal accounts in the appropriate ledger.
    NB Do not balance off any of your ledger accounts.
    VAT was 10 per cent rate.

20.2   Enter up a purchases analysis book with columns for the various expenses for M Barber for the month from the following information on credit items.

19X6			£
July	1	Bought goods from L Ogden	220
„	3	Bought goods from E Evans	390
„	4	Received electricity bill (lighting & heating from North Electricity Board)	88
„	5	Bought goods from H Noone	110
„	6	Motor lorry repaired, received bill from Kirk Motors	136
„	8	Bought stationery from Avon Enterprises	77
„	10	Motor van serviced, bill from Kirk Motors	55
„	12	Gas bill received from North Gas Board (lighting & heating)	134
„	15	Bought goods from A Dodds	200
„	17	Bought light bulbs (lighting & heating) from O Aspinall	24
„	18	Goods bought from J Kelly	310
„	19	Invoice for carriage inwards from D Adams	85
„	21	Bought stationery from J Moore	60
„	23	Goods bought from H Noone	116
„	27	Received invoice for carriage inwards from D Flynn	62
„	31	Invoice for motor spares supplied during the month received from Kirk Motors	185

20.3   Enter up the relevant accounts in the purchases and general ledgers from the purchases analysis book you have completed for question 20.2.

21

Employees' pay

Objectives

After you have studied this chapter, you should:

- *understand the basic outline of PAYE income tax*

- *be able to calculate the net pay of an employee given details of his or her gross pay and PAYE income tax and other deductions*

21.1 Introduction

In this chapter we will consider the calculation of the pay and the deductions that are made from it by the employer.

There is no exact definition of 'wages' and 'salaries'. In general it is accepted that wages are earnings paid on a weekly basis, whilst salaries are paid monthly.

The employer will have to make various deductions so that a distinction is made between:

- **Gross pay:** This is the amount of wages or salary *before* deductions are made; and
- **Net pay:** This is the amount of wages or salary *after* deductions.

Many employees talk about 'take-home pay'. This in fact is their net pay.

21.2 Methods of calculating gross pay

The methods can vary widely between employers and also as regards different employees in the same organisation. The main methods are:

- Fixed amount salaries or wages: these are an agreed annual amount.
- Piece rate: based on the number of units produced by the employee.
- Commission: a percentage based on the amount of sales made by the employee.
- Basic rate per hour: a fixed rate multiplied by number of hours worked.

Arrangements for rewarding people for working overtime (time exceeding normal hours worked) will vary widely. The rate will usually be in excess of that paid during normal working hours. People being paid salaries will often not be paid for overtime.

In addition bonuses may be paid on top of the above earnings. Bonus schemes will also vary widely, and may depend on the amount of net profit made by the company, or on the amount of work performed or production achieved, either by the whole company or else the department in which the employee works.

21.3 Income tax deductions

In the UK, the wages and salaries of all employees are liable to have income tax deducted from them. It does not mean that everyone will pay income tax – some may not earn enough to be liable for any tax. However, if income tax is found to be payable, the employer deducts the tax due from the employee's wages or salary and sends it to the Inland Revenue, the government department in charge of the collection of income tax. This system is known as 'pay-as-you-earn', or PAYE.

Each person in the UK is allowed to subtract various amounts from the earnings to see if he/she is liable to pay income tax. The amounts given for each person depend upon his or her personal circumstances. An extra amount can be deducted by a man who is married, as compared to a single man or woman. The total of these for a person is known as his or her 'personal reliefs', or 'personal allowances'. Once these have been deducted any balance will have to suffer income tax. It is:

	£
Gross pay	xxx
less reliefs	xxx
Pay which is taxable	xxx

Two people may, therefore, earn the same wages, but if one of them gets more allowances than the other. he or she will have less taxable pay, and so will pay less income tax than the other person.

Each year in his budget, the Chancellor of the Exchequer announces what the rates of income tax are going to be for the following year, and also how much is to be deducted in respect of each allowance. Because of the annual changes the rates of income tax now shown are for illustration only, they are *not necessarily* the actual rates of income tax at the time you are reading this book.

For instance, assume that the rates of income tax (on the amount actually exceeding the allowances for each person) are:

- On the first £3,000   Income Tax at 20%
- On the next £24,000   Income Tax at 25%
- On the remainder   Income Tax at 40%

The income tax payable by each of four persons can now be looked at.

1 Miss Brown earns £3,800 per annum. Her personal reliefs amount to £4,000. Income tax payable = Nil.

2 Mr Green earns £8,760 per annum. His personal reliefs amount to £4,000. Income tax is therefore payable on the excess of £4,760. This amounts to:

		£
On first £3,000 at 20%	=	600
On remaining £1,760 at 25%	=	440
Total income tax for the year		1,040

3 Mr Black earns £10,700 per annum. His personal reliefs amount to £5,300. Income tax is therefore payable on the excess of £5,400. This amounts to:

		£
On first £3,000 at 20%	=	600
On remaining £2,400 at 25%	=	600
		1,200

4   Mr White earns £39,700 per annum. His personal allowances amount to £5,200. Income tax is therefore payable on the excess of £34,500. This amounts to:

		£
On first £3,000 at 20%	=	600
On next £24,000 at 25%	=	6,000
On remaining £7,500 at 40%	=	3,000
		£9,600

Let us assume that Miss Brown and Mr Green are paid weekly, and Mr Black and Mr White are paid monthly. If each payment to them during the year was of equal amounts, then we can calculate the amount of PAYE deducted from each payment of earnings.

PAYE deducted on weekly basis:

1   Miss Brown. Tax for year = nil. Tax each week = nil.
2   Mr Green. Tax for year = £1,040. Tax each week £1,040 ÷ 52 = £20.

PAYE deducted on monthly basis:

3   Mr Black. Tax for year = £1,200. Tax each month £1,200 ÷ 12 = £100.
4   Mr White. Tax for year = £9,600. Tax each month £9,600 ÷ 12 = £800.

These examples were deliberately made easy to understand. In real life, earnings will change part way through a tax year, the amounts paid each week or monthmay be different, etc. The Inland Revenue issues employers with tax tables to help calculate the PAYE. Code numbers are used to deal with the different allowances employees may have, and we shall look at this next.

21.4 Tax code numbers

We have already seen that personal reliefs, which are deducted from gross pay to find taxable pay, will vary between workers.

When employers come to use the tax tables they need an easy method of knowing the amount of personal reliefs to which each of their employees is entitled. The Inland Revenue solve this for the employer by giving each employee a tax code number.

The tax code will incorporate all the tax reliefs to which the employee is entitled. This means that, should the worker receive extra reliefs for special clothing, or for being blind, or for being a single parent, these extra reliefs will be incorporated into the tax code.

To find the tax code the total of all the reliefs is calculated, and the tax code will consist of the total reliefs but not including the last digit. The number will also be followed by a letter.

L means a code incorporating a single person's relief.
H means a code incorporating a married person's relief.

For instance, in the case of the employees given in section 21.3:

- Miss Brown is unmarried. Her personal reliefs amounted to £4,000. Her tax code will be 400L.
- Mr Green is unmarried. His personal reliefs amounted to £4,000. His tax code will be 400L.
- Mr Black is married. His personal tax reliefs amounted to £5,300. His tax code will be 530H.
- Mr White is married. His personal tax reliefs amounted to £5,200. His tax code will be 520H.

21.5 National insurance

In the UK, national insurance contributions have to be paid for and by each employee. In return, the employee may claim benefits from the state, if and when required, e.g. for retirement or for unemployment benefits. The contributions are split into two parts:

1 The part that the employee has to suffer by it being deducted from his pay.
2 The part that the employer has to suffer. This is not deductible from pay.

The rates change from time to time but, assuming a total national insurance rate of 19 per cent, of which the employee's contribution is 9 per cent and the employer's contribution 10 per cent, then £38 total contribution will have to be paid in respect of an employee who has earned £200 in the period, i.e. £200 × 19% = £38.

Of this, £18 (9%) can be deducted from the employee's pay, whilst £20 (10%) is a cost of the employer.

Where the employee pays the full rate of national insurance he will be entitled to an extra pension on top of his retirement pension. This is known as SERPS, which means State Earnings Related Pension Scheme. The more that is paid in national insurance, the greater the amount of SERPS receivable at retirement age. These employees are known as 'non-contracted out' employees.

Where an employer has an approved pension scheme, the employee will pay lower rates of national insurance, but will not benefit from SERPS on retirement. These are known as 'contracted out' employees. This also applies where employees have decided to be 'contracted out' but provide their own properly approved private pension scheme.

21.6 Other deductions from pay

1 Pensions contributions

An employee may belong to a firm's private pension fund. The money paid into the fund will be paid partly by the firm and partly by the employee, e.g. in many employments the employee's contribution will be 6 per cent, with the firm paying whatever is necessary to give the employee the agreed amount of pension.

The amount of the contribution payable by the employee will therefore be deducted in calculating the net pay due to them. The term 'superannuation' is often used instead of 'pension'.

2 Voluntary contributions

These will include items such as charitable donations, subscriptions to the firm's social club, union subscriptions and payments under the government's Save as You Earn Scheme (SAYE).

21.7 Statutory Sick Pay and Statutory Maternity Pay

1 Statutory Sick Pay (SSP) is payments made to employees when they are ill and absent from work. At present it is not paid for the first three days of illness, and is limited to a total of 28 weeks maximum.
2 Statutory Maternity Pay (SMP) is payments made for up to 18 weeks to an employee away from work on maternity leave.

SSP and SMP are paid to employees in the same way as ordinary wages. They are both liable to have PAYE tax and national insurance deducted from them.

21.8 Calculation of net wages/salary payable

UK students who need to know how to use PAYE tax and national insurance tables will need to study this further.

For general guidance for all readers, and for those who do not want to know about the use of income tax and national insurance tables, we can look at two general examples of the calculation of net pay. The percentages used are for illustrative purposes only.

		£
(A) G Jarvis:	Gross earnings for the week ended 8 May 19X8	100
	Income tax: found by consulting tax tables	
	and employee's code number	12
	National insurance 9% of gross pay	9

G Jarvis: Payslip week ended 8 May 19X8

	£	£
Gross pay for the week		100
Less Income tax	12	
National insurance	9	21
Net pay		79

		£
(B) H Reddish:	Gross earnings for the month of May 19X8	800
	Income tax (from tax tables)	150
	Superannuation: 6% of gross pay	48
	National insurance 9% of gross pay	72

H Reddish: Payslip month ended 31 May 19X8

	£	£
Gross pay for the month		800
Less Income tax	150	
Superannuation	48	
National insurance	72	270
Net pay		530

The total costs to the employer in each of the above cases will be as follows, assuming the employer's part of national insurance contributions to be £10 for Jarvis and £81 for Reddish:

	G Jarvis £	H Reddish £
Gross pay	100	800
Employer's share of national insurance	10	81
Total cost to the employer	110	881

It will be the figures of £110 and £881 that will be incorporated in the profit and loss account as expenses shown under wages and salaries headings.

New terms

PAYE (p. 188): The system whereby income tax is deducted from wages and salaries by employers and sent to the Inland Revenue.

Personal allowances (p. 189): Amounts each person may subtract from income in order to arrive at taxable income. The value of each allowance is set by Parliament following the Budget each year. They are for things like being married, caring for a dependent relative, etc.

Tax code (p. 189): The number found by adding up an individual's personal allowances which is used to calculate that individual's tax liability.

Main point to remember

1 The PAYE system ensures that employees pay tax on their earnings and, consequently, that the Government receives the income it needs in order to perform its role.

Review questions

Note: These questions are for general use only. They have been designed to be able to be worked out without the use of tax and national insurance tables. The national insurance given is the employee's part only.

21.1 H Smith is employed at a rate of £5 per hour. During the week to 18 May 19X9 he worked his basic week of 40 hours. According to the requisite tables the income tax due on his wages was £27, and national insurance £16. Calculate his net wages.

21.2 B Charles has a basic working week of 40 hours, paid at the rate of £4 per hour. For hours worked in excess of this he is paid 1½ times basic rate. In the week to 12 March 19X6 he worked 45 hours. The first £80 per week is free of income tax, on the next £50 he pays at the 20% rate and above that he pays at the 25% rate. National insurance amounted to £17. Calculate his net wages.

21.3 B Croft has a job as a car salesman. He is paid a basic salary of £200 per month, with a commission extra of 2% on the value of his car sales. During the month of April 19X6 he sells £30,000 worth of cars. The first £450 per month is free of income tax, on the next £50 he pays at the 20% rate and above that he pays at the 25% rate. He also pays national insurance for the month of £66. Calculate his net pay for the month.

21.4 T Penketh is an accountant with a salary of £2,000 per month plus bonus, which for May 19X6 was £400. He pays superannuation contributions of 5% of gross pay, and these are allowed as reliefs against income tax. In addition to this he has further reliefs (free pay) of £430. The taxable pay is taxed at the rate of 20% on the first £250, whilst the remainder suffers the 25% tax rate. In addition he pays national insurance of £190. Calculate his net pay for the month.

21.5A K Blake is employed at the rate of £6 per hour. During the week to 25 May 19X6 he works 35 hours. According to the tax and national insurance tables he should pay income tax £28 and national insurance £18. Calculate his net wages.

21.6A R Kennedy is a security van driver. He has a wage of £200 per week, plus danger money of £2 per hour extra spent in transporting gold bullion. During the week ended 15 June 19X6 he spends 20 hours taking gold bullion to London Airport. The first £90 per week of his pay is free of income tax, whilst on the next £50 he pays at the 20% rate, and at the 25% rate above that figure. He pays national insurance for the week of £19. Calculate his net pay for the week.

21.7A Mrs T Hulley is paid monthly. For part of April 19X6 she earns £860 and then goes on maternity leave, her maternity pay for April being £90. She has pay free of tax £320, whilst on the next £250 she pays at the 20% tax rate, and 25% above that. She pays £79 national insurance. Calculate her net pay for the month.

21.8A P Urmston is paid monthly. For June 19X6 he earns £1,500 and also receives statutory sick pay of £150. He pays £90 superannuation which is allowed as a relief against income tax and he has further reliefs (free pay) of £350. The taxable pay is taxed at the rate of 20% on the first £250 and 25% thereafter. He pays national insurance of £130 for the month. Calculate his net pay for the month.

22

Computers and accounting

Objectives

After you have studied this chapter, you should:

- *appreciate that computerised accounting systems mimic manual accounting systems and do everything that is done by a manual accounting system*

- *appreciate that computerised accounting systems automate most of the entries required in a manual accounting system, other than an initial entry for each transaction*

- *be aware that different computer hardware configurations are used, depending largely upon company size*

- *be aware that accountants use spreadsheets to write many of their own computer programs, particularly for managerial accounting purposes*

- *appreciate that financial accounting packages tend to be bought 'off-the-shelf', possibly customised to the business, or the software (particularly in larger companies) may be commissioned from computer software specialists either within the business or from external agencies*

- *be aware of the advantages and pitfalls of using a computerised accounting system*

- *appreciate that the accounting information system is just one part of the management information system*

- *be aware of the structure and flexibility of spreadsheets*

- *be aware of why a database package is a useful tool*

- *be aware of the requirements and implications of the Data Protection Act 1998*

22.1 Introduction

Most businesses, except the very small firm, now use computers to handle their accounting data. When businesses embark on computerised accounts, they soon appreciate that bookkeeping and accounting skills are more important than computing ones. This is because many systems are now developed to be 'user friendly', in that they guide users through by presenting screens of 'what to do next' help.

The methods adopted in computer-based accounting adhere to the fundamental principles of accounting covered in this and other accounting textbooks. No matter how sophisticated and easy to use a computer system is, it will not overcome the need for bookkeeping and accounting knowledge by those in control. Apart from a knowledge of these principles in order to know how to best adapt a business from manual to computer-based accounting, accounting knowledge is required to help understand the significance of the outputs from a computer-based accounting system, just as it is required in respect of output from a manual accounting system.

22.2 Large versus small systems

The system used by a company will vary in size to meet the volume of data processing required by the business. Very large businesses may use a mainframe or minicomputer-based system for handling bulk data, frequently with personal computers (PCs) for a number of purposes such as departmental accounts and financial modelling. Others will use PCs for all accounting purposes. As the workstations used with mainframe and minicomputer-based systems are often 'dumb terminals' – i.e. they have no computing power of their own – the workstations will be networked (i.e. linked together through wires that run from their workstations to the mainframe or minicomputer). In some cases, these will be 'local area networks' or LANs (i.e. internal to the location); in others they will be part of a 'wide area network' or WAN (i.e. connected outwith the location of the workstation to, for example, a computer located at the business's head office in another city). It is quite common for a workstation to be connected to both a local area network and a wide area network. Being linked together has the advantage that data and information can be passed directly from one computer to another. Thus, although they can operate independently of any other computer, PC-based systems may also be connected together on a local area network, and have links to wide area networks.

The computer programs used may be developed 'in-house' (by the firm's own staff) or written under contract with an outside firm or agency. Such systems are tailored to exactly what the business wants and are sometimes referred to as 'bespoke' systems. A large supermarket chain, for example, would have software developed incorporating the electronic point of sale (EPOS) system now common at supermarket check-outs. These check-out systems not only keep an accurate check on what is sold, in the form of an electronic sales day book, but such information can be fed into the central computer to assist the reordering of stock from warehouses, and to keep a check on cash sales. They also provide data for stock analysis and marketing purposes.

Expensive, specially designed software (often called 'customised' software) of this type will be used, generally, by large businesses. Many medium and smaller firms will not require such special solutions, and will rely on software packages that can easily be bought (known generally as 'off-the-shelf' packages) and are flexible enough to be adapted to most businesses.

Most financial accounting and bookkeeping programs are purchased or developed 'in-house' by computer programmers. Besides this the accountant will want to tackle other problems not already discussed in this volume. These will include matters such as forecasting the cash flows of a business, stock ordering, deciding on capital expenditure investment, how to find the point at which the business moves into profit (breakeven analysis) and costing. For such purposes, irrespective of the size of the business, accountants can use the techniques of spreadsheets (*see* 22.8) generally available, such as Excel, Quattro Pro and Lotus 1–2–3, and databases such as Access, Paradox and DBase. Such systems will change fairly rapidly over the years as new ones are developed.

The cost of computer hardware and software has been falling in real terms for many years – it has been suggested that had the same relative cost reduction applied to a Rolls-Royce motor car, it would now be cheaper to throw the car away once it ran out of petrol than to fill up the petrol tank! Consequently, computerisation is now affordable for all businesses. In fact, such has been the increase in data processing and analysis as a result of businesses seeking to maximise the use of their computing power that many businesses now process such large volumes of data that they would find it impossible to revert to a manual system.

22.3 Benefits from computers

Time-saving with respect to transactions processing, increased accuracy and the production of a whole series of reports is an obvious desirable benefit when computerising an accounting system. The basic principle of any accounting system is depicted in Exhibit 22.1.

Exhibit 22.1

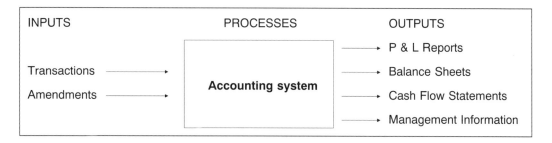

The aim of a computerised accounting system is to perform the processing stage electronically, much more quickly than if it were done manually. However, transactions and amendment details have to be input into the process in the correct form, in the correct order and in a timely manner. Although there is scope to use electronic methods of entering some of this information (e.g. EPOS systems), it requires a good deal of initiative and an organised way of doing things. Further time-saving can be achieved by automatic output of reports such as details about whether the firm is meeting sales targets, customer statements, purchase analysis, cash and bank statements. Such reports and statements can be produced by the computer searching through information generated and saved by the accounting system.

Effective reporting is often required in order to improve the decision-making process. For example, a computer system should be capable of detecting when a customer appears to be running up excessive debts with the company, offering the chance to take action. Another area is the need to remain within budgets. Many business expenses can get out of hand if they are not checked at regular intervals. What a computerised accounts system should be capable of is an activity called 'exception reporting': a process of issuing early warning messages to operators and managers when something appears to be out of order. In a manual system, the situation often occurs when many errors or unwanted transactions go unnoticed until the repercussions are too late or have already incurred unnecessary costs to the firm.

For many businesses, the need to produce monthly and annual returns, such as VAT, and processing payroll stoppages can be time-consuming, tedious and unrewarding. The use of a computer system can be an effective tool in speeding up the process and reducing the monotony of producing lengthy and uninteresting reports with large amounts of figure work. In many cases, firms find that they can use computer printouts or data on computer disks instead of having to complete official forms.

Improved accuracy may be one of the more obvious benefits of any kind of computer system, which is especially the case with accounting, where numerous calculations have to be carried out.

Increased job satisfaction and more effective use of operator time can be an added bonus of computerisation. For example, if a firm computerises its stock records, an operator's job of keeping records properly maintained will be much the same as in the manual system. However, with instant reporting facilities available, such as a list of all stock items that may be in short supply, the operator can produce details almost instantly. This will allow an operator the facility of keeping a much closer check on stock levels. Also, if time can be saved in producing stock reports, the operator may have more time to 'chase up' suppliers who are not delivering on time or 'shop around' the market for better suppliers and products.

Many more benefits of computerisation tend to become apparent as businesses develop their systems. It is worth noting that the extent of the benefits will vary from firm to firm, with each firm deriving different benefits. It may well be the case that a firm can derive no benefit at all from computerisation. Once a computer system is working properly, managers will often find themselves extracting reports that under a manual system could not be achieved within a timescale that would serve a useful purpose. The improved reporting and analysis that can be achieved by computerisation should improve the whole decision-making process within a firm.

22.4 Computerised ledgers

Many businesses now make good use of accounting packages which are readily available and have been well tested. Such packages are commonly modularised with typically the sales ledger, purchase ledger, nominal ledger, stock control, sales invoicing, sales order processing, purchases order processing, fixed assets, payroll, bill of materials, and job costing all being offered as separate modules in their own right. When a business decides to use a computer, it acquires only those modules it needs rather than a complete range of modules. For example, many businesses do not require a sales ledger because they do not sell to a large number of customers on credit.

The various ledgers and accounts maintained in a computerised accounting system mimic those kept in a manual system. The nominal ledger, for example, will adhere to the basic rules of double entry bookkeeping in that each debit entry has a corresponding credit entry – if a customer is issued with an invoice, the transaction giving precise details of the invoice will be stored in the credit sales records to form part of the customer history and then the nominal entry by crediting sales accounts and debiting a debtor's account. The difference lies in the method of entry – each transaction is entered only once and the software automatically completes the double entry. The information stored is available on-line and can be used to produce statements, ledger account details, analysis of how long debts have been outstanding, etc. virtually instantly. For example, the computerised sales ledger will hold all details about customers. The starting point would be to enter the details concerning the customer (name, address, etc.) along with the balance brought forward from the manual system (if such a transfer is occurring; otherwise, if it is a new customer, an opening zero balance will be created automatically by the software). All transactions that correspond to a customer, such as the issue of an invoice or receipt of payment, are entered into the system and automatically posted to the customer's account. Customers can, at any time, be issued with a statement of their account, and the business can always obtain an up-to-date and complete history of trading with any particular customer. The purchase ledger will operate exactly the same way in that supplier details are held and, once entered through the purchases module, all transactions relating to individual purchasers will automatically be posted to the appropriate creditor account.

Bank payments and receipts are a central feature of computerised accounting systems. The modules can be operated by someone with virtually no bookkeeping knowledge. For example, if an electricity bill is paid, the system will prompt for the details required in order to process and record the double entry.

In order to use the computerised accounting system efficiently and effectively, someone with both accounting skills and a good knowledge of the business will be required to organise the ledger in the first instance. Some of these packages are written for no specific business and need to be 'tailored' to the one that is going to use it. Most require businesses to define what accounts they are to have in their nominal ledger and how such accounts are to be grouped. For example, fixed asset accounts may have account references commencing with 'F', while expense accounts commence with 'E'; the package will probably have its own default set of account codes, and it may be necessary to override the defaults in order to use the business's own account. In addition, part of the setting up of a computer system will require the tailoring of the package for certain reports such as the profit and loss account and balance sheet.

Most packages are capable of allowing firms to set up methods for dealing with depreciation of fixed assets and regular payments of, for example, rent and rates. However, such packages do require a good 'knowledge' of double entry when making special adjustments through their journal entries. For example, the computer will not overcome some errors and omissions such as the operator misreading an amount on an invoice or crediting a payment to a wrong customer account. Such errors that will need correcting will require a full knowledge of the accounting system as well as bookkeeping and accounting principles. Most systems also post various amounts into suspense accounts when it is unclear as to where postings are to be made; these also require journal entries to adjust them.

22.5 Invoicing, stock and order processing

Automation of much of the data processing can be taken further when integrating other modules. Stock control offers the benefit of keeping very close tabs on stock levels. If an invoicing package is also in use, then an invoice can be generated in such a way that an operator can collect the details of the business or person to invoice from the sales ledger and details of all stock to be invoiced from the stock files. Once the invoice has been raised, the recorded stock levels fall accordingly, the sales ledger is updated and the nominal entries are made by crediting sales and debiting debtors' control.

Sales order processing allows an order to be placed into the system and can then be used at a later stage to generate an invoice. Sales order processing is important to many businesses as it gives them an indication about what stock levels are required. Having sales orders on computer also offers the advantage of being able to avoid any orders being left overdue and late. Computers can produce outstanding order reports and such things as 'picking lists' very quickly.

Purchase order processing allows an operator to print an order to send off to a supplier or, in some more advanced systems, it may be transmitted over a direct link into the supplier's accounting system where it will be recorded and converted into an issue from stock. The computerised purchase order system also serves the useful purpose of allowing instant access to information about what is on order. By entering stock on order against various stock records, it reduces the likelihood of issuing multiple orders for stock unnecessarily.

The full use of all modules in this integrated manner allows a business to access stock details and get a complete profile on its status in terms of what is left in stock, what is on order, what has been ordered by customers. Furthermore, most packages keep a history of stock movements helping the business to analyse specific stock turnovers. When integrated in this fashion, the processing structure may be as depicted in Exhibit 22.2.

Exhibit 22.2 An integrated accounts system

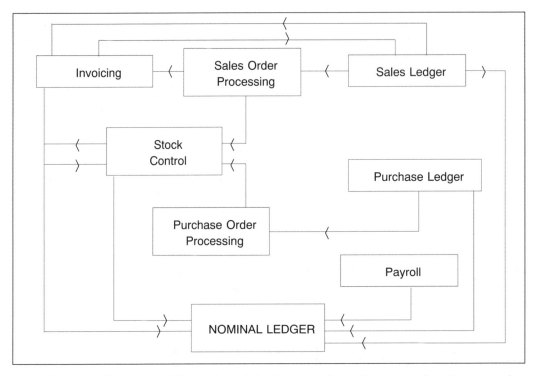

Exhibit 22.2 shows an additional module for payroll. Businesses with a large number of employees would find this particularly useful as payroll systems require a good deal of regular processing. Again, a reasonable knowledge of payroll is required in order to set up the system in the first place.

22.6 Accounting information systems

The accounting information system (AIS) comprises all these various modules. To operate effectively, all the modules need to be compatible with each other, so that data can be passed between them.

Output from an AIS need not be on paper – screen displays, disks or direct file transfer to another computer over a LAN or WAN are all commonplace alternatives. Where some organisations require that information be passed to them on their own forms, the IT revolution of the last few years has led to many organisations being willing to accept printout generated from a computer, even computer disks, instead of having their own forms completed and returned. For example, fairly standard and repetitive information generation such as VAT receipts and payments are common to most businesses, and Customs and Excise will accept computer-generated VAT returns in most cases. Also, if a payroll system is used, the Inland Revenue are willing to accept computer-generated reports.

Another fairly standard report obtainable from an AIS is a list of debtors showing how much they each owe, and for how long the amounts have been outstanding (aged debtors listing). Other examples of standard reports that a computerised AIS ought to be quite capable of providing include price lists, reordering stock quantities, lists of invoices and credit notes and audit trails.

22.7 Management information systems

All computer systems, whether in the form of a purchased package or bespoke for a particular firm, will need to supply information in a form that management can use to assist in its decision making. Whether the output is on paper, via computer screens, on disk, or available on-line, the information system centred upon the computer is generally referred to as the 'management information system' (MIS). The MIS contains far more information than the accounting information system – production data and marketing statistics, for example, would be included in the MIS. The accounting information system is a component within the MIS, and must be capable of integration with the other functional information systems that together comprise the rest of the MIS.

Beyond standard reports, systems are normally flexible enough to allow management to extract the kind of reports that may be unique to their business or department. These reports can be extracted in a very short time compared with a manual system and serve to enhance the control management have over their business.

However, two things should be emphasised:

1   The reports and information extracted from a computer can only be as good as the data placed into it. If the full benefits of computerisation are to be enjoyed, checks need to be regularly made to ensure that data input is accurate and timely.
2   Computerisation allows infinite instant access to data. It is a straightforward matter designing and producing a new report, and it can be easier to print all possible types of reports across all functions than to limit the reports produced to those actually needed by the people they are sent to. If report generation is not controlled, information overload will occur and decision makers may have difficulty seeing the wood because of all the trees.

22.8 Use of spreadsheets

A piece of software that has become popular as an accountant's tool is the spreadsheet. It divides a screen into vertical columns and horizontal rows to form a grid of cells. The name derives from the appearance of the computer *spreading* accounts on a *sheet*, allowing the user to directly enter numbers, formulae or text into the cells. Each cell is referred to by its co-ordinate, like a map reference or point on a graph. For example, cell C12 is in column C row 12. Formulae can be entered to link cells. An example of linking cells is where a cell entry reads:

B1 * C1

This makes the value of the contents of the cell equal to the value of cell B1 multiplied by the value of cell C1. The spreadsheet effectively becomes a screen-based calculator that is also capable of being printed and of being displayed as a graph.

Any figure can be changed at any time and the new results will instantly and automatically be shown. This makes it very easy to perform sensitivity, or what if, analysis (for example, *what* would the result be *if* sales were to increase by 10 per cent?)

and has led to a far higher level of understanding of the effects of decisions than was ever possible when all such recalculations could involve anything up to days of work. It is this facility of being able to quickly recalculate formulae that makes the spreadsheet a powerful, useful and popular analytical tool.

Spreadsheets can be used in order to seek goals. For example, spreadsheets can depict the sales and costs of a business where a model is set up to determine what price will be required in order to achieve a specific net profit.

Spreadsheets tend to be written by accountants for their own use, rather than by computer programmers. Some other examples of uses for spreadsheets are as follows:

- financial plans and budgets can be represented as a table, with columns for time periods (e.g. months) and rows for different elements of the plan (e.g. costs and revenue);
- tax, investment and loan calculations can be made with ease;
- statistics using built-in functions such as averages, standard deviations, time series and regression analysis can be calculated;
- consolidation – merging branch or departmental accounts to form group (consolidated) accounts – is possible. Three-dimensional spreadsheets facilitate this, but it is relatively straightforward to do using any spreadsheet;
- currency conversion is possible – useful for an organisation with overseas interests such as a multinational company;
- timetabling and roster planning of staff within organisations or departments can be achieved.

22.9 Use of databases

Instead of being specifically designed for accounting, databases are designed for a more general purpose. A database is organised into a collection of related files into which go records. For example, a stock system could be developed where a stock file contains a record for each item of stock. The records are further broken down into fields. Hence, there could be a field for reference, one for description, a quantity, reordering level and so on. The system would then be developed to keep such records updated.

This application is favoured by many businesses as it tends to be more flexible than an accounts package and easier and cheaper to put together than a set of programs specifically written for the business.

Such database packages require a little more computing expertise and a sound knowledge of the accounts system in order to create something appropriate. In such instances, while many would be written by an accountant, it is possible that computing and accounting personnel would work together on the development, particularly where the accountant had no previous experience of using the database software.

22.10 Data security and the Data Protection Act 1998

One of the most important principles in computing is the discipline of backing up data. This serves the purpose that, if anything ever goes wrong with the data, then the business can always revert to a back-up copy of the accounts, usually on computer disk. If, for example, a company backs up its data at midday and there is a loss of data later that afternoon, then the worst that could happen is that the company has to restore the data from the midday back-up and then re-enter the data since that time. Clearly, therefore, the more often a business backs up its data, the less work is needed in the event of data loss.

Most accounting packages allow a business to use passwords to restrict which personnel have access to which modules. Indeed, within a module, it is normally possible to restrict what certain users have access to. This assists management in maintaining tighter control on the system and avoids over-complicating operations for operators. It ensures that operators do not have access to those parts of a much wider system than they need in order to do their job adequately and avoids the risks inherent in exposing all parts of the system to all operators. As an extra benefit, by limiting the functions available to operators, it becomes easier and quicker to train them.

Most firms that make extensive use of computers for accounts, payroll, and any other applications that involve personal details of individuals, need to register with the **Data Protection Commissioner**.

The Data Protection Act defines a **data controller** as someone who determines how and for which purposes **personal data** is used. A **data subject** is anyone of whom data is held on a computer that can be identified as relating to them. Such data on a computer has to be processed by the computer's software before it can serve the purpose of information. It is this information that the **Data Protection Commissioner** wants to know about.

Essentially, data users must declare what information they have access to on data subjects and the uses they will put that information to. The main objective of the Act is to ensure that individuals are aware of what is being held about them on business computers and allow them access to this information.

If a firm is only using the sales ledger or purchase ledger for preparing and sending invoices and statements and does not use the comment details for a contact name then registration may not be necessary. Also, if customers and suppliers are companies, and individuals cannot be identified in the data, registration is not necessary. In the same way, if all a firm does with payroll data is to pay wages and prepare statutory returns, registration is not necessary.

If customer and supplier lists are used for sending out sales promotions, the firm must register; likewise registration is required if a firm uses data on the payroll for management information about staff sickness or any form of staff monitoring.

Forms for registration require the firm to reveal the kind of data it holds on individuals and the purpose for which it wants to use it. The firm must also give details on how data subjects can find out what data is held on computer about them.

In addition to the possible need to register, firms must comply with certain practices with regard to holding personalised data on computer. Many of these legal requirements simply define good computing practice and should be applied, where applicable, to all data used on a computer. These legal principles are contained in Schedule I of the Act:

1 Personal data shall be processed fairly and lawfully and, in particular, shall not be processed unless certain conditions contained in Schedules 2 and 3 of the Act have been met.
2 Personal data shall be obtained only for one or more specified and lawful purposes, and shall not be further processed in any manner incompatible with that purpose or those purposes.
3 Personal data shall be adequate, relevant and not excessive in relation to the purpose or purposes for which they are processed.
4 Personal data shall be accurate and, where necessary, kept up to date.
5 Personal data processed for any purpose or purposes shall not be kept for longer than is necessary for that purpose or those purposes.
6 Personal data shall be processed in accordance with the rights of data subjects under this Act.
7 Appropriate technical and organisational measures shall be taken against

unauthorised or unlawful processing of personal data and against accidental loss or destruction of, or damage to, personal data.

8 Personal data shall not be transferred to a country or territory outside the European Economic Area unless that country or territory ensures an adequate level of protection for the rights and freedoms of data subjects in relation to the processing of personal data.

New term

Accounting information system (p. 198): The infrastructure that supports the production and delivery of accounting information. Its objective is to collect and store data about accounting transactions in order to generate meaningful output for decision making.

Main points to remember

1 Accounting information systems are just one part of an overall management information system.

2 Output from an AIS can only be as good as the data that went into it.

3 Output need not be paper-based, and many organisations now accept output generated by computer in place of completed copies of their own pro formas.

4 Output can be excessive and cause information overload if not controlled to ensure it is useful to the person who receives it.

5 Spreadsheets are in general use by accountants who commonly develop their own software applications with them.

6 Databases are well suited to recording facts such as names and addresses and stock codes.

7 The Data Protection Act 1998 must be observed when personal data is held on computer.

Review questions

22.1 What are the legal principles underlying the protection of personal information kept on computers?

22.2 What benefits can flow from processing sales details on a computer?

22.3 For what type of activities in accounting is the use of spreadsheets particularly suitable?

22.4 What benefits for the whole accounting system can follow from using a computer for accounting work?

Part 4

ADJUSTMENTS BEFORE FINAL ACCOUNTS

Introduction

This part is concerned with all the adjustments that have to be made before final accounts can be prepared.

23

Capital and revenue expenditure

Objectives

After you have studied this chapter, you should:

- *be able to distinguish between expenditure that is capital in nature and that which is revenue expenditure*

- *understand that some expenditure is part capital expenditure and part revenue expenditure*

- *realise the effect on the final accounts, and the profits shown there, if revenue expenditure is wrongly treated as being capital expenditure, and vice versa*

23.1 Capital expenditure

Capital expenditure is made when a firm spends money either to:

1 Buy fixed assets, or
2 Add to the value of an existing fixed asset.

Included in such amounts should be those spent on:

1 Acquiring fixed assets.
2 Bringing them into the firm.
3 Legal costs of buying buildings.
4 Carriage inwards on machinery bought.
5 Any other cost needed to get the fixed asset ready for use.

23.2 Revenue expenditure

Expenditure which is not for increasing the value of fixed assets, but for running the business on a day-to-day basis, is known as **revenue expenditure**.

The difference between revenue and capital expenditure can be seen clearly with the total cost of using a motor van for a firm. To buy a motor van is capital expenditure. The motor van will be in use for several years and is, therefore, a fixed asset.

To pay for petrol to use in the motor van for the next few days is revenue expenditure. This is because the expenditure is used up in a few days and does not add to the value of fixed assets.

23.3 Differences between capital and revenue expenditure

A few instances listed in Exhibit 23.1 will demonstrate the difference.

You can see that revenue expenditure is that chargeable to the trading or profit and loss account, while capital expenditure will result in increased figures for fixed assets in the balance sheet.

Exhibit 23.1

Expenditure	Type of Expenditure
1 Buying motor van	Capital
2 Petrol costs for motor van	Revenue
3 Repairs to motor van	Revenue
4 Putting extra headlights on motor van	Capital
5 Buying machinery	Capital
6 Electricity costs of using machinery	Revenue
7 We spent £1,500 on machinery. £1,000 was for an item added to the machine: £500 for repairs	Capital £1,000 Revenue £500
8 Painting outside of new building	Capital
9 Three years later – repainting outside of building in (8)	Revenue

23.4 Capital expenditure: further analysis

Capital expenditure not only consists of the cost of purchasing the fixed asset, but also includes other costs necessary to get the fixed asset operational. Some of the possible additional costs are now given:

(a) Delivery cost;
(b) Installation costs;
(c) Inspection and testing the fixed asset before use;
(d) Legal costs in purchasing property and land;
(e) Architects' fees for building plans and for supervising construction of buildings;
(f) Demolition costs to remove something before new building can begin.

23.5 Joint expenditure

Sometimes one item of expenditure will need dividing between capital and revenue expenditure.

A builder was engaged to tackle some work on your premises, the total bill being for £3,000. If one-third of this was for repair work and two-thirds for improvements, £1,000 should be charged in the profit and loss account as revenue expenditure, and £2,000 identified as capital expenditure and, therefore, added to the value of premises and shown as such in the balance sheet.

23.6 Incorrect treatment of expenditure

If one of the following occurs:

1 capital expenditure is incorrectly treated as revenue expenditure, or
2 revenue expenditure is incorrectly treated as capital expenditure,

then both the balance sheet figures and trading and profit and loss account figures will be incorrect.

This means that the net profit figure will also be incorrect. If the expenditure affects items in the trading account, then the gross profit figure will also be incorrect.

23.7 Treatment of loan interest

If money is borrowed to finance the purchase of a fixed asset then interest will have to be paid on the loan. The loan interest however is *not* a cost of acquiring the asset, but is simply a cost of financing it. This means that loan interest is revenue expenditure and *not* capital expenditure.

23.8 Capital and revenue receipts

When an item of capital expenditure is sold, the receipt is called a capital receipt. Suppose a motor van is bought for £5,000, and sold five years later for £750. The £5,000 was treated as capital expenditure. The £750 received is treated as a capital receipt.

Revenue receipts are sales or other revenue items, such as rent receivable or commissions receivable.

New terms

Capital expenditure (p. 205): When a firm spends money to buy or add value to a fixed asset.

Revenue expenditure (p. 205): Expenses needed for the day-to-day running of the business.

Main points to remember

1 Some items are part capital expenditure and part revenue expenditure, and need to be apportioned accordingly.

2 If capital expenditure or revenue expenditure is mistaken one for the other, then gross or net profit figures (or both) will be incorrectly stated, as will balance sheet figures.

3 If capital receipts or revenue receipts are mistaken one for the other, then gross or net profit figures (or both) will be incorrectly stated, as will balance sheet figures.

Review questions

23.1
(a) What is meant by 'capital expenditure', and 'revenue expenditure'?
(b) Some of the following items should be treated as capital and some as revenue. For each of them state which classification applies:

  (i)   The purchase of machinery for use in the business.
  (ii) Carriage paid to bring the machinery in (i) above to the works.
  (iii) Complete redecoration of the premises at a cost of £1,500.
  (iv) A quarterly account for heating.
  (v)   The purchase of a soft drinks vending machine for the canteen with a stock of soft drinks.
  (vi) Wages paid by a building contractor to his own workmen for the erection of an office in the builder's stockyard.

23.2A   Indicate which of the following would be revenue items and which would be capital items in a wholesale bakery:

(a) Purchase of a new motor van.
(b) Purchase of replacement engine for existing motor van.
(c) Cost of altering interior of new van to increase carrying capacity.
(d) Cost of motor taxation licence for new van.
(e) Cost of motor taxation licence for existing van.
(f) Cost of painting firm's name on new van.
(g) Repair and maintenance of existing van.

23.3   Explain clearly the difference between capital expenditure and revenue expenditure. State which of the following you would classify as capital expenditure, giving your reasons:

(a) Cost of building extension to factory.
(b) Purchase of extra filing cabinets for sales office.
(c) Cost of repairs to accounting machine.
(d) Cost of installing reconditioned engine in delivery van.
(e) Legal fees paid in connection with factory extension.

23.4A   The data which follows was extracted from the books of account of H Kirk, an engineer, on 31 March 19X6, his financial year end.

		£
(a)	Purchase of extra milling machine (includes £300 for repair of an old machine)	2,900
(b)	Rent	750
(c)	Electrical expenses (includes new wiring £600, part of premises improvement)	3,280
(d)	Carriage inwards (includes £150 carriage on new cement mixer)	1,260
(e)	Purchase of extra drilling machine	4,100

You are required to allocate each or part of the items above to either 'capital' or 'revenue' expenditure.

23.5   For the business of J Charles, wholesale chemist, classify the following between 'capital' and 'revenue' expenditure:

(a) Purchase of an extra motor van.
(b) Cost of rebuilding warehouse wall which had fallen down.
(c) Building extension to the warehouse.
(d) Painting extension to warehouse when it is first built.
(e) Repainting extension to warehouse three years later than that done in (d).
(f) Carriage costs on bricks for new warehouse extension.
(g) Carriage costs on purchases.

(*h*)   Carriage costs on sales.
(*i*)   Legal costs of collecting debts.
(*j*)   Legal charges on acquiring new premises for office.
(*k*)   Fire insurance premium.
(*l*)   Costs of erecting new machine.

23.6A   For the business of H Ward, a food merchant, classify the following between 'capital' and 'revenue' expenditure:

(*a*)   Repairs to meat slicer.
(*b*)   New tyre for van.
(*c*)   Additional shop counter.
(*d*)   Renewing signwriting on shop.
(*e*)   Fitting partitions in shop.
(*f*)   Roof repairs.
(*g*)   Installing thief detection equipment.
(*h*)   Wages of shop assistant.
(*i*)   Carriage on returns outwards.
(*j*)   New cash register.
(*k*)   Repairs to office safe.
(*l*)   Installing extra toilet.

23.7
(*a*)   Distinguish between capital and revenue expenditure.
(*b*)   Napa Ltd took delivery of a microcomputer and printer on 1 July 19X6, the beginning of its financial year. The list price of the equipment was £4,999 but Napa Ltd was able to negotiate a price of £4,000 with the supplier. However, the supplier charged an additional £340 to install and test the equipment. The supplier offered a 5% discount if Napa Ltd paid for the equipment and the additional installation costs within seven days. Napa Ltd was able to take advantage of this additional discount. The installation of special electrical wiring for the computer cost £110. After initial testing certain modifications costing £199 proved necessary. Staff were sent on special training courses to operate the microcomputer and this cost £990. Napa Ltd insured the machine against fire and theft at a cost of £49 per annum. A maintenance agreement was entered into with Sonoma plc. Under this agreement Sonoma plc promised to provide 24 hour breakdown cover for one year. The cost of the maintenance agreement was £350.

Required:
Calculate the acquisition cost of the microcomputer to Napa Ltd.

(*c*)   The following costs were also incurred by Napa Ltd during the financial year ended 30 June 19X7:

(*1*)   Interest on loan to purchase microcomputer.
(*2*)   Cost of software for use with the microcomputer.
(*3*)   Cost of customising the software for use in Napa Ltd's business.
(*4*)   Cost of paper used by the computer printer.
(*5*)   Wages of computer operators.
(*6*)   Cost of ribbons used by the computer printer.
(*7*)   Cost of adding extra memory to the microcomputer.
(*8*)   Cost of floppy discs used during the year.
(*9*)   Costs of adding a manufacturer's upgrade to the microcomputer equipment.
(*10*)   Cost of adding air conditioning to the computer room.

Required:
Classify each of the above as capital expenditure or revenue expenditure.

(Association of Accounting Technicians)

23.8 At the beginning of the financial year on 1 April 19X5, a company had a balance on plant account of £372,000 and on provision for depreciation of plant account of £205,400.

The company's policy is to provide depreciation using the reducing balance method applied to the fixed assets held at the end of the financial year at the rate of 20% per annum.

On 1 September 19X5 the company sold for £13,700 some plant which it had acquired on 31 October 19X1 at a cost of £36,000. Additionally, installation costs totalled £4,000. During 19X3 major repairs costing £6,300 had been carried out on this plant and, in order to increase the capacity of the plant, a new motor had been fitted in December 19X3 at a cost of £4,400. A further overhaul costing £2,700 had been carried out during 19X4.

The company acquired new replacement plant on 30 November 19X5 at a cost of £96,000, inclusive of installation charges of £7,000.

Required:
Calculate:

(a) the balance of plant at cost at 31 March 19X6
(b) the provision for depreciation of plant at 31 March 19X6
(c) the profit or loss on disposal of the plant.

(Association of Chartered Certified Accountants)

23.9A Sema plc, a company in the heavy engineering industry, carried out an expansion programme in the 19X6 financial year, in order to meet a permanent increase in contracts.

The company selected a suitable site and commissioned a survey and valuation report, for which the fee was £1,500. On the basis of the report the site was acquired for £90,000.

Solicitor's fees for drawing up the contract and conveyancing were £3,000.

Fees of £8,700 were paid to the architects for preparing the building plans and overseeing the building work. This was carried out partly by the company's own workforce (at a wages cost of £11,600), using company building materials (cost £76,800), and partly by sub-contractors who charged £69,400, of which £4,700 related to the demolition of an existing building on the same site.

The completed building housed two hydraulic presses.

The cost of press A was £97,000 (ex works), payable in a single lump sum two months after installation. Sema was given a trade discount of 10% and a cash discount for prompt payment of 2%. Hire of a transporter to collect the press and to convey it to the new building was £2,900. Installation costs were £2,310, including hire of lifting gear, £1,400.

Press B would have cost £105,800 (delivered) if it had been paid in one lump sum. However, Sema opted to pay three equal annual instalments of £40,000, starting on the date of acquisition. Installation costs were £2,550, including hire of lifting gear, £1,750.

The whole of the above expenditure was financed by the issue of £500,000 7% Debentures (on which the annual interest payable was £35,000).

Before the above acquisitions were taken into account, the balances (at cost) on the fixed asset accounts for premises and plant were £521,100 and £407,500 respectively.

Required:

(a) Using such of the above information as is relevant, post and balance the premises and plant accounts for the 19X6 financial year.
(b) State, with reasons, which of the given information you have not used in your answer to (a) above.

(Association of Chartered Certified Accountants)

24

Bad debts, provisions for doubtful debts, provisions for discounts on debtors

Objectives

After you have studied this chapter, you should be able to:

* *understand how bad debts can be written off*

* *make provisions for possible bad debts*

* *calculate and make provisions for discounts on debtors*

24.1 Bad debts

With many businesses a large proportion, if not all, of the sales are on a credit basis. The business is therefore taking the risk that some of the customers may never pay for the goods sold to them on credit. This is a normal business risk and therefore **bad debts** as they are called are a normal business expense, and must be charged as such when calculating the profit or loss for the period.

When a debt is found to be bad, the asset as shown by the debtor's account is worthless, and must accordingly be eliminated as an asset account. This is done by crediting the debtor's account to cancel the asset and increasing the expenses account of bad debts by debiting it there. Sometimes the debtor will have paid part of the debt, leaving the remainder to be written off as a bad debt. The total of the bad debts account is later transferred to the profit and loss account.

An example of debts being written off as bad can now be shown in Exhibit 24.1.

Exhibit 24.1

C Bloom

19X5		£	19X5		£
Jan 8	Sales	50	Dec 31	Bad debts	50

R Shaw

19X5		£	19X5		£
Feb 16	Sales	240	Aug 17	Cash	200
			Dec 31	Bad debts	40
		240			240

Bad Debts

19X5		£	19X5		£
Dec 31 C Bloom		50	Dec 31 Profit and loss		90
„ „ R Shaw		40			
		90			90

Profit and Loss Account (extract) for the year ended 31 December 19X5

	£
Gross profit	xxx
Less Expenses:	
Bad debts	90

24.2 Provisions for doubtful debts

Why provisions are needed

When we are drawing up our final accounts we want to achieve the following objectives:

- to charge as expenses in the profit and loss account for that year an amount representing sales of *that year* for which we will never be paid;
- to show in the balance sheet as correct a figure as possible of the true value of debtors at the balance sheet date.

Out of the credit sales during a year, it may have become obvious by the year end that some will never be paid for. Taking the year ended 31 December 19X3, for example, three credit sales – £500 in January 19X3, £750 in March 19X3 and £200 in June 19X3 – may be known by the year end definitely to be bad debts. These can then be written off to the bad debts expense account during the year ended 31 December 19X3.

However, how about the sales much later in the year which have not been paid for by the year end? These have not been owing for so long, and it will be more difficult to determine which of them will be bad debts. For instance, suppose that a sale on 15 December 19X3 had not been paid by 31 December 19X3. How likely will it be that it will become a bad debt? Obviously, if you had known on 15 December 19X3 that it would become a bad debt then you would not have sold the buyer the goods on credit. But selling goods to people who *may* never pay is a normal business risk, no matter how hard you try to avoid it, if you have to sell on credit terms.

This means that it is impossible to determine with absolute accuracy at the year end what the amount is in respect of debtors who will never pay their accounts. However, you sold the goods in the year ended 31 December 19X3, and that is the year in which you took the risk of selling goods that might never be paid for. Therefore in the profit and loss account for 19X3 you want to show the full amount that has become bad debts or will prove to be so.

To overcome the problem of charging against profits for (*a*) debts that have proved to be bad, and (*b*) debts that are likely to be bad but have not yet been proved to be so, the basic idea has evolved of keeping (*a*) and (*b*) in two separate accounts:

(*a*) **Bad debts expense account:** This is used only when the debt has been proved to be a bad debt and is written off.

(*b*) **Provision for doubtful debts account:** This account is used only for estimates of the amount of the *debtors remaining at the year end **after** the bad debts have been written off* that are likely to finish up as bad debts. (This account can also be known as the 'provision for *bad* debts account'. In order that you may become used to both terms, either of which could appear in an examination, some of the examples in this book will use one, and some the other.)

By charging both (*a*) and (*b*) in the profit and loss account for the year, we get the full amount provided for in respect of bad and doubtful debts that are believed to have arisen from sales made during the year. These amounts are shown as deductions from the gross profit.

By showing (*b*) as a deduction from the figure of debtors in the balance sheet at the year end, we then get a net figure, which represents a more correct figure of the value of debtors. It may not be absolutely accurate – only time will tell which of the debtors will turn out to be bad debts – but it is better than not attempting to make an estimate.

You can see that the provision for doubtful debts is similar in a way to the provision for depreciation. It too could never be absolutely accurate, since only in several years' time, when the asset is put out of use, can it be determined whether or not the provisions had been appropriate. Having to accept estimates where absolute accuracy is impossible is a part of accounting.

In order to arrive at a figure for doubtful debts, a firm must first consider that some debtors will never pay any of the amount they owe, while others will pay a part of the amount owing only, leaving the remainder permanently unpaid. The estimated figure can be made:

1 by looking at each debt, and deciding to what extent it will be bad;
2 by estimating, on the basis of experience, what percentage of the total amount due from debtors will prove to be bad debts.

It is well known that the longer a debt is owing the more likely it is that it will become a bad debt. Some firms draw up an ageing schedule, showing how long debts have been owing. Older debtors need higher percentage estimates of bad debts than do newer debtors. Exhibit 24.2 gives an example of such an ageing schedule.

Exhibit 24.2

Ageing Schedule for Doubtful Debts			
Period debt owing	*Amount*	*Estimated percentage doubtful*	*Provision for doubtful debts*
	£	%	£
Less than one month	5,000	1	50
1 month to 2 months	3,000	3	90
2 months to 3 months	800	4	32
3 months to 1 year	200	5	10
Over 1 year	160	20	32
	9,160		214

Accounting entries for provisions for doubtful debts

When the decision has been taken as to the amount of the provision to be made, then the accounting entries needed for the provision are:

Year in which provision *first made*:

1 Debit profit and loss account with amount of provision (i.e. deduct from gross profit as expenses).
2 Credit provision for doubtful debts account.

Exhibit 24.3 shows the entries needed for a provision for doubtful debts.

Exhibit 24.3

At 31 December 19X3 the debtors figure amounted to £10,000. It is estimated that 2 per cent of debts (i.e. £200) will prove to be bad debts, and it is decided to make a provision for these. The accounts will appear as follows:

Profit and Loss Account (extract) for the year ended 31 December 19X3

	£
Gross profit	xxx
Less Expenses:	
Provision for doubtful debts	200

Provision for Doubtful Debts

			£
	19X3		
	Dec 31	Profit and loss	200

In the balance sheet the balance on the provision for doubtful debts will be deducted from the total of debtors:

Balance Sheet (extract) as at 31 December 19X3

Current assets	£	£
Debtors	10,000	
Less Provision for doubtful debts	200	9,800

24.3 Increasing the provision

Let us suppose that for the same firm as in Exhibit 24.3, at the end of the following year, 31 December 19X4, the doubtful debts provision needed to be increased. This was because the provision was kept at 2 per cent, but the debtors had risen to £12,000. A provision of £200 had been brought forward from the *previous* year, but we now want a total provision of £240 (i.e. 2 per cent of £12,000). All that is needed is a provision for an extra £40. The double entry will be:

1 Debit profit and loss account (i.e. deduct from gross profit as expenses).
2 Credit provision for doubtful debts account.

Profit and Loss Account (extract) for the year ended 31 December 19X4

	£
Gross profit	xxx
Less Expenses	
Provision for doubtful debts (increase)	40

Provision for Doubtful Debts

19X4		£	19X4		£
Dec 31	Balance c/d	240	Jan 1	Balance b/d	200
			Dec 31	Profit and loss	40
		240			240
			19X5		
			Jan 1	Balance b/d	240

The balance sheet as at 31 December 19X4 will appear as:

Balance Sheet (extract) as on 31 December 19X4

Current assets	£	£
Debtors	12,000	
Less Provision for doubtful debts	240	11,760

24.4 Reducing the provision

The provision is shown as a credit balance. Therefore, to reduce it we would need a debit entry in the provision account. The credit would be in the profit and loss account. Let us assume that at 31 December 19X5, in the firm already examined, the debtors figure had fallen to £10,500 but the provision remained at 2 per cent, i.e. £210 (2 per cent of £10,500).

As the provision had previously been £240, then it now needs a reduction of £30. The double entry is:

1 Debit provision for doubtful debts account.
2 Credit profit and loss account (i.e. add to gross profit).

Provision for Doubtful Debts

19X5		£	19X5		£
Dec 31	Profit and loss	30	Jan 1	Balance b/d	240
„ 31	Balance c/d	210			
		240			240
			19X6		
			Jan 1	Balance b/d	210

Profit and Loss Account (extract) for the year ended 31 December 19X5

	£
Gross profit	xxx
Add Reduction in provision for doubtful debts	30

The balance sheet will appear:

Balance Sheet (extract) as on 31 December 19X5

Current assets	£	£
Debtors	10,500	
Less Provision for doubtful debts	210	10,290

You will have noticed that increases in the provision for doubtful debts increase the total of expenses. On the other hand, a reduction in provision for doubtful debts will be added to the gross profit.

Let us now look at a comprehensive example, Exhibit 24.4.

Exhibit 24.4

A business starts on 1 January 19X2 and its financial year end is 31 December annually. A table of the debtors, the bad debts written off and the estimated bad debts at the rate of 2 per cent of debtors at the end of each year is now given. The double entry accounts and the extracts from the final accounts follow.

Year to 31 December	Debtors at end of year (after bad debts written off)	Bad debts written off during year	Debts thought at end of year to be impossible to collect: 2% of debtors
	£	£	£
19X2	6,000	423	120 (2% of £6,000)
19X3	7,000	510	140 (2% of £7,000)
19X4	7,750	604	155 (2% of £7,750)
19X5	6,500	610	130 (2% of £6,500)

Bad Debts

		£			£
19X2			19X2		
Dec 31	Various debtors	423	Dec 31	Profit and loss	423
19X3			19X3		
Dec 31	Various debtors	510	Dec 31	Profit and loss	510
19X4			19X4		
Dec 31	Various debtors	604	Dec 31	Profit and loss	604
19X5			19X5		
Dec 31	Various debtors	610	Dec 31	Profit and loss	610

Provision for Doubtful Debts

		£			£
			19X2		
			Dec 31	Profit and loss	120
19X3			19X3		
Dec 31	Balance c/d	140	Dec 31	Profit and loss	20
		140			140
19X4			19X4		
Dec 31	Balance c/d	155	Jan 1	Balance b/d	140
			Dec 31	Profit and loss	15
		155			155
19X5			19X5		
Dec 31	Profit and loss	25	Jan 1	Balance b/d	155
	Balance c/d	130			
		155			155
			19X6		
			Jan 1	Balance b/d	130

Profit and Loss Account(s) (extracts) for the year ended

		£	£
Gross profit for 19X2, 19X3, 19X4, 19X5			xxx
19X2	*Less* Expenses:		
	Bad debts	423	
	Provision for doubtful debts (increase)	120	543
19X3	*Less* Expenses:		
	Bad debts	510	
	Provision for doubtful debts (increase)	20	530
19X4	*Less* Expenses:		
	Bad debts	604	
	Provision for doubtful debts (increase)	15	619
19X5	*Add* Reduction in provision for doubtful debts		25
	Less Expenses:		
	Bad debts	610	585

Balance Sheets (extracts) as at 31 December

		£	£
19X2	Debtors	6,000	
	Less Provision for doubtful debts	120	5,880
19X3	Debtors	7,000	
	Less Provision for doubtful debts	140	6,860
19X4	Debtors	7,750	
	Less Provision for doubtful debts	155	7,595
19X5	Debtors	6,500	
	Less Provision for doubtful debts	130	6,370

24.5 Bad debts recovered

It is not uncommon for a debt written off in previous years to be recovered in later years. When this occurs, the bookkeeping procedures are:

1   Reinstate the debt by making the following entries:

>   *Dr* Debtor's account
>   *Cr* Bad debts recovered account

The reason for reinstating the debt in the ledger account of the debtor is to have a detailed history of his/her account as a guide for granting credit in future. By the time a debt is written off as bad, it will be recorded in the debtor's ledger account. Therefore when such a debt is recovered, it also must be shown in the debtor's ledger account.

2   When the cash/cheque is later received from the debtor in settlement of the account or part thereof:

>   *Dr* Cash/bank
>   *Cr* Debtor's account
> with the amount received.

At the end of the financial year, the credit balance in the bad debts recovered account will be transferred to either the bad debts account or direct to the credit side of the profit and loss account. The effect is the same since the bad debts account will in itself be transferred to the profit and loss account at the end of the financial year.

24.6 Provisions for discounts on debtors

Some firms create provisions for discounts to be allowed on the debtors outstanding at the balance sheet date. This, they maintain, is quite legitimate, as the amount of debtors less any doubtful debt provision is not the best estimate of collectable debts, owing to cash discounts which will be given to debtors if they pay within a given time. The cost of discounts, it is argued, should be charged in the period when the sales were made.

To do this the procedure is similar to the doubtful debts provision. It must be borne in mind that the estimate of discounts to be allowed should be based on the net figure of debtors less bad debts provision, as it is obvious that discounts are not allowed on bad debts! Let us look at the example in Exhibit 24.5.

Exhibit 24.5

Year ended 31 December	Debtors	Provision for bad debts	Provision for discounts allowed
	£	£	%
19X3	4,000	200	2
19X4	5,000	350	2
19X5	4,750	250	2

Provision for Discounts on Debtors

	£			£
		19X3		
		Dec 31 Profit and loss		76
19X4		19X4		
Dec 31 Balance c/d	93	Dec 31 Profit and loss		17
	93			93
19X5		19X5		
Dec 31 Profit and loss	3	Jan 1 Balance b/d		93
„ Balance c/d	90			
	93			93
		19X6		
		Jan 1 Balance b/d		90

Profit and Loss Account (extracts) for the year ended 31 December ...

	£	£
Gross profits (19X3 and 19X4 and 19X5)		xxx
Less Expenses:		
(19X3) Provision for discounts on debtors	76	
(19X4) Increase in provision for discounts on debtors	17	
Add (19X5) Reduction in provision for discounts on debtors		3

Balance Sheets (extracts) as at 31 December

		£	£	£
19X3	Debtors		4,000	
	Less Provision for doubtful debts	200		
	„ Provision for discounts on debtors	76		
			276	
				3,724
19X4	Debtors		5,000	
	Less Provision for doubtful debts	350		
	„ Provision for discounts on debtors	93		
			443	
				4,557
19X5	Debtors		4,750	
	Less Provision for doubtful debts	250		
	„ Provision for discounts on debtors	90		
			340	
				4,410

New terms

Bad debt (p. 211): A debt that we will not be able to collect.

Provision for doubtful debts (p. 212): An account showing the expected amounts of debtors at the balance sheet date who will not be able to pay their accounts.

Main points to remember

1 Debts that we are unable to collect are credited to the customer's account (to cancel them) and debited to a bad debts account.

2 Provisions for bad debts are needed, otherwise the value of the debtors on the balance sheet will be showing too high a value, and could mislead anyone looking at the balance sheet. Also, this allows for more accurate calculation of profit or losses.

3 Provision for doubtful debts accounts are kept separate from the bad debts account. The amount of the provision is on the basis of the best guess that can be made taking all the facts into account.

4 An increase in a provision will have a debit in the profit and loss account.

5 A reduction in a provision will have a credit in the profit and loss account.

6 A provision for doubtful debts is shown as a deduction from the debtors in the balance sheet.

Review questions

24.1 In a new business during the year ended 31 December 19X8 the following debts are found to be bad, and are written off on the dates shown:

30 April	H Gordon	£110
31 August	D Bellamy Ltd	£64
31 October	J Alderton	£12

On 31 December 19X8 the schedule of remaining debtors, amounting in total to £6,850, is examined, and it is decided to make a provision for doubtful debts of £220.

You are required to show:

(a) The Bad Debts Account, and the Provision for Doubtful Debts Account.
(b) The charge to the Profit and Loss Account.
(c) The relevant extracts from the Balance Sheet as at 31 December 19X8.

24.2 A business had always made a provision for doubtful debts at the rate of 5% of debtors. On 1 January 19X7 the provision for this, brought forward from the previous year, was £260.
   During the year to 31 December 19X7 the bad debts written off amounted to £540.
   On 31 December 19X7 the remaining debtors totalled £6,200 and the usual provision for doubtful debts is to be made.
   You are to show:

(a) The Bad Debts Account for the year ended 31 December 19X7.
(b) The Provision for Doubtful Debts Account for the year.
(c) Extract from the Profit and Loss Account for the year.
(d) The relevant extract from the Balance Sheet as at 31 December 19X7.

24.3 A business started trading on 1 January 19X6. During the two years ended 31 December 19X6 and 19X7 the following debts were written off to the Bad Debts Account on the dates stated:

31 August 19X6	W Best	£85
30 September 19X6	S Avon	£140
28 February 19X7	L J Friend	£180
31 August 19X7	N Kelly	£60
30 November 19X7	A Oliver	£250

On 31 December 19X6 there had been a total of debtors remaining of £40,500. It was decided to make a provision for doubtful debts of £550.
   On 31 December 19X7 there had been a total of debtors remaining of £47,300. It was decided to make a provision for doubtful debts of £600.

You are required to show:

(i) The Bad Debts Account and the Provision for Doubtful Debts Account for each of the two years.
(ii) The relevant extracts from the Balance Sheets as at 31 December 19X6 and 19X7.

24.4A A business, which started trading on 1 January 19X5, adjusted its bad debt provisions at the end of each year on a percentage basis, but each year the percentage rate is adjusted in accordance with the current 'economic climate'. The following details are available for the three years ended 31 December 19X5, 19X6 and 19X7.

	Bad debts written off year to 31 December	Debtors at 31 December	Per cent provision for bad debts
	£	£	
19X5	656	22,000	5
19X6	1,805	40,000	7
19X7	3,847	60,000	6

You are required to show:

(*a*) Bad Debts Accounts for each of the three years.
(*b*) Provision for Doubtful Debts Accounts for each of the three years.
(*c*) Balance Sheet extracts as at 31 December 19X5, 19X6 and 19X7.

24.5A

(*a*) Businesses often create a provision for bad debts.

  (*i*)   Of which concept (or convention) is this an example? Explain your answer.
  (*ii*) What is the purpose of creating a provision for bad debts?
  (*iii*) How might the amount of a provision for bad debts be calculated?

(*b*) On 1 January 19X8 there was a balance of £500 in the Provision for Bad Debts Account, and it was decided to maintain the provision at 5% of the debtors at each year end.

The debtors on 31 December each year were:

	£
19X8	12,000
19X9	8,000
19X0	8,000

Show the necessary entries for the **three** years ended 31 December 19X8 to 31 December 19X0 inclusive in the following:

(*i*)   the Provision for Bad Debts Account;
(*ii*) the Profit and Loss Accounts.

(*c*) What is the difference between bad debts and provision for bad debts?

(*d*) On 1 January 19X0 Warren Mair owed Jason Dalgleish £130. On 25 August 19X0 Mair was declared bankrupt. A payment of 30p in the £ was received in full settlement. The remaining balance was written off as a bad debt. Write up the account of Warren Mair in Jason Dalgleish's ledger.

(*Northern Examinations and Assessment Board: GCSE*)

24.6 The balance sheet as at 31 May 19X7 of Forest Traders Limited included a provision for doubtful debts of £2,300. The company's accounts for the year ended 31 May 19X8 are now being prepared. The company's policy now is to relate the provision for doubtful debts to the age of debts outstanding. The debts outstanding at 31 May 19X8 and the required provisions for doubtful debts are as follows:

Debts outstanding	Amount	Provision for doubtful debts
	£	%
Up to 1 month	24,000	1
More than 1 month and up to 2 months	10,000	2
More than 2 months and up to 3 months	8,000	4
More than 3 months	3,000	5

Customers are allowed a cash discount of 2½% for settlement of debts within one month. It is now proposed to make a provision for discounts to be allowed in the company's accounts for the year ended 31 May 19X8.

Required:
Prepare the following accounts for the year ended 31 May 19X8 in the books of Forest Traders Limited to record the above transactions:

(a) Provision for doubtful debts;
(b) Provision for discounts to be allowed on debtors.

(*Association of Accounting Technicians*)

24.7A A firm makes a provision for doubtful debts of 5% of debtors, also a provision of 2½% for discount on debtors.

On 1 January 19X7 the balances brought forward on the relevant accounts were provision for doubtful debts £672 and provision for discounts on debtors £631.

You are required to:

(a) Enter the balances in the appropriate accounts, using a separate Provision for Doubtful Debts Account.
(b) During 19X7 the firm incurred bad debts £2,960 and allowed discounts £6,578. On 31 December 19X7 debtors amounted to £25,600. Show the entries in the appropriate accounts for the year 19X7, assuming that the firm's accounting year ends on 31 December 19X7, also balance sheet extracts at 31 December 19X7.

24.8 E Chivers commenced business on 1 January 19X7 and makes his accounts to 31 December every year. For the year ended 31 December 19X7, bad debts written off amounted to £1,200. It was also found necessary to create a provision for doubtful debts of £2,000.

In 19X8, debts amounting to £1,600 proved bad and were written off. Mrs P Iles, whose debt of £350 was written off as bad in 19X7, settled her account in full on 30 November 19X8. As at 31 December 19X8 total debts outstanding were £56,000. It was decided to bring the provision up to 5% of this figure on that date.

In 19X9, £2,350 debts were written off during the year, and another recovery of £150 was made in respect of debts written off in 19X7. As at 31 December 19X9, total debts outstanding were £42,000. The provision for doubtful debts is to be maintained at 5% of this figure.

You are required to show for the years 19X7, 19X8 and 19X9, the

(a) Bad Debts Account.
(b) Bad Debts Recovered Account.
(c) Provision for Bad Debts Account.
(d) Extract from the Profit and Loss Account.

24.9

(A) Explain why a provision may be made for doubtful debts.

(B) Explain the procedure to be followed when a customer whose debt has been written off as bad subsequently pays the amount originally owing.

(C) On 1 January 19X7 D Watson had debtors of £25,000 on which he had made a provision for doubtful debts of 3%.

During 19X7,
(*i*) A Stewart who owed D Watson £1,200 was declared bankrupt and a settlement of 25p in the £ was made, the balance being treated as a bad debt.
(*ii*) Other bad debts written off during the year amounted to £2,300.

On 31 December 19X7 total debtors amounted to £24,300 but this requires to be adjusted as follows:

(a) J Smith, a debtor owing £600 was known to be unable to pay and this amount was to be written off.
(b) A cheque for £200 from S McIntosh was returned from the bank unpaid.

D Watson maintained his provision for doubtful debts at 3% debtors.

Required:
(1) For the financial year ended 31 December 19X7, show the entries in the following accounts:
    (*i*) Provision for doubtful debts
    (*ii*) Bad debts

(2) What is the effect on net profit of the change in the provision for doubtful debts?

(*Scottish Qualifications Authority*)

25

Depreciation of fixed assets: nature and calculations

Objectives

After you have studied this chapter, you should:

- *be able to explain the need for a charge for depreciation expense*

- *understand the causes of depreciation*

- *be able to calculate depreciation using both the straight line and the reducing balance methods*

- *know how to calculate depreciation on assets bought or sold within an accounting period*

25.1 Nature of fixed assets

Fixed assets are those assets of material value which are:
- of long life, and
- to be used in the business, and
- not bought with the main purpose of resale.

25.2 Depreciation of fixed assets

However, fixed assets such as machinery, motor vans, fixtures and even buildings do not last for ever. If the amount received (if any) on disposal is deducted from the cost of buying them, the difference is called depreciation.

The only time that depreciation can be calculated accurately is when the fixed asset is disposed of, and the difference between the cost to its owner and the amount received on disposal is then calculated. If a motor van was bought for £1,000 and sold five years later for £20, then the amount of depreciation is £1,000 – £20 = £980.

25.3 Depreciation is an expense

Depreciation is the part of the original cost of the fixed asset consumed during its period of use by the firm. It is an expense for services consumed in the same way as expenses for items such as wages, rent or electricity. Because it is an expense, depreciation will have to be charged to the profit and loss account, and will therefore reduce net profit.

You can see that the only real difference between the expense of depreciation for a motor vehicle and the expense of petrol for the motor vehicle is that the petrol expense is used up in a day or two, whereas the expense for the motor vehicle is spread over several years. Both expenses are expenses of the business.

25.4 Causes of depreciation

These can be divided up between 1 physical deterioration, 2 economic factors, 3 the time factor, 4 depletion. Let us look at these in more detail.

Physical deterioration

1 **Wear and tear**. When a motor vehicle or machinery or fixtures and fittings are used they eventually wear out. Some last many years, others last only a few years. This is true of buildings, although some may last for a long time.
2 **Erosion, rust, rot and decay**. Land may be eroded or wasted away by the action of wind, rain, sun and other elements of nature. Similarly, the metals in motor vehicles or machinery will rust away. Wood will rot eventually. Decay is a process which will also be present due to the elements of nature and the lack of proper attention.

Economic factors

These may be said to be the reasons for an asset being put out of use even though it is in good physical condition. The two main factors are usually **obsolescence** and **inadequacy**.

1 **Obsolescence**. This is the process of becoming out of date. For instance, over the years there has been great progress in the development of synthesisers and electronic devices used by leading commercial musicians. The old equipment will therefore have become obsolete, and much of it will have been taken out of use by such musicians.

    This does not mean that the equipment is worn out. Other people may well buy the old equipment and use it, possibly because they cannot afford to buy new up-to-date equipment.
2 **Inadequacy**. This arises when an asset is no longer used because of the growth and changes in the size of the firm. For instance, a small ferryboat that is operated by a firm at a coastal resort will become entirely inadequate when the resort becomes more popular. Then it will be found that it would be more efficient and economical to operate a large ferryboat, and so the smaller boat will be put out of use by the firm.

    In this case also it does not mean that the ferryboat is no longer in good working order. It may be sold to a firm at a smaller resort.

The time factor

Obviously time is needed for wear and tear, erosion, etc., and for obsolescence and inadequacy to take place. However, there are fixed assets to which the time factor is connected in a different way. These are assets which have a legal life fixed in terms of years.

For instance, you may agree to rent some buildings for 10 years. This is normally called a lease. When the years are finished the lease is worth nothing to you, as it has finished. Whatever you paid for the lease is now of no value.

A similar asset is where you buy a patent with complete rights so that only you are able to produce something. When the patent's time has finished it then has no value. The usual length of life of a patent is 16 years.

Instead of using the term depreciation, the term *amortisation* is often used for these assets.

Depletion

Other assets are of wasting character, perhaps due to the extraction of raw materials from them. These materials are then either used by the firm to make something else, or are sold in their raw state to other firms. Natural resources such as mines, quarries and oil wells come under this heading. To provide for the consumption of an asset of a wasting character is called provision for **depletion**.

25.5 Land and buildings

Prior to SSAP 12, which applied after 1977, freehold and long leasehold properties were very rarely subject to a charge for depreciation. It was contended that, as property values tended to rise instead of fall, it was inappropriate to charge depreciation.

However, SSAP 12 requires that depreciation be written off over the property's useful life, with the exception that freehold land will not normally require a provision for depreciation. This is because land does not normally depreciate. Buildings do, however, eventually fall into disrepair or become obsolete and must be subject to a charge for depreciation each year. When a revaluation of property takes place, the depreciation charge must be on the revalued figure.

An exception to all this is **investment properties**. These are properties owned not for use but simply for investment. In this case investment properties will be shown in the balance sheet at their open market value.

25.6 Appreciation

At this stage of the chapter readers may well begin to ask themselves about the assets that increase (appreciate) in value. The answer to this is that normal accounting procedure would be to ignore any such appreciation, as to bring appreciation into account would be to contravene both the cost concept and the prudence concept as discussed in Chapter 10. Nevertheless, in certain circumstances appreciation is taken into account in partnership and limited company accounts, but this is left until partnerships and limited companies are considered.

25.7 Provision for depreciation as allocation of cost

Depreciation in total over the life of an asset can be calculated quite simply as cost less amount receivable when the asset is put out of use by the firm. If the item is bought and sold within the one accounting period, then the depreciation for that period is charged as a revenue expense in arriving at that period's net profit. The difficulties start when the asset is used for more than one accounting period, and an attempt has to be made to charge each period with the depreciation for that period.

Even though depreciation provisions are now regarded as allocating cost to each accounting period (except for accounting for inflation), it does not follow that there is any 'true' method of performing even this task. All that can be said is that the cost should be allocated over the life of the asset in such a way as to charge it as equitably as possible to the periods in which the asset is used. The difficulties involved are considerable and some of them are now listed.

1   Apart from a few assets, such as a lease, how accurately can a firm assess an asset's useful life? Even a lease may be put out of use if the premises leased have become inadequate.
2   How does one measure use? A car owned by a firm for two years may have been driven one year by a very careful driver and another year by a reckless driver. The standard of driving will affect the motor car and also the amount of cash receivable on its disposal. How should such a firm apportion the car's depreciation costs?
3   There are other expenses besides depreciation, such as repairs and maintenance of the fixed asset. As both of these affect the rate and amount of depreciation should they not also affect the depreciation provision calculations?
4   How can a firm possibly know the amount receivable in x years' time when the asset is put out of use?

These are only some of the difficulties. Therefore, the methods of calculating provisions for depreciation are mainly accounting customs.

25.8 Methods of calculating depreciation charges

The two main methods in use are the **straight line method** and the **reducing balance method.** Most accountants think that, although other methods may be needed in certain cases, the straight line method is the one that is generally most suitable.

Straight line method

By this method, sometimes also called the fixed instalment method, the number of years of use is estimated. The cost is then divided by the number of years, to give the depreciation charge each year.

For instance, if a motor lorry was bought for £22,000 and we thought we would keep it for four years and then sell it for £2,000, the depreciation to be charged would be:

$$\frac{\text{Cost (£22,000)} - \text{Extimated disposal value (£2,000)}}{\text{Number of expected years of use (4)}} = \frac{£20,000}{4}$$

= £5,000 depreciation each year for four years.

If, after four years, the motor lorry had no disposal value, the charge for depreciation would have been:

$$\frac{\text{Cost (£22,000)}}{\text{Number of expected years of use (4)}} = \frac{£20,000}{4}$$

= £5,500 depreciation each year for four years.

Reducing balance method

By this method a fixed percentage for depreciation is deducted from the cost in the first year. In the second or later years the same percentage is taken of the reduced balance (i.e. cost *less* depreciation already charged). This method is also known as the diminishing balance method.

If a machine is bought for £10,000, and depreciation is to be charged at 20 per cent, the calculations for the first three years would be as follows:

	£
Cost	10,000
First year: depreciation (20%)	2,000
	8,000
Second year: depreciation (20% of £8,000)	1,600
	6,400
Third year: depreciation (20% of £6,400)	1,280
Cost not yet apportioned, end of Year 3	5,120

The basic formula used to find the requisite percentage to apply with this method is:

$$r = 1 - \sqrt[n]{\frac{s}{c}}$$

where n = the number of years
       s = the net residual value (this must be a significant amount or the answers will be absurd, since the depreciation rate would amount to nearly one)
       c = the cost of the asset
       r = the rate of depreciation to be applied.

Using, as an example, the figures:

$$n = 4 \text{ years}$$
$$s = \text{residual value } £256$$
$$c = \text{cost } £10,000$$

the calculations would appear as:

$$r = 1 - \sqrt[4]{\frac{256}{£10,000}} = 1 - \frac{4}{10} = 0.6 \text{ or } 60 \text{ per cent}$$

The depreciation calculation applied to each of the four years of use would be:

	£
Cost	10,000
Year 1: Depreciation provision 60% of £10,000	6,000
Cost not yet apportioned, end of Year 1	4,000
Year 2: Depreciation provision 60% of £4,000	2,400
Cost not yet apportioned, end of Year 2	1,600
Year 3: Depreciation provision 60% of £1,600	960
Cost not yet apportioned, end of Year 3	640
Year 4: Depreciation provision 60% of £640	384
Cost not yet apportioned, end of Year 4	256

In this case the percentage to be applied worked out conveniently to a round figure.

However, the answer will often come out to several places of decimals. In this case it would be usual to take the nearest whole figure as a percentage to be applied.

The percentage to be applied, assuming a significant amount for residual value, is usually between two and three times greater for the reducing balance method than for the straight line method.

The advocates of this method usually argue that it helps to even out the total charged as expenses for the use of the asset each year. They state that provisions for depreciation are not the only costs charged, that there are the running costs in addition and that the repairs and maintenance element of running costs usually increase with age. Therefore, to equate total usage costs for each year of use the depreciation provisions should fall as the repairs and maintenance element increases. However, as can be seen from the figures of the example already given, the repairs and maintenance element would have to be comparatively large to bring about an equal total charge for each year of use.

To summarise, the people who favour this method say that:

In the early years			In the later years
A higher charge for depreciation	will tend to be fairly equal to		A lower charge for depreciation
+			+
A lower charge for repairs and upkeep			A higher charge for repairs and upkeep

25.9 Choice of method

The purpose of depreciation is to spread the total cost of the asset over the periods in which it is available to be used. The method chosen should be that which allocates cost to each period in accordance with the amount of benefit gained from the use of the asset in the period.

If, therefore, the main value is to be obtained from the asset in its earliest years, it may be appropriate to use the reducing balance which charges more in the early years. If, on the other hand, the benefits are to be gained evenly over the years, then the straight line method would be more appropriate.

The repairs and maintenance factor also has to be taken into account. One argument has already been mentioned in the last section.

Exhibit 25.1 gives a comparison of the calculations using the two methods, if the same cost is given for the two methods.

Exhibit 25.1

A firm has just bought a machine for £8,000. It will be kept in use for four years, then it will be disposed of for an estimated amount of £500. They ask for a comparison of the amounts charged as depreciation using both methods.

For the straight line method a figure of $(£8,000 - £500) \div 4 = £7,500 \div 4 = £1,875$ per annum is to be used. For the reducing balance method a percentage figure of 50 per cent will be used.

	Method 1 Straight Line £		Method 2 Reducing Balance £
Cost	8,000		8,000
Depreciation: year 1	1,875	(50% of £8,000)	4,000
	6,125		4,000
Depreciation: year 2	1,875	(50% of £4,000)	2,000
	4,250		2,000
Depreciation: year 3	1,875	(50% of £2,000)	1,000
	2,375		1,000
Depreciation: year 4	1,875	(50% of £1,000)	500
Disposal value	500		500

This illustrates the fact that using the reducing balance method has a much higher charge for depreciation in the early years, and lower charges in the later years.

25.10 Depreciation provisions and assets bought or sold

There are two main methods of calculating depreciation provisions for assets bought or sold during an accounting period.

1 To ignore the dates during the year that the assets were bought or sold, merely calculating a full period's depreciation on the assets in use at the end of the period. Thus, assets sold during the accounting period will have had no provision for depreciation made for that last period irrespective of how many months they were in use. Conversely, assets bought during the period will have a full period of depreciation provision calculated even though they may not have been owned throughout the whole of the period.
2 Provision for depreciation made on the basis of one month's ownership, one month's provision for depreciation. Fractions of months are usually ignored. This is obviously a more scientific method than that already described.

For examination purposes, where the dates on which assets are bought and sold are shown, then Method 2 is the method expected by the examiner. If no such dates are given, then obviously Method 1 will have to be used.

25.11 Other methods of calculating depreciation

There are many more methods of calculating depreciation but they are outside the scope of this chapter. These are fully considered in Chapter 36. You will find the revaluation method, depletion unit method, machine hour method and the sum of the year's digits in that chapter.

New terms

Amortisation (p. 226): A term used instead of depreciation when assets are used up simply because of the time factor.

Depletion (p. 226): The wasting away of an asset as it is used up.

Depreciation (p. 225): The part of the cost of the fixed asset consumed during its period of use by the firm.

Obsolescence (p. 225): Becoming out of date.

Reducing balance method (p. 228): Depreciation calculation which is at a lesser amount every following period.

Straight line method (p. 227): Depreciation calculation which remains at an equal amount each year.

Main points to remember

1   Depreciation is an expense of the business and has to be charged against any period during which depreciation occurs.

2   The main causes of depreciation are: physical deterioration, economic factors, the time factor and depletion.

3   There are other methods of calculating depreciation in addition to the straight line and reducing balance methods. Special methods are used in particular industries.

Review questions

25.1   D Sankey, a manufacturer, purchases a lathe for the sum of £4,000. It has an estimated life of five years and a scrap value of £500.

Sankey is not certain whether he should use the straight line or the reducing balance basis for the purpose of calculating depreciation on the machine.

You are required to calculate the depreciation on the lathe using both methods, showing clearly the balance remaining in the lathe account at the end of each of the five years for each method. (Assume that 40 per cent per annum is to be used for the reducing balance method.)

25.2   A machine costs £12,500. It will be kept for four years, and then sold for an estimated figure of £5,120. Show the calculations of the figures for depreciation (to nearest £) for each of the four years using (*a*) the straight line method, (*b*) the reducing balance method, for this method using a depreciation rate of 20 per cent.

25.3   A motor vehicle costs £6,400. It will be kept for five years, and then sold for scrap £200. Calculate the depreciation for each year using (*a*) the reducing balance method, using a depreciation rate of 50 per cent, (*b*) the straight line method.

25.4A   A machine costs £5,120. It will be kept for five years, and then sold at an estimated figure of £1,215. Show the calculations of the figures for depreciation for each year using (*a*) the straight line method, (*b*) the reducing balance method, for this method using a depreciation rate of 25 per cent.

25.5A   A bulldozer costs £12,150. It will be kept for five years. At the end of that time agreement has already been made that it will be sold for £1,600. Show your calculations of the amount of depreciation each year if (a) the reducing balance method at a rate of 33⅓ per cent was used, (b) the straight line method was used.

25.6A   A motor tractor is bought for £6,000. It will be used for three years, and then sold back to the supplier for £3,072. Show the depreciation calculations for each year using (a) the reducing balance method with a rate of 20 per cent, (b) the straight line method.

25.7   A company, which makes up its accounts annually to 31 December, provides for depreciation of its machinery at the rate of 10 per cent per annum on the diminishing balance system.
On 31 December 19X9, the machinery consisted of three items purchased as under:

	£
On 1 January 19X7 Machine A	Cost 3,000
On 1 April 19X8 Machine B	Cost 2,000
On 1 July 19X9 Machine C	Cost 1,000

Required:

Your calculations showing the depreciation provision for the year 19X9.

26

Double entry records for depreciation

Objectives

After you have studied this chapter, you should be able to:

- *incorporate depreciation calculations into the accounting records*

- *record the disposal of fixed assets and the adjustments needed to the provision for depreciation accounts*

26.1 Recording depreciation

Looking back quite a few years, the charge for depreciation always used to be shown in the fixed asset accounts themselves. This method has now fallen into disuse.

The method now used is where the fixed assets accounts are always kept for showing the assets at cost price. The depreciation is shown accumulating in a separate 'provision for depreciation' account. This is the method used throughout this book. An illustration can now be looked at as in Exhibit 26.1.

No entry is made in the asset account for depreciation. Instead, the depreciation is shown accumulating in a separate account. The double entry is:

Debit the profit and loss account
Credit the provision for depreciation account

Exhibit 26.1

In a business with financial years ended 31 December a machine is bought for £2,000 on 1 January 19X5. It is to be depreciated at the rate of 20 per cent using the reducing balance method. The records for the first three years are now shown.

Machinery

19X5		£	
Jan	1 Cash	2,000	

Provision for Depreciation – Machinery

19X5		£	19X5		£
Dec 31 Balance c/d		400	Dec 31 Profit and Loss		400
19X6			19X6		
Dec 31 Balance c/d		720	Jan 1 Balance b/d		400
			Dec 31 Profit and Loss		320
		720			720
19X7			19X7		
Dec 31 Balance c/d		976	Jan 1 Balance b/d		720
			Dec 31 Profit and Loss		256
		976			976
			19X8		
			Jan 1 Balance b/d		976

Profit and Loss Account (extracts) for the year ended 31 December

		£
19X5	Depreciation	400
19X6	Depreciation	320
19X7	Depreciation	256

Now the balance on the Machinery Account is shown on the balance sheet at the end of each year less the balance on the Provision for Depreciation Account.

Balance Sheets (extracts)

	£	£
As at 31 December 19X5		
Machinery at cost	2,000	
Less Depreciation to date	400	
		1,600
As at 31 December 19X6		
Machinery at cost	2,000	
Less Depreciation to date	720	
		1,280
As at 31 December 19X7		
Machinery at cost	2,000	
Less Depreciation to date	976	
		1,024

26.2 The disposal of an asset

Reason for accounting entries

Upon the sale of an asset, we will want to delete it from our accounts. This means that the cost of that asset needs to be taken out of the asset account. In addition, the depreciation of the asset which has been sold will have to be taken out of the depreciation provision. Finally, the profit and loss on sale, if any, will have to be calculated.

When we charge depreciation on a fixed asset we are having to make guesses. We cannot be absolutely certain how long we will keep the asset in use, nor can we be certain at the date of purchase how much the asset will be sold for when we dispose of it. We will not often guess correctly. This means that when we dispose of an asset the cash received for it is usually different from our original guess.

Accounting entries needed

On the sale of a fixed asset, for instance machinery, the following entries are needed:

(A) Transfer the cost price of the asset sold to an assets disposal account (in this case a machinery disposals account):
Debit machinery disposals account.
Credit machinery account.

(B) Transfer the depreciation already charged to the assets disposal account:
Debit provision for depreciation: machinery.
Credit machinery disposals account.

(C) For remittance received on disposal:
Debit cash book.
Credit machinery disposals account.

(D) Transfer difference (amount to balance the account) to the profit and loss account. If the machinery disposals account shows a credit balance, it is a profit on sale:
Debit machinery disposals account.
Credit profit and loss account.
If the machinery disposals account shows a debit balance, it is a loss on sale:
Debit profit and loss account.
Credit machinery disposals account.

These entries can be illustrated by looking at those needed if the machinery already shown in Exhibit 26.1 was sold. To 31 December 19X7 the cost was £2,000 and a total of £976 had been written off as depreciation leaving a book value of £2,000 – £976 = £1,024. If therefore the machinery is sold in 19X8 for *more* than £1,024 a profit on sale will be made. If, on the other hand, the machinery is sold for *less* than £1,024 then a loss will be incurred.

Exhibit 26.2 shows the entries needed when the machinery has been sold for £1,070 and therefore a profit on sale has been made. Exhibit 26.3 shows where the machinery has been sold for £950, thus incurring a loss on sale. In both cases the sale is on 2 January 19X8 and no depreciation is to be charged for the two days' ownership in 19X8.

Exhibit 26.2 Asset sold at a profit

Machinery

19X5		£	19X8		£
Jan 1 Cash		2,000	Jan 2 Machinery disposals (A)		2,000

Provision for Depreciation: Machinery

19X8			£	19X8			£
Jan	2	Machinery disposals (B)	976	Jan	1	Balance b/d	976

Machinery Disposals

19X8				£	19X8				£
Jan	2	Machinery	(A)	2,000	Jan	2	Provision for		
Dec	31	Profit and loss	(D)	46			depreciation	(B)	976
					Jan	2	Cash	(C)	1,070
				2,046					2,046

Profit and Loss Account for the year ended 31 December 19X8

		£
Gross profit		xxx
Add Profit on sale of machinery	(D)	46

Exhibit 26.3   Asset sold at a loss

Machinery

19X5			£	19X8				£
Jan	1	Cash	2,000	Jan	2	Machinery disposals	(A)	2,000

Provision for Depreciation: Machinery

19X8				£	19X8			£
Jan	2	Machinery disposals	(B)	976	Jan	1	Balance b/d	976

Machinery Disposals

19X8				£	19X8				£
Jan	2	Machinery	(A)	2,000	Jan	2	Provision for		
							depreciation	(B)	976
					Jan	2	Cash	(C)	950
					Dec	31	Profit and loss	(D)	74
				2,000					2,000

Profit and Loss Account for the year ended 31 December 19X8

		£
Gross profit		xxx
Less Loss on sale of machinery	(D)	74

In many cases the disposal of an asset will mean that we have sold it. This will not always be the case. A car may be put in exchange against the purchase of a new car. Here the disposal value is the exchange value. If a new car costing £10,000 was to be paid for by £6,000 in cash and £4,000 for the old car put in exchange, then the disposal value of the old car is £4,000.

Similarly a car may have been in an accident and now be worthless. If insured, the disposal value will be the amount received from the insurance company. If an asset is scrapped, the disposal value is that received from the sale of the scrap, which may be nil.

26.3 Change of depreciation method

It is possible to make a change in the method of calculating depreciation. This should not be done frequently, and it should only be undertaken after a thorough review. Where a change is made the effect, if material (*see* Chapter 10 on materiality), should be shown as a note to the final accounts in the year of change.

Further examples

So far the examples shown have deliberately been kept simple. Only one item of an asset has been shown in each case. Exhibits 26.4 and 26.5 give examples of more complicated cases.

Exhibit 26.4

A machine is bought on 1 January 19X5 for £1,000 and another one on 1 October 19X6 for £1,200. The first machine is sold on 30 June 19X7 for £720. The firm's financial year ends on 31 December. The machinery is to be depreciated at 10 per cent, using the straight line method and based on assets in existence at the end of each year ignoring items sold during the year.

Machinery

	£			£
19X5				
Jan 1 Cash	1,000			
19X6		19X6		
Oct 1 Cash	1,200	Dec 31 Balance c/d		2,200
	2,200			2,200
19X7		19X7		
Jan 1 Balance b/d	2,200	Jun 30 Disposals		1,000
		Dec 31 Balance c/d		1,200
	2,200			2,200
19X8				
Jan 1 Balance b/d	1,200			

Provision for Depreciation: Machinery

	£		£
		19X5	
		Dec 31 Profit and loss	100
19X6		19X6	
Dec 31 Balance c/d	320	Dec 31 Profit and loss	220
	320		320
19X7		19X7	
Jun 30 Disposals of machinery		Jan 1 Balance b/d	320
(2 years ×10 per cent		Dec 31 Profit and loss	120
× £1,000)	200		
Dec 31 Balance c/d	240		
	440		440
		19X8	
		Jan 1 Balance b/d	240

Disposals of Machinery

19X7		£	19X7		£
Jun 30	Machinery	1,000	Jun 30	Cash	720
			Jun 30	Provision for depreciation	200
			Dec 31	Profit and loss	80
		1,000			1,000

Profit and Loss Account (extracts) for the year ended 31 December

		£
	Less Expenses:	
19X5	Provision for depreciation: Machinery	100
19X6	Provision for depreciation: Machinery	220
19X7	Provision for depreciation: Machinery	120
	Loss on machinery sold	80

Balance Sheet (extracts) as at 31 December

		£	£
19X5	Machinery at cost price	1,000	
	Less Depreciation to date	100	
			900
19X6	Machinery at cost	2,200	
	Less Depreciation to date	320	
			1,880
19X7	Machinery at cost	1,200	
	Less Depreciation to date	240	
			960

Another example can now be given. This is somewhat more complicated, first owing to a greater number of items, and second because the depreciation provisions are calculated on a proportionate basis, i.e. one month's depreciation for every one month's ownership.

Exhibit 26.5

A business with its financial year end being 31 December buys two motor vans, No 1 for £800 and No 2 for £500, both on 1 January 19X1. It also buys another motor van, No 3, on 1 July 19X3 for £900 and another, No 4, on 1 October 19X3 for £720. The first two motor vans are sold, No 1 for £229 on 30 September 19X4, and the other, No 2, was sold for scrap £5 on 30 June 19X5.

Depreciation is on the straight line basis, 20 per cent per annum, ignoring scrap value in this particular case when calculating depreciation per annum. Show the extracts from the assets account, provision for depreciation account, disposal account and profit and loss account for the years ended 31 December 19X1, 19X2, 19X3, 19X4, and 19X5, and the balance sheets as at those dates.

Motor Vans

19X1			£				£
Jan	1	Cash	1,300				
19X3							
July	1	Cash	900	19X3			
Oct	1	Cash	720	Dec	31	Balance c/d	2,920
			2,920				2,920
19X4				19X4			
Jan	1	Balance b/d	2,920	Sept	30	Disposals	800
				Dec	31	Balance c/d	2,120
			2,920				2,920
19X5				19X5			
Jan	1	Balance b/d	2,120	June	30	Disposals	500
				Dec	31	Balance c/d	1,620
			2,120				2,120
19X6							
Jan	1	Balance b/d	1,620				

Provision for Depreciation: Motor Vans

			£	19X1			£
				Dec	31	Profit and loss	260
19X2				19X2			
Dec	31	Balance c/d	520	Dec	31	Profit and loss	260
			520				520
19X3				19X3			
				Jan	1	Balance b/d	520
Dec	31	Balance c/d	906	Dec	31	Profit and loss	386
			906				906
19X4				19X4			
Sept	30	Disposals	600	Jan	1	Balance b/d	906
Dec	31	Balance c/d	850	Dec	31	Profit and loss	544
			1,450				1,450
19X5				19X5			
June	30	Disposals	450	Jan	1	Balance b/d	850
Dec	31	Balance c/d	774	Dec	31	Profit and loss	374
			1,224				1,224
				19X6			
				Jan	1	Balance b/d	774

Workings – depreciation provisions

		£	£
19X1	20% of £1,300		260
19X2	20% of £1,300		260
19X3	20% of £1,300 × 12 months	260	
	20% of £900 × 6 months	90	
	20% of £720 × 3 months	36	
			386
19X4	20% of £2,120 × 12 months		424
	20% of £800 × 9 months	120	
			544
19X5	20% of £1,620 × 12 months	324	
	20% of £500 × 6 months	50	
			374

Workings – transfers of depreciation provisions to disposal accounts

Van 1 Bought Jan 1 19X1 Cost £800
       Sold Sept 30 19X4
       Period of ownership $3\frac{3}{4}$ years
       Depreciation provisions $3\frac{3}{4} \times 20\% \times £800 = £600$
Van 2 Bought Jan 1 19X1 Cost £500
       Sold June 30 19X5
       Period of ownership $4\frac{1}{2}$ years
       Depreciation provisions $4\frac{1}{2} \times 20\% \times £500 = £450$

Disposals of Motor Vans

19X4			£	19X4			£
Sept	30	Motor van	800	Sept	30	Provision for depreciation	600
				,,	,,	Cash	229
Dec	31	Profit and loss	29				
			829				829
19X5				19X5			
Jun	30	Motor van	500	Jun	30	Provision for depreciation	450
				,,	,,	Cash	5
				Dec	31	Profit and loss	45
			500				500

Profit and Loss Account (extracts) for the year ended 31 December

		£	£
	Gross profit (each year 19X1, 19X2, 19X3)		xxx
	Less Expenses:		
19X1	Provision for depreciation: motor vans		260
19X2	Provision for depreciation: motor vans		260
19X3	Provision for depreciation: motor vans		386
19X4	Gross profit		xxx
	Add Profit on motor van sold		29
			xxx
	Less Expenses:		
	Provision for depreciation: motor vans		544
			xxx
19X5	Gross profit		xxx
	Less Expenses:		
	Provision for depreciation: motor vans	374	
	Loss on motor van sold	45	

Balance Sheets (extracts) as at 31 December

		£	£
19X1	Motor vans at cost	1,300	
	Less Depreciation to date	260	
			1,040
19X2	Motor vans at cost	1,300	
	Less Depreciation to date	520	
			780
19X3	Motor vans at cost	2,920	
	Less Depreciation to date	906	
			2,014
19X4	Motor vans at cost	2,120	
	Less Depreciation to date	850	
			1,270
19X5	Motor vans at cost	1,620	
	Less Depreciation to date	774	
			846

This chapter has covered all the principles involved. Obviously an examiner can present his questions in his own way, frequently devised by him to test your understanding by presenting them in different ways. Practice at the questions in this book and comparing them with the answers shown in full will demonstrate the truth of this statement.

26.4 Depreciation provisions and the replacement of assets

Making a provision for depreciation does not mean that money is invested somewhere to finance the replacement of the asset when it is put out of use. It is simply a bookkeeping entry, and the end result is that lower net profits are shown because the provisions have been charged to the profit and loss account.

It is not surprising to find that people who have not studied accounting misunderstand the situation. They often think that a provision is the same as money kept somewhere with which to replace the asset eventually.

On the other hand, lower net profits may also mean lower drawings by the proprietor. If this is so, then there will be more money in the bank with which to replace the asset. However, there is no guarantee that lower net profits mean lower drawings.

New term

Provision for depreciation account (p. 233): The account where depreciation is accumulated for balance sheet purposes. It is used in order to leave the cost figure as the balance in the fixed asset account.

Main points to remember

1   The method of showing depreciation in the assets account is now used only by some small organisations, and is outdated.

2   Using the modern method, asset accounts are kept at cost price, while the depreciation is credited to a provision for depreciation account.

3   When we sell a fixed asset, we must transfer both the cost and the accumulated depreciation to a separate disposal account.

4   Profit on disposal is transferred to the credit of the profit and loss account.

5   Loss on disposal is transferred to the debit of the profit and loss account.

Multiple-choice questions

Now attempt Set No. 3 consisting of 20 questions, shown on pp. 576–8.

Review questions

26.1   A company starts in business on 1 January 19X1. You are to write up the motor vans account and the provision for depreciation account for the year ended 31 December 19X1 from the information given below. Depreciation is at the rate of 20 per cent per annum, using the basis of one month's ownership needs one month's depreciation.

19X1   Bought two motor vans for £1,200 each on 1 January
       Bought one motor van for £1,400 on 1 July

26.2   A company starts in business on 1 January 19X3, the financial year end being 31 December. You are to show:

(a)   The machinery account.
(b)   The provision for depreciation account.
(c)   The balance sheet extracts for each of the years 19X3, 19X4, 19X5, 19X6.

The machinery bought was:

19X3	1 January	1 machine costing £800
19X4	1 July	2 machines costing £500 each
	1 October	1 machine costing £600
19X6	1 April	1 machine costing £200

Depreciation is at the rate of 10 per cent per annum, using the straight line method, machines being depreciated for each proportion of a year.

26.3A   A company maintains its fixed assets at cost. Depreciation provision accounts, one for each type of asset, are in use. Machinery is to be depreciated at the rate of $12\frac{1}{2}$ per cent per annum, and fixtures at the rate of 10 per cent per annum, using the reducing balance method. Depreciation is to be calculated on assets in existence at the end of each year, giving a full year's depreciation even though the asset was bought part of the way through the year. The following transactions in assets have taken place:

19X5	1 January	Bought machinery £640, fixtures £100
	1 July	Bought fixtures £200
19X6	1 October	Bought machinery £720
	1 December	Bought fixtures £50

The financial year end of the business is 31 December.

You are to show:
(a) The machinery account.
(b) The fixtures account.
(c) The two separate provision for depreciation accounts.
(d) The fixed assets section of the balance sheet at the end of each year, for the years ended 31 December 19X5 and 19X6.

26.4   A company depreciates its plant at the rate of 20 per cent per annum, straight line method, for each month of ownership. From the following details draw up the plant account and the provision for depreciation account for each of the years 19X4, 19X5, 19X6 and 19X7.

19X4	Bought plant costing £900 on 1 January.
	Bought plant costing £600 on 1 October.
19X6	Bought plant costing £550 on 1 July.
19X7	Sold plant which had been bought for £900 on 1 January 19X4 for the sum of £275 on 30 September 19X7.

You are also required to draw up the plant disposal account and the extracts from the balance sheet as at the end of each year.

26.5 A company maintains its fixed assets at cost. Depreciation provision accounts for each asset are kept.

At 31 December 19X8 the position was as follows:

	Total cost to date	Total depreciation to date
Machinery	52,590	25,670
Office furniture	2,860	1,490

The following additions were made during the financial year ended 31 December 19X9:

> Machinery £2,480, office furniture £320.
> Some old machines bought in 19X5 for £2,800 were sold for £800 during the year.
> The rates of depreciation are:
> Machinery 10 per cent, office furniture 5 per cent, using the straight line basis, calculated on the assets in existence at the end of each financial year irrespective of date of purchase.

You are required to show the asset and depreciation accounts for the year ended 31 December 19X9 and the balance sheet entries at that date.

26.6A
(a) What is the meaning of depreciation?
(b) Give **three** reasons why depreciation may occur.
(c) Name **two** methods of depreciation.
(d) In what way do you think the concept of consistency applies to depreciation?
(e) 'Since the calculation of depreciation is based on estimates, not facts, why bother to make the calculation?'
Explain briefly why you think that the calculation of depreciation is based on estimates.
(f) If depreciation was omitted, what effects would this have on the final accounts?
(g) 'Some assets increase (appreciate) in value, but normal accounting procedure would be to ignore any such appreciation.'
Explain why bringing appreciation into account would go against the prudence concept.
(h) A business whose financial year ends at 31 December purchased on 1 January 19X7 a machine for £5,000. The machine was to be depreciated by ten equal instalments. On 4 January 19X9 the machine was sold for £3,760.
Ignoring any depreciation in the year of sale, show the relevant entries for each of the following accounts for the years ended 31 December 19X7, 19X8 and 19X9:

(i) Machinery
(ii) Provision for depreciation of machinery
(iii) Machinery disposals
(iv) Profit and loss

(*Northern Examinations and Assessment Board: GCSE*)

26.7

(a) Identify the four factors which cause fixed assets to depreciate.

(b) Which one of these factors is the most important for each of the following assets?

(i) a gold mine,
(ii) a motor lorry,
(iii) a 50 year lease on a building,
(iv) land,
(v) a ship used to ferry passengers and vehicles across a river following the building of a bridge across the river,
(vi) a franchise to market a new computer software package in a certain country.

(c) The financial year of Ochre Ltd will end on 31 December 19X6. At 1 January 19X6 the company had in use equipment with a total accumulated cost of £135,620 which had been depreciated by a total of £81,374. During the year ended 31 December 19X6 Ochre Ltd purchased new equipment costing £47,800 and sold off equipment which had originally cost £36,000, and which had been depreciated by £28,224, for £5,700. No further purchases or sales of equipment are planned for December. The policy of the company is to depreciate equipment at 40% using the diminishing balance method. A full year's depreciation is provided for on all equipment in use by the company at the end of each year.

Required:
Show the following ledger accounts for the year ended 31 December 19X6:
(i) the Equipment Account;
(ii) the Provision for Depreciation on Equipment Account;
(iii) the Assets Disposals Account.

(*Association of Accounting Technicians*)

26.8A Mavron plc owned the following motor vehicles as at 1 April 19X6:

Motor Vehicle	Date Acquired	Cost £	Estimated Residual Value £	Estimated Life (years)
AAT 101	1 October 19X3	8,500	2,500	5
DJH 202	1 April 19X4	12,000	2,000	8

Mavron plc's policy is to provide at the end of each financial year depreciation using the straight line method applied on a month-by-month basis on all motor vehicles used during the year.

During the financial year ended 31 March 19X7 the following occurred:

(a) On 30 June 19X6 AAT 101 was traded in and replaced by KGC 303. The trade-in allowance was £5,000. KGC 303 cost £15,000 and the balance due (after deducting the trade-in allowance) was paid partly in cash and partly by a loan of £6,000 from Pinot Finance. KGC 303 is expected to have a residual value of £4,000 after an estimated economic life of 5 years.
(b) The estimated remaining economic life of DJH 202 was reduced from 6 years to 4 years with no change in the estimated residual value.

Required:
(a) Show any Journal entries necessary to give effect to the above.
(b) Show the Journal entry necessary to record depreciation on Motor Vehicles for the year ended 31 March 19X7.
(c) Reconstruct the Motor Vehicles Account and the Provision for Depreciation Account for the year ended 31 March 19X7.

Show the necessary calculations clearly.

(*Association of Accounting Technicians*)

26.9 A firm buys a fixed asset for £10,000. The firm estimates that the asset will be used for 5 years. After exactly $2\frac{1}{2}$ years, however, the asset is suddenly sold for £5,000. The firm always provides a full year's depreciation in the year of purchase and no depreciation in the year of disposal.

Required:

(a) Write up the relevant accounts (including disposal account but not profit and loss account) for each of Years 1, 2 and 3:
    (i)   Using the straight line depreciation method (assume 20% pa);
    (ii) Using the reducing balance depreciation method (assume 40% pa).

(b) (i)   What is the purpose of depreciation? In what circumstances would each of the two methods you have used be preferable?
    (ii) What is the meaning of the net figure for the fixed asset in the balance sheet at the end of Year 2?

(c) If the asset was bought at the beginning of Year 1, but was not used at all until Year 2 (and it is confidently anticipated to last until Year 6), state under each method the appropriate depreciation charge in Year 1, and briefly justify your answer.

(*Association of Chartered Certified Accountants*)

26.10A Contractors Ltd was formed on 1 January 19X6 and the following purchases and sales of machinery were made during the first 3 years of operations.

Date	Asset	Transaction	Price
1 January 19X6	Machines 1 and 2	purchase	£40,000 each
1 October 19X6	Machines 3 and 4	purchase	£15,200 each
30 June 19X6	Machine 3	sale	£12,640
1 July 19X8	Machine 5	purchase	£20,000

Each machine was estimated to last 10 years and to have a residual value of 5% of its cost price. Depreciation was by equal instalments, and it is company policy to charge depreciation for every month an asset is owned.

Required:

(a) Calculate
    (i) the total depreciation on Machinery for each of the years 19X6, 19X7, and 19X8;
    (ii) the profit or loss on the sale of Machine 3 in 19X8.

(b) Contractors Ltd depreciates its vehicles by 30% per annum using the diminishing balance method. What difference would it have made to annual reported profits over the life of a vehicle if it had decided instead to depreciate this asset by 20% straight line?

(*Scottish Qualifications Authority*)

27

Other adjustments for final accounts

Objectives

After you have studied this chapter, you should be able to:

- *adjust expense accounts for accruals and prepayments*

- *adjust revenue accounts for amounts owing*

- *show accruals, prepayments and revenue debtors in the balance sheet*

- *ascertain the amounts of expense and revenue items to be shown in the profit and loss account*

27.1 Final accounts so far

The trading and profit and loss accounts you have looked at have taken the sales for a period and deducted all the expenses for that period, the result being a net profit (or a net loss).

Up to this part of the book it has always been assumed that the expenses belonged exactly to the period of the trading and profit and loss account. If the trading and profit and loss account for the year ended 31 December 19X5 was being drawn up, then the rent paid as shown in the trial balance was exactly for 19X5. There was no rent owing at the beginning of 19X5 nor any owing at the end of 19X5, nor had any rent been paid in advance.

This was done to make your first meeting with final accounts much easier for you.

27.2 Adjustments needed

Let us look instead at two firms who pay rent for buildings in Oxford. The rent for each building is £1,200 a year.

1 Firm A pays £1,000 in the year. At the year end it owes £200 for rent.
  Rent expense used up   =   £1,200
  Rent paid for   =   £1,000

2 Firm B pays £1,300 in the year. This figure includes £100 in advance for the following year.
  Rent expense used up   =   £1,200
  Rent paid for   =   £1,300

A profit and loss account for 12 months needs 12 months' rent as an expense = £1,200. This means that in both **1** and **2** the double entry accounts will have to be adjusted.

In all the examples following in this chapter the trading and profit and loss accounts are for the year ended 31 December 19X5.

27.3 Accrued expenses

Assume that rent of £1,000 per year is payable at the end of every three months. The rent was not always paid on time. Details were:

Amount	Rent due	Rent paid
£250	31 March 19X5	31 March 19X5
£250	30 June 19X5	2 July 19X5
£250	30 September 19X5	4 October 19X5
£250	31 December 19X5	5 January 19X6

The rent account appeared as:

Rent

19X5		£	
Mar 31	Cash	250	
Jul 2	„	250	
Oct 4	„	250	

The rent paid 5 January 19X6 will appear in the books of the year 19X6 as part of the double entry.

The expense for 19X5 is obviously £1,000, as that is the year's rent, and this is the amount needed to be transferred to the profit and loss account. But if £1,000 was put on the credit side of the rent account (the debit being in the profit and loss account) the account would not balance. We would have £1,000 on the credit side of the account and only £750 on the debit side.

To make the account balance the £250 rent owing for 19X5, but paid in 19X6, must be carried down to 19X6 as a credit balance because it is a liability on 31 December 19X5. Instead of rent owing it could be called rent accrued or just simply an accrual. The completed account can now be shown:

Rent

19X5		£	19X5		£
Mar 31	Cash	250	Dec 31	Profit and loss	1,000
Jul 2	„	250			
Oct 4	„	250			
Dec 31	Accrued c/d	250			
		1,000			1,000
			19X6		
			Jan 1	Accrued b/d	250

The balance c/d has been described as accrued c/d, rather than as a balance. This is to explain what the balance is for; it is for an **accrued expense**.

27.4 Prepaid expenses

Insurance for a firm is at the rate of £840 a year, starting from 1 January 19X5. The firm has agreed to pay this at the rate of £210 every three months. However payments were not made at the correct times. Details were:

Amount	Insurance due	Insurance paid
£210	31 March 19X5	£210 28 February 19X5
£210 £210	30 June 19X5 30 September 19X5	£420 31 August 19X5
£210	31 December 19X5	£420 18 November 19X5

The insurance account for the year ended 31 December 19X5 will be shown in the books:

Insurance

19X5		£			
Feb 28	Bank	210			
Aug 31	,,	420			
Nov 18	,,	420			

Now the last payment of £420 is not just for 19X5; it can be split as £210 for the three months to 31 December 19X5 and £210 for the three months ended 31 March 19X6. For a period of 12 months the cost of insurance is £840 and this is, therefore, the figure needing to be transferred to the profit and loss account.

If this is entered then the amount needed to balance the account will therefore be £210 and at 31 December 19X5 this is a benefit paid for but not used up; it is an asset and needs carrying forward as such to 19X6, i.e. as a debit balance. It is a **prepaid expense**.

The account can now be completed:

Insurance

19X5		£	19X5		£
Feb 28	Bank	210	Dec 31	Profit and loss	840
Aug 31	,,	420			
Nov 18	,,	420	,, 31	Prepaid c/d	210
		1,050			1,050
19X6					
Jan 1	Prepaid b/d	210			

Prepayment will also happen when items other than purchases are bought for use in the business, and they are not fully used up in the period.

For instance, packing materials are normally not entirely used up over the period in which they are bought, there being a stock of packing materials in hand at the end of the period. This stock is, therefore, a form of prepayment and needs carrying down to the following period in which it will be used.

This can be seen in the following example:

> Year ended 31 December 19X5.
> Packing materials bought in the year £2,200.
> Stock of packing materials in hand as at 31 December 19X5 £400.

Looking at the example, it can be seen that in 19X5 the packing materials used up will have been £2,200 – £400 = £1,800. We will still have a stock of £400 packing materials at 31 December 19X5 to be carried forward to 19X6. The £400 stock of packing materials will be carried forward as an asset balance (debit balance) to 19X6.

Packing Materials

19X5		£	19X5			£
Dec 31 Bank		2,200	Dec 31	Profit and loss		1,800
			Dec 31	Stock c/d		400
		2,200				2,200
19X6						
Jan 1 Stock b/d		400				

The stock of packing materials is not added to the stock of unsold goods in hand in the balance sheet, but is added to the other prepayments of expenses.

27.5 Revenue owing at the end of period

The **revenue** owing for sales is already shown in the books. These are the debit balances on our customers' accounts, i.e. debtors. There may be other kinds of revenue, all of which has not been received by the end of the period, e.g. rent receivable. An example now follows:

Our warehouse is larger than we need. We rent part of it to another firm for £800 per annum. Details for the year ended 31 December were as follows:

Amount	Rent due	Rent received
£200	31 March 19X5	4 April 19X5
£200	30 June 19X5	6 July 19X5
£200	30 September 19X5	9 October 19X5
£200	31 December 19X5	7 January 19X6

The account for 19X5 will appear as:

Rent Receivable

			19X5			£
			Apr	4	Bank	200
			Jul	6	Bank	200
			Oct	9	Bank	200

The rent received of £200 on 7 January 19X6 will be entered in the books in 19X6.

Any rent paid by the firm would be charged as a debit to the profit and loss account. Any rent received, being the opposite, is transferred to the credit of the profit and loss account, as it is a revenue.

The amount to be transferred for 19X5 is that earned for the 12 months, i.e. £800. The rent received account is completed by carrying down the balance owing as a debit balance to 19X6. The £200 owing is an asset on 31 December 19X5.

The rent receivable account can now be completed:

Rent Receivable

19X5		£	19X5			£
Dec 31 Profit and loss		800	Apr	4	Bank	200
			Jul	6	Bank	200
			Oct	9	Bank	200
			Dec	31	Accrued c/d	200
		800				800
19X6						
Jan 1 Accrued b/d		200				

27.6 Expenses and revenue account balances and the balance sheet

In all the cases listed dealing with adjustments in the final accounts, there will still be a balance on each account after the preparation of the trading and profit and loss accounts. All such balances remaining should appear in the balance sheet. The only question left is where and how they shall be shown.

The amounts owing for expenses are usually added together and shown as one figure. These could be called expense creditors, expenses owing or accrued expenses. The item would appear under current liabilities as they are expenses which have to be discharged in the near future.

The items prepaid are also added together and called prepayments, prepaid expenses or payments in advance. They are shown next under the debtors. Amounts owing for rents receivable or other revenue owing are usually added to debtors.

The balance sheet in respect of the accounts so far seen in this chapter would appear:

Balance Sheet as at 31 December 19X5

	£	£	£
Current assets			
Stock		xxx	
Debtors		200	
Prepayments (400 + 210)		610	
Bank		xxx	
Cash		xxx	
		x,xxx	
Less Current liabilities			
Trade creditors	xxx		
Accrued expenses	250	xxx	
			x,xxx

27.7 Expenses and revenue accounts covering more than one period

Students are often asked to draw up an expense or revenue account for a full year, and there are amounts owing or prepaid at both the beginning and end of the year. We can now see how this is done.

Example A

The following details are available:

(A) On 31 December 19X4 three months rent of £3,000 was owing.
(B) The rent chargeable per year was £12,000.
(C) The following payments were made in the year 19X5:
6 January £3,000; 4 April £3,000; 7 July £3,000; 18 October £3,000.
(D) The final three months rent for 19X5 is still owing.

Now we can look at the completed rent account. The letters (A) to (D) give reference to the details above.

Rent

19X5			£	19X5			£
Jan 6	Bank	(C)	3,000	Jan 1	Owing b/d	(A)	3,000
Apr 4	Bank	(C)	3,000	Dec 31	Profit and loss	(B)	12,000
Jul 7	Bank	(C)	3,000				
Oct 18	Bank	(C)	3,000				
Dec 31	Accrued c/d	(D)	3,000				
			15,000				15,000
				19X6			
				Jan 1	Accrued b/d		3,000

Example B

The following details are available:

(A) On 31 December 19X4 packing materials in hand amounted to £1,850.
(B) During the year to 31 December 19X5 £27,480 was paid for packing materials.
(C) There were no stocks of packing materials on 31 December 19X5.
(D) On 31 December 19X5 we still owed £2,750 for packing materials already received and used.

The packing materials account will appear as:

Packing Materials

19X5			£	19X5		£
Jan 1	Stocks b/d	(A)	1,850	Dec 31	Profit and loss	32,080
Dec 31	Bank	(B)	27,480			
Dec 31	Owing c/d	(D)	2,750			
			32,080			32,080
				19X6		
				Jan 1	Owing b/d	2,750

The figure of £32,080 is the difference on the account, and is transferred to the profit and loss account.

We can prove it is correct:

	£	£
Stock at start of year		1,850
Add Bought and used:		
Paid for	27,480	
Still owed for	2,750	30,230
Cost of packing materials used in the year		32,080

Example C

Where different expenses are put together in one account, it can get even more confusing. Let us look at where rent and rates are joined together. Here are the details for the year ended 31 December 19X5:

(A) Rent is payable of £6,000 per annum.
(B) Rates of £4,000 per annum are payable by instalments.
(C) At 1 January 19X5 rent £1,000 had been prepaid in 19X4.
(D) On 1 January 19X5 rates were owed of £400.
(E) During 19X5 rent was paid £4,500.
(F) During 19X5 rates were paid £5,000.
(G) On 31 December 19X5 rent £500 was owing.
(H) On 31 December 19X5 rates of £600 had been prepaid.

A combined rent and rates account is to be drawn up for the year 19X5 showing the transfer to the profit and loss account, and balances are to be carried down to 19X6.

Rent and Rates

19X5			£	19X5			£
Jan 1	Rent prepaid b/d	(C)	1,000	Jan 1	Rates owing b/d	(D)	400
Dec 31	Bank: rent	(E)	4,500	Dec 31	Profit and loss a/c	(A) + (B)	10,000
Dec 31	Bank: rates	(F)	5,000				
Dec 31	Rent owing c/d	(G)	500	Dec 31	Rates prepaid c/d	(H)	600
			11,000				11,000
19X6				19X6			
Jan 1	Rates prepaid b/d	(H)	600	Jan 1	Rent owing b/d	(G)	500

27.8 Goods for own use

Traders will often take items out of their business stocks for their own use, without paying for them. There is nothing wrong about this, but an entry should be made to record the event. This is done by:

1 Credit purchases account, to reduce cost of goods available for sale.
2 Debit drawings account, to show that the proprietor has taken the goods for private use.

In the United Kingdom, an adjustment may be needed for value added tax. If goods supplied to a trader's customers have VAT added to their price, then any such goods taken for own use will need such an adjustment. This is because the VAT regulations state that VAT should be added to the cost of goods taken. The double entry for the VAT content would be:

1 Debit drawings account.
2 Credit VAT account.

Adjustments may also be needed for other private items. For instance, if a trader's private insurance had been incorrectly charged to the insurance account, then the correction would be:

1   Credit insurance account.
2   Debit drawings account.

27.9 Distinctions between various kinds of capital

The capital account represents the claim of the proprietor against the assets of the business at a point in time. The word **capital** is, however, often used in a specific sense. The main meanings are listed below.

Capital invested

This means the actual amount of money, or money's worth, brought into the business by the proprietor from his outside interests. The amount of capital invested is not disturbed by the amount of profits made by the business or losses incurred.

Capital employed

Candidates at an early stage in their studies are often asked to define this term. In fact, for those who progress to a more advanced stage, it will be seen in Volume 2 that it could have several meanings as the term is often used quite loosely. At an elementary level it is taken to mean the effective amount of money that is being used in the business. Thus, if all the assets were added together and the liabilities of the business deducted, the answer would be that the difference is the amount of money employed in the business. You will by now realise that this is the same as the closing balance of the capital account. It is also sometimes called **net assets**.

Working capital

This is a term for the excess of the current assets over the current liabilities of a business.

27.10 Final accounts in the services sector

So far we have looked at accounts for people who traded in some sort of goods. Because we wanted to be able to see what the gross profit on goods was for each firm we drew up a trading account for that purpose.

There are, however, many firms which do not deal in 'goods' but instead supply 'services'. This will include professional firms such as accountants, solicitors, doctors, estate agents, and the like, also firms with services such as television maintenance, window-cleaning, gardening, hairdressing, piano-tuning. As 'goods' are not dealt in there is no need for trading accounts to be drawn up. Instead a profit and loss account plus a balance sheet will be drafted.

The first item in the profit and loss account will be the revenue which might be called 'work done', 'fees', 'charges', 'accounts rendered', 'takings', etc., depending on the nature of the organisation. Any other items of income will be added, e.g. rent receivable, and then the expenses will be listed and deducted to arrive at a net profit or net loss.

An example of the profit and loss account of a solicitor might be as per Exhibit 27.1.

Exhibit 27.1

J Plunkett, Solicitor
Profit and Loss Account for the year ended 31 December 19X3

	£	£
Revenue:		
Fees charged		87,500
Insurance commissions		1,300
		88,800
Less Expenses:		
Wages and salaries	29,470	
Rent and rates	11,290	
Office expenses	3,140	
Motor expenses	2,115	
General expenses	1,975	
Depreciation	2,720	50,710
Net profit		38,090

27.11 Worksheets

Instead of drawing up a set of final accounts in the way already shown in this textbook, a worksheet could be drawn up instead. It may provide a useful aid where a large number of adjustments are needed.

Worksheets are usually drawn up on specially preprinted types of stationery with suitable columns printed on them. To provide such special stationery in an examination is difficult, also for students to draw up such a worksheet from scratch would be very time-consuming; therefore very few examinations will ask for worksheet operation. However, the examiner may ask you something about worksheets, if this is contained in the syllabus.

In Exhibit 27.2 the worksheet is shown (*see* p. 256) that would have been drawn up as an answer to Review question 27.10. Compare your answer to question 27.10 drawn up in the usual way with the worksheet. The gross profits and net profits are the same; it is simply the display that is different.

If you were an accountant working for John Brown, the final account given to him and to anyone else who was an interested party, such as the Inspector of Taxes or the bank, would be the same as the conventional type. They would not be given the worksheets.

27.12 Definition of accounting

In Chapter 1 we gave a definition of bookkeeping as being concerned with the work of entering information into accounting records and afterwards maintaining such records properly. This definition does not need to be amended.

However, accounting was not fully defined in Chapter 1. It would probably not have meant much to the reader at that stage in his/her studies. The following is the most widely used definition: '*The process of identifying, measuring, and communicating economic information to permit informed judgements and decisions by users of the information.*'

Exhibit 27.2

JOHN BROWN
WORKSHEET
See Review question 27.10

	Trial Balance		Adjustments		Trading Account		Profit & Loss Account		Balance Sheet	
	1 *Dr*	*2* *Cr*	*3* *Dr*	*4* *Cr*	*5* *Dr*	*6* *Cr*	*7* *Dr*	*8* *Cr*	*9* *Dr*	*10* *Cr*
Sales		400,000				400,000				
Purchases	350,000				350,000					
Sales returns	5,000				5,000					
Purchases returns		6,200				6,200				
Stock 1.1.19X7	100,000				100,000					
Provision for bad debt		800		180 (*iv*)						980
Wages & salaries	30,000		5,000 (*ii*)				35,000			
Rates	6,000			500 (*iii*)			5,500			
Telephone	1,000		220 (*v*)				1,220			
Shop fittings	40,000			4,000 (*vi*)					36,000	
Van	30,000			6,000 (*vi*)					24,000	
Debtors	9,800								9,800	
Creditors		7,000								7,000
Bad debts	200						200			
Capital		179,000								179,000
Bank	3,000								3,000	
Drawings	18,000								18,000	
	593,000	593,000								
Stock 31.12.19X7 – Asset			120,000 (*i*)						120,000	
Stock 31.12.19X7 – Cost of goods sold				120,000 (*i*)		120,000				
Accrued expenses				5,000 (*ii*) 220 (*v*)						5,000 220
Provision for bad debts			180 (*iv*)				180			
Prepaid expenses			500 (*iii*)						500	
Depreciation shop fittings			4,000 (*vi*)				4,000			
Depreciation van			6,000 (*vi*)				6,000			
			135,900	135,900						
Gross profit (balancing figure)					71,200			71,200		
					526,200	526,200				
Net profit (balancing figure)							19,100			19,100
							71,200	71,200	211,300	211,300

New terms

Accrued expense (p. 248): An expense which the firm has used up, but which has not yet been paid for.

Prepaid expense (p. 249): An expense to be used in a following period, which has been paid in advance.

Main points to remember

1   Adjustments are needed so that the expenses and income shown in the final accounts will equal the expenses incurred in the period and the revenue that has accrued.

2   The balances caused by the adjustments will be shown on the balance sheet at the end of the period.

3   Goods taken for own use without anything being recorded in the books will necessitate a transfer from purchases to the drawings account, plus an adjustment for VAT if appropriate.

4   Private expenses should not be charged as an expense in the trading and profit and loss accounts, but should instead be charged to drawings account.

Review questions

27.1   The financial year of H Saunders ended on 31 December 19X6. Show the ledger accounts for the following items including the balance transferred to the necessary part of the final accounts, also the balances carried down to 19X7:

(a)   Motor expenses: Paid in 19X6 £744; Owing at 31 December 19X6 £28.
(b)   Insurance: Paid in 19X6 £420; Prepaid as at 31 December 19X6 £35.
(c)   Stationery: Paid during 19X6 £1,800; Owing as at 31 December 19X5 £250; Owing as at 31 December 19X6 £490.
(d)   Rates: Paid during 19X6 £950; Prepaid as at 31 December 19X5 £220; Prepaid as at 31 December 19X6 £290.
(e)   Saunders sub-lets part of the premises. Receives £550 during the year ended 31 December 19X6. Tenant owed Saunders £180 on 31 December 19X5 and £210 on 31 December 19X6.

27.2A   J Owen's year ended on 30 June 19X8. Write up the ledger accounts, showing the transfers to the final accounts and the balances carried down to the next year for the following:

(a)   Stationery: Paid for the year to 30 June 19X8 £855; Stocks of stationery at 30 June 19X7 £290; at 30 June 19X8 £345.
(b)   General expenses: Paid for the year to 30 June 19X8 £590; Owing at 30 June 19X7 £64; Owing at 30 June 19X8 £90.
(c)   Rent and rates (combined account): Paid in the year to 30 June 19X8 £3,890; Rent owing at 30 June 19X7 £160; Rent paid in advance at 30 June 19X8 £250; Rates owing 30 June 19X7 £205; Rates owing 30 June 19X8 £360.
(d)   Motor expenses: Paid in the year to 30 June 19X8 £4,750; Owing as at 30 June 19X7 £180; Owing as at 30 June 19X8 £375.
(e)   Owen earns commission from the sales of one item. Received for the year to 30 June 19X8 £850; Owing at 30 June 19X7 £80; Owing at 30 June 19X8 £145.

27.3 On 1 January 19X8 the following balances, among others, stood in the books of M Baldock, a sole trader:

(*a*) Rates, £104 (Dr);
(*b*) Packing materials, £629 (Dr).

During the year ended 31 December 19X8 the information related to these two accounts is as follows:

(*i*) Rates of £1,500 were paid to cover the period 1 April 19X8 to 31 March 19X9;
(*ii*) £5,283 was paid for packing materials bought;
(*iii*) £357 was owing on 31 December 19X8 in respect of packing materials bought on credit;
(*iv*) Old materials amounting to £172 were sold as scrap for cash;
(*v*) Closing stock of packing materials was valued at £598.

You are required to write up the two accounts showing the appropriate amounts transferred to the Profit and Loss Account at 31 December 19X8, the end of the financial year of the trader.

Note: No separate accounts are opened for creditors for packing materials bought on credit.

27.4A On 1 January 19X6 the following balances, among others, stood in the books of T Thomas:

(*a*) Lighting and heating, (Dr) £277.
(*b*) Insurance, (Dr) £307.

During the year ended 31 December 19X6 the information related to these two accounts is as follows:

(*i*) Fire-insurance, £960, covering the year ended 31 April 19X7 was paid.
(*ii*) General insurance, £630, covering the year ended 31 August 19X7 was paid.
(*iii*) An insurance rebate of £55 was received on 30 June 19X6.
(*iv*) Electricity bills of £874 were paid.
(*v*) An electricity bill of £83 for December 19X6 was unpaid as on 31 December 19X6.
(*vi*) Oil bills of £1,260 were paid.
(*vii*) Stock of oil as on 31 December 19X6 was £92.

You are required to write up the accounts for lighting and heating, and for insurance, for the year to 31 December 19X6. Carry forward necessary balances to 19X7.

27.5 Three of the accounts in the ledger of Charlotte Williams indicated the following balances at 1 January 19X0:

Insurance paid in advance £562;
Wages outstanding £306;
Rent receivable, received in advance £36.

During 19X0 Charlotte:

Paid for insurance £1,019, by bank standing order;
Paid £15,000 wages, in cash;
Received £2,600 rent, by cheque, from the tenant.

At 31 December 19X0, insurance prepaid was £345. On the same day rent receivable in arrears was £105 and wages accrued amounted to £419.

(a) Prepare the insurance, wages and rent receivable accounts for the year ended 31 December 19X0, showing the year end transfers and the balances brought down.
(b) Prepare the profit and loss account extract showing clearly the amounts transferred from each of the above accounts for the year ended 31 December 19X0.
(c) Explain the effects on the final accounts of accounting for (i) expenses accrued and (ii) income received in advance at year end.
(d) What are the purposes of accounting for (i) expenses accrued and (ii) income received in advance at year end?

(*Edexcel Foundation, London Examinations: GCSE*)

27.6A The two accounts below were taken from the books of a retailer at the end of his financial year, 31 December 19X7.

Insurance Account

Dr					Cr
19X7		£	19X7		£
Jan 1	Balance	80	Dec 31	Profit and loss	530
Jan–Dec	Bank	540	Dec 31	Balance c/d	90
		620			620
Dec 31	Balance b/d	90			

Rent Receivable Account

Dr					Cr
19X7		£	19X7		£
Dec 31	Profit and loss	885	Jan 1	Balance	60
Dec 31	Balance c/d	75	Jan–Dec	Bank	900
		960			960
			Dec 31	Balance b/d	75

Required:

Answers to the following questions.

1   What type of account is the insurance account?
2   What type of account is the rent receivable account?
3   In which subdivision of the ledger will these accounts be found?
4   Under which heading will the closing balance of the insurance account be found on the balance sheet?
5   Under which heading will the closing balance of the rent receivable account be found on the balance sheet?
6   In which subsidiary book (book of prime entry) will the entries transferring amounts to the profit and loss account be found?
7   Which document will be the source of information for the entry in the insurance account 'bank £540'?
8   Which document will be the source of information for the entry in the rent receivable account 'bank £900'?
9   What amount for insurance will appear in the trial balance dated 31 December 19X7 prepared prior to the preparation of final accounts?
10 What amount for rent receivable will appear in the trial balance dated 31 December 19X7 prepared prior to the preparation of final accounts?
11 If the adjustment in the insurance account for £90 on 31 December had been overlooked, would the net profit have been under- or overstated and by how much?
12 If the adjustment in the rent receivable account for £75 on 31 December had been overlooked, would the net profit have been under- or overstated and by how much?

(Southern Examining Group: GCSE)

27.7A The owner of a small business selling and repairing cars which you patronise has just received a copy of his accounts for the current year.

He is rather baffled by some of the items and as he regards you as a financial expert, he has asked you to explain certain points of difficulty to him. This you have readily agreed to do. His questions are as follows:

(a) 'What is meant by the term "assets"? My mechanical knowledge and skill is an asset to the business but it does not seem to have been included.'
(b) 'The house I live in cost £30,000 five years ago and is now worth £60,000, but that is not included either.'
(c) 'What is the difference between "fixed assets" and "current assets"?'
(d) 'Why do amounts for "vehicles" appear under both fixed asset and current asset headings?'
(e) 'Why is the "bank and cash" figure in the balance sheet different from the profit for the year shown in the profit and loss account?'
(f) 'I see the profit and loss account has been charged with depreciation on equipment etc. I bought all these things several years ago and paid for them in cash. Does this mean that I am being charged for them again?'

Required:
Answer each of his questions in terms which he will be able to understand.

(*Association of Chartered Certified Accountants*)

27.8 The following trial balance was extracted from the books of A Scholes at the close of business on 28 February 19X7.

	Dr £	Cr £
Purchases and sales	11,280	19,740
Cash at bank	1,140	
Cash in hand	210	
Capital account 1 March 19X6		9,900
Drawings	2,850	
Office furniture	1,440	
Rent	1,020	
Wages and salaries	2,580	
Discounts	690	360
Debtors and creditors	4,920	2,490
Stock 1 March 19X6	2,970	
Provision for bad and doubtful debts 1 March 19X6		270
Delivery van	2,400	
Van running costs	450	
Bad debts written off	810	
	32,760	32,760

Notes:
(a) Stock 28 February 19X7 £3,510.
(b) Wages and salaries accrued at 28 February 19X7 £90.
(c) Rent prepaid at 28 February 19X7 £140.
(d) Van running costs owing at 28 February 19X7 £60.
(e) Increase the provision for bad and doubtful debts by £60.
(f) Provide for depreciation as follows: Office furniture £180; Delivery van £480.

Required:
Draw up the trading and profit and loss account for the year ending 28 February 19X7 together with a balance sheet as on 28 February 19X7, using vertical formats throughout.

27.9A T Morgan, a sole trader, extracted the following trial balance from his books at the close of business on 31 March 19X9:

	Dr £	Cr £
Purchases and sales	22,860	41,970
Stock 1 April 19X8	5,160	
Capital 1 April 19X8		7,200
Bank overdraft		4,350
Cash	90	
Discounts	1,440	930
Returns inwards	810	
Returns outwards		570
Carriage outwards	2,160	
Rent and insurance	1,740	
Provision for bad and doubtful debts		660
Fixtures and fittings	1,200	
Delivery van	2,100	
Debtors and creditors	11,910	6,060
Drawings	2,880	
Wages and salaries	8,940	
General office expenses	450	
	61,740	61,740

Notes:
(a) Stock 31 March 19X9 £4,290.
(b) Wages and salaries accrued at 31 March 19X9 £210; Office expenses owing £20.
(c) Rent prepaid 31 March 19X9 £180.
(d) Increase the provision for bad and doubtful debts by £150 to £810.
(e) Provide for depreciation as follows: Fixtures and fittings £120; Delivery van £300.

Required:

Prepare the trading and profit and loss accounts for the year ended 31 March 19X9 together with a balance sheet as at that date, using vertical formats.

27.10 This question also relates to worksheets – *see* p. 256.

From the following trial balance of John Brown, store owner, prepare a trading account and profit and loss account for the year ended 31 December 19X7, and a balance sheet as at that date, taking into consideration the adjustments shown below:

Trial Balance as at 31 December 19X7

	Dr £	Cr £
Sales		400,000
Purchases	350,000	
Sales returns	5,000	
Purchases returns		6,200
Opening stock at 1 January 19X7	100,000	
Provision for bad debts		800
Wages and salaries	30,000	
Rates	6,000	
Telephone	1,000	
Shop fittings at cost	40,000	
Van at cost	30,000	
Debtors and creditors	9,800	7,000
Bad debts	200	
Capital		179,000
Bank balance	3,000	
Drawings	18,000	
	593,000	593,000

(*i*)   Closing stock at 31 December 19X7 £120,000.
(*ii*) Accrued wages £5,000.
(*iii*) Rates prepaid £500.
(*iv*) The provision for bad debts to be increased to 10 per cent of debtors.
(*v*)   Telephone account outstanding £220.
(*vi*) Depreciate shop fittings at 10 per cent per annum, and van at 20 per cent per annum, on cost.

27.11A The following trial balance has been extracted from the ledger of Mr Yousef, a sole trader.

Trial Balance as at 31 May 19X6

	Dr £	Cr £
Sales		138,078
Purchases	82,350	
Carriage	5,144	
Drawings	7,800	
Rent, rates and insurance	6,622	
Postage and stationery	3,001	
Advertising	1,330	
Salaries and wages	26,420	
Bad debts	877	
Provision for bad debts		130
Debtors	12,120	
Creditors		6,471
Cash in hand	177	
Cash at bank	1,002	
Stock as at 1 June 19X5	11,927	
Equipment		
at cost	58,000	
accumulated depreciation		19,000
Capital		53,091
	216,770	216,770

The following additional information as at 31 May 19X6 is available:

(a) Rent is accrued by £210.
(b) Rates have been prepaid by £880.
(c) £2,211 of carriage represents carriage inwards on purchases.
(d) Equipment is to be depreciated at 15% per annum using the straight line method.
(e) The provision for bad debts to be increased by £40.
(f) Stock at the close of business has been valued at £13,551.

Required:
Prepare a trading and profit and loss account for the year ended 31 May 19X6 and a balance sheet as at that date.

(Association of Accounting Technicians)

27.12   Mr Chai has been trading for some years as a wine merchant. The following list of balances has been extracted from his ledger as at 30 April 19X7, the end of his most recent financial year.

	£
Capital	83,887
Sales	259,870
Trade creditors	19,840
Returns out	13,407
Provision for bad debts	512
Discounts allowed	2,306
Discounts received	1,750
Purchases	135,680
Returns inwards	5,624
Carriage outwards	4,562
Drawings	18,440
Carriage inwards	11,830
Rent, rates and insurance	25,973
Heating and lighting	11,010
Postage, stationery and telephone	2,410
Advertising	5,980
Salaries and wages	38,521
Bad debts	2,008
Cash in hand	534
Cash at bank	4,440
Stock as at 1 May 19X6	15,654
Trade debtors	24,500
Fixtures and fittings – at cost	120,740
Provision for depreciation on fixtures and fittings – as at 30 April 19X7	63,020
Depreciation	12,074

The following additional information as at 30 April 19X7 is available:

(*a*)   Stock at the close of business was valued at £17,750.
(*b*)   Insurances have been prepaid by £1,120.
(*c*)   Heating and lighting is accrued by £1,360.
(*d*)   Rates have been prepaid by £5,435.
(*e*)   The provision for bad debts is to be adjusted so that it is 3% of trade debtors.

Required:
Prepare Mr Chai's trading and profit and loss account for the year ended 30 April 19X7 and a balance sheet as at that date. *Note*: vertical style preferred.

(*Association of Accounting Technicians*)

28

The valuation of stock

Objectives

After you have studied this chapter, you should:

● *understand that there can be more than one way of valuing stocks*

● *be able to calculate the value of stock using the different methods*

● *be able to adjust stock valuations, where necessary, by a reduction to net realisable values*

● *understand the factors affecting the choice of method taken*

28.1 Different valuations of stock

Most people would think that there can be only one figure for the valuation of stock. This is not true. We will examine in this chapter how we can calculate different figures for stock.

Assume that a firm has just completed its first financial year and is about to value stock at cost price. It has dealt in only one type of goods. A record of the transactions is now shown in Exhibit 28.1.

Exhibit 28.1

Bought			Sold		
19X5		£	19X5		£
January	10 at £30 each	300	May	8 for £50 each	400
April	10 at £34 each	340	November	24 for £60 each	1,440
October	20 at £40 each	800			
	40	1,440		32	1,840

Still in stock at 31 December, 8 units.

The total figure of purchases is £1,440 and that of sales is £1,840. The trading account for the first year of trading can now be completed if the closing stock is brought into the calculations.

But what value do we put on each of the 8 units left in stock at the end of the year? If all of the units bought during the year had cost £30 each, then the closing stock would be 8 × £30 = £240. However, we have bought goods at different prices. This means that the valuation depends on which goods are taken for this calculation, the units at £30 or at £34, or at £40.

Many firms do not know exactly whether they have sold all the oldest units before they sell the newer units. For instance, a firm selling spanners may not know if the oldest spanners had been sold before the newest spanners.

The stock valuation will therefore be based on an accounting custom, and not on the facts of exactly which units were still in stock at the year end. The three main methods of doing this are now shown.

28.2 First in, first out method

This is usually known as **FIFO**, the first letters of each word. This method says that the first goods to be received are the first to be issued. Using the figures in Exhibit 28.1 we can now calculate the closing figure of stock as follows:

	Received	Issued	Stock after each transaction		
				£	£
19X5 January	10 at £30 each		10 at £30 each		300
April	10 at £34 each		10 at £30 each	300	
			10 at £34 each	340	640
May		8 at £30 each	2 at £30 each	60	
			10 at £34 each	340	400
October	20 at £40 each		2 at £30 each	60	
			10 at £34 each	340	
			20 at £40 each	800	1,200
November		2 at £30 each			
		10 at £34 each			
		12 at £40 each			
		24	8 at £40 each		320

The closing stock at 31 December 19X5 is therefore valued at £320.

28.3 Last in, first out method

This is usually known as **LIFO**. As each issue of goods is made they are said to be from the last lot of goods received before that date. Where there is not enough left of the last lot of goods, then the balance of goods needed is said to come from the previous lot still unsold.

From the information shown in Exhibit 28.1 the calculation can now be shown.

	Received	Issued	Stock after each transaction		
				£	£
19X5 January	10 at £30 each		10 at £30 each		300
April	10 at £34 each		10 at £30 each	300	
			10 at £34 each	340	640
May		8 at £34 each	10 at £30 each	300	
			2 at £34 each	68	368
October	20 at £40 each		10 at £30 each	300	
			2 at £34 each	68	
			20 at £40 each	800	1,168
November		20 at £40 each			
		2 at £34 each			
		2 at £30 each			
		24	8 at £30 each		240

The closing stock at 31 December 19X5 is therefore valued at £240.

28.4 Average cost method (AVCO)

Using the **AVCO** method, with each receipt of goods the average cost for each item of stock is recalculated. Further issues of goods are then at that figure, until another receipt of goods means that another recalculation is needed. From the information in Exhibit 28.1 the calculation can be shown.

Received		Issued	Average cost per unit of stock held	Number of units in stock	Total value of stock
			£		£
January	10 at £30		30	10	300
April	10 at £34		32*	20	640
May		8 at £32	32	12	384
October	20 at £40		37*	32	1,184
November		24 at £37	37	8	296

The closing stock at 31 December 19X5 is therefore valued at £296.

*In April, this is calculated as follows: stock 10 × £30 = £300 + stock received (10 × £34 × £340 = total £640. 20 units in stock, so the average is £640 ÷ 20 = £32. In October this is calculated as follows: stock 12 × £32 = £384 + stock received (20 × £40) £800 = £1,184. 32 units in stock, so the average is £1,184 ÷ 32 = £37.

28.5 Stock valuation and the calculation of profits

Using the figures from Exhibit 28.1 with stock valuations shown by the three methods of FIFO, LIFO, and AVCO, the trading accounts would appear:

Trading Account for the year ended 31 December 19X5							
	FIFO £	LIFO £	AVCO £		FIFO £	LIFO £	AVCO £
Purchases	1,440	1,440	1,440	Sales	1,840	1,840	1,840
less Closing stock	320	240	296				
Cost of goods sold							
Gross profit	1,120	1,200	1,144				
	720	640	696				
	1,840	1,840	1,840		1,840	1,840	1,840

As you can see, different methods of stock valuation will mean that different profits are shown.

28.6 Reduction to net realisable value

The **net realisable value** of stock is calculated as follows:

Saleable value – Expenses needed before completion of sale = Net realisable value.

The concept of prudence is used when stock is valued. Stock should not be over-valued, otherwise profits shown will be too high. Therefore, if the net realisable value of stock is less than the cost of the stock, then the figure to be taken for the final accounts is that of net realisable value.

A somewhat exaggerated example will show the necessity for this action. Assume that an art dealer has bought only two paintings during the financial year ended 31 December 19X8. He starts off the year without any stock, and then buys a genuine masterpiece for £6,000, selling this later in the year for £11,500. The other is a fake, but he does not realise this when he buys it for £5,100, only to discover during the year that in fact he had made a terrible mistake and that the net realisable value is £100. The fake remains unsold at the end of the year. The trading accounts, Exhibit 28.2, would appear as (*a*) if stock is valued at cost, and (*b*) if stock is valued at net realisable value.

Exhibit 28.2

		(a) £			(b) £
Sales		11,500			11,500
Purchases	11,100			11,100	
Closing stock	5,100	6,000		100	11,000
Gross profit		5,500			500

Trading Account for the year ended 31 December 19X8

Method (*a*) ignores the fact that the dealer had a bad trading year owing to his skill being found wanting in 19X8. If this method was used, then the loss on the fake would reveal itself in the following year's trading account. Method (*b*), however, realises that the loss really occurred at the date of purchase rather than at the date of sale. Following the concept of prudence accounting practice chooses method (*b*).

At one time the terminology was 'lower of cost or market value'. Changing it to 'lower of cost or net realisable value' gives a more precise definition to the terms used.

28.7 Stock groups and valuation

If there is only one sort of goods in stock, calculating the lower of cost or net realisable value is easy. If we have several or many types of goods in stock, we can use one of two ways of making the calculation.

From the information given in Exhibit 28.3 we will calculate the stock in two different ways.

Exhibit 28.3

Stock at 31 December 19X8			
Article	*Different categories*	*Cost*	*Net realisable value*
		£	£
1	A	100	80
2	A	120	150
3	A	300	400
4	B	180	170
5	B	150	130
6	B	260	210
7	C	410	540
8	C	360	410
9	C	420	310
		2,300	2,400

Articles 1, 2 and 3 are televisions. Articles 4, 5 and 6 are radios. Articles 7, 8 and 9 are videos.

The category method

The same sorts of items are put together in categories. Thus, articles 1, 2 and 3 are televisions and shown as category A. Articles 4, 5 and 6 are radios and shown as category B. Articles 7, 8 and 9 are videos and shown as category C.

A calculation showing a comparison of cost valuation and net realisable value for each category is now shown.

Category	*Cost*	*Net realisable value*
A	£100 + £120 + £300 = £520	£80 + £150 + £400 = £630
B	£180 + £150 + £260 = £590	£170 + £130 + £210 = £510
C	£410 + £360 + £420 = £1,190	£540 + £410 + £310 = £1,260

The lower of cost and net realisable value is, therefore:

		£
Category A: lower of £520 or £630	=	520
Category B: lower of £590 or £510	=	510
Category C: lower of £1,190 or £1,260	=	1,190
Stock is valued for final accounts at		2,220

Article method

By this method, the lower of cost or net realisable value for each article is compared and the lowest figure taken. From Exhibit 28.3 this gives us the following valuation:

Articles	Valuation
	£
1	80
2	120
3	300
4	170
5	130
6	210
7	410
8	360
9	310
	£2,090

28.8 Some other bases in use

Retail businesses often estimate the cost of stock by calculating it in the first place at selling price, and then deducting the normal margin of gross profit on such stock. Adjustment is made for items which are to be sold at other than normal selling prices.

Where standard costing is in use the figure of standard cost is frequently used.

28.9 Factors affecting the stock valuation decision

Obviously the overriding consideration applicable in all circumstances when valuing stock is the need to give a 'true and fair view' of the state of the affairs of the undertaking as on the balance sheet date and of the trend of the firm's trading results. There is, however, no precise definition of 'true and fair view'; it obviously rests on the judgement of the persons concerned. It would be necessary to study the behavioural sciences to understand the factors that affect judgement. However, it should be possible to state that the judgement of any two persons will not always be the same in the differing circumstances of various firms.

In fact, the only certain thing about stock valuation is that the concept of consistency should be applied, i.e. that once adopted, the same basis should be used in the annual accounts until some good reason occurs to change it. A reference should then be made in the final accounts as to the effect of the change on the reported profits, if the amount involved is material.

It will perhaps be useful to look at some of the factors which cause a particular basis to be chosen. The list is intended to be indicative rather than comprehensive, and is merely intended as a first brief look at matters which will have to be studied in depth by those intending to make a career in accountancy.

1 **Ignorance**
   The personalities involved may not appreciate the fact that there is more than one possible way of valuing stock.

2 **Convenience**
The basis chosen may not be the best for the purposes of profit calculation but it may be the easiest to calculate. It must always be borne in mind that the benefits which flow from possessing information should be greater than the costs of obtaining it. The only difficulty with this is actually establishing when the benefits do exceed the cost, but in some circumstances the decision not to adopt a given basis will be obvious.

3 **Custom**
It may be the particular method used in a certain trade or industry.

4 **Taxation**
The whole idea may be to defer the payment of tax for as long as possible. Because the stock figures affect the calculation of profits on which the tax is based the lowest possible stock figures may be taken to show the lowest profits up to the balance sheet date.

5 **The capacity to borrow money or to sell the business at the highest possible price**
The higher the stock value shown, then the higher will be the profits calculated to date, and therefore at first sight the business looks more attractive to a buyer or lender. Either of these considerations may be more important to the proprietors than anything else. It may be thought that those in business are not so gullible, but all business people are not necessarily well acquainted with accounting customs. In fact, many small businesses are bought, or money is lent to them, without the expert advice of someone well versed in accounting.

6 **Remuneration purposes**
Where someone managing a business is paid in whole or in part by reference to the profits earned, then one basis may suit them better than others. They may therefore strive to have that basis used to suit their own ends. The owner, however, may try to follow another course to minimise the remuneration that he/she will have to pay out.

7 **Lack of information**
If proper stock records have not been kept, then such bases as the average cost method or the LIFO method may not be calculable.

8 **Advice of the auditors**
Many firms use a particular basis because the auditors advised its use in the first instance. A different auditor may well advise that a different basis be used.

28.10 The conflict of aims

The list of some of the factors which affect decisions is certainly not exhaustive, but it does illustrate the fact that stock valuation is usually a compromise. There is not usually only one figure which is true and fair, there must be a variety of possibilities. Therefore the desire to borrow money, and in so doing to paint a good picture by being reasonably optimistic in valuing stock, will be tempered by the fact that this may increase the tax bill. Stock valuation is therefore a compromise between the various ends for which it is to be used.

28.11 Work in progress

The valuation of work in progress is subject to all the various criteria and methods used in valuing stock. Probably the cost element is more strongly pronounced than in stock valuation, as it is very often impossible or irrelevant to say what net realisable value or replacement price would be applicable to partly finished goods. Firms in industries such as those which have contracts covering several years have evolved their own methods.

Long-term contract work in progress will be dealt with in Volume 2.

28.12 Goods on sale or return

Goods received on sale or return

Sometimes we may receive goods from one of our suppliers on a **sale or return** basis. What this means is that we do not have to pay for the goods until we sell them. If we do not sell them we have to return them to our supplier.

This means that the goods do not belong to us. If we have some goods on sale or return at the stocktaking date, they should not be included in our stock valuation.

Goods sent to our customers on sale or return

We may send goods on a sale or return basis to our customers. The stock will belong to us until it is sold. At our stocktaking date any goods held by our customers on sale or return should be included in our stock valuation.

28.13 Stocktaking and the balance sheet date

Students often think that all the counting and valuing of stock is done on the last day of the accounting period. This might be true in a small business, but it is often impossible in larger businesses. There may be too many items of stock to do it so quickly.

This means that stocktaking may take place over a period of days. To get the figure of the stock valuation as on the last day of the accounting period, we will have to make adjustments. Exhibit 28.4 gives an example of such calculations.

Exhibit 28.4

Lee Ltd has a financial year which ends on 31 December 19X7. The stocktaking is not in fact done until 8 January 19X8. When the items in stock on that date are priced out, it is found that the stock value amounted to £28,850. The following information is available about transactions between 31 December 19X7 and 8 January 19X8:

1 Purchases since 31 December 19X7 amounted to £2,370 at cost.
2 Returns inwards since 31 December 19X7 were £350 at selling price.
3 Sales since 31 December 19X7 amounted to £3,800 at selling price.
4 The selling price is always cost price + 25 per cent.

Lee Ltd

Computation of stock as on 31 December 19X7

			£
Stock (at cost)			28,850
Add Items which were in stock on 31 December 19X7 (at cost)			
		£	
Sales		3,800	
Less Profit content (20 per cent of selling price)*		760	3,040
			31,890
Less Items which were not in stock on 31 December 19X7 (at cost)			
	£		
Returns inwards	350		
Less Profit content (20 per cent of selling price)*	70	280	
Purchases (at cost)		2,370	2,650
Stock in hand as on 31 December 19X7			29,240

*Stock at cost (or net realisable value), and not at selling price. As this calculation has a sales figure in it which includes profit, we must deduct the profit part to get to the cost price. This is true also for returns inwards.

At one time it was very rare for the auditors to attend at stocktaking time as observers. The professional accounting bodies now encourage the auditors to be present if at all possible.

28.14 Stock levels

One of the most common faults found in the running of a business is that too high a level of stock is maintained.

A considerable number of firms that have problems with a shortage of finance will find that they can help matters by having a sensible look at the amounts of stock they hold. It would be a very rare firm indeed which, if they had not investigated the matter previously, could not manage to let parts of their stock run down. As this would save spending cash on items not really necessary, this cash could be better utilised elsewhere.

New terms

AVCO (p. 268): A method by which the goods used are priced out at average cost.

FIFO (p. 267): A method by which the first goods to be received are said to be the first to be sold.

LIFO (p. 267): A method by which the goods sold are said to have come from the last lot of goods received.

Net realisable value (p. 269): The value of goods calculated as the selling price less expenses before sale.

Sale or return (p. 273): Goods that do not belong to the person holding them.

Main points to remember

1 The methods of pricing out stocks, e.g. FIFO or LIFO, are methods of pricing out stocks only. It does not mean that goods are physically handed out on a FIFO or LIFO basis.

2 Different stock valuing methods mean that different amounts of profit will be shown for a particular period.

3 Using the net realisable value when this is lower than cost is an example of the prudence concept in accounting, so that profits are not overstated.

4 Without stock records of quantities of items, it would be very difficult to track down theft or losses or to detect wastage of goods.

Review questions

28.1 From the following figures calculate the closing stock-in-trade that would be shown using (*i*) FIFO, (*ii*) LIFO, (*iii*) AVCO methods.

	Bought		*Sold*
January	10 at £30 each	April	8 for £46 each
March	10 at £34 each	December	12 for £56 each
September	20 at £40 each		

28.2 For question 28.1 draw up the trading account for the year showing the gross profits that would have been reported using (*i*) FIFO, (*ii*) LIFO, (*iii*) AVCO methods.

28.3A From the following figures calculate the closing stock-in-trade that would be shown using (*i*) FIFO, (*ii*) LIFO, (*iii*) AVCO methods on a perpetual inventory basis.

	Bought		*Sold*
January	24 at £10 each	June	30 at £16 each
April	16 at £12.50 each	November	34 at £18 each
October	30 at £13 each		

28.4A Draw up trading accounts using each of the three methods from the details in question 28.3A.

28.5 The sixth formers at the Broadway School run a tuck shop business. They began trading on 1 December 19X9 and sell two types of chocolate bar, 'Break' and 'Brunch'.

Their starting capital was a £200 loan from the School Fund.

Transactions are for cash only.

Each Break costs the sixth form 16p and each Brunch costs 12p.

25% is added to the cost to determine the selling price.

Transactions during December are summarised as follows:

December 6	Bought 5 boxes, each containing 48 bars, of Break; and 3 boxes, each containing 36 bars, of Brunch.
December 20	The month's sales amounted to 200 Breaks and 90 Brunches.

(*a*) Record the above transactions in the cash, purchases and sales accounts.
    All calculations must be shown.

(b) On 20 December (the final day of term) a physical stocktaking showed 34 Break and 15 Brunch in stock. Using these figures calculate the value of the closing stock, and enter the amount in the stock account.

(c) Prepare a trading account for the tuck shop, calculating the gross profit/loss for the month of December 19X9.

(d) Calculate the number of each item that **should** have been in stock. Explain why this information should be a cause for concern.

(*Edexcel Foundation, London Examinations: GCSE*)

28.6 Thomas Brown and Partners, a firm of practising accountants, have several clients who are retail distributors of the Allgush Paint Spray guns.

The current price list of Gushing Sprayers Limited, manufacturers, quotes the following wholesale prices for the Allgush Paint Spray guns:

Grade A distributors   £500 each
Grade B distributors   £560 each
Grade C distributors   £600 each

The current normal retail price of the Allgush Paint Spray gun is £750.

Thomas Brown and Partners are currently advising some of their clients concerning the valuation of stock in trade of Allgush Paint Spray guns.

1   Charles Gray – Grade B distributor
On 30 April 19X9, 15 Allgush Paint Spray guns were in stock, including 1 gun which was slightly damaged and expected to sell at half the normal retail price. Charles Gray considers that this gun should remain in stock at cost price until it is sold.

K. Peacock, a customer of Charles Gray, was expected to purchase a spray gun on 30 April 19X9, but no agreement was reached owing to the customer being involved in a road accident and expected to remain in hospital until late May 19X9.

Charles Gray argues that he is entitled to regard this as a sale during the year ended 30 April 19X9.

2   Jean Kim – Grade C distributor
On 31 May 19X9, 22 Allgush Paint Spray guns were in stock. Unfortunately Jean Kim's business is suffering a serious cash flow crisis. It is very doubtful that the business will survive and therefore a public auction of the stock in trade is likely. Reliable sources suggest that the spray guns may be auctioned for £510 each; auction fees and expenses are expected to total £300.

Jean Kim has requested advice as to the basis upon which her stock should be valued at 31 May 19X9.

3   Peter Fox – Grade A distributor
Peter Fox now considers that stock valuations should be related to selling prices because of the growing uncertainties of the market for spray guns.

Alternatively, Peter Fox has suggested that he uses the cost prices applicable to Grade C distributors as the basis for stock valuations – 'after all this will establish consistency with Grade C distributors'.

Required:
A brief report to each of Charles Gray, Jean Kim and Peter Fox concerning the valuation of their stocks in trade.
Note: Answers should include references to appropriate accounting concepts.

(*Association of Accounting Technicians*)

28.7A Mary Smith commenced trading on 1 September 19X9 as a distributor of the Straight Cut garden lawn mower, a relatively new product which is now becoming increasingly popular.

Upon commencing trading, Mary Smith transferred £7,000 from her personal savings to open a business bank account.

Mary Smith's purchases and sales of the Straight Cut garden lawn mower during the three months ended 30 November 19X9 are as follows:

19X9	Bought	Sold
September	12 machines at £384 each	–
October	8 machines at £450 each	4 machines at £560 each
November	16 machines at £489 each	20 machines at £680 each

Assume all purchases are made in the first half of the month and all sales are in the second half of the month.

At the end of October 19X9, Mary Smith decided to take one Straight Cut garden lawn mower out of stock for cutting the lawn outside her showroom. It is estimated that this lawn mower will be used in Mary Smith's business for 8 years and have a nil estimated residual value. Mary Smith wishes to use the straight line basis of depreciation.

Additional information:
1 Overhead expenses paid during the three months ended 30 November 19X9 amounted to £1,520.
2 There were no amounts prepaid on 30 November 19X9, but sales commissions payable of $2\frac{1}{2}$% of the gross profit on sales were accrued due on 30 November 19X9.
3 Upon commencing trading, Mary Smith resigned a business appointment with a salary of £15,000 per annum.
4 Mary Smith is able to obtain interest of 10% per annum on her personal savings.
5 One of the lawn mowers not sold on 30 November 19X9 has been damaged in the showroom and is to be repaired in December 19X9 at a cost of £50 before being sold for an expected £400.

Note: Ignore taxation.

Required:
(a) Prepare, in as much detail as possible, Mary Smith's trading and profit and loss account for the quarter ended 30 November 19X9 using:
   (i) the first in first out basis of stock valuation, and
   (ii) the last in first out basis of stock valuation.
(b) Using the results in (a) (i) above, prepare a statement comparing Mary Smith's income for the quarter ended 30 November 19X9 with that for the quarter ended 31 August 19X9.
(c) Give one advantage and one disadvantage of each of the bases of stock valuations used in (a) above.

(Association of Accounting Technicians)

28.8 'The idea that stock should be included in accounts at the lower of historical cost and net realisable value follows the prudence convention but not the consistency convention.'

Required:
(a) Do you agree with the quotation?
(b) Explain, with reasons, whether you think this idea (that stocks should be included in accounts at the lower of historical cost and net realisable value) is a useful one. Refer to at least two classes of user of financial accounting reports in your answer.

(Association of Chartered Certified Accountants)

28.9A After stocktaking for the year ended 31 May 19X9 had taken place, the closing stock of Cobden Ltd was aggregated to a figure of £87,612.

During the course of the audit which followed, the undernoted facts were discovered:

(a) Some goods stored outside had been included at their normal cost price of £570. They had, however, deteriorated and would require an estimated £120 to be spent to restore them to their original condition, after which they could be sold for £800.

(b) Some goods had been damaged and were now unsaleable. They could, however, be sold for £110 as spares after repairs estimated at £40 had been carried out. They had originally cost £200.

(c) One stock sheet had been over-added by £126 and another under-added by £72.

(d) Cobden Ltd had received goods costing £2,010 during the last week of May 19X9 but, because the invoices did not arrive until June 19X9, they have not been included in stock.

(e) A stock sheet total of £1,234 had been transferred to the summary sheet as £1,243.

(f) Invoices totalling £638 arrived during the last week of May 19X9 (and were included in purchases and in creditors) but, because of transport delays, the goods did not arrive until late June 19X9 and were not included in closing stock.

(g) Portable generators on hire from another company at a charge of £347 were included, at this figure, in stock.

(h) Free samples sent to Cobden Ltd by various suppliers had been included in stock at the catalogue price of £63.

(i) Goods costing £418 sent to customers on a sale or return basis had been included in stock by Cobden Ltd at their selling price, £602.

(j) Goods sent on a sale or return basis to Cobden Ltd had been included in stock at the amount payable (£267) if retained. No decision to retain had been made.

Required:
Using such of the above information as is relevant, prepare a schedule amending the stock figure as at 31 May 19X9. State your reason for each amendment or for not making an amendment.

(*Association of Chartered Certified Accountants*)

29

Bank reconciliation statements

Objectives

After you have studied this chapter, you should:

- *be able to reconcile cash book balances with bank statement balances*

- *understand how bank overdrafts affect the reconciliation process*

- *be able to make necessary entries for dishonoured cheques*

- *be able to reconcile ledger accounts to suppliers' statements*

29.1 Completing entries in the cash book

In our own books we will enter up the bank columns of our cash book, showing monies banked and paid out. Our bank will also record items paid into and out of our bank account with them.

If all the items entered in our cash book were the same as those entered in our account with the bank, then obviously the bank balance per our books and the bank balance per the bank's books would equal each other.

On the other hand, there may be items paid into and out of our account at the bank which have not been recorded by us in our cash book. To see what these are, if any, we will need a copy of our account as kept at the bank. They will give us such a copy, known as a bank statement. Let us look at an example of a cash book and a bank statement in Exhibit 29.1. We will tick off the items that are the same in both sets of records.

Exhibit 29.1

Cash Book (bank columns only: *before* balancing on 31.12.19X8)

19X8				£	19X8				£
Dec	1	Balance b/d	✓	250	Dec	5	J Gordon	✓	65
,,	20	P Thomas	✓	100	,,	27	K Hughes	✓	175
,,	28	D Jones	✓	190					

Bank Statement

19X8			Withdrawals £	Deposits £	Balance £
Dec	1	Balance b/d ✓			250
,,	8	10625* ✓	65		185
,,	21	Deposit ✓		100	285
,,	28	Deposit ✓		190	475
,,	29	10626* ✓	175		300
,,	30	Bank Giro credit: P Smith		70	370
,,	31	Bank charges	50		320

*10625 and 10626 refer to the serial numbers on the cheques paid out.

It is now possible to see that the two items not shown in our cash book are:

Bank Giro credit: P Smith	£70
Bank charges	£50

P Smith had paid us £70, but instead of sending us a cheque he had paid the money by credit transfer direct into our bank account, using the bank's services. We did not know of this until we received the bank statement.

The other item was in respect of bank charges. The bank had charged us £50 for keeping our bank account and all the work connected with it. Instead of sending us an invoice they have simply taken the money out of our bank account.

As we have now identified the items missing from our cash book we can now complete writing it up as follows:

Cash Book (bank columns only: *after* balancing on 31.12.19X8)

19X8			£	19X8			£
Dec	1	Balance b/d	250	Dec	5	J Gordon	65
,,	20	P Thomas	100	,,	27	K Hughes	175
,,	28	D Jones	190	,,	31	Bank charges	50
,,	30	P Smith	70	,,	31	Balance c/d	320
			610				610
19X9							
Jan	1	Balance b/d	320				

Both closing balances are now shown as being £320.

29.2 Where closing balances differ

Although a cash book may be written up to date by us, we obviously cannot alter the bank's own records. Even after writing up entries in our cash book there may still be a difference between our cash book balance and the bank statement balance. Exhibit 29.2 shows such a case.

Exhibit 29.2

Cash Book (after being completed to date)

19X9			£	19X9			£
Jan	1	Balance b/d	320	Jan	10	C Morgan	110
„	16	R Lomas	160	„	20	M McCarthy	90
„	24	V Verity	140	„	28	Cheshire CC rates	180
„	31	J Soames (B)	470	„	30	M Peck (A)	200
„	31	R Johnson	90	„	31	Balance c/d	600
			1,180				1,180
Feb	1	Balance b/d	600				

Bank Statement

19X9			Withdrawals £	Deposits £	Balance £
Jan	1	Balance b/d			320
„	12	10627	110		210
„	16	Deposit		160	370
„	23	10628	90		280
„	24	Deposit		140	420
„	28	Direct debit: Cheshire CC	180		240
„	31	Bank Giro credit: R Johnson		90	330

You can see that two items are in the cash book but are not shown on the bank statement. These are:

(A) A cheque had been paid to M Peck on January 30. He banked it at his bank on January 31 but it was not presented to our bank until February 2. This is known as an **'unpresented cheque'**.

(B) Although we had received a cheque for £470 from J Soames on January 31, we did not bank it until February 1. This will be known as a 'bank lodgement not yet credited' to our bank's account.

The balance per our cash book on January 31 was £600, whereas our bank statement shows a balance of £330. To prove that although the balances are different they can be 'reconciled' with each other, a **bank reconciliation statement** will be drawn up. It will either start with the bank statement balance and then reconcile it to the cash book balance, or it will start with the cash book balance and then reconcile it to the bank statement balance. If the second approach is adopted, it would appear as:

Bank Reconciliation Statement as at 31 December 19X8

		£
Balance as per cash book		600
Add Unpresented cheque	(A)	200
		800
Less Bank lodgement not credited	(B)	470
Balance per bank statement		330

If the two balances cannnot be reconciled then there will be an error somewhere. This will have to be located and then corrected.

This reconciliation technique is also used when dealing with other statements drawn up outside the firm. For example, when reconciling ledger accounts to suppliers' statements.

29.3 The bank balance in the balance sheet

The balance to be shown in the balance sheet is that per the cash book after it has been written up to date. In Exhibit 29.2 the balance sheet figure would be £600.

29.4 Other terms used in banking

1 **Standing Orders.** A firm can instruct its bank to pay regular amounts of money at stated dates to persons or firms. For instance, you may ask your bank to pay £200 a month to a building society to repay a mortgage.
2 **Direct Debits.** These are payments which have to be made, such as rates, insurance premiums and similar items. Instead of asking the bank to pay the money, as with standing orders, you give permission to the creditor to obtain the money directly from your bank account. This is particularly useful if the amounts payable may vary from time to time, as it is the creditor who changes the payments, not you. With standing orders, if the amount is ever to be changed then you have to inform the bank. With direct debits it is the creditor who arranges that, not you.

Both of these items will be written up in your cash book before attempting a reconciliation.

29.5 Bank overdrafts

The adjustment needed to reconcile the bank overdraft (shown by a credit balance in the cash book) according to the firm's books with that shown in the bank's books are the complete opposite of that needed when the account is not overdrawn.

Exhibit 29.3 is of a cash book and a bank statement showing an overdraft. Only the cheque for G Cumberbatch (A) £106 and the cheque paid to J Kelly (B) £63 need adjusting. Work through the reconciliation statement and then see the note after it.

Exhibit 29.3

Cash Book

19X8			£	19X8				£
Dec	5	I Howe	308	Dec	1	Balance b/d		709
,,	24	L Mason	120	,,	9	P Davies		140
,,	29	K King	124	,,	27	J Kelly	(B)	63
,,	31	G Cumberbatch (A)	106	,,	29	United Trust		77
,,	31	Balance c/d	380	,,	31	Bank charges		49
			1,038					1,038

Bank Statement

19X8			Dr £	Cr £	Balance £
Dec	1	Balance b/d			709 O/D
"	5	Cheque		308	401 O/D
"	14	P Davies	140		541 O/D
"	24	Cheque		120	421 O/D
"	29	K King: Credit transfer		124	297 O/D
"	29	United Trust: Standing order	77		374 O/D
"	31	Bank charges	49		423 O/D

Note: An overdraft is often shown with the letters O/D following the amount.

Bank Reconciliation Statement as on 31 December 19X8

	£
Overdraft as per cash book	380
Add Bank lodgements not on bank statement	106
	486
Less Unpresented cheque	63
Overdraft per bank statement	423

Note: Now compare the reconciliation statements in Exhibits 29.2 and 29.3. This shows:

	Balances	Overdrafts
Balance/overdraft per cash book	xxxx	xxxx
Adjustments		
Unpresented cheque	Plus	Less
Banking not entered	Less	Plus
Balance/overdraft per bank statement	xxxx	xxxx

Adjustments are, therefore, made in the opposite way when there is an overdraft.

29.6 Dishonoured cheques

When a cheque is received from a customer and paid into the bank, it is recorded on the debit side of the cash book. It is also shown on the bank statement as a banking by the bank. However, at a later date it may be found that his bank will not pay us the amount due on the cheque. The bank has failed to honour the cheque. It is known as a **dishonoured cheque**.

There are several possible reasons for this. Let us suppose that K King gave us a cheque for £5,000 on 20 May 19X9. We bank it, but a few days later our bank returns the cheque to us. Typical reasons are:

1 King had put £5,000 in figures on the cheque, but had written it in words as five thousand five hundred pounds. You will have to give the cheque back to King for amendment.
2 Normally cheques are considered *stale* six months after the date on the cheque. In other words the banks will not pay cheques over six months old. If King had put the year 19X8 on the cheque instead of 19X9, then the cheque would be returned to us by our bank.

3   King simply did not have sufficient funds in his bank account. Suppose he had previously a balance of only £2,000 and yet he has given us a cheque for £5,000. His bank has not allowed him to have an overdraft. In such a case the cheque would be dishonoured. The bank would write on the cheque '*refer to drawer*', and we would have to get in touch with King to see what he was going to do about it.

In all of these cases the bank would show the original banking as being cancelled by showing the cheque paid out of our bank account. As soon as this happens they will notify us. We will then also show the cheque as being cancelled by a credit in the cash book. We will then debit that amount to King's account.

When King originally paid his account our records would have appeared as:

K King

19X9		£	19X9		£
May 1 Balance b/d		5,000	May 20 Bank		5,000

Bank Account

19X9		£		
May 20 K King		5,000		

After our recording the dishonour, the records will appear as:

K King

19X9		£	19X9		£
May 1 Balance b/d		5,000	May 20 Bank		5,000
May 25 Bank: cheque dishonoured		5,000			

Bank Account

19X9		£	19X9		£
May 20 K King		5,000	May 25 K King: cheque dishonoured		5,000

In other words King is once again shown as owing us £5,000.

New terms

Bank Giro credit (p. 280): An amount paid by someone direct into our bank account.

Bank reconciliation statement (p. 281): A calculation comparing the cash book balance with the bank statement balance.

Direct debits (p. 282): Where we give permission for an organisation to collect amounts owing direct from our account.

Dishonoured cheque (p. 283): A cheque which is found to be worth nothing.

Standing order (p. 282): Instructions to our bank to pay specified amounts at given dates.

Unpresented cheque (p. 281): A cheque which has been sent but has not yet gone through the bank account of the receiver of it.

Main points to remember

1 A bank reconciliation statement should show whether or not errors have been made either in the bank columns of the cash book or on the bank statement.

2 It is best to update the cash book before attempting a bank reconciliation.

3 In the case of bank overdrafts, the reconciliation statements show adjustments that are the opposite to those shown with positive bank balances.

Review questions

29.1 From the following draw up a bank reconciliation statement from details as on 31 December 19X6:

	£
Cash at bank as per bank column of the cash book	678
Unpresented cheques	256
Cheques received and paid into the bank, but not yet entered on the bank statement	115
Credit transfers entered as banked on the bank statement but not entered in the cash book	56
Cash at bank as per bank statement	875

29.2A Draw up a bank reconciliation statement, after writing the cash book up to date, ascertaining the balance on the bank statement, from the following as on 31 March 19X9:

	£
Cash at bank as per bank column of the cash book (Dr)	3,896
Bankings made but not yet entered on bank statement	606
Bank charges on bank statement but not yet in cash book	28
Unpresented cheques C Clarke	117
Standing order to ABC Ltd entered on bank statement, but not in cash book	55
Credit transfer from A Wood entered on bank statement, but not yet in cash book	189

29.3 The following are extracts from the cash book and the bank statement of J Roche.
You are required to:

(a) Write the cash book up to date, and state the new balance as on 31 December 19X9, and

(b) Draw up a bank reconciliation statement as on 31 December 19X9.

Cash Book

19X9	Dr	£	19X9	Cr	£
Dec 1	Balance b/d	1,740	Dec 8	A Dailey	349
Dec 7	T J Masters	88	Dec 15	R Mason	33
Dec 22	J Ellis	73	Dec 28	G Small	115
Dec 31	K Wood	249	Dec 31	Balance c/d	1,831
Dec 31	M Barrett	178			
		2,328			2,328

Bank Statement

19X9			Dr £	Cr £	Balance £
Dec	1	Balance b/d			1,740
Dec	7	Cheque		88	1,828
Dec	11	A Dailey	349		1,479
Dec	20	R Mason	33		1,446
Dec	22	Cheque		73	1,519
Dec	31	Credit transfer: J Walters		54	1,573
Dec	31	Bank charges	22		1,551

29.4A The bank columns in the cash book for June 19X7 and the bank statement for that month for C Grant are as follows:

Cash Book

19X7		Dr	£	19X7		Cr	£
Jun	1	Balance b/d	2,379	Jun	5	D Blake	150
Jun	7	B Green	158	Jun	12	J Gray	433
Jun	16	A Silver	93	Jun	16	B Stephens	88
Jun	28	M Brown	307	Jun	29	Orange Club	57
Jun	30	K Black	624	Jun	30	Balance c/d	2,833
			3,561				3,561

Bank Statement

19X7			Dr £	Cr £	Balance £
Jun	1	Balance b/d			2,379
Jun	7	Cheque		158	2,537
Jun	8	D Blackness	150		2,387
Jun	16	Cheque		93	2,480
Jun	17	J Gray	433		2,047
Jun	18	B Stephens	88		1,959
Jun	28	Cheque		307	2,266
Jun	29	UDT standing order	44		2,222
Jun	30	Johnson: trader's credit		90	2,312
Jun	30	Bank charges	70		2,242

You are required to:

(a) Write the cash book up to date to take the above into account, and then

(b) Draw up a bank reconciliation statement as on 30 June 19X7.

29.5   Read the following and answer the questions below.

On 31 December 19X8 the bank column of C Tench's cash book showed a debit balance of £1,500.

The monthly bank statement written up to 31 December 19X8 showed a credit balance of £2,950.

On checking the cash book with the bank statement it was discovered that the following transactions had not been entered in the cash book:

Dividends of £240 had been paid directly to the bank.
A credit transfer – Customs and Excise VAT refund of £260 – had been collected by the bank.
Bank charges £30.
A direct debit of £70 for the RAC subscription had been paid by the bank.
A standing order of £200 for C Tench's loan repayment had been paid by the bank.
C Tench's deposit account balance of £1,400 was transferred into his bank current account.

A further check revealed the following items:

Two cheques drawn in favour of T Cod £250 and F Haddock £290 had been entered in the cash book but had not been presented for payment.
Cash and cheques amounting to £690 had been paid into the bank on 31 December 19X8 but were not credited by the bank until 2 January 19X9.

(*a*)   Starting with the debit balance of £1,500, bring the cash book (bank columns) up to date and then balance the bank account.
(*b*)   Prepare a bank reconciliation statement as at 31 December 19X8.

(*Midland Examining Group: GCSE*)

29.6A   In the draft accounts for the year ended 31 October 19X9 of Thomas P Lee, garage proprietor, the balance at bank according to the cash book was £894.68 in hand.

Subsequently the following discoveries were made:

(1)   Cheque number 176276 dated 3 September 19X9 for £310.84 in favour of G Lowe Limited has been correctly recorded in the bank statement, but included in the cash book payments as £301.84.
(2)   Bank commission charged of £169.56 and bank interest charged of £109.10 have been entered in the bank statement on 23 October 19X9, but not included in the cash book.
(3)   The recently received bank statement shows that a cheque for £29.31 received from T Andrews and credited in the bank statements on 9 October 19X9 has now been dishonoured and debited in the bank statement on 26 October 19X9. The only entry in the cash book for this cheque records its receipt on 8 October 19X9.
(4)   Cheque number 177145 for £15.10 has been recorded twice as a credit in the cash book.
(5)   Amounts received in the last few days of October 19X9 totalling £1,895.60 and recorded in the cash book have not been included in the bank statements until 2 November 19X9.
(6)   Cheques paid according to the cash book during October 19X9 and totalling £395.80 were not presented for payment to the bank until November 19X9.
(7)   Traders' credits totalling £210.10 have been credited in the bank statement on 26 October 19X9, but not yet recorded in the cash book.
(8)   A standing order payment of £15.00 on 17 October 19X9 to Countryside Publications has been recorded in the bank statement but is not mentioned in the cash book.

Required:
(*a*)   Prepare a computation of the balance at bank to be included in Thomas P Lee's balance sheet as at 31 October 19X9.
(*b*)   Prepare a bank reconciliation statement as at 31 October 19X9 for Thomas P Lee.
(*c*)   Briefly explain why it is necessary to prepare bank reconciliation statements at accounting year ends.

(*Association of Accounting Technicians*)

29.7 The bank statement for G Greene for the month of March 19X6 is:

19X6			Dr £	Cr £	Balance £
Mar	1	Balance			5,197 O/D
Mar	8	L Tulloch	122		5,319 O/D
Mar	16	Cheque		244	5,075 O/D
Mar	20	A Bennett	208		5,283 O/D
Mar	21	Cheque		333	4,950 O/D
Mar	31	M Turnbull: trader's credit		57	4,893 O/D
Mar	31	BKS: standing order	49		4,942 O/D
Mar	31	Bank charges	28		4,970 O/D

The cash book for March 19X6 is:

19X6	Dr	£	19X6	Cr	£
Mar 16	N Marsh	244	Mar 1	Balance b/d	5,197
Mar 21	K Alexander	333	Mar 6	L Tulloch	122
Mar 31	U Sinclair	160	Mar 30	A Bennett	208
Mar 31	Balance c/d	5,280	Mar 30	J Shaw	490
		6,017			6,017

You are to:
(a) Write the cash book up to date, and
(b) Draw up a bank reconciliation statement as on 31 March 19X6.

29.8A Following is the cash book (bank columns) of E Flynn for December 19X7:

19X7	Dr	£	19X7	Cr	£
Dec 6	J Hall	155	Dec 1	Balance b/d	3,872
Dec 20	C Walters	189	Dec 10	P Wood	206
Dec 31	P Miller	211	Dec 19	M Roberts	315
Dec 31	Balance c/d	3,922	Dec 29	P Phillips	84
		4,477			4,477

The bank statement for the month is:

19X7			Dr £	Cr £	Balance £
Dec	1	Balance			3,872 O/D
Dec	6	Cheque		155	3,717 O/D
Dec	13	P Wood	206		3,923 O/D
Dec	20	Cheque		189	3,734 O/D
Dec	22	M Roberts	315		4,049 O/D
Dec	30	Mercantile: standing order	200		4,249 O/D
Dec	31	K Saunders: trader's credit		180	4,069 O/D
Dec	31	Bank charges	65		4,134 O/D

You are required to:

(a) Write the cash book up to date to take the necessary items into account, and
(b) Draw up a bank reconciliation statement as on 31 December 19X7.

30

Control accounts

Objectives

After you have studied this chapter, you should:

- *be able to draw up sales ledger control accounts*

- *be able to draw up purchases ledger control accounts*

- *know the sources of information for control accounts*

- *be able to reconcile the purchase ledger and the sales ledger with their respective control accounts*

30.1 Need for control accounts

When all the accounts were kept in one ledger a trial balance could be drawn up as a test of the arithmetical accuracy of the accounts. It must be remembered that certain errors were not revealed by such a trial balance. If the trial balance totals disagreed, for a small business the books could easily and quickly be checked so as to find the errors.

However, when the firm has grown and the accounting work has been so divided up that there are several or many ledgers, any errors could be very difficult to find. We could have to check every item in every ledger. What is required is a type of trial balance for each ledger, and this requirement is met by the **control account**. Thus, it is only the ledgers whose control accounts do not balance that need detailed checking to find errors.

30.2 Principle of control accounts

The principle on which the control account is based is simple and is as follows. If the opening balance of an account is known, together with information of the additions and deductions entered in the account, the closing balance can be calculated.

Applying this to a complete ledger, the total of opening balances together with the additions and deductions during the period should give the total of closing balances. This can be illustrated by reference to a sales ledger for entries for a month.

	£
Total of opening balances, 1 January 19X6	3,000
Add Total of entries which have increased the balances	9,500
	12,500
Less Total of entries which have reduced the balances	8,000
Total of closing balances should be	4,500

Because totals are used, the accounts are often known as *total accounts*. Thus, a control account for a sales ledger could be known as either a sales ledger control account or as a total debtors account.

Similarly, a control account for a purchases ledger could be known either as a purchases ledger control account or as a total creditors account.

In larger organisations the control accounts are often part of the double entry system, with the individual personal accounts for debtors and creditors being treated for memorandum purposes only. In smaller firms, the control account is often seen as a form of trial balance for each ledger.

30.3 Information for control accounts

Exhibits 30.1 and 30.2 list from where information is obtained with which to draw up control accounts.

Exhibit 30.1

Sales Ledger Control	Source
1 Opening debtors	List of debtors' balances drawn up at the end of the previous period
2 Credit sales	Total from sales journal
3 Returns inwards	Total of returns inwards journal
4 Cheques received	Cash book: bank column on received side. List extracted or total of a special column which has been included in the cash book
5 Cash received	Cash book: cash column on received side. List extracted or total of a special column which has been included in the cash book
6 Closing debtors	List of debtors' balances drawn up at the end of the period

Exhibit 30.2

Purchases Ledger Control	Source
1 Opening creditors	List of creditors' balances drawn up at the end of the previous period
2 Credit purchases	Total from purchases journal
3 Returns outwards	Total of returns outwards journal
4 Cheques paid	Cash book: bank column on payments side. List extracted or total of a special column which has been included in the cash book
5 Cash paid	Cash book: cash column on payments side. List extracted or total of a special column which has been included in the cash book
6 Closing creditors	List of creditors' balances drawn up at the end of the period

30.4 Form of control accounts

It is usual to find control accounts in the same form as an account, with the totals of the debit entries in the ledger on the left-hand side of the control account, and the totals of the various credit entries in the ledger on the right-hand side of the control account.

Exhibit 30.3 shows an example of a sales ledger control account for a sales ledger in which all the entries are arithmetically correct.

Exhibit 30.3

	£
Sales ledger	
Debit balances on 1 January 19X6	1,894
Total credit sales for the month	10,290
Cheques received from customers in the month	7,284
Cash received from customers in the month	1,236
Returns inwards from customers during the month	296
Debit balances on 31 January as extracted from the sales ledger	3,368

Sales Ledger Control

19X6		£	19X6		£
Jan	1 Balances b/d	1,894	Jan	31 Bank	7,284
„	31 Sales	10,290	„	31 Cash	1,236
			„	31 Returns inwards	296
			„	31 Balances c/d	3,368
		12,184			12,184

We have proved the ledger to be arithmetically correct, because the totals of the control account equal each other. If the totals are not equal, then this proves there is an error somewhere.

Exhibit 30.4 shows an example where an error is found to exist in a purchases ledger. The ledger will have to be checked in detail, the error found, and the control account then corrected.

Exhibit 30.4

Purchases ledger	£
Credit balances on 1 January 19X6	3,890
Cheques paid to suppliers during the month	3,620
Returns outwards to suppliers in the month	95
Bought from suppliers in the month	4,936
Credit balances on 31 January as extracted from the purchases ledger	5,151

Purchases Ledger Control

19X6			£	19X6			£
Jan	31	Bank	3,620	Jan	1	Balances b/d	3,890
,,	31	Returns outwards	95	,,	31	Purchases	4,936
,,	31	Balances c/d	5,151				
			8,866*				8,826*

*There is a £40 error in the purchases ledger. We will have to check that ledger in detail to find the error. A double line has not yet been drawn under the totals. We will do this (known as 'ruling off the account') when the error has been found and the totals corrected.

30.5 Other advantages of control accounts

Control accounts have merits other than that of locating errors. Normally the control accounts are under the charge of a responsible official, and fraud is made more difficult because transfers made (in an effort) to disguise frauds will have to pass the scrutiny of this person.

For management purposes the balances on the control account can always be taken to equal debtors and creditors without waiting for an extraction of individual balances. Management control is thereby aided, for the speed at which information is obtained is one of the prerequisites of efficient control.

30.6 Other sources of information for control accounts

With a large organisation there may well be more than one sales ledger or purchases ledger. The accounts in the sales ledgers may be divided up in ways such as:

- Alphabetically. Thus we may have three sales ledgers split A–F, G–O and P–Z.
- Geographically. This could be split: Europe, Far East, Africa, Australasia, North and South America.

For each ledger we must therefore have a separate control account. An example of an analytical sales book is shown as Exhibit 30.5.

Exhibit 30.5

Sales Book

Date	Details		Total	Ledgers		
				A–F	G–O	P–Z
19X6			£	£	£	£
Feb 1	J Archer		58	58		
" 3	G Gaunt		103		103	
" 4	T Brown		116	116		
" 8	C Dunn		205	205		
" 10	A Smith		16			16
" 12	P Smith		114			114
" 15	D Owen		88		88	
" 18	B Blake		17	17		
" 22	T Green		1,396		1,396	
" 27	C Males		48		48	
			2,161	396	1,635	130

The totals of the A–F column will be the total sales figures for the sales ledger A–F control account, the total of the G–O column for the G–O control account and so on.

A similar form of analysis can be used in the purchases book, returns inwards book, returns outwards book and the cash book. The *totals* necessary for each of the control accounts can be obtained from the appropriate columns in these books.

Other items, such as bad debts written off or transfers from one ledger to another, will be found in the journal where such items are recorded.

30.7 Other transfers

Transfers to bad debt accounts will have to be recorded in the sales ledger control account as they involve entries in the sales ledgers.

Similarly, a contra account, whereby the same firm is both a supplier and a customer, and inter-indebtedness is set off, will also need entering in the control accounts. An example of this follows:

(A) The firm has sold A Hughes £600 goods.
(B) Hughes has supplied the firm with £880 goods.
(C) The £600 owing by Hughes is set off against £880 owing to him.
(D) This leaves £280 owing to Hughes.

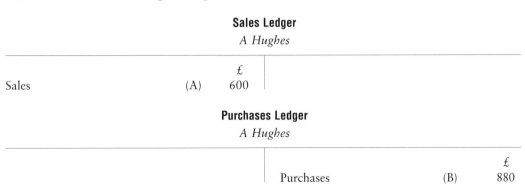

Sales Ledger

A Hughes

			£	
Sales		(A)	600	

Purchases Ledger

A Hughes

				£
	Purchases		(B)	880

The set-off now takes place.

Sales Ledger
A Hughes

		£				£
Sales	(A)	600	Set-off: Purchases ledger	(C)		600

Purchases Ledger
A Hughes

		£				£
Set-off: Sales ledger	(C)	600	Purchases	(B)		880
Balance c/d	(D)	280				
		880				880
			Balance b/d	(D)		280

The transfer of the £600 will therefore appear on the credit side of the sales ledger control account and on the debit side of the purchases ledger control account.

30.8 A more complicated example

Exhibit 30.6 shows a worked example of a more complicated control account.

You will see that there are sometimes credit balances in the sales ledger as well as debit balances. Suppose for instance we sold £500 goods to W Young, he then paid in full for them, and then afterwards he returned £40 goods to us. This would leave a credit balance of £40 on the account, whereas usually the balances in the sales ledger are debit balances.

Exhibit 30.6

19X6			£
Aug 1		Sales ledger – debit balances	3,816
„ 1		Sales ledger – credit balances	22
„ 31		Transactions for the month:	
		Cash received	104
		Cheques received	6,239
		Sales	7,090
		Bad debts written off	306
		Discounts allowed	298
		Returns inwards	664
		Cash refunded to a customer who had overpaid his account	37
		Dishonoured cheques	29
		Interest charged by us on overdue debt	50
	At the end of the month:		
		Sales ledger – debit balances	3,429
		Sales ledger – credit balances	40

Sales Ledger Control Account

19X6			£	19X6			£
Aug	1	Balances b/d	3,816	Aug	1	Balances b/d	22
„	31	Sales	7,090	„	31	Cash	104
		Cash refunded	37			Bank	6,239
		Bank: dishonoured cheques	29			Bad debts	306
		Interest on debt	50			Discounts allowed	298
		Balances c/d	40			Returns inwards	664
						Balances c/d	3,429
			11,062				11,062

30.9 Control accounts as part of double entry

In larger organisations it would be normal to find that control accounts are an integral part of the double entry system, the balances of the control accounts being taken for the purpose of extracting a trial balance. In this case the personal accounts are being used as subsidiary records.

30.10 Self-balancing ledgers and adjustment accounts

Because ledgers which have a control account system are proved to be correct as far as the double entry is concerned they used to be called **self-balancing ledgers**. The control accounts where such terminology were in use were then often called **adjustment accounts**. These terms are very rarely used nowadays.

30.11 Reconciliation of control accounts

Errors and omissions can occur when entering information into the accounting records. We have seen in Chapter 29 how these are identified and used to reconcile differences between the bank account and the bank statement balances. When a ledger control account is not in balance, it indicates that something has gone wrong with the entries made to the accounting records. This leads to an investigation which (hopefully) reveals the cause(s). Then, in order to verify whether the identified item(s) caused the failure to balance the control account, a reconciliation is carried out.

Exhibit 30.7 shows an example of a **purchases ledger control account reconciliation**. It takes the original control account balance and adjusts it to arrive at an amended balance which should equal the revised total of the source amounts that, together, equal the control account balance.

It can be seen that the general approach is similar to that adopted for bank reconciliation statements. However, as each control account may be constructed using information from a number of sources (*see* section 30.3) the extent of the investigation to identify the cause of the control account imbalance is likely to be far greater than that undertaken when performing a bank reconciliation.

Exhibit 30.7

An example of a Purchase Ledger Control Account Reconciliation

	£
Original purchase ledger control account balance	xxx
Add Invoice omitted from control account, but entered in purchase ledger	xxx
Supplier balance excluded from purchase ledger total because the account had been included in the sales ledger by mistake	xxx
Credit sale posted in error to the debit of a purchase ledger account instead of the debit of an account in the sales ledger	xxx
Under-casting error in calculation of total end of period creditors' balances	xxx
	xxx
Less Customer account with a credit balance included in the purchase ledger that should have been included in the sales ledger	xxx
Return inwards posted in error to the credit of a purchase ledger account instead of the credit of an account in the sales ledger	xxx
Credit note entered in error in the returns outwards day book as £223 instead of £332	xxx
Revised purchase ledger control account balance obtained from revised source amounts	xxx

New term

Control account (p. 289): An account which checks the arithmetical accuracy of a ledger.

Main points to remember

1 Control accounts enable errors to be traced down to the ledger that does not balance; thus there will be no need to check all the books in full to find an error.

2 Transfers between sales and purchases ledgers should be shown in the control accounts.

Review questions

30.1 You are required to prepare a sales ledger control account from the following for the month of May:

19X6		£
May 1	Sales ledger balances	4,936
	Totals for May:	
	Sales journal	49,916
	Returns inwards journal	1,139
	Cheques and cash received from customers	46,490
	Discounts allowed	1,455
May 31	Sales ledger balances	5,768

30.2A   You are required to prepare a purchases ledger control account from the following for the month of June. The balance of the account is to be taken as the amount of creditors as on 30 June.

19X6		£
June 1	Purchases ledger balances	3,676
	Totals for June:	
	Purchases journal	42,257
	Returns outwards journal	1,098
	Cheques paid to suppliers	38,765
	Discounts received from suppliers	887
June 30	Purchases ledger balances	?

30.3   Prepare a sales ledger control account from the following:

19X5		£
May 1	Debit balances	6,420
	Totals for May:	
	Sales journal	12,800
	Cash and cheques received from debtors	10,370
	Discounts allowed	395
	Debit balances in the sales ledger set off against	
	credit balances in the purchases ledger	145
May 31	Debit balances	?
	Credit balances	50

30.4A   Prepare a sales ledger control account from the following information for July 19X9, carrying down the balance at 31 July:

19X9		£
July 1	Sales ledger balances	9,700
July 31	Sales journal	99,280
	Bad debts written off	279
	Cheques received from debtors	95,120
	Discounts allowed	1,285
	Cheques dishonoured	226
	Returns inwards	3,170
	Set-offs against balances in purchases ledger	400

30.5   The trial balance of Queen and Square Ltd revealed a difference in the books. In order that the error(s) could be located it was decided to prepare purchases and sales ledger control accounts.
   From the following prepare the control accounts and show where an error may have been made:

19X6		£
Jan 1	Purchases ledger balances	11,874
	Sales ledger balances	19,744
	Totals for the year 19X6	
	Purchases journal	154,562
	Sales journal	199,662
	Returns outwards journal	2,648
	Returns inwards journal	4,556
	Cheques paid to suppliers	146,100
	Petty cash paid to suppliers	78
	Cheques and cash received from customers	185,960
	Discounts allowed	5,830
	Discounts received	2,134
	Balances on the sales ledger set off against	
	balances in the purchases ledger	1,036
Dec 31	The list of balances from the purchases ledger shows a total	
	of £14,530 and that from the sales ledger a total of £22,024	

30.6A The following extracts have been taken from the subsidiary books of the business owned by D Jenkinson for the month of April 19X0.

Purchases Day Book

		£
Apr	3 W Allen	480
	7 J Morris	270
	17 T Sage	410
	24 F Wilding	650

Returns Out Day Book

		£
Apr	14 W Allen	50
	29 T Sage	80

Cash Book (Credit side)

		Discounts received	Bank
		£	£
Apr	9 T Sage	30	690
	18 F Wilding	5	195
	24 J Morris	31	389
	27 W Allen	18	322

General Journal

			£	£
Apr	30	Creditor W Allen	180	
		Debtor W Allen		180
		being transfer from		
		sales ledger to		
		purchases ledger		

It should be noted that the balances in the accounts of D Jenkinson's suppliers on 1 April 19X0 were as follows:

	£
W Allen	360
J Morris	140
T Sage	720
F Wilding	310

Required:
(a) The name of the source document which will have been used for making entries in the
   (i)   purchases day book
   (ii)   returns out day book.
(b) The name of **two** subsidiary books (other than those shown in the extracts above) which could form part of D Jenkinson's accounting system. In the case of **one** of the subsidiary books chosen, explain its purpose.
(c) The account of T Sage in D Jenkinson's purchases ledger for the month of April 19X0. (The account should be balanced at the end of the month.)
(d) D Jenkinson's purchases ledger control account for the month of April 19X0. (The account should be balanced at the end of the month.)
(e) Advice for D Jenkinson on **two** ways in which he might find the purchases ledger control account useful.

(Southern Examining Group: GCSE)

30.7 The financial year of The Better Trading Company ended on 30 November 19X7. You have been asked to prepare a Total Debtors Account and a Total Creditors Account in order to produce end-of-year figures for Debtors and Creditors for the draft final accounts.

You are able to obtain the following information for the financial year from the books of original entry:

		£
Sales	– cash	344,890
	– credit	268,187
Purchases	– cash	14,440
	– credit	496,600
Total receipts from customers		600,570
Total payments to suppliers		503,970
Discounts allowed (all to credit customers)		5,520
Discounts received (all from credit suppliers)		3,510
Refunds given to cash customers		5,070
Balance in the sales ledger set off against balance in the purchases ledger 70		
Bad debts written off		780
Increase in the provision for bad debts		90
Credit notes issued to credit customers		4,140
Credit notes received from credit suppliers		1,480

According to the audited financial statements for the previous year debtors and creditors as at 1 December 19X6 were £26,555 and £43,450 respectively.

Required:
Draw up the relevant Total Accounts entering end-of-year totals for debtors and creditors.

(*Association of Accounting Technicians*)

30.8

(a) Why are many accounting systems designed with a purchase ledger (creditors ledger) control account, as well as with a purchase ledger (creditors ledger)?

(b) The following errors have been discovered:
   (i)   An invoice for £654 has been entered in the purchase day book as £456;
   (ii) A prompt payment discount of £100 from a creditor had been completely omitted from the accounting records;
   (iii) Purchases of £250 had been entered on the wrong side of a supplier's account in the purchase ledger;
   (iv) No entry had been made to record an agreement to contra an amount owed to X of £600 against an amount owed by X of £400;
   (v)   A credit note for £60 had been entered as if it was an invoice.

   State the numerical effect on the purchase ledger control account balance of correcting each of these items (treating each item separately).

(c) Information technology and computerised systems are rapidly increasing in importance in data recording. Do you consider that this trend will eventually remove the need for control accounts to be incorporated in the design of accounting systems? Explain your answer briefly.

(*Association of Chartered Certified Accountants*)

30.9A The trial balance of Happy Bookkeeper Ltd, as produced by its bookkeeper, includes the following items:

Sales ledger control account	£110,172
Purchase ledger control account	£78,266
Suspense account (debit balance)	£2,315

You have been given the following information:

(*i*)   The sales ledger debit balances total £111,111 and the credit balances total £1,234.

(*ii*)   The purchase ledger credit balances total £77,777 and the debit balances total £1,111.

(*iii*)   The sales ledger includes a debit balance of £700 for business X, and the purchase ledger includes a credit balance of £800 relating to the same business X. Only the net amount will eventually be paid.

(*iv*)   Included in the credit balance on the sales ledger is a balance of £600 in the name of H Smith. This arose because a sales invoice for £600 had earlier been posted in error from the sales day book to the debit of the account of M Smith in the purchase ledger.

(*v*)   An allowance of £300 against some damaged goods had been omitted from the appropriate account in the sales ledger. This allowance had been included in the control account.

(*vi*)   An invoice for £456 had been entered in the purchase day book as £654.

(*vii*)   A cash receipt from a credit customer for £345 had been entered in the cash book as £245.

(*viii*)   The purchase day book had been overcast by £1,000.

(*ix*)   The bank balance of £1,200 had been included in the trial balance, in error, as an overdraft.

(*x*)   The bookkeeper had been instructed to write off £500 from customer Y's account as a bad debt, and to reduce the provision for doubtful debts by £700. By mistake, however, he had written off £700 from customer Y's account and *increased* the provision for doubtful debts by £500.

(*xi*)   The debit balance on the insurance account in the nominal ledger of £3,456 had been included in the trial balance as £3,546.

Required:

Record corrections in the control and suspense accounts. Attempt to reconcile the sales ledger control account with the sales ledger balances, and the purchase ledger control account with the purchase ledger balances. What further action do you recommend?

(*Association of Chartered Certified Accountants*)

31

Errors not affecting trial balance agreement

Objectives

After you have studied this chapter, you should be able to:

- *correct all errors which do not affect trial balance totals being equal*
- *distinguish between the different kinds of errors*

31.1 Types of error

In Chapter 6 it was seen that if we followed these rules:

- Every debit entry needs a corresponding credit entry.
- Every credit entry needs a corresponding debit entry.

and entered up our books using these rules, then when we extracted the trial balance its totals would agree, i.e. it would 'balance'.

Suppose we correctly entered cash sales £70 to the debit of the cash book, but did not enter the £70 to the credit of the sales account. If this were the only error in the books, the trial balance totals would differ by £70. However, there are certain kinds of error which would not affect the agreement of the trial balance totals, and we will now consider these:

1 **Errors of omission** — where a transaction is completely omitted from the books. If we sold £90 goods to J Brewer, but did not enter it in either the sales or Brewer's personal account, the trial balance would still 'balance'.
2 **Errors of commission** — this type is where the correct amount is entered but in the wrong person's account, e.g. where a sale of £11 to C Green is entered in the account of K Green. It will be noted that the correct class of account was used, both the accounts concerned being personal accounts.
3 **Errors of principle** — where an item is entered in the wrong class of account, e.g. if a fixed asset such as a motor van is debited to an expenses account such as motor expenses account.
4 **Compensating errors** — where errors cancel out each other. If the sales account was added up to be £10 too much and the purchases account was also added up to be £10 too much, then these two errors would cancel out in the trial balance. This is because the totals both of the debit side of the trial balance and of the credit side will be £10 too much.
5 **Errors of original entry** — where the original figure is incorrect, yet double entry is still observed using this incorrect figure. An instance of this could be where there were sales of £150 goods but an error is made in calculating the sales invoice. If it

were calculated as £130, and £130 were credited as sales and £130 were debited to the personal account of the customer, the trial balance would still 'balance'.

6 **Complete reversal of entries** — where the correct accounts are used but each item is shown on the wrong side of the account. Suppose we had paid a cheque to D Williams for £200, the double entry of which is Cr Bank £200, Dr D Williams £200. In error it is entered as Cr D Williams £200, Dr Bank £200. The trial balance totals will still agree.

7 **Transposition errors** — where the wrong sequence of the individual characters within a number was entered. For example, £142 entered instead of £124. This is quite a common error and is very difficult to spot when the error has occurred in both the debit and the credit entries, as the trial balance would still balance. (It is more common for this error to occur on one side of the double entry only.)

31.2 Correction of errors

Most errors are found at a date later than the one on which they are first made. When we correct them we should not do so by crossing out items, tearing out accounts and throwing them away, or using chemicals to make the writing disappear.

We have to do corrections in double entry accounts by writing in the corrections in a double entry fashion. We should:

1 Show the corrections by means of journal entries, and then
2 Show the corrections in the double entry set of accounts, by posting these journal entries to the ledger accounts affected.

1 Error of omission

The sale of goods, £59 to E George, has been completely omitted from the books. We must correct this by entering the sale in the books. The journal entries for the correction are now shown:

The Journal

	Dr	Cr
	£	£
E George	59	
Sales account		59

Correction of omission of Sales Invoice No.......
from sales journal

2 Error of commission

A purchase of goods, £44 from C Simons, was entered in error in C Simpson's account. To correct this, it must be cancelled out of C Simpson's account, and then entered where it should be in C Simons' account. The double entry will be:

C Simpson

19X5	£	19X5	£
Sept 30 C Simons: Error corrected	44	Sept 30 Purchases	44

C Simons

		£
	19X5	
	Sept 30 Purchases:	
	Entered originally in	
	C Simpson's account	44

The Journal entry will be:

The Journal

	Dr	Cr
	£	£
C Simpson	44	
C Simons		44
Purchase Invoice No ... entered in wrong		
personal account, now corrected		

In fact, the journal entry should be made before double entry in the accounts is completed. The example was shown as above to make it easier to understand.

3 Error of principle

The purchase of a machine, £200, is debited to purchases account instead of being debited to a machinery account. We therefore cancel the item out of the purchases account by crediting that account. It is then entered where it should be by debiting the machinery account.

The Journal

	Dr	Cr
	£	£
Machinery account	200	
Purchases account		200
Correction of error: purchase of fixed asset debited		
to purchases account.		

4 Compensating error

The sales account is overcast by £200, as also is the wages account. The trial balance therefore still 'balances'. This assumes that these are the only two errors found in the books.

The Journal

	Dr	Cr
	£	£
Sales account	200	
Wages account		200
Correction of overcasts of £200 each in the sales account and the wages		
account which compensated for each other.		

5 Error of original entry

A sale of £38 to A Smailes was entered in the books as £28. It needs another £10 of sales entering now.

The Journal

	Dr	Cr
	£	£
A Smailes	10	
Sales account		10
Correction of error whereby sales were understated by £10		

6 Complete reversal of entries

A payment of cash of £16 to M Dickson was entered on the receipts side of the cash book in error and credited to M Dickson's account. This is somewhat more difficult to adjust. First must come the amount needed to cancel the error, then comes the actual entry itself. Because of this, the correcting entry is double the actual amount first recorded. We can now look at why this is so:

What we should have had:

Cash

			£
		M Dickson	16

M Dickson

	£		
Cash	16		

was entered as:

Cash

	£		
M Dickson	16		

M Dickson

			£
		Cash	16

We can now see that we have to enter double the original amount to correct the error:

Cash

	£		£
M Dickson	16	M Dickson (error corrected)	32

M Dickson

	£		£
Cash (error corrected)	32	M Dickson	16

Overall, when corrected, the cash account showing £16 debit and £32 credit means a net credit of £16. Similarly, Dickson's account shows £32 debit and £16 credit, a net debit of £16. As the final (net) answer is the same as what should have been entered originally, the error is now corrected.

The Journal entry appears:

The Journal

	Dr	Cr
	£	£
M Dickson	32	
Cash		32
Payment of cash £16 debited to cash and credited to		
M Dickson in error on .... Error now corrected.		

7 Transposition error

A credit purchase from P Maclaran costing £56 was entered in the books as £65. The £9 error needs to be removed.

The Journal

	Dr	Cr
	£	£
P Maclaran	9	
Purchases account		9
Correction of error whereby purchases were overstated by £9		

31.3 Casting

You will often notice the use of the expression 'to cast', which means 'to add up'. **Overcasting** means incorrectly adding up a column of figures to give an answer which is greater than it should be. **Undercasting** means incorrectly adding up a column of figures to give an answer which is less than it should be.

New terms

Casting (p. 305): Adding up figures.

Compensating error (p. 303): Where two errors of equal amounts, but on opposite sides of the accounts, cancel out each other.

Error of commission (p. 302): Where a correct amount is entered, but in the wrong person's account.

Error of omission (p. 302): Where a transaction is completely omitted from the books.

Error of original entry (p. 304): Where an item is entered, but both the debit and credit entries are of the same incorrect amount.

Error of principle (p. 303): Where an item is entered in the wrong type of account, e.g. a fixed asset in an expense account.

Transposition error (p. 305): Where the characters within a number are entered in the wrong sequence.

Main points to remember

1   When errors are found, they should be amended by using proper double entry procedures.

2   All corrections of errors should take place via the journal, where entries are first recorded before being posted to the appropriate ledger accounts.

Review questions

31.1   Show the journal entries necessary to correct the following errors:

(a)   A sale of goods £678 to J Harris had been entered in J Hart's account.

(b)   The purchase of a machine on credit from L Pyle for £4,390 had been completely omitted from our books.

(c)   The purchase of a motor van £3,800 had been entered in error in the Motor Expenses account.

(d)   A sale of £221 to E Fitzwilliam had been entered in the books, both debit and credit, as £212.

(e)   Commission received £257 had been entered in error in the Sales account.

(f)   A receipt of cash from T Heath £77 had been entered on the credit side of the cash book and the debit side of T Heath's account.

(g)   A purchase of goods £189 had been entered in error on the debit side of the Drawings account.

(h)   Discounts Allowed £366 had been entered in error on the debit side of the Discounts Received account.

31.2A Show the journal entries needed to correct the following errors:

(a) Purchases £699 on credit from K Ward had been entered in H Wood's account.
(b) A cheque of £189 paid for advertisements had been entered in the cash column of the cash book instead of in the bank column.
(c) Sale of goods £443 on credit to B Gordon had been entered in error in B Gorton's account.
(d) Purchase of goods on credit K Isaacs £89 entered in two places in error as £99.
(e) Cash paid to H Moore £89 entered on the debit side of the cash book and the credit side of H Moore's account.
(f) A sale of fittings £500 had been entered in the Sales account.
(g) Cash withdrawn from bank £100, had been entered in the cash column on the credit side of the cash book, and in the bank column on the debit side.
(h) Purchase of goods £428 has been entered in error in the Fittings account.

31.3 After preparing its draft final accounts for the year ended 31 March 19X6 and its draft balance sheet as at 31 March 19X6 a business discovered that the stock lists used to compute the value of stock as at 31 March 19X6 contained the following entry:

Stock item	Number	Cost per unit	Total cost
Y 4003	100	£1.39	£1,390

Required:
(a) What is wrong with this particular entry?
(b) What would the effect of the error have been on
    (i) the value of stock as at 31 March 19X6?
    (ii) the cost of goods sold for the year ended 31 March 19X6?
    (iii) the net profit for the year ended 31 March 19X6?
    (iv) the total for Current Assets as at 31 March 19X6?
    (v) the Owner's Capital as at 31 March 19X6?

(*Association of Accounting Technicians*)

31.4 Give the journal entries needed to record the corrections of the following. Narratives are not required.

(a) Extra capital of £10,000 paid into the bank had been credited to Sales account.
(b) Goods taken for own use £700 had been debited to General Expenses.
(c) Private insurance £89 had been debited to Insurance account.
(d) A purchase of goods from C Kelly £857 had been entered in the books as £587.
(e) Cash banked £390 had been credited to the bank column and debited to the cash column in the cash book.
(f) Cash drawings of £400 had been credited to the bank column of the cash book.
(g) Returns inwards £168 from M McCarthy had been entered in error in J Charlton's account.
(h) A sale of a motor van £1,000 had been credited to Motor Expenses.

31.5A Journal entries to correct the following are required, but the narratives can be omitted.

(a) Commissions Received £880 have been credited to Rent Received account.
(b) Bank charges £77 have been debited to Rent account.
(c) Completely omitted from the books is a payment of Sundry Expenses by cheque £23.
(d) A purchase of fixtures £478 has been entered in Purchases account.
(e) Returns inwards £833 have been entered on the debit side of the Returns Outwards account.
(f) A loan from R Smiley £5,000 has been entered on the credit side of the Capital account.
(g) Loan interest of £500 has been debited to Premises account.
(h) Goods taken for own use £250 have been debited to Purchases account and credited to Drawings.

31.6A Thomas Smith, a retail trader, has very limited accounting knowledge. In the absence of his accounting technician, he extracted the following trial balance as at 31 March 19X8 from his business's accounting records:

	£	£
Stock in trade at 1 April 19X7		10,700
Stock in trade at 31 March 19X8	7,800	
Discounts allowed		310
Discounts received	450	
Provision for doubtful debts	960	
Purchases	94,000	
Purchases returns	1,400	
Sales		132,100
Sales returns	1,100	
Freehold property: at cost	70,000	
Provision for depreciation	3,500	
Motor vehicles: at cost	15,000	
Provision for depreciation	4,500	
Capital — Thomas Smith		84,600
Balance at bank	7,100	
Trade debtors		11,300
Trade creditors	7,600	
Establishment and administrative expenditure	16,600	
Drawings	9,000	
	£239,010	£239,010

Required:

(a) Prepare a corrected trial balance as at 31 March 19X8.

  After the preparation of the above trial balance, but before the completion of the final accounts for the year ended 31 March 19X8, the following discoveries were made:

  (i) The correct valuation of the stock in trade at 1 April 19X7 is £12,000; apparently some stock lists had been mislaid.

  (ii) A credit note for £210 has now been received from J Hardwell Limited; this relates to goods returned in December 19X7 by Thomas Smith. However, up to now J Hardwell Limited had not accepted that the goods were not of merchantable quality and Thomas Smith's accounting records did not record the return of the goods.

  (iii) Trade sample goods were sent to John Grey in February 19X8. These were free samples, but were charged wrongly at £1,000 to John Grey. A credit note is now being prepared to rectify the error.

  (iv) In March 19X8, Thomas Smith painted the inside walls of his stockroom using materials costing £150 which were included in the purchases figure in the above trial balance. Thomas Smith estimates that he saved £800 by doing all the painting himself.

(b) Prepare the journal entries necessary to amend the accounts for the above discoveries. *Note:* narratives are required.

(*Association of Accounting Technicians*)

32

Suspense accounts and errors

Objectives

After you have studied this chapter, you should be able to:

- *correct errors using a suspense account*
- *recalculate profits after errors have been corrected*

32.1 Errors and the trial balance

In the last chapter we looked at errors which still left equal totals in the trial balance. However, many errors will mean that trial balance totals will not be equal. Let us now look at some of these:

- Incorrect additions in any account.
- Making an entry on only one side of the accounts, e.g. a debit but no credit; a credit but no debit.
- Entering a different amount on the debit side from the amount on the credit side.

32.2 Suspense account

We should try very hard to find errors immediately when the trial balance totals are not equal. When they cannot be found, the trial balance totals should be made to agree with each other by inserting the amount of the difference between the two sides in a **suspense account**. This occurs in Exhibit 32.1 where there is a £40 difference.

Exhibit 32.1

Trial Balance as on 31 December 19X5

	Dr	Cr
	£	£
Totals after all the accounts have been listed	100,000	99,960
Suspense account		40
	100,000	100,000

To make the two totals the same, a figure of £40 for the suspense account has been shown on the credit side. A suspense account is opened and the £40 difference is also shown there on the credit side:

Suspense Account

				19X5		£
				Dec 31 Difference per trial balance		40

32.3 Suspense account and the balance sheet

If the errors are not found before the final accounts are prepared, the suspense account balance will be included in the balance sheet. Where the balance is a credit balance, it should be included on the capital and liabilities side of the balance sheet. When the balance is a debit balance it should be shown on the assets side of the balance sheet.

32.4 Correction of errors

When the errors are found they must be corrected, using double entry. Each correction must first have an entry in the journal describing it, and then be posted to the accounts concerned.

One error only

We will look at two examples:

1 Assume that the error of £40 as shown in Exhibit 32.1 is found in the following year on 31 March 19X6. The error was that the sales account was undercast by £40. The action taken to correct this is:

   Debit suspense account to close it: £40.
   Credit sales account to show item where it should have been: £40.

The accounts now appear as Exhibit 32.2.

Exhibit 32.2

Suspense Account

19X6		£	19X5		£
Mar 31 Sales		40	Dec 31 Difference per trial balance		40

Sales

			19X6		£
			Mar 31 Suspense		40

This can be shown in journal form as:

The Journal

	Dr	Cr
19X6	£	£
Mar 31 Suspense	40	
Sales		40
Correction of undercasting of sales by £40 in last year's accounts		

2 The trial balance on 31 December 19X6 had a difference of £168. It was a shortage on the debit side.

A suspense account is opened, the difference of £168 is entered on the debit side. On 31 May 19X7 the error was found. We had made a payment of £168 to K Leek to close his account. It was correctly entered in the cash book, but it was not entered in K Leek's account.

First of all, (A) the account of K Leek is debited with £168, as it should have been in 19X6. Second (B) the suspense account is credited with £168 so that the account can be closed.

K Leek

19X7			£	19X7		£
May 31 Bank		(A)	168	Jan 1 Balance b/d		168

The account of K Leek is now correct.

Suspense Account

19X7		£	19X7		£
Jan 1 Difference per trial balance		168	May 31 K Leek	(B)	168

The Journal entries are:

The Journal

	Dr	Cr
19X7	£	£
May 31 K Leek	168	
Suspense		168
Correction of non-entry of payment last year in K Leek's account		

More than one error

We can now look at Exhibit 32.3 where the suspense account difference was caused by more than one error.

Exhibit 32.3

The trial balance at 31 December 19X7 showed a difference of £77, being a shortage on the debit side. A suspense account is opened, and the difference of £77 is entered on the debit side of the account.

On 28 February 19X8 all the errors from the previous year were found.

(A) A cheque of £150 paid to L Kent had been correctly entered in the cash book, but had not been entered in Kent's account.
(B) The purchases account had been undercast by £20.
(C) A cheque of £93 received from K Sand had been correctly entered in the cash book, but had not been entered in Sand's account.

These three errors resulted in a net error of £77, shown by a debit of £77 on the debit side of the suspense account. These are corrected as follows:

(*a*) Make correcting entries in accounts for (A), (B) and (C).
(*b*) Record double entry for these items in the suspense account.

L Kent

19X8			£		
Feb 28 Suspense	(A)	150			

Purchases

19X8			£		
Feb 28 Suspense	(B)	20			

K Sand

			19X8		£
			Feb 28 Suspense	(C)	93

Suspense Account

19X8			£	19X8			£
Jan 1 Balance b/d		77		Feb 28 L Kent	(A)	150
Feb 28 K Sand	(C)	93		Feb 28 Purchases	(B)	20
		170				170

The Journal

		Dr	Cr
19X8		£	£
Feb 28 L Kent		150	
Suspense			150
Cheque paid omitted from Kent's account			
Feb 28 Purchases		20	
Suspense			20
Undercasting of purchases by £20 in last year's accounts			
Feb 28 Suspense		93	
K Sand			93
Cheque received omitted from Sand's account			

Only those errors which make the trial balance totals different from each other have to be corrected via the suspense account.

32.5 The effect of errors on profits

Some of the errors will have meant that original profits calculated will be wrong. Other errors will have no effect upon profits. We will use Exhibit 32.4 to illustrate the different kinds of errors.

Exhibit 32.4 shows a set of accounts in which errors have been made.

Exhibit 32.4

K Davis

Trading and Profit and Loss Account for the year ended 31 December 19X5

		£	£
Sales			8,000
Less	Cost of goods sold:		
	Opening stock	500	
	Add Purchases	6,100	
		6,600	
	Less Closing stock	700	5,900
Gross profit			2,100
Add Discounts received			250
			2,350
Less	Expenses:		
	Rent	200	
	Insurance	120	
	Lighting	180	
	Depreciation	250	750
Net profit			1,600

Balance Sheet as at 31 December 19X5

	£	£
Fixed assets		
Fixtures at cost	2,200	
Less Depreciation to date	800	1,400
Current assets		
Stock	700	
Debtors	600	
Bank	340	
	1,640	
Less Current liabilities		
Creditors	600	1,040
Suspense account		60
		2,500
Capital		
Balance as at 1.1.19X5		1,800
Add Net profit		1,600
		3,400
Less Drawings		900
		2,500

1 Errors which do not affect profit calculations

If an error affects items only in the balance sheet, then the original calculated profit will not need altering. Exhibit 32.5 shows this:

Exhibit 32.5

Assume that in Exhibit 32.4 the £60 debit balance on the suspense account was because of the following error:

1 November 19X5 we paid £60 to a creditor T Monk. It was correctly entered in the cash book. It was not entered anywhere else. The error was found on 1 June 19X6.

The journal entries to correct it will be:

The Journal

	Dr	Cr
19X6	£	£
June 1 T Monk	60	
Suspense account		60
Payment to T Monk on 1 November 19X5 not		
entered in his account. Correction now made		

Both of these accounts appeared in the balance sheet only with T Monk as part of creditors. The net profit of £1,600 does not have to be changed.

2 Errors which do affect profit calculations

If the error is in one of the figures shown in the trading and profit and loss account, then the original profit will need altering. Exhibit 32.6 shows this:

Exhibit 32.6

Assume that in Exhibit 32.4 the £60 debit balance was because the rent account was added up incorrectly. It should be shown as £260 instead of £200. The error was found on 1 June 19X6. The journal entries to correct it are:

The Journal

	Dr	Cr
19X6	£	£
Jun 1 Rent	60	
Suspense		60
Correction of rent undercast last year		

Rent last year should have been increased by £60. This would have reduced net profit by £60. A statement of corrected profit for the year is now shown.

K Davis

Statement of Corrected Net Profit for the year ended 31 December 19X5

	£
Net profit per the accounts	1,600
Less Rent understated	60
	1,540

3 Where there have been several errors

If in Exhibit 32.4 there had been four errors in the accounts of K Davis, found on 31 March 19X6, their correction can now be seen. Assume that the net difference had also been £60.

		£
(A)	Sales overcast by	£70
(B)	Insurance undercast by	£40
(C)	Cash received from a debtor entered in the cash book only	£50
(D)	A purchase of £59 is entered in the books, debit and credit entries as	£95

Note: Error (D) is known as an error of transposition, as the correct figures have been shown in the wrong order, i.e. they have been 'transposed'.

The entries in the suspense account and the journal entries will be as follows:

Suspense Account

19X6			£	19X6				£
Jan	1	Balance b/d	60	Mar	31	Sales	(A)	70
Mar	31	Debtor (C)	50	,,	31	Insurance	(B)	40
			110					110

The Journal

			Dr	Cr
19X6			£	£
1 Mar 31	Sales		70	
	Suspense			70
	Sales overcast of £70 in 19X5			
2 Mar 31	Insurance		40	
	Suspense			40
	Insurance expense undercast by £40 in 19X5			
3 Mar 31	Suspense		50	
	Debtor's account			50
	Cash received omitted from debtor's account in 19X5			
4 Mar 31	Creditor's account		36	
	Purchases			36
	Credit purchase of £59 entered both as debit and credit as £95 in 19X5			

Note: In (D), the correction of the overstatement of purchases does not pass through the suspense account.

Now we can calculate the corrected net profit for the year 19X5. Only items (A), (B) and (D) affect figures in the trading and profit and loss account. These are the only adjustments to be made to profit.

K Davis

Statement of corrected net profit for the year ended 31 December 19X5

			£
Net profit per the accounts			1,600
Add Purchases overstated	(D)		36
			1,636
Less Sales overcast	(A)	70	
Insurance undercast	(B)	40	110
Corrected net profit for the year			1,526

Error (C), the cash not posted to a debtor's account, did not affect profit calculations.

32.6 Suspense accounts: businesses and examinations

Businesses

Every attempt should be made to find errors. A suspense account should be opened only if all other efforts have failed.

Examinations

Unless it is part of a question, *do not* make your balance sheet totals agree by using a suspense account. The same applies to trial balances. Examiners are very likely to penalise you for showing a suspense account when it should not be required.

New term

Suspense account (p. 309): Account showing balance equal to difference in trial balance.

Main points to remember

1   Some of the errors made, but not all, will mean that the profits originally calculated were incorrect.

2   Errors that do not affect profit calculations will have an effect only on items in the balance sheet.

Multiple-choice questions

Now attempt Set No 4, consisting of 20 questions, shown on pp. 578–81.

Review questions

32.1   Your bookkeeper extracted a trial balance on 31 December 19X8 which failed to agree by £330, a shortage on the credit side of the trial balance. A suspense account was opened for the difference.

In January 19X9 the following errors made in 19X8 were found:

(*i*)   Sales day book had been undercast by £100.
(*ii*)   Sales of £250 to J Cantrell had been debited in error to J Cochrane's account.
(*iii*)   Rent account had been undercast by £70.
(*iv*)   Discounts Received account had been undercast by £300.
(*v*)   The sale of a motor vehicle at book value had been credited in error to Sales account £360.

You are required to:
(*a*)   Show the journal entries necessary to correct the errors.
(*b*)   Draw up the suspense account after the errors described have been corrected.
(*c*)   If the net profit had previously been calculated at £7,900 for the year ended 31 December 19X8, show the calculations of the corrected net profit.

32.2A You have extracted a trial balance and drawn up accounts for the year ended 31 December 19X6. There was a shortage of £292 on the credit side of the trial balance, a suspense account being opened for that amount.

During 19X7 the following errors made in 19X6 were located:

(*i*) £55 received from sales of old office equipment has been entered in the sales account.
(*ii*) Purchases day book had been overcast by £60.
(*iii*) A private purchase of £115 had been included in the business purchases.
(*iv*) Bank charges £38 entered in the cash book have not been posted to the bank charges account.
(*v*) A sale of goods to B Cross £690 was correctly entered in the sales book but entered in the personal account as £960.

Required:
(*a*) Show the requisite journal entries to correct the errors.
(*b*) Write up the suspense account showing the correction of the errors.
(*c*) The net profit originally calculated for 19X6 was £11,370. Show your calculation of the correct figure.

32.3 Show how each of the following errors would affect trial balance agreement:

(*i*) Equipment repairs £720 was debited to the equipment account.
(*ii*) £1,700 discounts allowed credited to discounts received account.
(*iii*) Stock at close overvalued by £2,000.
(*iv*) £750 commission received was debited to the sales account.
(*v*) Drawings £305 credited to the capital account.
(*vi*) Cheque paying £170 to C Charles entered in cash book but not in personal account.
(*vii*) Cheque £248 from L Barnes credited to L Barrett.

Format should be as follows:

Item	If no effect state 'No'	Debit side exceeds credit side by amount shown	Credit side exceeds debit side by amount shown
(*i*)			
(*ii*)			
(*iii*)			
(*iv*)			
(*v*)			
(*vi*)			
(*vii*)			

32.4 The following is a trial balance which has been incorrectly drawn up:

Trial Balance – 31 January 19X9

	£	£
Capital 1 February 19X8	5,500	
Drawings	2,800	
Stock 1 February 19X8		2,597
Trade debtors		2,130
Furniture and fittings	1,750	
Cash in hand	1,020	
Trade creditors		2,735
Sales		7,430
Returns inwards		85
Discount received	46	
Business expenses	950	
Purchases	4,380	
	16,446	14,977

In addition to the mistakes evident above, the following errors were also discovered:

1 A payment of £75 made to a creditor had not been posted from the cash book into the purchases ledger.
2 A cheque for £56 received from a customer had been correctly entered in the cash book but posted to the customer's account as £50.
3 A purchase of fittings £120 had been included in the purchases account.
4 The total of the discounts allowed column in the cash book of £38 had not been posted into the general ledger.
5 A page of the sales day book was correctly totalled as £564 but carried forward as £456.

Show the trial balance as it would appear after all the errors had been corrected. You are required to show all workings.

32.5 Study the following and answer the questions below.

The trial balance of Mary Harris (Gowns) as at 31 December 19X8 showed a difference which was posted to a suspense account. Draft final accounts for the year ended 31 December 19X8 were prepared showing a net profit of £47,240. The following errors were subsequently discovered:

- Sales of £450 to C Thomas had been debited to Thomasson Manufacturing Ltd.
- A payment of £275 for telephone charges had been entered on the debit side of the Telephone account as £375.
- The sales journal had been undercast by £2,000.
- Repairs to a machine, amounting to £390, had been charged to Machinery account.
- A cheque for £1,500, being rent received from Atlas Ltd, had only been entered in the cash book.
- Purchases from P Brooks, amounting to £765, had been received on 31 December 19X8 and included in the closing stock at that date, but the invoice had not been entered in the purchases journal.

Questions
(a) (i) Give the journal entries, without narratives, necessary to correct the above errors.
     (ii) Show the effect of each of these adjustments on the net profit in the draft accounts and the correct profit for the year ended 31 December 19X8.
(b) (i) State briefly the purpose of the journal, giving a suitable example of its use.
     (ii) State why it is necessary to distinguish between capital and revenue expenditure.

(Midland Examining Group: GCSE)

32.6A Gail Dawson is the owner of a retail business. She has employed an inexperienced bookkeeper to maintain her accounting records.

(a) On 31 March 19X9, the end of the business's accounting year, the bookkeeper extracted the following trial balance from the business's records:

Trial Balance at 31 March 19X9	Dr £	Cr £
Fixed assets at cost	18,300	
Provision for depreciation of fixed assets, 1 April 19X8	2,800	
Stocks		
1 April 19X8	3,700	
31 March 19X9		2,960
Trade debtors		1,825
Trade creditors	864	
Balance at bank (overdrawn)	382	
Capital		26,860
Drawings	7,740	
Sales	26,080	
Purchases		18,327
Running expenses	6,904	
Provision for doubtful debts	90	
Suspense		16,888
	£66,860	£66,860

Required:

1 A corrected version of Gail Dawson's trial balance dated 31 March 19X9 based on the above information, but with an amended figure for the suspense account.

(b) The following errors were found in the accounting system after a corrected version of the trial balance above was prepared.

(i) The total of the sales day book for December 19X8 had been overstated by £120.

(ii) In January 19X9 some new office equipment had been purchased for £360; this had been debited to the purchases account.

(iii) A payment by cheque to a creditor, £216, had been entered in the books as £261.

(iv) A credit note for £37 sent to a customer had been overlooked.

(v) The owner had withdrawn a cheque for £80 for private use in October 19X8; both the bank and drawings account had been credited with this amount.

Required:

In the books of Gail Dawson

2 Journal entries to correct each of these errors.
(**Note:** narratives are NOT required.)

3 The suspense account. (Start with the amount in the corrected trial balance given in answer to Required 1 above, and include any entries arising from the correction of the errors.)

4 An explanation of the term 'error of commission'. (Give an example of such an error to illustrate your answer.)

(*Southern Examining Group: GCSE*)

32.7 The trial balance as at 30 April 19X7 of Timber Products Limited was balanced by the inclusion of the following debit balance:

Difference on trial balance suspense account £2,513.

Subsequent investigations revealed the following errors:

(*i*) Discounts received of £324 in January 19X7 have been posted to the debit of the discounts allowed account.
(*ii*) Wages of £2,963 paid in February 19X7 have not been posted from the cash book.
(*iii*) A remittance of £940 received from K Mitcham in November 19X6 has been posted to the credit of B Mansell Limited.
(*iv*) In December 19X6, the company took advantage of an opportunity to purchase a large quantity of stationery at a bargain price of £2,000. No adjustments have been made in the accounts for the fact that three-quarters, in value, of this stationery was in stock on 30 April 19X7.
(*v*) A payment of £341 to J Winters in January 19X7 has been posted in the personal account as £143.
(*vi*) A remittance of £3,000 received from D North, a credit customer, in April 19X7 has been credited to sales.

The draft accounts for the year ended 30 April 19X7 of Timber Products Limited show a net profit of £24,760.

Timber Products Limited has very few personal accounts and therefore does not maintain either a purchases ledger control account or a sales ledger control account.

Required:
(*a*) Prepare the difference on trial balance suspense account showing, where appropriate, the entries necessary to correct the accounting errors.
(*b*) Prepare a computation of the corrected net profit for the year ended 30 April 19X7 following corrections for the above accounting errors.
(*c*) Outline the principal uses of trial balances.

(*Association of Accounting Technicians*)

32.8A Chi Knitwear Ltd is an old-fashioned firm with a handwritten set of books. A trial balance is extracted at the end of each month, and a profit and loss account and balance sheet are computed. This month, however, the trial balance will not balance, the credits exceeding debits by £1,536.

You are asked to help and after inspection of the ledgers discover the following errors.

(*i*) A balance of £87 on a debtor's account has been omitted from the schedule of debtors, the total of which was entered as debtors in the trial balance.
(*ii*) A small piece of machinery purchased for £1,200 had been written off to repairs.
(*iii*) The receipts side of the cash book had been undercast by £720.
(*iv*) The total of one page of the sales day book had been carried forward as £8,154, whereas the correct amount was £8,514.
(*v*) A credit note for £179 received from a supplier had been posted to the wrong side of his account.
(*vi*) An electricity bill in the sum of £152, not yet accrued for, is discovered in a filing tray.
(*vii*) Mr Smith, whose past debts to the company had been the subject of a provision, at last paid £731 to clear his account. His personal account has been credited but the cheque has not yet passed through the cash book.

Required:
(*a*) Write up the suspense account to clear the difference, and
(*b*) State the effect on the accounts of correcting each error.

(*Association of Chartered Certified Accountants*)

Part 5

SPECIAL ACCOUNTING PROCEDURES

Introduction

This part is concerned with the accounting procedures that have to be followed with different forms of organisations, and commences with a chapter outlining the basic ratios which may be found necessary at this stage.

33

Introduction to accounting ratios

Objectives

After you have studied this chapter, you should:

- *be able to calculate some basic accounting ratios*
- *be able to use accounting ratios to calculate missing or forecasted figures*
- *understand the reasons behind a change in the ratios*

33.1 The need for accounting ratios

We will see in Chapter 48, that accounting ratios are used to enable us to analyse and interpret accounting statements.

The current chapter has been inserted here simply so that we will be able to deal with Chapter 34 which includes the drawing up of accounts from incomplete records. The ratios described in this chapter will be sufficient for us to deduce the data needed to make the incomplete records into a complete set of records, so that we can then draw up the final accounts. Without the use of such accounting ratios the construction of final accounts from incomplete records would often be impossible.

33.2 Mark-up and margin

The purchase and sale of goods may be shown as:

> **Cost Price + Profit = Selling Price**

The profit when shown as a fraction, or percentage, of the cost price is known as the **mark-up**.

The profit when shown as a fraction, or percentage, of the selling price is known as the **margin**.

We can now calculate these using this example:

Cost Price + Profit = Selling Price
$£4$ + $£1$ = $£5$.

Mark-up = $\dfrac{\text{Profit}}{\text{Cost Price}}$ as a fraction, or if required as a percentage, multiply by 100:

$$£\frac{1}{4} = \frac{1}{4}, \text{ or } \frac{1}{4} \times 100 = 25 \text{ per cent.}$$

Margin = $\dfrac{\text{Profit}}{\text{Selling Price}}$ as a fraction, or if required as a percentage, multiply by 100:

$$£\frac{1}{5} = \frac{1}{5}, \text{ or } \frac{1}{5} \times 100 = 20 \text{ per cent.}$$

33.3 Calculating missing figures

Now we can use these ratios to complete trading accounts where some of the figures are missing. All examples in this chapter:

- assume that all the goods in a firm have the same rate of mark-up, and
- ignore wastages and theft of goods.

Example 1

The following figures are for the year 19X5:

	£
Stock 1.1.19X5	400
Stock 31.12.19X5	600
Purchases	5,200

A uniform rate of mark-up of 20% is applied.

Find the gross profit and the sales figure:

Trading Account for the year ended 31 December 19X5

	£	£
Sales		?
Less Cost of goods sold:		
Stock 1.1.19X5	400	
Add Purchases	5,200	
	5,600	
Less Stock 31.12.19X5	600	5,000
Gross profit		?

Answer:
It is known that: Cost of goods sold + Profit = Sales
and also that: Cost of goods sold + Percentage Mark-up = Sales

The following figures are also known: £5,000 + 20% = Sales

After doing the arithmetic: £5,000 + £1,000 = £6,000

The trading account can be completed by inserting the gross profit £1,000 and £6,000 for Sales.

Example 2

Another firm has the following figures for 19X6:

	£
Stock 1.1.19X6	500
Stock 31.12.19X6	800
Sales	6,400

A uniform rate of margin of 25% is in use.

Find the gross profit and the figure of purchases:

Trading Account for the year ended 31 December 19X6

	£	£
Sales		6,400
Less Cost of goods sold:		
Stock 1.1.19X6	500	
Add Purchases	?	
	?	
Less Stock 31.12.19X6	800	?
Gross profit		?

Answer:	Cost of goods sold	+ Gross profit	= Sales
Therefore	Sales	– Gross profit	= Cost of goods sold
	Sales	– 25% margin	= Cost of goods sold
	£6,400	– £1,600	= £4,800

Now the following figures are known:

		£	£
Cost of goods sold:			
Stock 1.1.19X6		500	
Add Purchases	(1)	?	
	(2)	?	
Less Stock 31.12.19X6		800	4,800

The two missing figures are found by normal arithmetical deduction:

	No (2) less £800	= £4,800
	Therefore No (2)	= £5,600
So that: £500 opening stock + No (1)		= £5,600
	Therefore No (1)	= £5,100

The completed trading account can now be shown:

Trading Account for the year ended 31 December 19X6

	£	£
Sales		6,400
Less Cost of goods sold:		
Stock 1.1.19X6	500	
Add Purchases	5,100	
	5,600	
Less Stock 31.12.19X6	800	4,800
Gross profit		1,600

This technique is found very useful by retail stores when estimating the amount to be bought if a certain sales target is to be achieved. Alternatively, stock levels or sales figures can be estimated given information as to purchases and opening stock figures.

33.4 The relationship between mark-up and margin

As both of these figures refer to the same profit, but expressed as a fraction or a percentage of different figures, there is bound to be a relationship. If one is known as a fraction, the other can soon be found.

If the mark-up is known, to find the margin take the same numerator to be numerator of the margin, then for the denominator of the margin take the total of the mark-up's denominator plus the numerator. An example can now be shown:

Mark-up   *Margin*

$$\frac{1}{4} \quad \frac{1}{4+1} = \frac{1}{5}$$

$$\frac{2}{11} \quad \frac{2}{11+2} = \frac{2}{13}$$

If the margin is known, to find the mark-up take the same numerator to be the numerator of the mark-up, then for the denominator of the mark-up take the figure of the margin's denominator less the numerator:

Margin   *Mark-up*

$$\frac{1}{6} \quad \frac{1}{6-1} = \frac{1}{5}$$

$$\frac{3}{13} \quad \frac{3}{13-3} = \frac{3}{10}$$

33.5 Manager's commission

Managers of businesses are very often remunerated by a basic salary plus a percentage of profits. It is quite common to find the percentage expressed not as a percentage of profits before such commission has been deducted, but as a percentage of the amount remaining after deduction of the commission.

For example, assume that profits before the manager's commission was deducted amounted to £8,400, and that the manager was entitled to 5% of the profits remaining after such commission was deducted. If 5% of £8,400 was taken, this amounts to £420, and the profits remaining would amount to £7,980. However, 5% of £7,980 amounts to £399 so that the answer of £420 is wrong.

The formula to be used to arrive at the correct answer is:

$$\frac{\text{Percentage commission}}{100 + \text{Percentage commission}} \times \text{Profit before commission.}$$

In the above problem this would be used as follows:

$$\frac{5}{100 + 5} \times £8,400 = £400 \text{ manager's commission.}$$

The profits remaining are £8,000 and as £400 represents 5% of it the answer is verified.

33.6 Commonly used accounting ratios

There are some ratios that are in common use for the purpose of comparing one period's results against those of a previous period. Two of those most in use are the ratio of gross profit to sales, and the rate of turnover or stockturn.

Gross profit as percentage of sales

The basic formula is:

$$\frac{\text{Gross Profit}}{\text{Sales}} \times \frac{100}{1} = \text{Gross Profit as percentage of sales.}$$

Put another way, this represents the amount of gross profit for every £100 of sales. If the answer turned out to be 15%, this would mean that for every £100 of sales £15 gross profit was made before any expenses were paid.

This ratio is used as a test of the profitability of the sales. Just because the sales are increased does not of itself mean that the gross profit will increase. The trading accounts in Exhibit 33.1 illustrate this.

Exhibit 33.1

Trading Accounts for the year ended 31 December

	£	19X6 £	£	19X7 £
Sales		7,000		8,000
Less Cost of goods sold:				
Opening stock	500		900	
Add Purchases	6,000		7,200	
	6,500		8,100	
Less Closing stock	900	5,600	1,100	7,000
Gross profit		1,400		1,000

In the year 19X6 the gross profit as a percentage of sales was:

$$\frac{1,400}{7,000} \times \frac{100}{1} = 20 \text{ per cent}$$

In the year 19X7 it became:

$$\frac{1,000}{8,000} \times \frac{100}{1} = 12\frac{1}{2} \text{ per cent}$$

Sales had increased, but as the gross profit percentage had fallen by a relatively greater amount the gross profit has fallen. There can be many reasons for such a fall in the gross profit percentage. Some are now listed:

1 Perhaps the goods being sold have cost more, but the selling price of the goods has not risen to the same extent.
2 Perhaps in order to increase sales, reductions have been made in the selling price of goods.
3 There could be a difference in how much has been sold of each sort of goods, called the sales-mix, between this year and last, with different kinds of goods carrying different rates of gross profit per £100 of sales.
4 There may have been a greater wastage or theft of goods.

These are only some of the possible reasons for the decrease. The idea of calculating the ratio is to show that the profitability per £100 of sales has changed. The firm would then try to find out why and how such a change has taken place.

As the figure of sales less returns inwards is also known as **turnover**, the ratio is also known as the **gross profit percentage on turnover**.

Stockturn or rate of turnover

If we always kept just £100 of stock at cost, which when we sold it would sell for £125, then if we sold this amount eight times in a year we would make 8 × £25 = £200 gross profit. The quicker we sell our stock (we could say the quicker we turn over our stock) the more the profit we will make, if our gross profit percentage stays the same.

To check on how quickly we are turning over our stock we can use the formula:

$$\frac{\text{Cost of goods sold}}{\text{Average stock}} = \text{Number of times stock is turned over within a period.}$$

It would be best if the average stock held could be calculated by valuing the stock quite a few times each year, then dividing the totals of the figures obtained by the number of valuations. For instance, monthly stock figures are added up and then divided by twelve. However, it is quite common, especially in examinations or in cases where no other information is available, to calculate the average stock as the opening stock plus the closing stock and the answer divided by two. Using the figures in Exhibit 33.1 we can calculate the **stockturn** for 19X6 and 19X7:

$$19X6 \quad \frac{5{,}600}{(500 + 900) \div 2} = 8 \text{ times per annum}$$

$$19X7 \quad \frac{7{,}000}{(900 + 1{,}100) \div 2} = 7 \text{ times per annum}$$

Instead of saying that the stockturn is so many times per annum, we could instead say on average how long we keep stock before we sell it. We do this by the formula:

To express it in months: 12 ÷ Stockturn = x months
To express it in days: 365 ÷ Stockturn = x days

From Exhibit 33.1:

	19X6		19X7	
In months	$\dfrac{12}{8}$ =	1.5 months	$\dfrac{12}{7}$ =	1.7 months
In days	$\dfrac{365}{8}$ =	45.6 days	$\dfrac{365}{7}$ =	52.1 days

All the above figures are rounded off to the nearest decimal point.

When the rate of stockturn is falling it can be due to such causes as a slowing down of sales activity, or to keeping a higher figure of stock than is really necessary. The ratio does not prove anything by itself, it merely prompts inquiries as to why it should be changing.

This chapter has only looked at ratios so as to help with the content of the next chapter. Later on in the book, in Chapter 48, we turn again to ratios, this time a more advanced and detailed survey.

New terms

Margin (p. 323): Profit shown as a percentage or fraction of selling price.

Mark-up (p. 323): Profit shown as a percentage or fraction of cost price.

Stockturn (p. 328): Number of times we sell our stock in an accounting period.

Main points to remember

1   Accounting ratios can be used to deduce missing figures, given certain assumptions.

2   If the mark-up is known as a fraction, then the margin as a fraction can easily be calculated.

3   If the margin is known as a fraction, then the mark-up as a fraction can easily be calculated.

Review questions

33.1   R Stubbs is a trader who sells all of his goods at 25% above cost. His books give the following information at 31 December 19X9:

	£
Stock 1 January 19X9	9,872
Stock 31 December 19X9	12,620
Sales for year	60,000

You are required to:
(*a*)   Ascertain cost of goods sold.
(*b*)   Show the value of purchases during the year.
(*c*)   Calculate the profit made by Stubbs.

Show your answer in the form of a trading account.

33.2A   C White gives you the following information as at 30 June 19X7:

	£
Stock 1 July 19X6	6,000
Purchases	54,000

White's mark-up is 50% on 'cost of goods sold'. His average stock during the year was £12,000. Draw up a trading and profit and loss account for the year ended 30 June 19X7.

(*a*)   Calculate the closing stock as at 30 June 19X7.
(*b*)   State the total amount of profit and loss expenditure White must not exceed if he is to maintain a *net* profit on sales of 10%.

33.3   J Green's business has a rate of turnover of 7 times. Average stock is £12,600. Trade discount (i.e. margin allowed) is $33\frac{1}{3}$% off all selling prices. Expenses are $66\frac{2}{3}$% of gross profit.

   You are to calculate:

(*a*)   Cost of goods sold.

(*b*)   Gross profit margin.

(*c*)   Turnover.

(*d*)   Total expenses.

(*e*)   Net profit.

33.4A The following figures relate to the retail business of J Clarke for the month of May 19X9. Goods which are on sale fall into two categories, A and B.

	Category A	Category B
Sales to the public at manufacturer's recommended list price	£6,000	£14,000
Trade discount allowed to retailers	20%	25%
Total expenses as a percentage of sales	10%	10%
Annual rate of stock turnover	12	20

Calculate for each category:
(a) Cost of goods sold
(b) Gross profit
(c) Total expenses
(d) Net profit
(e) Average stock at cost, assuming that sales are distributed evenly over the year, and that there are twelve equal months in the year.

33.5 The following trading account for the year ended 31 December 19X8 is given to you by H Rayner:

	£	£
Sales		150,000
Less Cost of goods sold:		
Opening stock	20,100	
Add Purchases	129,900	
	150,000	
Less Closing stock	28,500	
		121,500
Gross profit		28,500

Rayner says that normally he adds 25% to the cost of goods to fix the sales price. However, this year saw some arithmetical errors in these calculations.

(a) Calculate what his sales would have been if he had not made any errors.
(b) Given that his expenses remain constant at 7% of his sales, calculate his net profit for the year 19X8.
(c) Work out the rate of stockturn for 19X8.
(d) He thinks that next year he can increase his mark-up to $27\frac{1}{2}\%$, selling goods which will cost him £140,000. If he does not make any more errors in calculating selling prices, you are to calculate the expected gross and net profits for 19X9.

33.6A   *Trading Account for the year ended 31 December 19X9*

	£		£
Stock 1 January 19X9	3,000	Sales	60,000
Purchases	47,000		
	50,000		
Stock 31 December 19X9	4,500		
Cost of sales	45,500		
Gross profit	14,500		
	60,000		60,000

R Sheldon presents you with the trading account set out above. He always calculates his selling price by adding 33⅓% of cost on to the cost price.

(a) If he has adhered strictly to the statement above, what should be the percentage of gross profit to sales?
(b) Calculate his actual percentage of gross profit to sales.
(c) Give two reasons for the difference between the figures you have calculated above.
(d) His suppliers are proposing to increase their prices by 5%, but R Sheldon considers that he would be unwise to increase his selling price. To obtain some impression of the effect on gross profit if his costs should be increased by 5% he asks you to reconstruct his trading account to show the gross profit if the increase had applied from 1 January 19X9.
(e) Using the figures given in the trading account at the beginning of the question, calculate R Sheldon's rate of stock turnover.
(f) R Sheldon's expenses amount to 10% of his sales. Calculate his net profit for the year ended 31 December 19X9.
(g) If all expenses remained unchanged, but suppliers of stock increased their prices by 5% as in (d) above, calculate the percentage reduction in the amount of net profit which R Sheldon's accounts would have shown.

(Edexcel Foundation, London Examinations)

34

Single entry and incomplete records

Objectives

After you have studied this chapter, you should be able to:

- *deduce the figure of profits where only the increase in capital and details of drawings are known*

- *draw up a trading and profit and loss account and balance sheet from records not kept on a double entry system*

- *deduce the figures of sales and purchases from incomplete records*

34.1 Why double entry is not used

For every small shopkeeper, market stall or other small business to keep its books using a full double entry system would be ridiculous. First of all, a large number of the owners of such firms would not know how to write up double entry records, even if they wanted to.

It is more likely that they would enter details of a transaction once only, using a single entry system. Also many of them would fail to record every transaction, resulting in incomplete records.

It is perhaps only fair to remember that accounting is after all supposed to be an aid to management; it is not something to be done as an end in itself. Therefore, many small firms, especially retail shops, can have all the information they want by merely keeping a cash book and having some form of record, not necessarily in double entry form, of their debtors and creditors.

Somehow, however, the profits will have to be calculated. This could be for the purpose of calculating income tax payable. How can profits be calculated if the bookkeeping records are inadequate or incomplete?

34.2 Profit as an increase in capital

Probably the way to start is to recall that, unless there has been an introduction of extra cash or resources into the firm, the only way that capital can be increased is by making profits. Therefore, profits can be found by comparing capital at the end of the last period with that at the end of this period.

Let us look at a firm where capital at the end of 19X4 was £2,000. During 19X5 there have been no drawings, and no extra capital has been brought in by the owner. At the end of 19X5 the capital was £3,000.

	This year's capital		Last year's capital	
Net profit =	£3,000	–	£2,000	= £1,000

If on the other hand the drawings had been £700, the profits must have been £1,700, calculated thus:

Last year's Capital + Profits – Drawings = This year's Capital
£2,000   +   ?   –   £700   =   £3,000

We can see that £1,700 profits was the figure needed to complete the formula, filling in the missing figure by normal arithmetical deduction:

$$£2,000 + £1,700 - £700 = £3,000$$

Exhibit 34.1 shows the calculation of profit where insufficient information is available to draft a trading and profit and loss account, only information of assets and liabilities being known.

Exhibit 34.1

H Taylor has not kept proper bookkeeping records, but he has kept notes in diary form of the transactions of his business. He is able to give you details of his assets and liabilities as at 31 December 19X5 and at 31 December 19X6 as follows:

At 31 December 19X5. *Assets*: Motor van £1,000; Fixtures £700; Stock £850; Debtors £950; Bank £1,100; Cash £100. *Liabilities*: Creditors £200; Loan from J Ogden £600.

At 31 December 19X6. *Assets*: Motor van (after depreciation) £800; Fixtures (after depreciation) £630; Stock £990; Debtors £1,240; Bank £1,700; Cash £200. *Liabilities*: Creditors £300; Loan from J Ogden £400; Drawings were £900.

First of all a **Statement of Affairs** is drawn up as at 31 December 19X5. This is the name given to what would have been called a balance sheet if it had been drawn up from a set of records. The capital is the difference between the assets and liabilities.

H Taylor

Statement of Affairs as at 31 December 19X5

	£	£
Fixed assets		
Motor van		1,000
Fixtures		700
		1,700
Current assets		
Stock	850	
Debtors	950	
Bank	1,100	
Cash	100	
	3,000	
Less Current liabilities		
Creditors	200	
Working capital		2,800
		4,500
Financed by:		
Capital (difference)		3,900
Long-term liability: Loan from J Ogden		600
		4,500

A statement of affairs is now drafted up as at the end of 19X6. The formula of Opening Capital + Profit – Drawings = Closing Capital is then used to deduce the figure of profit.

H Taylor

Statement of Affairs as at 31 December 19X6

		£		£
Fixed assets				
Motor van				800
Fixtures				630
				1,430
Current assets				
Stock		990		
Debtors		1,240		
Bank		1,700		
Cash		200		
		4,130		
Less Current liabilities				
Creditors		300		3,830
				5,260
Financed by:				
Capital				
Balance at 1.1.19X6		3,900		
Add Net profit	(C)	?		
	(B)	?		
Less Drawings		900	(A)	?
Long-term liability: Loan from J Ogden				400

Deduction of net profit:

Opening Capital + Net Profit − Drawings = Closing Capital. Finding the missing figures (A), (B) and (C) by deduction:

(A) is the figure needed to make the balance sheet totals equal, i.e. £4,860;

(B) is therefore £4,860 + £900 = £5,760;

(C) is therefore £5,760 − £3,900 = £1,860.

To check:

			£		£
Capital			3,900		
Add Net profit		(C)	1,860		
		(B)	5,760		
Less Drawings			900	(A)	4,860

Obviously, this method of calculating profit is very unsatisfactory as it is much more informative when a trading and profit and loss account can be drawn up. Therefore, whenever possible the comparisons of capital method of ascertaining profit should be avoided and a full set of final accounts drawn up from the available records.

It is important to realise that a business would have exactly the same trading and profit and loss account and balance sheet whether they kept their books by single entry or double entry. However, as you will see, whereas the double entry system uses the trial balance in preparing the final accounts, the single entry system will have to arrive at the same answer by different means.

34.3 Drawing up the final accounts

The following example shows the various stages of drawing up final accounts from a single entry set of records.

The accountant discerns the following details of transactions for J Frank's retail store for the year ended 31 December 19X5.

(*a*) The sales are mostly on a credit basis. No record of sales has been made, but £10,000 has been received, £9,500 by cheque and £500 by cash, from persons to whom goods have been sold.

(*b*) Amount paid by cheque to suppliers during the year = £7,200.

(*c*) Expenses paid during the year: by cheque, Rent £200, General Expenses £180; by cash, Rent £50.

(*d*) J Frank took £10 cash per week (for 52 weeks) as drawings.

(*e*) Other information is available:

	At 31.12.19X4	*At 31.12.19X5*
	£	£
Debtors	1,100	1,320
Creditors for goods	400	650
Rent owing	–	50
Bank balance	1,130	3,050
Cash balance	80	10
Stock	1,590	1,700

(*f*) The only fixed asset consists of fixtures which were valued at 31 December 19X4 at £800. These are to be depreciated at 10 per cent per annum.

Stage 1: Draw up a Statement of Affairs on the closing day of the last accounting period. This is now shown:

J Frank

Statement of Affairs as at 31 December 19X4

	£	£
Fixed assets		
Fixtures		800
Current assets		
Stock	1,590	
Debtors	1,100	
Bank	1,130	
Cash	80	
	3,900	
Less Current liabilities		
Creditors	400	
Working capital		3,500
		4,300
Financed by:		
Capital (difference)		4,300
		4,300

All of these opening figures are then taken into account when drawing up the final accounts for 19X5.

Stage 2: Next a cash and bank summary, showing the totals of each separate item, plus opening and closing balances, is drawn up.

	Cash	Bank		Cash	Bank
	£	£		£	£
Balances 31.12.19X4	80	1,130	Suppliers		7,200
Receipts from debtors	500	9,500	Rent	50	200
			General Expenses		180
			Drawings	520	
			Balances 31.12.19X5	10	3,050
	580	10,630		580	10,630

Stage 3: Calculate the figures for purchases and sales to be shown in the trading account. Remember that the figures needed are the same as those which would have been found if double entry records had been kept.

Purchases: In double entry, purchases means the goods that have been bought in the period irrespective of whether they have been paid for or not during the period. The figure of payments to suppliers must therefore be adjusted to find the figure for purchases.

	£
Paid during the year	7,200
Less Payments made, but which were for goods which were purchased in a previous year (creditors 31.12.19X4)	400
	6,800
Add Purchases made in this year, but for which payment has not yet been made (creditors 31.12.19X5)	650
Goods bought in this year, i.e. purchases	7,450

The same answer could have been obtained if the information had been shown in the form of a total creditors account, the figure for purchases being the amount required to make the account totals agree.

Total Creditors

	£		£
Cash paid to suppliers	7,200	Balances b/d	400
Balances c/d	650	Purchases (missing figure)	7,450
	7,850		7,850

Sales: The sales figure will only equal receipts where all the sales are for cash. Therefore, the receipts figures need adjusting to find sales. This can only be done by constructing a total debtors account, the sales figure being the one needed to make the totals agree.

Total Debtors

	£		£
Balances b/d	1,100	Receipts: Cash	500
		Cheque	9,500
Sales (missing figure)	10,220	Balances c/d	1,320
	11,320		11,320

Stage 4: Expenses. Where there are no accruals or prepayments either at the beginning or end of the accounting period, then expenses paid will equal expenses used up during the period. These figures will be charged to the trading and profit and loss account.

On the other hand, where such prepayments or accruals exist, then an expense account should be drawn up for that particular item. When all known items are entered, the missing figure will be the expenses to be charged for the accounting period. In this case only the rent account needs to be drawn up.

Rent Account

	£		£
Cheques	200	Rent (missing figure)	300
Cash	50		
Accrued c/d	50		
	300		300

Stage 5: Now draw up the final accounts.

J Frank

Trading and Profit and Loss Account for the year ended 31 December 19X5

	£	£
Sales (stage 3)		10,220
Less Cost of goods sold:		
Stock at 1.1.19X5	1,590	
Add Purchases (stage 3)	7,450	
	9,040	
Less Stock at 31.12.19X5	1,700	7,340
Gross profit		2,880
Less Expenses:		
Rent (stage 4)	300	
General expenses	180	
Depreciation: Fixtures	80	560
Net profit		2,320

Balance Sheet as at 31 December 19X5

	£	£	£
Fixed assets			
Fixtures at 1.1.19X5		800	
Less Depreciation		80	720
Current assets			
Stock		1,700	
Debtors		1,320	
Bank		3,050	
Cash		10	
		6,080	
Less Current liabilities			
Creditors	650		
Rent owing	50	700	
Working capital			5,380
			6,100
Financed by:			
Capital			
Balance 1.1.19X5 (per Opening Statement of Affairs)			4,300
Add Net profit			2,320
			6,620
Less Drawings			520
			6,100

34.4 Incomplete records and missing figures

In practice, part of the information relating to cash receipts or payments is often missing. If the missing information is in respect of one type of payment, then it is normal to assume that the missing figure is the amount required to make both totals agree in the cash column of the cash and bank summary. This does not happen with bank items owing to the fact that another copy of the bank statement can always be obtained from the bank. Exhibit 34.2 shows an example when the drawings figure is unknown; Exhibit 34.3 is an example where the receipts from debtors had not been recorded.

Exhibit 34.2

The following information on cash and bank receipts and payments is available:

	Cash	Bank
	£	£
Cash paid into the bank during the year	5,500	
Receipts from debtors	7,250	800
Paid to suppliers	320	4,930
Drawings during the year	?	–
Expenses paid	150	900
Balances at 1.1.19X5	35	1,200
Balances at 31.12.19X5	50	1,670

	Cash	Bank		Cash	Bank
	£	£		£	£
Balances 1.1.19X5	35	1,200	Bankings C	5,500	
Received from debtors	7,250	800	Suppliers	320	4,930
Bankings C		5,500	Expenses	150	900
			Drawings	?	
			Balances 31.12.19X5	50	1,670
	7,285	7,500		7,285	7,500

The amount needed to make the two sides of the cash columns agree is £1,265. Therefore, this is taken as the figure of drawings.

Exhibit 34.3

Information of cash and bank transactions is available as follows:

	Cash	Bank
	£	£
Receipts from debtors	?	6,080
Cash withdrawn from the bank for business use (this is the amount which is used besides cash receipts from debtors to pay drawings and expenses)		920
Paid to suppliers		5,800
Expenses paid	640	230
Drawings	1,180	315
Balances at 1.1.19X5	40	1,560
Balances at 31.12.19X5	70	375

	Cash	Bank		Cash	Bank
	£	£		£	£
Balances 1.1.19X5	40	1,560	Suppliers		5,800
Received from debtors	?	6,080	Expenses	640	230
Withdrawn from Bank C	920		Withdrawn from Bank C		920
			Drawings	1,180	315
			Balances 31.12.19X5	70	375
	1,890	7,640		1,890	7,640

Receipts from debtors is, therefore, the amount needed to make each side of the cash column agree, £930.

It must be emphasised that balancing figures are acceptable only when all the other figures have been verified. Should, for instance, a cash expense be omitted when cash received from debtors is being calculated, then this would result in an understatement not only of expenses but also ultimately of sales.

34.5 Where there are two missing pieces of information

If both cash drawings and cash receipts from debtors were not known, it would not be possible to deduce both of these figures. The only course lying open would be to estimate whichever figure was more capable of being accurately assessed, use this as a known figure, then deduce the other figure. However, this is a most unsatisfactory position as both of the figures are no more than pure estimates, the accuracy of each one relying entirely upon the accuracy of the other.

34.6 Cash sales and purchases for cash

Where there are cash sales as well as sales on credit terms, then the cash sales must be added to sales on credit to give the total sales for the year. This total figure of sales will be the one shown in the trading account.

Similarly, purchases for cash will need adding to credit purchases to give the figure of total purchases for the trading account.

34.7 Goods stolen or lost by fire, etc

When goods are stolen, destroyed by fire, or lost in some other way, then the value of them will have to be calculated. This could be needed to substantiate an insurance claim or to settle problems concerning taxation, etc.

If the stock had been properly valued immediately before the fire, burglary, etc, then the stock loss would obviously be known. Also if a full and detailed system of stock records were kept, then the value would also be known. However, as the occurrence of fires or burglaries cannot be foreseen, and not many businesses keep full and proper stock records, the stock loss will have to be calculated in some other way.

The methods described in this chapter and Chapter 33 are used instead. The only difference is that instead of computing closing stock at a year end, for example, the closing stock will be that as at immediately before the fire consumed it or it was stolen.

Exhibits 34.4 and 34.5 will now be looked at. The first exhibit will be a very simple case, where figures of purchases and sales are known and all goods are sold at a uniform profit ratio. The second exhibit is rather more complicated.

Exhibit 34.4

J Collins lost the whole of his stock by fire on 17 March 19X9. The last time that a stocktaking had been done was on 31 December 19X8, the last balance sheet date, when it was £1,950 at cost. Purchases from then to 17 March 19X9 amounted to £6,870 and Sales for the period were £9,600. All sales were made at a uniform profit margin of 20 per cent.

First, the trading account can be drawn up with the known figures included. Then the missing figures can be deduced afterwards.

J Collins

Trading Account for the period 1 January 19X9 to 17 March 19X9

		£		£
Sales				9,600
Less Cost of goods sold:				
Opening stock		1,950		
Add Purchases		6,870		
		8,820		
Less Closing stock	(C)	?		
			(B)	?
Gross profit			(A)	?

Now the missing figures can be deduced.

It is known that the gross profit margin is 20 per cent, therefore gross profit (A) is 20% of £9,600 = £1,920.

Now (B) ? + (A) £1,920 = £9,600, so that (B) is the difference, i.e. £7,680.

Now that (B) is known, (C) can be deduced: £8,820 – (C) ? = £7,680, so (C) is the difference, i.e. £1,140.

The figure for goods destroyed by fire, at cost, is therefore £1,140.

Exhibit 34.5

T Scott had the whole of his stock stolen from his warehouse on the night of 20 August 19X6. Also destroyed were his sales and purchases journals, but the sales and purchases ledgers were salvaged. The following facts are known:

(a) Stock was known at the last balance sheet date, 31 March 19X6, to be £12,480 at cost.
(b) Receipts from debtors during the period 1 April to 20 August 19X6 amounted to £31,745. Debtors were: at 31 March 19X6 £14,278, at 20 August 19X6 £12,333.
(c) Payments to creditors during the period 1 April to 20 August 19X6 amounted to £17,270. Creditors were: at 31 March 19X6 £7,633, at 20 August 19X6 £6,289.
(d) The margin on sales has been constant at 25 per cent.

Before we can start to construct a trading account for the period, we need to find out the figures of sales and of purchases. These can be found by drawing up total debtors and total creditors accounts, sales and purchases figures being the difference on the accounts.

Total Creditors

	£		£
Cash and bank	17,270	Balances b/d	7,633
Balances c/d	6,289	Purchases (difference)	15,926
	23,559		23,559

Total Debtors

	£		£
Balances b/d	14,278	Cash and bank	31,745
Sales (difference)	29,800	Balances c/d	12,333
	44,078		44,078

The trading account can now show the figures already known.

Trading Account for the period 1 April to 20 August 19X6

		£	£
Sales			29,800
Less Cost of goods sold:			
Opening stock		12,480	
Add Purchases		15,926	
		28,406	
Less Closing stock	(C)	?	
	(B)		?
Gross profit	(A)		?

Gross profit can be found, as the margin on sales is known to be 25%, therefore (A) = 25% of £29,800 = £7,450.

Cost of goods sold (B) ? + Gross profit £7,450 = £29,800, therefore (B) is £22,350.

£28,406 – (C) ? = (B) £22,350, therefore (C) is £6,056.

The figure for cost of goods stolen is therefore £6,056.

New term

Statement of affairs (p. 333): A statement from which the capital of the owner is deducted by estimating assets and liabilities. Then Capital = Assets – Liabilities.

Main points to remember

1 If the increase in capital over a period is known, and also details of drawings, then the net profit can be deduced without double entry records.

2 The figures needed for purchases and sales can be deduced from a total creditors account and a total debtors account.

Review questions

34.1 B Arkwright started in business on 1 January 19X5 with £10,000 in a bank account. Unfortunately he did not keep proper books of account.

He is forced to submit a calculation of profit for the year ended 31 December 19X5 to the Inspector of Taxes. He ascertains that at 31 December 19X5 he had stock valued at cost £3,950, a motor van which had cost £2,800 during the year and which had depreciated by £550, debtors of £4,970, expenses prepaid of £170, bank balance £2,564, cash balance £55, trade creditors £1,030, and expenses owing £470.

His drawings were: cash £100 per week for 50 weeks, cheque payments £673.

Draw up statements to show the profit or loss for the year.

34.2A J Kirkwood is a dealer who has not kept proper books of account. At 31 August 19X6 his state of affairs was as follows:

	£
Cash	115
Bank balance	2,209
Fixtures	4,000
Stock	16,740
Debtors	11,890
Creditors	9,052
Motor van (at valuation)	3,000

During the year to 31 August 19X7 his drawings amounted to £7,560. Winnings from a football pool £2,800 were put into the business. Extra fixtures were bought for £2,000.

At 31 August 19X7 his assets and liabilities were: Cash £84; Bank overdraft £165; Stock £21,491; Creditors for goods £6,002; Creditors for expenses £236; Fixtures to be depreciated £600; Motor van to be valued at £2,500; Debtors £15,821; Prepaid expenses £72.

Draw up a statement showing the profit and loss made by Kirkwood for the year ended 31 August 19X7.

34.3 Following is a summary of Kelly's bank account for the year ended 31 December 19X7:

	£		£
Balance 1.1.19X7	405	Payments to creditors for goods	29,487
Receipts from debtors	37,936	Rent	1,650
Balance 31.12.19X7	602	Rates	890
		Sundry expenses	375
		Drawings	6,541
	38,943		38,943

All of the business takings have been paid into the bank with the exception of £9,630. Out of this, Kelly has paid wages of £5,472, drawings of £1,164 and purchase of goods £2,994.
The following additional information is available:

	31.12.19X6	31.12.19X7
Stock	13,862	15,144
Creditors for goods	5,624	7,389
Debtors for goods	9,031	8,624
Rates prepaid	210	225
Rent owing	150	–
Fixtures at valuation	2,500	2,250

You are to draw up a set of final accounts for the year ended 31 December 19X7. Show all of your workings.

34.4A J Evans has kept records of his business transactions in a single entry form, but he did not realise that he had to record cash drawings. His bank account for the year 19X8 is as follows:

	£		£
Balance 1.1.19X8	1,890	Cash withdrawn from bank	5,400
Receipts from debtors	44,656	Trade creditors	31,695
Loan from T Hughes	2,000	Rent	2,750
		Rates	1,316
		Drawings	3,095
		Sundry expenses	1,642
		Balance 31.12.19X8	2,648
	48,546		48,546

Records of cash paid were: Sundry expenses £122; Trade creditors £642. Cash sales amounted to £698.
The following information is also available:

	31.12.19X7	31.12.19X8
	£	£
Cash in hand	48	93
Trade creditors	4,896	5,091
Debtors	6,013	7,132
Rent owing	–	250
Rates in advance	282	312
Motor van (at valuation)	2,800	2,400
Stock	11,163	13,021

You are to draw up a trading and profit and loss account for the year ended 31 December 19X8, and a balance sheet as at that date. Show all of your workings.

34.5 On 1 May 19X8 Jenny Barnes, who is a retailer, had the following balances in her books: Premises £70,000; Equipment £8,200; Vehicles £5,100; Stock £9,500; Trade debtors £150.
Jenny does not keep proper books of account, but bank statements covering the 12 months from 1 May 19X8 to 30 April 19X9 were obtained from the bank and summarised as follows:

	£
Money paid into bank:	
Extra capital	8,000
Shop takings	96,500
Received from debtors	1,400
Payments made by cheque:	
Paid for stock purchased	70,500
Purchase of delivery van	6,200
Vehicle running expenses	1,020
Lighting and heating	940
Sales assistants' wages	5,260
Miscellaneous expenses	962

It has been discovered that, in the year ending 30 April 19X9, the owner had paid into bank all shop takings apart from cash used to pay (i) £408 miscellaneous expenses and (ii) £500 per month drawings.

At 30 April 19X9:

£7,600 was owing to suppliers for stock bought on credit.
The amount owed by trade debtors is to be treated as a bad debt. Assume that there had been no sales on credit during the year.
Stock was valued at £13,620.

Depreciation for the year was calculated at £720 (equipment) and £1,000 (vehicles).

You are asked to prepare trading and profit and loss accounts for the year ended 30 April 19X9. (Show all necessary workings separately.)

(*Edexcel Foundation, London Examinations: GCSE*)

34.6A Bill Smithson runs a second-hand furniture business from a shop which he rents. He does not keep complete accounting records, but is able to provide you with the following information about his financial position at 1 April 19X8: Stock of furniture £3,210; Trade debtors £2,643; Trade creditors £1,598; Motor vehicle £5,100; Shop fittings £4,200; Motor vehicle expenses owing £432.

He has also provided the following summary of his bank account for the year ended 31 March 19X9:

	£		£
Balance at 1 Apr 19X8	2,420	Payments of trade creditors	22,177
Cheques received from trade debtors	44,846	Electricity	1,090
Cash sales	3,921	Telephone	360
		Rent	2,000
		Advertising	1,430
		Shop fittings	2,550
		Insurance	946
		Motor vehicle expenses	2,116
		Drawings	16,743
		Balance at 31 Mar 19X9	1,775
	£51,187		£51,187

All cash and cheques received were paid into the bank account immediately.
You find that the following must also be taken into account:

- Depreciation is to be written off the motor vehicle at 20% and off the shop fittings at 10%, calculated on the book values at 1 April 19X8 plus additions during the year.
- At 31 March 19X9 motor vehicle expenses owing were £291 and insurance paid in advance was £177.
- Included in the amount paid for shop fittings were:
  a table bought for £300, which Smithson resold during the year at cost,
  some wooden shelving (cost £250), which Smithson used in building an extension to his house.
  Other balances at 31 March 19X9 were:

	£
Trade debtors	4,012
Trade creditors	2,445
Stock of furniture	4,063

Required:
(*a*) For the year ended 31 March 19X9
    (*i*) calculate Smithson's sales and purchases,
    (*ii*) prepare his trading and profit and loss account.
(*b*) Prepare Smithson's balance sheet as at 31 March 19X9.

(*Midland Examining Group: GCSE*)

34.7 Although Janet Lambert has run a small business for many years, she has never kept adequate accounting records. However, a need to obtain a bank loan for the expansion of the business has necessitated the preparation of 'final' accounts for the year ended 31 August 19X9. As a result, the following information has been obtained after much careful research:

1   Janet Lambert's business assets and liabilities are as follows:

As at	1 September 19X8	31 August 19X9
	£	£
Stock in trade	8,600	16,800
Debtors for sales	3,900	4,300
Creditors for purchases	7,400	8,900
Rent prepaid	300	420
Electricity accrued due	210	160
Balance at bank	2,300	1,650
Cash in hand	360	330

2   All takings have been banked after deducting the following payments:

Cash drawings – Janet Lambert has not kept a record of cash drawings, but suggests these will be in the region of	£8,000
Casual labour	£1,200
Purchase of goods for resale	£1,800

Note: Takings have been the source of all amounts banked.

3   Bank payments during the year ended 31 August 19X9 have been summarised as follows:

	£
Purchases	101,500
Rent	5,040
Electricity	1,390
Delivery costs (to customers)	3,000
Casual labour	6,620

4   It has been established that a gross profit of $33\frac{1}{3}\%$ on cost has been obtained on all goods sold.

5   Despite her apparent lack of precise accounting records, Janet Lambert is able to confirm that she has taken out of the business during the year under review goods for her own use costing £600.

Required:
(a) Prepare a computation of total purchases for the year ended 31 August 19X9.
(b) Prepare a trading and profit and loss account for the year ended 31 August 19X9 and a balance sheet as at that date, both in as much detail as possible.
(c) Explain why it is necessary to introduce accruals and prepayments into accounting.

(*Association of Accounting Technicians*)

34.8A Jean Smith, who retails wooden ornaments, has been so busy since she commenced business on 1 April 19X5 that she has neglected to keep adequate accounting records. Jean's opening capital consisted of her life savings of £15,000 which she used to open a business bank account. The transactions in this bank account during the year ended 31 March 19X6 have been summarised from the bank account as follows:

	£
Receipts:	
Loan from John Peacock, uncle	10,000
Takings	42,000
Payments:	
Purchases of goods for resale	26,400
Electricity for period to 31 December 19X5	760
Rent of premises for 15 months to 30 June 19X6	3,500
Rates of premises for the year ended 31 March 19X6	1,200
Wages of assistants	14,700
Purchase of van, 1 October 19X5	7,600
Purchase of holiday caravan for Jean Smith's private use	8,500
Van licence and insurance, payments covering a year	250

According to the bank account, the balance in hand on 31 March 19X6 was £4,090 in Jean Smith's favour.

While the intention was to bank all takings intact, it now transpires that, in addition to cash drawings, the following payments were made out of takings before bankings:

	£
Van running expenses	890
Postages, stationery and other sundry expenses	355

On 31 March 19X6, takings of £640 awaited banking; this was done on 1 April 19X6. It has been discovered that amounts paid into the bank of £340 on 29 March 19X6 were not credited to Jean's bank account until 2 April 19X6 and a cheque of £120, drawn on 28 March 19X6 for purchases, was not paid until 10 April 19X6. The normal rate of gross profit on the goods sold by Jean Smith is 50% on sales. However, during the year a purchase of ornamental goldfish costing £600 proved to be unpopular with customers and therefore the entire stock bought had to be sold at cost price.

Interest at the rate of 5% per annum is payable on each anniversary of the loan from John Peacock on 1 January 19X6.

Depreciation is to be provided on the van on the straight line basis; it is estimated that the van will be disposed of after five years' use for £100.

The stock of goods for resale at 31 March 19X6 has been valued at cost at £1,900.

Creditors for purchases at 31 March 19X6 amounted to £880 and electricity charges accrued due at that date were £180.

Trade debtors at 31 March 19X6 totalled £2,300.

Required:
Prepare a trading and profit and loss account for the year ended 31 March 19X6 and a balance sheet as at that date.

(Association of Accounting Technicians)

34.9 David Denton set up in business as a plumber a year ago, and he has asked you to act as his accountant. His instructions to you are in the form of the following letter.

Dear Henry,

I was pleased when you agreed to act as my accountant and look forward to your first visit to check my records. The proposed fee of £250 p.a. is acceptable. I regret that the paperwork for the work done during the year is incomplete. I started my business on 1 January last, and put £6,500 into a business bank account on that date. I brought my van into the firm at that time, and reckon that it was worth £3,600 then. I think it will last another three years after the end of the first year of business use.

I have drawn £90 per week from the business bank account during the year. In my trade it is difficult to take a holiday, but my wife managed to get away for a while. The travel agent's bill for £280 was paid out of the business account. I bought the lease of the yard and office for £6,500. The lease has ten years to run, and the rent is only £300 a year payable in advance on the anniversary of the date of purchase, which was 1 April. I borrowed £4,000 on that day from Aunt Jane to help pay for the lease. I have agreed to pay her 10% interest per annum, but have been too busy to do anything about this yet.

I was lucky enough to meet Miss Prism shortly before I set up on my own, and she has worked for me as an office organiser right from the start. She is paid a salary of £3,000 p.a. All the bills for the year have been carefully preserved in a tool box, and we analysed them last week. The materials I have bought cost me £9,600, but I reckon there was £580 worth left in the yard on 31 December. I have not yet paid for them all yet, I think we owed £714 to the suppliers on 31 December. I was surprised to see that I had spent £4,800 on plumbing equipment, but it should last me five years or so. Electricity bills received up to 30 September came to £1,122; but motor expenses were £912, and general expenses £1,349 for the year. The insurance premium for the year to 31 March next was £800. All these have been paid by cheque but Miss Prism has lost the rate demand. I expect the Local Authority will send a reminder soon since I have not yet paid. I seem to remember that rates came to £180 for the year to 31 March next.

Miss Prism sent out bills to my customers for work done, but some of them are very slow to pay. Altogether the charges made were £29,863, but only £25,613 had been received by 31 December. Miss Prism thinks that 10% of the remaining bills are not likely to be paid. Other customers for jobs too small to bill have paid £3,418 in cash for work done, but I only managed to bank £2,600 of this money. I used £400 of the difference to pay the family's grocery bills, and Miss Prism used the rest for general expenses, except for £123 which was left over in a drawer in the office on 31 December.

Kind regards,

Yours sincerely,

David.

You are required to draw up a profit and loss account for the year ended 31 December, and a balance sheet as at that date.

(*Association of Chartered Certified Accountants*)

34.10 The following are summaries of the cash book and bank accounts of J Duncan who does not keep his books using the double entry system.

Bank Summary	£	£
Balance on 1 January 19X8		8,000
Receipts		
Debtors	26,000	
Cash banked	4,100	30,100
		38,100
Payments		
Trade creditors	18,500	
Rent	1,400	
Machinery	7,500	
Wages	6,100	
Insurance	1,450	
Debtors (dishonoured cheque)	250	
Loan Interest	300	35,500
Balance on 31 December 19X8		2,600

Cash Summary	£	£
Balance on 1 January 19X8		300
Receipts		
Cash sales	14,000	
Debtors	400	14,400
		14,700
Payments		
Drawings	9,500	
Repairs	300	
Electricity	750	
Cash Banked	4,100	14,650
Balance on 31 December 19X8		50

The following referred to 19X8	£
Bad debts written off	400
Discount received	350
Goods withdrawn by J Duncan for own use	300
Credit note issued	1,200

The following additional information is available.	1 January 19X8 £	31 December 19X8 £
Stocks	4,100	3,200
Machinery	12,600	15,900
Rent prepaid	200	
Rent owing		250
Debtors	6,300	5,000
Creditors	2,400	2,500
Loan from Bank at 8%	5,000	5,000
Loan interest owing		100

You are required to:
(*a*) Calculate the value of J Duncan's capital on 1 January 19X8.
(*b*) Prepare the Trading and Profit and Loss Accounts for the year ended 31 December 19X8.

(*Scottish Qualifications Authority*)

34.11 Using the information in Question 34.10, prepare J Duncan's Balance Sheet as at 31 December 19X8.

34.12A The following are summaries of the cash book and bank accounts of P Maclaran who does not keep her books using the double entry system.

Bank Summary	£	£
Balance on 1 January 19X8		6,000
Receipts		
Debtors	35,000	
Cash banked	2,200	37,200
		43,200
Payments		
Trade creditors	31,000	
Rent	1,100	
Machinery	3,400	
Wages	9,200	
Insurance	850	
Debtors (dishonoured cheque)	80	
Loan Interest	500	46,130
Balance on 31 December 19X8		(2,930)

Cash Summary	£	£
Balance on 1 January 19X8		60
Receipts		
Cash sales	9,700	
Debtors	1,100	10,800
		10,860
Payments		
Drawings	6,600	
Repairs	1,400	
Electricity	570	
Cash Banked	2,200	10,770
Balance on 31 December 19X8		90

The following referred to 19X8	£
Bad debts written off	240
Discount received	600
Goods withdrawn by P Maclaran for own use	1,200
Credit note issued	640

The following additional information is available.	1 January 19X8	31 December 19X8
	£	£
Stocks	2,300	5,400
Machinery	9,800	10,400
Rent prepaid		100
Rent owing	150	
Debtors	8,100	9,200
Creditors	5,700	4,800
Loan from Bank at 10%	7,000	7,000
Loan interest owing		200

You are required to:
(a) Calculate the value of P Maclaran's capital on 1 January 19X8.
(b) Prepare the Trading and Profit and Loss Accounts for the year ended 31 December 19X8.

34.13A Using the information in Question 34.12, prepare P Maclaran's Balance Sheet as at 31 December 19X8.

35

Receipts and payments accounts and income and expenditure accounts

Objectives

After you have studied this chapter, you should:

- *be able to draw up income and expenditure accounts and balance sheets for non-trading organisations*

- *be able to calculate profit and losses from special activities and incorporate them into the final accounts*

- *understand that various forms of revenue may need special treatment*

35.1 Non-trading organisations

Clubs, associations and other non-profit-making organisations do not have trading and profit and loss accounts drawn up for them, as their main purpose is not trading or profit making. They are run so that their members can do things such as play football or chess. The kind of final accounts prepared by these organisations are either **receipts and payments accounts** or **income and expenditure accounts**.

35.2 Receipts and payments accounts

Receipts and payments accounts are a summary of the cash book for the period. Exhibit 35.1 is an example.

Exhibit 35.1

The Homers Running Club

Receipts and Payments Account for the year ended 31 December 19X5

Receipts	£	Payments	£
Bank balance 1.1.19X5	236	Groundsman's wages	728
Subscriptions received in 19X5	1,148	Sports stadium expenses	296
Rent received	116	Committee expenses	58
		Printing and stationery	33
		Bank balance 31.12.19X5	385
	1,500		1,500

35.3 Income and expenditure accounts

When assets are owned, and there are liabilities, the receipts and payments account is not a good way of drawing up final accounts. Other than the cash received and paid out, it shows only the cash balances. The other assets and liabilities are not shown at all. What is required is:

1 a balance sheet, and
2 an account showing whether the association's capital has increased.

In a profit-making firm, **2** would be a trading and profit and loss account. In a non-profit organisation, **2** would be an income and expenditure account.

An income and expenditure account follows the same rules as trading and profit and loss accounts. The only differences are the terms used. A comparison now follows:

Terms used

Profit-making firm	Non-profit organisation
1 Trading and Profit and Loss Account	1 Income and Expenditure Account
2 Net Profit	2 Surplus of Income over Expenditure
3 Net Loss	3 Excess of Expenditure over Income

35.4 Profit or loss for a special purpose

Sometimes there are reasons why a non-profit-making organisation would want a profit and loss account.

This is where something is done to make a profit. The profit is not to be kept, but used to pay for the main purpose of the organisation.

For instance, a football club may have discos or dances which people pay to go to. Any profit from these helps to pay football expenses. For these discos and dances a trading and profit and loss account would be drawn up. Any profit (or loss) would be transferred to the income and expenditure account.

35.5 Accumulated fund

A sole trader or a partnership would have capital accounts. A non-profit-making organisation would instead have an **accumulated fund**. It is in effect the same as a capital account, as it is the difference between assets and liabilities.

In a sole trader or partnership:

Capital + Liabilities = Assets

In a non-profit-making organisation:

Accumulated Fund + Liabilities = Assets

35.6 Drawing up income and expenditure accounts

We can now look at the preparation of an income and expenditure account and a balance sheet of a club in Exhibit 35.2. A separate trading account is to be prepared for a bar, where refreshments are sold to make a profit.

Probably the majority of clubs and associations keep their accounts using single entry methods. This example will therefore be from single entry records, using the principles described in the last chapter.

Exhibit 35.2

Long Lane Football Club

Receipts and Payments Account for the year ended 31 December 19X6

Receipts		£	Payments		£
Bank balance 1.1.19X6		524	Payment for bar supplies		3,962
Subscriptions received for			Wages:		
19X5 (arrears)		55	Groundsman and assistant		939
19X6		1,236	Barman		624
19X7 (in advance)		40	Bar expenses		234
Bar sales		5,628	Repairs to stands		119
Donations received		120	Ground upkeep		229
			Secretary's expenses		138
			Transport costs		305
			Bank balance 31.12.19X6		1,053
		7,603			7,603

The treasurer of the Long Lane Football Club has prepared a receipts and payments account, but members have complained about the inadequacy of such an account. He therefore asks an accountant to prepare a trading account for the bar, and an income and expenditure account and a balance sheet. The treasurer gives the accountant a copy of the receipts and payments account together with information of assets and liabilities at the beginning and end of the year:

Notes:		*31.12.19X5*	*31.12.19X6*
1		£	£
	Stocks in the bar – at cost	496	558
	Owing for bar supplies	294	340
	Bar expenses owing	25	36
	Transport costs	–	65

2   The land and football stands were valued at 31 December 19X5 at: land £4,000; football stands £2,000; the stands are to be depreciated by 10 per cent per annum.

3   The equipment at 31 December 19X5 was valued at £550, and is to be depreciated at 20 per cent per annum.

4   Subscriptions owing by members amounted to £55 on 31 December 19X5, and £66 on 31 December 19X6.

From this information the accountant drew up the following accounts and statements.

Stage 1: Draw up a Statement of Affairs as at 31 December 19X5.

Statement of Affairs as at 31 December 19X5

	£	£	£
Fixed assets			
Land			4,000
Stands			2,000
Equipment			550
			6,550
Current assets			
Stock in bar		496	
Debtors for subscriptions		55	
Cash at bank		524	
		1,075	
Less Current liabilities			
Creditors	294		
Bar expenses owing	25	319	
Working capital			756
			7,306
Financed by:			
Accumulated fund (difference)			7,306
			7,306

Stage 2: Draw up a Bar Trading Account.

Long Lane Football Club

Bar Trading Account for the year ended 31 December 19X6

	£	£
Sales		5,628
Less Cost of goods sold:		
Stock 1.1.19X6	496	
Add Purchases*	4,008	
	4,504	
Less Stock 31.12.19X6	558	3,946
Gross profit		1,682
Less Bar expenses*	245	
Barman's wages	624	869
Net profit to income and expenditure account		813

*Workings on purchases and bar expenses figures:

Purchases Control

	£		£
Cash	3,962	Balances (creditors) b/d	294
Balances c/d	340	Trading account (difference)	4,008
	4,302		4,302

Bar Expenses

	£		£
Cash	234	Balance b/d	25
Balance c/d	36	Trading account (difference)	245
	270		270

Stage 3: Draw up the Final Accounts.

Long Lane Football Club

Income and Expenditure Account for the year ended 31 December 19X6

Income	£	£	£
Subscriptions for 19X6*			1,302
Profit from the bar			813
Donations received			120
			2,235
Less Expenditure			
Wages – Groundsman and assistant		939	
Repairs to stands		119	
Ground upkeep		229	
Secretary's expenses		138	
Transport costs*		370	
Depreciation			
Stands	200		
Equipment	110	310	2,105
Surplus of income over expenditure			130

*Workings on transport costs and subscriptions received figures:

Transport Costs

	£		£
Cash	305	Income and expenditure	
Accrued c/d	65	account	370
	370		370

Subscriptions Received

	£		£
Balance (debtors) b/d	55	Cash 19X5	55
Income and expenditure		19X6	1,236
account (difference)	1,302	19X7	40
Balance (in advance) c/d	40	Balance (owing) c/d	66
	1,397		1,397

It will be noted that subscriptions received in advance are carried down as a credit balance to the following period.

The Long Lane Football Club

Balance Sheet as at 31 December 19X6

	£	£	£
Fixed assets			
Land at valuation			4,000
Pavilion at valuation		2,000	
Less Depreciation		200	1,800
Equipment at valuation		550	
Less Depreciation		110	440
Current assets			6,240
Stock of bar supplies		558	
Debtors for subscriptions		66	
Cash at bank		1,053	
		1,677	
Less Current liabilities			
Creditors for bar supplies	340		
Bar expenses owing	36		
Transport costs owing	65		
Subscriptions received in advance	40	481	
Working capital			1,196
			7,436
Financed by:			
Accumulated fund			
Balance as at 1.1.19X6			7,306
Add Surplus of income over expenditure			130
			7,436

35.7 Outstanding subscriptions and the prudence concept

So far we have treated subscriptions owing as being an asset. However, as any treasurer of a club would tell you, most subscriptions that have been owing for a long time are never paid. A lot of clubs do not therefore bring in unpaid subscriptions as an asset in the balance sheet. This is obviously keeping to the prudence concept which states that assets should not be over-valued. They are therefore ignored by these clubs for final accounts purposes.

However, in an examination a student should assume that subscriptions owing are to be brought into the final accounts unless instructions to the contrary are given.

Exhibit 35.3 shows an instance where subscriptions in arrears and in advance occur at the beginning and close of a period.

Exhibit 35.3

An amateur theatre organisation charges its members an annual subscription of £20 per member. It accrues for subscriptions owing at the end of each year and also adjusts for subscriptions received in advance.

(A) On 1 January 19X2, 18 members owed £360 for the year 19X1.
(B) In December 19X1, 4 members paid £80 for the year 19X2.

(C) During the year 19X2 we received cash for subscriptions £7,420.

For 19X1	£360	
For 19X2	£6,920	
For 19X3	£140	£7,420

(D) At close of 31 December 19X2, 11 members had not paid their 19X2 subscriptions.

Subscriptions

19X2			£	19X2			£
Jan 1	Owing b/d	(A)	360	Jan 1	Prepaid b/d	(B)	80
Dec 31	Income and expenditure		*7,220	Dec 31	Bank	(C)	7,420
Dec 31	Prepaid c/d	(C)	140	Dec 31	Owing c/d	(D)	220
			7,720				7,720
19X3				19X3			
Jan 1	Owing b/d	(D)	220	Jan 1	Prepaid b/d	(C)	140

* Difference between two sides of the account.

35.8 Life membership

In some clubs and societies members can make a payment for life membership. This means that by paying a fairly substantial amount now the member can enjoy the facilities of the club for the rest of his life.

Such a receipt should not be treated as income in the income and expenditure account solely in the year in which the member paid the money. It should be credited to a life membership account, and transfers should be made from that account to the credit of the income and expenditure account of an appropriate amount annually.

Exactly what is meant by an appropriate amount is decided by the committee of the club or society. The usual basis is to establish, on average, how long members will continue to use the benefits of the club. To take an extreme case, if a club was in existence which could not be joined until one achieved the age of 70, then the expected number of years' use of the club on average per member would be relatively few. Another club, such as a golf club, where a fair proportion of the members joined when reasonably young, and where the game is capable of being played by members until and during old age, would expect a much higher average of years of use per member. The simple matter is that the club should decide for itself.

In an examination the candidate has to follow the instructions set for him by the examiner. The credit balance remaining on the account, after the transfer of the agreed amount has been made to the credit of the income and expenditure account, should be shown on the balance sheet as a liability. It is, after all, the liability of the club to provide amenities for the member without any further payment by him.

35.9 Donations

Any donations received are usually shown as income in the year that they are received.

35.10 Entrance fees

New members often have to pay an entrance fee in the year that they join, in addition to the membership fee for that year. Entrance fees are normally included as income in the year that they are received. The club could, however, decide to treat them differently. It all depends on the circumstances.

New terms

Accumulated fund (p. 353): A form of capital account for a non-profit-making organisation.

Income and expenditure account (p. 352): An account for a non-profit-making organisation to find the surplus or loss made during a period.

Receipts and payments account (p. 351): A summary of the cash book of a non-profit-making organisation.

Main points to remember

1   A receipts and payments account does not show the full financial position of an organisation, except for one where the only asset is cash.

2   An income and expenditure account is drawn up to show either the surplus of income over expenditure or the excess of expenditure over income. These are the same as 'profit' or 'loss' in a profit-based organisation.

3   The accumulated fund is basically the same as a capital account.

4   Although the main object of the organisation is non-profit making, certain activities may be run at a profit (or may lose money) in order to help finance the main objects.

5   In an examination you should treat subscriptions owing at the end of a period in the same way as debtors, unless told otherwise.

6   Donations are usually treated as income in the period in which they are received.

7   Entrance fees are usually treated as income in the year in which they are received.

8   The treatment of life membership fees is purely at the discretion of the organisation.

Review questions

35.1 A summary of the Uppertown Football Club is shown below. From it, and the additional information, you are to construct an income and expenditure account for the year ended 31 December 19X4, and a balance sheet as at that date.

Cash Book Summary

	£		£
Balance 1.1.19X4	180	Purchase of equipment	125
Collections at matches	1,650	Rent for football pitch	300
Profit on sale of refreshments	315	Printing and stationery	65
		Secretary's expenses	144
		Repairs to equipment	46
		Groundsman's wages	520
		Miscellaneous expenses	66
		Balance 31.12.19X4	879
	2,145		2,145

Further information:
(*i*)   At 1.1.19X4 equipment was valued at £500.
(*ii*) Depreciate all equipment 20 per cent for the year 19X4.
(*iii*) At 31.12.19X4 rent paid in advance was £60.
(*iv*) At 31.12.19X4 there was £33 owing for printing.

35.2A The following trial balance of Haven Golf Club was extracted from the books as on 31 December 19X8:

	Dr £	Cr £
Clubhouse	21,000	
Equipment	6,809	
Profits from raffles		4,980
Subscriptions received		18,760
Wages of bar staff	2,809	
Bar stocks 1 January 19X8	1,764	
Bar purchases and sales	11,658	17,973
Greenkeepers' wages	7,698	
Golf professional's salary	6,000	
General expenses	580	
Cash at bank	1,570	
Accumulated fund at 1 January 19X8		18,175
	59,888	59,888

Notes:
(*i*)   Bar purchases and sales were on a cash basis. Bar stocks at 31 December 19X8 were valued at £989.
(*ii*) Subscriptions paid in advance by members at 31 December 19X8 amounted to £180.
(*iii*) Provide for depreciation of equipment £760.

You are required to:
(*a*) Draw up the bar trading account for the year ended 31 December 19X8.
(*b*) Draw up the income and expenditure account for the year ended 31 December 19X8, and a balance sheet as at 31 December 19X8.

35.3 Read the following and answer the questions below.

On 1 January 19X8 The Happy Haddock Angling Club had the following assets:

	£
Cash at bank	200
Snack bar stocks	800
Club house buildings	12,500

During the year to 31 December 19X8 the Club received and paid the following amounts:

Receipts	£	Payments	£
Subscriptions 19X8	3,500	Rent and rates	1,500
Subscriptions 19X9	380	Extension to club house	8,000
Snack bar income	6,000	Snack bar purchases	3,750
Visitors' fees	650	Secretarial expenses	240
Loan from bank	5,500	Interest on loan	260
Competition fees	820	Snack bar expenses	600
		Games equipment	2,000

Notes: The snack bar stock on 31 December 19X8 was £900.
The games equipment should be depreciated by 20%.

(a) Prepare an income and expenditure account for the year ended 31 December 19X8. Show, either in this account or separately, the snack bar profit or loss.
(b) Prepare a balance sheet as at 31 December 19X8.

(*Midland Examining Group: GCSE*)

35.4A The treasurer of the City Sports Club has produced the following receipts and payments account for the year ended 31 December 19X7:

Receipts	£	Payments	£
Balance at bank 1 January 19X7	1,298	Coffee supplies bought	1,456
Subscriptions received	3,790	Wages of attendants and cleaners	1,776
Profits and dances	186	Rent of rooms	887
Profit on exhibition	112	New equipment bought	565
Coffee bar takings	2,798	Travelling expenses of teams	673
Sale of equipment	66	Balance at bank 31 December 19X7	2,893
	8,250		8,250

Notes:
(i) Coffee bar stocks were valued: 31 December 19X6 £59, 31 December 19X7 £103. There was nothing owing for coffee bar stocks on either of these dates.
(ii) On 1 January 19X7 the club's equipment was valued at £2,788. Included in this figure, valued at £77, was the equipment sold during the year for £66.
(iii) The amount to be charged for depreciation of equipment for the year is £279. This is in addition to the loss on equipment sold during the year.
(iv) Subscriptions owing by members 31 December 19X6 nil, at 31 December 19X7 £29.

You are required to:
(a) Draw up the coffee bar trading account for the year ended 31 December 19X7. For this purpose £650 of the wages is to be charged to this account; the remainder will be charged in the income and expenditure account.
(b) Calculate the accumulated fund as at 1 January 19X7.
(c) Draw up the income and expenditure account for the year ended 31 December 19X7, and a balance sheet as at 31 December 19X7.

35.5   The following is a summary of the receipts and payments of the Miniville Rotary Club during the year ended 31 July 19X9.

Miniville Rotary Club

Receipts and Payments Account for the year ended 31 July 19X9

	£		£
Cash and bank balances b/f	210	Secretarial expenses	163
Sales of competition tickets	437	Rent	1,402
Members' subscriptions	1,987	Visiting speakers' expenses	1,275
Donations	177	Donations to charities	35
Refund of rent	500	Prizes for competitions	270
Balance c/f	13	Stationery and printing	179
	£3,324		£3,324

The following valuations are also available:

as at 31 July	19X8	19X9
	£	£
Equipment (original cost £1,420)	975	780
Subscriptions in arrears	65	85
Subscriptions in advance	10	37
Owing to suppliers of competition prizes	58	68
Stocks of competition prizes	38	46

Required:
(a) Calculate the value of the accumulated fund of the Miniville Rotary Club as at 1 August 19X8.
(b) Reconstruct the following accounts for the year ended 31 July 19X9:
   (i)   the subscriptions account,
   (ii) the competition prizes account.
(c) Prepare an income and expenditure account for the Miniville Rotary Club for the year ended 31 July 19X9 and a balance sheet as at that date.

(*Association of Accounting Technicians*)

35.6A   The Milham Theatre Club has been in existence for a number of years. Members pay an annual subscription of £15 which entitles them to join trips to professional productions at a reduced rate.

On 1 February 19X9 the Club's assets and liabilities were as follows:

Cash in hand £80, Bank balance (overdrawn) £180, Subscriptions in arrears £150, Savings account with local building society £1,950, Amount owing for coach hire £60.

Required:
(a) A *detailed* calculation of the Milham Theatre Club's accumulated fund at 1 February 19X9.

The Club's treasurer was able to present the following information at 31 January 19X8:

Receipts and Payments Accounts for year ended 31 January 19X8

	£	£
Opening balances		
Cash in hand	80	
Cash at bank (overdrawn)*	(180)	
		(100)
Receipts		
Subscriptions		
for year ended 31 January 19X7	120	
for year ended 31 January 19X8	1,620	
for year ended 31 January 19X9	165	
Gift from member	1,000	
Interest on Building Society Account	140	
Theatre outings		
receipts from members for theatre tickets	2,720	
receipts from members for coach travel	1,240	
		7,005
		6,905
Payments		
Transfer to Building Society Account	1,210	
Theatre trips		
tickets	3,120	
coach hire	1,540	
Secretarial and administrative expenses	55	
		5,925
		980
Closing balances		
cash in hand	35	
cash at bank	945	
		980

- On 31 January 19X8 the club committee decided to write off any arrears of subscriptions for the year ended 31 January 19X7; the membership secretary reported that £75 is due for subscriptions for the year ended 31 January 19X8.
- The treasurer has calculated that the full amount of interest receivable on the building society account for the year ended 31 January 19X8 is £155.
- The club committee has decided that the gift should be capitalised.

Required:
(b) An account showing the surplus or deficit made by the Milham Theatre Club on theatre trips.
(c) An income and expenditure account for the Milham Theatre Club for the year ended 31 January 19X8.
(d) An *extract* from the Milham Theatre Club's balance sheet as at 31 January 19X8, showing the accumulated fund and current liability sections only.

The club committee have been concerned by the fact that the club's income has been steadily declining over recent years.

Required:
(e) Advice for the committee on *four* ways in which they could improve the club's income.

(Southern Examining Group: GCSE)

*Note: Figures in brackets represent minus amounts.

35.7   The accounting records of the Happy Tickers Sports and Social Club are in a mess. You manage to find the following information to help you prepare the accounts for the year to 31 December 19X8.

Summarised Balance Sheet 31 December 19X7

	£		£
Half-share in motorised roller	600	Insurance (3 months)	150
New sports equipment unsold	1,000	Subscriptions 19X8	120
Used sports equipment at valuation	700	Life subscriptions	1,400
Rent (2 months)	200		1,670
Subscriptions 19X7	60	Accumulated fund	2,900
Café stocks	800		
Cash and bank	1,210		
	4,570		4,570

Receipts in the year to 31 December 19X8:	£
Subscriptions – 19X7	40
– 19X8	1,100
– 19X9	80
– Life	200
From sales of new sports equipment	900
From sales of used sports equipment	14
Café takings	4,660
	6,994

Payments in the year to 31 December 19X8:	£
Rent (for 12 months)	1,200
Insurance (for 18 months)	900
To suppliers of sports equipment	1,000
To café suppliers	1,900
Wages of café manager	2,000
Total cost of repairing motorised roller	450
	7,450

Notes:

(*i*)   Ownership and all expenses of the motorised roller are agreed to be shared equally with the Carefree Conveyancers Sports and Social Club which occupies a nearby site. The roller cost a total of £2,000 on 1 January 19X6 and had an estimated life of 10 years.

(*ii*)   Life subscriptions are brought into income equally over 10 years, in a scheme begun 5 years ago in 19X3. Since the scheme began the cost of £200 per person has been constant. Prior to 31 December 19X7 10 life subscriptions had been received.

(*iii*)   Four more annual subscriptions of £20 each had been promised relating to 19X8, but not yet received. Annual subscriptions promised but unpaid are carried forward for a maximum of 12 months.

(*iv*)   New sports equipment is sold to members at cost plus 50%. Used equipment is sold off to members at book valuation. Half the sports equipment bought in the year (all from a cash and carry supplier) has been used within the club, and half made available for sale, new, to members. The 'used equipment at valuation' figure in the 31 December 19X8 balance sheet is to remain at £700.

(*v*)   Closing café stocks are £850, and £80 is owed to suppliers at 31 December 19X8.

Required:

(*a*) Calculate the profit on café operations and the profit on sale of sports equipment.

(*b*) Prepare a statement of subscription income for 19X8.

(*c*) Prepare an income and expenditure statement for the year to 31 December 19X8, and balance sheet as at 31 December 19X8.

(*d*) Why do life subscriptions appear as a liability?

(*Association of Chartered Certified Accountants*)

36

Manufacturing accounts

Objectives

After you have studied this chapter, you should be able to:

- *calculate prime cost and production cost of goods manufactured*
- *draw up manufacturing accounts*
- *adjust the accounts in respect of work in progress*
- *understand and calculate a further five methods of provisions for depreciation*

36.1 Manufacturing: not retailing

We now have to deal with firms which are manufacturers. For these firms a **manufacturing account** is prepared in addition to the trading and profit and loss accounts.

36.2 Divisions of costs

In a manufacturing firm the costs are divided into different types. These may be summarised in chart form as follows:

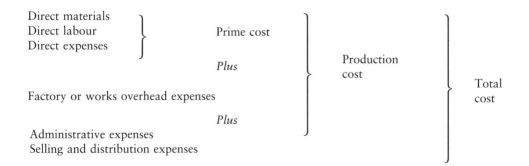

Direct materials
Direct labour
Direct expenses
} Prime cost

Plus

Factory or works overhead expenses

Plus

Administrative expenses
Selling and distribution expenses

Production cost

Total cost

36.3 Direct and indirect costs

When you see the words **direct costs** you know that it has been possible to trace the costs of making an item to the item being manufactured. If it cannot easily be traced to the item being manufactured, then it is an indirect expense and will be included under factory overhead expenses.

For example, the wages of a machine operator making a particular item will be direct labour. The wages of a foreman in charge of many men on different jobs will be indirect labour, and will be part of factory overhead expenses. Other instances of costs being direct costs:

1 Cost of direct materials will include carriage inwards on raw materials.
2 Hire of special machinery for a job.

36.4 Factory overhead expenses

Factory overhead costs are all those costs which occur in the factory where production is being done, but which cannot easily be traced to the items being manufactured. Examples are:

- Wages of cleaners.
- Wages of crane drivers.
- Rent and rates of the factory.
- Depreciation of plant and machinery.
- Costs of operating fork-lift trucks.
- Factory power.
- Factory lighting.

36.5 Administration expenses

Administration expenses consist of such items as managers' salaries, legal and accountancy charges, the depreciation of accounting machinery and secretarial salaries.

36.6 Selling and distribution expenses

Selling and distribution expenses are items such as sales staff's salaries and commission, carriage outwards, depreciation of delivery vans, advertising and display expenses.

36.7 Format of final accounts

Manufacturing account part

This is debited with the production cost of goods completed during the accounting period. It contains costs of:

- Direct materials.
- Direct labour.
- Direct expenses.
- Factory overhead expenses.

When completed this account will show the total of production cost. This figure will then be transferred down to the trading account.

Trading account part

This account includes:

- Production cost brought down from the manufacturing account.
- Opening and closing stocks of finished goods.
- Sales.

When completed this account will disclose the gross profit. This will then be carried down to the profit and loss account part.

The manufacturing account and the trading account can be shown in the form of a diagram:

Manufacturing Account

	£
Production costs for the period:	
Direct materials	xxx
Direct labour	xxx
Direct expenses	xxx
Production cost of goods completed c/d to trading account	xxx

Trading Account

		£	£
Sales			
Less Production cost of goods sold:			
Opening stock of finished goods	(A)	xxx	
Add Production costs of goods completed b/d		xxx	
		xxx	
Less Closing stock of finished goods	(B)	xxx	xxx
Gross profit			xxx

(A) is production costs of goods unsold in previous period
(B) is production costs of goods unsold at end of the period

Profit and loss account part

This account includes:

- Gross profit brought down from the trading account.
- All administration expenses.
- All selling and distribution expenses.

When completed, this account will show the net profit.

36.8 A worked example of a manufacturing account

Exhibit 36.1 shows the necessary details for a manufacturing account. It has been assumed that there were no partly completed units (known as **work in progress**) either at the beginning or end of the period.

Exhibit 36.1

Details of production cost for the year ended 31 December 19X7:

	£
1 January 19X7, stock of raw materials	500
31 December 19X7, stock of raw materials	700
Raw materials purchased	8,000
Manufacturing (direct) wages	21,000
Royalties	150
Indirect wages	9,000
Rent of factory – excluding administration and selling and distribution blocks	440
Depreciation of plant and machinery in factory	400
General indirect expenses	310

Manufacturing Account for the year ended 31 December 19X7

	£	£
Stock of raw materials 1.1.19X7		500
Add Purchases		8,000
		8,500
Less Stock of raw materials 31.12.19X7		700
Cost of raw materials consumed		7,800
Manufacturing wages		21,000
Royalties		150
Prime cost		28,950
Factory overhead expenses		
Rent	440	
Indirect wages	9,000	
General expenses	310	
Depreciation of plant and machinery	400	10,150
Production cost of goods completed c/d		39,100

Sometimes, if a firm has produced less than the customers have demanded, then the firm may well have bought an outside supply of finished goods. In this case, the trading account will have both a figure for purchases and a figure for production cost of goods completed.

36.9 Work in progress

The production cost to be carried down to the trading account is that of production cost of goods completed during the period. If items have not been completed, they cannot be sold. Therefore, they should not appear in the trading account.

For instance, if we have the following information, we can calculate the transfer to the trading account:

	£
Total production costs expended during the year	5,000
Production costs last year on goods not completed last year, but completed in this year (work in progress)	300
Production costs this year on goods which were not completed by the year end (work in progress)	440

The calculation is:

	£
Total production costs expended this year	5,000
Add Costs from last year, in respect of goods completed in this year (work in progress)	300
	5,300
Less Costs in this year, for goods to be completed next year (work in progress)	440
Production costs expended on goods completed this year	4,860

36.10 Another worked example

Exhibit 36.2

	£
1 January 19X7, Stock of raw materials	800
31 December 19X7, Stock of raw materials	1,050
1 January 19X7, Work in progress	350
31 December 19X7, Work in progress	420
Year to 31 December 19X7:	
Wages: Direct	3,960
Indirect	2,550
Purchase of raw materials	8,700
Fuel and power	990
Direct expenses	140
Lubricants	300
Carriage inwards on raw materials	200
Rent of factory	720
Depreciation of factory plant and machinery	420
Internal transport expenses	180
Insurance of factory buildings and plant	150
General factory expenses	330

Manufacturing Account for the year ended 31 December 19X7

	£	£
Stock of raw materials 1.1.19X7		800
Add Purchases		8,700
" Carriage inwards		200
		9,700
Less Stock of raw materials 31.12.19X7		1,050
Cost of raw materials consumed		8,650
Direct wages		3,960
Direct expenses		140
Prime cost		12,750
Factory overhead expenses:		
Fuel and power	990	
Indirect wages	2,550	
Lubricants	300	
Rent	720	
Depreciation of plant	420	
Internal transport expenses	180	
Insurance	150	
General factory expenses	330	5,640
		18,390
Add Work in progress 1.1.19X7		350
		18,740
Less Work in progress 31.12.19X7		420
Production cost of goods completed c/d		18,320

The trading account is concerned with finished goods. If in the foregoing exhibit there had been £3,500 stock of finished goods at 1 January 19X7 and £4,400 at 31 December 19X7, and the sales of finished goods amounted to £25,000, then the trading account would appear:

Trading Account for the year ended 31 December 19X7

	£	£
Sales		25,000
Less Cost of goods sold:		
Stock of finished goods 1.1.19X7	3,500	
Add Production cost of goods completed b/d	18,320	
	21,820	
Less Stock of finished goods 31.12.19X7	4,400	17,420
Gross profit c/d		7,580

The profit and loss account is then constructed in the normal way.

36.11 Apportionment of expenses

Quite often expenses will have to be split between

- Factory overhead expenses: to be charged in the manufacturing account section
- Administration expenses: } to be charged in the profit and
- Selling and distribution expenses: } loss account section

An instance of this could be the rent expense. If the rent is paid separately for each part of the organisation, then it is easy to charge the rent to each sort of expense. However, only one figure of rent may be paid, without any indication as to how much is for the factory part, how much is for the selling and distribution part and that for the administration buildings.

How the rent expense will be apportioned in the latter case will depend on circumstances, using the most equitable way of doing it. For instance, one of the following methods may be used:

- by floor area;
- by property valuations of each part of the buildings and land.

36.12 Full set of final accounts

A complete worked example is now given. Note that in the profit and loss account the expenses have been separated so as to show whether they are administration expenses, selling and distribution expenses, or financial charges.

The trial balance in Exhibit 36.3 has been extracted from the books of J Jarvis, Toy Manufacturer, as on 31 December 19X7:

Exhibit 36.3

J Jarvis

Trial Balance as on 31 December 19X7

	Dr	Cr
	£	£
Stock of raw materials 1.1.19X7	2,100	
Stock of finished goods 1.1.19X7	3,890	
Work in progress 1.1.19X7	1,350	
Wages (direct £18,000; factory indirect £14,500)	32,500	
Royalties	700	
Carriage inwards (on raw materials)	350	
Purchases of raw materials	37,000	
Productive machinery (cost £28,000)	23,000	
Accounting machinery (cost £2,000)	1,200	
General factory expenses	3,100	
Lighting	750	
Factory power	1,370	
Administrative salaries	4,400	
Sales reps' salaries	3,000	
Commission on sales	1,150	
Rent	1,200	
Insurance	420	
General administration expenses	1,340	
Bank charges	230	
Discounts allowed	480	
Carriage outwards	590	
Sales		100,000
Debtors and creditors	14,230	12,500
Bank	5,680	
Cash	150	
Drawings	2,000	
Capital as at 1.1.19X7		29,680
	142,180	142,180

Notes at 31.12.19X7:

1 Stock of raw materials £2,400, stock of finished goods £4,000, work in progress £1,500.

2 Lighting, and rent and insurance are to be apportioned: factory ⅚ths, administration ⅙th.

3 Depreciation on productive and accounting machinery at 10 per cent per annum on cost.

J Jarvis

Manufacturing, Trading and Profit and Loss Account for the year ended 31 December 19X7

	£	£	£
Stock of raw materials 1.1.19X7			2,100
Add Purchases			37,000
„ Carriage inwards			350
			39,450
Less Stock raw materials 31.12.19X7			2,400
Cost of raw materials consumed			37,050
Direct labour			18,000
Royalties			700
Prime cost			55,750
Factory overhead expenses:			
General factory expenses		3,100	
Lighting ⅚ths		625	
Power		1,370	
Rent ⅚ths		1,000	
Insurance ⅚ths		350	
Depreciation of plant		2,800	
Indirect labour		14,500	23,745
			79,495
Add Work in progress 1.1.19X7			1,350
			80,845
Less Work in progress 31.12.19X7			1,500
Production cost of goods completed c/d			79,345
Sales			100,000
Less Cost of goods sold:			
Stock of finished goods 1.1.19X7		3,890	
Add Production cost of goods completed		79,345	
		83,235	
Less Stock of finished goods 31.12.19X7		4,000	79,235
Gross profit			20,765
Administration expenses			
Administrative salaries	4,400		
Rent ⅙th	200		
Insurance ⅙th	70		
General expenses	1,340		
Lighting ⅙th	125		
Depreciation of accounting machinery	200	6,335	
Selling and distribution expenses			
Sales rep's salaries	3,000		
Commission on sales	1,150		
Carriage outwards	590	4,740	
Financial charges			
Bank charges	230		
Discounts allowed	480	710	11,785
Net profit			8,980

J Jarvis

Balance Sheet as at 31 December 19X7

	£	£
Fixed assets		
Productive machinery at cost	28,000	
Less Depreciation to date	7,800	20,200
Accounting machinery at cost	2,000	
Less Depreciation to date	1,000	1,000
		21,200
Current assets		
Stock		
Raw materials	2,400	
Finished goods	4,000	
Work in progress	1,500	
Debtors	14,230	
Bank	5,680	
Cash	150	
	27,960	
Less Current liabilities		
Creditors	12,500	
Working capital		15,460
		36,660
Financed by		
Capital		
Balance as at 1.1.19X7		29,680
Add Net profit		8,980
		38,660
Less Drawings		2,000
		36,660

36.13 Market value of goods manufactured

The accounts of Jarvis, just illustrated, are subject to the limitation that the respective amounts of the gross profit which are attributable to the manufacturing side or to the selling side of the firm are not known. A technique is sometimes used to bring out this additional information. By this method the cost which would have been involved if the goods had been bought in their finished state instead of being manufactured by the firm is brought into account. This is credited to the manufacturing account and debited to the trading account so as to throw up two figures of gross profit instead of one. It should be pointed out that the net profit will remain unaffected. All that will have happened will be that the figure of £20,765 gross profit will be shown as two figures instead of one.

The accounts in summarised form will appear:

*Manufacturing, Trading and Profit and Loss Account for the year ended
31 December 19X7*

	£	£
Market value of goods completed c/d		95,000
Less Production cost of goods completed (as before)		79,345
Gross profit on manufacture c/d		15,655
Sales		100,000
Stock of finished goods 1.1.19X7	3,890	
Add Market value of goods completed b/d	95,000	
	98,890	
Less Stock of finished goods 31.12.19X7	4,000	94,890
Gross profit on trading c/d		5,110
Gross profit		
On manufacturing	15,655	
On trading	5,110	20,765

36.14 Further methods of providing for depreciation

In Chapter 25 the straight line and reducing balance methods were examined. We can now look at some further methods.

There is no information easily available to show how many organisations are using each method. It is possible to devise one's own special method. If it brings about an equitable charge for depreciation for that organisation, then the method will be suitable.

36.15 The revaluation method

When there are a few expensive items of fixed assets, it is not difficult to draw up the necessary accounts for depreciation. For each item we:

(*a*) Find its cost.
(*b*) Estimate its years of use to the firm.
(*c*) Calculate and provide depreciation.
(*d*) Make the adjustments when the asset is disposed of.
(*e*) Calculate profit or loss on disposal.

This is worth doing for expensive items. There are, however, many examples of fixed assets for which the calculation would not be worth doing, and in fact may be impossible.

Some firms will have many low cost fixed assets. Garages or engineering works will have a lot of spanners, screwdrivers and other small tools; brewers will have crates; laboratories will have many small, low cost glass instruments.

It would be impossible to follow procedures (*a*) to (*e*) above for every screwdriver or crate. Instead the revaluation method is used.

The method is not difficult to use. An example is shown in Exhibit 36.4.

Exhibit 36.4

A firm has a lot of steel containers. These are not sold but are used by the firm.

	£
On 1 January 19X6 the containers were valued at	3,500
During the year to 31 December containers were purchased costing	1,300
On 31 December 19X6 the containers were valued at	3,800

The depreciation is calculated:

	£
Value at start of period	3,500
Add Cost of items bought during period	1,300
	4,800
Less Value at close of period	3,800
Depreciation for year to 31 December 19X6	1,000

The depreciation figure £1,000 will be charged as an expense. Using this idea, we can look at Exhibit 36.5, where depreciation is entered in the books for the first three years of a firm starting trading.

Exhibit 36.5

The firm starts in business on 1 January 19X6.

	£
In its first year it buys crates costing	800
Their estimated value at 31 December 19X6	540
Crates bought in the year ended 31 December 19X7	320
Estimated value of all crates in hand on 31 December 19X7	530
Crates bought in the year ended 31 December 19X8	590
Estimated value of all crates in hand on 31 December 19X8	700

Crates

19X6	£	19X6	£
Dec 31 Cash (during the year)	800	Dec 31 Profit and loss	260
		„ 31 Stock c/d	540
	800		800
19X7		19X7	
Jan 1 Stock b/d	540	Dec 31 Profit and loss	330
Dec 31 Cash (during the year)	320	„ 31 Stock c/d	530
	860		860
19X8		19X8	
Jan 1 Stock b/d	530	Dec 31 Profit and loss	420
Dec 31 Cash (during the year)	590	„ 31 Stock c/d	700
	1,120		1,120
19X9			
Jan 1 Stock b/d	700		

Profit and Loss Account for the year ended 31 December

		£
19X6	Use of crates	260
19X7	Use of crates	330
19X8	Use of crates	420

The balance of the crates account at the end of each year is shown as a fixed asset in the balance sheet.

Sometimes the firm may make its own items such as tools or crates. In these instances the tools account or crates account should be debited with labour costs and material costs.

Revaluation is also used, for instance, by farmers for their cattle. Like other fixed assets depreciation should be provided for, but during the early life of an animal it will be appreciating in value, only to depreciate later. The task of calculating the cost of an animal becomes virtually impossible if it has been born on the farm, and reared on the farm by grazing on the pasture land and being fed on other foodstuffs, some grown on the farm and others bought by the farmer.

To get over this problem the revaluation method is used. Because of the difficulty of calculating the cost of the animals, they are valued at the price which they would fetch if sold at market. This is an exception to the general rule of assets being shown at cost price.

36.16 Depletion unit method

With fixed assets such as a quarry from which raw materials are dug out to be sold to the building industry, a different method is needed.

If a quarry was bought for £5,000 and it was expected to contain 1,000 tonnes of saleable materials, then for each tonne taken out we would depreciate it by £5, i.e. £5,000 ÷ 1,000 = £5.

This can be shown as:

$$\frac{\text{Cost of fixed asset}}{\text{Expected total contents in units}} \times \text{Number of units taken in period}$$

$$= \text{Depreciation for that period.}$$

36.17 Machine hour method

With a machine the depreciation provision may be based on the number of hours that the machine was operated during the period compared with the total expected running hours during the machine's life with the firm. A firm which bought a machine costing £2,000 having an expected running life of 1,000 hours, and no scrap value, could provide for depreciation of the machine at the rate of £2 for every hour it was operated during a particular accounting period.

36.18 Sum of the years' digits

This method is popular in the USA but not common in the UK. It provides for higher depreciation to be charged early in the life of an asset with lower depreciation in later years.

Given an asset costing £3,000 which will be in use for 5 years, the calculations will be:

From purchase the asset will last for	5 years
From the second year the asset will last for	4 years
From the third year the asset will last for	3 years
From the fourth year the asset will last for	2 years
From the fifth year the asset will last for	1 year
Sum of these digits	15

	£
1st year 5/15ths of £3,000 is charged =	1,000
2nd year 4/15ths of £3,000 is charged =	800
3rd year 3/15ths of £3,000 is charged =	600
4th year 2/15ths of £3,000 is charged =	400
5th year 1/15th of £3,000 is charged =	200
	3,000

36.19 Units of output method

This method establishes the total expected units of output expected from the asset. Depreciation, based on cost less salvage value, is then calculated for the period by taking that period's units of output as a proportion of the total expected output over the life of the asset.

An instance of this could be a machine which is expected to be able to produce 10,000 widgets over its useful life. It has cost £6,000 and has an expected salvage value of £1,000. In year 1 a total of 1,500 widgets are produced, and in year 2 the production is 2,500 widgets.

The depreciation per period is calculated :

$$\left(Cost - salvage\ value \right) \times \left(\frac{period's\ production}{total\ expected\ production} \right)$$

$$Year\ 1:\ £5,000 \times \frac{1,500}{10,000} = £750\ depreciation$$

$$Year\ 2:\ £5,000 \times \frac{2,500}{10,000} = £1,250\ depreciation$$

New terms

Direct costs (p. 366): Costs that can be traced to the item being manufactured.

Factory overhead costs (p. 366): Production costs in the factory which cannot be traced to the item being manufactured.

Manufacturing account (p. 366): An account in which production cost is calculated.

Prime cost (p. 365): Direct materials plus direct labour plus direct expenses.

Production cost (p. 365): Prime cost plus factory overhead costs.

Total cost (p. 365): Production cost plus administration, selling and distribution expenses.

Work in progress (p. 368): Items not completed at the end of a period.

Main points to remember

1 The trading account is used for calculating the gross profit made by selling the goods manufactured.

2 The profit and loss account shows as net profit what is left of gross profit after all administration, selling and distribution costs incurred have been deducted.

3 Work in progress, both at the start and the close of a period, must be adjusted to ascertain the production costs of goods completed in the period.

Review questions

36.1 A firm both buys loose tools and also makes some itself. The following data is available concerning the years ended 31 December 19X4, 19X5 and 19X6.

19X4		£
Jan 1	Stock of loose tools	1,250
	During the year:	
	Bought loose tools from suppliers	2,000
	Made own loose tools: the cost of wages of employees being £275 and the materials cost £169	
Dec 31	Loose tools valued at	2,700
19X5		
	During the year:	
	Loose tools bought from suppliers	1,450
	Made own loose tools: the cost of wages of employees being £495 and the materials cost £390	
Dec 31	Loose tools valued at	3,340
19X6		
	During the year:	
	Loose tools bought from suppliers	1,890
	Made own loose tools: the cost of wages of employees being £145 and the materials cost £290. Received refund from a supplier for faulty tools returned to him	88
Dec 31	Loose tools valued at	3,680

You are to draw up the Loose Tools Account for the three years, showing the amount transferred as an expense in each year to the Manufacturing Account.

36.2 On 1 April 19X6 a business purchased a machine costing £112,000. The machine can be used for a total of 20,000 hours over an estimated life of 48 months. At the end of that time the machine is expected to have a trade-in value of £12,000.

The financial year of the business ends on 31 December each year. It is expected that the machine will be used for:

4,000 hours during the financial year ending 31 December 19X6
5,000 hours during the financial year ending 31 December 19X7
5,000 hours during the financial year ending 31 December 19X8
5,000 hours during the financial year ending 31 December 19X9
1,000 hours during the financial year ending 31 December 19X0

Required:
(a) Calculate the annual depreciation charges on the machine on each of the following bases for each of the financial years ending on 31 December 19X6, 19X7, 19X8, 19X9 and 19X0:
   (i) the straight line method applied on a month for month basis,
   (ii) the diminishing balance method at 40% per annum applied on a full year basis, and
   (iii) the units of output method.
(b) Suppose that during the financial year ended 31 December 19X7 the machine was used for only 1,500 hours before being sold for £80,000 on 30 June.
   Assuming that the business has chosen to apply the straight line method on a month for month basis, show the following accounts for 19X7 only:
   (i) the Machine account,
   (ii) the Provision for Depreciation – Machine account, and
   (iii) the Assets Disposals account.

(Association of Accounting Technicians)

36.3A On 1 January 19X1 a business purchased a laser printer costing £1,800. The printer has an estimated life of 4 years after which it will have no residual value.

It is expected that the output from the printer will be:

Year	Sheets printed
19X1	35,000
19X2	45,000
19X3	45,000
19X4	55,000
	180,000

Required:
(a) Calculate the annual depreciation charges for 19X1, 19X2, 19X3 and 19X4 on the laser printer on the following bases:
   (i) the straight line basis,
   (ii) the diminishing balance method at 60% per annum, and
   (iii) the units of output method.
   Note: Your workings should be to the nearest £.
(b) Suppose that in 19X4 the laser printer were to be sold on 1 July for £200 and that the business had chosen to depreciate it at 60% per annum using the diminishing balance method applied on a month for month basis.
   Reconstruct the following accounts for 19X4 only:
   (i) the Laser Printer account,
   (ii) the Provision for Depreciation – Laser Printer account, and
   (iii) the Assets Disposals account.

(Association of Accounting Technicians)

36.4 Prepare manufacturing, trading and profit and loss accounts from the following balances of T Jackson for the year ended 31 December 19X7.

	£
Stocks at 1 January 19X7:	
Raw materials	18,450
Work in progress	23,600
Finished goods	17,470
Purchases: Raw materials	64,300
Carriage on raw materials	1,605
Direct labour	65,810
Office salaries	16,920
Rent	2,700
Office lighting and heating	5,760
Depreciation: Works machinery	8,300
Office equipment	1,950
Sales	200,600
Factory fuel and power	5,920

Rent is to be apportioned: Factory $\frac{2}{3}$; Office $\frac{1}{3}$. Stocks at 31 December 19X7 were: Raw materials £20,210, Work in progress £17,390, Finished goods £21,485.

36.5A Chesterton Plc are manufacturers. At the end of their accounting year, 30 April 19X9, the following information was available:

	£
Stocks at 1 May 19X8:	
Raw materials	17,500
Finished goods	24,800
Work in progress	15,270
Wages and salaries	
Factory direct	138,500
Factory indirect	27,200
Purchases of raw materials	95,600
Power and fuel (indirect)	18,260
Sales	410,400
Insurance	3,680
Returns inwards (finished goods)	5,200
Stocks at 30 April 19X9:	
Raw materials	13,200
Finished goods	14,600
Work in progress	15,700

Notes:
- The company's machinery cost £82,000 and the provision for depreciation on 1 May 19X8 was £27,000. Machinery is to be depreciated by 20% per annum using reducing balance method.
- Fuel and power £390 in arrears at 30 April 19X9; at the same date insurance £240 is prepaid.
- Insurance is to be allocated: $\frac{5}{8}$ factory; $\frac{3}{8}$ administration.

Required:
For Chesterton Plc
(a) A manufacturing account for the year ended 30 April 19X9, showing clearly:
    (i)   cost of raw materials consumed
    (ii) prime cost
    (iii) total cost of production.
(b) A trading account for the year ended 30 April 19X9 showing clearly:
    (i)   cost of sales of finished goods
    (ii) gross profit.
(*Southern Examining Group: GCSE*)

36.6 D Saunders is a manufacturer. His trial balance at 31 December 19X6 is as follows:

	£	£
Delivery van expenses	2,500	
Lighting and heating: Factory	2,859	
Office	1,110	
Manufacturing wages	45,470	
General expenses: Factory	5,640	
Office	3,816	
Sales reps: commission	7,860	
Purchase of raw materials	39,054	
Rent: Factory	4,800	
Office	2,200	
Machinery (cost £50,000)	32,500	
Office equipment (cost £15,000)	11,000	
Office salaries	6,285	
Debtors	28,370	
Creditors		19,450
Bank	13,337	
Sales		136,500
Premises (cost £50,000)	40,000	
Stocks at 31 December 19X5:		
Raw materials	8,565	
Finished goods	29,480	
Drawings	8,560	
Capital		137,456
	293,406	293,406

Prepare the manufacturing, trading and profit and loss accounts for the year ended 31 December 19X6 and a balance sheet as at that date. Give effect to the following adjustments:

1 Stocks at 31 December 19X6: raw materials £9,050, finished goods £31,200. There is no work in progress.
2 Depreciate machinery £2,000, office equipment £1,500, premises £1,000.
3 Manufacturing wages due but unpaid at 31 December 19X6 £305, office rent prepaid £108.

36.7A Jean Marsh owns a small business making and selling children's toys. The following trial balance was extracted from her books on 31 December 19X9.

	Dr £	Cr £
Capital		15,000
Drawings	2,000	
Sales		90,000
Stocks at 1 January 19X9:		
Raw materials	3,400	
Finished goods	6,100	
Purchases of raw materials	18,000	
Carriage inwards	800	
Factory wages	18,500	
Office salaries	16,900	
J Marsh: salary and expenses	10,400	
General expenses:		
Factory	1,200	
Office	750	
Lighting	2,500	
Rent	3,750	
Insurance	950	
Advertising	1,400	
Bad debts	650	
Discount received		1,600
Carriage outwards	375	
Plant and machinery, at cost less depreciation	9,100	
Motor car, at cost less depreciation	4,200	
Bank	3,600	
Cash in hand	325	
Debtors and creditors	7,700	6,000
	112,600	112,600

You are given the following additional information.
1 Stocks at 31 December 19X9
    Raw materials   £2,900
    Finished goods   £8,200
    There was no work in progress.
2 Depreciation for the year is to be charged as follows:
    Plant and machinery   £1,500
    Motor car   £ 500
3 At 31 December 19X9 Insurance paid in advance was £150 and Office general expenses unpaid were £75.
4 Lighting and rent are to be apportioned
    $\frac{4}{5}$ Factory, $\frac{1}{5}$ Office
    Insurance is to be apportioned
    $\frac{3}{4}$ Factory, $\frac{1}{4}$ Office
5 Jean is the firm's salesperson and her salary and expenses are to be treated as a selling expense. She has sole use of the firm's car.

Questions:
For the year ended 31 December 19X9 prepare
(a) a manufacturing account showing prime cost and factory cost of production.
(b) a trading account.
(c) a profit and loss account, distinguishing between administrative and selling costs.
(d) a balance sheet as at 31 December 19X9.*

(*Midland Examining Group: GCSE*)

*Part (d) of the question was not in the original examination question. It has been added to give you further practice.

36.8 The following list of balances as at 31 July 19X6 has been extracted from the books of Jane Seymour who commenced business on 1 August 19X5 as a designer and manufacturer of kitchen furniture:

	£
Plant and machinery, at cost on 1 August 19X5	60,000
Motor vehicles, at cost on 1 August 19X5	30,000
Loose tools, at cost	9,000
Sales	170,000
Raw materials purchased	43,000
Direct factory wages	39,000
Light and power	5,000
Indirect factory wages	8,000
Machinery repairs	1,600
Motor vehicle running expenses	12,000
Rent and insurances	11,600
Administrative staff salaries	31,000
Administrative expenses	9,000
Sales and distribution staff salaries	13,000
Capital at 1 August 19X5	122,000
Sundry debtors	16,500
Sundry creditors	11,200
Balance at bank	8,500
Drawings	6,000

Additional information for the year ended 31 July 19X6:

(*i*)   It is estimated that the plant and machinery will be used in the business for 10 years and the motor vehicles used for 4 years: in both cases it is estimated that the residual value will be nil. The straight line method of providing for depreciation is to be used.

(*ii*)   Light and power charges accrued due at 31 July 19X6 amounted to £1,000 and insurances prepaid at 31 July 19X6 totalled £800.

(*iii*)   Stocks were valued at cost at 31 July 19X6 as follows:

Raw materials	£ 7,000
Finished goods	£10,000

(*iv*)   The valuation of work in progress at 31 July 19X6 included variable and fixed factory overheads and amounted to £12,300.

(*v*)   Two-thirds of the light and power and rent and insurances costs are to be allocated to the factory costs and one-third to general administration costs.

(*vi*)   Motor vehicle costs are to be allocated equally to factory costs and general administration costs.

(*vii*)   Goods manufactured during the year are to be transferred to the trading account at £95,000.

(*viii*)   Loose tools in hand on 31 July 19X6 were valued at £5,000.

Required:

(*a*)   Prepare a manufacturing, trading and profit and loss account for the year ended 31 July 19X6 of Jane Seymour.

(*b*)   An explanation of how each of the following accounting concepts have affected the preparation of the above accounts:

- conservatism,
- matching,
- going concern.

(*Association of Accounting Technicians*)

37

Departmental accounts

Objectives

After you have studied this chapter, you should:

- *be able to draw up departmental trading and profit and loss accounts*

- *be able to calculate the contributions made by each section of a business*

- *appreciate that departmental accounts can be more meaningful to management than a single set of trading and profit and loss accounts*

- *be able to apportion expenses between departments on a logical basis*

37.1 Use of departmental accounts

Some items of accounting information are more useful than others. For a retail store with five departments, it is better to know that the store has made £10,000 gross profit than not to know what the gross profit was. Obviously it would be better if we knew how much gross profit was made in each department.

Assume that the gross profits and losses of a firm's departments were as follows:

Department	Gross profit	Gross loss
	£	£
A	4,000	
B	3,000	
C	5,000	
D		8,000
E	6,000	
	18,000	8,000

Gross profit of the firm, £10,000.

If we knew the above, we could see how well, or how badly, each part of the business was doing. If we closed down department D we could make a greater total gross profit of £18,000. Perhaps we could replace department D with a department which would make a gross profit instead of a loss.

You would have to know more about the business before you could be certain what the figures mean. Some stores deliberately allow parts of their business to lose money, so that customers come to the store to buy the cheap goods and then spend money in the other departments.

Accounting information therefore seldom tells all the story. It serves as one measure, but there are other non-accounting factors to be considered before a relevant decision for action can be made.

The various pros and cons of the actions to be taken to increase the overall profitability of the business cannot therefore be properly considered until the departmental gross profits or losses are known. It must not be thought that departmental accounts refer only to departmental stores. They refer to the various facets of a business.

The reputation of many a successful business person has been built up on an ability to utilise the departmental account principle to guide their actions to increase the profitability of a firm. The lesson still has to be learned by many medium-sized and small firms. It is one of accounting's greatest, and simplest, aids to business efficiency.

To find out how profitable each part of the business is, we will have to prepare departmental accounts to give us the facts for each department.

37.2 Allocation of expenses

The expenses of the firm are often split between the various departments, and the net profit for each department then calculated. Each expense is divided between the departments on what is considered to be the most logical basis. This will differ considerably between businesses. An example of a trading and profit and loss account drawn up in such a manner is shown in Exhibit 37.1.

Exhibit 37.1

Northern Stores have three departments in their store:

	(a) Jewellery	(b) Ladies hairdressing	(c) Clothing
	£	£	£
Stock of goods or materials, 1 January 19X8	2,000	1,500	3,000
Purchases	11,000	3,000	15,000
Stock of goods or materials, 31 December 19X8	3,000	2,500	4,000
Sales and work done	18,000	9,000	27,000
Wages of assistants in each department	2,800	5,000	6,000

The following expenses cannot be traced to any particular department:

	£
Rent	3,500
Administration expenses	4,800
Air conditioning and lighting	2,000
General expenses	1,200

It is decided to apportion rent together with air conditioning and lighting in accordance with the floor space occupied by each department. These were taken up in the ratios of (a) one-fifth, (b) half, (c) three-tenths. Administration expenses and general expenses are to be split in the ratio of sales and work done.

The Northern Stores

Trading and Profit and Loss Account for the year ended 31 December 19X8

	(a) Jewellery £	(a) Jewellery £	(b) Hairdressing £	(b) Hairdressing £	(c) Clothing £	(c) Clothing £
Sales and work done		18,000		9,000		27,000
Cost of goods or materials:						
Stock 1.1.19X8	2,000		1,500		3,000	
Add Purchases	11,000		3,000		15,000	
	13,000		4,500		18,000	
Less Stock 31.12.19X8	3,000	10,000	2,500	2,000	4,000	14,000
Gross profit		8,000		7,000		13,000
Less Expenses:						
Wages	2,800		5,000		6,000	
Rent	700		1,750		1,050	
Administration expenses	1,600		800		2,400	
Air conditioning and lighting	400		1,000		600	
General expenses	400	5,900	200	8,750	600	10,650
Net profit/loss		2,100		(1,750)		2,350

This way of calculating net profits and losses seems to imply a precision that is lacking in fact, and would often lead to an interpretation that the hairdressing department has lost £1,750 this year, and that this amount would be saved if the department were closed down. It has already been stated that different departments are very often dependent on one another; therefore it will be realised that this would not necessarily be the case.

The calculation of net profits and losses is also dependent on the arbitrary division of overhead expenses. It is by no means obvious that the overheads of department (b) would be avoided if it were closed down. Assuming that the sales staff of the department could be discharged without compensation, then £5,000 would be saved in wages. The other overhead expenses shown under department (b) would not, however, necessarily disappear. The rent may still be payable in full even though the department were closed down. The administration expenses may turn out to be only slightly down, say from £4,800 to £4,600, a saving of £200; air conditioning and lighting down to £1,500, a saving of £500; general expenses down to £1,100, a saving of £100. Therefore the department, when open, costs an additional £5,800 compared with when the department is closed. This is made up as follows:

	£
Administration expenses	200
Air conditioning and lighting	500
General expenses	100
Wages	5,000
	5,800

But when open, assuming this year is typical, the department makes £7,000 gross profit. The firm is therefore £1,200 a year better off when the department is open than when it is closed, subject to certain assumptions. These are:

(a) That the remaining departments would not be profitably expanded into the space vacated to give greater proportionate benefits than the hairdressing department.

(b) That a new type of department which would be more profitable than hairdressing could not be set up.

(c) That the department could not be leased to another firm at a more profitable figure than that shown by hairdressing.

There are also other factors which, though not easily seen in an accounting context, are still extremely pertinent. They are concerned with the possible loss of confidence in the firm by customers generally; what appears to be an ailing business does not usually attract good customers. Also the effect on the remaining staff should not be ignored. The fear that the dismissal of the hairdressing staff may also happen to themselves may result in the loss of staff, especially the most competent members who could easily find work elsewhere, and so the general quality of the staff may decline with serious consequences for the firm.

37.3 Allocation of expenses: a better method

It is less misleading to show costs split as follows:

First section of trading and profit and loss account	Direct costs allocated entirely to the department and which would *not* be paid if department closed down
Second section of trading and profit and loss account	Costs not directly traceable to the department or which would still be payable even if the department closed down

The *surpluses* brought down from the first section represent the **contribution** that each department has made to cover the expenses, the remainder being the net profit for the whole of the firm. If expenses were greater than the sales figure then the result would be a **negative contribution**.

From the figures given in Exhibit 37.1 the accounts would appear as in Exhibit 37.2.

Exhibit 37.2

The Northern Stores

Trading and Profit and Loss Account for the year ended 31 December 19X8

	(a) Jewellery		(b) Hairdressing		(c) Clothing	
	£	£	£	£	£	£
Sales and work done		18,000		9,000		27,000
Less cost of goods or materials:						
Stock 1.1.19X8	2,000		1,500		3,000	
Add Purchases	11,000		3,000		15,000	
	13,000		4,500		18,000	
Less Stock 31.12.19X8	3,000		2,500		4,000	
	10,000		2,000		14,000	
Wages	2,800	12,800	5,000	7,000	6,000	20,000
Surpluses c/d		5,200		2,000		7,000

All Departments

	£	£
Surpluses b/d:		
Jewellery	5,200	
Hairdressing	2,000	
Clothing	7,000	14,200
Less		
Rent	3,500	
Administration expenses	4,800	
Air conditioning and lighting	2,000	
General expenses	1,200	11,500
Net profit		2,700

The contribution of a department is the result of activities which are under the control of a departmental manager. The efficiency of their control will affect the amount of the contribution.

The costs in the second section, such as rent, insurance or lighting cannot be affected by the departmental manager. It is therefore only fair if the departmental manager is judged by the *contribution* of his department rather than the net profit of his department.

In examinations students must answer the questions as set, and not give their own interpretations of what the question should be. Therefore if an examiner gives details of the methods of apportionment of expenses, then he is really looking for an answer in the same style as Exhibit 37.1.

37.4 The balance sheet

The balance sheet does not usually show assets and liabilities split between different departments.

37.5 Inter-departmental transfers

Purchases made for one department may be subsequently sold in another department. In such a case the items should be deducted from the figure for purchases of the original purchasing department, and added to the figure for purchases for the subsequent selling department.

New terms

Contribution (p. 388): The surplus of revenue over expenses allocated to a section of a business.

Negative contribution (p. 388): The excess of expenses allocated to a section of a business over the revenue from that section.

Main points to remember

1 It is desirable for the contribution of each section of a business to be calculated to aid management decisions.

2 Expenses should be divided between those which can logically be allocated to departments and those which cannot.

3 A negative contribution is only one guide as to whether a section of a business should be closed. There may be other factors which would go against such a closure.

Review questions

37.1 From the following you are to draw up the trading account for Charnley's Department Store for the year ended 31 December 19X8.

Stocks:	1.1.19X8	31.12.19X8
	£	£
Electrical Department	6,080	7,920
Furniture Department	17,298	16,150
Leisure Goods Department	14,370	22,395

Sales for the year:	£
Electrical Department	29,840
Furniture Department	73,060
Leisure Goods Department	39,581

Purchases for the year:	
Electrical Department	18,195
Furniture Department	54,632
Leisure Goods Department	27,388

37.2 J Spratt is the proprietor of a shop selling books, periodicals, newspapers and children's games and toys. For the purposes of his accounts he wishes the business to be divided into two departments:

Department A   Books, periodicals and newspapers.
Department B   Games, toys and fancy goods.

The following balances have been extracted from his nominal ledger at 31 March 19X9:

	Dr	Cr
	£	£
Sales Department A		15,000
Sales Department B		10,000
Stocks Department A, 1 April 19X8	250	
Stocks Department B, 1 April 19X8	200	
Purchases Department A	11,800	
Purchases Department B	8,200	
Wages of sales assistants Department A	1,000	
Wages of sales assistants Department B	750	
Newspaper delivery wages	150	
General office salaries	750	
Rates	130	
Fire insurance – buildings	50	
Lighting and air conditioning	120	
Repairs to premises	25	
Internal telephone	25	
Cleaning	30	
Accountancy and audit charges	120	
General office expenses	60	

Stocks at 31 March 19X9 were valued at:
Department A £300
Department B £150

The proportion of the total floor area occupied by each department was:
Department A one-fifth
Department B four-fifths

Prepare J Spratt's trading and profit and loss account for the year ended 31 March 19X9, apportioning the overhead expenses, where necessary, to show the Department profit or loss. The apportionment should be made by using the methods as shown:

Area – Rates, Fire insurance, Lighting and air conditioning, Repairs, Telephone, Cleaning; Turnover – General office salaries, Accountancy, General office expenses.

37.3A From the following list of balances you are required to prepare a departmental trading and profit and loss account in columnar form for the year ended 31 March 19X9, in respect of the business carried on under the name of Ivor's Superstores:

			£	£
Rent and rates				4,200
Delivery expenses				2,400
Commission				3,840
Insurance				900
Purchases:	Dept.	A	52,800	
		B	43,600	
		C	34,800	131,200
Discounts received				1,968
Salaries and wages				31,500
Advertising				1,944
Sales:	Dept.	A	80,000	
		B	64,000	
		C	48,000	192,000
Depreciation				2,940
Opening stock:	Dept.	A	14,600	
		B	11,240	
		C	9,120	34,960
Administration and general expenses				
7,890				
Closing stock:	Dept.	A	12,400	
		B	8,654	
		C	9,746	30,800

Except as follows, expenses are to be apportioned equally between the departments.

Delivery expenses – proportionate to sales.
Commission – 2 per cent of sales.
Salaries and wages; Insurance – in the proportion of 6:5:4.
Discounts received – 1.5 per cent of purchases.

38

Cash flow statements

Objectives

After you have studied this chapter, you should:

- *be able to draw up a cash flow statement for any type of organisation*

- *realise that cash flow statements can give a different view of a business to that simply concerned with profits*

- *understand the basic outline of Financial Reporting Standards 1 (FRS 1) and the format to be used*

- *appreciate some of the uses which can be made of cash flow statements*

38.1 Need for cash flow statements

For any business it is important to ensure that:

- Sufficient profits are made to finance the business.
- Sufficient cash funds are available as and when needed.

We ascertain the amount of profits in a profit and loss account. We also show what the assets, capital and liabilities are at a given date by drawing up a balance sheet. Although the balance sheet shows the cash balance (see definition later) at a given date, it does not show us how we have used our cash funds during the accounting year.

What we really need, to help throw some light on to the cash situation, is some form of statement which shows us exactly where the cash has come from during the year, and exactly what we have done with it. The statement that fulfils these needs is called a **cash flow statement**.

We take the word 'cash' to mean cash balances, plus bank balances, plus 'cash equivalents'. These cash equivalents consist of the temporary investments of cash not required at present by the business. Such investments must be readily convertible into cash, or would mature within three months if left as investments.

38.2 Financial Reporting Standard 1: Cash Flow Statements

In 1991, the Accounting Standards Board issued the first Financial Reporting Standard (FRS 1). It was revised and reissued in 1996. The standard, as its title suggests, supports the use of cash flow statements.

This had not always been the case. An earlier SSAP had favoured the use of 'source and application of funds statements'. These funds were concerned with working capital and not cash. FRS 1 changed all of this, with cash as the central item. This book will therefore deal with cash flow statements and not with the statements centred on working capital.

The Accounting Standards Board in fact requires only certain companies to include cash flow statements with their published final accounts and other matter. It does, however, encourage other companies to use them.

38.3 Businesses other than companies

Although small companies, partnerships and sole traders do not have to prepare them, cash flow statements can be of considerable use to them.

FRS 1 prescribes a format for cash flow statements. An example is shown later in Exhibit 38.6. This is suitable for a company, but obviously there are factors concerning partnerships and sole traders which do not occur in companies. It will be of help to students if the cash flow statements for sole traders and partnerships are fashioned to be as like those for companies as is possible. Such layouts will be followed in this book.

38.4 Profit and liquidity not directly related

Many people think that if we are making profits then there should be no shortage of cash. This is not necessarily so. Let us look at a few instances where, although reasonable profits are being made by each of the following firms, they could find themselves short of cash; if not now then they may do so in future.

- A sole trader is making £40,000 a year profits. However, his drawings have been over £60,000 a year for some time.
- A company has been over-generous with credit terms to debtors, and last year extended the time in which debtors could pay from one month to three months. In addition it has taken on quite a few extra customers who are not creditworthy and such sales may result in bad debts in the future.
- A partnership whose products will not be on the market for quite a long time has invested in some very expensive machinery. A lot of money has been spent now, but no income will result in the near future.

In all of these cases, each of the firms could easily run out of cash. In fact many businesses fail and are wound up because of cash shortages, despite adequate profits being made. Cash flow statements can help to show up such problems.

38.5   Where from: where to

Basically a cash flow statement shows where the cash funds came from, and where they have gone to. Exhibit 38.1 shows details of such cash flows.

Exhibit 38.1

Cash comes from (sources)	Cash funds		Cash goes to (applications)
	In	Out	
1 Profits	→	→	1 Losses
2 Sales of Fixed Assets	→	→	2 Purchase Fixed Assets
3 Decrease in Stock	→	→	3 Increase in Stock
4 Decrease in Debtors	→	→	4 Increase in Debtors
5 Capital Introduced	→	→	5 Drawings/Dividends
6 Loans Received	→	→	6 Loans Repaid
7 Increase in Creditors	→	→	7 Decrease in Creditors

These can be explained as:

1   Profits bring a flow of cash into the firm. Losses take cash out of it.
2   The cash received from sales of fixed assets comes into the firm. A purchase of fixed assets takes it out.
3   Reducing stock in the normal course of business means turning it into cash. An increase in stock ties up cash funds.
4   A reduction in debtors means that the extra amount paid comes into the firm as cash. Letting debtors increase stops that extra amount of cash coming in.
5   An increase in a sole proprietor's capital, or issues of shares in a company, brings cash in. Drawings or dividends take it out.
6   Loans received bring in cash, while their repayment reduces cash.
7   An increase in creditors keeps the extra cash in the firm. A decrease in creditors means that the extra payments take cash out.

If therefore we take the cash (and bank) balances at the start of a financial period, and adjust for cash flows in and out during the financial period, then we would arrive at the cash (and bank) balances at the end of the period. This can be shown as:

Cash per balance sheet (figures end of previous period)   +   Changes – which must be because of cash flows during intervening period   =   Cash per balance sheet (figures end of following period)

38.6   Construction of a cash flow statement

We will first of all look at a cash flow statement drawn up for a sole trader's business, as this will be easier than looking at the more complicated example of a limited company.

We will start from Exhibit 38.2 and construct Exhibit 38.3, a cash flow statement.

Exhibit 38.2

The following are the balance sheets of T Holmes as at 31 December 19X6 and 31 December 19X7:

	31.12.19X6		31.12.19X7	
	£	£	£	£
Fixed assets				
Premises at cost		25,000		28,800
Current assets				
Stock	12,500		12,850	
Debtors	21,650		23,140	
Cash and bank balances	4,300		5,620	
	38,450		41,610	
Less Current liabilities				
Creditors	11,350		11,120	
Working capital		27,100		30,490
		52,100		59,290
Financed by:				
Capital				
Opening balances b/fwd		52,660		52,100
Add Net profit for year		16,550		25,440
		69,210		77,540
Less Drawings		17,110		18,250
		52,100		59,290

Note: No depreciation has been charged in the accounts.

Exhibit 38.3

T Holmes

Cash Flow Statement for the year ended 31 December 19X7

	£
Net cash flow from operating activities (*see* Note 1)	23,370
Capital expenditure and financial investment	
Payment to acquire extra premises	3,800
Financing	
Drawings	
18,250	
Increase in cash	1,320

Notes:

1 Reconciliation of net profit to net cash inflow:

	£	£
Net profit		25,440
Less cash used for:		
Increase in stock	350	
Increase in debtors	1,490	
Decrease in creditors	230	2,070
Net cash flow from operating activities		23,370

2 Analysis of changes in cash during the year:

	£
Balance at 1 January 19X7	4,300
Net cash inflow	1,320
Balance at 31 December 19X7	5,620

38.7 Note on the use of brackets

In accounting, it is customary to show a figure in brackets if it is a minus figure. This would be deducted from the other figures to arrive at the total of the column. These are seen very frequently in cash flow statements. For example, Note 1 accompanying Exhibit 38.3 would have been shown as:

	£
Net profit	25,440
Increase in stock	(350)
Increase in debtors	(1,490)
Decrease in creditors	(230)
	23,370

38.8 Adjustments needed to net profit

When net profit is included as a source of cash funds, we usually have to adjust the net profit figure to take account of items included which do not involve a movement of cash *in the period covered by the cash flow statement.*

38.9 Depreciation

For instance, suppose we bought equipment costing £3,000 in the year ended 31 December 19X6. It is depreciated at £1,000 per annum for 3 years and then scrapped, disposal value being nil. This would result in the following:

	Years to 31 December		
	19X6	*19X7*	*19X8*
	£	£	£
(*i*) Item involving flow of cash:			
Cost of equipment	3,000		
(*ii*) Items not involving flow of cash:			
Depreciation	1,000	1,000	1,000
(*iii*) Net profit before depreciation	12,000	13,000	15,000
(*iv*) Net profit after depreciation	11,000	12,000	14,000

Now the question arises as to which of figures (*i*) to (*iv*) are the ones to be used in cash flow statements. Let us examine items (*i*) to (*iv*) accordingly.

(*i*)   A payment of £3,000 is made to buy equipment. This *does* involve a flow of cash and should therefore be included in the cash flow statement for 19X6.

(*ii*) Depreciation is represented by a bookkeeping entry:

Debit profit and loss: Credit provision for depreciation.

This does not involve any outflow of cash and should not be shown in a cash flow statement.

(*iii*) Net profit before depreciation. This brings cash flowing into the firm and therefore should be shown in cash flow statements.

(*iv*) Net profit after depreciation. Depreciation does not involve cash flow, and therefore (*iii*) is the net profit we need.

In most examination questions (*iii*) will not be shown. As we will show you, the figure for net profit before depreciation will be calculated in the cash flow statement itself.

38.10 Bad debts provisions

If a debt is written off as bad, then that involves a flow of cash. A debt would have become cash when paid. Now you are saying that this will not happen and have written it off to profit and loss account.

On the other hand a provision for bad debts is similar in this respect to a provision for depreciation. The cash flow occurs *when* a bad debt *is* written off, and not when provisions are made in case there may be bad debts in the future.

If an examination question gives you the net profits *after* bad debts provision, then the provision has to be added back to exclude it from the profit calculations.

38.11 Book profit/loss on sales of fixed assets

If a fixed asset with a book value (after depreciation) of £5,000 is sold for £6,400 cash, then the flow of cash is £6,400. The fact that there has been a book profit of £1,400 does not provide any more cash above the figure of £6,400. Similarly, the sale of an asset with a book value of £3,000 for £2,200 cash produces a flow of cash of £2,200. The £800 book loss does mean that there has been a further overflow.

38.12 Example of adjustments

As the net profit figure in accounts is:

(*i*)   *after* adjustments for depreciation
(*ii*) *after* provisions for bad debts adjustments
(*iii*) *after* book profits/losses on sales of fixed assets

profits need to be adjusted in cash flow statements. However, the adjustments are only for depreciation in *that period*, and for fixed asset book profits/losses for *that period*. No adjustments are needed with reference to previous periods. Exhibit 38.4 shows examples of three firms.

Exhibit 38.4

	Firm A £	Firm B £	Firm C £
Depreciation for year	2,690	4,120	6,640
Increases in bad debt provision	540	360	
Decrease in bad debt provision			200
Book loss on sale of fixed assets	1,200		490
Book profit on sale of fixed assets		750	
Net profit after the above items included	16,270	21,390	32,410

Reconciliation of net profit to net cash inflow

	£	£	£
Net profit	16,270	21,390	32,410
Adjustment for items not involving the movement of funds:			
Depreciation	2,690	4,120	6,640
Book profit on sale of fixed assets		(750)	
Book loss on sale of fixed assets	1,200		490
Increase in bad debt provision	540	360	
Decrease in bad debt provision			(200)
Net cash flow from operating activities	20,700	25,120	39,340

You will notice that the items in brackets, i.e. (750) and (200), had been credits in the profit and loss accounts and need deducting, while the other items were debits and need adding back.

38.13 A comprehensive example

Exhibit 38.5

The balance sheets of R Lester are as follows:

	31.12.19X7			31.12.19X8		
	£	£	£	£	£	£
Fixed assets						
Equipment at cost		28,500			26,100	
Less Depreciation to date		11,450	17,050		13,010	13,090
Current assets						
Stock		18,570			16,250	
Debtors	8,470			14,190		
Less Bad debts provision	420	8,050		800	13,390	
Cash and bank balances		4,060			3,700	
		30,680			33,340	
Less Current liabilities						
Creditors		4,140			5,730	
Working capital			26,540			27,610
			43,590			40,700
Financed by:						
Capital						
Opening balances b/d			35,760			33,590
Add Net profit			10,240			11,070
Add Cash introduced			–			600
			46,000			45,260
Less Drawings			12,410			8,560
			33,590			36,700
Loan from J Gorsey			10,000			4,000
			43,590			40,700

Notes: Equipment with a book value of £1,350 was sold for £900. Depreciation written off equipment during the year was £2,610.

The cash flow statement will be as follows:

R Lester

Cash Flow Statement for the year ended 31 December 19X8

	£	£
Net cash flow from operating activities (*see* Note 1)		12,700
Capital expenditure and financial investment		
Receipts from sale of fixed assets		900
Financing		
Capital introduced	600	
Loan repaid to J Gorsey	(6,000)	
Drawings	(8,560)	(13,960)
Decrease in cash		(360)

Notes:

1 Reconciliation of net profit to net cash inflow:

	£	£
Net profit		11,070
Depreciation	2,610	
Loss on sale of fixed assets	450	
Increase in bad debts provision	380	
Decrease in stock	2,320	
Increase in creditors	1,590	
Increase in debtors	(5,720)	1,630
Net cash flow from operating activities		12,700

2 Analysis of changes in cash during the year:

	£
Balance at 1 January 19X8	4,060
Net cash inflow	(360)
Balance at 31 December 19X8	3,700

38.14 UK companies and FRS 1

We have already stated that UK companies, except the very smallest, have to publish a cash flow statement for each accounting period. Students whose level of studies terminates with the conclusion of Volume 1 will not normally need to know more than has already been written in this chapter. However, some will need to know the basic layout in FRS 1. For these students, the basic layout is shown in Exhibit 38.6.

Exhibit 38.6

X LIMITED

Cash Flow Statement for the year ended 31 December 19X7

	£000	£000
1 Net cash inflow/(outflow) from operating activities (*see* Note 1)		XXX
2 *Returns on investments and servicing of finance*		
Interest received	XXX	
Interest paid	(XXX)	
Preference dividends paid	(XXX)	
Net cash inflow/(outflow) from returns on investments and servicing of finance		XXX
3 *Taxation*		XXX
4 *Capital expenditure and financial investment*		
Payments to acquire intangible fixed assets	XXX	
Payments to acquire tangible fixed assets	XXX	
Receipts from sales of tangible fixed assets	XXX	
Net cash inflow/(outflow) from capital expenditure and financial investment		XXX
5 *Acquisitions and disposals*		
Purchase of subsidiary undertaking	(XXX)	
Sale of business	XXX	
Net cash inflow/(outflow) from acquisitions and disposals		XXX
6 *Equity dividends paid*		(XXX)
7 *Management of liquid resources*		
Cash withdrawn from 7 day deposit	XXX	
Purchase of government securities	(XXX)	
Sale of corporate bonds	XXX	
Net cash inflow/(outflow) from management of liquid resources		XXX
8 *Financing*		
Issue of ordinary share capital	XXX	
Repurchase of debenture loan	(XXX)	
Expenses paid in connection with share issues	(XXX)	
Increase/(decrease) in cash in the period		XXX

Reconciliation of net cash flow to movement in net debt/funds

Increase/(decrease) in cash in the period	XXX	
Cash inflow/(outflow) from increase/decrease in debt and lease financing	XXX	
Cash inflow/(outflow) from decrease/increase in liquid resources	XXX	
Change in net debt resulting from cash flows		XXX
Loans and finance leases acquired with subsidiary		(XXX)
New finance leases		(XXX)
Exchange rate translation differences		XXX
Movement in net debt in the period		XXX
Net funds at 1 January 19X7		XXX
Net debt at 31 December 19X7		(XXX)

...tatement

...perating profit to net cash inflow/(outflow) from operating activities

	£000
	XXX
	XXX
of tangible fixed assets	XXX
...i stocks	XXX
...i debtors	XXX
...i creditors	XXX
...ash inflow/(outflow) from operating activities	XXX

Each of the eight headings of the cash flow statement can be shown as one line in the statement and the detail in a note. (The numbers have been shown in Exhibit 38.6 in order to make it clear what the eight headings are. These line numbers would not normally be included in the cash flow statement.)

The reconciliation to net debt does not form part of the statement, nor does the reconciliation of operating profit to net cash flow from operating activities. Either can be shown in a separate note (as the reconciliation of operating profit to net cash flow from operating activities is shown above) or adjoining the statement (as in the case of the reconciliation of the movement of cash to net debt above).

38.15 Uses of cash flow statements

Cash flow statements have many uses other than the legal need for some companies to prepare them.

Let us first of all list a few cases where a business might find them useful in helping to answer their queries:

(a) One small businessman wants to know why he now has an overdraft. He started off the year with money in the bank, he has made profits, and yet he now has a bank overdraft.

(b) Another businessman wants to know why the bank balance has risen even though the firm is losing money.

(c) The partners in a business have put in additional capital this last year. Even so, the bank balance fell dramatically during the year. They want an explanation as to how this has happened.

A study of the cash flow statement in each case would reveal to them the answers to their questions. A study of the final accounts themselves would not give them the information that they needed.

Besides the answers to such specific queries, cash flow statements should also help businesses to assess the following:

- the cash flows which the business may be able to generate in the future;
- how far the business will be able to meet future commitments, such as taxation due, loan repayments, interest payments, contracts which could possibly lose quite a lot of money;
- how far future share issues may be needed, or additional capital in the case of sole traders or partnerships;
- a valuation of the business.

New term

Cash flow statement (p. 394): A statement showing how cash has been generated and disposed of by an organisation.

Main points to remember

1   By law, large companies have to draw up and publish cash flow statements.

2   FRS 1 is the accounting standard which governs the drafting of cash flow statements in companies.

3   Net profit has to be adjusted for non-cash items to find the net cash flow from operating activities.

4   Depreciation, bad debt provisions, and book profits/losses on sales of assets are all examples of non-cash items needing adjustment.

Review questions

38.1   The balance sheets of M Daly, a sole trader, for two successive years are shown below. You are required to draw up a cash flow statement for the year ended 31 December 19X4.

Balance Sheets as at 31 December

	19X3	19X4		19X3	19X4
	£	£		£	£
Land and premises			Capital account:		
(cost £3,000)	2,600	2,340	1 January	4,200	4,700
Plant and machinery			*Add* Net profit for		
(cost £2,000)	1,500	–	the year	1,800	2,200
(cost £3,000)	–	2,300		6,000	6,900
Stocks	660	630			
Trade debtors	1,780	1,260	Deduct drawings	1,300	1,500
Bank	–	710		4,700	5,400
			Trade creditors	1,200	840
			Bank overdraft	640	–
			Loan (repayable		
			December 19X9)	–	1,000
	6,540	7,240		6,540	7,240

38.2A

John Flynn

Balance Sheets as at 31 December

	19X8 £	19X9 £		19X8 £	19X9 £
Buildings	5,000	5,000	Capital at 1 January	15,500	16,100
Fixtures *Less* Depreciation	1,800	2,000	*Add* Cash introduced	–	2,500
			„ Net profit for year	6,800	7,900
Motor van *Less* Depreciation	2,890	5,470		22,300	26,500
Stock	3,000	8,410	*Less* Drawings	6,200	7,800
Debtors	4,860	5,970		16,100	18,700
Bank	3,100	–	Creditors	2,900	2,040
Cash	350	150	Bank overdraft	–	1,260
			Loan (repayable in 10 years' time)	2,000	5,000
	21,000	27,000		21,000	27,000

Draw up a cash flow statement for John Flynn for the year ended 31 December 19X9. You are told that fixtures bought in 19X9 cost £400, whilst a motor van was bought for £4,000.

38.3 Malcolm Phillips is a sole trader who prepares his accounts annually to 30 April. His summarised balance sheets for the last two years are shown below.

Balance Sheets as at 30 April

	19X8 £	19X9 £		19X8 £	19X9 £
Capital at 1 May	20,000	20,500	Fixed assets, at cost	15,500	18,500
Add			*Less* Provision for		
Profit for year	7,000	8,500	depreciation	1,500	1,700
Additional capital introduced	–	2,000		14,000	16,800
	27,000	31,000			
Less Drawings	6,500	8,000			
	20,500	23,000	Stock	3,100	5,900
Trade creditors	2,000	2,200	Debtors	3,900	3,400
Bank overdraft	–	900	Bank	1,500	–
	22,500	26,100		22,500	26,100

Malcolm is surprised to see that he now has an overdraft, in spite of making a profit and bringing in additional capital during the year.

Questions:

(*a*) Draw up a suitable financial statement which will explain to Malcolm how his overdraft has arisen.

(*b*) The following further information relates to the year ended 30 April 19X9.

	£
Sales (all on credit)	30,000
Cost of sales	22,500

Calculate Malcolm's
(*i*) gross profit margin
(*ii*) rate of stock turnover (stock-turn).

(*Midland Examining Group GCSE*)

38.4 From the following details you are to draft a cash flow statement for C Willis for the year ended 31 December 19X8:

C Willis

Profit and Loss Account for the year ended 31 December 19X8

	£	£
Gross profit		29,328
Add Discounts received	298	
„ Profit on sale of motor van	570	868
		30,196
Less Expenses		
Motor expenses	1,590	
Wages	8,790	
General expenses	2,144	
Bad debts	340	
Increase in bad debt provision	120	
Depreciation: Motor van	1,090	14,074
		16,122

Balance Sheets at 31 December

	19X7		19X8	
	£	£	£	£
Fixed assets				
Motor vans at cost	11,200		7,200	
Less Depreciation to date	4,160	7,040	2,980	4,220
Current assets				
Stock	10,295		17,150	
Debtors *less* provision*	5,190		3,380	
Bank	1,568		2,115	
	17,053		22,645	
Less Current liabilities				
Creditors	2,770	14,283	2,920	19,725
		21,323		23,945
Less Long-term liability				
Loan from P Bond		6,000		5,000
		15,323		18,945
Capital				
Opening balance b/d	12,243		15,323	
Add Net profit	14,080		16,122	
	26,323		31,445	
Less Drawings	11,000	15,323	12,500	18,945

* Debtors 19X7 £5,490 – provision £300.
  Debtors 19X8 £3,800 – provision £420.

Note: The motor van was sold for £2,300 during 19X8.

38.5A You are required to draw up a cash flow statement for S Markham for the year ended 30 June 19X8 from the following information:

S Markham
Profit and Loss Account for the year ended 30 June 19X8

	£	£
Gross profit		139,940
Add Reduction in bad debt provision		170
		140,110
Less Expenses:		
Wages and salaries	49,220	
General trading expenses	14,125	
Equipment running costs	16,040	
Motor vehicle expenses	8,110	
Depreciation: Motor vehicles	3,090	
Equipment	2,195	
Loss on sale of equipment	560	93,340
Net profit		46,770

Balance Sheets at 30 June

	19X7		19X8	
	£	£	£	£
Fixed assets				
Equipment at cost	31,150		20,100	
Less Depreciation to date	18,395	12,755	14,600	5,500
Motor vehicles at cost	22,510		22,510	
Less Depreciation to date	7,080	15,430	10,170	12,340
		28,185		17,840
Current assets				
Stock	28,970		32,005	
Debtors *less* provision*	16,320		15,050	
Bank	9,050		28,225	
	54,340		75,280	
Less Current liabilities				
Creditors	11,350	42,990	14,360	60,920
		71,175		78,760
Less Long-term liability				
Loan from A White		21,185		10,000
		49,990		68,760
Capital				
Opening balance	38,340		49,990	
Add Net profit		36,150		46,770
	74,490		96,760	
Less Drawings	24,500	49,990	28,000	68,760

* Debtors 19X7 £17,000 – provision £680.
  Debtors 19X8 £15,560 – provision £510.

Note: The equipment was sold for £4,500.

39

Joint venture accounts

Objectives

After you have studied this chapter, you should:

- *understand what is meant by the term 'joint venture'*

- *know how to make the entries in the accounts for a joint venture*

39.1 Nature of joint ventures

Sometimes a particular business venture can best be done by two or more firms joining together to do it instead of doing it separately. The joining together is for that one venture only, it is not joining together to make a continuing business.

Such projects are known as **joint ventures**. For instance, a merchant might provide the capital, the transport to the markets and the selling skills. The farmer grows the produce. The profits or losses are then shared between them in agreed ratios. It is like a partnership, but only for this one transaction. There may be several joint ventures between the same firms, but each one is a separate venture. The agreements for each venture may be different from each other.

39.2 Accounting for large joint ventures

For large-scale joint ventures, a separate bank account and separate set of books are kept. In such cases the calculation of profit is not difficult. It is similar to preparing a set of final accounts in an ordinary firm.

39.3 Accounting for smaller joint ventures

No separate set of books or separate bank accounts are kept for smaller joint ventures. Each party will record in his own books only those transactions with which he has been concerned. Exhibit 39.1 gives an example of such a joint venture.

Exhibit 39.1

White of London and Green of Glasgow enter into a joint venture. White is to supply the goods and pay some of the expenses. Green is to sell the goods and receive the cash, and pay the remainder of the expenses. Profits are to be shared equally.

Details of the transactions are as follows:

	£
White supplied the goods costing	1,800
White paid wages	200
White paid for storage expenses	160
Green paid transport expenses	120
Green paid selling expenses	320
Green received cash from sales of all the goods	3,200

Stage 1

White and Green will each have entered up his part of the transactions. White will have opened an account named 'Joint Venture with Green'. Similarly, Green will have opened a 'Joint Venture with White' account. The double entry to these joint venture accounts will be:

In White's books:

Payments by White:	Debit joint venture with Green
	Credit cash book
Good supplied:	Debit joint venture with Green
	Credit purchases

In Green's books:

Payments by Green:	Debit joint venture with White
	Credit cash book
Cash received by Green:	Debit cash book
	Credit joint venture with White

At this point the joint venture accounts in each of their books will appear as follows:

White's books (in London)

Joint Venture with Green

	£		
Purchases	1,800		
Cash: wages	200		
Cash: storage expenses	160		

Green's books (in Glasgow)

Joint Venture with White

	£		£
Cash: transport expenses	120	Cash: sales	3,200
Cash: selling expenses	320		

Stage 2

At this stage, White and Green know only the details in their own set of books. They do not yet know what the details are in the other person's books.

This means that they cannot yet calculate profits, or find out how much cash has to be paid or received to close the venture. To do this they must each send a copy of their joint venture accounts to the other person.

Each person will then draw up a memorandum joint venture account, to include all the details from each joint venture account. This is now shown:

White and Green
Memorandum Joint Venture Account

	£	£		£
Purchases		1,800	Sales	3,200
Wages		200		
Storage expenses		160		
Transport expenses		120		
Selling expenses		320		
Net profit:				
White (one-half)	300			
Green (one-half)	300	600		
		3,200		3,200

The memorandum joint venture account is not a double entry account. It is drawn up only (*a*) to find out the shares of net profit or loss, and (*b*) to help calculate the amounts payable and receivable to close the venture.

Stage 3

The net profit shares for White and Green need to be brought into their books. This is as follows:

White's books
   Debit share of profit to joint venture with Green's account
      Credit White's profit and loss account

Green's books
   Debit share of profit to joint venture with White's account
      Credit Green's profit and loss account

After these entries the joint venture accounts are balanced down. These will show:

(*a*) If the balance carried down is a credit balance, the person has received more from the joint venture than he should keep. He will then have to pay that amount to the other person to close the venture.
(*b*) If the balance carried down is a debit balance, the person has received less from the joint venture than he should get. He will then need to receive cash from the other person to close the venture.

The joint venture accounts now completed can be shown.

White's books (in London)

Joint Venture with Green

	£		£
Purchases	1,800	Balance c/d	2,460
Cash: wages	200		
Cash: storage expenses	160		
Share of profit transferred			
to profit and loss account	300		
	2,460		2,460
Balance b/d	2,460	Cash in settlement from Green	2,460

Green's books (in Glasgow)

Joint Venture with White

	£		£
Cash: transport expenses	120	Cash: sales	3,200
Cash: selling expenses	320		
Share of profit transferred			
to profit and loss account	300		
Balance c/d	2,460		
	3,200		3,200
Cash in settlement to White	2,460	Balance b/d	2,460

New term

Joint ventures (p. 407): Business agreements under which two businesses join together for a set of activities and agree to share the profits.

Main points to remember

1 When two or more businesses join together for a particular business venture, and do not form a permanent business entity, they have entered into a joint venture.

2 Larger joint ventures operate a separate bank account and books dedicated to the project.

3 The participants in smaller joint ventures rely on their own bank accounts and books to run and record their part of the project, using a *memorandum joint venture account* to pass the details of their part of the project to the other participant(s).

Review questions

39.1 Ollier and Avon enter a joint venture, to share profits or losses equally, resulting from dealings in second-hand cars. Both parties take an active part in the business, each recording his own transactions. They have no joint banking account or separate set of books.

19X9
Jan 1 Ollier buys three cars for £900.
 „ 31 Ollier pays for repairs and respraying of vehicles £60.
Mar 1 Avon pays garage rental £20 and advertising expenses £10.
Apr 12 Avon pays for licence and insurance renewal of vehicles £36.
Aug 10 Avon buys a vehicle in excellent condition for £100.
 „ 31 Ollier sells the four vehicles, to various clients, the sales being completed on this date, totalling £1,600.

Show the relevant accounts in the books of both partners.

39.2A Mr Carter entered into a joint venture with Mr Thomas for the purchase and sale of bicycles. They agreed that profits and losses should be shared equally.
   The following transactions took place:

(a) Mr Carter purchased bicycles for £88,900 and paid carriage £273.
(b) Mr Thomas purchased bicycles for £7,560 and paid carriage £51.

(c) Mr Thomas paid to Mr Carter £40,000.

(d) Mr Carter sold bicycles for £73,400 and sent a cheque for £30,000 to Mr Thomas.

(e) Mr Thomas sold for £10,230 all the bicycles he had purchased.

(f The unsold bicycles in the possession of Mr Carter were taken over by him at a valuation of £26,000.

(g) The amount due from one venturer to the other was paid and the joint venture was dissolved.

You are required to prepare:

(i) a statement to show the net profit or loss of the joint venture, and

(ii) the accounts for the joint venture in the books of Mr Carter and Mr Thomas.

39.3 Plant, Hoe & Reap entered into a joint venture for dealing in carrots. The transactions connected with this venture were:

19X9

Jan	8	Plant rented land cost £156.
„	10	Hoe supplied seeds cost £48.
„	17	Plant employed labour for planting £105.
„	19	Hoe charged motor expenses £17.
„	30	Plant employed labour for fertilising £36.
Feb	28	Plant paid the following expenses: Sundries £10, Labour £18, Fertiliser £29.
Mar	17	Reap employed labour for lifting carrots £73.
„	30	Sale expenses London paid by Reap £39.
„	31	Reap received cash from sale proceeds gross £987.

Required:

Show the joint venture accounts in the books of Plant, Hoe & Reap. Also show in full the method of arriving at the profit on the venture which is to be apportioned: Plant seven-twelfths; Hoe three-twelfths; Reap two-twelfths.

Any outstanding balances between the parties are settled by cheque on 30 April.

39.4A Wild, Wood and Bine enter into a joint venture for dealing in antique brass figures. The following transactions took place:

19X8

Mar	1	Wild rented a shop, paying 3 months' rent £150.
„	2	Wood bought a motor van for £2,700.
„	4	Wood bought antiques for £650.
„	15	Bine received cash from sale proceeds of antiques £3,790.
„	28	Wild bought antiques for £1,200.
Apr	11	Motor van broke down. Bine agreed to use his own van for the job, until cessation of the joint venture, at an agreed charge of £400.
„	13	Motor van bought on Mar 2 was sold for £2,100. Proceeds were kept by Wild.
„	15	Sales of antiques, cash being kept by Wood £780.
„	18	Lighting bills paid for shop by Bine £120.
„	30	Bine bought antiques for £440.
May	4	General expenses of shop paid for £800, Bine and Wild paying half each.
„	19	Antiques sold by Bine £990, proceeds being kept by him.
„	31	Joint venture ended. The antiques still in stock were taken over at an agreed valuation of £2,100 by Wood.

Required:

Show the joint venture accounts in the books of each of the three parties. Show in full the workings needed to arrive at the profit on the venture. The profit or loss was to be split: Wood one-half; Wild one-third; Bine one-sixth. Any outstanding balances between the parties were settled on 31 May 19X8.

40

Bills of exchange

Objectives

After you have studied this chapter, you should:

- *understand what is meant by the term 'bill of exchange', how they are used, and by whom*

- *know how to make the entries in the accounts for a bill of exchange*

40.1 Nature of bills of exchange

When goods are supplied to someone on credit, or services performed for him, then that person becomes a **debtor**. The creditor firm would normally wait for payment by the debtor. Until payment is made the money owing is of no use to the creditor firm as it is not being used in any way. This can be remedied by **factoring** the debtors, which involves passing the debts over to a finance firm. They will pay an agreed amount for the legal rights to the debts.

Another possibility is that of obtaining a bank overdraft, with the debtors accepted as part of the security on which the overdraft has been granted.

Yet another way that can give the creditor effective use of the money owing to him is for him to draw a **bill of exchange** on the debtor. This means that a document is drawn up requiring the debtor to pay the amount owing to the creditor, or to anyone nominated by him at any time, on or by a particular date. He sends this document to the debtor who, if he agrees to it, is said to 'accept' it by writing on the document that he will comply with it and appends his signature. The debtor then returns the bill of exchange to the creditor. This document is then legal proof of the debt. The debtor is not then able to contest the validity of the debt except for any irregularity in the bill of exchange itself.

40.2 How bills of exchange are used

The creditor can now act in one of three ways:

1   He can negotiate the bill to another person in payment of a debt. That person may also renegotiate it to someone else. The person who possesses the bill at maturity, i.e. the date for payment of the bill, will present it to the debtor for payment.
2   He may 'discount' it with a bank. 'Discount' here means that the bank will take the bill of exchange and treat it in the same manner as money deposited in the bank account. The bank will then hold the bill until maturity when it will present it to the debtor for payment. The bank will make a charge to the creditor for this service, known as a **discounting charge**.
3   The third way open to the creditor is for him to hold the bill until maturity when he

will present it to the debtor for payment. In this case, apart from having a document which is legal proof of the debt and could therefore save legal costs if a dispute arose, no benefit has been gained from having a bill of exchange. However, action **1** or **2** could have been taken if the need had arisen.

40.3 The parties to a bill of exchange

The creditor who draws up the bill of exchange is known as the **drawer**. The debtor on whom it is drawn is the **drawee**, when accepted he becomes the **acceptor**, while the person to whom the bill is to be paid is the **payee**. In fact, it may be recognised that a cheque is a special type of bill of exchange where the drawee is always a bank and, in addition, is payable on demand. This chapter, however, refers to bills of exchange other than cheques.

To the person who is to receive the money on maturity of the bill of exchange the document is known as a **bill receivable**, while to the person who is to pay the sum due on maturity it is known as a **bill payable**.

40.4 Dishonoured bills

When the debtor fails to make payment on maturity the bill is said to be dishonoured. If the holder is someone other than the drawer then he will have recourse against the person who has negotiated the bill to him, that person will then have recourse against the one who negotiated it to him, and so on until final recourse is had against the drawer of the bill for the amount of money due on the bill. The drawer's right of action is then against the acceptor.

On dishonour, a bill is often **noted**. This means that the bill is handed to a lawyer acting in his capacity as a notary public, who then re-presents the bill to the acceptor. The notary public then records the reasons for it not being discharged. The notary public's fee is known as a **noting charge**. With a foreign bill, in addition to the bill being noted, it is necessary to **protest** the bill in order to preserve the holder's rights against the drawer and previous endorsers. **Protest** is the term which covers the legal formalities needed.

The action to be taken by the drawer depends entirely upon circumstances. Often the lack of funds on the acceptor's part is purely temporary. In this case the drawer will negotiate with the acceptor and agree to draw another bill, or substitute several bills of smaller amounts with different maturity dates, for the amount owing, frequently with an addition for interest to compensate for the extended period of credit. Negotiation is the keynote; it must not be thought that acceptors are always sued when they fail to make payment. They are customers, and where future dealings with them are expected to be profitable harsh measures are certainly to be avoided. Legal action should be the last action to be considered. Any interest charged to the acceptor would be debited to his account and credited to an Interest Receivable Account.

40.5 Discounting charges and noting charges

From the acceptor's point of view the discounting of a bill is a matter wholly for the drawer or holder to decide. He, the acceptor, has been allowed a term of credit and will pay the agreed price on the maturity of the bill. Therefore the discounting charge is not one that he should suffer; this should be borne wholly by the person discounting the bill.

On the other hand, the noting charge has been brought about by the acceptor's default. It is equitable that his account should be charged with the amount of the expense of **noting** and **protesting**.

40.6 Retired bills

Instead of waiting until maturity, bills may be retired, i.e. not allowed to run until maturity. They may be paid off before maturity, in which case a rebate is often allowed because the full term of credit has not been taken; or else renewed by fresh bills being drawn and the old ones cancelled. The new bills often include interest because the term of credit has been extended.

40.7 Examples of bookkeeping entries

Exhibit 40.1

1 Drawer's Books

Goods had been sold by D Jarvis to J Burgon on 1 January 19X6 for £400. A bill of exchange is drawn by Jarvis and accepted by Burgon on 1 January 19X6, the date of maturity being 31 March 19X6. The following accounts show the entries necessary:

(*a*) If the bill is held by the drawer until maturity when the drawee makes payment.

J Burgon

19X6		£	19X6		£
Jan	1 Sales	400	Jan	1 Bill receivable	400

Bills Receivable

19X6		£	19X6		£
Jan	1 J Burgon	400	Mar	31 Bank	400

Bank

19X6		£		
Mar	31 Bills receivable	400		

(*b*) Where the bill is negotiated to another party by the drawer, in this case to IDT Ltd on 3 January 19X6.

J Burgon

19X6		£	19X6		£
Jan	1 Sales	400	Jan	1 Bill receivable	400

Bills Receivable

19X6		£	19X6		£
Jan	1 J Burgon	400	Jan	3 IDT Ltd	400

(c) If the bill is discounted with the bank, in this case on 2 January 19X6, the discounting charges being £6.

J Burgon

19X6			£	19X6			£
Jan	1	Sales	400	Jan	1	Bill receivable	400

Bills Receivable

19X6			£	19X6			£
Jan	1	J Burgon	400	Jan	2	Bank	400

Bank

19X6			£	19X6			£
Jan	2	Bills receivable	400	Jan	2	Discounting charges	6

Discounting Charges

19X6			£				
Jan	2	Bank	6				

2   Acceptor's Books

The instances (a), (b) and (c) in the drawer's books will result in similar entries in the acceptor's books. From the acceptor's point of view two things have happened, first the acceptance of the bill, and second its discharge by payment. The fact that (a), (b) and (c) would result in different payees is irrelevant so far as the acceptor is concerned.

D Jarvis

19X6			£	19X6			£
Jan	1	Bills payable	400	Jan	1	Purchases	400

Bills Payable

19X6			£	19X6			£
Mar	31	Bank	400	Jan	1	D Jarvis	400

Bank

				19X6			£
				Mar	31	Bill payable	400

40.8 Dishonoured bills and accounting entries

These can be illustrated by reference to Exhibit 40.2.

Exhibit 40.2

On 1 April 19X7 A Grant sells goods for £600 to K Lee, a bill with a maturity date of 30 June 19X7 being drawn by Grant and accepted by Lee on 2 April 19X7. On 30 June

19X7 the bill is presented to Lee, but he fails to pay it and it is therefore dishonoured. The bill is noted, the cost of £2 being paid by Grant on 7 July 19X7.

The entries needed will depend on whether or not the bill had been discounted by Grant.

1 Drawer's Books

Where the bill had not been discounted or renegotiated:

K Lee

19X7		£	19X7		£
Apr	1 Sales	600	Apr	2 Bills receivable	600
Jun	30 Bill receivable – dishonoured	600			
Jul	7 Bank: Noting charge (*a*)	2			

Bills Receivable

19X7		£	19X7		£
Apr	2 K Lee	600	Jun	30 K Lee – bill dishonoured	600

Bank

			19X7		£
			Jul	7 Noting charges – K Lee (*a*)	2

Note:

(*a*) As the noting charges are directly incurred as the result of Lee's default, then Lee must suffer the cost by his account being debited with that amount.

Where the bill has been discounted with a bank:

The entries can now be seen as they would have appeared if the bill had been discounted on 5 April 19X7, discounting charges being £9.

K Lee

19X7		£	19X7		£
Apr	1 Sales	600	Apr	2 Bill receivable	600
Jun	30 Bank – bill dishonoured (*c*)	600			
Jul	7 Bank: Noting charge	2			

Bills Receivable

19X7		£	19X7		£
Apr	2 K Lee	600	Apr	5 Bank	600

Bank

19X7		£	19X7		£
Apr	5 Bills receivable	600	Apr	5 Discounting charges (*b*)	9
			Jun	30 K Lee – bill dishonoured (*c*)	600
			Jul	7 Noting charges – K Lee	2

Discounting Charges

19X7			£	
Apr	5	Bank (b)	9	

Notes:

(b) The discounting charges are wholly an expense of A Grant. They are therefore charged to an expense account. Contrast this with the treatment of the noting charges.

(c) On maturity the bank will present the bill to Lee. On its dishonour the bank will hand the bill back to Grant, and will cancel out the original amount shown as being deposited in the bank account. This amount is then charged to Lee's personal account to show that he is still in debt.

2 Acceptor's Books

The entries in the acceptor's books will not be affected by whether or not the drawer has discounted the bill.

A Grant

19X7			£	19X7			£
Apr	1	Bill payable	600	Apr	1	Purchases	600
				Jun	30	Bill payable – dishonoured	600
				Jul	7	Noting charge (d)	2

Bills Payable

19X7			£	19X7			£
Jun	30	A Grant – bill dishonoured	600	Apr	1	A Grant	600

Noting Charges

19X7			£	
Jul	7	A Grant (d)	2	

Note:

(d) The noting charges will have to be reimbursed to A Grant. To show this fact A Grant's account is credited while the Noting Charges Account is debited to record the expense.

40.9 Bills receivable as contingent liabilities

The fact that bills had been discounted, but had not reached maturity by the balance sheet date, could give an entirely false impression of the financial position of the business unless a note to this effect is made on the balance sheet. That such a note is necessary can be illustrated by reference to the following balance sheets.

Balance Sheet as at 31 December 19X7

	(a) £	(a) £	(b) £	(b) £
Fixed assets		3,500		3,500
Current assets:				
Stock	1,000		1,000	
Debtors	1,200		1,200	
Bills receivable	1,800		–	
Bank	500		2,300	
	4,500		4,500	
Less Current liabilities	3,000		3,000	
Working capital		1,500		1,500
		5,000		5,000
		£		£
Financed by:				
Capital		5,000		5,000

Balance sheet (a) shows the position if £1,800 of bills receivable were still in hand. Balance sheet (b) shows the position if the bills had been discounted, ignoring discounting charges. To an outsider, balance sheet (b) seems to show a much stronger liquid position with £2,300 in the bank. However, should the bills be dishonoured on maturity the bank balance would slump to £500. The appearance of balance sheet (b) is therefore deceptive unless a note is added, e.g. 'Note: There is a contingent liability of £1,800 on bills discounted at the balance sheet date.' This note enables the outsider to view the bank balance in its proper perspective of depending on the non-dishonour of the bills discounted.

New terms

Bill of exchange (p. 412): A document drawn up by the drawer which requires his debtor, the drawee, to accept the bill, agreeing to pay a specified sum to the person called the payee on the due date specified.

Acceptor (p. 413): The drawee, when he accepts the bill, becomes the acceptor, thereby accepting liability to pay the debt.

Dishonoured bill (p. 413): Where the acceptor fails to pay his debt on the due date.

Contingent liability (p. 417): Until the acceptor pays his debt owing on the bill, the drawer will have a liability for the contingency that the bill will be dishonoured.

Factoring (p. 412): Passing the legal right to debts to a finance firm for an agreed amount.

Main points to remember

1   Bills of exchange enable businesses to obtain money owing to them in advance of the date when the debtor is expected to clear his debt.

2   They are also a form of evidence should the amount due be disputed later.

3   Bills of exchange are not a guarantee that a debt will be honoured.

Review questions

40.1 N Gudgeon sells goods to two companies on July 1 19X7.

To R Johnson Ltd	£2,460
To B Scarlet & Co Ltd	£1,500

He draws bills of exchange on each of them and they are both accepted.

He discounts both of the bills with the bank on July 4 19X7, and suffers discounting charges of £80 on Johnson's bill and £65 on Scarlet's bill. On September 1 19X7 the bills mature and Johnson Ltd meets its liability. Scarlet's bill is dishonoured and is duly noted on September 4, the noting charge being £6.

Show the above in the necessary accounts:

(*a*) In the books of Gudgeon.
(*b*) In the books of Scarlet Ltd and of Johnson Ltd.

40.2A P Cummings buys goods from T Victor Ltd on January 21 19X7 for £2,900 and from C Bellamy & Co for £4,160. Bills are drawn on him and he accepts them.

T Victor Ltd discount their bill with their bank on January 29, the discounting charge being £110.

C Bellamy & Co simply keep their bill waiting for maturity.

On maturity of the bills on April 21 19X7, Cummings duly meets (pays) Bellamy's bill. He is unable to pay Victor's bill and it is accordingly dishonoured. Victor duly has it noted on April 28 19X7, the noting charge being £10.

Show the entries necessary in:

(*a*) The books of P Cummings.
(*b*) The books of T Victor Ltd.
(*c*) The books of C Bellamy & Co.

40.3 KC owed TM £960. KC accepted a bill of exchange at three months' date for this amount. TM discounted it for £948.

Before the due date of the bill TM was informed that KC was unable to meet the bill and was offering a composition of 37.5 per cent of each £ to his creditors. This offer was accepted and cash equivalent to the composition was received.

Show the ledger entries to record the above in TM's ledger.

40.4 Draw up a sales ledger control account for the month of August 19X6 from the following:

19X6			£
Aug	1	Balances (Dr)	12,370
		Balances (Cr)	105
		Totals for the month:	
		Sales journal	16,904
		Returns inwards journal	407
		Cheques received from customers	15,970
		Bills receivable accepted	1,230
		Cash received from customers	306
		Bad debts written off	129
		Cash discounts allowed	604
		Bill receivable dishonoured	177
Aug	31	Balances (Cr)	88
		Balances (Dr)	?

Note: This question is being asked because it contains entries for bills of exchange.

40.5 A purchases ledger control account should be drawn up for February 19X7 from the following:

19X7			£
Feb	1	Balances (Dr)	33
		Balances (Cr)	8,570
		Totals for month:	
		Purchases journal	11,375
		Returns outwards journal	568
		Bills payable accepted by us	1,860
		Cheques paid to suppliers	9,464
		Cash paid to suppliers	177
		We were unable to meet a bill payable on maturity and it was	
		therefore dishonoured	800
		We agreed to suffer noting charge on dishonoured bill	20
Feb	28	Balances (Dr)	47
		Balances (Cr)	?

Note: This question is being asked because it contains entries for bills of exchange.

40.6A Prepare journal entries to indicate how the following would appear in the ledger accounts of (*a*) Noone, (*b*) Iddon.

19X8

Jan   1   Iddon sells goods £420 to Noone, and Noone sends to Iddon a three months' acceptance for this amount.

  ,,   1   Iddon discounts the acceptance with the Slough Discount Co. Ltd, receiving its cheque for £412.

Feb 29   One-third of Noone's stock, valued at £3,600, is destroyed by fire. Noone claims on the underwriters at Lloyds with whom he is insured.

Apr   1   The underwriters admit the claim for £3,000 only as the total stock was only insured for £9,000.

  ,,   4   In view of Noone's difficulties Iddon meets the acceptance due today by giving his cheque for £420 to the Slough Discount Co. Ltd; he draws on Noone a further bill for one month for £430 (to include £10 interest) which Noone accepts.

  ,,   9   Noone receives cheque from the underwriters in settlement of the admitted claim.

May   7   Noone's bank honours the acceptance presented by Iddon as due today.

40.7A Enter the following in the appropriate ledger accounts of R Smith:

19X9

Jan   5   R Smith sold goods to P Thomas, £320, and Thomas accepted Smith's bill for three months for this amount.

  ,,   6   R Smith discounted Thomas's bill at the London Discount Co. for £304, and pays this amount into his account at the bank.

Apr   8   The London Discount Co. notified Smith that Thomas's bill had been dishonoured. Smith at once sent a cheque to the London Discount Co. for the full amount of the bill plus £3 charges.

  ,, 14   Smith agreed that Thomas's bankers should accept a further bill for one month for the total amount owing plus £10 interest, and received the new acceptance.

May 18   Smith's bank informed him the new bill had been paid.

40.8A
- On 1 June 19X8, X purchased goods from Y for £860 and sold goods to Z for £570.
- On the same date, X drew a bill (No. 1) at three months on Z for £400 and Z accepted it.
- On 12 June 19X2, Z drew a bill (No. 2) at three months on Q for £150 which Q accepted.
- On 14 June, Z endorsed bill No. 2 over to X and, on 16 June, X endorsed this bill over to Y.
- On 20 June, X accepted a bill (No. 3) at three months for £720 drawn by Y in full settlement of his account, including interest. On 23 June, Y discounted bill No. 3 at his bank.
- On 17 September, Y informed X that Q's acceptance had been dishonoured and X sent a cheque for £150 to Y. The other bills were paid on the due dates.
- On 20 September, X received a cheque from Z for half the amount due from him.

Required:
Show the entries to record these transactions in the ledger and cash book of X.

40.9A Balances and transactions affecting a company's control accounts for the months of May 19X8 are listed below:

	£	
Balances at 1 May 19X8:		
Sales ledger	9,123	(debit)
	211	(credit)
Purchases ledger	4,490	(credit)
	88	(debit)
Transactions during May 19X8:		
Purchases on credit	18,135	
Allowances from suppliers	629	
Receipts from customers by cheque	27,370	
Sales on credit	36,755	
Discounts received	1,105	
Payments to creditors by cheque	15,413	
Contra settlements	3,046	
Allowances to customers	1,720	
Bills of exchange receivable	6,506	
Customers' cheques dishonoured	489	
Cash receipts from credit customers	4,201	
Refunds to customers for overpayment of accounts	53	
Discounts allowed	732	
Balances at 31 May 19X8:		
Sales ledger	136	(credit)
Purchases ledger	67	(debit)

Required:
(a) Explain the purposes for which control accounts are prepared.
(b) Post the sales ledger and purchases ledger control accounts for the month of May 19X2 and derive the respective debit and credit closing balances on 31 May 19X8.

Note: This question is being asked because it contains entries for bills of exchange.

(Association of Chartered Certified Accountants)

41

Consignment accounts

Objectives

After you have studied this chapter, you should:

- *understand what is meant by the term 'consignment account', how such accounts are used, and by whom*

- *know how to record the entries for consignment accounts*

41.1 Nature of a consignment

When a trader sells goods directly to customers, whether they are in his home country or overseas, these are ordinary sales. However, a trader may send goods to an agent to sell them for him. These goods are said to be sent on **consignment**. The main features are:

(a) The trader sends the goods to the agent. The goods do not belong to the agent; his job is to sell them for the trader. The goods are owned by the trader until they are sold. The trader sending the goods is called the **consignor**. The agent is called the **consignee**.

(b) The agent will store the goods until they are sold by him. He will have to pay some expenses, but these will later be refunded by the trader.

(c) The agent will receive a commission from the trader for his work.

(d) The agent will collect the money from the customers to whom he sells the goods. He will pay this over to the trader after deducting his expenses and commission. The statement from the agent to the trader showing this is known as the *account sales*.

Consignment accounts are to be found mainly in overseas trade.

41.2 Consignor's (the trader's) records

For each consignment to an agent a separate consignment account is opened. Think of it as a trading and profit and loss account for each consignment. The purpose is to calculate the net profit or loss on each consignment.

Goods consigned and expenses paid by the consignor

Double entry needed:

Goods consigned (a)   Debit consignment account
                           Credit goods sent on consignment account

Expenses paid (b)   Debit consignment account
                           Credit cash book

Expenses of the agent (consignee) and sales receipts

When the sales have been completed the consignee will send an account sales to the consignor. This will show:

	£	£
Sales		xxx
Less Expenses	xxx	
Commission	xxx	
		xxx
Balance now paid		xxx

The consignor enters these details in his books. The double entry needed is:

Sales (c):   Debit consignee's account
                                  Credit consignment account

Expenses of consignee (d):   Debit consignment account
                                  Credit consignee's account

Commission of consignee (e):   Debit consignment account
                                  Credit consignee's account

Cash received from consignee (f): Debit cash
                                  Credit consignee's account

Against each type of entry needed, (a) to (f) are shown. These will be used in Exhibit 41.1.

Exhibit 41.1

Wills of London, whose financial year ends on 31 December, consigned goods to Adams, his agent in Canada. All transactions were started and completed in 19X8.

(a) January 16: Wills consigned goods costing £500 to Adams.
(b) February 28: Wills paid carriage to Canada, £50.

Adams, the consignee, sends an account sales on 31 July when all the goods have been sold. It shows:

(c) Sales amounted to £750.
(d) Adams' expenses were: Import duty, £25.
                        Distribution expenses, £30.
(e) Commission had been agreed at 6 per cent of sales. This amounted to £41.
(f) Adams paid balance owing, £650.

Wills' books:

Consignment to Adams, Ottawa, Canada

19X8			£	19X8			£
Jan	16	Goods sent on		Jul	31	Sales (c)	750
		consignment (a)	500				
Feb	28	Bank: carriage (b)	50				
Jul	31	Adams: Import duty (d)	25				
		Distribution (d)	30				
„	31	Adams: Commission (e)	45				
„	31	Profit on consignment					
		(transferred to profit					
		and loss account)	100				
			750				750

Goods sent on Consignment

		19X8	£
		Jan 16 Consignment to Adams (a)	500

Cash Book

19X8		£	19X8		£
Jul 31 Adams (consignee) (f)		650	Feb 28 Consignment to Adams:		
			Carriage (b)		50

Adams (Consignee)

19X8		£	19X8		£
Jul 31 Consignment: Sales (c)		750	Jul 31 Consignment:		
			„ 31 Import duty (d)		25
			„ 31 Distribution (d)		30
			„ 31 Commission (e)		45
			„ 31 Bank (f)		650
		750			750

You can see that the main features are:

(a) The consignment account is a trading and profit and loss account for one consignment.

(b) The consignee's (Adams) personal account is used to show double entry for items concerning him. All of these details have been shown on the account sales he sent after selling the goods.

41.3 Consignee's (the agent's) records

The only items needed in the consignee's records will be found from the account sales he sent to the consignor after the goods have been sold.

He does not enter, in his double entry, the goods received on consignment. They never belong to him. His job is to sell the goods. Of course he will keep a note of the goods, but not in his double entry account records.

The double entry needed is:

Cash from sales of consignment (c)   Debit cash book
         Credit consignor's account

Payment of consignment expenses (d):   Debit consignor's account
         Credit cash book

Commission earned (e):   Debit consignor's account
         Credit profit and loss account

Cash to settle balance shown on account sales (f):   Debit consignor's account
         Credit cash book

Exhibit 41.2

Taking the details shown in Exhibit 41.1 the account sales sent by Adams (consignee) to Wills (consignor) would appear as follows:

Account Sales (converted into £ sterling)

Adams,
Ottawa,
Canada.
31 July 19X8

To   Wills
        London.

	£	£
Sale of goods received on consignment (c)		750
Less Charges:		
Import duty (d)	25	
Distribution costs (d)	30	
Commission (e)	45	100
Bank draft enclosed (f)		650

The double entry accounts in the books of the consignee (Adams) follow:

Wills (Consignor)

19X8		£	19X8		£
Jul 31	Bank:		Jul 31	Bank: Sales (c)	750
	Import duty (d)	25			
	Distribution (d)	30			
„ 31	Commission transferred				
	to profit and loss (e)	45			
„ 31	Bank (f)	650			
		750			750

Cash Book

19X8		£	19X8		£
Jul 31	Wills: Sales (c)	750	Jul 31	Wills: Import duty (d)	25
			„ 31	Wills: Distribution (d)	30
			„ 31	Wills: To settle account (f)	650

Profit and Loss Account (Adams)

		£
	Commission on consignment	
	from Wills (e)	45

You will see that the account of Wills in Adams' books in Exhibit 41.2 contains exactly the same details as that of Adams in Wills' books in Exhibit 41.1. Obviously the debits and credits are on opposite sides in the two sets of accounts.

41.4 Bad debts and consignments

Normally, when an agent sells the goods of the consignor he will collect the sale money from the customer. If the customer does not pay his account, the money in respect of this does not have to be paid by the agent to the consignor.

To make certain he does not have such bad debts, the consignor may pay an extra commission to the agent. When this happens the money for the debt will have to be paid by the agent even though he has not collected it. This extra commission is called **del credere commission**.

41.5 Consignor's accounting period and incomplete consignments

In this chapter we have looked at consignments which were all sold by the agent before the financial year end of the consignor. For instance, if a consignor's account year ends annually on 31 December, all goods consigned in 19X7 will have been sold by 31 December 19X7.

Sometimes this will not be true. We could have sent goods to the agent in September 19X7, and the final sales may be in March 19X8. When the consignor prepares his final accounts up to 31 December 19X7, there will be an incomplete consignment at the date of the balance sheet.

41.6 Accounting for incomplete consignments

The main difference between a completed consignment at the balance sheet date and an uncompleted one is that the unsold stock has to be valued and carried down to the following period. This stock will appear in the balance sheet of the consignor as a current asset. Such a case is shown in Exhibit 41.3.

Exhibit 41.3

(a) Farr of Chester consigns 10 cases of goods costing £200 per case to Moore in Nairobi on 1 July 19X7.
(b) Farr pays £250 for carriage and insurance for the whole consignment on 1 July 19X7.

Farr receives an interim account sales with a bank draft from Moore on 28 December 19X7. It shows (converted into £ sterling):

(c) Moore has sold 8 cases of goods for £400 each = £3,200.
(d) Moore has paid a total of £150 for landing charges and import duties on receipt of the whole consignment.
(e) Moore has paid selling costs, in respect of the 8 cases sold, of £160.
(f) Moore has deducted his commission of 10 per cent in respect of the 8 cases sold = 10% × £3,200 = £320.
(g) Moore encloses bank draft of £2,570. This is made up of (c) £3,200 – (d) £150 – (e) £160 – (f) £320 = £2,570.

Farr now wishes to balance off his consignment account at his financial year end, 31 December 19X7, and to transfer the profit to date to his profit and loss account.

The consignment account will appear as follows:

Farr's books:

Consignment to Moore

19X7		£	19X7		£
Jul 1	Goods on consignment (a)	2,000	Dec 28	Moore: Sale of part consignment (c)	3,200
„ 1	Bank: Carriage and insurance (b)	250	„ 31	Value of unsold stock (h) c/d	480
Dec 28	Moore:				
	Landing charges and import duties (d)	150			
	Selling costs (e)	160			
	Commission (f)	320			
„ 31	Profit on consignment to profit and loss	800			
		3,680			3,680

19X8			
Jan 1	Value of unsold stock (b) b/d	480	

Note:	(h)	Value of unsold stock at 31 December 19X7:	£	£
		Goods: 2 cases × £200 each		400
		Add Proportion of expenses belonging to 2 unsold cases out of 10 received		
		(b) Carriage 2/10 × £250	50	
		(d) Landing charges and duties 2/10 × £150	30	80
				480

There is no proportion of (e) selling costs £160 or (f) commission £320 added to the valuation of the 2 unsold cases. This is because both of these expenses were only for the sale of the 8 cases, and nothing to do with the 2 unsold cases.

The profit and loss account for Farr for the year ended 31 December 19X7 will include the consignment profit of £800. The balance sheet as at 31 December 19X7 will include the consignment stock of £480 as a current asset.

The consignee's account, Moore's, can be shown in Farr's books as:

Moore

19X7		£	19X7		£
Dec 28	Consignment: Sales (c)	3,200	Dec 28	Consignment expenses:	
				Landing charges etc. (d)	150
				Selling costs (e)	160
				Commission (f)	320
				Bank (g)	2,570
		3,200			3,200

41.7 Final completion of consignment

When the remainder of the consignment is sold, the consignment account can be closed. This will be done by transferring the final portion of profit or loss to the consignor's profit and loss account. The details will be found in the final account sales which the consignee will have sent to the consignor.

Taking the completion of the consignment in Exhibit 41.3 as an example, the following details were obtained from the final account sales dated 31 March 19X8.

(*i*)   The final 2 cases of goods were sold for £380 each = £760.
(*j*)   Selling costs for these 2 cases were £70.
(*k*)   Commission deducted at 10 per cent = 10%× £760 = £76.
(*l*)   Bank draft sent for £614. Made up of (*i*) £760 – (*j*) £70 – (*k*) £76 = £614.

The consignment account can now be shown.

Farr's books:

Consignment to Moore

19X8		£	19X8		£
Jan 1	Value of unsold stock (*h*) b/d	480	Mar 31 Moore: Sale of remainder (*i*)		760
Mar 31	Moore:				
	Selling costs (*j*)	70			
	Commission (*k*)	76			
„ 31	Profit to profit and loss	134			
		760			760

New terms

Consignment (p. 422): Selling goods through an agent.

Consignor (p. 422): The person sending goods on consignment.

Consignee (p. 422): The person receiving the goods on consignment.

Del credere commission (p. 426): Extra commission payable to an agent who will promise to pay for any bad debts.

Main points to remember

1   Goods sent to an agent on consignment continue to belong to the consignor until they are sold.

2   The consignee, or agent, sells the goods and collects the money due from customers.

3   The money collected is passed to the consignor after deduction of expenses and commission.

Review questions

41.1   On 8 February 19X8 PJ, a London trader, consigned 120 cases of goods to MB, an agent in New Zealand.
    The cost of the goods was £25 a case. PJ paid carriage to the port £147 and insurance £93.
    On 31 March 19X8 PJ received an *account sales* from MB, showing that 100 cases had been sold for £3,500 and MB had paid freight, at the rate of £2 a case, and port charges amounting to £186. MB was entitled to a commission of 5 per cent on sales. A *sight draft* for the net amount due was enclosed with the *account sales*.
    You are required to show the accounts for the above transactions in the ledger of PJ and to show the transfer to profit and loss account at 31 March 19X8.

(Institute of Chartered Secretaries and Administrators)

41.2A

(*a*)   Explain the differences between a consignment and a sale.

(*b*)   100 cases of goods costing £3,500 were sent on consignment by X Limited to Y Limited on 1 February 19X7. At the same time, X Limited paid delivery expenses of £100 and insurance of £20. On 1 March 19X7 an interim account sales was received from Y Limited showing that 80 cases had been sold for £63 each and that storage charges of £180 and selling expenses of £100 had been deducted from the account. After also deducting the commission on sales which was agreed at 5 per cent of the gross sales, Y Limited settled the balance due to X Limited for goods sold by a bank draft.

Required:

(*i*) Prepare the interim account sales, and
(*ii*) Prepare the consignment account in the books of X Limited.

41.3   On 15 November 19X8, Hughes consigned 300 cases of wooden items to Galvez of Madrid. On 31 December 19X8, Galvez forwarded an account sales, with a draft for the balance, showing the following transactions:

1   250 cases sold at £20 each and 50 at £18 each.
2   Port and duty charges £720.
3   Storage and carriage charges £410.
4   Commission on sales 5% + 1% del credere.

Required:
(*a*)   Prepare the account sales, and
(*b*)   Show the consignment inward account in the books of Galvez. Ignore interest.

41.4   Stone consigned goods to Rock on 1 January 19X8, their value being £12,000, and it was agreed that Rock should receive a commission of 5 per cent on gross sales. Expenses incurred by Stone for freight and insurance amount to £720. Stone's financial year ended on 31 March 19X8, and an account sales made up to that date was received from Rock. This showed that 70 per cent of the goods had been sold for £10,600 but that up to 31 March 19X8, only £8,600 had been received by Rock in respect of these sales. Expenses in connection with the goods consigned were shown as being £350, and it was also shown that £245 had been incurred in connection with the goods sold. With the account sales, Rock sent a sight draft for the balance shown to be due, and Stone incurred bank charges of £12 on 10 April 19X8, in cashing same.

Stone received a further account sales from Rock made up to 30 June 19X8, and this showed that the remainder of the goods had been sold for £4,800 and that £200 had been incurred by way of selling expenses. It also showed that all cash due had been received with the exception of a debt for £120 which had proved to be bad. A sight draft for the balance due was sent with the account sales and the bank charged Stone £9 on 1 July 19X8, for cashing same. You are required to write up the necessary accounts in Stone's books to record these transactions.

(*Institute of Chartered Accountants in England and Wales*)

41.5A Fleet is a London merchant. During the financial year to 31 March 19X8, he sent a consignment of goods to Sing, his agent in Bali. The details of the transaction were as follows:

(a) On 1 April 19X7, 1,000 boxes were sent to Sing. These boxes had originally cost Fleet £20 each.
(b) Fleet's carriage, freight and insurance costs of the consignment paid on 30 April 19X7 amounted to £2,000.
(c) During the voyage to Bali, ten boxes were lost. On 30 September 19X7, Fleet received a cheque for £220 as compensation from his insurance company for the loss of the boxes.
(d) On 1 March 19X8, Fleet received £20,000 from Sing.
(e) Both Fleet and Sing's accounting year end is 31 March.
(f) On 15 April 19X8, Fleet received the following interim account sales from Sing:

Interim Account Sales

The Water Front
Gama
Bali

31 March 19X8
Consignment of goods sold on behalf of Fleet, London: 950 boxes of merchandise.

	£	£	£
Sales:			
950 boxes at £30 each			28,500
Charges:			
Distribution expenses (at £2 per box)		1,900	
Landing charges and import duty (at £1 per box)		990	
Commission (5% × £28,500)		1,425	4,315
			24,185
Less amount previously sent			20,000
Net proceeds per draft enclosed			£4,185

31 March 19X8
Sing (signed)
Bali

Required:
Prepare the following ledger accounts for the year to 31 March 19X8:

(a) in Fleet's books of account:
    (i) goods sent on consignment account;
    (ii) consignment to Sing's account;
    (iii) Sing (consignee) account;

   and,

(b) in Sing's books of account:
    (i) Fleet (London) account;
    (ii) commission account.

(Association of Accounting Technicians)

Part 6

PARTNERSHIP ACCOUNTS AND COMPANY ACCOUNTS

Introduction

This part is concerned with accounting procedures, particularly those affecting partnerships; gives an introduction to goodwill in relation to partnerships and other business organisations; and introduces the accounts of limited liability companies.

42

Partnership accounts: an introduction

Objectives

After you have studied this chapter, you should:

- *understand exactly what a partnership is*

- *be able to distinguish between limited partners and the ones with unlimited liability*

- *know what the main features of a partnership agreement should be*

- *realise what will happen if no agreement has been made to share profits or losses*

- *be able to draw up the final accounts of a partnership*

42.1 The need for partnerships

So far we have mainly considered businesses owned by only one person. Businesses set up to make a profit can often have more than one owner. There are various reasons for multiple ownership:

1 The capital required is more than one person can provide.
2 The experience or ability required to manage the business cannot be found in one person alone.
3 Many people want to share management instead of doing everything on their own.
4 Very often the partners will be members of the same family.

There are two types of multiple ownership; **partnerships** and limited companies. This chapter deals only with partnerships. Limited companies will be the subject of later chapters.

42.2 Nature of a partnership

A partnership has the following characteristics:

1 It is formed to make profits.
2 It must obey the law as given in the Partnership Act 1890. If there is a limited partner, as described in 42.3, there is also the Limited Partnership Act of 1907 to

comply with as well.

3   Normally there can be a minimum of two partners and a maximum of 20 partners. Exceptions are banks, where there cannot be more than ten partners; also there is no maximum limit for firms of accountants, solicitors, stock exchange members or other professional bodies receiving the approval of the Board of Trade for this purpose.

4   Each partner (except for limited partners described below) must pay their share of any debts that the partnership could not pay. If necessary, they could be forced to sell all their private possessions to pay their share of the debts. This can be said to be unlimited liability.

42.3 Limited partners

Limited partners are not liable for the debts as in section 42.2 (4) above. They have the following characteristics:

1   Their liability for the debts of the partnership is limited to the capital they have put in. They can lose that capital, but they cannot be asked for any more money to pay the debts.

2   They are not allowed to take part in the management of the partnership business.

3   All the partners cannot be limited partners, so that there must be at least one partner with unlimited liability.

42.4 Partnership agreements

Agreements in writing are not necessary. However, it is better if a proper written agreement is drawn up by a lawyer or accountant. Where there is a proper written agreement there will be fewer problems between partners. A written agreement means less confusion about what has been agreed.

42.5 Contents of partnership agreements

The written agreement can contain as much, or as little, as the partners want. The law does not say what it must contain. The usual accounting contents are:

1   The capital to be contributed by each partner.
2   The ratio in which profits (or losses) are to be shared.
3   The rate of interest, if any, to be paid on capital before the profits are shared.
4   The rate of interest, if any, to be charged on partners' drawings.
5   Salaries to be paid to partners.
6   Arrangements for the admission of new partners.
7   Procedures to be carried out when a partner retires or dies.

Points **1** to **5** in the list above are now examined in detail. Points **6** and **7** will be taken up in later chapters.

1 Capital contributions

Partners need *not* contribute equal amounts of capital. What matters is how much capital each partner *agrees* to contribute.

2 Profit (or loss) sharing ratios

Partners can agree to share profits/losses in any ratio or any way that they may wish. However, it is often thought by students that profits should be shared in the same ratio as that in which capital is contributed. For example, suppose the capitals were Allen £2,000 and Beet £1,000, many people would share the profits in the ratio of two-thirds to one-third, even though the work to be done by each partner is similar. A look at the division of the first few years' profits on such a basis would be:

Years	1	2	3	4	5	Total
	£	£	£	£	£	£
Net profits	1,800	2,400	3,000	3,000	3,600	
Shared:						
Allen $\frac{2}{3}$	1,200	1,600	2,000	2,000	2,400	9,200
Beet $\frac{1}{3}$	600	800	1,000	1,000	1,200	4,600

It can now be seen that Allen would receive £9,200, or £4,600 more than Beet. To treat each partner fairly, the difference between the two shares of profit in this case, as the duties of the partners are the same, should be adequate to compensate Allen for putting extra capital into the firm. It is obvious that £4,600 extra profits is far more than adequate for this purpose, as Allen only put in an extra £1,000 as capital.

Consider too the position of capital ratio sharing of profits if one partner put in £99,000 and the other put in £1,000 as capital.

To overcome the difficulty of compensating for the investment of extra capital, the concept of interest on capital was devised.

3 Interest on capitals

If the work to be done by each partner is of equal value but the capital contributed is unequal, it is reasonable to grant interest on the partners' capitals. This interest is treated as a deduction prior to the calculation of profits and their distribution according to the profit-sharing ratio.

The rate of interest is a matter of agreement between the partners, but it should equal the return which they would have received if they had invested the capital elsewhere.

Taking Allen and Beet's firm again, but sharing the profits equally after charging 5 per cent per annum interest on capital, the division of profits would become:

Years	1	2	3	4	5	Total
	£	£	£	£	£	£
Net profit	1,800	2,400	3,000	3,000	3,600	
Interest on capitals						
Allen	100	100	100	100	100 =	500
Beet	50	50	50	50	50 =	250
Remainder shared:						
Allen $\frac{1}{2}$	825	1,125	1,425	1,425	1,725 =	6,525
Beet $\frac{1}{2}$	825	1,125	1,425	1,425	1,725 =	6,525

Summary	Allen	Beet
	£	£
Interest on capital	500	250
Balance of profits	6,525	6,525
	7,025	6,775

Allen has thus received £250 more than Beet, this being adequate return (in the partners' estimation) for having invested an extra £1,000 in the firm for five years.

4 Interest on drawings

It is obviously in the best interests of the firm if cash is withdrawn from the firm by the partners in accordance with the two basic principles of: (*a*) as little as possible, and (*b*) as late as possible. The more cash that is left in the firm the more expansion can be financed, the greater the economies of having ample cash to take advantage of bargains and of not missing cash discounts because cash is not available and so on.

To deter the partners from taking out cash unnecessarily the concept can be used of charging the partners interest on each withdrawal, calculated from the date of withdrawal to the end of the financial year. The amount charged to them helps to swell the profits divisible between the partners. The rate of interest should be sufficient to achieve this without being too harsh.

Suppose that Allen and Beet have decided to charge interest on drawings at 5 per cent per annum, and that their year end was 31 December. The following drawings are made:

Allen

Drawings		Interest		
				£
1 January	£100	£100 × 5% × 12 months	=	5
1 March	£240	£240 × 5% × 10 months	=	10
1 May	£120	£120 × 5% × 8 months	=	4
1 July	£240	£240 × 5% × 6 months	=	6
1 October	£ 80	£ 80 × 5% × 3 months	=	1
		Interest charged to Allen	=	26

Beet

Drawings		Interest		
				£
1 January	£ 60	£ 60 × 5% × 12 months	=	3
1 August	£480	£480 × 5% × 5 months	=	10
1 December	£240	£240 × 5% × 1 month	=	1
		Interest charged to Beet	=	14

5 Salaries to partners

One partner may have more responsibility or tasks than the others. As a reward for this, rather than change the profit and loss sharing ratio, he may have a salary which is deducted before sharing the balance of profits.

6 Performance-related payments to partners

Partners may agree that commission or performance-related bonuses be payable to some or all the partners linked to their individual performance. As with salaries, these would be deducted before sharing the balance of profits.

42.6 An example of the distribution of profits

Taylor and Clarke have been in partnership for one year sharing profits and losses in the ratio of Taylor $\frac{3}{5}$ths, Clarke $\frac{2}{5}$ths. They are entitled to 5 per cent per annum interest on capitals, Taylor having £2,000 capital and Clarke £6,000. Clarke is to have a salary of £500. They charge interest on drawings, Taylor being charged £50 and Clarke £100. The net profit, before any distributions to the partners, amounted to £5,000 for the year ended 31 December 19X7.

	£	£	£
Net profit			5,000
Add Charged for interest on drawings:			
Taylor		50	
Clarke		100	
			150
			5,150
Less Salary: Clarke		500	
Interest on capital:			
Taylor	100		
Clarke	300		
		400	
			900
			4,250
Balance of profits			
Shared:			
Taylor $\frac{3}{5}$ths		2,550	
Clarke $\frac{2}{5}$ths		1,700	
			4,250

The £5,000 net profits have therefore been shared:

	Taylor	*Clarke*
	£	*£*
Balance of profits	2,550	1,700
Interest on capital	100	300
Salary	–	500
	2,650	2,500
Less Interest on drawings	50	100
	2,600	2,400

£5,000

42.7 The final accounts

If the sales, stock and expenses of partnership were exactly the same as that of a sole trader, then the trading and profit and loss account would be identical with that as prepared for the sole trader. However, a partnership would have an extra section shown under the profit and loss account. This section is called the profit and loss appropriation account, and it is in this account that the distribution of profits is shown. The heading to the trading and profit and loss account does not include the words 'appropriation account'. It is purely an accounting custom not to include it in the heading.

The trading and profit and loss account of Taylor and Clarke from the details given would appear:

Taylor and Clarke

Trading and Profit and Loss Account for the year ended 31 December 19X7

(Trading Account – same as for sole trader)

(Profit and Loss Account – same as for sole trader)

	£	£	£
Net profit			5,000
Interest on drawings:			
Taylor		50	
Clarke		100	150
			5,150
Less:			
Interest on capitals			
Taylor	100		
Clarke	300	400	
Salary: Clarke		500	900
			4,250
Balance of profits shared:			
Taylor ⅗ths		2,550	
Clarke ⅖ths		1,700	4,250

42.8   Fixed and fluctuating capital accounts

There is a choice open in partnership accounts as follows.

Fixed capital accounts plus current accounts

The capital account for each partner remains year by year at the figure of capital put into the firm by the partners. The profits, interest on capital and the salaries to which the partner may be entitled are then credited to a separate current account for the partner, and the drawings and the interest on drawings are debited to it. The balance of the current account at the end of each financial year will then represent the amount of undrawn (or withdrawn) profits. A credit balance will be undrawn profits, while a debit balance will be drawings in excess of the profits to which the partner was entitled.

For Taylor and Clarke, capital and current accounts, assuming drawings of £2,000 each, will appear:

Taylor – *Capital*

		£
19X7		
Jan 1 Bank		2,000

Clarke – *Capital*

		£
19X7		
Jan 1 Bank		6,000

Taylor – *Current Account*

19X7		£	19X7		£
Dec 31	Cash: Drawings	2,000	Dec 31	Profit and loss	
„ 31	Profit and loss			appropriation account:	
	appropriation account:			Interest on capital	100
	Interest on drawings	50		Share of profits	2,550
„ 31	Balance c/d	600			
		2,650			2,650
			19X8		
			Jan 1	Balance b/d	600

Clarke – *Current Account*

19X7		£	19X7		£
Dec 31	Cash: Drawings	2,000	Dec 31	Profit and loss	
„ 31	Profit and loss			appropriation account:	
	appropriation account:			Interest on capital	300
	Interest on drawings	100		Share of profits	1,700
„ 31	Balance c/d	400		Salary	500
		2,500			2,500
			19X8		
			Jan 1	Balance b/d	400

Notice that the salary of Clarke was not paid to him, it was merely credited to his account. If in fact it was paid in addition to his drawings, the £500 cash paid would have been debited to the current account, changing the £400 credit balance into a £100 debit balance.

Examiners often ask for the capital accounts and current accounts to be shown in columnar form. For the previous accounts of Taylor and Clarke these would appear as follows:

Capital Accounts

		Taylor	Clarke				Taylor	Clarke
		£	£	19X7			£	£
				Jan 1	Bank		2,000	6,000

Current Accounts

		Taylor	Clarke				Taylor	Clarke
19X7		£	£	19X7			£	£
Dec 31	Cash: Drawings	2,000	2,000	Dec 31	Interest on capital		100	300
„ 31	Interest on drawings	50	100	„ 31	Share of profits		2,550	1,700
„ 31	Balances c/d	600	400	„ 31	Salary			500
		2,650	2,500				2,650	2,500
				19X8				
				Jan 1	Balances b/d		600	400

Fluctuating capital accounts

The distribution of profits would be credited to the capital account, and the drawings and interest on drawings debited. Therefore the balance on the capital account will change each year, i.e. it will fluctuate.

If fluctuating capital accounts had been kept for Taylor and Clarke they would have appeared:

Taylor – *Capital*

19X7		£	19X7		£
Dec 31	Cash: Drawings	2,000	Jan 1	Bank	2,000
„ 31	Profit and loss		Dec 31	Profit and loss	
	appropriation account:			appropriation account:	
	Interest on drawings	50		Interest on capital	100
„ 31	Balance c/d	2,600		Share of profits	2,550
		4,650			4,650
			19X8		
			Jan 1	Balance b/d	2,600

Clarke – *Capital*

19X7		£	19X7		£
Dec 31	Cash: Drawings	2,000	Jan 1	Bank	6,000
„ 31	Profit and loss		Dec 31	Profit and loss	
	appropriation account:			appropriation account:	
	Interest on			Interest on capital	300
	drawings	100		Salary	500
„ 31	Balance c/d	6,400		Share of profit	1,700
		8,500			8,500
			19X8		
			Jan 1	Balance b/d	6,400

Fixed capital accounts preferred

The keeping of fixed capital accounts plus current accounts is considered preferable to fluctuating capital accounts. When partners are taking out greater amounts than the share of the profits that they are entitled to, this is shown up by a debit balance on the current account and so acts as a warning.

42.9 Where no partnership agreement exists

Where no agreement exists, express or implied, Section 24 of the Partnership Act 1890 governs the situation. The accounting content of this section states:

(a) Profits and losses are to be shared equally.
(b) There is to be no interest allowed on capital.
(c) No interest is to be charged on drawings.
(d) Salaries are not allowed.
(e) If a partner puts a sum of money into a firm in excess of the capital he has agreed to subscribe, he is entitled to interest at the rate of 5 per cent per annum on such an advance.

This section applies where there is no agreement. There may be an agreement not by a partnership deed but in a letter, or it may be implied by conduct, for instance when a partner signs a balance sheet which shows profits shared in some other ratio than equally. Where a dispute arises as to whether agreement exists or not, and this cannot be resolved by the partners, only the courts will be competent to decide.

42.10 The balance sheet

The capital part side of the balance sheet will appear:

Balance Sheet as at 31 December 19X7

			£	£
Capital accounts		Taylor	2,000	
		Clarke	6,000	
				8,000

Current accounts	*Taylor*	*Clarke*		
	£	£		
Interest on capital	100	300		
Share of profits	2,550	1,700		
Salary	–	500		
	2,650	2,500		
Less Drawings	(2,000)	(2,000)		
Interest on drawings	(50)	(100)		
	(2,050)	(2,100)		
	600	400		
				1,000

If one of the current accounts had finished in debit, for instance if the current account of Clarke had finished up as £400 debit, the figure of £400 would appear in brackets and the balances would appear net in the totals column:

	Taylor	*Clarke*	
	£	£	£
Closing balance	600	(400)	200

If the net figure turned out to be a debit figure then this would be deducted from the total of the capital accounts.

New terms

Fixed capital accounts (p. 438): Capital accounts which consist only of the amounts of capital actually paid into the firm.

Fluctuating capital accounts (p. 438): Capital accounts whose balances change from one period to the next.

Interest on capital (p. 435): An amount at an agreed rate of interest which is credited to a partner based on the amount of capital contributed by him/her.

Interest on drawings (p. 436): An amount at an agreed rate if interest, based on the drawings taken out, which is debited to the partners.

Limited partner (p. 434): A partner whose liability is limited to the capital he or she has put into the firm.

Partnership (p. 433): A firm in which two or more are working together as owners wth a view to making profits.

Partnership salaries (p. 436): Agreed amounts payable to partners in respect of duties undertaken by them.

Main points to remember

1   There is no limited liability in partnerships except for 'limited partners'.

2   The contents of a partnership agreement will override anything written in this chapter. Partners can agree to anything they want to, in as much or as little detail as they wish.

3   If there is no partnership agreement, then the provisions of the Partnership Act (details shown in section 42.9) will apply.

4   Partners can agree to show their capital accounts using either the fixed capital or fluctuating capital methods.

5   If more than 20 owners of an organisation are needed, then a partnership would not be suitable; instead, a limited company would be preferable.

Review questions

42.1 Stephens, Owen and Jones are partners. They share profits and losses in the ratios of $\frac{2}{5}$, $\frac{2}{5}$ and $\frac{1}{5}$ respectively.

For the year ended 31 December 19X6, their capital accounts remained fixed at the following amounts:

	£
	£
Stephens	6,000
Owen	4,000
Jones	2,000

They have agreed to give each other 10 per cent interest per annum on their capital accounts.

In addition to the above, partnership salaries of £3,000 for Owen and £1,000 for Jones are to be charged.

The net profit of the partnership, before taking any of the above into account was £25,200.

You are required to draw up the appropriation account of the partnership for the year ended 31 December 19X6.

42.2 Read the following and answer the questions below.

Roach and Salmon own a grocery shop. Their first financial year ended on 31 December 19X9.

The following balances were taken from the books on that date:

Capital:	Roach – £60,000;	Salmon – £48,000.
Partnership salaries:	Roach – £9,000;	Salmon – £6,000.
Drawings:	Roach – £12,860;	Salmon – £13,400.

The firm's net profit for the year was £32,840.
Interest on capital is to be allowed at 10% per year.
Profits and losses are to be shared equally.

(*a*) From the information above prepare the firm's appropriation account and the partners' current accounts.
(*b*) If there is no partnership agreement, to which Act of Parliament do the partners then refer?

(*Midland Examining Group: GCSE*)

42.3 Draw up a profit and loss appropriation account for the year ended 31 December 19X7 and balance sheet extracts at that date, from the following:

(*i*)   Net profits £30,350.
(*ii*)   Interest to be charged on capitals: Williams £2,000; Powell £1,500; Howe £900.
(*iii*) Interest to be charged on drawings: Williams £240; Powell £180; Howe £130.
(*iv*)   Salaries to be credited: Powell £2,000; Howe £3,500.
(*v*)   Profits to be shared: Williams 50%; Powell 30%; Howe 20%.
(*vi*)   Current accounts: balances b/fwd Williams £1,860; Powell £946; Howe £717.
(*vii*) Capital accounts: balances b/fwd Williams £40,000; Powell £30,000; Howe £18,000.
(*viii*) Drawings: Williams £9,200; Powell £7,100; Howe £6,900.

42.4A Penrose and Wilcox are in partnership, sharing profits and losses in the ratio 3:2. The following information was taken from their books for the year ended 31 December 19X9, before the completion of their profit and loss appropriation account.

		£	
Current accounts (1 January 19X9)			
	Penrose	640	*(Dr)*
	Wilcox	330	*(Cr)*
Drawings	Penrose	3,000	
	Wilcox	2,000	
Net trading profit		6,810	
Interest on capital	Penrose	540	
	Wilcox	720	
Salary	Penrose	2,000	
Interest on drawings	Penrose	270	
	Wilcox	180	

(a) Prepare, for the year ended 31 December 19X9:
   (i) the profit and loss appropriation account of Penrose and Wilcox;
   (ii) the current accounts in the ledger for Penrose and Wilcox.
(b) Why in many partnerships are current accounts prepared as well as capital accounts?
(c) At 1 January 19X9 Penrose had a debit balance in his current account. What does this mean?
(d) In partnership accounts what is the purpose of preparing:
   (i) a profit and loss account?
   (ii) a profit and loss appropriation account?
(e) In partnership accounts why is:
   (i) interest allowed on capital?
   (ii) interest charged on drawings?

(Northern Examinations and Assessment Board: GCSE)

42.5 Bee, Cee and Dee have been holding preliminary discussions with a view to forming a partnership to buy and sell antiques.

The position has now been reached where the prospective partners have agreed the basic arrangements under which the partnership will operate.

Bee will contribute £40,000 as capital, and up to £10,000 as a long-term loan to the partnership, if needed. He has extensive other business interests and will not therefore be taking an active part in the running of the business.

Cee is unable to bring in more than £2,000 as capital initially, but, because he has an expert knowledge of the antique trade, will act as the manager of the business on a full-time basis.

Dee is willing to contribute £10,000 as capital. He will also assist in running the business as the need arises. In particular, he is prepared to attend auctions anywhere within the United Kingdom in order to acquire trading stock which he will transport back to the firm's premises in his van. On occasions he may also help Cee to restore the articles prior to sale to the public.

At the meeting, the three prospective partners intend to decide upon the financial arrangements for sharing out the profits (or losses) made by the firm, and have approached you for advice.

You are required to prepare a set of explanatory notes, under suitable headings, of the considerations which the prospective partners should take into account in arriving at their decisions at the next meeting.

(Association of Chartered Certified Accountants)

42.6 Mendez and Marshall are in partnership sharing profits and losses equally. The following is their trial balance as at 30 June 19X9.

	Dr £	Cr £
Buildings (cost £75,000)	50,000	
Fixtures at cost	11,000	
Provision for depreciation: Fixtures		3,300
Debtors	16,243	
Creditors		11,150
Cash at bank	677	
Stock at 30 June 19X8	41,979	
Sales		123,650
Purchases	85,416	
Carriage outwards	1,288	
Discounts allowed	115	
Loan interest: King	4,000	
Office expenses	2,416	
Salaries and wages	18,917	
Bad debts	503	
Provision for bad debts		400
Loan from J King		40,000
Capitals: Mendez		35,000
Marshall		29,500
Current accounts: Mendez		1,306
Marshall		298
Drawings: Mendez	6,400	
Marshall	5,650	
	244,604	244,604

Required:
Prepare a trading and profit and loss appropriation account for the year ended 30 June 19X9, and a balance sheet as at that date.

(a) Stock, 30 June 19X9, £56,340.
(b) Expenses to be accrued: Office Expenses £96; Wages £200.
(c) Depreciate fixtures 10 per cent on reducing balance basis, buildings £1,000.
(d) Reduce provision for bad debts to £320.
(e) Partnership salary: £800 to Mendez. Not yet entered.
(f) Interest on drawings: Mendez £180; Marshall £120.
(g) Interest on capital account balances at 10 per cent.

42.7A Oscar and Felix are in partnership. They share profits in the ratio: Oscar 60 per cent; Felix 40 per cent. The following trial balance was extracted as at 31 March 19X9.

	Dr £	Cr £
Office equipment at cost	6,500	
Motor vehicles at cost	9,200	
Provision for depreciation at 31.3.19X8:		
Motor vehicles		3,680
Office equipment		1,950
Stock at 31 March 19X8	24,970	
Debtors and creditors	20,960	16,275
Cash at bank	615	
Cash in hand	140	
Sales		90,370
Purchases	71,630	
Salaries	8,417	
Office expenses	1,370	
Discounts allowed	563	
Current accounts at 31.3.19X8		
Oscar		1,379
Felix		1,211
Capital accounts: Oscar		27,000
Felix		12,000
Drawings: Oscar	5,500	
Felix	4,000	
	153,865	153,865

Required:
Draw up a set of final accounts for the year ended 31 March 19X9 for the partnership. The following notes are applicable at 31 March 19X9.

(a) Stock 31 March 19X9 £27,340.
(b) Office expenses owing £110.
(c) Provide for depreciation: motor 20 per cent of cost, office equipment 10 per cent of cost.
(d) Charge interest on capitals at 10 per cent.
(e) Charge interest on drawings: Oscar £180; Felix £210.

42.8 The following list of balances as at 30 September 19X9 has been extracted from the books of Brick and Stone, trading in partnership, sharing the balance of profits and losses in the proportions 3:2 respectively.

	£
Printing, stationery and postages	3,500
Sales	322,100
Stock in hand at 1 October 19X8	23,000
Purchases	208,200
Rent and rates	10,300
Heat and light	8,700
Staff salaries	36,100
Telephone charges	2,900
Motor vehicle running costs	5,620
Discounts allowable	950
Discounts receivable	370
Sales returns	2,100
Purchases returns	6,100
Carriage inwards	1,700
Carriage outwards	2,400
Fixtures and fittings: at cost	26,000
provision for depreciation	11,200
Motor vehicles: at cost	46,000
provision for depreciation	25,000
Provision for doubtful debts	300
Drawings: Brick	24,000
Stone	11,000
Current account balances at 1 October 19X8:	
Brick	3,600 credit
Stone	2,400 credit
Capital account balances at 1 October 19X8:	
Brick	33,000
Stone	17,000
Debtors	9,300
Creditors	8,400
Balance at bank	7,700

Additional information:

1   £10,000 is to be transferred from Brick's capital account to a newly opened Brick Loan Account on 1 July 19X9.
    Interest at 10 per cent per annum on the loan is to be credited to Brick.
2   Stone is to be credited with a salary at the rate of £12,000 per annum from 1 April 19X9.
3   Stock in hand at 30 September 19X9 has been valued at cost at £32,000.
4   Telephone charges accrued due at 30 September 19X9 amounted to £400 and rent of £600 prepaid at that date.
5   During the year ended 30 September 19X9 Stone has taken goods costing £1,000 for his own use.
6   Depreciation is to be provided at the following annual rates on the straight line basis:

Fixtures and fittings	10%
Motor vehicles	20%

Required:

(a) Prepare a trading and profit and loss account for the year ended 30 September 19X9.

(b) Prepare a balance sheet as at 30 September 19X9 which should include summaries of the partners' capital and current accounts for the year ended on that date.

Note: In both (a) and (b) vertical forms of presentation should be used.

(*Association of Accounting Technicians*)

42.9A Menzies, Whitlam and Gough share profits and losses in the ratios 5:3:2 respectively. Their trial balance as at 30 September 19X9 was as follows:

	Dr £	Cr £
Sales		210,500
Returns inwards	6,800	
Purchases	137,190	
Carriage inwards	1,500	
Stock 30 September 19X8	42,850	
Discounts allowed	110	
Salaries and wages	18,296	
Bad debts	1,234	
Provision for bad debts 30.9.19X8		800
General expenses	945	
Rent and rates	2,565	
Postages	2,450	
Motor expenses	3,940	
Motor vans at cost	12,500	
Office equipment at cost	8,400	
Provisions for depreciation at 30.9.19X8:		
Motor vans		4,200
Office equipment		2,700
Creditors		24,356
Debtors	37,178	
Cash at bank	666	
Drawings: Menzies	12,610	
Whitlam	8,417	
Gough	6,216	
Current accounts: Menzies		1,390
Whitlam	153	
Gough		2,074
Capital accounts: Menzies		30,000
Whitlam		16,000
Gough		12,000
	304,020	304,020

Draw up a set of final accounts for the year ended 30 September 19X9. The following notes are relevant at 30 September 19X9:

(i) Stock 30 September 19X9, £51,060.

(ii) Rates in advance £120; Stock of postage stamps £190.

(iii) Increase provision for bad debts to £870.

(iv) Salaries: Whitlam £1,200; Gough £700. Not yet recorded.

(v) Interest on Drawings: Menzies £170; Whitlam £110; Gough £120.

(vi) Interest on Capitals at 10 per cent.

(vii) Depreciate Motor vans £2,500, Office equipment £1,680.

43

Goodwill for sole traders and partnerships

Objectives

After you have studied this chapter, you should:

- *understand why goodwill exists*

- *realise that it has a monetary value*

- *be able to calculate the amount of adjustments needed when there is some form of change in a partnership*

- *be able to make the adjustments for goodwill in the books of a partnership*

43.1 Nature of goodwill

Suppose you have been in a business for some years and you wanted to sell it. How much would you ask as the total sale price of the business? You decide to list how much you could get for each asset if sold separately. This list might be as follows:

	£
Buildings	225,000
Machinery	75,000
Debtors	60,000
Stock	40,000
	400,000

Instead you sell the whole of the business as a going concern to Mr Lee for £450,000. He has therefore paid £50,000 more than the total for all the assets. This extra payment of £50,000 is called **goodwill**. He has paid this because he wanted to take over the business as a going concern. Thus:

Purchased Goodwill = Total Price *less* value of identifiable assets.

43.2 Reasons for payment of goodwill

In buying an existing business which has been established for some time there may be quite a few possible advantages. Some of them are listed here:

- A large number of regular customers who will continue to deal with the new owner.
- The business has a good reputation.
- It has experienced, efficient and reliable employees.
- The business is situated in a good location.
- It has good contacts with suppliers.

None of these advantages is available to completely new businesses. For this reason, many people would decide to buy an existing business and pay an amount for goodwill.

43.3 Existence of goodwill

Goodwill does not necessarily exist in a business. If the business had a bad reputation, an inefficient labour force or other negative factors, the owner might be unlikely to be paid for goodwill on selling the business.

43.4 Methods of calculating goodwill

There is no single way of calculating goodwill to which everyone can agree. The seller will probably want more for the goodwill than the buyer will want to pay. All that is certain is that when an agreement is reached between buyer and seller, then that is the amount of goodwill. Various methods are used to help buyer and seller come to an agreed figure. The calculations give buyer and seller a figure with which to begin discussions of the value.

Very often each industry or occupation has its own customary way of calculating goodwill:

(a) In more than one type of retail business it has been the custom to value goodwill at the average weekly sales for the past year multiplied by a given figure. The given figure will, of course, differ between different types of businesses, and often changes gradually in the same types of business in the long term.

(b) With many professional firms, such as accountants in public practice, it is the custom to value goodwill as being the gross annual fees times a given number. For instance, what is termed a two years' purchase of a firm with gross fees of £6,000 means goodwill = 2 × £6,000 = £12,000.

(c) The average net annual profit for a specified past number of years multiplied by an agreed number. This is often said to be x years' purchase of the net profits.

(d) The super-profits method.

It may be argued, as in the case of a sole trader for example, that the net profits are not 'true profits'. This is because the sole trader has not charged for the following expenses:

(a) Services of the proprietor. He has worked in the business, but he has not charged for such services. Any drawings he makes are charged to a capital account, not to the profit and loss account.

(b) The use of the money he has invested in the business. If he had invested his money elsewhere he would have earned interest or dividends on such investments.

Super profits are what is left of the net profits after allowances have been made for (a) services of the proprietor and (b) the use of the capital.

They are usually calculated as:

		£	£
Annual net profits			80,000
Less	(*i*) Remuneration proprietor would have earned for		
	similar work elsewhere	20,000	
	(*ii*) Interest that would have been earned if capital had		
	been invested elsewhere	10,000	30,000
Annual super profits			50,000

The annual super profits are then multiplied by a number agreed by seller and purchaser of the business.

43.5 Sole trader's books

Goodwill is not entered in a sole trader's accounts unless he has actually bought it. This will show that he did not start the business himself, but bought an existing business.

43.6 Partnership books

Although goodwill is not normally entered in the accounts unless it has been purchased, sometimes it is necessary in partnerships.

Unless it has been agreed differently, a partner will own a share in the goodwill in the same ratio in which he shares profits. For instance, if A takes one-quarter of the profits he will be the owner of one-quarter of the goodwill. This is true even if there is no goodwill account.

This means that when something happens such as:

(*a*) existing partners decide to change profit and loss sharing ratios, or
(*b*) a new partner is introduced, or
(*c*) a partner retires or dies,

then the ownership of goodwill by partners changes in some way.

The change may involve cash passing from one partner to another, or an adjustment in the books, so that the changes in ownership do not lead to a partner (or partners) giving away his share of ownership for nothing.

43.7 Change in profit-sharing ratios of existing partners

Sometimes the profit and loss sharing ratios have to be changed. Typical reasons are:

- A partner may not work as much as he used to do, possibly because of old age or ill-health.
- His skills and ability may have changed.
- He may be doing much more for the business than he used to do.

If the partners decide to change their profit-sharing ratios, an adjustment will be needed.

To illustrate why this is so, let us look at the following example of a partnership in which goodwill is not already shown in a goodwill account at its correct value.

(*a*) A, B and C are in partnership, sharing profits and losses equally.
(*b*) On 31 December 19X5 they decide to change this to A one half, B one-quarter and C one-quarter.

(*c*) On 31 December 19X5 the goodwill, which had never been shown in the books, was valued at £60,000. If, just before the profit-sharing change, the firm had been sold and £60,000 received for goodwill, then each partner would have received £20,000 as they shared profits equally.

(*d*) At any time after 31 December 19X5, once the profit sharing has changed, their ownership of goodwill is worth A £30,000, B £15,000 and C £15,000. If goodwill is sold for that amount then those figures will be received by the partners for goodwill.

(*e*) If, when (*b*) above happened there had been no change made to A by B and C, or no other form of adjustment, then B and C would each have given away a £5,000 share of the goodwill for nothing. This would not be sensible.

We can now look at how the adjustments can be made when a goodwill account with the correct valuation does not already exist.

Exhibit 43.1

E, F and G have been in business for ten years. They have always shared profits equally. No goodwill account has ever existed in the books. On 31 December 19X6 they agree that G will take only a one-fifth share of the profits as from 1 January 19X7, because he will be devoting less of his time to the business in the future. E and F will each take two-fifths of the profits. The summarised balance sheet of the business on 31 December 19X6 appears as follows:

Balance Sheet as at 31 December 19X6

	£			£
Net Assets	7,000	Capital:	E	3,000
			F	1,800
			G	2,200
	7,000			7,000

The partners agree that the goodwill should be valued at £3,000. Answer (1) shows the solution when a goodwill account is opened. Answer (2) is the solution when a goodwill account is not opened.

1 Goodwill account opened. Open a goodwill account. Then make the following entries:
Debit goodwill account: total value of goodwill.
Credit partners' capital accounts: each one with his share of goodwill in old profit-sharing ratio.

The goodwill account will appear as:

Goodwill

	£		£
Capitals: valuation shared		Balance c/d	3,000
E	1,000		
F	1,000		
G	1,000		
	3,000		3,000

The capital accounts may be shown in columnar fashion as:

Capital Accounts

	E £	F £	G £		E £	F £	G £
Balances c/d	4,000	2,800	3,200	Balances b/d	3,000	1,800	2,200
				Goodwill: old ratios	1,000	1,000	1,000
	4,000	2,800	3,200		4,000	2,800	3,200

The balance sheet items before and after the adjustments will appear as:

	Before £	After £			Before £	After £
Goodwill	–	3,000	Capitals:	E	3,000	4,000
				F	1,800	2,800
Other assets	7,000	7,000		G	2,200	3,200
	7,000	10,000			7,000	10,000

2 Goodwill account not opened. The effect of the change of ownership of goodwill may be shown in the following form:

Before		After		Loss or Gain	Action Required
	£		£		
E One-third	1,000	Two-fifths	1,200	Gain £200	Debit E's capital account £200
F One-third	1,000	Two-fifths	1,200	Gain £200	Debit F's capital account £200
G One-third	1,000	One-fifth	600	Loss £400	Credit G's capital account £400
	3,000		3,000		

The column headed 'Action Required' shows that a partner who has gained goodwill because of the change must be charged for it by having his capital account debited with the value of the gain. A partner who has lost goodwill must be compensated for it by having his capital account credited.

The capital accounts will appear as:

Capital Accounts

	E £	F £	G £		E £	F £	G £
Goodwill adjustments	200	200		Balances b/d	3,000	1,800	2,200
Balances c/d	2,800	1,600	2,600	Goodwill adjustments			400
	3,000	1,800	2,600		3,000	1,800	2,600

As there is no goodwill account the balance sheet items before and after the adjustments will therefore appear as:

	Before	After			Before	After
	£	£			£	£
Net assets	7,000	7,000	Capitals: E		3,000	2,800
			F		1,800	1,600
			G		2,200	2,600
	7,000	7,000			7,000	7,000

Comparison of methods 1 and 2

Let us see how the methods compare. Assume that shortly afterwards the assets in 1 and 2 are sold for £7,000 and the goodwill for £3,000. The total of £10,000 would be distributed as follows, using each of the methods:

Method 1 The £10,000 is exactly the amount needed to pay the partners according to the balances on their capital accounts. The payments are therefore made of

Capitals paid to	E		4,000
	F		2,800
	G		3,200
Total cash paid			£10,000

Method 2 First of all the balances on capital accounts, totalling £7,000, are to be paid. Then the £3,000 received for goodwill will be split between the partners in their profit and loss ratios. This will result in payments as follows:

	Capitals	Goodwill Shared		Total Paid
E	2,800	(2/5ths)	1,200	4,000
F	1,600	(2/5ths)	1,200	2,800
G	2,600	(1/5th)	600	3,200
	£7,000		£3,000	£10,000

You can see that the final amounts paid to the partners are the same whether a goodwill account is opened or not.

43.8 Admission of new partners

New partners may be admitted, usually for one of two reasons:

1 As an extra partner, either because the firm has grown or someone is needed with different skills.
2 To replace partners who are leaving the firm. This might be because of retirement or death of a partner.

43.9 Goodwill on admission of new partners

The new partner will be entitled to a share in the profits. Normally, he will also be entitled to the same share of the value of goodwill. It is correct to charge him for his taking over that share of the goodwill.

43.10 Goodwill adjustments when new partners admitted

This calculation is done in three stages:

1 Show value of goodwill divided between old partners in old profit and loss sharing ratios.
2 Then show value of goodwill divided between partners (including new partner) in new profit and loss sharing ratio.
3 Goodwill gain shown: charge these partners for the gain.
4 Goodwill loss shown: give these partners an allowance for their losses.

This is illustrated in Exhibits 43.2 and 43.3.

Exhibit 43.2

A and B are in partnership, sharing profits and losses equally. C is admitted as a new partner. The three partners will share profits and losses one-third each.

Total goodwill is valued at £60,000.

Stage 1			Stage 2		Stage 3	
Partners	Old profit shares	Share of goodwill £	New profit shares	Share of goodwill £	Gain or loss £	Adjustment needed
A	1/2	30,000	1/3	20,000	10,000 Loss	Cr A Capital
B	1/2	30,000	1/3	20,000	10,000 Loss	Cr B Capital
C		–	1/3	20,000	20,000 Gain	Dr C Capital
		60,000		60,000		

This means that A and B need to have their capitals increased by £10,000 each. C needs his capital reducing by £20,000.

Note that A and B have kept their profits in the same ratio to each other. While they used to have one-half each, now they have one-third each.

We will now see in Exhibit 43.3 that the method shown is the same even when existing partners take a different share of the profit to that before the change.

Exhibit 43.3

D and E are in partnership sharing profits one-half each. A new partner F is admitted. Profits will now be shared D one-fifth, and E and F two-fifths each. D and E have therefore not kept their shares equal to each other. Goodwill is valued at £60,000.
D needs his capital increased by £18,000. E's capital is to be increased by £6,000.
F needs his capital reduced by £24,000.

Stage 1			Stage 2		Stage 3	
Partners	*Old profit shares*	*Share of goodwill* £	*New profit shares*	*Share of goodwill* £	*Gain or loss* £	*Adjustment needed*
D	1/2	30,000	1/5	12,000	18,000 Loss	Cr D Capital
E	1/2	30,000	2/5	24,000	6,000 Loss	Cr E Capital
F	–		2/5	24,000	24,000 Gain	Dr F Capital
		60,000		60,000		

43.11 Accounting entries for goodwill adjustments

These depend on how the partners wish to arrange the adjustment. Three methods are usually used:

1 Cash is paid by the new partner privately to the old partners for his share of the goodwill. No goodwill account is to be opened.

   In Exhibit 43.3, F would therefore give £24,000 in cash, being £18,000 to D and £6,000 to E. They would bank these amounts in their private bank accounts. No entry is made for this in the accounts of the partnership.

2 Cash is paid by the new partner into the business bank account for his share of the goodwill. No goodwill account is to be opened. Assume that the capital balances before F was admitted were D £50,000, E £50,000, and F was to pay in £50,000 as capital plus £24,000 for goodwill.

   In Exhibit 43.3, the entries would be shown in the capital accounts as:

Capital Accounts

	D £	E £	F £		D £	E £	F £
Adjustments for goodwill			24,000	Balances b/d	50,000	50,000	
				Cash for capital			50,000
				Cash for goodwill			24,000
Balances c/d	68,000	56,000	50,000	loss of goodwill	18,000	6,000	
	68,000	56,000	74,000		68,000	56,000	74,000

3 Goodwill account to be opened. No extra cash to be paid in by the new partner for goodwill.

   In Exhibit 43.3, the opening capitals were D £50,000, E £50,000. F paid in £50,000 as capital.

Here the action required is:

- Debit goodwill account: with total value of goodwill.
- Credit capitals of old partners: with their shares of goodwill in old profit-sharing ratios.

No adjustments for goodwill gains and losses are required as the capital accounts of D and E have been increased by the full value of the goodwill at the time of F's admission to partnership.

For Exhibit 43.3, the entries would appear as:

Goodwill

	£		£
Value divided:		Balance c/d	60,000
D Capital	30,000		
E Capital	30,000		
	60,000		60,000

Capital Accounts

	D £	E £	F £		D £	E £	F £
				Balances b/d	50,000	50,000	
				Cash for capital			50,000
Balances c/d	80,000	80,000	50,000	Goodwill	30,000	30,000	
	80,000	80,000	50,000		80,000	80,000	50,000

As stated in Section 43.7, were the partnership dissolved and realised the £210,000 it was valued at when F was admitted, it would first be used to repay the capital account balances. D and F would, therefore, be fully compensated for the value of the goodwill at the time of F's admission to partnership, and F would receive exactly the amount of his investment.

43.12 Where new partners pay for share of goodwill

Unless otherwise agreed, the assumption is that the total value of goodwill is directly proportionate to the amount paid by the new partner for the share taken by him. If a new partner pays £1,200 for a one-fifth share of the profits, then goodwill is taken to be £6,000. A sum of £800 for a one-quarter share of the profits would therefore be taken to imply a total value of £3,200 for goodwill.

43.13 Goodwill on withdrawal or death of partners

This depends on whether or not a goodwill account exists.

If there was no goodwill account

If no goodwill account already existed the partnership goodwill should be valued because the outgoing partner is entitled to his share of its value. This value is entered in double entry accounts:

- Debit goodwill account with valuation.
- Credit each old partner's capital account in profit-sharing ratios.

Exhibit 43.4

H, I and J have been in partnership for many years sharing profit and losses equally. No goodwill account has ever existed.

J is leaving the partnership. The other two partners are to take over his share of profits equally. Capitals entered before goodwill were £50,000 each. The goodwill is valued at £45,000.

Goodwill

		£		£
Valuation:	Capital H	15,000	Balance c/d	45,000
	Capital I	15,000		
	Capital J	15,000		
		45,000		45,000
Balance b/d		45,000		

Capital Accounts

	H £	I £	J £		H £	I £	J £
Balances c/d	65,000	65,000	65,000	Balances b/d	50,000	50,000	50,000
				Goodwill shares	15,000	15,000	15,000
	65,000	65,000	65,000		65,000	65,000	65,000
				Balances b/d	65,000	65,000	65,000

When J leaves the partnership, his capital balance of £65,000 will be paid to him.

If a goodwill account exists

1 If a goodwill account exists with the correct valuation of goodwill entered in it, no further action is needed.
2 If the valuation in the goodwill account needs to be changed, the following will apply:

Goodwill undervalued: Debit increase needed to goodwill account.
                                      Credit increase to old partners' capital accounts in their old profit-sharing ratios.

Goodwill overvalued: Debit reduction to old partners' capital accounts in their old profit-sharing ratios.
                                        Credit reduction needed to goodwill account.

43.14 Depreciation of goodwill in company accounts

This will be dealt with in section 46.14.

New terms

Goodwill (p. 449): The excess amount that has to be paid to acquire a part or the whole of a business as a going concern, over and above the value of the net assets owned by the business.

Super profits (p. 450): Net profits less allowance for alternative earnings and alternative return on capital invested.

Main points to remember

1   The true value of goodwill can be established only when the business is sold, but for various reasons of fairness between partners it is valued the best way possible when there is no imminent sale of a business.

2   If the old partners agree, a new partner can be admitted without paying anything in as capital.

3   Goodwill is usually owned by the partners in the ratio in which they share profits.

4   If there is a change in partnership without adjustments for goodwill, then some partners will make an unfair gain while others will quite unfairly lose money.

5   If a new partner pays a specific amount for his or her share of the goodwill, then that payment is said to be a 'premium'.

Review questions

43.1   The partners have always shared their profits in the ratios of X4: Y3: Z1. They are to alter their profit ratios to X3: Y5: Z2. The last balance sheet before the change was:

Balance Sheet as at 31 December 19X7

	£
Net Assets (not including goodwill)	14,000
	14,000
Capitals:	
X	6,000
Y	4,800
Z	3,200
	14,000

The partners agree to bring in goodwill, being valued at £12,000 on the change.

Show the balance sheets on 1 January 19X8 after goodwill has been taken into account if:

(*a*)   Goodwill account was opened.
(*b*)   Goodwill account was not opened.

43.2A The partners are to change their profit ratios as shown:

	Old ratio	New ratio
A	2	3
B	3	4
C	4	3
D	1	2

They decide to bring in a goodwill amount of £18,000 on the change. The last balance sheet before any element of goodwill has been introduced was:

Balance Sheet as at 30 June 19X8

	£
Net assets (not including goodwill)	18,800
	18,800
Capitals:	
A	7,000
B	3,200
C	5,000
D	3,600
	18,800

Show the balance sheets on 1 July 19X8 after necessary adjustments have been made if:

(a) Goodwill account was opened.
(b) Goodwill account was not opened.

43.3 X and Y are in partnership, sharing profits and losses equally. They decide to admit Z. By agreement, goodwill valued at £6,000 is to be introduced into the business books. Z is required to provide capital equal to that of Y after he has been credited with his share of goodwill. The new profit-sharing ratio is to be 4:3:3 respectively for X, Y and Z.

The balance sheet before admission of Z showed:

	£
Fixed and current assets	15,000
Cash	2,000
	17,000
Capital X	8,000
Capital Y	4,000
Current liabilities	5,000
	17,000

Show:
(a) Journal entries for admission of Z.
(b) Opening balance sheet of new business.
(c) Journal entries for writing off the goodwill which the new partners decided to do soon after the start of the new business.

43.4A L, M and S are in partnership. They shared profits in the ratio 2:5:3. It is decided to admit R. It is agreed that goodwill was worth £10,000, but that this is not to be brought into the business records. R will bring £4,000 cash into the business for capital. The new profit-sharing ratio is to be L 3: M 4: S 2: R 1.

The balance sheet before R was introduced was as follows:

	£
Assets (other than in cash)	11,000
Cash	2,500
	13,500
Capitals: L	3,000
M	5,000
S	4,000
Creditors	1,500
	13,500

Show:
(*a*) The entries in the capital accounts of L, M, S and R, the accounts to be in columnar form.
(*b*) The balance sheet after R has been introduced.

43.5 T, U and V are in partnership. They shared profits in the ratio 4:5:1. It is decided to admit W. It is agreed that goodwill was worth £30,000 and that it was to be brought into the business records. W will bring £20,000 cash into the business for capital. The new profit-sharing ratio is to be T 6: U 7: V 2: W 5.

The balance sheet before W was introduced was as follows:

	£
Assets (other than in cash)	40,000
Cash	6,000
	46,000
Capitals: T	14,000
U	18,000
V	5,000
Liabilities	9,000
	46,000

Show:
(*a*) The entries in the capital accounts of T, U, V, and W, the accounts to be in columnar form.
(*b*) The balance sheet after W has been introduced.

43.6 A new partner has joined the business during the year and has paid in £10,000 for 'goodwill'. This £10,000 has been credited by the bookkeeper to the account of the new partner. The senior partner had objected to this, but the bookkeeper had replied: 'Why not credit the £10,000 to the account of the new partner? It is his money after all.'

Required:
Give your advice as to the proper treatment of this £10,000. Explain your reasons fully.

(*Association of Chartered Certified Accountants*)

43.7 Owing to staff illnesses, the draft final accounts for the year ended 31 March 19X9 of Messrs Stone, Pebble and Brick, trading in partnership as the Bigtime Building Supply Company, have been prepared by an inexperienced, but keen, clerk. The draft summarised balance sheet as at 31 March 19X9 is as follows:

	£	£
Tangible fixed assets: At cost less depreciation to date		45,400
Current assets	32,290	
Less: Trade creditors	6,390	25,900
		£71,300

Represented by:	*Stone*	*Pebble*	*Brick*	*Total*
	£	£	£	£
Capital accounts: at 1 April 19X8	26,000	18,000	16,000	60,000
Current accounts:				
Share of net profit for the year ended				
31 March 19X9	12,100	12,100	12,100	
Drawings year ended 31 March 19X9	(8,200)	(9,600)	(7,200)	
At 31 March 19X9	3,900	2,500	4,900	11,300
				£71,300

The partnership commenced on 1 April 19X8 when each of the partners introduced, as their partnership capital, the net tangible fixed and current assets of their previously separate businesses. However, it has now been discovered that, contrary to what was agreed, no adjustments were made in the partnership books for the goodwill of the partners' former businesses now incorporated in the partnership. The agreed valuations of goodwill at 1 April 19X8 are as follows:

	£
Stone's business	30,000
Pebble's business	20,000
Brick's business	16,000

It is agreed that a goodwill account should not be opened in the partnership's books.

It has now been discovered that effect has not been given in the accounts to the following provisions in the partnership agreement effective from 1 January 19X9:

1 Stone's capital to be reduced to £20,000, the balance being transferred to a loan account upon which interest at the rate of 11% per annum will be paid on 31 December each year.
2 Partners to be credited with interest on their capital account balances at the rate of 5% per annum.
3 Brick to be credited with a partner's salary at the rate of £8,500 per annum.
4 The balance of the net profit or loss to be shared between Stone, Pebble and Brick in the ratio 5:3:2 respectively.

Notes:
1 It can be assumed that the net profit indicated in the draft accounts accrued uniformly throughout the year.
2 It has been agreed between the partners that no adjustments should be made for any partnership goodwill as at 1 January 19X9.

Required:
(*a*) Prepare the profit and loss appropriation account for the year ended 31 March 19X9.
(*b*) Prepare a corrected statement of the partners' capital and current accounts for inclusion in the partnership balance sheet as at 31 March 19X9.

(*Association of Accounting Technicians*)

44

Revaluation of partnership assets

Objectives

After you have studied this chapter, you should:

- *understand the need for revaluation of assets in a partnership*
- *be able to make the necessary adjustments when assets are revalued*

44.1 Need for revaluation

When a business is sold, and the sale price of the assets exceeds their book values, there will be a profit on the sale. This profit will be shared between the partners in their profit and loss sharing ratios. Any loss on sale would be shared in the same way. This means that whenever one of the following happens:

- A new partner is admitted;
- A partner leaves the firm;
- The partners change profit and loss sharing ratios;

the assets will have to be revalued.

If this were not done the new partner admitted would benefit from increases in value before he joined the firm, without having to pay anything for it.

Similarly, if the value of assets had fallen before he had joined the firm, and no revaluation took place, he would share that loss of value without any adjustment being made for it.

Partners who leave or change their profit and loss sharing ratios would also be affected, if there were no payments or allowances for such gains or losses.

44.2 Profit or loss on revaluation

We have already seen that there should be a revaluation when there is a change in partners or a change in profit-sharing ratios.

If the revaluation shows no difference in asset values, no further action is needed. This will not happen very often, especially if assets include buildings. These are normally shown at cost, but this is very rarely the actual value after the buildings have been owned for a few years.

		£
If:	New total valuation of assets	90,000
Is more than:	Old total valuation of assets	60,000
The result is:	Profit on revaluation	30,000

		£
If:	Old total valuation of assets	50,000
Is more than:	New total valuation of assets	40,000
The result is:	Loss on revaluation	10,000

44.3 Accounting for revaluation

Revaluation account is opened

1 For each asset showing a gain on revaluation:
   Debit asset account with gain.
   Credit revaluation account.
2 For each asset showing a loss on revaluation:
   Debit revaluation account.
   Credit asset account with loss.
3 If there is an increase in total valuation of assets:
   Debit profit to revaluation account.
   Credit old partners' capital accounts in old profit and loss sharing ratios.*
4 If there is a fall in total valuations of assets:
   Debit old partners' capital accounts in old profit and loss sharing ratios.*
   Credit loss to revaluation account.

*If partners' current accounts are kept, then the entries should be made in their current accounts.

Exhibit 44.1

Following is the balance sheet as at 31 December 19X5 of W and Y, who shared profit and losses in the ratios W two-thirds; Y one-third. From 1 January 19X6 the profit and loss sharing ratios are to be altered to W one-half; Y one-half.

Balance Sheet as at 31 December 19X5

	£		£
Premises at cost	6,500	Capitals: W	7,000
Fixtures (at cost less depreciation)	1,500	Y	5,000
Stock	2,000		
Debtors	1,200		
Bank	800		
	12,000		12,000

The assets were revalued on 1 January 19X6 to be: Premises £9,000, Fixtures £1,100. Other assets remained at the same values.

Accounts to show the assets at revalued amounts follow:

Revaluation

	£	£		£
Assets reduced in value:			Assets increased in value:	
Fixtures		400	Premises	2,500
Profit on revaluation carried to				
Capital accounts:				
W two-thirds	1,400			
Y one-third	700	2,100		
		2,500		2,500

Premises

	£		£
Balance b/d	6,500	Balance c/d	9,000
Revaluation: Increase	2,500		
	9,000		9,000
Balance b/d	9,000		

Fixtures

	£		£
Balance b/d	1,500	Revaluation: Reduction	400
		Balance c/d	1,100
	1,500		1,500
Balance b/d	1,100		

Capital: W

	£		£
Balance c/d	8,400	Balance b/d	7,000
		Revaluation: Share of profit	1,400
	8,400		8,400
		Balance b/d	8,400

Capital: Y

	£		£
Balance c/d	5,700	Balance b/d	5,000
		Revaluation: Share of profit	700
	5,700		5,700
		Balance b/d	5,700

44.4 Revaluation of goodwill

This chapter deals with the revaluation of all assets other than goodwill. The revaluation of goodwill has already been dealt with in Chapter 43.

New term

Revaluation account (p. 464): An account used to record gains and losses when assets are revalued.

Main points to remember

1 When a new partner joins a firm, or a partner retires or dies, the partnership assets should be revalued.

2 Revaluation of assets should also occur when there is a change in the profit and loss sharing ratios of partners.

3 Profits on revaluation of assets are credited to the old partners' capital accounts in the old profit and loss sharing ratios.

4 Losses on revaluation of assets are debited to the old partners' capital accounts in the old profit and loss sharing ratios.

5 The asset accounts also show the revalued amounts. Losses will have been credited to them and profits debited.

Review questions

44.1

Hughes, Allen and Elliott

Balance Sheet as at 31 December 19X8

	£
Buildings at cost	8,000
Motor vehicles (at cost *less* depreciation)	3,550
Office fittings (at cost *less* depreciation)	1,310
Stock	2,040
Debtors	4,530.
Bank	1,390
	20,820

	£
Capitals:	
Hughes	9,560
Allen	6,420
Elliott	4,840
	20,820

The above partners have always shared profits and losses in the ratio: Hughes 5, Allen 3, Elliott 2.

From 1 January the assets were to be revalued as the profit-sharing ratios are to be altered soon. The following assets are to be revalued to the figures shown: Buildings £17,500, Motor vehicles £2,600, Stock £1,890, Office fittings £1,090.

Required:
(*a*) You are required to show all the ledger accounts necessary to record the revaluation.
(*b*) Draw up a balance sheet as at 1 January 19X9.

44.2A Avon and Brown have been in partnership for many years sharing profits and losses in the ratio 3:2 respectively. The following was their balance sheet as at 31 December 19X6.

	£
Goodwill	2,000
Plant and machinery	1,800
Stock	1,960
Debtors	2,130
Cash at bank	90
	£7,980
Capital: Avon	4,000
Brown	3,000
	7,000
Sundry creditors	980
	£7,980

On 1 January 19X7, they decided to admit Charles as a partner on the condition that he contributed £2,000 as his capital but that the plant and machinery and stock should be revalued at £2,000 and £1,900 respectively, the other assets, excepting goodwill, remaining at their present book values. The goodwill was agreed to be valueless.

You are required to show:
(*a*) The ledger entries dealing with the above in the following accounts:
    (*i*) Goodwill account,
    (*ii*) Revaluation accounts,
    (*iii*) Capital accounts;
(*b*) The balance sheet of the partnership immediately after the admission of Charles.

44.3 Alan, Bob and Charles are in partnership sharing profits and losses in the ratio 3:2:1 respectively.

The balance sheet for the partnership as at 30 June 19X6 is as follows:

Fixed assets	£	£
Premises		90,000
Plant		37,000
Vehicles		15,000
Fixtures		2,000
		144,000
Current assets		
Stock	62,379	
Debtors	34,980	
Cash	760	98,119
		£242,119
Capital		
Alan		85,000
Bob		65,000
Charles		35,000
		185,000
Current account		
Alan	3,714	
Bob	(2,509)	
Charles	4,678	5,883
Loan – Charles		28,000
Current liabilities		
Creditors		19,036
Bank overdraft		4,200
		£242,119

Charles decides to retire from the business on 30 June 19X6, and Don is admitted as a partner on that date. The following matters are agreed:

(a) Certain assets were revalued:
  – Premises £120,000
  – Plant £35,000
  – Stock £54,179
(b) Provision is to be made for doubtful debts in the sum of £3,000.
(c) Goodwill is to be recorded in the books on the day Charles retires in the sum of £42,000. The partners in the new firm do not wish to maintain a goodwill account so that amount is to be written back against the new partners' capital accounts.
(d) Alan and Bob are to share profits in the same ratio as before, and Don is to have the same share of profits as Bob.
(e) Charles is to take his car at its book value of £3,900 in part payment, and the balance of all he is owed by the firm in cash except £20,000 which he is willing to leave as a loan account.
(f) The partners in the new firm are to start on an equal footing so far as capital and current accounts are concerned. Don is to contribute cash to bring his capital and current accounts to the same amount as the original partner from the old firm who has the lower investment in the business.

The original partner in the old firm who has the higher investment will draw out cash so that his capital and current account balances equal those of his new partners.

Required:
(a) Account for the above transactions, including goodwill and retiring partners' accounts.
(b) Draft a balance sheet for the partnership of Alan, Bob and Don as at 30 June 19X6.

(*Association of Accounting Technicians*)

45

Partnership dissolution

Objectives

After you have studied this chapter, you should:

- *know what happens upon dissolution of a partnership*
- *know how to record the entries relating to the dissolution of a partnership*

45.1 Need for dissolution

Reasons for dissolution include the following:

(*a*) The partnership is no longer profitable, and there is no longer any reason to carry on trading.
(*b*) The partners cannot agree between themselves how to operate the partnership. They therefore decide to finish the partnership.
(*c*) Factors such as ill-health or old age may bring about the close of the partnership.

45.2 What happens upon dissolution

Upon **dissolution** the partnership firm stops trading or operating. Then, in accordance with the Partnership Act 1890:

(*a*) the assets are disposed of;
(*b*) the liabilities of the firm are paid to everyone other than partners;
(*c*) the partners are repaid their advances and current balances – advances are the amounts they have put in above and beyond the capital;
(*d*) the partners are paid the final amounts due to them on their capital accounts.

Any profit or loss on dissolution would be shared by all the partners in their profit and loss sharing ratios. Profits would increase capitals repayable to partners. Losses would reduce the capitals repayable.

   If a partner's final balance on his capital and current accounts is in deficit, he will have to pay that amount into the partnership bank account.

45.3 Disposal of assets

The assets do not have to be sold to external parties. Quite often one or more existing partners will take assets at values agreed by all the partners. In such a case the partner may not pay in cash for such assets; instead they will be charged to his capital account.

45.4 Accounting for partnership dissolution

The main account around which the dissolution entries are made is known as the realisation account. It is this account in which it is calculated whether the realisation of the assets is at a profit or at a loss.

Exhibit 45.1 shows the simplest of partnership dissolutions. We will then look at a more difficult example in Exhibit 45.2.

Exhibit 45.1

The last balance sheet of A and B, who share profits A two-thirds : B one-third is shown below. On this date they are to dissolve the partnership.

Balance Sheet at 31 December 19X9

	£	£		£
Fixed assets				
Buildings		10,000	Capitals: A	12,000
Motor vehicle		2,000	B	6,000
		12,000		18,000
Current assets			*Current liabilities*	
Stock	3,000		Creditors	2,000
Debtors	4,000			
Bank	1,000	8,000		
		20,000		20,000

The buildings were sold for £10,500 and the stock for £2,600. £3,500 was collected from debtors. The motor vehicle was taken over by A at an agreed value of £1,700, but he did not pay any cash for it. £2,000 was paid to creditors. The costs of the dissolution were paid which were £200.

The accounting entries needed are:

(A) Transfer book values of all assets to the realisation account:
        Debit realisation account
          Credit asset accounts
(B) Amounts received from disposal of assets:
        Debit bank
          Credit realisation account
(C) Values of assets taken over by partner without payment:
        Debit partner's capital account
          Credit realisation account
(D) Creditors paid:
        Debit creditors' accounts
          Credit bank
(E) Costs of dissolution:
        Debit realisation account
          Credit bank
(F) Profit or loss on realisation to be shared between partners in profit and loss sharing ratios:
    If a profit: Debit realisation account
                    Credit partners' capital accounts
    If a loss: Debit partners' capital accounts
                    Credit realisation account

(G) Pay to the partners their final balances on their capital accounts:
     Debit capital accounts
      Credit bank

The entries are now shown. The letters (A) to (G) as above are shown against each entry:

Buildings

		£			£
Balance b/d		10,000	Realisation	(A)	10,000

Motor Vehicle

		£			£
Balance b/d		2,000	Realisation	(A)	2,000

Stock

		£			£
Balance b/d		3,000	Realisation	(A)	3,000

Debtors

		£			£
Balance b/d		4,000	Realisation	(A)	4,000

Realisation

		£				£
Assets to be realised:			Bank: Assets sold			
Buildings	(A)	10,000	Buildings	(B)		10,500
Motor vehicle	(A)	2,000	Stock	(B)		2,600
Stock	(A)	3,000	Debtors	(B)		3,500
Debtors	(A)	4,000	Taken over by partner A:			
Bank:			Motor vehicle	(C)		1,700
Dissolution costs	(E)	200	Loss on realisation		£	
			A 2/3	(F)	600	
			B 1/3	(F)	300	900
		19,200				19,200

Bank

		£			£
Balance b/d		1,000	Creditors	(D)	2,000
Realisation: Assets sold			Realisation: Costs	(E)	200
Buildings	(B)	10,500	Capitals: to clear		
Stock	(B)	2,600	A	(G)	9,700
Debtors	(B)	3,500	B	(G)	5,700
		17,600			17,600

Creditors

		£			£
Bank	(D)	2,000	Balance b/d		2,000

A: Capital

		£		£
Realisation: Motor	(C)	1,700	Balance b/d	12,000
Realisation: Share of loss	(F)	600		
Bank: to close	(G)	9,700		
		12,000		12,000

B: Capital

		£		£
Realisation: Share of loss	(F)	300	Balance b/d	6,000
Bank: to close	(G)	5,700		
		6,000		6,000

The final balances on the partners' capital accounts should always equal the amount in the bank account from which they are to be paid. For instance, in the above exhibit there was £15,400 in the bank from which to pay A £9,700 and B £5,700. If the final bank balance does not pay out the partners' capital accounts exactly, you will have made a mistake somewhere.

45.5 A more detailed example

Exhibit 45.1 did not show the more difficult accounting entries. A more difficult example appears in Exhibit 45.2.

The extra information is:

(a) Any provision such as bad debts or depreciation is to be transferred to the credit of the asset account: see entries (A) in Exhibit 45.2.
(b) Discounts on creditors – to balance the creditors' account, transfer the discounts on creditors to the credit of the realisation account: see entries (F) in the exhibit.
(c) Transfer the balances on the partners' current accounts to their capital accounts: see entries (I) of the exhibit.
(d) A partner who owes the firm money because his capital account is in deficit must now pay the money owing: see entries (J) of the exhibit.

Exhibit 45.2

On 31 December 19X8, P, Q and R decided to dissolve their partnership. They had always shared profits in the ratio of P 3 : Q 2 : R 1.

Their goodwill was sold for £3,000, the machinery for £1,800 and the stock for £1,900. There were three motor cars, all taken over by the partners at agreed values, P taking one for £800, Q one for £1,000 and R one for £500. The premises were taken over by R at an agreed value of £5,500. The amounts collected from debtors amounted to £2,700 after bad debts and discounts had been deducted. The creditors were discharged for £1,600, the difference being due to discounts received. The costs of dissolution amounted to £1,000.

Their last balance sheet is summarised as:

Balance Sheet as at 31 December 19X8

	£	£	£			£	£
Fixed assets				Capital accounts:	P		6,000
Premises			5,000		Q		5,000
Machinery			3,000		R		3,000
Motor vehicles			2,500				14,000
			10,500				
				Current accounts:	P	200	
Current assets					Q	100	
Stock		1,800			R	500	800
Debtors	3,000			*Current liabilities*			
Less Provision				Creditors			1,700
for bad debts	200	2,800					
Bank		1,400	6,000				
			16,500				16,500

The accounts recording the dissolution are shown below. A description of each entry follows the accounts, the letters (A) to (K) against each entry indicating the relevant descriptions.

Premises

	£			£
Balance b/d	5,000	Realisation	(B)	5,000

Machinery

	£			£
Balance b/d	3,000	Realisation	(B)	3,000

Motor Vehicles

	£			£
Balance b/d	2,500	Realisation	(B)	2,500

Stock

	£			£
Balance b/d	1,800	Realisation	(B)	1,800

Debtors

	£			£
Balance b/d	3,000	Provisions for bad debts	(A)	200
		Realisation	(B)	2,800

Realisation

		£			£
Assets to be realised:			Bank: Assets sold		
Premises	(B)	5,000	Goodwill	(C)	3,000
Machinery	(B)	3,000	Machinery	(C)	1,800
Motor vehicles	(B)	2,500	Stock	(C)	1,900
Stock	(B)	1,800	Debtors	(C)	2,700
Debtors	(B)	2,800	Taken over by partners:		
Bank: Costs	(G)	1,000	P: Motor car	(D)	800
Profit on realisation:	(H)		Q: Motor car	(D)	1,000
		£	R: Motor car	(D)	500
P		600	R: Premises	(D)	5,500
Q		400	Creditors: Discounts	(F)	100
R		200 1,200			
		17,300			17,300

Creditors

		£		£
Bank	(E)	1,600	Balance b/d	1,700
Realisation (Discounts)	(F)	100		
		1,700		1,700

Bank

		£			£
Balance b/d		1,400	Creditors	(E)	1,600
Realisation: Assets sold			Realisation: Costs	(G)	1,000
Goodwill	(C)	3,000	P: Capital	(K)	6,000
Machinery	(C)	1,800	Q: Capital	(K)	4,500
Stock	(C)	1,900			
Debtors	(C)	2,700			
R: Capital	(J)	2,300			
		13,100			13,100

P Capital

		£		£
Realisation: Motor car	(D)	800	Balance b/d	6,000
Bank	(K)	6,000	Current account transferred (I)	200
			Realisation: Share of profit (H)	600
		6,800		6,800

Provision for Bad Debts

		£		£
Debtors	(A)	200	Balance b/d	200

P Current Account

		£			£
P: Capital	(I)	200	Balance b/d		200

Q Current Account

		£			£
Q: Capital	(I)	100	Balance b/d		100

Q Capital

		£			£
Realisation: Motor car	(D)	1,000	Balance b/d		5,000
Bank	(K)	4,500	Current account transferred (I)		100
			Realisation: Share of profit (H)		400
		5,500			5,500

R Capital

		£			£
Realisation: Motor car	(D)	500	Balance b/d		3,000
Realisation: Premises	(D)	5,500	Current account transferred (I)		500
			Realisation: Share of profit (H)		200
			Bank	(J)	2,300
		6,000			6,000

R Current Account

		£			£
R: Capital	(I)	500	Balance b/d		500

Description of transactions:

(A) The provision accounts are transferred to the relevant asset accounts so that the net balance on the asset accounts may be transferred to the realisation account. Debit provision accounts. Credit asset accounts.

(B) The net book values of the assets are transferred to the realisation account. Debit realisation account. Credit asset accounts.

(C) Assets sold. Debit bank account. Credit realisation account.

(D) Assets taken over by partners. Debit partners' capital accounts. Credit realisation account.

(E) Liabilities discharged. Credit bank account. Debit liability accounts.

(F) Discounts on creditors. Debit creditors' account. Credit realisation account.

(G) Costs of dissolution. Credit bank account. Debit realisation account.

(H) Profit or loss split in profit/loss-sharing ratio. Profit – debit realisation account. Credit partners' capital accounts. The opposite if a loss.

(I) Transfer the balances on the partners' current accounts to their capital accounts.

(J) Any partner with a capital account in deficit, i.e. debits exceeding credits, must now pay in the amount needed to cancel his indebtedness to the partnership firm. Debit bank account. Credit capital account.

(K) The credit balances on the partners' capital accounts can now be paid to them. Credit bank account. Debit partners' capital accounts.

The payments made under (K) should complete the payment of all the balances in the partnership books.

45.6 The rule in *Garner* v *Murray*

It sometimes happens that a partner's capital account finishes up with a debit balance. Normally the partner will pay in an amount to clear his indebtedness to the firm. However, sometimes he will be unable to pay all, or part, of such a balance. In the case of *Garner* v *Murray* in 1904 (a case in England) the court ruled that, subject to any agreement to the contrary, such a deficiency was to be shared by the other partners *not* in their profit-and-loss-sharing ratios but in the ratio of their 'last agreed capitals'. By 'their last agreed capitals' is meant the credit balances on their capital accounts in the normal balance sheet drawn up at the end of their last accounting period.

It must be borne in mind that the balances on their capital accounts after the assets have been realised may be far different from those on the last balance sheet. Where a partnership deed is drawn up it is commonly found that agreement is made to use normal profit-and-loss-sharing ratios instead, thus rendering the *Garner* v *Murray* rule inoperative. **The *Garner* v *Murray* rule does not apply to partnerships in Scotland.**

Before reading further you should check whether or not this topic is in the requirements for your examinations.

Exhibit 45.3

After completing the realisation of all the assets, in respect of which a loss of £4,200 was incurred, but before making the final payments to the partners, the balance sheet appears:

Balance Sheet

	£	£
Cash at bank		6,400
		6,400
Capitals: R	5,800	
S	1,400	
T	400	
	7,600	
Less Q (debit balance)	1,200	6,400
		6,400

According to the last balance sheet drawn up before the dissolution, the partners' capital account credit balances were: Q £600; R £7,000; S £2,000; T £1,000; while the profits and losses were shared Q 3 : R 2 : S 1 : T 1.

Q is unable to meet any part of his deficiency. Each of the other partners therefore suffer the deficiency as follows:

$$\frac{\text{Own capital per balance sheet before dissolution}}{\text{Total of all solvent partners' capitals per same balance sheet}} \times \text{Deficiency}$$

This can now be calculated.

$$R \quad \frac{£7,000}{£7,000 + £2,000 + £1,000} \times £1,200 = £840$$

$$S \quad \frac{£2,000}{£7,000 + £2,000 + £1,000} \times £1,200 = £240$$

$$T \quad \frac{£1,000}{£7,000 + £2,000 + £1,000} \times £1,200 = \frac{£120}{£1,200}$$

When these amounts have been charged to the capital accounts, then the balances remaining on them will equal the amount of the bank balance. Payments may therefore be made to clear their capital accounts.

	Credit balance b/d		Share of deficiency now debited		Final credit balances
	£		£		£
R	5,800	–	840	=	4,960
S	1,400	–	240	=	1,160
T	400	–	120	=	280
Equals the bank balance					6,400

45.7 Piecemeal realisation of assets

Frequently the assets may take a long time to realise. The partners will naturally want payments made to them on account as cash is received. They will not want to wait for payments until the dissolution is completed just for the convenience of the accountant. There is, however, a danger that if too much is paid to a partner, and he is unable to repay it, then the person handling the dissolution could be placed in a very awkward position.

To counteract this, the concept of prudence is brought into play. This is done by:

(a) Treating each receipt of sale money as being the final receipt, even though more could be received.
(b) Any loss then calculated so far to be shared between partners in profit-and-loss-sharing ratios.
(c) Should any partner's capital account after each receipt show a debit balance, then he is assumed to be unable to pay in the deficiency. This deficit will be shared (failing any other agreement) between the partners using the *Garner* v *Murray* rule.
(d) After payments of liabilities and the costs of dissolution the remainder of the cash is then paid to the partners.
(e) In this manner, even if no further money were received, or should a partner become insolvent, the division of the available cash would be strictly in accordance with the legal requirements. Exhibit 45.4 shows such a series of calculations.

Exhibit 45.4

The following is the summarised balance sheet of H, I, J and K as at 31 December 19X8. The partners had shared profits in the ratios H 6:I 4:J 1:K1.

Balance Sheet as at 31 December 19X8

	£
Assets	8,400
	8,400
Capitals:	
H	600
I	3,000
J	2,000
K	1,000
Creditors	1,800
	8,400

On 1 March 19X9 some of the assets were sold for cash £5,000. Out of this the creditors' £1,800 and the cost of dissolution £200 are paid, leaving £3,000 distributable to the partners.

On 1 July 19X9 some more assets are sold for £2,100. As all of the liabilities and the costs of dissolution have already been paid, then the whole of the £2,100 is available for distribution between the partners.

On 1 October 19X9 the final sale of the assets realised £1,200.

First distribution: 1 March 19X9	H	I	J	K
	£	£	£	£
Capital balances before dissolution	600	3,000	2,000	1,000
Loss if no further assets realised: Assets £8,400				
– Sales £5,000 = £3,400 + Costs £200 = £3,600				
loss				
Loss shared in profit/loss ratios	1,800	1,200	300	300
	1,200Dr	1,800Cr	1,700Cr	700Cr
H's deficiency shared in *Garner v Murray*	³⁄₆	600 ²⁄₆	400 ¹⁄₆	200
ratios				
Cash paid to partners (£3,000)		1,200	1,300	500

Second distribution: 1 July 19X9	H	I	J	K
	£	£	£	£
Capital balances before dissolution	600	3,000	2,000	1,000
Loss if no further assets realised:				
Assets £8,400 – Sales (£5,000 + £2,100)				
= £1,300 + Costs £200 = £1,500 loss				
Loss shared in profit/loss ratios	750	500	125	125
	150Dr	2,500Cr	1,875Cr	875Cr
H's deficiency shared in *Garner v Murray* ratios		75	50	25
		2,425	1,825	850
Less First distribution already paid		1,200	1,300	500
Cash now paid to partners (£2,100)		1,225	525	350

Third and final distribution: 1 October 19X9	H	I	J	K
	£	£	£	£
Capital balances before dissolution	600	3,000	2,000	1,000
Loss finally ascertained:				
Assets £8,400 – Sales (£5,000 + £2,100				
+ £1,200) = £100 + Costs £200 = £300 loss				
Loss shared in profit/loss ratios	150	100	25	25
	450Cr	2,900Cr	1,975Cr	975Cr
(No deficiency now exists on any capital account)				
Less First and second distributions	–	2,425	1,825	850
Cash now paid to partners (£1,200)	450	475	150	125

In any subsequent distribution following that in which all the partners have shared, i.e. no partner could then have had a deficiency left on his capital account, all receipts of cash are divided between the partners in their profit-and-loss-sharing ratios. Following the above method would give the same answer for these subsequent distributions but obviously an immediate division in the profit-and-loss-sharing ratios would be quicker. The reader is invited to try it to satisfy him/herself that it would work out at the same answer.

New terms

Dissolution (p. 469): When a partnership firm ceases operations and its assets are disposed of.

The *Garner* v *Murray* rule (p. 476): If one partner is unable to make good a deficit on his capital account, the remaining partners will share the loss in proportion to their last agreed capitals, not in the profit/loss-sharing ratio.

Main points to remember

1 Upon dissolution, a partnership firm stops trading or operating, any profit or loss on dissolution being shared by the partners in their profit-sharing ratio.

2 The *Garner* v *Murray* rule does not apply to partnerships in Scotland.

Review questions

45.1 S, W and M are partners. They share profits and losses in the ratios of $\frac{2}{5}$, $\frac{2}{5}$ and $\frac{1}{5}$ respectively.

For the year ended 31 December 19X9 their capital accounts remained fixed at the following amounts:

	£
S	6,000
W	4,000
M	2,000

They have agreed to give each other 10 per cent interest per annum on their capital accounts.

In addition to the above, partnership salaries of £3,000 for W and £1,000 for M are to be charged.

The net profit of the partnership before taking any of the above into account was £25,200.

You are required to draw up the appropriation account of the partnership for the year ended 31 December 19X9.

45.2A Draw up a profit and loss appropriation account for Winn, Pool and Howe for the year ended 31 December 19X7, and balance sheet extracts at that date, from the following:

(i)   Net profits £30,350.
(ii)   Interest to be charged on capitals: Winn £2,000; Pool £1,500; Howe £900.
(iii)   Interest to be charged on drawings: Winn £240; Pool £180; Howe £130.
(iv)   Salaries to be credited: Pool £2,000; Howe £3,500.
(v)   Profits to be shared: Winn 50%; Pool 30%; Howe 20%.
(vi)   Current accounts: Winn £1,860; Pool £946; Howe £717.
(vii)   Capital accounts: Winn £40,000; Pool £30,000; Howe £18,000.
(viii) Drawings: Winn £9,200; Pool £7,100; Howe £6,900.

45.3 Moore and Stephens, who share profits and losses equally, decide to dissolve their partnership as at 31 March 19X9. Their balance sheet on that date was as follows:

	£		£
Buildings	800	Capital account: Moore	2,000
Tools and fixtures	850	Stephens	1,500
			3,500
Debtors	2,800		
Cash	1,800	Sundry creditors	2,750
	6,250		6,250

The debtors realised £2,700, the buildings £400 and the tools and fixtures £950. The expenses of dissolution were £100 and discounts totalling £200 were received from creditors.

Required:
Prepare the accounts necessary to show the results of the realisation and of the disposal of the cash.

45.4 X, Y and Z have been in partnership for several years, sharing profits and losses in the ratio 3:2:1. Their last balance sheet which was prepared on 31 October 19X9 is as follows:

Balance Sheet of X, Y and Z
as at 31 October 19X9

	£			£		
Fixed assets			Capital X			4,000
At cost	20,000		Y			4,000
Less Depreciation	6,000		Z			2,000
		14,000				10,000
Current assets			*Current liabilities*			
Stock	5,000		Bank	13,000		
Debtors	21,000		Creditors	17,000		
		26,000				30,000
		£40,000				£40,000

Despite making good profits during recent years they had become increasingly dependent on one credit customer, Smithson, and in order to retain his custom they had gradually increased his credit limit until he owed the partnership £18,000. It has now been discovered that Smithson is insolvent and that he is unlikely to repay any of the money owed by him to the partnership. Reluctantly X, Y and Z have agreed to dissolve the partnership on the following terms:

(*i*)   The stock is to be sold to Nelson Ltd for £4,000.
(*ii*) The fixed assets will be sold for £8,000 except for certain items with a book value of £5,000 which will be taken over by X at an agreed valuation of £7,000.
(*iii*) The debtors, except for Smithson, are expected to pay their accounts in full.
(*iv*) The costs of dissolution will be £800 and discounts received from creditors will be £500.
   Z is unable to meet his liability to the partnership out of his personal funds.

Required:
(*a*) the realisation account;
(*b*) the capital accounts to the partners recording the dissolution of the partnership.

(*Associated Examining Board*)

45.5A The following trial balance has been extracted from the books of Gain and Main as at 31 March 19X8; Gain and Main are in partnership sharing profits and losses in the ratio 3 to 2:

	£	£
Capital accounts:		
Gain		10,000
Main		5,000
Cash at bank	1,550	
Creditors		500
Current accounts:		
Gain		1,000
Main	2,000	
Debtors	2,000	
Depreciation: Fixtures and fittings		1,000
Motor vehicles		1,300
Fixtures and fittings	2,000	
Land and buildings	30,000	
Motor vehicles	4,500	
Net profit (for the year to 31 March 19X8)		26,250
Stock, at cost	3,000	
	£45,050	£45,050

In appropriating the net profit for the year, it has been agreed that Main should be entitled to a salary of £9,750. Each partner is also entitled to interest on his opening capital account balance at the rate of 10 per cent per annum.

Gain and Main have decided to convert the parnership into a limited company, Plain Limited, as from 1 April 19X8. The company is to take over all the assets and liabilities of the partnership, except that Gain is to retain for his personal use one of the motor vehicles at an agreed transfer price of £1,000.

The purchase consideration will consist of 40,000 ordinary shares of £1 each in Plain Limited, to be divided between the partners in profit-sharing ratio. Any balance on the partners' current accounts is to be settled in cash.

You are required to:
Prepare the main ledger accounts of the partnership in order to close off the books as at 31 March 19X8.

(*Association of Accounting Technicians*)

45.6A A, B & C are partners sharing profits and losses in the ratio 2:2:1. The balance sheet of the partnership as at 30 September 19X7 was as follows:

	£		£	£
Freehold premises	18,000	Capital accounts		
Equipment and machinery	12,000	A	22,000	
Motor cars	3,000	B	18,000	
Inventory*	11,000	C	10,000	
Debtors	14,000			50,000
Bank	9,000	Loan account – A		7,000
		Creditors		10,000
	£67,000			£67,000

* *Author's note*: Inventory is another word for stock.

The partners agreed to dispose of the business to CNO Limited with effect from 1 October 19X7 under the following conditions and terms:

(*i*)   CNO Limited will acquire the goodwill, all fixed assets and the inventory for the purchase consideration of £58,000. This consideration will include a payment of £10,000 in cash and the issue of 12,000 10 per cent preference shares of £1 each at par, and the balance by the issue of £1 ordinary shares at £1.25 per share.

(*ii*)   The partnership business will settle amounts owing to creditors.

(*iii*)   CNO Limited will collect the debts on behalf of the vendors.

Purchase consideration payments and allotments of shares were made on 1 October 19X7.

The partnership creditors were paid off by 31 October 19X7 after the taking of cash discounts of £190.

CNO Limited collected and paid over all partnership debts by 30 November 19X7 except for bad debts amounting to £800. Discounts allowed to debtors amounted to £400.

Required:

(*a*)   Journal entries (including those relating to cash) necessary to close the books of the partnership, and

(*b*)   Set out the basis on which the shares in CNO Limited are allotted to partners.
     Ignore interest.

(*Institute of Chartered Secretaries and Administrators*)

45.7 Amis, Lodge and Pym were in partnership sharing profits and losses in the ratio 5:3:2. The following trial balance has been extracted from their books of account as at 31 March 19X8:

	£	£
Bank interest received		750
Capital accounts (as at 1 April 19X7):		
Amis		80,000
Lodge		15,000
Pym		5,000
Carriage inwards	4,000	
Carriage outwards	12,000	
Cash at bank	4,900	
Current accounts:		
Amis	1,000	
Lodge	500	
Pym	400	
Discounts allowed	10,000	
Discounts received		4,530
Drawings:		
Amis	25,000	
Lodge	22,000	
Pym	15,000	
Motor vehicles:		
at cost	80,000	
accumulated depreciation (at 1 April 19X7)		20,000
Office expenses	30,400	
Plant and machinery:		
at cost	100,000	
accumulated depreciation (at 1 April 19X7)		36,600
Provision for bad and doubtful debts (at 1 April 19X7)		420
Purchases	225,000	
Rent, rates, heat and light	8,800	
Sales		404,500
Stock (at 1 April 19X7)	30,000	
Trade creditors		16,500
Trade debtors	14,300	
	£583,300	£583,300

Additional information:
(*a*) Stock at 31 March 19X8 was valued at £35,000.
(*b*) Depreciation on the fixed assets is to be charged as follows:
　　Motor vehicles – 25 per cent on the reduced balance.
　　Plant and machinery – 20 per cent on the original cost.
　　There were no purchases or sales of fixed assets during the year to 31 March 19X8.
(*c*) The provision for bad and doubtful debts is to be maintained at a level equivalent to 5 per cent of the total trade debtors as at 31 March 19X8.
(*d*) An office expense of £405 was owing at 31 March 19X8, and some rent amounting to £1,500 had been paid in advance as at that date. These items had not been included in the list of balances shown in the trial balance.
(*e*) Interest on drawings and on the debit balance on each partner's current account is to be charged as follows:

	£
Amis	1,000
Lodge	900
Pym	720

(*f*) According to the partnership agreement, Pym is allowed a salary of £13,000 per annum. This amount was owing to Pym for the year to 31 March 19X8, and needs to be accounted for.

(*g*) The partnership agreement also allows each partner interest on his capital account at a rate of 10 per cent per annum. There were no movements on the respective partners' capital accounts during the year to 31 March 19X8, and the interest had not been credited to them as at that date.

Note: The information given above is sufficient to answer part (*a*) (*i*) and (*ii*) of the question, and notes (*h*) and (*i*) below are pertinent to requirements (*b*) (*i*), (*ii*) and (*iii*) of the question.

(*h*) On 1 April 19X8, Fowles Limited agreed to purchase the business on the following terms:

   (*i*)   Amis to purchase one of the partnership's motor vehicles at an agreed value of £5,000, the remaining vehicles being taken over by the company at an agreed value of £30,000;

   (*ii*)   the company agreed to purchase the plant and machinery at a value of £35,000 and the stock at a value of £38,500;

   (*iii*)   the partners to settle the trade creditors: the total amount agreed with the creditors being £16,000;

   (*iv*)   the trade debtors were not to be taken over by the company, the partners receiving cheques on 1 April 19X8 amounting to £12,985 in total from the trade debtors in settlement of the outstanding debts;

   (*v*)   the partners paid the outstanding office expense on 1 April 19X8, and the landlord returned the rent paid in advance by cheque on the same day;

   (*vi*)   as consideration for the sale of the partnership, the partners were to be paid £63,500 in cash by Fowles Limited, and to receive 75,000 in £1 ordinary shares in the company, the shares to be apportioned equally amongst the partners.

(*i*) Assume that all the matters relating to the dissolution of the partnership and its sales to the company took place on 1 April 19X8.

Required:

(*a*) Prepare:

   (*i*)   Amis', Lodge's and Pym's trading, profit and loss and profit and loss appropriation account for the year to 31 March 19X8;

   (*ii*)   Amis', Lodge's and Pym's current accounts (in columnar format) for the year to 31 March 19X8 (the final balance on each account is to be then transferred to each partner's respective capital account);

   and

(*b*) Compile the following accounts:

   (*i*)   the partnership realisation account for the period up to and including 1 April 19X8;

   (*ii*)   the partners' bank account for the period up to and including 1 April 19X8; and

   (*iii*) the partners' capital accounts (in columnar format) for the period up to and including 1 April 19X8.

Note: Detailed workings should be submitted with your answer.

(*Association of Accounting Technicians*)

45.8A Proudie, Slope and Thorne were in partnership sharing profits and losses in the ratio 3:1:1. The draft balance sheet of the partnership as at 31 May 19X9 is shown below:

	£000	£000	£000
	Cost	Depreciation	Net book
Fixed assets			value
Land and buildings	200	40	160
Furniture	30	18	12
Motor vehicles	60	40	20
	£290	£98	192
Current assets			
Stocks		23	
Trade debtors		42	
Less Provision for doubtful debts	1		
		41	
Prepayments			2
Cash		10	
		76	
Less Current liabilities			
Trade creditors	15		
Accruals	3		
		18	
			58
			£250
Financed by:			
Capital accounts			
Proudie		100	
Slope		60	
Thorne		40	
			200
Current accounts			
Proudie		24	
Slope		10	
Thorne		8	
			42
			242
Loan			
Proudie			8
			£250

Additional information:

1 Proudie decided to retire on 31 May 19X9. However, Slope and Thorne agreed to form a new partnership out of the old one, as from 1 June 19X9. They agreed to share profits and losses in the same ratio as in the old partnership.

2 Upon the dissolution of the old partnership, it was agreed that the following adjustments were to be made to the partnership balance sheet as at 31 May 19X9.
(a) Land and buildings were to be revalued at £200,000.
(b) Furniture was to be revalued at £5,000.
(c) Proudie agreed to take over one of the motor vehicles at a value of £4,000, the remaining motor vehicles being revalued at £10,000.
(d) Stocks were to be written down by £5,000.
(e) A bad debt of £2,000 was to be written off, and the provision for doubtful debts was then to be adjusted so that it represented 5 per cent of the then outstanding trade debtors as at 31 May 19X9.

(*f*) A further accrual of £3,000 for office expenses was to be made.

(*g*) Professional charges relating to the dissolution were estimated to be £1,000.

3 It has not been the practice of the partners to carry goodwill in the books of the partnership, but on the retirement of a partner it had been agreed that goodwill should be taken into account. Goodwill was to be valued at an amount equal to the average annual profits of the three years expiring on the retirement. For the purpose of including goodwill in the dissolution arrangement when Proudie retired, the net profits for the last three years were as follows:

	£000
Year to 31 May 19X7	130
Year to 31 May 19X8	150
Year to 31 May 19X9	181

The net profit for the year to 31 May 19X9 had been calculated before any of the items listed in 2 above were taken into account. The net profit was only to be adjusted for items listed in 2(*d*), 2(*e*) and 2(*f*) above.

4 Goodwill is not to be carried in the books of the new partnership.

5 It was agreed that Proudie's old loan of £8,000 should be repaid to him on 31 May 19X9, but any further amount owing to him as a result of the dissolution of the partnership should be left as a long-term loan in the books of the new partnership.

6 The partners' current accounts were to be closed and any balances on them as at 31 May 19X9 were to be transferred to their respective capital accounts.

Required:

(*a*) Prepare the revaluation account as at 31 May 19X9.

(*b*) Prepare the partners' capital accounts as at the date of dissolution of the partnership, and bring down any balances on them in the books of the new partnership.

(*c*) Prepare Slope and Thorne's balance sheet as at 1 June 19X9.

(*Association of Accounting Technicians*)

45.9 Lock, Stock and Barrel have been in partnership as builders and contractors for many years. Owing to adverse trading conditions it has been decided to dissolve the partnership. Profits are shared Lock 40 per cent, Stock 30 per cent, Barrel 30 per cent. The partnership deed also provides that in the event of a partner being unable to pay off a debit balance the remaining partners will treat this as a trading loss.

The latest partnership balance sheet was as follows:

	Cost	Depreciation	
Fixed tangible assets	£	£	£
Freehold yard and buildings	20,000	3,000	17,000
Plant and equipment	150,000	82,000	68,000
Motor vehicles	36,000	23,000	13,000
	206,000	108,000	98,000
Current assets			
Stock of land for building		75,000	
Houses in course of construction		115,000	
Stocks of materials		23,000	
Debtors for completed houses		62,000	
		275,000	
Current liabilities			
Trade creditors		77,000	
Deposits and progress payments		82,000	
Bank overdraft		132,500	
		291,500	
Excess of current liabilities over current assets			(16,500)
			81,500
Partners' capital accounts			
Lock		52,000	
Stock		26,000	
Barrel		3,500	
			81,500

During the six months from the date of the latest balance sheet to the date of dissolution the following transactions have taken place:

	£
Purchase of materials	20,250
Materials used for houses in course of construction	35,750
Payments for wages and subcontractors on building sites	78,000
Payments to trade creditors for materials	45,000
Sales of completed houses	280,000
Cash received from customers for houses	225,000
Payments for various general expenses	12,500
Payments for administration salaries	17,250
Cash withdrawn by partners: Lock	6,000
Stock	5,000
Barrel	4,000

All deposits and progress payments have been used for completed transactions.

Depreciation is normally provided each year at £600 on the freehold yard and buildings, at 10 per cent on cost for plant and equipment and 25 per cent on cost for motor vehicles.

The partners decide to dissolve the partnership on 1 February 19X7 and wish to take out the maximum cash possible, as items are sold. At this date there are no houses in course of construction and one-third of the stock of land had been used for building.

It is agreed that Barrel is insolvent and cannot bring any money into the partnership. The partners take over the partnership cars at an agreed figure of £2,000 each. All other vehicles were sold on 28 February 19X7 for £6,200. At the same date stocks of materials were sold for £7,000, and the stock of the land realised £72,500. On 30 April 19X7 the debtors paid in full and all the plant and equipment was sold for £50,000.

The freehold yard and buildings realised £100,000 on 1 June 19X7, on which date all remaining cash was distributed.

There are no costs of realisation or distribution.

Required:

(a) Prepare a partnership profit and loss account for the six months to 1 February 19X7, partners' capital accounts for the same period and a balance sheet at 1 February 19X7.

(b) Show calculations of the amounts distributable to the partners.

(c) Prepare a realisation account and the capital accounts of the partners to the final distribution.

(*Association of Chartered Certified Accountants*)

45.10A Grant and Herd are in partnership sharing profits and losses in the ratio 3 to 2. The following information relates to the year to 31 December 19X8:

	Dr £000	Cr £000
Capital accounts (at 1 January 19X8):		
Grant		300
Herd		100
Cash at bank	5	
Creditors and accruals		25
Debtors and prepayments	18	
Drawings during the year: Grant (all at 30 June 19X8)	40	
Herd (all at 31 March 19X8)	40	
Fixed assets: at cost	300	
accumulated depreciation (at 31 December 19X8)		100
Herd – salary	10	
Net profit (for the year to 31 December 19X8)		60
Stocks at cost (at 31 December 19X8)	90	
Trade creditors		141
Trade debtors	223	
	£726	£726

Additional information:

1 The partnership agreement allows for Herd to be paid a salary of £20,000 per annum, and for interest of 5 per cent per annum to be paid on the partners' capital account balances as at 1 January in each year. Interest at a rate of 10 per cent per annum is charged on the partners' drawings.

2 The partners decide to dissolve the partnership as at 31 December 19X8, and the business was then sold to Valley Limited. The purchase consideration was to be 400,000 £1 ordinary shares in Valley at a premium of 25p per share. The shares were to be issued to the partners on 31 December 19X8, and they were to be shared between them in their profit-sharing ratio.

The sale agreement allowed Grant to take over one of the business cars at an agreed valuation of £10,000. Apart from the car and the cash and bank balances, the company took over all the other partnership assets and liabilities at their book values as at 31 December 19X8.

3 Matters relating to the appropriation of profit for the year to 31 December 19X8 are to be dealt with in the partners' capital accounts, including any arrears of salary owing to Herd.

Required:

(a) Write up the following accounts for the year to 31 December 19X8:
    (i) the profit and loss appropriation account;
    (ii) Grant and Herd's capital accounts; and
    (iii) the realisation account.

(b) Prepare Valley's balance sheet as at 1 January 19X9 immediately after the acquisition of the partnership and assuming that no further transactions have taken place in the meantime.

(*Association of Accounting Technicians*)

45.11 Dinho and Manueli are in partnership sharing profits and losses equally after interest of 10% on each partner's capital account in excess of £100,000. At 31 December 19X8, the partnership trial balance was:

	Dr £	Cr £
Bank		56,700
Capital accounts: Dinho		194,000
Manueli		123,000
Creditors		85,800
Debtors	121,000	
Equipment, at cost	85,000	
Long-term loan		160,000
Freehold property	290,000	
Provision for depreciation on equipment		20,000
Stocks	143,500	
	639,500	639,500

On 31 December 19X8, the partnership was converted to a limited company, Bin Ltd. All the partnership assets and liabilities were taken over by the company in exchange for shares in Bin Ltd valued at £304,000. The share capital was allocated so as to preserve the rights previously enjoyed by the partners under their partnership agreement.

The assets and liabilities and shares issued were all entered in the books of Bin Ltd at 31 December. In the company's books, the debtors were recorded at £116,000 and the freehold property was valued at £260,000.

On 1 January 19X9, Pa invested £120,000 in the company and was issued shares on the same basis as had been applied when deciding the share allocations to Dinho and Manueli – i.e. as if he had been an equal partner in the partnership.

Pa had previously been an employee of the partnership earning £40,000 per annum. The £120,000 he invested in the company had been earning interest of 6% per annum from the bank. His salary will continue to be paid.

Assume that all profits will be paid as dividends. Ignore taxation.

Required:
(a) Prepare the partnership realisation account after the sale of the business to Bin Ltd had been completed and recorded in the partnership books.
(b) Prepare Bin Ltd's balance sheet as at 1 January 19X9 after the purchase of shares by Pa.
(c) Calculate the annual profit that Bin Ltd needs to make before it pays any dividends if Pa is to receive the same amount of income as he was receiving before buying shares in Bin Ltd.

46

An introduction to the final accounts of limited liability companies

Objectives

After you have studied this chapter, you should:

- *understand how limited companies differ from other organisations*
- *be able to calculate how distributable profits available for dividends are divided between the different classes of shares*
- *realise the differences between shares and debentures*
- *be able to draw up the trading and profit and loss accounts for a limited company*
- *be able to draw up a balance sheet for a limited company*

46.1 Need for limited companies

Limited companies came into existence originally because of the growth in the size of businesses, and the need to have a lot of people investing in the business who would not be able to take part in its management. Partnerships were not suitable for such businesses because:

- Normally they cannot have more than 20 partners, not counting limited partners.
- If a partnership business fails, a partner could lose part, or all, of his private assets to pay the debts of the business.

The form of organisation which does not have these limitations is the limited liability company, normally known as the limited company. The law governing the preparation and publication of the final accounts of limited companies in the United Kingdom is contained in two Acts of Parliament. These are the Companies Acts of 1985 and 1989. Both Acts are in force for this purpose, the 1989 Act adding to and amending the 1985 Act.

46.2 Limited liability

The capital of a limited company is divided into **shares**. These can be shares of £1 each, £5 each, £10 each or any other amount per share. To become a member of a limited company, or a shareholder, a person must buy one or more of the shares.

If the shareholder has paid in full for the shares, his liabilit
If a company loses all its assets, all the shareholder can lose
forced to pay anything out of his private money in respect of t

If the shareholder has only partly paid for the shares, he
balance owing on the shares. Apart from that he cannot be
private money for company losses.

This is known as limited liability and the company is knov
You can see that these limited companies meet the need for
owners, and make it possible to have a large amount of capital.

There are in fact a few companies which have unlimited liabil
the scope of this book.

46.3 Public and private companies

There are two classes of company, the public company and the private company. In the
UK private companies far outnumber public companies. In the Companies Acts a public
company is defined as one which fulfils the following conditions:

- Its memorandum states that it is a public company, and has registered as such.
- It has an authorised share capital of at least £50,000.
- Minimum membership is two. There is no maximum.
- Its name must end with the words 'public limited company' or the abbreviation plc. It
  can have the Welsh equivalent if registered in Wales.

A private company is usually, but not always, a smaller business, and may be formed by
one or more persons. It is defined by the Act as a company which is not a public
company. The main differences between a private company and a public company are
that a private company:

- can have an authorised capital of less than £50,000,
- cannot offer its shares for subscription to the public at large, whereas public
  companies can.

This means that if you were to walk into a bank, or similar public place, and see a
prospectus offering anyone the chance to take up shares in a company, then that
company would be a public company.

The shares that are dealt in on the Stock Exchange are all of public limited companies.
This does not mean that all public companies' shares are traded on the Stock Exchange,
as for various reasons some public companies have either chosen not to, or not been
allowed to, have their shares traded there. The ones that are traded in are known as
'quoted companies' meaning that their shares have prices quoted on the Stock Exchange.
They have to comply with Stock Exchange requirements.

46.4 Directors of the company

The day-to-day business of a company is not carried out by the shareholders. The
possession of a share normally confers voting rights on the holder, who is then able to
attend general meetings of the company. At one of these the shareholders will meet and
will vote for **directors**, these being the people who will be entrusted with the running of
the business. At each **Annual General Meeting** the directors will have to report on their
stewardship, and this report is accompanied by a set of final accounts for the year.

company is said to possess a 'separate legal identity' from that of its lders. Put simply, this means that a company is not seen as being exactly the as its shareholders. For instance, a company can sue one or more of its lareholders, and similarly, a shareholder can sue the company. This would not be the case if the company and its shareholders were exactly the same thing, as one cannot sue oneself.

46.6 Share capital

A shareholder of a limited company obtains their reward in the form of a share of the profits, known as a **dividend**. The directors consider the amount of profits and decide on the amount of profits which are placed to reserves. Out of the profits remaining the directors then propose the payment of a certain amount of dividend to be paid. It is important to note that the shareholders cannot propose a higher dividend for themselves than that already proposed by the directors. They can, however, propose that a lesser dividend should be paid, although this action is very rare indeed. If the directors propose that no dividend be paid, then the shareholders are powerless to alter the decision.

The decision by the directors as to the amount proposed as dividends is a very complex one and cannot be fully discussed here. Such points as government directives to reduce dividends, the effect of taxation, the availability of bank balances to pay the dividends, the possibility of takeover bids and so on will all be taken into account.

The dividend is usually expressed as a percentage. Ignoring income tax, a dividend of 10 per cent in Firm A on 500,000 Ordinary Shares of £1 each will amount to £50,000, or a dividend of 6 per cent in Firm B on 200,000 Ordinary Shares of £2 each will amount to £24,000. A shareholder having 100 shares in each firm would receive £10 from Firm A and £12 from Firm B. There are two main types of shares:

1 **Preference shares.** These get an agreed percentage rate of dividend before the ordinary shareholders receive anything.
2 **Ordinary shares.** These receive the remainder of the total profits available for dividends. There is no upper limit to the amounts of dividends they can receive.

For example, if a company had 10,000 5 per cent preference shares of £1 each and 20,000 ordinary shares of £1 each, then the dividends would be payable as in Exhibit 46.1.

Exhibit 46.1

Year	1	2	3	4	5
	£	£	£	£	£
Profits appropriated for dividends	900	1,300	1,600	3,100	2,000
Preference dividends (5%)	500	500	500	500	500
Ordinary dividends	(2%)400	(4%)800	(5½%)1,100	(13%)2,600	(7½%)1,500

The two main types of preference shares are non-cumulative preference shares and cumulative preference shares:

1   **Non-cumulative preference shares**
These can receive a dividend up to an agreed percentage each year. If the amount paid is less than the maximum agreed amount, the shortage is lost by the shareholder. He cannot carry forward that shortage and get it in a future year.

2   **Cumulative preference shares**
These also have an agreed maximum percentage dividend. However, any shortage of dividend paid in a year can be carried forward. These arrears of preference dividends will have to be paid before the ordinary shareholders receive anything.

Exhibit 46.2

A company has 5,000 £1 ordinary shares and 2,000 5 per cent non-cumulative preference shares of £1 each. The profits available for dividends are: year 1 £150, year 2 £80, year 3 £250, year 4 £60, year 5 £500.

Year	1	2	3	4	5
	£	£	£	£	£
Profits	150	80	250	60	500
Preference dividend (non-cumulative)					
(limited in years 2 and 4)	100	80	100	60	100
Dividends on ordinary shares	50	–	150	–	400

Exhibit 46.3

Assume that the preference shares in Exhibit 46.2 had been cumulative. The dividends would have been:

Year	1	2	3	4	5
	£	£	£	£	£
Profits	150	80	250	60	500
Preference dividend	100	80	120*	60	140*
Dividends on ordinary shares	50	–	130	–	360

*including arrears.

46.7 Share capital: different meanings

The term 'share capital' can have any of the following meanings:

1   **Authorised share capital.** Sometimes known as registered capital or nominal capital. This is the total of the share capital which the company is allowed to issue to shareholders.

2   **Issued share capital.** This is the total of the share capital actually issued to shareholders.

If all of the authorised share capital has been issued, then 1 and 2 above would be the same amount.

3   **Called-up capital.** Where only part of the amounts payable on each share has been asked for, the total amount asked for on all the shares is known as the called-up capital.

4   **Uncalled capital.** This is the total amount which is to be received in future, but which has not yet been asked for.

5   **Calls in arrears.** The total amount for which payment has been asked (i.e. called for), but has not yet been paid by shareholders.

6 **Paid-up capital.** This is the total of the amount of share capital which has been paid for by shareholders.

Exhibit 46.4 illustrates these different meanings.

Exhibit 46.4

1 Better Enterprises Ltd was formed with the legal right to be able to issue 100,000 shares of £1 each.
2 The company has actually issued 75,000 shares.
3 None of the shares has yet been fully paid up. So far the company has made calls of 80p (£0.80) per share.
4 All the calls have been paid by shareholders except for £200 owing from one shareholder.

(a) Authorised or nominal share capital is:	1 £100,000.
(b) Issued share capital is:	2 £75,000.
(c) Called-up capital is:	3 75,000 × £0.80 = £60,000.
(d) Calls in arrear amounted to:	4 £200.
(e) Paid-up capital is:	(c) £60,000 less (d) £200 = £59,800.

46.8 Debentures

The term debenture is used when a limited company receives money on loan, and certificates called debenture certificates are issued to the lender. Interest will be paid to the holder, the rate of interest being shown on the certificate. Instead of always being called debentures they are often known as loan stock or as loan capital.

Debenture interest has to be paid whether profits are made or not. They are therefore different from shares, where dividends depend on profits being made. A debenture may be either:

- Redeemable, i.e. repayable at or by a particular date, or
- Irredeemable, normally repayable only when the company is officially terminated, known as liquidation.

If a date is shown behind a debenture, e.g. 2001/2008, it means that the company can redeem it in any of the years 2001 to 2008 inclusive.

People lending money to companies in the form of debentures will obviously be interested in how safe their investment will be. Some debentures are given the legal right that on certain happenings the debenture holders will be able to take control of specific assets, or of the whole of the assets. They can then sell the assets and recoup the amount due under their debentures, or deal with the assets in ways specified in the deed under which the debentures were issued. Such debentures are known as being secured against the assets, the term 'mortgage' debenture often being used. Other debentures have no prior right to control the assets under any circumstances. These are known as **simple** or **naked** debentures.

46.9 Trading and profit and loss accounts

The trading and profit and loss accounts for both private and public companies are drawn up in exactly the same way.

The trading account of a limited company is no different from that of a sole trader or a partnership. However, some differences may be found in the profit and loss account.

The two main expenses that would be found only in company accounts are:

Directors' remuneration

As directors exist only in companies, this type of expense is found only in company accounts.

Directors are legally employees of the company, appointed by the shareholders. Their remuneration is charged to the main profit and loss account.

Debenture interest

The interest payable for the use of the money is an expense of the company, and is payable whether profits are made or not. This means that debenture interest is charged as an expense in the profit and loss account itself. Contrast this with dividends which are dependent on profits having been made.

46.10 The appropriation account

Next under the profit and loss account is a section called the profit and loss appropriation account. The appropriation account shows how the net profits are to be appropriated, i.e. how the profits are to be used.

We may find any of the following in the appropriation account:

Credit side

1   **Net profit for the year**
    This is the net profit brought down from the main profit and loss account.
2   **Balance brought forward from last year**
    As you will see, all the profits may not be appropriated during a period. This then will be the balance on the appropriation account, as brought forward from the previous year. They are usually called retained profits.

Debit side

3   **Transfers to reserves**
    The directors may decide that some of the profits should not be included in the calculation of how much should be paid out as dividends. These profits are transferred to **reserve accounts**.

    There may be a specific reason for the transfer such as a need to replace fixed assets. In this case an amount would be transferred to a fixed assets replacement reserve.

    Or the reason may not be specific. In this case an amount would be transferred to a general reserve account.
4   **Amounts written off as goodwill**
    Goodwill, in a company, may have amounts written off it from time to time. When this is done the amount written off should be shown in the appropriation account and not in the main profit and loss account. (*See* also section 46.14.)
5   **Preliminary expenses**
    When a company is formed, there are many kinds of expenses concerned with its

formation. These include, for example, legal expenses and various government taxes. Since 1981 these cannot be shown as an asset in the balance sheet, and can be charged to the appropriation account.

6   **Taxation payable on profits**

At this point in your studies you do not need to know very much about taxation. However, it does affect the preparation of accounts, and so we will tell you here as much as you need to know now. Sole traders and partnerships pay income tax based on their profits. Such income tax, when paid, is simply charged as drawings – it is not an expense.

In the case of companies, the taxation levied upon them is called **corporation tax**. It is also based on the amount of profits made. In the later stages of your examinations you will learn how to calculate it. At this point you will be told how much it is, or be given a simple arithmetical way of ascertaining the amount.

Corporation tax is *not* an expense, it is an appropriation of profits. This was established by two legal cases many years ago. However, for the sake of presentation and to make the accounts more understandable to the general reader, it is not shown with the other appropriations. Instead, as in Exhibit 46.5 it is shown as a deduction from profit for the year before taxation (i.e. this is the net profit figure) to show the net result, i.e. profit for the year after taxation.

7   **Dividends**

Out of the remainder of the profits the directors propose what dividends should be paid.

8   **Balance carried forward to next year**

After the dividends have been proposed there will probably be some profits that have not been appropriated. These retained profits will be carried forward to the following year.

Exhibit 46.5 shows the profit and loss appropriation account of a new business for its first three years of trading.

Exhibit 46.5

IDC Ltd has an ordinary share capital of 40,000 ordinary shares of £1 each and 20,000 5 per cent preference shares of £1 each.

- The net profits for the first three years of business ended 31 December are: 19X4, £10,967; 19X5, £14,864; and 19X6, £15,822.
- Transfers to reserves are made as follows: 19X4 nil; 19X5, general reserve, £1,000; and 19X6, fixed assets replacement reserve, £2,250.
- Dividends were proposed for each year on the preference shares at 5 per cent and on the ordinary shares at: 19X4, 10 per cent; 19X5, 12.5 per cent; 19X6, 15 per cent.
- Corporation tax, based on the net profits of each year, is 19X4 £4,100; 19X5 £5,250; 19X6 £6,300.

IDC Ltd

Profit and Loss Appropriation Accounts
(1) For the year ended 31 December 19X4

	£	£
Profit for the year before taxation		10,967
Less Corporation tax		4,100
Profit for the year after taxation		6,867
Less Proposed dividends:		
Preference dividend of 5%	1,000	
Ordinary dividend of 10%	4,000	5,000
Retained profits carried forward to next year		1,867

(2) For the year ended 31 December 19X5

	£	£
Profit for the year before taxation		14,864
Less Corporation tax		5,250
Profit for the year after taxation		9,614
Add Retained profits from last year		1,867
		11,481
Less Transfer to general reserve	1,000	
Proposed dividends:		
Preference dividend of 5%	1,000	
Ordinary dividend of 12½%	5,000	7,000
Retained profits carried forward to next year		4,481

(3) For the year ended 31 December 19X6

	£	£
Profit for the year before taxation		15,822
Less Corporation tax		6,300
Profit for the year after taxation		9,522
Add Retained profits from last year		4,481
		14,003
Less Transfer to fixed assets		
replacement reserve	2,250	
Proposed dividends:		
Preference dividend of 5%	1,000	
Ordinary dividend of 15%	6,000	9,250
Retained profits carried forward to next year		4,753

In a balance sheet, corporation tax owing can normally be found as a current liability.

46.11 The balance sheet

Prior to the UK Companies Act 1981, a company could, provided it disclosed the necessary information, draw up its balance sheet and profit and loss account for publication in any way that it wished. The 1981 Act, however, stopped such freedom of display, and laid down the precise details to be shown. These have been repeated in the Companies Acts of 1985 and 1989.

As many of the readers of this book will not be sitting UK examinations they will not have to comply with the UK Companies Acts. We are therefore showing two specimen balance sheets containing the same facts:

1 Exhibit 46.6 for students sitting examinations based on UK laws. The specimen shown does not contain all the possible items which could be shown, as this chapter is an introduction to the topic only. Volume 2 of this book gives a greater insight into company accounts.
2 Exhibit 46.7 is for students sitting local overseas examinations not based on UK legislation.

Exhibit 46.6 (for students sitting examinations based on UK company legislation)

Letters in brackets (A) to (G) refer to notes following the balance sheet.

Balance Sheet as at 31 December 19X7

		£	£	£
Fixed assets				
Intangible assets	(A)			
Goodwill			10,000	
Tangible assets	(B)			
Buildings		9,000		
Machinery		5,600		
Motor vehicles		2,400	17,000	27,000
Current assets				
Stock		6,000		
Debtors		3,000		
Bank		4,000	13,000	
Creditors: Amounts falling due within one year	(C)			
Proposed dividend		1,000		
Creditors		3,000		
Corporation tax owing		2,000	6,000	
Net current assets	(D)			7,000
Total assets less current liabilities				34,000
Creditors: amounts falling due after more than one year	(E)			
Debenture loans				8,000
				26,000
Capital and reserves				
Called-up share capital	(F)			20,000
Share premium account	(G)			1,200
Other reserves				
General reserve				3,800
Profit and loss account				1,000
				26,000

Notes:
(A) Intangible assets are those not having a 'physical' existence; for instance, you can see and touch tangible assets under (B), i.e. buildings, machinery etc., but you cannot see and touch goodwill.
(B) Tangible fixed assets under a separate heading. Notice that figures are shown net after depreciation. In a note accompanying the accounts the cost and depreciation on these assets would be given.

(C) Only items payable within one year go under this heading.

(D) The term 'net current assets' replaces the more familiar term of 'working capital'.

(E) These particular debentures are repayable several years hence. If they had been payable within one year they would have been shown under (C).

(F) An analysis of share capital will be given in supplementary notes to the balance sheet.

(G) One reserve that is in fact not labelled with the word 'reserve' in its title is the share premium account. For various reasons (discussed fully in Volume 2) shares can be issued for more than their face or nominal value. The excess of the price at which they are issued over the nominal value of the shares is credited to a share premium account. This is then shown with the other reserves in the balance sheet.

Exhibit 46.7 (for local overseas examinations)

Balance Sheet as at 31 December 19X7

		Cost	Depreciation to date (b)	Net
Fixed assets	(a)	£	£	£
Goodwill		15,000	5,000	10,000
Buildings		15,000	6,000	9,000
Machinery		8,000	2,400	5,600
Motor vehicles		4,000	1,600	2,400
		42,000	15,000	27,000
Current assets				
Stock			6,000	
Debtors			3,000	
Bank			4,000	
			13,000	
Less Current liabilities				
Proposed dividend		1,000		
Creditors		3,000		
Corporation tax owing		2,000	6,000	
Working capital				7,000
				34,000
Financed by:				
Share capital				
Authorised 30,000 shares of £1 each	(c)			30,000
Issued 20,000 ordinary shares of £1 each, fully paid	(d)			20,000
Reserves	(e)			
Share premium			1,200	
General reserve			3,800	
Profit and loss account			1,000	
				6,000
	(f)			26,000
Debentures				
Six per cent debentures: repayable 19X3				8,000
				34,000

Notes:

(a) Fixed assets should normally be shown either at cost or alternatively at some other valuation. In either case, the method chosen should be clearly stated.

(b) The total depreciation from date of purchase to the date of the balance sheet should be shown.

(c) The authorised share capital, where it is different from the issued share capital, is shown as a note.

(d) Where shares are only partly called up, then it is the amount actually called up that appears in the balance sheet and not the full amount.

(e) Reserves consist either of those unused profits remaining in the appropriation account, or those transferred to a reserve account appropriately titled, e.g. general reserve, fixed assets replacement reserve. At this juncture all that needs to be said is that any account labelled as a reserve has originated by being charged as a debit in the appropriation account and credited to a reserve account with an appropriate title. These reserves are shown in the balance sheet after share capital under the heading of 'Reserves'.

(f) The share capital and reserves should be totalled so as to show the book value of all the shares in the company. Either the term 'shareholders' funds' or 'members' equity' is often given to the total of share capital plus reserves.

In Volume 2 you will be told more about the differences between 'revenue reserves' and 'capital reserves'. The main importance about the distinction is in deciding how much can be treated as being available for paying out to shareholders by cheque in the form of dividends. 'Revenue reserves', which include the appropriation account balance and the general reserve can be treated as available for such dividends. 'Capital reserves' which will include revaluation reserves on property and land, also some reserves (which you have not yet met) which have to be created to meet some legal statutory need, cannot be treated as available for payment out as dividends.

A term which sometimes appears in examinations is that of 'fungible assets'. Fungible assets are assets which are substantially indistinguishable one from another.

A fully worked example

Exhibit 46.8

The following trial balance is extracted from the books of FW Ltd as on 31 December 19X5:

Trial balance as on 31 December 19X5

	Dr £	Cr £
10% preference share capital		20,000
Ordinary share capital		70,000
10% debentures (repayable 19X9)		30,000
Goodwill at cost	15,500	
Buildings at cost	95,000	
Equipment at cost	8,000	
Motor vehicles at cost	17,200	
Provision for depreciation: equipment 1.1.19X5		2,400
Provision for depreciation: motors 1.1.19X5		5,160
Stock 1.1.19X5	22,690	
Sales		98,200
Purchases	53,910	
Carriage inwards	1,620	
Salaries and wages	9,240	
Directors' remuneration	6,300	
Motor expenses	8,120	
Rates and insurances	2,930	
General expenses	560	
Debenture interest	1,500	
Debtors	18,610	
Creditors		11,370
Bank	8,390	
General reserve		5,000
Share premium account		14,000
Interim ordinary dividend paid	3,500	
Profit and loss account 31.12.19X4		16,940
	273,070	273,070

The following adjustments are needed:

(*i*)   Stock at 31.12.19X5 was £27,220.
(*ii*)   Depreciate Motors £3,000, Equipment £1,200.
(*iii*) Accrue Debenture interest £1,500.
(*iv*) Provide for Preference dividend £2,000 and Final ordinary dividend of 10 per cent.
(*v*)   Transfer £2,000 to General reserve.
(*vi*) Write off Goodwill £3,000.
(*vii*) Authorised share capital is £20,000 in Preference shares and £100,000 in Ordinary shares.
(*viii*) Provide for Corporation tax £5,000.

The final accounts will now be shown using a vertical form. The profit and loss account will be suitable both for those sitting UK examinations, and those sitting local overseas examinations. The balance sheets will be shown separately for both kinds of students.

Note that the profit and loss account is not restricted to that which must be published by companies.

(a) Trading and profit and loss accounts suitable both for UK and overseas examinations. For internal use only, not for publication.

F W Ltd

Trading & Profit & Loss Account for the year ended 31 December 19X5

	£	£	£
Sales			98,200
Less Cost of goods sold:			
Opening stock		22,690	
Add Purchases	53,910		
Add Carriage inwards	1,620	55,530	
		78,220	
Less Closing stock		27,220	51,000
Gross profit			47,200
Less Expenses:			
Salaries and wages		9,240	
Motor expenses		8,120	
Rates and insurances		2,930	
General expenses		560	
Directors' remuneration (A)		6,300	
Debenture interest (B)		3,000	
Depreciation: Motors		3,000	
Equipment		1,200	34,350
Profit for the year before taxation			12,850
Less Corporation tax			5,000
Profit for the year after taxation			7,850
Add Retained profits from last year			16,940
			24,790
Less Appropriations:			
Transfer to general reserve		2,000	
Goodwill part written off		3,000	
Preference share dividend		2,000	
Ordinary share dividends:			
Interim	3,500		
Final (C)	7,000	10,500	17,500
Retained profits carried forward to next year			7,290

Notes:

(A) As stated earlier, directors' remuneration is shown as an expense in the profit and loss account itself.

(B) As stated earlier, debenture interest is an expense to be shown in the profit and loss account itself.

(C) The final dividend of 10 per cent is based on the issued ordinary share capital and *not* on the authorised ordinary share capital.

(b) Balance sheet based on UK legislation

F W Ltd
Balance Sheet as at 31 December 19X7

		£	£	£
Fixed assets				
Intangible assets				
Goodwill			12,500	
Tangible assets	(A)			
Buildings		95,000		
Equipment		4,400		
Motors		9,040	108,440	120,940
Current assets				
Stock		27,220		
Debtors		18,610		
Bank		8,390	54,220	
Creditors: amounts falling due within one year				
Creditors		11,370		
Proposed dividend		9,000		
Debenture interest accrued		1,500		
Taxation		5,000	26,870	
Net current assets				27,350
Total assets less current liabilities				148,290
Creditors: amounts falling due after more than one year				
Debentures				30,000
				118,290
Capital and reserves	(B)			
Called-up share capital	(C)			90,000
Share premium account				14,000
Other reserves				
General reserve				7,000
Profit and loss account				7,290
				118,290

(A) Notes to be given in an appendix as to cost, acquisitions and sales in the year and depreciation.

(B) Reserves consist either of those unused profits remaining in the appropriation account, or those transferred to a reserve account appropriately titled, e.g. general reserve, fixed assets replacement reserve, etc.

One reserve that is in fact not labelled with the word 'reserve' in its title is the share premium account. This is shown with the other reserves in the balance sheet.

The closing balance on the profit and loss appropriation account is shown under reserves. These are profits not already appropriated, and therefore 'reserved' for future use.

(C) The authorised share capital, where it is different from the issued share capital, is shown as a note. Notice that the total figure of £120,000 for authorised capital is not included when adding up the balance sheet sides. Only the issued capital figures are included in balance sheet totals.

(c) Balance sheet for students sitting local overseas examinations.

Balance Sheet as at 31 December 19X5

Fixed assets	Costs £	Depreciation to date £	Net £
Goodwill	15,500	3,000	12,500
Buildings	95,000	–	95,000
Equipment	8,000	3,600	4,400
Motors	17,200	8,160	9,040
	135,700	14,760	120,940
Current assets			
Stock		27,220	
Debtors		18,610	
Bank		8,390	
		54,220	
Less Current liabilities			
Creditors	11,370		
Dividends owing	9,000		
Debenture interest owing	1,500		
Taxation	5,000	26,870	
Working capital			27,350
			148,290

Financed by: Share Capital	Authorised £	Issued £	£
Preference shares	20,000	20,000	
Ordinary shares	100,000	70,000	90,000
	120,000		
Reserves			
Share premium		14,000	
General reserve		7,000	
Profit and loss		7,290	28,290
			118,290
Loan capital			
10% debentures			30,000
			148,290

46.12 Bonus shares

The issue of bonus shares would appear to be outside the scope of syllabuses at this level. However, some examinations have included a minor part of a question concerned with bonus shares. All that is needed here is a very brief explanation only, leaving further explanations at a later stage.

Bonus shares are 'free' shares issued to shareholders without any cash being paid for them. The reserves are utilised for the purpose. Thus, if before the bonus issue there were £20,000 share capital and £12,000 reserves, and then a bonus issue of 1 for 4 were made (i.e. 1 bonus share for every 4 shares already held) the bonus issue would amount to £5,000. The share capital then becomes £25,000 and the reserves become £7,000.

A proper and fuller explanation appears in Volume 2 of this book. A bonus issue is often known as a 'scrip' issue.

46.13 FRS 3: Reporting Financial Performance

Accounting is not a static subject. Changes occur over the years as they are seen to be necessary, and also get general agreement as to their usefulness. Since the advent of SSAPs (Statements of Standard Accounting Practice) and FRSs (Financial Reporting Standards), the number of changes that practitioners and students have had to learn has increased at a very fast rate. A prime example of this is the introduction of FRS 3, which necessitates changes to the formats of company profit and loss accounts when certain events have occurred.

Suppose that you are considering the affairs of a business over the years. The business has not changed significantly, there have been no acquisitions, no discontinued operations, no fundamental reorganisation or restructuring of the business, nor have there been any extraordinary items affecting the accounts. In these circumstances, when comparing the accounts over the years, you are comparing like with like, subject to the problem of the effects of inflation or deflation.

On the other hand, suppose that some of the things mentioned have occurred. When trying to see what the future might hold for the company, simply basing your opinions on what has happened in the past can be very confusing.

To help you to distinguish the past and the future, and to give you some idea as to what changes have occurred, FRS 3 requires that the following are highlighted in the profit and loss account if they are material in amount:

(a) *What the results of continuing operations are, including the results of acquisitions.* Obviously acquisitions affect future results, and are therefore included in continuing operations.

(b) *What the results have been of discontinued operations.* This should help distinguish the past from the future.

(c) *The profits or losses on the sale or termination of an operation, the costs of fundamental reorganisation or restructuring* and *the profits and losses on the disposal of fixed assets.* The profits and losses concerning these matters are not going to happen again, and so this also helps us distinguish the past from the future.

We can see in Exhibit 46.9 how FRS 3 requires (a), (b) and (c) to be shown on the face of the profit and loss account. Not only is the turnover split to show the figures relevant to continuing operations, acquisitions and discontinued operations, the operating profit is split in a similar fashion. In addition any profit or loss on the disposal of the discontinued operations would also be shown.

Exhibit 46.9

Block plc

Profit and Loss Account for the year ending 31 December 19X6 (extract)

		£000	£000
1	Turnover		
	Continuing operations	520	
	Acquisitions	110	
		630	
	Discontinued operations	170	
			800
2	Cost of sales		500
3	Gross profit		300
4	Distribution costs	60	
5	Administrative expenses	40	
			100
	Operating profit		
	Continuing operations	160	
	Acquisitions	60	
	(A)	220	
	Discontinued operations (loss) (B)	(20)	
			200
	Profit on disposal of discontinued operations (C)		10
			210
6	Other operating income		20
	Profit or loss on ordinary activities before interest		230

The items marked (A), (B) and (C) can be described as exceptional items. They are material in amount, they fall within the ordinary activities of the firm, and need to be shown so that the accounts will give a 'true and fair view'.

They are exceptional in that they are not the ordinary daily occurrence, but remember that they fall within the ordinary activities of the company. FRS 3 requires that three categories of exceptional items be shown separately on the face of the profit and loss account after operating profit and before interest, and included under the appropriate heading of continued or discontinued operations:

- profits or losses on the sale or termination of an operation;
- costs of a fundamental reorganisation or restructuring having a material effect on the nature and focus of the reporting entity's operations;
- profits or losses on the disposal of fixed assets.

Other exceptional items should be credited or charged in arriving at the profit or loss on ordinary activities by inclusion under the heading to which they relate. The amount of each exceptional item should be disclosed in a note, or on the face of the profit and loss account, if necessary, in order to give a true and fair view.

Some other items are also contained in FRS 3. These are:

(a) Where assets have been revalued there may be a material difference in the results shown in the accounts using such revalued figures, which obviously affects depreciation. If this is the case, then FRS 3 requires that there should also be shown as a note what the profit and loss account would have been if the account had been shown using historical (i.e. not revalued) figures.

There should also be a statement which shows how the reported profit on ordinary activities (using accounts with revalued assets) can be reconciled with that calculated using historical figures.

(b) A note should be given reconciling the opening and closing totals of shareholders' funds of the period. This shows how such items as the profit for the year or a new share issue have increased the funds, whereas dividends and items written off capital reserves have reduced the funds.

46.14 FRS 10: Goodwill and intangible assets (companies)

This standard was issued in December 1997, replacing SSAP 22. It requires that:

1 Purchased goodwill and purchased intangible assets (e.g. patents, trade marks, etc.) should be capitalised as assets.
2 If goodwill has not been purchased then there should not be any entry of it in the company's books. (This is different from the situation applicable to partnerships.)
3 Internally developed intangible assets should be capitalised (i.e. entered in the company's books as an asset) only when they have a readily ascertainable market value.
4 The calculation of goodwill should be the excess of the value of the consideration given (the price paid) over the total of the fair values of the net assets acquired.

FRS 10 requires that goodwill and intangible assets are amortised (i.e. depreciated) over their useful economic life. However, when goodwill or intangible assets are regarded as having indefinite useful economic lives, they should not be amortised.

New terms

Debenture (p. 494): Loan to a company.

Directors (p. 491): Officials appointed by shareholders to manage the company for them.

Dividends (p. 492): The amount given to shareholders as their share of the profits of the company.

Limited company (p. 490): An organisation owned by its shareholders, whose liability is limited to their share capital.

Ordinary shares (p. 492): Shares entitled to dividends after the preference shareholders have been paid their dividends.

Preference shares (p. 492): Shares that are entitled to an agreed rate of dividend before the ordinary shareholders receive anything.

Preliminary expenses (p. 496): All the costs that are incurred when a company is formed.

Private company (p. 491): A limited company that must issue its shares privately.

Public company (p. 491): A company that can issue its shares publicly, and for which there is no maximum number of shareholders.

Reserve accounts (p. 495): The transfer of apportioned profits to accounts for use in future years.

Shares (p. 490): The division of the capital of a limited company into parts.

Main points to remember

1 Limited companies exist because of the disadvantages and constraints arising from partnerships.

2 A fully paid-up shareholder's liability is limited to the shares he or she holds in the company. Shareholders cannot then be asked to pay any other company debt from their private resources.

3 There are far more private companies than public companies.

4 A limited company has a 'separate legal entity' from that of its members.

5 Directors' remuneration is charged to the main part of the profit and loss account.

6 Debenture interest is charged to the main part of the profit and loss account.

7 Transfers to reserves, dividends and taxation are charged to the appropriation part of the profit and loss account.

8 Any balance of profits unappropriated at the end of a period is carried forward as a balance to the next period.

Multiple-choice questions

Now attempt Set No 5 of the multiple-choice questions on pp. 581–3.

Review questions

46.1 GWR Ltd started in business on 1 January 19X6. Its issued share capital was 100,000 ordinary shares of £1 each and 50,000 10 per cent preference shares of £1 each.

Its net profits for the first two years of business were: 19X6 £42,005; 19X7 £34,831.

Preference dividends were paid for each of these years, whilst ordinary dividends were proposed as 19X6 12 per cent and 19X7 9 per cent.

Corporation tax, based on the profits of these two years, was: 19X6 £13,480; 19X7 £11,114.

Transfers to general reserve took place as: 19X6 £6,000; 19X7 £4,000.

Draw up profit and loss appropriation accounts for each of the years ended 31 December 19X6 and 19X7.

46.2 LMS Ltd has an authorised capital of £200,000, consisting of 160,000 ordinary shares of £1 each and 40,000 8 per cent preference shares of £1 each. Of these 120,000 ordinary shares had been issued and all the preference shares when the business first started trading.

The business has a financial year end of 31 December. The first three years of business resulted in net profit as follows: 19X7 £27,929; 19X8 £32,440; 19X9 £36,891.

Dividends were paid each year on the preference shares. Dividends on the ordinary shares were proposed as follows: 19X7 8 per cent; 19X8 10 per cent; 19X9 11 per cent.

Corporation tax, based on the profits of each year, was: 19X7 £8,331; 19X8 £10,446; 19X9 £12,001.

Transfers to reserves were made as: General reserve 19X7 £3,000, 19X8 £4,000, and Foreign exchange reserve 19X9 £2,000.

You are to show the profit and loss appropriation accounts for each of the years 19X7, 19X8 and 19X9.

46.3 A balance sheet is to be drawn up from the following as at 30 June 19X6:

	£
Issued share capital: ordinary shares £1 each	100,000
Authorised share capital: ordinary shares of £1 each	200,000
10 per cent debentures (repayable 30 June 19X9)	40,000
Buildings at cost	105,000
Motor vehicles at cost	62,500
Fixtures at cost	11,500
Profit and loss account	5,163
Fixed assets replacement reserve	8,000
Stock	16,210
Debtors	14,175
General reserve	6,000
Creditors	9,120
Proposed dividend	5,000
Depreciation to date: Motor vehicles	15,350
Premises	22,000
Fixtures	3,750
Bank (balancing figure for you to ascertain)	?

46.4A From the information given below you are required to prepare for Streamline plc:

(a) a profit and loss appropriation account for the year ended 31 December 19X9;
(b) a balance sheet as at 31 December 19X9.

Streamline plc has an authorised share capital of £520,000, divided into 500,000 £1 ordinary shares and 20,000 5% preference shares of £1 each. Of these shares, 300,000 ordinary shares and all of the 5% preference shares have been issued and are fully paid.
   In addition to the above information, the following balances remained in the accounts after the profit and loss account had been prepared for the year ended 31 December 19X9.

	Dr £	Cr £
Plant and machinery, at cost	140,000	
Provision for depreciation on plant and machinery		50,000
Premises at cost	250,000	
Profit and loss account balance (1 January 19X9)		34,000
Net trading profit for year ended 31 December 19X9		15,000
Wages owing		3,900
Bank balance	15,280	
Stock (31 December 19X9)	16,540	
Trade debtors and creditors	12,080	3,000
Advertising prepaid	2,000	
General reserve		10,000

The directors have proposed the payment of the preference share dividend, and an ordinary share dividend of 6%. They also recommend a transfer of £20,000 to the general reserve.

(*Northern Examinations and Assessment Board: GCSE*)

46.5 The trial balance extracted from the books of Chang Ltd at 31 December 19X8 was as follows:

	£	£
Share capital		100,000
Profit and loss account 31 December 19X7		34,280
Freehold premises at cost	65,000	
Machinery at cost	55,000	
Provision for depreciation on machinery account as at 31 December 19X7		15,800
Purchases	201,698	
Sales		316,810
General expenses	32,168	
Wages and salaries	54,207	
Rent	4,300	
Lighting expenses	1,549	
Bad debts	748	
Provision for doubtful debts at 31 December 19X7		861
Debtors	21,784	
Creditors		17,493
Stock in trade 31 December 19X7	25,689	
Bank balance	23,101	
	485,244	485,244

You are given the following additional information:
(*i*)   The authorised and issued share capital is divided into 100,000 shares of £1 each.
(*ii*)   Stock in trade at 31 December 19X8, £29,142.
(*iii*) Wages and salaries due at 31 December 19X8 amounted to £581.
(*iv*) Rent paid in advance at 31 December 19X8 amounted to £300.
(*v*)   A dividend of £10,000 is proposed for 19X8.
(*vi*) The provision for doubtful debts is to be increased to £938.
(*vii*) A depreciation charge is to be made on machinery at the rate of 10 per cent per annum on cost.

Required:
A trading and profit and loss account for 19X8 and a balance sheet as at 31 December 19X8.

46.6A The following is the trial balance of B.B.C. Ltd as on 31 December 19X7:

	Dr £	Cr £
Share capital issued: ordinary shares £1		75,000
Debtors and creditors	28,560	22,472
Stock 31 December 19X6	41,415	
Bank	16,255	
Machinery at cost	45,000	
Motor vehicles at cost	28,000	
Depreciation provisions at 31.12.19X6:		
Machinery		18,000
Motor vehicles		12,600
Sales		97,500
Purchases	51,380	
Motor expenses	8,144	
Repairs to machinery	2,308	
Sundry expenses	1,076	
Wages and salaries	11,372	
Directors' remuneration	6,200	
Profit and loss account as at 31.12.19X6		6,138
General reserve		8,000
	239,710	239,710

Given the following information, you are to draw up a trading and profit and loss account for the year ended 31 December 19X7, and a balance sheet as at that date:

(*i*)   Authorised share capital: £100,000 in ordinary shares of £1.
(*ii*) Stock at 31 December 19X7 £54,300
(*iii*) Motor expenses owing £445.
(*iv*) Ordinary dividend proposed of 20 per cent.
(*v*)   Transfer £2,000 to general reserve.
(*vi*) Provide for depreciation of all fixed assets at 20 per cent reducing balance method.

Required:
A trading and profit and loss account for 19X7 and a balance sheet as at 31 December 19X7.

46.7 You are to draw up a trading and profit and loss account for the year ended 31 December 19X8, and a balance sheet as at that date from the following trial balance and details of T Howe Ltd:

	Dr £	Cr £
Bank	6,723	
Debtors	18,910	
Creditors		12,304
Stock at 31 December 19X7	40,360	
Buildings at cost	100,000	
Equipment at cost	45,000	
Profit and loss account as at 31.12.19X7		15,286
General reserve		8,000
Foreign exchange reserve		4,200
Authorised and issued share capital		100,000
Purchases	72,360	
Sales		135,486
Carriage inwards	1,570	
Carriage outwards	1,390	
Salaries	18,310	
Rates and occupancy expenses	4,235	
Office expenses	3,022	
Sundry expenses	1,896	
Provisions for depreciation at 31.12.19X7:		
Buildings		32,000
Equipment		16,000
Directors' remuneration	9,500	
	323,276	323,276

Notes at 31 December 19X8:

(*i*)   Stock at 31 December 19X8 £52,360.
(*ii*) Rates owing £280; Office expenses owing £190.
(*iii*) Dividend of 10 per cent proposed.
(*iv*) Transfers to reserves: General £1,000; Foreign exchange £800.
(*v*)   Depreciation on cost: Buildings 5 per cent; Equipment 20 per cent.

46.8A Here is the trial balance of RF Ltd as at 30 June 19X8:

	Dr £	Cr £
Share capital: authorised and issued		50,000
Stock as at 30 June 19X7	38,295	
Debtors	26,890	
Creditors		12,310
10% debentures		20,000
Fixed assets replacement reserve		10,000
General reserve		6,000
Profit and loss account as at 30 June 19X7		3,964
Debenture interest	1,000	
Equipment at cost	35,000	
Motor vehicles at cost	28,500	
Bank	3,643	
Cash	180	
Sales		99,500
Purchases	66,350	
Returns inwards	1,150	
Carriage inwards	240	
Wages and salaries	10,360	
Rent, rates and insurance	5,170	
Discounts allowed	1,246	
Directors' remuneration	2,500	
Provision for depreciation at 30 June 19X7:		
Equipment		8,400
Motors		10,350
	220,524	220,524

Given the following information as at 30 June 19X8, draw up a set of final accounts for the year to that date:

(*i*) Stock 30 June 19X8 £49,371.
(*ii*) The share capital consisted of 25,000 ordinary shares of £1 each and 25,000 10 per cent preference shares of £1 each. The dividend on the preference shares was proposed to be paid as well as a dividend of 20 per cent on the ordinary shares.
(*iii*) Accrued rent £700; Directors' remuneration £2,500.
(*iv*) Debenture interest ½ year's interest owing.
(*v*) Depreciation on cost: Equipment 10 per cent; Motors 20 per cent.
(*vi*) Transfers to reserves: General reserve £2,000; Fixed assets replacement reserve £1,000.

46.9 Burden plc has an authorised capital of 500,000 ordinary shares of £0.50 each.

(a) At the end of its financial year, 31 May 19X9, the following balances appeared in the company's books:

	£
Issued capital: 400,000 shares fully paid	200,000
Freehold land and buildings at cost	320,000
Stock in trade	17,800
10% debentures	30,000
Trade debtors	6,840
Trade creditors	8,500
Expenses prepaid	760
Share premium	25,000
General reserve	20,000
Expenses outstanding	430
Profit and loss account balance (1 June 19X8)	36,200
Bank overdrawn	3,700
Fixtures, fittings and equipment	
at cost	54,000
provision for depreciation	17,500

The company's trading and profit and loss accounts had been prepared and revealed a net profit of £58,070. However, this figure and certain balances shown above needed adjustment in view of the following details which had not been recorded in the company's books.

(i) It appeared that a trade debtor who owed £300 would not be able to pay. It was decided to write his account off as a bad debt.

(ii) An examination of the company's stock on 31 May 19X9 revealed that some items shown in the accounts at a cost of £1,800 had deteriorated and had a resale value of only £1,100.

(iii) At the end of the financial year some equipment which had cost £3,600 and which had a net book value of £800 had been sold for £1,300. A cheque for this amount had been received on 31 May 19X9.

Required:
1 A statement which shows the changes which should be made to the net profit of £58,070 in view of these unrecorded details.

(b) The directors proposed to pay a final dividend of 10% and to transfer £50,000 to general reserve on 31 May 19X9.

Required:
For Burden plc (taking account of *all* the available information)
2 The profit and loss appropriation account for the year ended 31 May 19X9.
3 Two *extracts* from the company's balance sheet as at 31 May 19X9, showing in detail:
   (i) the current assets, current liabilities and working capital
   (ii) the items which make up the shareholders' funds.

(c) The directors are concerned about the company's liquidity position.

Required:
4 **THREE** transactions which will increase the company's working capital. State which balance sheet items will change as a result of each transaction and whether the item will increase or decrease in value.

(*Southern Examining Group: GCSE*)

46.10A The accountant of Fiddles plc has begun preparing final accounts but the work is not yet complete. At this stage the items included in the trial balance are as follows:

	£000
Land	100
Buildings	120
Plant and machinery	170
Depreciation provision	120
Share capital	100
Profit and loss balance brought forward	200
Debtors	200
Creditors	110
Stock	190
Operating profit	80
Debentures (16%)	180
Provision for doubtful debts	3
Bank balance (asset)	12
Suspense	1

Notes (*i*) to (*vii*) below are to be taken into account:

(*i*) The debtors control account figure, which is used in the trial balance, does not agree with the total of the debtors ledger. A contra of £5,000 has been entered correctly in the individual ledger accounts but has been entered on the wrong side of both control accounts.

A batch total of sales of £12,345 had been entered in the double entry system as £13,345, although individual ledger account entries for these sales were correct. The balance of £4,000 on sales returns account has inadvertently been omitted from the trial balance, though correctly entered in the ledger records.

(*ii*) A standing order received from a regular customer for £2,000, and bank charges of £1,000, have been completely omitted from the records.

(*iii*) A debtor for £1,000 is to be written off. The provision for doubtful debts balance is to be adjusted to 1% of debtors.

(*iv*) The opening stock figure had been overstated by £1,000 and the closing stock figure had been understated by £2,000.

(*v*) Any remaining balance on suspense account should be treated as purchases if a debit balance and as sales if a credit balance.

(*vi*) The debentures were issued three months before the year end. No entries have been made as regards interest.

(*vii*) A dividend of 10% of share capital is to be proposed.

Required:
(*a*) Prepare journal entries to cover items in notes (*i*) to (*v*) above. You are NOT to open any new accounts and may use only those accounts included in the trial balance as given.
(*b*) Prepare final accounts for internal use in good order within the limits of the available information. For presentation purposes all the items arising from notes (*i*) to (*vii*) above should be regarded as material.

(*Association of Chartered Certified Accountants*)

46.11 'The historical cost convention looks backwards but the going concern convention looks forwards.'

Required:
(a) Explain clearly what is meant by:
    (i) the historical cost convention;
    (ii) the going concern convention.
(b) Does traditional financial accounting, using the historical cost convention, make the going concern convention unnecessary? Explain your answer fully.
(c) Which do you think a shareholder is likely to find more useful – a report on the past or an estimate of the future? Why?

(*Association of Chartered Certified Accountants*)

46.12 The chairman of a public limited company has written his annual report to the shareholders, extracts of which are quoted below.

Extract 1
'In May 19X6, in order to provide a basis for more efficient operations, we acquired PAG Warehousing and Transport Ltd. The agreed valuation of the net tangible assets acquired was £1.4 million. The purchase consideration, £1.7 million, was satisfied by an issue of 6.4 million equity shares, of £0.25 per share, to PAG's shareholders. These shares do not rank for dividend until 19X7.'

Extract 2
'As a measure of confidence in our ability to expand operations in 19X7 and 19X8, and to provide the necessary financial base, we issued £0.5 million 8% Redeemable Debenture Stock, 2000/2007, 20 million 6% £1 Redeemable Preference Shares and 4 million £1 equity shares. The opportunity was also taken to redeem the whole of the 5 million 11% £1 Redeemable Preference Shares.'

Required:
Answer the following questions on the above extracts.

Extract 1
(a) What does the difference of £0.3 million between the purchase consideration (£1.7m) and the net tangible assets value (£1.4m) represent?
(b) What does the difference of £0.1 million between the purchase consideration (£1.7m) and the nominal value of the equity shares (£1.6m) represent?
(c) What is the meaning of the term 'equity shares'?
(d) What is the meaning of the phrase 'do not rank for dividend'?

Extract 2
(e) In the description of the debenture stock issue, what is the significance of
    (i) 8%?
    (ii) 2000/2007?
(f) In the description of the preference share issue, what is the significance of
    (i) 6%?
    (ii) Redeemable?
(g) What is the most likely explanation for the company to have redeemed existing preference shares but at the same time to have issued others?
(h) What effect will these structural changes have had on the gearing of the company?*
(j) Contrast the accounting treatment, in the company's profit and loss accounts, of the interest due on the debentures with dividends proposed on the equity shares.
(k) Explain the reasons for the different treatments you have outlined in your answer to (j) above.

(*Association of Chartered Certified Accountants*)

* This part of the question is covered in the text on pp. 538–539.

46.13 The directors of the company by which you are employed as an accountant have received the forecast profit and loss account for 19X9 which disclosed a net profit for the year of £36,000.

This is considered to be an unacceptably low figure and a working party has been set up to investigate ways and means of improving the forecast profit.

The following suggestions have been put forward by various members of the working party:

(a) 'Every six months we deduct income tax of £10,000 from the debenture interest and pay it over to the Inland Revenue. If we withhold these payments, the company's profit will be increased considerably.'

(b) 'I see that in the three months August to October 19X9 we have forecast a total amount of £40,000 for repainting the exterior of the company's premises. If, instead, we charge this amount as capital expenditure, the company's profit will be increased by £40,000.'

(c) 'In November 19X9, the replacement of a machine is forecast. The proceeds from the sale of the old machinery should be credited to profit and loss account.'

(d) 'There is a credit balance of £86,000 on general reserve account. We can transfer some of this to profit and loss account to increase the 19X9 profit.'

(e) 'The company's £1 ordinary shares, which were originally issued at £1 per share, currently have a market value of £1.60 per share and this price is likely to be maintained. We can credit the surplus £0.60 per share to the 19X9 profit and loss account.'

(f) 'The company's premises were bought many years ago for £68,000, but following the rise in property values, they are now worth at least £300,000. This enhancement in value can be utilised to increase the 19X9 profit.'

You are required, as the accounting member of the working party, to comment on the feasibility of each of the above suggestions for increasing the 19X9 forecast profit.

(*Association of Chartered Certified Accountants*)

46.14 Explain what you understand by the accounting term 'debentures' and indicate the circumstances under which a debenture issue would or would not be an appropriate form of financing.

(*Scottish Qualifications Authority*)

47

Purchase of existing partnership and sole traders' businesses

Objectives

After you have studied this chapter, you should be able to:

- *enter up the purchase of a business in the purchaser's books*

- *draw up the balance sheet of the purchaser after taking over the assets and liabilities of the vendor*

47.1 Types of purchase

Quite frequently an existing partnership or sole trader's business is taken over as a going concern. At this juncture several methods of how this is done can be considered:

(*a*) An individual purchases the business of a sole trader.
(*b*) A partnership acquires the business of a sole trader.
(*c*) Existing businesses of sole traders join together to form a partnership.
(*d*) A limited company takes over the business of a sole trader or partnership.

47.2 Value of assets bought in purchaser's books

It must not be thought that because the assets bought are shown in the selling firm's books at one value, that the purchaser(s) must record the assets taken over in its own books at the same value. The values shown in the books of the purchaser(s) are those values at which it is buying the assets, such values being frequently quite different from those shown in the selling firm's books. As an instance of this, the selling firm may have bought premises many years ago for £10,000, but they may now be worth £50,000. The purchaser buying the premises will obviously have to pay £50,000, and it is therefore this value that is recorded in the books of the purchaser(s).

47.3 Goodwill on purchase

Where the total purchase price is greater than the new valuation made by the purchaser of the assets taken over, the excess is the amount paid for goodwill. This can be shown as:

	£
Total purchase consideration	90,000
Less New valuation of assets taken over	
(not usually the same values as per the old balances)	75,000
Goodwill	15,000

The revised balance sheet of the purchaser will include goodwill as an asset at the calculated figure, and the assets bought at the new valuations.

47.4 Capital reserve on purchase

Where the total purchase price is less than the new valuations of the assets taken over, the difference can either be treated as negative goodwill or as a capital reserve. (Companies must treat it as negative goodwill.) When treated as a capital reserve, it can be shown as:

	£
Total new valuations of assets taken over	70,000
(not usually the same values as per the old balance sheet)	
Less Total purchase consideration	50,000
Capital reserve	20,000

The new valuations of the assets will appear in the revised balance sheet of the purchaser.

The capital reserve will be shown as a reserve on the capital and liabilities side of the balance sheet.

47.5 Taking over a sole trader's business

It is easier to start with the takeover of the simplest sort of business unit, that of a sole trader. Some of the balance sheets shown will be deliberately simplified so that the principles involved are not hidden behind a mass of complicated calculations.

To illustrate the takeover of a business, given varying circumstances, the same business will be assumed to be taken over in different ways. The balance sheet of this business is that of A Brown, Exhibit 47.1.

Exhibit 47.1

A Brown

Balance Sheet as at 31 December 19X6

	£
Fixtures	30,000
Stock	8,000
Debtors	7,000
Bank	1,000
	46,000
Capital	43,000
Creditors	3,000
	46,000

An individual purchases business of sole trader

1 Assume that the assets and liabilities of A Brown, with the exception of the bank balance, are taken over by D Towers. He is to take over the assets and liabilities at the valuations as shown. The price to be paid is £52,000. The opening balance sheet of Towers will be as in Exhibit 47.2.

Exhibit 47.2

D Towers

Balance Sheet as at 1 January 19X7

	£
Goodwill	10,000
Fixtures	30,000
Stock	8,000
Debtors	7,000
	55,000
Capital	52,000
Creditors	3,000
	55,000

As £52,000 has been paid for net assets (assets less liabilities) valued at £30,000 + £8,000 + £7,000 − £3,000 = £42,000, the excess £10,000 represents the amount paid for goodwill.

2 Suppose that, instead of the information just given, the same amount has been paid by Towers, but the assets were taken over at a value of Fixtures £37,000; Stock £7,500; Debtors £6,500. The opening balance sheet of D Towers would have been as in Exhibit 47.3.

Exhibit 47.3

D Towers

Balance Sheet as at 1 January 19X7

	£
Goodwill	4,000
Fixtures	37,000
Stock	7,500
Debtors	6,500
	55,000
Capital	52,000
Creditors	3,000
	55,000

As £52,000 had been paid for net assets valued at £37,000 + £7,500 + £6,500 − £3,000 = £48,000, the excess £4,000 represents the amount paid for goodwill. The other assets are shown at their value to the purchaser, Towers.

Partnership acquires business of a sole trader

Assume instead that the business of Brown had been taken over by M Ukridge and D Allen. The partners are to introduce £30,000 each as capital. The price to be paid for the net assets, other than the bank balance, is £52,000. The purchasers placed the following values on the assets taken over: Fixtures £40,000; Stock £7,000; Debtors £6,000.

The opening balance sheet of Ukridge and Allen will be as in Exhibit 47.4.

Exhibit 47.4

M Ukridge and D Allen
Balance Sheet as at 1 January 19X7

	£
Goodwill	2,000
Fixtures	40,000
Stock	7,000
Debtors	6,000
Bank	8,000
	63,000
Capitals:	
M Ukridge	30,000
D Allen	30,000
	60,000
Creditors	3,000
	63,000

The sum of £52,000 has been paid for net assets of £40,000 + £7,000 + £6,000 − £3,000 = £50,000. This makes goodwill to be the excess of £2,000.

The bank balance is made up of £30,000 + £30,000 introduced by the partners, less £52,000 paid to Brown = £8,000.

Amalgamation of existing sole traders

Now assume that Brown was to enter into partnership with T Owens whose last balance sheet is shown in Exhibit 47.5.

Exhibit 47.5

T Owens
Balance Sheet as at 31 December 19X6

	£
Premises	20,000
Fixtures	5,000
Stock	6,000
Debtors	9,000
Bank	2,000
	42,000
Capital	37,000
Creditors	5,000
	42,000

1 If the two traders were to amalgamate all their business assets and liabilities, at the values as shown, the opening balance sheet of the partnership would be as in Exhibit 47.6.

Exhibit 47.6

A Brown & T Owens

Balance Sheet as at 1 January 19X7

	£
Premises	20,000
Fixtures	35,000
Stock	14,000
Debtors	16,000
Bank	3,000
	88,000
Capitals:	
Brown	43,000
Owens	37,000
Creditors	8,000
	88,000

2 Suppose that instead of both parties agreeing to amalgamation at the asset values as shown, the following values had been agreed to:

Owens' premises to be valued at £25,000, and his stock at £5,500; other items as per last balance sheet. Brown's fixtures to be valued at £33,000, his stock at £7,200 and debtors at £6,400. It is also to be taken that Brown has goodwill, value £7,000, whereas Owens' goodwill was considered valueless. Other items as per last balance sheet.

The opening balance sheet will be at the revised figures, and is shown as Exhibit 47.7.

Exhibit 47.7

A Brown & T Owens

Balance Sheet as at 1 January 19X7

	£
Goodwill	7,000
Premises	25,000
Fixtures	38,000
Stock	12,700
Debtors	15,400
Bank	3,000
	101,100
Capitals:	
Brown	51,600
Owen	41,500
Creditors	8,000
	101,100

Brown's capital can be seen to be £43,000 + £3,000 (fixtures) − £800 (stock) − £600 (debtors) + £7,000 (goodwill) = £51,600.

Owens' capital is £37,000 + £5,000 (premises) − £500 (stock) = £41,500.

Limited company acquires business of sole trader

In this book, only an elementary treatment will be considered. More complicated examples will be examined in *Business Accounting 2*.

Before the acquisition the balance sheet of D Lucas Ltd was as shown in Exhibit 47.8.

Exhibit 47.8

D Lucas Ltd

Balance Sheet as at 1 January 19X7

	£
Fixtures	36,000
Stock	23,000
Debtors	14,000
Bank	6,000
	79,000

	£
Share capital:	
Preference shares	20,000
Ordinary shares	40,000
Profit and loss	8,000
Creditors	11,000
	79,000

1 Assume that Brown's business had been acquired, except for the bank balance, goodwill being valued at £8,000 and the other assets and liabilities at balance sheet values. Lucas Ltd is to issue an extra 32,000 £1 ordinary shares at par and 18,000 £1 preference shares at par to Brown, in full settlement of the £50,000 net assets taken over.

Exhibit 47.9 shows the balance sheet of the company before and after the acquisition.

Exhibit 47.9

Lucas Ltd

Balance Sheets

	Before £	+ or – £	After £
Goodwill	–	+8,000	8,000
Fixtures	36,000	+30,000	66,000
Stock	23,000	+8,000	31,000
Debtors	14,000	+7,000	21,000
Bank	6,000		6,000
	79,000		132,000

	Before £	+ or – £	After £
Share capital:			
Preference	20,000	+18,000	38,000
Ordinary	40,000	+32,000	72,000
Profit and loss	8,000		8,000
Creditors	11,000	+3,000	14,000
	79,000		132,000

2 If instead we assume that the business of Brown was acquired as follows:

The purchase price to be satisfied by Brown being given £5,000 cash and issue an extra 50,000 ordinary shares at par and £10,000 debentures at par. The assets taken over to be valued at Fixtures £28,000; Stock £7,500; Debtors £6,500. The bank balance is not taken over.

Exhibit 47.10 shows the balance sheet of the company after the acquisition.

Exhibit 47.10

Lucas Ltd

Balance Sheets

	Before £	+ or − £	After £
Goodwill		+26,000	26,000
Fixtures	36,000	+28,000	64,000
Stock	23,000	+7,500	30,500
Debtors	14,000	+6,500	20,500
Bank	6,000	−5,000	1,000
	79,000		142,000

	Before £	+ or − £	After £
Share capital:			
Preference	20,000		20,000
Ordinary	40,000	+50,000	90,000
Debentures		+10,000	10,000
Profit and loss	8,000		8,000
Creditors	11,000	+3,000	14,000
	79,000		142,000

Goodwill is calculated: Purchase consideration is made up of ordinary shares £50,000 + debentures £10,000 + bank £5,000 = £65,000.

Net assets bought are: Fixtures £28,000 + Stock £7,500 + Debtors £6,500 − Creditors £3,000 = £39,000.

Therefore Goodwill is £65,000 − £39,000 = £26,000.

47.6 Business purchase account

In this chapter, to economise on space and descriptions, only the balance sheets have been shown. However, in the books of the purchaser the purchase of a business should pass through a 'Business Purchase Account'.

This would be as follows:

Business Purchase Account

Debit		*Credit*	
Each liability taken over	(B)	Each asset taken over	
Vendor: net amount of		at values placed on it,	
purchase price	(C)	including goodwill	(A)

Vendor's Account (Name of seller/s)

Debit		*Credit*	
Bank (or share capital)		Amount to be paid	
Amount paid	(D)	for business	(C)

Various Asset Accounts

Debit			
Business purchase (value placed			
on asset taken over)	(A)		

Various Liability Accounts

		Credit	
		Amount of liability	
		taken over	(B)

Bank (or Share Capital)

		Credit	
		Amount paid to vendor	(D)

New term

Capital Reserve (p. 519): An account that can be used by sole traders and partnerships when the total purchase price is less than the valuation of the assets at that time.

Main points to remember

1 The assets purchased are shown in the purchaser's balance sheet at their valuation, not at the value per the closing balance sheet of the vendor.

2 Where a greater price is paid than the total valuation of identifiable net assets then the difference is shown as goodwill.

3 Where the purchase price is less than the total valuation of identifiable net assets then the difference is shown as a capital reserve or as negative goodwill.

4 A limited company may use shares or debentures, as well as cash, to pay for the acquisition of another business.

Review questions

47.1

C Allen

Balance Sheet as at 31 December 19X8

	£
Premises	21,000
Stock	9,600
Debtors	6,300
Bank	1,700
	£38,600
Capital	31,800
Creditors	6,800
	£38,600

(a) The business of Allen is taken over by S Walters in its entirety. The assets are deemed to be worth the balance sheet values as shown. The price paid by Walters is £40,000. Show the opening balance sheet of Walters.

(b) Suppose instead that R Jones had taken over Allen's business. He does not take over the bank balance, and values premises at £28,000 and stock at £9,200. The price paid by him is £46,000. Show the opening balance sheet of Jones.

47.2A I Dodgem's balance sheet on 31 December 19X8 was as follows:

	£
Premises	55,000
Plant and machinery at cost	
Less Depreciation	21,000
Fixtures and fittings at cost *less* depreciation	4,000
Stock	17,000
Trade debtors	9,500
Cash	4,500
	£111,000
Capital	87,000
Trade creditors	8,000
Bank overdraft	15,800
Expenses owing	200
	£111,000

An opportunity had arisen for Dodgem to acquire the business of A Swing who is retiring.

A Swing
Balance Sheet as at 31 December 19X8

	£
Premises	25,000
Plant	9,000
Motor vehicle	3,500
Stock	11,000
Trade debtors	6,000
Bank	8,000
Cash	500
	£63,000
Capital	54,000
Trade creditors	9,000
	£63,000

Dodgem agreed to take over Swing's premises, plant, stock, trade debtors and trade creditors.

For the purpose of his own records Dodgem valued the premises at £35,000, plant at £6,000 and stock at £8,000.

The agreed purchase price was £50,000 and in order to finance the purchase Dodgem had obtained a fixed loan for 5 years from his bank, for one half of the purchase price on the condition that he contributed the same amount from his own private resources in cash. The purchase price was paid on 1 January 19X9.

Dodgem also decided to scrap some of his oldest plant and machinery which cost £9,000 with depreciation to date £8,000. This was sold for scrap for £300 cash on 1 January 19X9. On the same date he bought one new plant for £4,000, paying in cash.

Required:
(*a*) The purchase of business account in I Dodgem's books.
(*b*) I Dodgem's balance sheet as at 1 January 19X9 after all the above transactions have been completed.

(*Associated Examining Board*)

47.3 Spectrum Ltd is a private company with an authorised capital of £700,000 divided into shares of £1 each. 500,000 shares have been issued and are fully paid. The company has been formed to acquire small retail shops and establish a chain of outlets.

The company made offers to three sole traders and purchased the businesses run by Red, Yellow and Blue.

The assets acquired, liabilities taken over, and prices paid are listed below:

	Red	Yellow	Blue
	£	£	£
Premises	75,000	80,000	90,000
Delivery vans	7,000	–	10,000
Furniture and fittings	12,000	13,000	13,000
Stock	8,000	7,000	12,000
Creditors	6,000	8,000	7,000
Purchase price	120,000	130,000	150,000

The company also purchased a warehouse to be used as a central distribution store for £60,000. This has been paid.

Preliminary expenses (formation expenses) of £15,000 have also been paid.

The company took over the three shops outlined above and started trading on 1 January 19X2.

Approaches have also been made to Green for the purchase of his business for £100,000. Green has accepted the offer and the company will take over in the near future the following assets and liabilities:

	£
Premises	70,000
Stock	18,000
Creditors	3,000

The transaction had not been completed on 1 January 19X2 and Green was still running his own business.

(a) Prepare the opening balance sheet of Spectrum Ltd as at 1 January 19X2.

(b) How would you advise Spectrum Ltd to finance the purchase of Green's business when the deal is completed?

(Edexcel Foundation, London Examinations (University of London))

Part 7

AN INTRODUCTION TO FINANCIAL ANALYSIS

48 An introduction to the analysis and interpretation of accounting statements

Introduction

This part deals with the interpretation and understanding of financial accounts.

48

An introduction to the analysis and interpretation of accounting statements

Objectives

After you have studied this chapter, you should:

- *understand how the use of ratios can help to analyse the effectiveness of businesses*

- *be able to calculate the main accounting ratios*

48.1 The need for ratios

Let us take the performance of four companies, all dealing in the same type of goods.

	Gross profit £	Sales £
Company A	10,000	84,800
Company B	15,000	125,200
Company C	25,000	192,750
Company D	17,500	146,840

Suppose you want to know which company gets the best profit margins. Simply inspecting these figures and trying to decide which performance was the best, and which was the worst, is virtually impossible. To bring the same basis of comparison to each company we need some form of common measure. As you have already seen earlier in this manual, the common measure used would be a ratio – the amount of gross profit on sales as a percentage. The comparison now becomes:

	%
Company A	11.79
Company B	11.98
Company C	12.97
Company D	11.91

Company C, with 12.97%, or in other words £12.97 gross profit per £100 sales, has performed better than the other companies.

48.2 How to use ratios

You can only sensibly compare like with like. There is not much point in comparing the gross profit percentage of a wholesale chemists with that of a restaurant, for example.

Similarly, figures are only comparable if they have been built up on a similar basis. The sales figures of Company X which treats items as sales only when cash is received cannot be properly compared with Company Z which treats items as sales as soon as they are invoiced.

Another instance of this could be that of stockturn, if Company K is compared with Company L. They are both toy shops so would seem to be comparable. However, although both companies have sales of £100,000 the average stock of K is £40,000 whilst that of L is £10,000. Cost of sales is £50,000, so stockturn ratios are:

$$\begin{array}{ccc}
 & K & L \\
\dfrac{\text{Cost of sales}}{\text{Average stock}} & \dfrac{50{,}000}{40{,}000} = 1.25 & \dfrac{50{,}000}{10{,}000} = 5
\end{array}$$

It looks as though L has managed to turn its stock over five times during the year compared with K, 1.25 times. Is it true? In fact you were not told that K had a financial year end of 31 October, just before Christmas, so toy stocks would be extremely high. On the other hand, L had a year end of 31 January, when after Christmas sales the stock had dropped to the year's lowest figures. In fact, if stock had been valued at 31 October in Company L, then the average stock would also have been £40,000.

Ratios therefore need very careful handling. They are extremely useful if used properly, and very misleading otherwise.

48.3 Types of ratio

Liquidity ratios

The return of profit on capital employed, as you will see, gives an overall picture of profitability. It cannot always be assumed, however, that profitability is everything that is desirable. It must be stressed that accounting is needed, not just to calculate profitability, but also to know whether or not the business will be able to pay its creditors, expenses, loans falling due, etc. at the correct times. Failure to ensure that these payments are covered effectively could mean that the business would have to be closed down. Being able to pay one's debts as they fall due is known as being 'liquid'.

The two main measures of liquidity are the **current ratio** and the **acid test ratio**.

1 Current ratio

$$\text{Current ratio} = \frac{\text{Current assets}}{\text{Current liabilities}}$$

This compares assets which will become liquid within approximately 12 months with liabilities which will be due for payment in the same period.

2 Acid test ratio

$$\text{Acid test ratio} = \frac{\text{Current assets - stock}}{\text{Current liabilities}}$$

This shows that provided creditors and debtors are paid at approximately the same time, a view might be made as to whether the business has sufficient liquid resources to meet its current liabilities.

Exhibit 48.1 shows how two businesses may have similar profitability, yet their liquidity positions may be quite different.

Exhibit 48.1

	E		F	
	£	£	£	£
Fixed assets		40,000		70,000
Current assets				
Stock	30,000		50,000	
Debtors	45,000		9,000	
Bank	15,000		1,000	
	90,000		60,000	
Less Current liabilities: creditors	30,000	60,000	30,000	30,000
		100,000		100,000
Capital				
Opening capital		80,000		80,000
Add Net profit		36,000		36,000
		116,000		116,000
Less Drawings		16,000		16,000
		100,000		100,000

Notes: Sales for both E and F amounted to £144,000. Gross profits for E and F were identical at £48,000.

Profitability: this is the same for both businesses. However, there is a vast difference in the liquidity of the two businesses.

$$\text{Current ratios } E = \frac{90,000}{30,000} = 3 \quad F = \frac{60,000}{30,000} = 2$$

This looks adequate on the face of it, but the acid test ratio reveals that F is in distress, as it will probably find it difficult to pay its current liabilities on time.

$$\text{Acid test ratio } E = \frac{60,000}{30,000} = 2 \quad F = \frac{10,000}{30,000} = 0.33$$

Therefore, for a business to be profitable is not enough, it should also be adequately liquid as well.

However, although a business should be adequately liquid, it is possible for it to have too high a current ratio or an acid test ratio. If too much was being kept as current assets, which would raise the ratios, then those assets may not be being used profitably. For instance, a high stock figure would increase the current ratio, but we may have more money tied up in stock than is necessary, meaning that we are not using our money to best effect. Too high a balance in the bank account could also mean that the money is just lying there not being used properly.

3 Stockturn

Stockturn has already been described in Chapter 33. A reduction in stockturn can mean that the business is slowing down. Stocks may be piling up and not being sold. This could lead to a liquidity crisis, as money may be being taken out of the bank simply to increase stocks which are not then sold quickly enough.

For Exhibit 48.1 the cost of sales for each company was £144,000 − £48,000 = £96,000. If opening stocks had been E £34,000 and F £46,000, then stockturns would have been:

	E	F
Cost of sales / Average stock	$\dfrac{96{,}000}{(34{,}000 + 30{,}000) \div 2}$	$\dfrac{96{,}000}{(46{,}000 + 50{,}000) \div 2}$
	$= \dfrac{96{,}000}{32{,}000} = 3 \text{ times}$	$= \dfrac{96{,}000}{48{,}000} = 2 \text{ times}$

It appears that F's stock is starting to pile up, because it is having difficulty selling it compared with E.

4 Debtor/sales ratio

The resources tied up in debtors is an important ratio subject. Money tied up unnecessarily in debtors is unproductive money. In the example in Exhibit 48.1 this can be calculated for the two companies as:

	E	F
Debtor/sales	45,000/144,000 = 1:3.2	9,000/144,000 = 1:16

This relationship is often translated into the length of time a debtor takes to pay. This turns out to be:

$$E \qquad 365 \times \frac{1}{3.2} = 114 \text{ days} \qquad\qquad F \qquad 365 \times \frac{1}{16} = 22.8 \text{ days}$$

Why Company E should have allowed so much time for its debtors to pay is a matter for investigation. Possibly the company was finding it harder to sell goods, and to sell at all was eventually forced to sell to customers on long credit terms. It could well be that E has no proper credit control system, whereas F has an extremely efficient one.

5 Creditor/purchases ratio

Assuming that purchases for E amounted to £92,000 and for F £100,000 then the ratios are:

	E	F
Creditor/purchases	30,000/92,000 = 1:3.07	30,000/100,000 = 1:3.3

This also is often translated into the length of time we take to pay our creditors. This turns out to be:

$$E \qquad 365 \times \frac{1}{3.07} = 118.9 \text{ days} \qquad\qquad F \qquad 365 \times \frac{1}{3.3} = 110.6 \text{ days}$$

48.4 Profitability ratios

1 Rate of return to net profit on capital employed (ROCE)

This is the most important of all profitability ratios, as it encompasses all the other ratios, and an adequate return on capital employed is why the person(s) invested their money in the first place.

Sole traders

In an earlier chapter it was stated that the term 'capital employed' had not been standardised. In this chapter the average of the capital account will be used, i.e. (opening balance + closing balance) ÷ 2.

In businesses C and D in Exhibit 48.2 the same amount of net profits has been made, but capitals employed are different.

Exhibit 48.2

Balance Sheets

	C £	D £
Fixed + Current assets – Current liabilities	10,000	16,000
Capital accounts		
Opening balance	8,000	14,000
Add Net profits	3,600	3,600
	11,600	17,600
Less Drawings	1,600	1,600
	10,000	16,000

Return on capital employed is:

$$\frac{\text{Net Profit}}{\text{Capital employed}} \times 100$$

$$C \quad \frac{3,600}{(8,000 + 10,000) \div 2} \times \frac{100}{1} = 40\%$$

$$D \quad \frac{3,600}{(14,000 + 16,000) \div 2} \times \frac{100}{1} = 24\%$$

The ratio illustrates that what is important is not simply how much profit has been made but how well the capital has been employed. Business C has made far better use of its capital, achieving a return of £40 net profit for every £100 invested, whereas D has received only a net profit of £24 per £100.

Limited companies

Again, different meanings are attached to **capital employed**. The main ones are:

(a) return on capital employed by ordinary shareholders;
(b) return on capital employed by all long-term suppliers of capital.

To distinguish between these two meanings, in a limited company (a) is usually known as 'Return on Owners' Equity' (ROOE). The word 'Return' in this case is the net profit for the period. The words 'Owners' Equity' mean the book value of all things owned by the owners of the ordinary share capital. This is calculated: Ordinary Share Capital + all Reserves including Profit and Loss Account.

In the case of (b) this is often known simply as 'Return on Capital Employed' (ROCE). The word 'Return' in this case means net profit + any preference share dividends + debenture and long-term loan interest. The word 'Capital' means Ordinary Share Capital + Reserves including Profit and Loss Account + Preference Shares + Debentures and Long-term Loans.

Given the following balance sheets of two companies, P Ltd and Q Ltd, the calculations of (a) and (b) can be attempted:

Balance Sheets as at 31 December

	P Ltd		Q Ltd	
	£	£	£	£
	19X8	*19X9*	*19X8*	*19X9*
Fixed assets	5,200	5,600	8,400	9,300
Net current assets	2,800	3,400	1,600	2,700
	8,000	9,000	10,000	12,000
Share capital (ordinary)	3,000	3,000	5,000	5,000
Reserves	5,000	6,000	3,800	5,800
	8,000	9,000	8,800	10,800
10% debentures			1,200	1,200
			10,000	12,000

Profit and Loss Accounts for years to 31 December 19X9

	P Ltd	Q Ltd
	£	£
Net profit	2,200	3,800
Dividends	1,200	1,800
	1,000	2,000

Return on Owners' Equity (ROOE)

P Ltd   *Q Ltd*

$$\frac{2,200}{(8,000 + 9,000) \div 2} \times \frac{100}{1} = 25.9\% \qquad \frac{3,800}{(8,800 + 10,800) \div 2} \times \frac{100}{1} = 38.8\%$$

The return on capital employed by all long-term suppliers of capital is not relevant in the case of *P Ltd*, as there are only ordinary shareholders in *P Ltd*.

$$\text{ROCE: Q Ltd} = \frac{3,800 + 120^*}{(10,000 + 12,000) \div 2} \times \frac{100}{1} = 35.6\%$$

*The debenture interest 10% of £1,200 = £120 must be added back here, as it was an expense in calculating the £3,800 net profit.

2 Gross profit as percentage of sales

The formula is $\dfrac{\text{Gross profit}}{\text{Sales}} \times 100$

This was dealt with in Chapter 33.

3 Net profit as a percentage of sales

The formula is $\dfrac{\text{Net profit}}{\text{Sales}} \times 100$

48.5 Other ratios

There are a large number of other ratios which could be used, far more than can be mentioned in a textbook such as this. It will depend on the type of company exactly which ratios are the most important and it is difficult to generalise too much.

Different users of the accounts will want to use the ratio analysis which is of vital concern to them. If we can take a bank as an example, which lends money to a company, it will want to ensure two things:

(*a*) that the company will be able to pay interest on the loan as it falls due; *and*
(*b*) that it will be able to repay the loan on the agreed date.

The bank is therefore interested in:

(*a*) short-term liquidity, concerning payment of loan interest; and
(*b*) long-term solvency for eventual repayment of the loan.

Possible ratios would be:

1 Short-term liquidity

This could include mainly the *acid test ratio* and the *current ratio*, already described.

2 Long-term solvency

This might include:

(a) Operating profit/loan interest. This indicates how much of the profits are taken up by paying loan interest. Too great a proportion would mean that the company was borrowing more than was sensible, as a small fall in profits could mean the company operating at a loss with the consequent effect upon long-term solvency.

(b) Total external liabilities/shareholders' funds. This ratio measures how much financing is done via share capital and retained profits, and how much is from external sources. Too high a proportion of external liabilities could bring about long-term solvency problems if the company's profit-making capacity falls by a relatively small amount, as outside liabilities still have to be met.

(c) Shareholders' funds/total assets (excluding intangibles). This highlights the proportion of assets financed by the company's own funds. Large falls in this ratio will tend to show a difficulty with long-term solvency. Similarly, investors will want to see ratios suitable for their purposes, which are not the same as those for the bank. These will not only be used on a single company comparison, but probably with the average of the same type of ratios for other companies in the same industry.

These will include the following ratios. Note that **price** means the price of the shares on the stock exchange.

(i) Price/earnings ratio (P/E)
The formula is:

$$\text{Price/earnings ratio} = \frac{\text{Market price per share}}{\text{Earnings per share}}$$

This puts the price into context as a multiple of the earnings. The greater the P/E ratio, the greater the demand for the shares. A low P/E means there is little demand for shares.

(ii) Earnings per share (EPS)

The formula is:

$$\text{Earnings per share} = \frac{\text{Net profit after tax and preference dividends}}{\text{Number of ordinary shares issued}}$$

This gives the shareholder (or prospective shareholder) a chance to compare one year's earnings with another in terms easily understood.

(iii) Dividend cover

This is found by the formula:

$$\text{Dividend cover} = \frac{\text{Net profit after tax and preference dividends}}{\text{Ordinary dividends paid and proposed}}$$

This gives the shareholder some idea as to the proportion that the ordinary dividends bear to the amount available for distribution to ordinary shareholders. Usually, the dividend is described as being so many times covered by profits made. If therefore the dividend is said to be *three times covered*, it means that one-third of the available profits is being distributed as dividends.

3 Capital gearing ratio

The relationship of equity shares (ordinary shares) to other forms of long-term financing (long-term loans plus preference shares) can be extremely important. Analysts are therefore keen to ascertain a ratio to express this relationship.

There is more than one way of calculating this ratio. The most widely used method is as follows:

$$\frac{\text{Long-term loans} + \text{Preference shares}}{\text{Total shareholders' funds} + \text{Long-term loans} + \text{Preference shares}} \times \frac{100}{1}$$

Long-term loans include debentures. Total shareholders' funds include preference shares and ordinary shares and all the reserves.

Let us look at the calculations of the gearing of two companies, A Ltd and B Ltd in Exhibit 48.3. Both have already been trading for five years.

Exhibit 48.3

Year 5: items per balance sheet	A Ltd £	B Ltd £
10% debentures	10,000	100,000
10% preference shares	20,000	50,000
Ordinary shares	100,000	20,000
Reserves	70,000	30,000
	200,000	200,000

Gearing ratios:

A Ltd:
$$\frac{10,000 + 20,000}{10,000 + 20,000 + 100,000 + 70,000} \times \frac{100}{1} = 15\% \text{ (low gearing)}$$

B Ltd:
$$\frac{100,000 + 50,000}{100,000 + 50,000 + 20,000 + 30,000} \times \frac{100}{1} = 75\% \text{ (high gearing)}$$

Now let us look at how dividends are affected, given the same level of profits made before payment of debenture interest and preference dividends. All the profits made in these years are to be distributed.

A Ltd: Low gearing

		Year 6 £	Year 7 £	Year 8 £	Year 9 £
Profits before deducting the following:		20,000	15,000	30,000	40,000
Debenture interest	1,000				
Preference dividend	2,000	3,000	3,000	3,000	3,000
Profits left for ordinary dividend		17,000	12,000	27,000	37,000
Rate of ordinary dividend		17%	12%	27%	37%

B Ltd: High gearing

		Year 6 £	Year 7 £	Year 8 £	Year 9 £
Profits before deducting the following:		20,000	15,000	30,000	40,000
Debenture interest	10,000				
Preference dividend	5,000	15,000	15,000	15,000	15,000
Profits left for ordinary dividend		5,000	–	15,000	25,000
Rate of ordinary dividend		25%	–	75%	125%

A company with a high percentage gearing ratio is said to be *high geared*, whereas one with a low percentage gearing is said to be *low geared*. As you can see from the above example, the proportionate effect gearing has upon ordinary shareholders is far greater in a high geared company, ranging from 0 to 125 per cent dividend for B Ltd, whilst the range of ordinary dividends for A Ltd varied far less and lay between 17 and 37 per cent.

A high rate of debt (i.e. long-term loans and preference shares) means that in bad times very little might be left over for ordinary shareholders after payment of interest on the debt items and also preference dividends. In good times, however, the ordinary shareholders will enjoy a far higher return than in a low geared company.

This means that people investing in ordinary shares in a high geared company are taking a far greater risk with their money than if they had invested instead in a low geared company. It would have only required a drop of profits of £5,000 in Year 6 for B Ltd to find that there would be no ordinary dividends at all for both Years 6 and 7. Such a drop in Year 6 for A Ltd would still have allowed a dividend of 12 per cent for both of Years 6 and 7. Investors therefore who are prepared to risk their money in the hope of large dividends would have chosen B Ltd, whilst those who wanted to cut down on their risk and be more certain about receiving dividends would choose A Ltd.

48.6 Changing the gearing of a company

The management might decide that for various reasons it would like to change the gearing of the company. It can do this as follows:

To reduce gearing
1 By issuing new ordinary shares
2 By redeeming debentures
3 By retaining profits

To increase gearing
1 By issuing debentures
2 By buying back ordinary shares in issue
3 By issuing new preference shares

Such changes will be influenced by what kinds of investors the company wishes to attract. A highly geared company will attract risk-taking buyers of ordinary shares, whilst a low geared company will be more attractive to potential ordinary shareholders who wish to minimise risk.

48.7 The investor: choosing between shares and debentures

The choice of an investor will always be related to the amount of acceptable risk. We can list the possible investments under the headings of risk.

Lowest risk

Debenture holders have their interest paid to them whether or not profits are made. This contrasts with shares, both preference and ordinary, where there have to be profits available for distribution as dividends.

In addition, should there be insufficient cash funds available to pay debenture dividends, many debentures give their holders the right to sell off some or all of the assets of the company, and to recoup the amount of their debentures before anyone else has a claim. Such an investment does not have as much security as, say, government stocks, but it certainly ranks above the shares of that same company.

Medium risk

Preference shares have their dividends paid after the debenture interest has been paid, but before the ordinary shareholders. They still are dependent upon profits being available for distribution. If they are of the cumulative variety then any shortfall can be carried forward to future years and paid before any ordinary dividends are taken.

Highest risk

Ordinary shares have the highest risk. They must give way to both debenture holders and to preference shares for interest and dividends. However, should the remaining profits for distribution be very high then they may get a high return on their money.

48.8 Fixed and variable expenses

Some expenses will remain constant whether activity increases or falls, at least within a given range of change of activity. These expenses are called **fixed expenses**. An example of this would be the rent of a shop which would remain at the same figure, whether sales increased 10 per cent or fell 10 per cent. The same would remain true of such things as rates, fire insurance and so on.

Wages of shop assistants could also remain constant in such a case. If, for instance, the shop employed two assistants, then it would probably keep the same two assistants, on the same wages, whether sales increased or fell by 10 per cent.

Of course, such 'fixed expenses' can only be viewed as fixed in the short term. If sales doubled, then the business might well need a larger shop or more assistants. A larger shop would also certainly mean higher rates, higher fire insurance and so on, and with more assistants the total wage bill would be larger.

Variable expenses on the other hand will change with swings in activity. Suppose that wrapping materials are used in the shop, then it could well be that an increase in sales of 10 per cent may see ten per cent more wrapping materials used. Similarly an increase of 10 per cent of sales, if all sales are despatched by parcel post, could well see delivery charges increase by 10 per cent.

Some expenses could be part fixed and part variable. Suppose that because of an increase in sales of 10 per cent, telephone calls made increased by 10 per cent. With telephone bills the cost falls into two parts, one for the rent of the phone and the second part corresponding to the actual number of calls made. The rent would not change in such a case, and therefore this part of telephone expense would be 'fixed' whereas the calls part of the expense could increase by 10 per cent.

This means that the effect of a percentage change in activity could have a more, or less, percentage change in net profit, because the fixed expenses (within that range of activity) may not alter.

Exhibit 48.4 shows the change in net profit in Business A which has a low proportion of its expenses as 'fixed' expenses, whereas in Business B the 'fixed' expenses are a relatively high proportion of its expenses.

Exhibit 48.4

Business A

			(a) If sales fell 10%		(b) If sales rose 10%	
	£	£	£	£	£	£
Sales		50,000		45,000		55,000
Less Cost of goods sold		30,000		27,000		33,000
		20,000		18,000		22,000
Gross profit						
Less Expenses:						
Fixed	3,000		3,000		3,000	
Variable	13,000	16,000	11,700	14,700	14,300	17,300
Net profit		4,000		3,300		4,700

Business B

			(a) If sales fell 10%		(b) If sales rose 10%	
	£	£	£	£	£	£
Sales		50,000		45,000		55,000
Less Cost of goods sold		30,000		27,000		33,000
		20,000		18,000		22,000
Gross profit						
Less Expenses:						
Fixed	12,000		12,000		12,000	
Variable	4,000	16,000	3,600	15,600	4,400	16,400
Net profit		4,000		2,400		5,600

The comparison of percentage changes in net profit therefore works out as follows:

$$A \qquad\qquad B$$

Decrease of 10% sales

$$\frac{\text{Reduction in profit}}{\text{Original profit}} \times \frac{100}{1} \qquad \frac{700}{4,000} \times \frac{100}{1} = 17.5\% \qquad \frac{1,600}{4,000} \times \frac{100}{1} = 40\%$$

Increase of 10% sales

$$\frac{\text{Increase in profit}}{\text{Original profit}} \times \frac{100}{1} \qquad \frac{700}{4,000} \times \frac{100}{1} = 17.5\% \qquad \frac{1,600}{4,000} \times \frac{100}{1} = 40\%$$

It can be seen that a change in activity in Business *B*, which has a higher fixed expense content, will result in greater percentage changes in profit: 40% in *B* compared with 17.5% in *A*.

48.9 Trend figures

In examinations a student is often given just one year's accounting figures and asked to comment on them. Obviously, lack of space on an examination paper may preclude several years' figures being given, also the student lacks the time to prepare a comprehensive survey of several years' accounts.

In real life, however, it would be extremely stupid for anyone to base decisions on just one year's accounts, if more information was available. What is important for a business is not just what, say, accounting ratios are for one year, but what the trend has been.

Given two similar types of businesses *G* and *H*, both having existed for 5 years, if both of them had exactly the same ratios in year 5, are they both equally desirable as investments? Given one year's accounts it may appear so, but if one had all the 5 years' figures it may not give the same picture, as Exhibit 48.5 illustrates.

Exhibit 48.5

		Years				
		1	2	3	4	5 (current)
Gross profit as % of sales	*G*	40	38	36	35	34
	H	30	32	33	33	34
Net profit as % of sales	*G*	15	13	12	12	11
	H	10	10	10	11	11
Net profit as % of capital employed	*G*	13	12	11	11	10
	H	8	8	9	9	10
Liquidity	*G*	3	2.8	2.6	2.3	2.0
	H	1.5	1.7	1.9	1.0	2.0

From these figures *G* appears to be the worse investment for the future, as the trend appears to be downwards. If the trend for *G* is continued it could be in a very dangerous financial situation in a year or two. Business *H*, on the other hand, is strengthening its position all the time.

Of course, it would be ridiculous to assert that *H* will continue on an upward trend. One would have to know more about the business to be able to judge whether or not that could be true.

However, given all other desirable information, trend figures would be an extra important indicator.

48.10 Limitations of accounting statements

Final accounts are only partial information. They show the reader of them, in financial terms, what has happened *in the past*. This is better than having no information at all, but one needs to know much more.

First, it is impossible to sensibly compare two businesses which are completely unlike one another. To compare a supermarket's figures with those of a chemical factory would be rather pointless. It would be like comparing a lion with a lizard.

Second, there are a whole lot of factors that the past accounts do not disclose. The desire to keep to the money measurement concept, and the desire to be objective, both dealt with in Chapter 10, exclude a great deal of desirable information. Some typical desirable information can be listed, but beware, the list is indicative rather than exhaustive.

(a) What are the future plans of the business? Without this an investment in a business would be sheer guesswork.
(b) Has the firm got good quality staff?
(c) Is the business situated in a location desirable for such a business? A shipbuilding business situated a long way up a river which was becoming unnavigable, to use an extreme example, could soon be in trouble.
(d) What is its position as compared with its competitors? A business manufacturing a single product, which has a foreign competitor which has just invented a much improved product which will capture the whole market, is obviously in for a bad time.
(e) Will future government regulations affect it? Suppose that a business which is an importer of goods from Country X, which is outside the EU, finds that the EU is to ban all imports from Country X?
(f) Is its plant and machinery obsolete? If so, the business may not have sufficient funds to be able to replace it.
(g) Is the business of a high-risk type or in a relatively stable industry?
(h) Has the business got good customers? A business selling largely to Country Y, which is getting into trouble because of shortage of foreign exchange, could soon lose most of its trade. Also if one customer was responsible for, say, 60 per cent of sales, then the loss of that one customer would be calamitous.
(i) Has the business got good suppliers of its needs? A business in wholesaling could, for example, be forced to close down if manufacturers decided to sell direct to the general public.
(j) Problems concerned with the effects of distortion of accounting figures caused by inflation (or deflation).

The reader can now see that the list would have to be an extremely long one if it was intended to cover all possibilities.

48.11 SSAP 2: Disclosure of Accounting Policies

Users of accounts want to analyse and evaluate financial statements issued by organisations. They cannot do this effectively unless they know which accounting policies have been used when preparing such statements. This SSAP, which refers to companies, was issued to help bring about an improvement in the quality of financial reporting.

The SSAP begins by distinguishing between three terms, namely fundamental accounting concepts, accounting bases and accounting policies.

Fundamental accounting concepts

These are said to be the broad basic assumptions used in preparing the periodic financial accounts of a business. The SSAP singles out four concepts for special mention. These are:

- going concern concept;
- accruals concept;
- consistency concept;
- prudence concept.

We have already examined each of these concepts in Chapter 10. The SSAP says that they are so important that it presumed that the concepts have been observed unless stated otherwise. The Companies Act 1985 also recognises these four fundamental concepts although the Act refers to them as '**accounting principles**'.

Obviously there are other concepts in use besides these four; it is simply that the SSAP focuses on these four as being of overriding importance.

The SSAP does state that where there is a conflict between the use of the accruals concept and the prudence concept, then observance of the prudence concept must be followed.

To some extent, SSAP 2 has been superseded by the Companies Act and by other accounting standards. As discussed in Chapter 10, the Companies Act names a fifth fundamental accounting concept – separate determination – and FRS 5 deals with a sixth – substance over form.

The FRSSE (*Financial Reporting Standard for Smaller Entities*) issued in 1997 went further, following the terminology of the Companies Act by using the term 'accounting principle', rather than 'accounting concept'. It also referred to the Companies Act 1985 as the source for the principles, rather than SSAP 2. Nevertheless, the definitions of the four original fundamental accounting concepts and of the other terms contained in SSAP 2 still apply. These terms include:

Accounting bases

These are the methods for applying fundamental accounting concepts to financial transactions and items in financial accounts. In particular they must be used for:

- determining the periods in which revenue and costs should be recognised in the profit and loss account;
- determining the amounts at which material items should be shown in the balance sheet.

Instances where accounting bases are important concerning the above, and the main bases available, are:

- stock and work in progress (bases available include FIFO, LIFO, AVCO);
- depreciation of fixed assets (bases available include straight line method, reducing balance method, depletion unit method, revaluation method and so on).

Accounting policies

These constitute the bases which have been consistently used by a business. One example might be a business which has used the straight line method of depreciation for several years. This therefore has become its accounting policy for depreciation.

48.12 Further thoughts on concepts and conventions

In Chapter 10, you were introduced to the concepts and conventions used in accounting. Since then further chapters have consolidated your knowledge on specific points.

In recent years there has been a considerable change in the style of examinations in accounting at all levels. At one time nearly every examination question was simply of a computational nature, requiring you to prepare final accounts, draft journal entries, extract a trial balance and so on. Now, *in addition* to all that (which is still important) there are quite a lot of questions asking such things as:

- Why do we do it?
- What does it mean?
- How does it relate to the concepts and conventions?

Such questions depend very much on the interests and ingenuity of examiners. They like to set questions worded to find out those who can understand and interpret financial information, and eliminate those who cannot and simply try to repeat information learned by rote.

The examiners will often draw on knowledge from any part of the syllabus. It is therefore impossible for a student (or an author) to guess exactly how an examiner will select a question and how he will word it.

An example of this is where the examiner could ask you to show how different concepts contradict one another. Someone who has just read about the concepts, and memorised them, could not answer this unless they had thought further about it. Think about whether or not you could have answered that question before you read further.

One instance is the use of the concept of consistency. Basically it says that one should keep to the same method of entering an item each year. Yet if the net realisable value of stock is less than cost, then the normal method of showing it at cost should be abandoned and the net realisable value used instead. Thus, at the end of one period, stock may be shown at cost and at the end of the next period it will be shown at net realisable value. In this case the concept of prudence has overridden the concept of consistency.

Another instance of this is that of calculating profit based on sales whether they have been paid for or not. If the prudence concept were taken to extremes, then profit would only be calculated on a sale when the sale had been paid for. Instead the realisation concept has overridden the prudence concept.

Review questions 48.11 to 48.20 are typical examination questions which obviously relate to concepts and conventions, and to general understanding of the subject.

48.13 Other accounting standards

As well as the accounting standards that you have read about in this book, there are some other standards which may appear in the examinations of some of the professional bodies. We will cover them here briefly.

SSAP 13: Research and Development

Money spent on research and development presents a problem for accountants. You could argue that:

- Such costs are incurred so that profits can be earned in the future, and should therefore be carried forward to those future periods.
- Just because you have incurred such costs, you cannot be certain about future profitability occurring. It should therefore be written off as an expense in the period when the costs are incurred.

The costs can be divided between:

- **Pure (basic) research.** This is carried out to advance scientific and technical knowledge, but without any specific objective.
- **Applied research.** This utilises pure research undertaken so that a specific objective can be attained.

- **Development**. Work undertaken to develop new or existing products or services. This has to be carried out before commercial operations can begin.

SSAP 13 requires that both pure research and applied research costs be written off in the year they are incurred.

However, with development costs, if certain conditions are met, then they may be carried forward to future periods.

SSAP 17: Accounting for Post Balance Sheet Events

The balance sheet is supposed to reflect the financial position of a business at the balance sheet date. However, between the balance sheet date and its later approval by the board of directors, certain events may occur. These may mean that the balance sheet figures need amending.

The events can be divided between:

- **Adjusting events**. When these happen the balance sheet needs to be amended.
- **Non-adjusting events**. These do not lead to amendments of the balance sheet, but they may be shown as notes accompanying the balance sheet.

SSAP 18: Accounting for Contingencies

A contingency is defined as: 'a condition which exists at the balance sheet date, where the outcome will be confirmed only on the occurrence or non-occurrence of one or more uncertain events'.

An example of this could be where a legal action is being carried on, but the case has not yet been decided. For instance, a company may have been sued for £10 million damages, but the case is not yet over. The company may, or may not, have to pay the damages.

There is a vital difference in the treatment of a contingent loss as compared with a contingent gain. If such a loss can be estimated with reasonable accuracy, then a provision for it should be made in the accounts. However, a contingent profit should never be incorporated into the accounts. This obviously satisfies the concept of prudence.

FRSSE: Financial Reporting Standard for Smaller Entities

This accounting standard was issued in November 1997. It provides a simplified version of the body of accounting standards and is for use by 'smaller entities', i.e. small companies and other organisations that would be classified as 'small' were they companies. The standard quotes from sections 247–249 of the Companies Act 1985 in defining a 'small' company as one that does not exceed two or more of the following criteria:

Turnover	£2.8 million
Balance sheet total	£1.4 million
Average number of employees	50

The FRSSE is applicable to the great majority of companies and will, undoubtedly, feature increasingly in both examinations and in the work undertaken by accountants.

New terms

Accounting principles (p. 544): The current term for accounting concepts.

Acid test ratio (p. 532): A ratio comparing current assets *less* stock with current liabilities.

Creditor : purchases ratio (p. 534): A ratio assessing how long we take to pay creditors.

Current ratio (p. 532): A ratio comparing current assets with current liabilities.

Debtor : sales ratio (p. 534): A ratio assessing how long it takes our debtors to pay us.

Fixed expenses (p. 540): Expenses which remain constant whether activity rises or falls, within a given range of activity.

Gearing (p. 538): The ratio of long-term loans and preference shares shown as a percentage of total shareholders' funds, long-term loans, and preference shares.

Liquidity ratios (p. 532): Those ratios that relate to the cash position in an organisation and hence its ability to pay liabilities when due.

Return on capital employed (p. 534): Net profit as a percentage of capital employed, often abbreviated as ROCE.

Return on owners' equity (p. 535): Net profit as a percentage of ordinary share capital plus all reserves, often abbreviated as ROOE.

Variable expenses (p. 540): Expenses which change with swings in activity.

Main points to remember

1   A business must be both profitable *and* sufficiently liquid to be successful. One factor without the other can lead to serious trouble.

2   Careful credit control to ensure that the debtor : sales ratio is not too high is usually essential to the well-being of any business.

3   Comparing the trends to see if the ratios are getting better or worse as each period passes is essential for proper control. Prompt action needs to be taken where the trend in a ratio is deteriorating.

4   The most important ratio is return on capital employed (ROCE).

5   Gearing affects the risk factor for ordinary share investors. Higher gearing means greater risk whilst low gearing means lesser risks.

6   The relative amounts of fixed and variable expenses can affect profit significantly when there are swings in business activity.

Review questions

48.1 You are to study the following financial statements for two similar types of retail store and then answer the questions which follow.

Financial Statements

	A £	A £	B £	B £
Profit and loss accounts				
Sales		80,000		120,000
Less Cost of goods sold				
Opening stock	25,000		22,500	
Add Purchases	50,000		91,000	
	75,000		113,500	
Less Closing stock	15,000	60,000	17,500	96,000
Gross profit		20,000		24,000
Less Depreciation	1,000		3,000	
Other expenses	9,000	10,000	6,000	9,000
Net profit		10,000		15,000
Balance sheets				
Fixed assets				
Equipment at cost	10,000		20,000	
Less Depreciation to date	8,000	2,000	6,000	14,000
Current assets				
Stock	15,000		17,500	
Debtors	25,000		20,000	
Bank	5,000		2,500	
	45,000		40,000	
Less Current liabilities				
Creditors	5,000	40,000	10,000	30,000
		42,000		44,000
Financed by:				
Capitals				
Balance at start of year		38,000		36,000
Add Net profit		10,000		15,000
		48,000		51,000
Less Drawings		6,000		7,000
		42,000		44,000

Required:

(a) Calculate the following ratios:

- (i) gross profit as percentage of sales;
- (ii) net profit as percentage of sales;
- (iii) expenses as percentage of sales;
- (iv) stockturn;
- (v) rate of return of net profit on capital employed (use the average of the capital account for this purpose);
- (vi) current ratio;
- (vii) acid test ratio;
- (viii) debtor/sales ratio;
- (ix) creditor/purchases ratio.

(b) Drawing upon all your knowledge of accounting, comment upon the differences and similarities of the accounting ratios for A and B. Which business seems to be the most efficient? Give possible reasons.

48.2A Study the following financial statements of two companies and then answer the questions which follow. Both companies are stores selling textile goods.

Financial Statements

	R Ltd £	R Ltd £	T Ltd £	T Ltd £
Profit and loss accounts				
Sales		250,000		160,000
Less Cost of goods sold				
Opening stock	90,000		30,000	
Add Purchases	210,000		120,000	
	300,000		150,000	
Less Closing stock	110,000	190,000	50,000	100,000
Gross profit		60,000		60,000
Less Expenses				
Wages and salaries	14,000		10,000	
Directors' remuneration	10,000		10,000	
Other expenses	11,000	35,000	8,000	28,000
Net profit		25,000		32,000
Add Balance from last year		15,000		8,000
		40,000		40,000
Less Appropriations				
General reserve	2,000		2,000	
Dividend	25,000	27,000	20,000	22,000
Balance carried to next year		13,000		18,000
Balance sheets				
Fixed assets				
Equipment at cost	20,000		5,000	
Less Depreciation to date	8,000	12,000	2,000	3,000
Motor lorries	30,000		20,000	
Less Depreciation to date	12,000	18,000	7,000	13,000
		30,000		16,000
Current assets				
Stock	110,000		50,000	
Debtors	62,500		20,000	
Bank	7,500		10,000	
	180,000		80,000	
Less Current liabilities				
Creditors	90,000		16,000	
		90,000		64,000
		120,000		80,000
Financed by:				
Issued share capital		100,000		50,000
Reserves				
General reserve	7,000		12,000	
Profit and loss	13,000	20,000	18,000	30,000
		120,000		80,000

Required:

(a) Calculate the following ratios for each of *R Ltd* and *T Ltd*:

(i)	gross profit as percentage of sales;	(vi)	current ratio;
(ii)	net profit as percentage of sales;	(vii)	acid test ratio;
(iii)	expenses as percentage of sales;	(viii)	debtor/sales ratio;
(iv)	stockturn;	(ix)	creditor/purchases ratio.
(v)	rate of return of net profit on capital employed (for the purpose of this question only, take capital as being total of share capitals + reserves at the balance sheet date);		

(b) Comment briefly on the comparison of each ratio as between the two companies. State which company appears to be the most efficient, giving what you consider to be possible reasons.

48.3 Durham Limited had an authorised capital of £200,000 divided into 100,000 ordinary shares of £1 each and 200,000 8% preference shares of 50p each. The following balances remained in the accounts of the company after the trading and profit and loss accounts had been prepared for the year ended 30 April 19X9.

	Debit £	Credit £
Premises at cost	86,000	
General reserve		4,000
Ordinary shares: fully paid		100,000
8% Preference shares: fully paid		50,000
Electricity		100
Cash at bank	13,100	
Profit and loss account balance 1 May 19X8		14,500
Debtors and creditors	20,000	12,900
Net profit (year ended 30 April 19X9)		16,500
Machinery and plant at cost	60,000	
Provision for depreciation on machinery and plant		40,000
Stock	60,000	
Provision for bad debts		4,000
Insurance	900	
Preference share dividend paid	2,000	
	242,000	242,000

The Directors have recommended:
  a transfer of £5,000 to general reserve;
  an ordinary dividend of £0.15p per share; and
  a provision for the unpaid preference share dividend.

(a) Prepare the profit and loss appropriation account for year ended 30 April 19X9.
(b) Prepare the balance sheet as at 30 April 19X9, in a form which shows clearly the **working capital** and the **shareholders' funds.**
(c) Identify and calculate:
  (i) one ratio indicating the firm's profitability;
  (ii) two ratios indicating the firm's liquidity position.
(d) Make use of your calculations in (c) above to comment on the firm's financial position.
(e) Name two points of comparison which are not available from the information above in this question but which could make your comments in (d) above more meaningful.

(Edexcel Foundation, London Examinations: GCSE)

48.4 The summarised accounts of Hope (Eternal Springs) Ltd for the years 19X8 and 19X9 are given below.

Trading and Profit and Loss Accounts for the year ended 31 December

	19X8 £000	19X9 £000	19X9 £000
Sales	200		280
Less Cost of sales	150		210
Gross profit	50		70
Less			
Administration expenses	38	46	
Debenture interest	–	4	50
Net profit	12		20

Balance Sheets as at 31 December

	19X8 £000	19X9 £000		19X8 £000	19X9 £000
Ordinary share capital	100	100	Fixed assets, at cost		
Profit and Loss Account	30	41	*Less* Depreciation	110	140
8% Debentures	–	50			
Creditors	15	12	Stock	20	30
Bank	10	–	Debtors	25	28
			Bank	–	5
	155	203		155	203

Stock at 1 January 19X8 was £50,000

Required:

(a) Calculate the following ratios for 19X8 **and** 19X9:
   (i)   Gross profit: Sales
   (ii) Stock turnover
   (iii) Net profit: Sales
   (iv) Quick ('acid test')
   (v)   Working capital
   (vi) Net profit: Capital employed

(b) State the possible reasons for and significance of any changes in the ratios shown by your calculations.

(*Midland Examining Group: GCSE*)

48.5A The following figures are for AB Engineering Supplies Ltd at 31 December 19X9:

	£'000
Turnover	160
Gross profit	40
Average stock at cost price	10
Expenses	8

		£'000
Fixed assets		108
Current assets		
Stock	10	
Debtors	8	
Bank	2	20
		128
Current liabilities		10
Capital		118
		128

(a) Calculate:
   (i) gross profit as a percentage of the sales;
   (ii) rate of stock turnover;
   (iii) net profit as a percentage of sales;
   (iv) net profit as a percentage of total capital employed (fixed assets plus current assets);
   (v) current ratio;
   (vi) quick asset (acid test) ratio.

(b) The following figures are for another firm in the same line of business, CD Engineering Services Ltd, for the year ended 31 December 19X9.

	CD Engineering Services Ltd
Gross profit as a percentage of the sales	25%
Rate of stock turnover	9
Net profit as a percentage of sales	10%
Net profit as a percentage of total capital employed	12½%
Current ratio	1 : 1
Quick asset (acid test) ratio	0.5 : 1

Compare your results in (a) with those given for CD Engineering Services Ltd.
   As a result of your comparison, say which you think was the more successful business during 19X9, giving your reasons.

(*Northern Examinations and Assessment Board: GCSE*)

48.6A Galloway Ltd has an authorised capital of 250,000 ordinary shares of £1 each.

(a) At the end of its financial year, 30 April 19X8, the following balances remained in the company's books after preparation of trading and profit and loss accounts.

	£
Motor vehicles:	
at cost	38,400
provision for depreciation	16,300
Net profit for year	36,600
Freehold premises at cost	190,000
Stock in trade	32,124
Share capital: 200,000 ordinary shares of £1 each, fully paid	200,000
Insurance prepaid	280
Profit and loss account balance brought forward	3,950
Wages and salaries due	774
General reserve	24,000
Trade creditors	3,847
Trade debtors	4,782
8% Debentures	15,000
Rent receivable outstanding	175
Bank overdraft	1,830
Furniture and equipment:	
at cost	44,000
provision for depreciation	7,460

The directors have proposed

(i)   the transfer of £5,000 to the general reserve
(ii) a final dividend on the ordinary shares of 12.5%.

(b) Galloway Ltd's directors are making an assessment of the company's performance for the year. They are concerned by a decline in both profitability and liquidity despite an increase in turnover.

Required:
1   THREE significant differences between ordinary shares and debentures.
2   For Galloway Ltd
    (i)   a profit and loss appropriation account for the year ended 30 April 19X8
    (ii) a balance sheet as at 30 April 19X8 in a form which shows clearly:
    total shareholders' funds
    working capital.
3   Concerning the company's performance
    (i)   Name ONE ratio which could be used to assess profitability.
    (ii) State TWO possible reasons why the profitability ratio may have declined despite increased turnover.
    (iii) Name ONE ratio, other than working capital ratio, which could be used to assess liquidity.
    (iv) Give FOUR suggestions as to how working capital could be increased during the year ahead.

(Southern Examining Group: GCSE)

48.7 The trading stock of Joan Street, retailer, has been reduced during the year ended 31 March 19X8 by £6,000 from its commencing figure of £21,000.

A number of financial ratios and related statistics have been compiled relating to the business of Joan Street for the year ended 31 March 19X8; these are shown below alongside comparative figures for a number of retailers who are members of the trade association to which Joan Street belongs:

	Joan Street	Trade association
	%	%
Net profit as % net capital employed*	15	16
$\dfrac{\text{Net profit}}{\text{Sales}}$	9	8
$\dfrac{\text{Sales}}{\text{Net capital employed}}$	166⅔	200
$\dfrac{\text{Fixed assets}}{\text{Sales}}$	45	35
Working capital ratio:		
$\dfrac{\text{Current assets}}{\text{Current liabilities}}$	400	287½
Acid test ratio:		
$\dfrac{\text{Bank + Debtors}}{\text{Current liabilities}}$	275	187½
$\dfrac{\text{Gross profit}}{\text{Sales}}$	25	26
Debtors collection period:		
$\dfrac{\text{Debtors} \times 365}{\text{Sales}}$	36½ days	32¹⁷⁄₂₀ days
Stock turnover (based on average stock for the year)	10 times	8 times

Joan Street has supplied all the capital for her business and has had no drawings from the business during the year ended 31 March 19X8.

Required:
(a) Prepare the trading and profit and loss account for the year ended 31 March 19X8 and balance sheet as at that date of Joan Street in as much detail as possible.
(b) Identify two aspects of Joan Street's results for the year ended 31 March 19X8 which compare favourably with the trade association's figures and identify two aspects which compare unfavourably.
(c) Outline two drawbacks of the type of comparison used in this question.

(*Association of Accounting Technicians*)

Note from the authors: take the closing figure at 31 March 19X8.

48.8A   Harold Smart, who is a small manufacturer trading as Space Age Projects, is very pleased with his recently completed financial results which show that a planned 20% increase in turnover has been achieved in the last accounting year.

The summarised results relating to the last three financial years are as follows:

Year ended 30 September		19X7	19X8	19X9
		£	£	£
Sales		90,000	100,000	120,000
Cost of sales		74,000	75,000	92,000
Gross profit		16,000	25,000	28,000
Administrative overheads		3,000	5,000	6,000
Net profit		13,000	20,000	22,000

As at 30 September	19X6	19X7	19X8	19X9
	£	£	£	£
Fixed assets:				
At cost	155,000	165,000	190,000	206,000
Provision for depreciation	42,000	45,000	49,000	53,000
	113,000	120,000	141,000	153,000
Current assets:				
Stock	3,000	4,000	7,000	30,000
Debtors	14,000	19,000	15,000	10,000
Balance at bank	2,000	1,000	3,000	–
	19,000	24,000	25,000	40,000
Current liabilities:				
Creditors	5,000	4,000	6,000	9,000
Bank overdraft	–	–	–	2,000
	5,000	4,000	6,000	11,000

Since 30 September 19X6, Harold Smart has not taken any drawings from the business.

Harold Smart has been invited recently to invest £150,000 for a 5-year fixed term in government loan stock earning interest at 12½% per annum.

Note: Taxation is to be ignored.

Notwithstanding his response to these financial results, Harold Smart is a very cautious person and therefore has asked a financial consultant for a report.

Required:
(a)   A schedule of six accounting ratios or measures of resource utilisation covering each of the three years ended 30 September 19X9 of Space Age Projects.
(b)   As financial consultant prepare a report to Harold Smart on the financial results of Space Age Projects given above including comments on the alternative future actions that he might take.

Note: Reports should utilise the information given in answers to part (a) of this question.

(Association of Accounting Technicians)

48.9 Business A and Business B are both engaged in retailing, but seem to take a different approach to this trade according to the information available. This information consists of a table of ratios, shown below:

Ratio	Business A	Business B
Current ratio	2:1	1.5:1
Quick assets (acid test) ratio	1.7:1	0.7:1
Return on capital employed (ROCE)	20%	17%
Return on owners' equity (ROOE)	30%	18%
Debtors turnover	63 days	21 days
Creditors turnover	50 days	45 days
Gross profit percentage	40%	15%
Net profit percentage	10%	10%
Stock turnover	52 days	25 days

Required:
(a) Explain briefly how each ratio is calculated.
(b) Describe what this information indicates about the differences in approach between the two businesses. If one of them prides itself on personal service and one of them on competitive prices, which do you think is which and why?

(Association of Chartered Certified Accountants)

48.10A You are given summarised information about two firms in the same line of business, A and B, as follows.

Balance sheets at 30 June	£000	A £000	£000	£000	B £000	£000
Land			80			260
Buildings		120			200	
Less: Depreciation		40	80		–	200
Plant		90			150	
Less: Depreciation		70	20		40	110
			180			570
Stocks		80			100	
Debtors		100			90	
Bank		–			10	
		180			200	
Creditors	110			120		
Bank	50			–		
	160			120		
		20			80	
		200			650	
Capital b/forward		100			300	
Profit for year		30			100	
		130			400	
Less: Drawings		30			40	
		100			360	
Land revaluation		–			160	
Loan (10% p.a.)		100			130	
		200			650	
Sales		1,000			3,000	
Cost of sales		400			2,000	

Required:

(a) Produce a table of eight ratios calculated for both businesses.

(b) Write a report briefly outlining the strengths and weaknesses of the two businesses. Include comment on any major areas where the simple use of the figures could be misleading.

(*Association of Chartered Certified Accountants*)

48.11 The following letter has been received from a client. 'I gave my bank manager those audited accounts you prepared for last year. But he says he needs more information before he will agree to increase my overdraft. What could he possibly want to know that he can't get from those accounts? If they are not good enough why bother to prepare them?'

Required:
Outline the major points which should be included in a reply to this letter.

(*Association of Chartered Certified Accountants*)

48.12 An acquaintance of yours, H Gee, has recently set up in business for the first time as a general dealer.

   The majority of his sales will be on credit to trade buyers but he will sell some goods to the public for cash.

   He is not sure at which point of the business cycle he can regard his cash and credit sales to have taken place.

   After seeking guidance on this matter from his friends, he is thoroughly confused by the conflicting advice he has received. Samples of the advice he has been given include:

The sale takes place when:

(*i*) 'you have bought goods which you know you should be able to sell easily';

(*ii*) 'the customer places the order';

(*iii*) 'you deliver the goods to the customer';

(*iv*) 'you invoice the goods to the customer';

(*v*) 'the customer pays for the goods';

(*vi*) 'the customer's cheque has been cleared by the bank'.

He now asks you to clarify the position for him.

Required:

(a) Write notes for Gee, setting out, in as easily understood a manner as possible, the accounting conventions and principles which should generally be followed when recognising sales revenue.

(b) Examine each of the statements (*i*) to (*vi*) above and advise Gee (stating your reasons) whether the method advocated is appropriate to the particular circumstances of his business.

(*Association of Chartered Certified Accountants*)

48.13 The annual final accounts of businesses are normally prepared on the assumption that the business is a going concern.

Required:
Explain and give a simple illustration of

(a) the effect of this convention on the figures which appear in those final accounts.

(b) the implications for the final accounts figures if this convention were deemed to be inoperative.

(*Association of Chartered Certified Accountants*)

48.14 One of the well known accounting concepts is that of materiality.

Required:
(a) Explain what is meant by this concept.
(b) State and explain three types of situation to which this concept might be applicable.
(c) State and explain two specific difficulties in applying this concept.

(Association of Chartered Certified Accountants)

48.15 State three classes of people, other than managers and owners, who are likely to need to use financial accounting information. Discuss whether you think their requirements are compatible.

(Association of Chartered Certified Accountants)

48.16 A firm produces a standard manufactured product. The stages of the production and sale of the product may be summarised as follows:

Stage	**A**	**B**	**C**	**D**
Activity	*Raw material*	*WIP-I*	*WIP-II*	*Finished product*
	£	£	£	£
Costs to date	100	120	150	170
Net realisable value	80	130	190	300

Stage	**E**	**F**	**G**	**H**
Activity	*For sale*	*Sale agreed*	*Delivered*	*Paid for*
	£	£	£	£
Costs to date	170	170	180	180
Net realisable value	300	300	300	300

Required:
(a) What general rule do accountants apply when deciding when to recognise revenue on any particular transaction?
(b) Apply this rule to the above situation. State and explain the stage at which you think revenue will be recognised by accountants.
(c) How much would the gross profit on a unit of this product be? Why?
(d) Suggest arguments in favour of delaying the recognition of revenue until stage H.
(e) Suggest arguments in favour of recognising revenue in appropriate successive amounts at stages B, C and D.

(Association of Chartered Certified Accountants)

48.17

(a) In accounting practice a distinction is drawn between the terms 'reserves' and 'provisions' and between 'accrued expenses' and 'creditors'.

Required:
Briefly define each of the four terms quoted and explain the effect of each on the preparation of accounts.

(b) While preparing the final accounts for year ended 30 September 19X7, the accountant of Lanep Lighting Ltd had to deal with the following matters:

(i) the exterior of the company's premises was being repaired. The contractors had started work in August but were unlikely to finish before the end of November 19X7. The total cost would not be known until after completion. Cost of work carried out to 30 September 19X7 was estimated at £21,000;

(ii) the company rented a sales showroom from Commercial Properties plc at a rental of £6,000 per annum payable half yearly in arrears on 1 August and 1 February;

(iii) on 3 October 19X7 an invoice was received for £2,500, less a trade discount of 30 per cent, from Lucifer Ltd for goods for resale supplied during September 19X7;

(iv) the directors of Lanep Lighting Ltd have decided that an annual amount of £5,000 should be set aside, starting with year ended 30 Sept 19X7, for the purpose of plant replacement.

Required:
State the accounting treatment which should be accorded to each of the above matters in the Lanep Lighting Ltd profit and loss account for year ended 30 September 19X7 and balance sheet at that date.

(*Association of Chartered Certified Accountants*)

48.18 Bradwich plc is a medium-sized engineering company whose shares are listed on a major Stock Exchange.

It has recently applied to its bankers for a 7-year loan of £500,000 to finance a modernisation and expansion programme.

Mr Whitehall, a recently retired civil servant, is contemplating investing £10,000 of his lump sum pension in the company's ordinary shares in order to provide both an income during his retirement and a legacy to his grandchildren after his death.

The bank and Mr Whitehall have each acquired copies of the company's most recent annual report and accounts.

Required:
(a) State, separately for each of the two parties, those aspects of the company's performance and financial position which would be of particular interest and relevance to their respective interests.
(b) State, separately for each of the two parties, the formula of four ratios which would assist in measuring or assessing the matters raised in your answer to (a).

(*Association of Chartered Certified Accountants*)

48.19 Explain what you understand by the accounting term 'capital gearing', showing clearly the benefits of, and the potential problems associated with high gearing.

(*Scottish Qualifications Authority*)

48.20A What benefits can result through the use of ratios and what limitations should be imposed on any conclusions drawn from their use?

Appendix I

Review questions: the best approach

At the ends of chapters we have set review questions for you to attempt. If you simply read the text without attempting the questions then we can tell you now that you will not pass your examinations. You should first of all attempt the question, and then check it fully against the answers at the back of the book.

What you should not do is perform a 'ticking' exercise. By this we mean that you should not simply compare the question with the answer and tick off the bits of the answer which compare with the question. No one ever learned to do accounting properly that way. It is tempting to save time in so doing, but believe us you will regret it eventually. We have deliberately had the answers printed using a different page layout to try to stop you indulging in a 'ticking' exercise.

Need for practice

You should also try to find the time to answer as many exercises as possible. Our reasons for saying this are as follows:

1   Even though you may think you understand the text, when you come to answer the questions you may often find your understanding incomplete. The true test of understanding is whether or not you can tackle the questions competently.
2   It is often said that practice makes perfect, a sentiment we don't fully agree with. There is enough sense in it, however, in that if you don't do quite a lot of accounting questions you will almost certainly not become good at accounting.
3   You simply have got to get up to a good speed in answering questions: you will always fail accounting examinations if you are a very slow worker. The history of accountancy examinations so far has always been that a ridiculously large amount of work has been expected from a student during a short time. However, examining boards maintain that the examination could be completed in the time by an adequately prepared student. You can take it for granted that *adequately prepared students* are those who not only have the knowledge, but have also been trained to work quickly and at the same time maintain accuracy and neatness.
4   Speed itself is not enough; you also have to be neat and tidy, and follow all the proper practices and procedures while working at speed. Fast but really scruffy work can also mean failing the exam. Why is this so? At this level the examiner is very much concerned with your practical ability in the subject. Accounting is a practical subject, and your practical competence is about to be tested. The examiner will therefore expect the answers to be neat and well set out. Untidy work with figures spread over the sheet in a haphazard way, badly written figures, and columns of figures in which the vertical columns are not set down in straight lines, will incur the examiner's displeasure.

Need for headings

The next thing is that work should not only be neat and well laid out. Headings should always be given, and any dates needed should be inserted. The test you should apply is to imagine that you are a partner in a firm of professional accountants and you are away on holiday for a few weeks. During that time your assistants have completed all sorts of work including reports, drafting final accounts, various forms of other computations and so on. All of this work is deposited on your desk while you are away. When you return you look at each item in the pile awaiting your attention. Suppose the first item looks like a balance sheet as at 31 December in respect of one of your clients. When you looked at it you could see that it was a balance sheet, but you didn't know for which client, neither did you know which year it was for. Would you be annoyed with your staff? Of course you would. So therefore in an examination why should the examiner accept as a piece of your work a balance sheet answer without either the date or the name of the business or the fact that it is a balance sheet written clearly across the top? If proper headings are not given you will lose a lot of marks. Always therefore put in the headings properly; don't wait until your examination to start this correct practice. Similar attention should be paid to sub-totals which need showing, e.g. for Fixed assets, Current assets.

We will be looking at examination techniques later on, in Appendix II. There is no point in dealing with that important topic at this juncture.

The examiner's attitude

Really, what you should say to yourself is: 'Suppose I were in charge of an office, doing this type of accounting work, what would I say if one of my assistants put on my desk a sheet of paper with accounting entries on it written in the same manner as my own efforts in attempting this question?' Just look at some of the work you have done in the past. Would you have told your assistant to go back and do the work again because it is untidy? If you say that about your own work, why should the examiner think any differently?

Anyone who works in accounting knows well that untidy work leads to completely unnecessary errors. Therefore the examiner's insistence on clear, tidy, well laid-out work is not an outdated approach; they want to ensure that you are not going to mess up the work of an accounting department. Imagine going to the savings bank and the manager says to you: 'We don't know whether you've got £5 in the account or £5,000. You see, the work of our clerks is so untidy that we can never sort out exactly how much is in anybody's account.' We would guess that you would not want to put a lot of money into an account at that bank. How would you feel if someone took you to court for not paying a debt of £100 when in fact you owed them nothing? This sort of thing would happen all the time if we simply allowed people to keep untidy accounts. The examiner is there to ensure that the person to whom they give a certificate will be worthy of it, and will not continually mess up the work of any firm at which they may work in the future.

We can imagine quite a few of you groaning at all this, and if you do not want to pass the examination please give up reading here. If you do want to pass, and your work is untidy, what can you do about it? Well, the answer is simple enough: start right now to be neat and orderly in your work. Quite a lot of students have said to me over the years: 'I may be giving you untidy work now, but when I actually get in the exam room I will then do my work neatly enough.' This is as near impossible as anything can be. You cannot suddenly become able to do accounting work neatly, and certainly not when you are under the stress and strain of an examination. Even the neatest worker may well find in an examination that their work may not be of its usual standard as nervousness will cause them to make mistakes. If this is true, then if you are an untidy worker now your work in an examination is likely to be even more untidy. Have we convinced you yet?

The structure of the questions

Finally, we have attempted to build up the review questions in a structured way, starting with the easiest and then going on to more difficult questions. We would like to have omitted all complicated questions, on the basis that you may well waste a lot of time doing them without adding to your knowledge. On the other hand, if all the questions were very easy ones, then the shock of meeting more complicated questions for the first time in an examination could lead you to fail it. We have therefore tried to get a mixture of questions to give you the maximum benefit.

Now tackle the review questions.

Appendix II
Examination techniques

As authors we can change our writing style here into that of the first person, as we want to put across to you a message about examinations, and we want you to feel that we are writing this for you as an individual rather than simply as one of the considerable number of people who have read the technical part of the book.

When you think about it, you have spent a lot of hours trying to master such things as double entry, balance sheets, suspense accounts and goodness knows what else. Learning accounting/bookkeeping does demand a lot of discipline and practice. Compared with the many hours learning the subject, most students spend very little time actually considering in detail how to tackle the examination. You are probably one of them, and we would like you to take some time away from your revision of the various topics in the syllabus, and instead we want you to think about the examination.

Understanding examiners

Let us start by saying that if you want to understand anything about examinations then you have got to understand examiners, so let us look together at what these peculiar creatures get up to in an examination. The first thing is that when they set an examination they are looking at it on the basis that they want good students to get a pass mark. Obviously anyone who doesn't achieve the pass mark will fail, but the object of the exercise is to find those who will pass rather than to find the failures. This means that if you have done your work properly, and if you are not sitting for an examination well above your intellectual capabilities, then you should manage to get a pass mark. It is important for us to stress that before we get down to the details of setting about the task.

There are, however, quite a large number of students who will fail, not because they haven't put in enough hours on their studies, nor because they are unintelligent, but simply because they throw away marks unnecessarily by poor examination technique. If you can read the rest of this piece, and then say honestly that you wouldn't have committed at least one of the mistakes that we are going to mention, then you are certainly well outside the ordinary range of students.

Punctuality

Before thinking about the examination paper itself, let us think about how you are going to get to the examination room. If it is at your own college then you have no problems as to how you will get there. On the other hand it may be an external centre. Do you know exactly where the place is? If not, you had better have a trip there if possible. How are you going to get there? If you are going by bus or train, do you know which bus or train to catch? Will it be the rush hour when it may well take you much longer than if it were held at midday?

Quite a large proportion of students lose their way to the examination room, or else arrive, breathless and flustered, at the very last minute. They then start off the attempt at the examination in a somewhat nervous state, a recipe for disaster for a lot of students. So plan how you are going to get there and give yourself enough time.

Last minute learning for your examination will be of little use to you. The last few days before the examination should not be spent cramming. You can look at past examination papers and rework some of them. This is totally different from trying to cram new facts into your head.

On your way to the examination, if you can, try relaxation exercises. Deep breathing exercises in particular will put you into a relaxed mood. If you can't do anything like this then try reading the newspaper. Granted you will need the adrenalin to spur you into action when you actually start answering the examination paper, but you do not want to waste it before the examination instead and then put yourself into a highly nervous state.

Read the rubric carefully and follow its instructions

The rubric appears at the start of the examination paper, and says something such as:

'Attempt five questions only: the *three* questions in Section A and *two* from Section B.'

That instruction from the examiner is to be followed exactly. The examinee cannot change the instruction – it means what it says.

Now you may think that that is so simple that it is not worthwhile our forcibly pointing it out to you. We wish that was the case for all students. However, you would be amazed at the quite high percentage of students who do not follow the instructions given in the rubric. Having been examiners for many years for examining bodies all over the world we can assure you that we are not overstating the case. Let us look at two typical examples where students have ignored the rubric above:

(*a*) A student answered *two* questions from Section A and *three* from Section B. Here the examiner will mark the two Section A answers plus the first two answers shown on the examinee's script in respect of Section B. He will not read any part of the third displayed answer to Section B. The student can therefore only get marks for four answers.

(*b*) A student answered *three* questions from Section A and *three* from Section B. Here he will mark the three answers to Section A plus the first two displayed answers to Section B. He will not look at the third answer to Section B.

In the case of (*b*), the student may have done it that way deliberately, thinking that the examiner would mark all three Section B answers, and then award the student the marks from the best two answered questions. There is no way that an examiner will waste his time (and not get paid for it as well) by marking an extra answer. Students have argued that examiners would do that, but they are simply deluding themselves.

If you have time, and want to give an extra answer, thinking that you will get better marks than one answered previously, then do so. You must, however, make certain that the examiner is fully aware that you have deleted the answer that you do not want to have marked. Strike lines right through it, and also state that you wish to delete it. Otherwise the first answers only will be marked.

Always remember in examinations that you should always try to make life easier for the examiner. Give him what he wants, in the way that he wants it. If you do you will get better marks. Make his job harder than it needs to be and you will suffer. Examiners are only human beings after all!

Time planning

We must now look at the way in which you should tackle the examination paper when the time comes. One of the troubles about bookkeeping/accounting examinations is that the student is expected to do a lot of work in a relatively short time. We have campaigned against this attitude, but the tradition is long standing and here to stay. It will be the same for every other student taking your examination, so it is not unfair so far as any one student is concerned. Working at speed does bring about various disadvantages, and makes the way you tackle the examination of even greater importance than for examinations where the pace is more leisurely.

Time per question

The marks allotted to each question will indicate how long you should take in tackling the question. Most examinations are of 3 hours' duration, i.e. 180 minutes. This means that in a normal examination, with 100 marks in total, a 20-mark question should be allocated 20 per cent of the time, i.e. 20% × 180 = 36 minutes. Similarly, a question worth 30 marks should take up 30 per cent of the time, i.e. 30% × 180 = 54 minutes, and so on. Alternatively it is 1.8 minutes for each mark awarded for the question.

If the question is in parts, and the marks awarded are shown against each part, then that will give you a clue as to the time to be spent on each part. If part of the question asks for a description, for instance, and only 3 marks are awarded to that part, then you should not spend 20 minutes on a long and detailed description. Instead a brief description, taking about 5 minutes, is what is required.

Do the easiest questions first

Always tackle the easiest question first, then the next easiest question and so on; leave the most difficult question as the last one to be attempted. Why is this good advice? The fact is that most examiners usually set what might be called 'warm up' questions. These are usually fairly short, and not very difficult questions, and the examiner will expect you to tackle these first of all.

You may be able to do the easiest question in less than the time allocated. The examiner is trying to be kind to you. He knows that there is a certain amount of nervousness on the part of a student taking an examination, and he wants to give you the chance to calm down by letting you tackle these short, relatively easy questions first of all, and generally settle down to your work.

Even where all the questions are worth equal marks, you are bound to find some easier than others. It is impossible for an examiner to set questions which are equally as difficult as each other. So, remember, start with the easiest question. This will give you a feeling of confidence; it is very desirable to start off in this way.

Do not expect that these 'warm up' questions will be numbered 1 and 2 on your examination paper. Most accounting examinations start off with a rather long question, worth quite a lot of marks, as question number 1 on the paper. Over the years we have advised students not to tackle these questions first. A lot of students are fascinated by the fact that such a question is number 1, that it is worth a lot of marks, and their thinking runs: 'If I do this question first, and make a good job of it, then I am well on the way to passing the examination.'

There is no doubt that a speedy and successful attempt at such a question could possibly lead to a pass. The trouble is that this doesn't usually happen, and many students have admitted afterwards that their failure could be put down to simply ignoring this advice. What happens very often, is that the student starts off on such a question, things don't go very well, a few mistakes are made, the student then looks at the clock and sees that they are not 'beating the clock' in terms of possible marks, and then panic descends on them. Leaving that question very hastily, the student then proceeds to the next question, which normally might have been well attempted but, because of the state of mind, a mess is made of that one as well, and so you may fail an examination which you had every right to think you could pass.

Attempt every required question

The last point concerning time allocation which we want to get through to you is that you should attempt each and every question as required. On each question the first few marks are the easiest to get. For instance, on an essay question it is reasonably easy to get, say, the first 5 marks in a 20-mark question. Managing to produce a perfect answer to get the last 5 marks, from 15 to 20, is extremely difficult. This applies also to computational questions.

This means that, in an examination of, say, 5 questions with 20 marks possible for each question, there is not much point in tackling 3 questions only and trying to make a good job of them. The total possible marks would be 60 marks, and if you had not achieved full marks for each question, in itself extremely unlikely, you could easily fall below the pass mark of, say, 50 marks. It is better to leave questions unfinished when your allotted time, calculated as shown earlier, has expired, and to then go on immediately to the other questions. It is so easy, especially in an accounting examination, to find that one has exceeded the time allowed for a question by a considerable margin. So, although you may find it difficult to persuade yourself to do so, move on to the next question when your time for a question has expired.

Computations

One golden rule which should always be observed is: 'Show all of your workings.' Suppose for instance you have been asked to work out the Cost of Goods Sold, not simply as part of a Trading Account but for some other reason. On a scrap of paper you work out the answers below:

	£
Opening stock	4,000
Add Purchases	11,500
	15,500
Less Closing stock	3,800
	12,700

You put down the answer as £12,700. The scrap of paper with your workings on it is then crumpled up by you and thrown in the wastepaper basket as you leave the room. You may have noticed in reading this that in fact the answer should have been 11,700 and not 12,700, as the arithmetic was incorrect. The examiner may well have allocated, say, 4 marks for this bit of the question. What will he do when he simply sees your answer as £12,700? Will he say: 'I should imagine that the candidate mis-added to the extent of £1,000, and as I am not unduly penalising for arithmetic, I will give the candidate 3½ marks'? I'm afraid the examiner cannot do this; the candidate has got the answer wrong, there is no supporting evidence, and so the examiner gives marks as nil. If you had only attached the workings to your answer, then we have no doubt that you would have got 3½ marks at least.

It is often better to put the workings on the face of the final accounts, if appropriate. For instance, if rent paid is £1,900 and of that £300 has been paid in advance, you can show it on the face of the profit and loss account as:

Rent (1,900 – 300)   £1,600

By showing the workings in brackets you are demonstrating that you realise that they would not be shown on the published accounts. It also makes it easier for the examiner to mark.

Do balance sheets have to balance?

Many students ask: 'What should I do if my balance sheet doesn't balance?' The answer is quite simple: leave it alone and get on with answering the rest of the examination paper.

One of the reasons for this is to try and ensure that you answer the full required number of questions. You might spend 20 minutes to find the error, which might save you 1 mark. In that time you might have gained, say, 10 marks, if instead you had tackled the next question, for which you would not have had time if you had wasted it by searching for the error(s). That assumes that you actually find the error(s). Suppose you don't, you have spent 20 minutes looking for it, have not found it, so how do you feel now? The answer is, of course: quite terrible. You may make an even bigger mess of the rest of the paper than you would have done if you had simply ignored the fact that the balance sheet did not balance. In any case, it is quite possible to get, say, 29 marks out of 30 even though the balance sheet does not balance. The error may be a very minor case for which the examiner deducts one mark only.

Of course, if you have finished all of the questions, then by all means spend the rest of your time tracing the error and correcting it. Be certain, however, that your corrections are carried out neatly, as untidy crossings-out can result in the loss of marks. So, sometimes, an error found can get back one mark, which is then lost again because the corrections make an untidy mess of your paper, and examiners usually do deduct marks, quite rightly so, for untidy work. It might be better to write against the error 'see note', indicating exactly where the note is shown. You can then illustrate to the examiner that you know what the error is and how to correct it.

Essay questions

Quite a few years ago there were not many essay questions in accounting examinations at this level. This has changed, and you therefore need to know the approach to use in answering such questions.

Typical questions

Before discussing these, we want you to look at two recent examination questions. Having done that, visualise carefully what you would write in answer to them. Here they are:

(a) You are employed as a bookkeeper by G Jones, a trader. State briefly what use you would make of the following documents in relation to your bookkeeping records.

(i) A bank statement.

(*ii*) A credit note received to correct an overcharge on an invoice.
(*iii*) A paying-in slip.
(*iv*) Petty cash voucher.

(*b*) Explain the term 'depreciation'. Name and describe briefly two methods of providing for depreciation of fixed assets.

Now we can test whether or not you would have made a reasonably good attempt at the questions. With question (*a*) a lot of students would have written down what a bank statement is, what a paying-in slip is, what a petty cash voucher is and so on. Marks gained by you for an answer like that would be . . . nil. Why is this? Well you simply have not read the question properly. The question asked what *use* you would make of the documents, not *to describe* what the documents were. The bank statement would be used to check against the bank column in the cash book or cash records to see that the bank's entries and your own are in accordance with one another, with a bank reconciliation statement being drawn up to reconcile the two sets of records. The petty cash voucher would be used as a basis for entering up the payments columns in the petty cash book. Therefore the *use* of the items was asked for, not the *descriptions* of the items.

Let us see if you have done better on question (*b*). Would you have written down how to calculate two methods of depreciation, probably the reducing balance method and the straight line method? But have you remembered that the question also asked you to *explain the term depreciation*? In other words, what is depreciation generally? A fair number of students will have omitted that part of the question. My own guess is that far more students would have made perhaps a poor attempt at question (*a*) rather than doing question (*b*).

Underline the key words

We have already illustrated that a large percentage of students fail to answer the question set, instead answering the question they imagine it to be. Too many students write down everything they know about a topic, rather than what the examiner has asked for.

To remedy this defect, *underline the key words* in a question. This brings out the meaning so that it is difficult to misunderstand the question. For instance, let us look at the following question:

'Discuss the usefulness of departmental accounts to a business.'

Many students will write down all they know about departmental accounts, how to draw them up, how to apportion overheads between departments, how to keep columnar sales purchases journals to find the information etc.
Number of marks gained . . . nil.
Now underline the key words. They will be:

Discuss   usefulness   departmental accounts

The question is now seen to be concerned not with *describing* departmental accounts, but instead discussing the *usefulness* of departmental accounts.

Lastly, if the question says 'Draft a report on . . .' then the answer should be in the form of a *report*; if it says 'List the . . .' then the answer should consist of a *list*. Similarly 'Discuss . . .' asks for a *discussion*. 'Describe . . .' wants you to *describe* something, and so on.

You should therefore ensure that you are going to give the examiner:

(*i*) What he is asking for   *plus*   (*ii*) In the way that he wants it.

If you do not comply with (*i*) you may lose all the marks. If you manage to fulfil (*i*) but do not satisfy the examiner on (*ii*) you will still lose a lot of marks.

It is also just as important in computational questions to underline the key words to get at the meaning of a question, and then answer it in the manner required by the examiner. With computational questions it is better to look at what is required first before reading all of the rest of the question. That way, when you are reading the rest of the question, you are able to decide how to tackle it.

Never write out the question

Often – too often – students spend time writing out the text of essay questions before they set about answering them. This is a complete waste of time. It will not gain marks and should never be done.

Running out of time?

If your plans don't work out, you may find yourself with a question you could answer, but simply have not got the time to do it properly. It is better to write a short note to the examiner to that effect, and put down what you can of the main points in an abbreviated fashion. This will show that you have the knowledge and should gain you some marks.

Summary

Remember:

(*a*) Tackle the easiest questions first.
(*b*) Finish off answering each question when your time allocation for the question is up.
(*c*) Hand in all your workings.
(*d*) Do remember to be neat, also include all proper headings, dates, sub-totals, etc. A lot of marks can be lost here.
(*e*) Only answer as many questions as you are asked to tackle by the examiner. Extra answers will not be marked.
(*f*) Underline the *key* words in each question to ensure that you answer the question set, and not the question you wrongly take it to be.
(*g*) Never write out the text of essay questions.

Best of luck with your examination. We hope you get the rewards you deserve!

Appendix III
Multiple-choice questions

Each multiple-choice question usually has four suggested answers, letter (A), (B), (C) or (D). You should read each question and then decide which choice is best, either (A) or (B) or (C) or (D). On a separate piece of paper you should then write down your choice. Unless the textbook you are reading belongs to you, you should not make a mark against your choice in the textbook.

Answers to multiple-choice questions are given on p. 645 of this book.

Set No 1: 20 questions

MC1 Which of the following statements is incorrect?
(A) Assets – Capital = Liabilities
(B) Liabilities + Capital = Assets
(C) Liabilities + Assets = Capital
(D) Assets – Liabilities = Capital.

MC2 Which of the following is not an asset?
(A) Buildings
(B) Cash balance
(C) Debtors
(D) Loan from K Harris.

MC3 Which of the following is a liability?
(A) Machinery
(B) Creditors for goods
(C) Motor Vehicles
(D) Cash at Bank.

MC4 Which of the following is incorrect?

	Assets £	Liabilities £	Capital £
(A)	7,850	1,250	6,600
(B)	8,200	2,800	5,400
(C)	9,550	1,150	8,200
(D)	6,540	1,120	5,420

MC5 Which of the following statements is correct?

		Effect upon	
		Assets	Liabilities
(A)	We paid a creditor by cheque	−Bank	−Creditors
(B)	A debtor paid us £90 in cash	+Cash	+Debtors
(C)	J Hall lends us £500 by cheque	+Bank	−Loan from Hall
(D)	Bought goods on credit	+Stock	+Capital

MC6 Which of the following are correct?

	Accounts	To record	Entry in the account
(i)	Assets	an increase	Debit
		a decrease	Credit
(ii)	Capital	an increase	Debit
		a decrease	Credit
(iii)	Liabilities	an increase	Credit
		a decrease	Debit

(A) (i) and (ii)
(B) (ii) and (iii)
(C) (i) and (iii)
(D) None of them.

MC7 Which of the following are correct?

		Account to be debited	Account to be credited
(i)	Bought office furniture for cash	Office furniture	Cash
(ii)	A debtor, P Sangster, pays us by cheque	Bank	P Sangster
(iii)	Introduced capital by cheque	Capital	Bank
(iv)	Paid a creditor, B Lee, by cash	B Lee	Cash

(A) (i), (ii) and (iii) only
(B) (ii), (iii) and (iv) only
(C) (i), (ii) and (iv) only
(D) (i) and (iv) only.

MC8 Which of the following are incorrect?

		Account to be debited	Account to be credited
(i)	Sold motor van for cash	Cash	Motor van
(ii)	Returned some of Office Equipment to Suppliers Ltd	Office Equipment	Suppliers Ltd
(iii)	Repaid part of loan from C Charles by cheque	Loan from C Charles	Bank
(iv)	Bought machinery on credit from Betterways Ltd	Betterways Ltd	Machinery

(A) (ii) and (iv) only
(B) (iii) and (iv) only
(C) (ii) and (iii) only
(D) (i) and (iii) only.

MC9 Which of the following best describes the meaning of 'Purchases'?
(A) Items bought
(B) Goods bought on credit
(C) Goods bought for resale
(D) Goods paid for.

MC10 Which of the following should not be called 'Sales'?
(A) Office fixtures sold
(B) Goods sold on credit
(C) Goods sold for cash
(D) Sale of item previously included in 'Purchases'.

MC11 Of the following, which are correct?

		Account to be debited	Account to be credited
(i)	Goods sold on credit to R Williams	R Williams	Sales
(ii)	S Johnson returns goods to us	Returns inwards	S Johnson
(iii)	Goods bought for cash	Cash	Purchases
(iv)	We returned goods to A Henry	A Henry	Returns inwards

(A) (i) and (iii) only
(B) (i) and (ii) only
(C) (ii) and (iv) only
(D) (iii) and (iv) only.

MC12 Which of the following are incorrect?

		Account to be debited	Account to be credited
(i)	Goods sold for cash	Cash	Sales
(ii)	Goods bought on credit from T Carter	Purchases	T Carter
(iii)	Goods returned by us to C Barry	C Barry	Returns outwards
(iv)	Motor van bought for cash	Purchases	Cash

(A) (i) and (iii) only
(B) (iii) only
(C) (ii) and (iv) only
(D) (iv) only.

MC13 Given the following, what is the amount of Capital? Assets: Premises £20,000, Stock £8,500, Cash £100. Liabilities: Creditors £3,000, Loan from A Adams £4,000
(A) £21,100
(B) £21,600
(C) £32,400
(D) None of the above.

MC14 Which of the following is correct?
(A) Profit does not alter capital
(B) Profit reduces capital
(C) Capital can only come from profit
(D) Profit increases capital.

MC15 Which of the following are correct?

		Account to be debited	Account to be credited
(i)	Received commission by cheque	Bank	Commission received
(ii)	Paid rates by cash	Rates	Cash
(iii)	Paid motor expenses by cheque	Motor expenses	Bank
(iv)	Received refund of insurance by cheque	Insurance	Bank

(A) (i) and (ii) only
(B) (i), (ii) and (iii) only
(C) (ii), (iii) and (iv) only
(D) (i), (ii) and (iv) only.

MC16 Of the following, which are incorrect?

		Account to be debited	*Account to be credited*
(*i*)	Sold motor van for cash	Cash	Sales
(*ii*)	Bought stationery by cheque	Stationery	Bank
(*iii*)	Took cash out of business for private use	Cash	Drawings
(*iv*)	Paid general expenses by cheque	General expenses	Bank

(A) (*ii*) and (*iv*) only
(B) (*i*) and (*ii*) only
(C) (*i*) and (*iii*) only
(D) (*ii*) and (*iii*) only.

MC17 What is the balance on the following account on 31 May 19X5?

C De Freitas

19X5			£	19X5			£
May	1	Sales	205	May	17	Cash	300
„	14	Sales	360	„	28	Returns	50
„	30	Sales	180				

(A) A credit balance of £395
(B) A debit balance of £380
(C) A debit balance of £395
(D) There is a nil balance on the account.

MC18 What would have been the balance on the account of C De Freitas in MC17 on 19 May 19X5?
(A) A debit balance of £265
(B) A credit balance of £95
(C) A credit balance of £445
(D) A credit balance of £265.

MC19 Which of the following best describes a trial balance?
(A) Shows the financial position of a business
(B) It is a special account
(C) Shows all the entries in the books
(D) It is a list of balances on the books.

MC20 Is it true that the trial balance totals should agree?
(A) No, there are sometimes good reasons why they differ
(B) Yes, except where the trial balance is extracted at the year end
(C) Yes, always
(D) No, because it is not a balance sheet.

Set No 2: 20 questions

Answers on p. 645.

MC21 Gross profit is
(A) Excess of sales over cost of goods sold
(B) Sales less Purchases
(C) Cost of goods sold + Opening stock
(D) Net profit less expenses of the period.

MC22 Net profit is calculated in the
(A) Trading account
(B) Profit and loss account
(C) Trial balance
(D) Balance sheet.

MC23 To find the value of closing stock at the end of a period we
(A) do this by stocktaking
(B) look in the stock account
(C) deduct opening stock from cost of goods sold
(D) deduct cost of goods sold from sales.

MC24 The credit entry for net profit is on the credit side of
(A) The trading account
(B) The profit and loss account
(C) The drawings account
(D) The capital account.

MC25 Which is the best definition of a balance sheet?
(A) An account proving the books balance
(B) A record of closing entries
(C) A listing of balances
(D) A statement of assets.

MC26 The descending order in which current assets should be shown in the balance sheet is
(A) Stock, Debtors, Bank, Cash
(B) Cash, Bank, Debtors, Stock
(C) Debtors, Stock, Bank, Cash
(D) Stock, Debtors, Cash, Bank.

MC27 Which is the best description of fixed assets?
(A) Are bought to be used in the business
(B) Are items which will not wear out quickly
(C) Are expensive items bought for the business
(D) Are of long-life and are not bought specifically for resale.

MC28 Carriage inwards is charged to the trading account because
(A) It is an expense connected with buying goods
(B) It should not go in the balance sheet
(C) It is not part of motor expenses
(D) Carriage outwards goes in the profit and loss account.

MC29 Given figures showing: Sales £8,200; Opening stock £1,300; Closing stock £900; Purchases £6,400; Carriage inwards £200, the cost of goods sold figure is
(A) £6,800
(B) £6,200
(C) £7,000
(D) Another figure.

MC30 The costs of putting goods into a saleable condition should be charged to
(A) Trading account
(B) Profit and loss account
(C) Balance sheet
(D) None of these.

MC31 Suppliers' personal accounts are found in
(A)   Nominal ledger
(B)   General ledger
(C)   Purchases ledger
(D)   Sales ledger.

MC32 The Sales Journal is best described as
(A)   Part of the double entry system
(B)   Containing customers' accounts
(C)   Containing real accounts
(D)   A list of credit sales.

MC33 Of the following which are Personal Accounts?
(*i*)   Buildings
(*ii*)   Wages
(*iii*)   Debtors
(*iv*)   Creditors.

(A)   (*i*) and (*iv*) only
(B)   (*ii*) and (*iii*) only
(C)   (*iii*) and (*iv*) only
(D)   (*ii*) and (*iv*) only.

MC34 When Lee makes out a cheque for £50 and sends it to Young, then Lee is known as
(A)   The payee
(B)   The banker
(C)   The drawer
(D)   The creditor.

MC35 If you want to make sure that your money will be safe if cheques sent are lost in the post, you should
(A)   Not use the Postal Service in future
(B)   Always pay by cash
(C)   Always take the money in person
(D)   Cross your cheques 'Account Payee only, Not Negotiable'.

MC36 When banking money in to your current account you should always use
(A)   A cheque book
(B)   A paying-in slip
(C)   A cash book
(D)   A general ledger.

MC37 A debit balance of £100 in a cash account shows that
(A)   There was £100 cash in hand
(B)   Cash has been overspent by £100
(C)   £100 was the total of cash paid out
(D)   The total of cash received was less than £100.

MC38 £50 cash taken from the cash till and banked is entered
(A)   Debit cash column £50: Credit bank column £50
(B)   Debit bank column £50: Credit cash column £50
(C)   Debit cash column £50: Credit cash column £50
(D)   Debit bank column £50: Credit bank column £50.

MC39 A credit balance of £200 on the cash columns of the cash book would mean
(A)   We have spent £200 more than we have received
(B)   We have £200 cash in hand
(C)   The bookkeeper has made a mistake
(D)   Someone has stolen £200 cash.

MC40 'Posting' the transactions in bookkeeping means
(A)   Making the first entry of a double entry transaction
(B)   Entering items in a cash book
(C)   Making the second entry of a double entry transaction
(D)   Something other than the above.

Set No 3: 20 questions

Answers on p. 645.

MC41 A cash discount is best described as a reduction in the sum to be paid
(A)   If payment is made within a previously agreed period
(B)   If payment is made by cash, not cheque
(C)   If payment is made either by cash or cheque
(D)   If purchases are made for cash, not on credit.

MC42 Discounts received are
(A)   Deducted when we receive cash
(B)   Given by us when we sell goods on credit
(C)   Deducted by us when we pay our accounts
(D)   None of these.

MC43 The total of the 'Discounts Allowed' column in the Cash Book is posted to
(A)   The debit of the Discounts Allowed account
(B)   The debit of the Discounts Received account
(C)   The credit of the Discounts Allowed account
(D)   The credit of the Discounts Received account.

MC44 Sales invoices are first entered in
(A)   The Cash Book
(B)   The Purchases Journal
(C)   The Sales Account
(D)   The Sales Journal.

MC45 The total of the Sales Journal is entered on
(A)   The credit side of the Sales Account in the General Ledger
(B)   The credit side of the General Account in the Sales Ledger
(C)   The debit side of the Sales Account in the General Ledger
(D)   The debit side of the Sales Day Book.

MC46 Given a purchases invoice showing 5 items of £80 each, less trade discount of 25 per cent and cash discount of 5 per cent, if paid within the credit period, your cheque would be made out for
(A)   £285
(B)   £280
(C)   £260
(D)   None of these.

MC47 An alternative name for a Sales Journal is
(A) Sales Invoice
(B) Sales Day Book
(C) Daily Sales
(D) Sales Ledger.

MC48 Entered in the Purchases Journal are
(A) Payments to suppliers
(B) Trade discounts
(C) Purchases invoices
(D) Discounts received.

MC49 The total of the Purchases Journal is transferred to the
(A) Credit side of the Purchases Account
(B) Debit side of the Purchases Day Book
(C) Credit side of the Purchases Book
(D) Debit side of the Purchases Account.

MC50 Credit notes issued by us will be entered in our
(A) Sales Account
(B) Returns Inwards Account
(C) Returns Inwards Journal
(D) Returns Outwards Journal.

MC51 The total of the Returns Outwards Journal is transferred to
(A) The credit side of the Returns Outwards Account
(B) The debit side of the Returns Outwards Account
(C) The credit side of the Returns Outwards Book
(D) The debit side of the Purchases Returns Book.

MC52 We originally sold 25 items at £12 each, less $33\frac{1}{3}$ per cent trade discount. Our customer now returns 4 of them to us. What is the amount of credit note to be issued?
(A) £48
(B) £36
(C) £30
(D) £32.

MC53 Depreciation is
(A) The amount spent to buy a fixed asset
(B) The salvage value of a fixed asset
(C) The part of the cost of the fixed asset consumed during its period of use by the firm
(D) The amount of money spent in replacing assets.

MC54 A firm bought a machine for £3,200. It is to be depreciated at a rate of 25 per cent using the Reducing Balance Method. What would be the remaining book value after 2 years?
(A) £1,600
(B) £2,400
(C) £1,800
(D) Some other figure.

MC55 A firm bought a machine for £16,000. It is expected to be used for 5 years then sold for £1,000. What is the annual amount of depreciation if the straight line method is used?
(A)   £3,200
(B)   £3,100
(C)   £3,750
(D)   £3,000.

MC56 At the balance sheet date the balance on the Provision for Depreciation Account is
(A)   Transferred to Depreciation Account
(B)   Transferred to Profit and Loss Account
(C)   Simply deducted from the asset in the Balance Sheet
(D)   Transferred to the Asset Account.

MC57 In the trial balance the balance on the Provision for Depreciation Account is
(A)   Shown as a credit item
(B)   Not shown, as it is part of depreciation
(C)   Shown as a debit item
(D)   Sometimes shown as a credit, sometimes as a debit.

MC58 If a provision for depreciation account is in use then the entries for the year's depreciation would be
(A)   Credit Provision for Depreciation Account, debit Profit and Loss Account
(B)   Debit Asset Account, credit Profit and Loss Account
(C)   Credit Asset Account, debit Provision for Depreciation Account
(D)   Credit Profit and Loss Account, debit Provision for Depreciation Account.

MC59 When the final accounts are prepared the Bad Debts Account is closed by a transfer to the
(A)   Balance Sheet
(B)   Profit and Loss Account
(C)   Trading Account
(D)   Provision for Bad Debts Account.

MC60 A Provision for Bad Debts is created
(A)   When debtors become bankrupt
(B)   When debtors cease to be in business
(C)   To provide for possible bad debts
(D)   To write off bad debts.

Set No 4: 20 questions

Answers on p. 645.

MC61 Working Capital is a term meaning
(A)   The amount of capital invested by the proprietor
(B)   The excess of the current assets over the current liabilities
(C)   The capital less drawings
(D)   The total of Fixed Assets – Current Assets.

MC62 A credit balance brought down on a Rent Account means
(A)   We owe that rent at that date
(B)   We have paid that rent in advance at that date
(C)   We have paid too much rent
(D)   We have paid too little in rent.

MC63 A debit balance brought down on a Packing Materials Account means
(A) We owe for packing materials
(B) We are owed for packing materials
(C) We have lost money on packing materials
(D) We have a stock of packing materials unused.

MC64 If we take goods for own use we should
(A) Debit Drawings Account: Credit Purchases Account
(B) Debit Purchases Account: Credit Drawings Account
(C) Debit Drawings Account: Credit Stock Account
(D) Debit Sales Account: Credit Stock Account.

MC65 Capital Expenditure is
(A) The extra capital paid in by the proprietor
(B) The costs of running the business on a day-to-day basis
(C) Money spent on buying fixed assets or adding value to them
(D) Money spent on selling fixed assets.

MC66 In the business of C Sangster, who owns a clothing store, which of the following are Capital Expenditure?
(*i*) Shop fixtures bought
(*ii*) Wages of assistants
(*iii*) New motor van bought
(*iv*) Petrol for motor van.

(A) (*i*) and (*iii*)
(B) (*i*) and (*ii*)
(C) (*ii*) and (*iii*)
(D) (*ii*) and (*iv*).

MC67 If £500 was shown added to Purchases instead of being added to a fixed asset
(A) Net profit only would be understated
(B) Net profit only would be overstated
(C) It would not affect net profit
(D) Both gross and net profits would be understated.

MC68 A cheque paid by you, but not yet passed through the banking system, is
(A) A standing order
(B) A dishonoured cheque
(C) A credit transfer
(D) An unpresented cheque.

MC69 A Bank Reconciliation Statement is a statement
(A) Sent by the bank when the account is overdrawn
(B) Drawn up by us to verify our cash book balance with the bank statement balance
(C) Drawn up by the bank to verify the cash book
(D) Sent by the bank when we have made an error.

MC70 Which of the following are not true? A Bank Reconciliation Statement is
(*i*) Part of the double entry system
(*ii*) Not part of the double entry system
(*iii*) Sent by the firm to the bank
(*iv*) Posted to the ledger accounts.

(A) (*i*), (*iii*) and (*iv*)
(B) (*i*) and (*ii*)
(C) (*i*), (*ii*) and (*iv*)
(D) (*ii*), (*iii*) and (*iv*).

MC71 Which of the following should be entered in the Journal?
(*i*)   Payment for cash purchases
(*ii*) Fixtures bought on credit
(*iii*) Credit sale of goods
(*iv*) Sale of surplus machinery.

(A)   (*i*) and (*iv*)
(B)   (*ii*) and (*iii*)
(C)   (*iii*) and (*iv*)
(D)   (*ii*) and (*iv*).

MC72 The Journal is
(A)   Part of the double entry system
(B)   A supplement to the Cash Book
(C)   Not part of the double entry system
(D)   Used when other journals have been mislaid.

MC73 Given a desired cash float of £200, if £146 is spent in the period, how much will be reimbursed at the end of the period?
(A)   £200
(B)   £54
(C)   £254
(D)   £146.

MC74 When a petty cash book is kept there will be
(A)   More entries made in the general ledger
(B)   Fewer entries made in the general ledger
(C)   The same number of entries in the general ledger
(D)   No entries made at all in the general ledger for items paid by petty cash.

MC75 Which of the following do *not* affect trial balance agreement?
(*i*)   Sales £105 to A Henry entered in P Henry's account
(*ii*) Cheque payment of £134 for Motor expenses entered only in Cash Book
(*iii*) Purchases £440 from C Browne entered in both accounts as £404
(*iv*) Wages account added up incorrectly, being totalled £10 too much.

(A)   (*i*) and (*iv*)
(B)   (*i*) and (*iii*)
(C)   (*ii*) and (*iii*)
(D)   (*iii*) and (*iv*).

MC76 Which of the following are *not* errors of principle?
(*i*)   Motor expenses entered in Motor Vehicles account
(*ii*) Purchases of machinery entered in Purchases account
(*iii*) Sale of £250 to C Phillips completely omitted from books
(*iv*) Sale to A Henriques entered in A Henry's account.

(A)   (*ii*) and (*iii*)
(B)   (*i*) and (*ii*)
(C)   (*iii*) and (*iv*)
(D)   (*i*) and (*iv*).

MC77 Errors are corrected via the Journal because
(A)   It saves the bookkeeper's time
(B)   It saves entering them in the ledger
(C)   It is much easier to do
(D)   It provides a good record explaining the double entry records.

MC78 Which of these errors would be disclosed by the trial balance?
(A)   Cheque £95 from C Smith entered in Smith's account as £59
(B)   Selling expenses had been debited to Sales Account
(C)   Credit sales of £300 entered in both double entry accounts as £30
(D)   A purchase of £250 was omitted entirely from the books.

MC79 If a trial balance totals do *not* agree, the difference must be entered in
(A)   The Profit and Loss Account
(B)   A Suspense Account
(C)   A Nominal Account
(D)   The Capital Account.

MC80 What should happen if the balance on Suspense Account is of a material amount?
(A)   Should be written off to the balance sheet
(B)   Carry forward the balance to the next period
(C)   Find the error(s) before publishing the final accounts
(D)   Write it off to Profit and Loss Account.

Set No 5: 20 questions

Answers on p. 645.

MC81 Given opening debtors of £11,500, Sales £48,000 and receipts from debtors £45,000, the closing debtors should total
(A)   £8,500
(B)   £14,500
(C)   £83,500
(D)   £18,500.

MC82 In a Sales Ledger Control Account the Bad Debts written off should be shown in the account
(A)   As a debit
(B)   As a credit
(C)   Both as a debit and as a credit
(D)   As a balance carried down.

MC83 If cost price is £90 and selling price is £120, then
(*i*)   Mark-up is 25 per cent
(*ii*)   Margin is $33\frac{1}{3}$ per cent
(*iii*) Margin is 25 per cent
(*iv*)   Mark-up is $33\frac{1}{3}$ per cent.

(A)   (*i*) and (*ii*)
(B)   (*i*) and (*iii*)
(C)   (*iii*) and (*iv*)
(D)   (*ii*) and (*iv*).

MC84 Given cost of goods sold £16,000 and margin of 20 per cent, then sales figure is
(A)   £20,160
(B)   £13,600
(C)   £21,000
(D)   None of these.

MC85 If opening stock is £3,000, closing stock £5,000, sales £40,000 and margin 20 per cent, then stockturn is
(A) 8 times
(B) 7½ times
(C) 5 times
(D) 6 times.

MC86 If creditors at 1 January 19X3 were £2,500, creditors at 31 December 19X3 £4,200 and payments to creditors £32,000, then purchases for 19X3 are
(A) £30,300
(B) £33,700
(C) £31,600
(D) None of these.

MC87 Given opening capital of £16,500, closing capital as £11,350 and drawings were £3,300, then
(A) Loss for the year was £1,850
(B) Profit for the year was £1,850
(C) Loss for the year was £8,450
(D) Profit for the year was £8,450.

MC88 A Receipts and Payments Account is one
(A) Which is accompanied by a balance sheet
(B) In which the profit is calculated
(C) In which the opening and closing cash balances are shown
(D) In which the surplus of income over expenditure is calculated.

MC89 Prime cost includes
(*i*) Direct labour
(*ii*) Factory overhead expenses
(*iii*) Raw materials consumed
(*iv*) Direct expenses.

(A) (*i*), (*ii*) and (*iii*)
(B) (*ii*), (*iii*) and (*iv*)
(C) (*i*), (*iii*) and (*iv*)
(D) (*i*), (*ii*) and (*iv*).

MC90 Which of the following should be charged in the Profit and Loss Account?
(A) Office rent
(B) Work in progress
(C) Direct materials
(D) Carriage on raw materials.

MC91 In the Manufacturing Account is calculated
(A) The production costs paid in the year
(B) The total cost of goods produced
(C) The production cost of goods completed in the period
(D) The gross profit on goods sold.

MC92 The best method of departmental accounts is
(A) To allocate expenses in proportion to sales
(B) To charge against each department its controllable costs
(C) To allocate expenses in proportion to purchases
(D) To charge against each department its uncontrollable costs.

MC93 Where there is no partnership agreement then profits and losses
(A) Must be shared in same proportion as capitals
(B) Must be shared equally
(C) Must be shared equally after adjusting for interest on capital
(D) None of these.

MC94 If it is required to maintain fixed capitals then the partners' shares of profits must be
(A) Debited to capital accounts
(B) Credited to capital accounts
(C) Debited to partners' current accounts
(D) Credited to partners' current accounts.

MC95 You are to buy an existing business which has assets valued at buildings £50,000, Motor vehicles £15,000, Fixtures £5,000 and Stock £40,000. You are to pay £140,000 for the business. This means that
(A) You are paying £40,000 for Goodwill
(B) Buildings are costing you £30,000 more than their value
(C) You are paying £30,000 for Goodwill
(D) You have made an arithmetical mistake.

MC96 Assets can be revalued in a partnership change because
(A) The law insists upon it
(B) It helps prevent injustice to some partners
(C) Inflation affects all values

MC97 Any loss on revaluation is
(A) Credited to old partners in old profit-sharing ratios
(B) Credited to new partners in new profit-sharing ratios
(C) Debited to old partners in old profit-sharing ratios
(D) Debited to new partners in new profit-sharing ratios.

MC98 In a limited company which of the following are shown in the Appropriation Account?
(*i*) Debenture interest
(*ii*) Proposed dividend
(*iii*) Transfers to reserves
(*iv*) Directors' remuneration.

(A) (*i*) and (*ii*)
(B) (*ii*) and (*iii*)
(C) (*i*) and (*iv*)
(D) (*ii*) and (*iv*).

MC99 The Issued Capital of a company is
(A) Always the same as the Authorised Capital
(B) The same as Preference Share Capital
(C) Equal to the reserves of the company
(D) None of the above.

MC100 A company wishes to pay out all available profits as dividends. Net profit is £26,600. There are 20,000 8% Preference shares of £1 each, and 50,000 Ordinary shares of £1 each. £5,000 is to be transferred to General Reserve. What Ordinary dividends are to be paid, in percentage terms?
(A) 20 per cent
(B) 40 per cent
(C) 10 per cent
(D) 60 per cent.

Appendix IV Answers to review questions

(*Note*: All the answers are the work of the author. None has been supplied by an examining body.
The examining bodies accept no responsibility whatsoever for the accuracy or method of working in the answers given.)
(*Note*: In order to save space, £ signs have been omitted from columns of figures, except where the figures refer to £000, or where the denomination needs to be specified.)

1.1 (a) 10,700 (b) 23,100 (c) 4,300 (d) 3,150
    (e) 25,500 (f) 51,400

1.3 (a) Asset (b) Liability (c) Asset
    (d) Asset (e) Liability (f) Asset

1.5 Wrong: Assets: Loan from C Smith, Creditors; Liabilities: Stock of goods, Debtors.

1.7 Assets: Motor 2,000; Premises 5,000; Stock 1,000; Bank 700; Cash 100 = total 8,800.
Liabilities: Loan from Bevan 3,000; Creditors 400 = total 3,400. Capital 8,800 − 3,400 = 5,400.

1.9 (Horizontal)

A Foster
Balance Sheet as at 31 December 19X8

Fixtures	5,500	Capital	23,750
Motor vehicles	5,700	Creditors	2,450
Stock of goods	8,800		
Debtors	4,950		
Cash at bank	1,250		
	26,200		26,200

(Vertical)

A Foster
Balance Sheet as at 31 December 19X8

Fixed assets		
Fixtures	5,500	
Motor vehicles	5,700	11,200
Current assets		
Stock of goods	8,800	
Debtors	4,950	
Cash at bank	1,250	
	15,000	
Less Current liabilities		
Creditors	2,450	
		12,550
		23,750
Capital		23,750

1.11

	Assets	Liabilities	Capital
(a)	− Cash	− Creditors	
(b)	− Bank		
	+ Fixtures		
(c)	+ Stock	+ Creditors	
(d)	+ Cash		
(e)	+ Cash	+ Loan from J Walker	+ Capital
(f)	+ Bank		
	− Debtors		
(g)	− Stock	− Creditors	
(h)	+ Premises		
	− Bank		

1.13 (Horizontal)

C Sangster
Balance Sheet as at 7 May 19X8

Assets		Capital and Liabilities	
Fixtures	4,500	Capital	20,900
Motor vehicle	4,200	Creditors	2,370
Stock	5,720		
Debtors	3,000		
Bank	5,450		
Cash	400		
	23,270		23,270

(Vertical)

C Sangster
Balance sheet as at 7 May 19X8

Fixed assets		
Fixtures	4,500	
Motor vehicle	4,200	8,700
Current assets		
Stock	5,720	
Debtors	3,000	
Bank	5,450	
Cash	400	
	14,570	
Less current liabilities		
Creditors	2,370	12,200
		20,900
Capital		20,900

2.1

Debited	Credited
(a) Office machinery	D Isaacs Ltd
(b) C Jones	Capital
(c) Cash	N Fox
(d) Loan: P Exeter	Bank
(e) D Isaacs Ltd	Office machinery
(f) Bank	N Lyn
(g) Motor van	Cash

2.3

Bank

(1) Capital	2,500	(2) Office furn.	150
		(5) Motor van	600
		(15) Planers	750
		(31) Machinery	280
(23) J Walker	60		

Capital

| | | (1) Bank | 2,500 |

Office Furniture

| (2) Bank | 150 | (8) J Walker | 60 |

Machinery

| (3) Planers Ltd | 750 | | |
| (31) Bank | 280 | | |

Cash

| (23) J Walker | 60 | | |

Planers Ltd

| (15) Bank | 750 | (3) Machinery | 750 |

Motor Van

| (5) Bank | 600 | | |

J Walker & Sons

| (8) Off. furn. | 60 | (23) Cash | 60 |

2.4

Bank

(1) Capital	1,800	(8) Motor Van	950
(30) J Smith	500	(26) Betta-Built	58
		(28) Cash	100

Cash

(1) Capital	2,000	(2) Bank	75
		(25) W Machinery	75
		(28) Bank	100

Betta-Built Ltd

| (18) Office furn. | 62 | (5) Office furn. | 120 |
| (26) Bank | 58 | | |

Capital

| | | (1) Cash | 2,000 |

Office Furniture

| (5) Betta-Built | 120 | (18) B Built | 62 |

Motor Van

| (8) Bank | 950 | | |

Works Machinery

| (12) Evans & Sons | 560 | (25) Cash | 560 |

Evans & Sons

| | | (12) Works machinery | 560 |

J Smith (Loan)

| | 75 | (30) Bank | 500 |

3.1

Debited	Credited
(a) Purchases	J Reid
(b) B Perkins	Sales
(c) Motor Van	H Thomas
(d) Bank	Returns Inwards
(e) Cash	Sales
(f) H Hardy	Returns Outwards
(g) Cash	Machinery
(h) Returns Inwards	J Nelson
(i) Purchases	D Simpson
(i) H Forbes	Returns Outwards

3.3

Cash

(1) Capital	500	(3) Purchases	85
(10) Sales	42	(25) E Morgan	88
(31) A Knight	55		

Purchases

(3) Cash	85		
(7) E Morgan	116		
(18) A Moses	98		

Sales

| | | (10) Cash | 42 |
| | | (24) A Knight | 55 |

Returns Outwards

| | | (14) E Morgan | 28 |
| | | (21) A Moses | 19 |

A Knight

| (24) Sales | 55 | (31) Cash | 55 |

E Morgan

| (14) Returns | 28 | (7) Purchases | 116 |
| (25) Cash | 88 | | |

A Moses

| (25) Cash | 88 | (18) Purchases | 98 |
| (21) Returns | 19 | | |

Capital

| | | (1) Cash | 500 |

3.5

Bank

Dr		Cr	
(1) Capital	10,000	(25) F Jones	250
(6) Cash	250	(29) Manchester M	2,600

Cash

Dr		Cr	
(2) T Cooper (Loan)	400	(6) Bank	250
(4) Sales	500	(20) Purchases	220
		(31) Office Furn	100
		(24) Sales	70

Sales

Dr		Cr	
		(4) Cash	200
		(8) C Moody	180
		(10) J Newman	220
		(14) H Morgan	190
		(14) J Peat	320
		(24) Cash	70

Purchases

Dr		Cr	
(3) F Jones	840		
(3) S Charles	3,600		
(11) F Jones	370		
(20) Cash	220		

Returns Inwards

Dr		Cr	
(12) C Moody	40		
(26) H Morgan	30		

Returns Outwards

Dr		Cr	
		(15) F Jones	140
		(19) S Charles	110

Motor Van

Dr		Cr	
(17) Manchester Motors	2,600		

Manchester Motors

Dr		Cr	
(29) Bank	2,600	(17) Motor van	2,600

Office Furniture

Dr		Cr	
(18) Faster S	600	(27) Faster S	160
(31) Cash	100		

Faster Supplies Ltd

Dr		Cr	
(27) Office furn.	160	(18) Office furn.	600

Capital

Dr		Cr	
		(1) Bank	10,000

F Jones

Dr		Cr	
(15) Returns	140	(3) Purchases	840
(25) Bank	250	(11) Purchases	370

S Charles

Dr		Cr	
(19) Returns	110	(3) Purchases	3,600

T Cooper (Loan)

Dr		Cr	
		(2) Cash	400

J Newman

Dr		Cr	
		(10) Sales	220

H Morgan

Dr		Cr	
(26) Returns	30	(14) Sales	190

C Moody

Dr		Cr	
(12) Returns	40	(8) Sales	180

J Peat

Dr		Cr	
		(14) Sales	320

4.1

Capital

Dr		Cr	
		(1) Bank	2,000

Bank

Dr		Cr	
(1) Capital	2,000	(3) Fixtures	150
(21) Rent	5	(24) Motor van	300

M Mills

Dr		Cr	
(18) Returns out	23	(2) Purchases	175

Cash

Dr		Cr	
(5) Sales	275	(10) Rent	15
		(12) Stationery	27
		(30) Wages	117
		(31) Drawings	44

S Waites

Dr		Cr	
		(6) Purchases	114

Purchases

Dr		Cr	
(2) D Miller	175		
(6) S Waites	114		

U Henry

Dr		Cr	
		(23) Sales	77

Rent Received

Dr		Cr	
		(21) Bank	5

Sales

Dr		Cr	
		(5) Cash	275
		(23) U Henry	77

Stationery

Dr		Cr	
(12) Cash	27		

Returns Out

Dr		Cr	
		(18) M Mills	23

Fixtures

Dr		Cr	
(3) Bank	150		

Motor Van

Dr		Cr	
(24) Bank	300		

Rent

Dr		Cr	
(10) Cash	15		

Wages

Dr		Cr	
(30) Cash	117		

Drawings

Dr		Cr	
(31) Cash	44		

4.2

Capital

Dr		Cr	
		(1) Cash	1,500

Cash

Dr		Cr	
(1) Capital	1,500	(3) Rent	28
(11) Sales	49	(4) Bank	1,000
		(20) B Repairs	18
		(28) Purchases	125
		(30) Motor exps	15

Rent

Dr		Cr	
(3) Cash	28		

Building Repairs

Dr		Cr	
(20) Cash	18		

Motor Expenses

Dr		Cr	
(30) Cash	15		

Bank

Dr		Cr	
(4) Cash	1,000	(7) Stationery	15
		(27) A Hanson	279
		(29) Motor van	395

Motor Van

Dr		Cr	
(29) Bank	395		

A Hanson

Dr		Cr	
(14) Returns out	17	(2) Purchases	296
(27) Bank	279		

Purchases

Dr		Cr	
(2) A Hanson	296		
(28) Cash	125		

Sales

Dr		Cr	
		(5) E Linton	54
		(11) Cash	49
		(17) S Morgan	29

E Linton

Dr		Cr	
(5) Sales	54	(22) Returns in	14
(11) Cash	49		

S Morgan

Dr		Cr	
		(17) Sales	29

Stationery

Dr		Cr	
(7) Bank	15		

Returns Inwards

Dr		Cr	
(22) E Linton	14		

Returns Outwards

Dr		Cr	
		(14) A Hanson	17

A Webster

Dr		Cr	
		(31) Fixtures	120

Fixtures

Dr		Cr	
(31) A Webster	120		

4.5

(A) Bought motor vehicle £5,000, paying by bank.
(B) Paid off £4,000 creditors in cash.
(C) Lee lent us £150,000, this being paid into the bank.
(D) Bought land and buildings £125,000, paying by bank.
(E) Debtors paid cheques £80,000, being paid into bank.
(F) Land and buildings sold for £300,000, the proceeds being paid into the bank.
(G) Loan from Lee repaid out of the bank.
(H) Creditors £8,000 paid in cash.
(I) Stock costing £17,000 sold for £12,000 on credit. Loss of £5,000 shown deducted from Capital.

5.1

N Morgan

(1) Sales	153	(18) Bank	153	

J Lindo

(1) Sales	420	(10) Returns	20	
		(20) Bank	400	
	420		420	

L Masters

(4) Sales	418	(31) Balance c/d	621	
(31) Sales	203			
	621		621	
(1) Balance b/d	621			

5.2

H Harvey

(1) Sales	690	(10) Returns	40	
(4) Sales	66	(24) Cash	300	
		(31) Balance c/d	416	
	756		756	
(1) Balance b/d	416			

J Young

(10) Returns	55	(1) Purchases	458	
(28) Cash	250	(15) Purchases	80	
(30) Balance c/d	233			
	538		538	
		(1) Balance b/d	233	

L Williams

(10) Returns	17	(1) Purchases	120	
(30) Balance c/d	180	(1) Purchases	77	
	197		197	
		(1) Balance b/d	180	

G Norman

(10) Returns	22	(1) Purchases	708	
(30) Balance c/d	686			
	708		708	
		(1) Balance b/d	686	

T Harris

(19) Bank	880	(3) Purchases	880	

5.3

H Harvey

19X6		Dr	Cr	Balance	
May 1	Sales	690		690	Dr
May 4	Sales	66		756	Dr
May 10	Returns		40	716	Dr
May 24	Cash		300	416	Dr

5.4

N Morgan

19X6		Dr	Cr	Balance	
May 1	Sales	153		153	Dr
May 18	Bank		153	0	

J Lindo

19X6		Dr	Cr	Balance	
May 1	Sales	420		420	Dr
May 10	Returns		20	400	Dr
May 20	Bank		400	0	

L Masters

19X6		Dr	Cr	Balance	
May 4	Sales	418		418	Dr
May 31	Sales	203		621	Dr

J Young

19X8		Dr	Cr	Balance	
Jun 1	Purchases		458	458	Cr
Jun 10	Returns	55		403	Cr
Jun 15	Purchases		80	483	Cr
Jun 28	Cash	250		233	Cr

L Williams

19X8		Dr	Cr	Balance	
Jun 1	Purchases		120	120	Cr
Jun 3	Purchases		77	197	Cr
Jun 30	Returns	17		180	Cr

G Norman

19X8		Dr	Cr	Balance	
Jun 1	Purchases		708	708	Cr
Jun 10	Returns	22		686	Cr

T Harris

19X8		Dr	Cr	Balance	
Jun 3	Purchases		880	880	Cr
Jun 19	Bank	880		0	

5.5

D Williams

(1) Sales	458	(20) Bank	300	
		(28) Cash	100	
		(30) Balance c/d	58	
	458		458	
(1) Balance b/d	58			

A White

		Cr	Balance	
(2) Purchases		77	77	Cr

H Samuels

(17) Returns	24	(2) Purchases	231	
(30) Balance c/d	219	(10) Purchases	12	
	243		243	
		(1) Balance b/d	219	

P Owen

		Cr	Balance	
(2) Purchases		65	65	Cr

G Grant

(1) Sales	98	(12) Returns	9
		(30) Balance c/d	89
	98		98
(1) Balance b/d	89		

F Franklin

(8) Sales	249	(30) Bank	249

O Oliver

(17) Returns	12	(10) Purchases	222
(26) Cash	210		
	222		222

6.1

Cash

(1) Capital	250	(6) Rent	12
		(15) Carriage	23
		(31) Balance c/d	215
	250		250

Bank

(9) C Bailey	43	(12) K Gibson	25
(10) H Spencer	150	(12) D Ellis	54
		(31) Rent	18
		(31) Balance c/d	96
	193		193

Capital

		(1) Cash	250

Rent

(6) Cash	12		
(31) Bank	18		

Carriage

(15) Cash	23		

D Ellis

(12) Bank	54	(2) Purchases	54

C Mendez

		(2) Purchases	87
		(18) Purchases	43

K Gibson

(12) Bank	25	(2) Purchases	25

D Booth

		(2) Purchases	76
		(18) Purchases	110

L Lowe

		(2) Purchases	64

C Bailey

(4) Sales	43	(9) Bank	43

B Hughes

(4) Sales	62		
(21) Sales	67		

H Spencer

(4) Sales	176	(10) Bank	150

Purchases

(2) D Ellis	54		
(2) C Mendez	87		
(2) K Gibson	25		
(2) D Booth	76		
(2) L Lowe	64		
(18) C Mendez	43		
(18) D Booth	110		

Sales

		(4) C Bailey	43
		(4) B Hughes	62
		(4) H Spencer	176
		(21) B Hughes	67

Trial Balance as at 31 May 19X6

	Dr	Cr
Cash	215	
Bank	96	
Capital		250
Rent	30	
Carriage	23	
C Mendez		130
D Booth		186
L Lowe		64
B Hughes	129	
H Spencer	26	
Purchases	459	
Sales		348
	978	978

6.2

Bank

(1) Capital	800	(17) M Hyatt	84
(24) J Carlton	95	(21) Betta Ltd	50
		(31) Motor van	400
		(31) Balance c/d	361
	895		895

Cash

(5) Sales	87	(6) Wages	14
(30) J King (Loan)	60	(9) Purchases	46
		(12) Wages	14
		(31) Balance c/d	73
	147		147

Capital

		(1) Bank	800

Motor Van

(31) Bank	400		

Wages

(6) Cash	14		
(12) Cash	14		

Shop Fixtures

(15) Betta Ltd	50		

J King (Loan)

		(30) Cash	60

H Elliott

(7) Sales	35		

L Lane

(7) Sales	42		
(13) Sales	32		

J Carlton

(7) Sales	72	(24) Bank	95
(13) Sales	23		

K Henriques

(27) Returns	24	(2) Purchases	76

M Hyatt

(17) Bank	84	(2) Purchases	27
		(10) Purchases	57

T Braham

(18) Returns	20	(2) Purchases	56
		(10) Purchases	98

Betta Ltd

(21) Bank	50	(15) S. Fixtures	50

Sales

		(5) Cash	87
		(7) H Elliott	35
		(7) L Lane	42
		(7) J Carlton	72
		(13) L Lane	32
		(13) J Carlton	23

Purchases

(2) K Henriques	76		
(2) M Hyatt	27		
(2) T Braham	56		
(9) Cash	46		
(10) M Hyatt	57		
(10) T Braham	98		

Returns Outwards

		(18) T Braham	20
		(27) K Henriques	24

Trial Balance as on 31 March 19X6

	Dr	Cr
Bank	361	
Cash	73	
Capital		800
Motor van	400	
Wages	28	
Shop fixtures	50	
J King (Loan)		60
H Elliott	35	
L Lane	74	
K Henriques		52
T Braham		134
Sales		291
Purchases	360	
Returns outwards		44
	1,381	1,381

7.1

(Horizontal)

B Webb

Trading and Profit and Loss Account for the year ended 31 December 19X6

Purchases	14,629	Sales	18,462
Less Closing stock	2,548		
	12,081		
Cost of goods sold	6,381		
Gross profit c/d	6,381		
	18,462		18,462
Salaries	2,150	Gross profit b/d	6,381
Motor expenses	520		
Rent and Rates	670		
Insurance	111		
General expenses	105		
Net profit	2,825		
	6,381		6,381

(Vertical)

B Webb

Trading and Profit and Loss Account for the year ended 31 December 19X6

Sales		18,462
Less Cost of goods sold:		
Purchases	14,629	
Less Closing stock	2,548	
		12,081
Gross profit		6,381
Less Expenses:		
Salaries	2,150	
Motor expenses	520	
Rent and rates	670	
Insurance	111	
General expenses	105	
		3,556
Net profit		2,825

7.2

(Horizontal)

C Worth

Trading and Profit and Loss Account for the year ended 30 June 19X8

Purchases	23,803	Sales	28,794
Less Closing stock	4,166		
	19,637		
Cost of goods sold	9,157		
Gross profit c/d	9,157		
	28,794		28,794
Salaries	3,164	Gross profit b/d	9,157
Rent	854		
Lighting	422		
Insurance	105		
Motor expenses	1,133		
Sundry expenses	506		
Net profit	2,973		
	9,157		9,157

(Vertical)

C Worth

Trading and Profit and Loss Account for the year ended 30 June 19X8

Sales		28,794
Less Cost of goods sold:		
Purchases	23,803	
Less Closing stock	4,166	
		19,637
Gross profit c/d		9,157
Less Expenses:		
Salaries	3,164	
Rent	854	
Lighting	422	
Insurance	105	
Motor expenses	1,133	
Sundry expenses	506	
		6,184
Net profit		2,973

8.1

B Webb

Balance Sheet as at 31 December 19X6

Fixed assets		
Premises	1,500	
Motors	1,200	
		2,700
Current assets		
Stock	2,548	
Debtors	1,950	
Bank	1,654	
Cash	40	
	6,192	
	8,892	
Capital		
Balance at 1.1.19X6	5,424	
Add Net profit	2,825	
	8,249	
Less Drawings	895	
		7,354
Current liabilities		
Creditors		1,538
		8,892

8.2

(Vertical)

B Webb
Balance Sheet as at 31 December 19X6

Fixed assets		
Premises	1,500	
Motors	1,200	2,700
Current assets		
Stock	2,548	
Debtors	1,950	
Bank	1,654	
Cash	40	
	6,192	
Less Current liabilities		
Creditors	1,538	4,654
		7,354
Capital		
Balance at 1.1.19X6		5,424
Add Net profit		2,825
		8,249
Less Drawings		895
		7,354

(Vertical)

C Worth
Balance Sheet as at 30 June 19X8

Fixed assets		
Buildings	50,000	
Fixtures	1,000	
Motors	5,500	56,500
Current assets		
Stock	4,166	
Debtors	3,166	
Bank	3,847	
	11,179	
Less Current liabilities		
Creditors	1,206	9,973
		66,473
Capital		
Balance at 1.7.19X7		65,900
Add Net profit		2,973
		68,873
Less Drawings		2,400
		66,473

(Horizontal)

C Worth
Balance Sheet as at 30 June 19X8

Capital			Fixed assets		
Balance at 1.7.19X7		50,000	Buildings		65,900
Add Net profit		1,000	Fixtures		2,973
		5,500	Motors		68,873
		56,500			2,400
Current liabilities			Current assets		
Creditors		11,179	Stock	4,166	
		67,679	Debtors	3,166	
			Bank	3,847	66,473
					1,206
					67,679

9.1

(Horizontal)

T Clarke
Trading Account for the year ended 31 December 19X7

Purchases	33,333		Sales		38,742
Less Returns out	495	32,838	Less Returns in		890
Carriage inwards		670			37,852
		33,508			
Less Closing stock		7,489			
Cost of goods sold		26,019			
Gross profit		11,833			
		37,852			37,852

(Vertical)

T Clarke
Trading Account for the year ended 31 December 19X7

Sales		38,742
Less Returns in		890
		37,852
Less Cost of goods sold:		
Purchases		33,333
Less Returns out		495
		32,838
Carriage inwards		670
		33,508
Less Closing stock		7,489
		26,019
Gross profit		11,833

9.3

(Horizontal)

R Graham
Trading and Profit and Loss Account for the year ended 30 September 19X9

Opening stock		2,368		Sales	18,600	
Add Purchases	11,874			Less Returns in	205	18,395
Less Returns out	322	11,552				
Carriage inwards		310				
		14,230				
Less Closing stock		2,946				
Cost of goods sold		11,284				
Gross profit c/d		7,111				
		18,395				18,395

Salaries and wages	3,862	Gross profit b/d	7,111
Rent and rates	304		
Carriage out	200		
Insurance	78		
Motor expenses	664		
Office expenses	216		
Lighting and heating	166		
General expenses	314		
Net profit	1,307		
	7,111		7,111

Balance Sheet as at 30 September 19X9

Capital				*Fixed assets*		
Balance at 1.10.19X8		12,636		Premises		5,000
Add Net profit		1,307		Fixtures		350
		13,943		Motor vehicles		1,800
Less Drawings		1,200				7,150
		12,743		*Current assets*		
Current liabilities				Stock	2,946	
Creditors		1,731		Debtors	3,896	
		14,474		Bank	482	7,324
						14,474

(Vertical)

R Graham
Trading and Profit and Loss Account for the year ended 30 September 19X9

Sales		18,600	
Less Returns in		205	
			18,395
Less Cost of goods sold:			
Opening stock		2,368	
Add Purchases	11,874		
Less Returns out	322	11,552	
Carriage inwards		310	
		14,230	
Less Closing stock		2,946	11,284
Gross profit			7,111
Less Expenses:			
Salaries and wages		3,862	
Rent and rates		304	
Carriage out		200	
Insurance		78	
Motor expenses		664	
Office expenses		216	
Lighting and heating		166	
General expenses		314	5,804
Net profit			1,307

Balance Sheet as at 30 September 19X9

Fixed assets			
Premises		5,000	
Fixtures		350	
Motor vehicles		1,800	7,150
Current assets			
Stock		2,946	
Debtors		3,896	
Bank		482	
		7,324	
Less Current liabilities			
Creditors		1,731	5,593
			12,743
Capital			
Balance at 1.10.19X8		12,636	
Add Net profit		1,307	
		13,943	
Less Drawings		1,200	12,743

9.4

(Horizontal)

B Jackson

Trading and Profit and Loss Account for the year ended 30 April 19X7

Opening stock		3,776	Sales	18,600
Add Purchases	11,556		Less Returns in	440
Less Returns out	355	11,201		18,160
		234		
Carriage inwards		15,211		
		4,998		
Less Closing stock		10,213		
		7,947		
Gross profit c/d		18,160		18,160
Salaries and wages		2,447	Gross profit b/d	7,947
Motor expenses		664		
Rent		576		
Carriage out		326		
Sundry expenses		1,202		
Net profit		2,732		
		7,947		7,947

Balance Sheet as at 30 April 19X7

Fixed assets			*Capital*		
Fixtures		600	Balance as at 1.5.19X6		12,844
Motors		2,400	Add Net profit		2,732
		3,000			15,576
			Less Drawings		2,050
Current Assets					13,526
Stock	4,998				
Debtors	4,577		*Current liabilities*		
Bank	3,876		Creditors		3,045
Cash	120	13,571			16,571
		16,571			

(Vertical)

B Jackson

Trading and Profit and Loss Account for the year ended 30 April 19X7

Sales			18,600
Less Returns in			440
			18,160
Less Cost of goods sold:			
Opening stock		3,776	
Add Purchases	11,556		
Less Returns out	355	11,201	
		234	
Carriage inwards		15,211	
		4,998	
Less Closing stock		10,213	
Gross profit			7,947
Less Expenses:			
Salaries and wages		2,447	
Motor expenses		664	
Rent		576	
Carriage out		326	
Sundry expenses		1,202	5,215
Net profit			2,732

Balance Sheet as at 30 April 19X7

Fixed assets			
Fixtures		600	
Motors		2,400	3,000
Current assets			
Stock		4,998	
Debtors		4,577	
Bank		3,876	
Cash		120	
		13,571	
Less Current Liabilities			
Creditors		3,045	10,526
			13,526
Capital			
Balance as at 1.5.19X6			12,844
Add Net profit			2,732
			15,576
Less Drawings			2,050
			13,526

13.1

Cash Book

	Cash	Bank			Cash	Bank
(1) Capital	100		(2) Rent		10	65
(3) F Lake (Loan)		500	(4) B McKenzie			
(5) Sales	98		(9) B Burton			
(7) N Miller		62	(16) Bank C		22	
(11) Sales		53	(19) F Lake (Loan)		50	
(15) G Moores	65		(16) Bank C			100
(16) Cash C						12
(22) Sales			(26) Motor Expenses			100
(30) Bank C	100		(30) Cash C			
			(31) Wages		97	100
			(31) Balances c/d		184	454
	363	**731**			**363**	**731**

13.3

Cash Book

	Disc	Cash	Bank			Disc	Cash	Bank
(1) Balance b/d		230	4,756	(4) Rent				120
(2) R Burton	7		133	(8) N Black		9		351
(2) E Taylor	11		209	(8) P Towers		12		468
(2) R Harris	15		285	(8) C Rowse		20		780
(6) J Cotton: loan			1,000	(10) Motor expenses			44	
(12) H Hankins	3		74	(15) Wages			160	
(18) C Winston	13		247	(21) Cash				350
(18) R Wilson & Son	17		323	(24) Drawings			120	
(18) H Winter	23		437	(25) T Briers		7	133	
(21) Bank		350		(29) Fixtures				650
(31) Commission			88	(31) Balances c/d			123	4,833
	89	**580**	**7,552**			**48**	**580**	**7,552**

Discounts Received
(31) Total for month 48

Discounts Allowed
(31) Total for month 89

14.1

Sales Journal

(1) J Gordon	187
(3) G Abrahams	166
(6) V White	12
(10) J Gordon	55
(17) F Williams	289
(19) U Richards	66
(27) V Wood	28
(31) L Simes	78
(31) Total for month	**881**

Sales Ledger

J Gordon
(1) Sales 187
(10) Sales 55

G Abrahams
(3) Sales 166

V White
(6) Sales 12

F Williams
(17) Sales 289

U Richards
(19) Sales 66

V Wood
(27) Sales 28

L Simes
(31) Sales 78

General Ledger
Sales Account
(31) Total for month 881

14.3

Sales Journal

(1) F Gray	60
(4) A Gray	120
(8) E Hines	20
(20) M Allen	180
(31) B Cooper	160
(31) Total for month	**540**

Sales Ledger

F Gray
(1) Sales 60

A Gray
(4) Sales 120

E Hines
(8) Sales 20

M Allen
(20) Sales 180

B Cooper
(31) Sales 160

General Ledger
Sales Account
(31) Total for month 540

Workings of invoices:

(1) F Gray
3 rolls white tape × 10 = 30
5 sheets blue cotton × 6 = 30
1 dress length × 20 = 20
[80]
Less trade discount 2.5% 20
60

(4) A Gray
6 rolls white tape × 10 = 60
30 metres green baize × 4 = 120
180
Less trade discount 33⅓%
60
120

(8) E Hines
1 dress length black silk × 20 = 20

(20) M Allen
10 rolls white tape × 10 = 100
6 sheets blue cotton × 6 = 36
3 dress lengths black silk × 20 = 60
11 metres green baize × 4 = 44
240
Less trade discount 25% 60
180

(31) B Cooper
12 rolls white tape × 10 = 120
14 sheets blue cotton × 6 = 84
9 metres green baize × 4 = 36
240
Less trade discount 33⅓% 80
160

15.1

Workings of purchases invoices

(1) K King
4 radios × 30 =	120	
3 music centres × 160 =	480	
	600	
Less trade discount 25%	150	
		450

(3) A Bell
2 washing machines × 200 =	400	
5 vacuum cleaners × 60 =	300	
2 dishwashers × 150 =	300	
	1,000	
Less trade discount 20%	200	
		800

(15) J Kelly
1 music centre × 300 =	300	
2 washing machines × 250 =	500	
	800	
Less trade discount 25%	200	
		600

(20) B Powell
6 radios × 70	420	
Less trade discount 33⅓%	140	
		280

(30) B Lewis
4 dishwashers × 200	800	
Less trade discount 20%	160	
		640

Purchases Journal
(1) K King	450
(3) A Bell	800
(15) J Kelly	600
(20) B Powell	280
(30) B Lewis	640
	2,770

General Ledger
Purchases Account
(31) Total for month 2,770

Purchases Ledger

K King
(1) Purchases 450

A Bell
(3) Purchases 800

J Kelly
(15) Purchases 600

B Powell
(20) Purchases 280

B Lewis
(30) Purchases 640

15.3

Purchases Journal
(1) Smith Stores	90
(23) C Kelly	105
(31) J Hamilton	180
	375

Sales Journal
(8) A Grantley	90	72
(15) A Henry	105	240
(24) D Sangster	180	81
	375	393

Purchases Ledger

Smith Stores
(1) Purchases 90

C Kelly
(23) Purchases 105

J Hamilton
(31) Purchases 180

Sales Ledger

A Grantley
(8) Sales 90

A Henry
(15) Sales 105

D Sangster
(24) Sales 180

General Ledger
Sales Account
(31) Total for month 393
Purchases Account
(31) Total for month 375

16.1

Purchases Journal
(1) H Lloyd	119
(4) D Scott	98
(4) A Simpson	114
(4) A Williams	25
(4) S Wood	56
(10) A Simpson	59
(18) M White	89
(18) J Wong	67
(18) H Miller	196
(18) H Lewis	119
(31) A Williams	56
(31) C Cooper	98
	1,096

Returns Outwards Journal
(7) H Lloyd	16
(7) D Scott	14
(25) J Wong	5
(25) A Simpson	11
	46

General Ledger
Purchases Account
(31) Total for month 1,096
Returns Outwards Account
(31) Total for month 46

Purchases Ledger

H Lloyd
(7) Returns 16 | (1) Purchases 119

D Scott
(7) Returns 14 | (4) Purchases 98

A Simpson
(25) Returns 11 | (4) Purchases 114
| (10) Purchases 59

A Williams
| (4) Purchases 25
| (31) Purchases 56

S Wood
| (4) Purchases 56

M White
| (18) Purchases 89

J Wong
(25) Returns 5 | (18) Purchases 67

H Miller
| (18) Purchases 196

H Lewis
| (18) Purchases 119

C Cooper
| (31) Purchases 98

16.3

Sales Journal
(1) T Thompson	56
(1) L Rodriguez	148
(1) K Barton	145
(7) K Kelly	89
(7) N Mendes	78
(7) N Lee	257
(24) K Mohammed	57
(24) K Kelly	65
(24) O Green	112
(31) N Lee	55
	1,062

Purchases Journal
(3) P Potter	144
(3) H Harris	25
(3) B Spencer	76
(9) B Perkins	24
(9) H Harris	58
(9) H Miles	123
(17) H Harris	54
(17) B Perkins	65
(17) L Nixon	75
	644

Returns Inwards Journal
(14) T Thompson	5
(14) K Barton	11
(14) K Kelly	14
(28) N Mendes	24
	54

Returns Outwards Journal
(11) P Potter	12
(11) B Spencer	22
(20) B Spencer	14
	48

Sales Ledger

T Thompson
(1) Sales	56	(14) Returns	5

L Rodriguez
(1) Sales	148

K Barton
(1) Sales	145	(14) Returns	11

K Kelly
(1) Sales	89	(14) Returns	14
(24) Sales	65		

N Mendes
(7) Sales	78	(28) Returns	24

N Lee
(7) Sales	257		
(31) Sales	55		

K Mohammed
(24) Sales	57

O Green
(24) Sales	112

Purchases Ledger

P Potter
(11) Returns	12	(3) Purchases	144

H Harris
		(3) Purchases	25
		(9) Purchases	58
		(17) Purchases	54

B Spencer
(11) Returns	22	(3) Purchases	76
(20) Returns	14		

B Perkins
		(9) Purchases	24
		(17) Purchases	65

H Miles
		(9) Purchases	123

L Nixon
		(17) Purchases	75

General Ledger

Purchases
(31) Total for month	644

Returns Inwards
(31) Total for month	54

Sales
		(31) Total for month	1,062

Returns Outwards
		(31) Total for month	48

Returns Inwards Journal
(11) K O'Connor	16
(11) L Staines	18
	34

Returns Outwards Journal
(19) N Lee	9

T Best
(22) Purchases	72	(16) Bank & disct	72

N Hardy
(1) Balance	40	(16) Bank & disct	40

M Nelson
(1) Balance	180	(16) Bank & disct	180
(3) Sales	40		40
	220		220

K O'Connor
(3) Sales	56	(11) Returns	16
		(16) Bank & disct	40
	56		56

J Johnson
(22) Purchases	89

Trial Balance as at 31 May 19X9

C Harris	56	
H Gordon	38	
J Johnson	89	
T Best	72	
M Benjamin	100	
N Duffy	48	
B Green	118	
L Pearson	67	
Capital		5,598
Rent	15	
Motor expenses	13	
Drawings	20	
Salaries	56	
Rates	66	
Sales		527
Purchases	344	
Returns inwards	34	
Returns outwards		9
Premises	2,000	
Motor vans	750	
Fixtures	600	
Stock	1,289	
Discounts allowed	19	
Discounts received		17
Bank	855	
Cash	12	
	6,406	6,406

Cash Book

	Disc	Cash	Bank		Disc	Cash	Bank
(1) Balances		45	1,254	(1) Rent			15
(16) N Hardy	2		38	(4) Motor expenses		13	
(16) M Nelson	11		209	(7) Drawings		20	
(16) K O'Connor	2		38	(24) B Blake	4		76
(16) L Staines	4		76	(24) V Reagan	10		190
				(24) N Lee	3		57
				(27) Salaries			56
				(30) Rates			66
				(31) Better Motors			300
				(31) Balance c/d		12	855
	19	45	1,615		17	45	1,615

17.1

The Journal

(1) Premises	2,000	
Motor van	450	
Fixtures	600	
Stock	1,289	
Debtors: N Hardy	40	
M Nelson	180	
Bank	1,254	
Cash	45	
Creditors: B Blake		60
V Reagan		200
Capital		5,598
	5,858	5,858
(14) Motor van	300	
Better Motors		300

Purchases Journal
(2) B Blake	20
(2) C Harris	56
(2) H Gordon	38
(2) N Lee	69
(22) J Johnson	89
(22) T Best	72
	344

Sales Journal
(3) K O'Connor	56
(3) M Benjamin	78
(3) L Staines	98
(3) N Duffy	48
(3) B Green	118
(3) M Nelson	40
(9) M Benjamin	22
(9) L Pearson	67
	527

17.2

(a) Motor vehicles	Dr	6,790	: Kingston	Cr	6,790
(b) Bad debts	Dr	34	: H Newman	Cr	34
(c) Unique Offices	Dr	490	: Office furniture	Cr	490
(d) (i) Bank	Dr	39	: W Charles	Cr	39
(ii) Bad debts	Dr	111	: W Charles	Cr	111
(e) Drawings	Dr	45	: Purchases	Cr	45
(f) Drawings	Dr	76	: Insurance	Cr	76
(g) Machinery	Dr	980	: Systems Accelerated	Cr	980

18.1

Petty Cash Book

Receipts		Total	Cleaning	Motor Expenses	Postages	Stationery	Travelling
300	(1) Balance b/d						
	(2) Postages	18			18		
	(3) Travelling	12					12
	(4) Cleaning	15	15				
	(7) Petrol	22		22			
	(8) Travelling	25					25
	(9) Stationery	17				17	
	(11) Cleaning	18	18				
	(14) Postages	5			5		
	(15) Travelling	8					8
	(18) Stationery	9				9	
	(18) Cleaning	23	23				
	(20) Postages	13			13		
	(24) Motor service	43		43			
	(26) Petrol	18		18			
	(27) Cleaning	21	21				
	(29) Postages	5			5		
	(30) Petrol	14		14			
		286	77	97	41	26	45
286	(31) Cash						
586	(31) Balance c/d	300					
		586					

Purchases Ledger

B Blake

(24) Bank	60	(1) Balance	76
(24) Discount	20	(2) Purchases	4
	80		80

V Reagan

(24) Bank & disct.	200	(1) Balance b/d	200
	200		200

C Harris

	(2) Purchases	56

H Gordon

	(2) Purchases	38

N Lee

(19) Returns	9	(2) Purchases	69
(24) Bank & disct	60		
	69		69

Sales Ledger

M Benjamin

(3) Sales	78
(9) Sales	22

L Staines

(3) Sales	98	(11) Returns	18
		(16) Bank & disct	80
	98		98

N Duffy

(3) Sales	48

B Green

(3) Sales	118

L Pearson

(9) Sales	67

General Ledger

Capital

	(1) Balance	5,598

Rent

(1) Bank	15

Motor Expenses

(4) Cash	13

Drawings

(7) Cash	20

Salaries

(27) Bank	56

Rates

(30) Bank	66

Sales

	(31) Total for month	527

Purchases

(31) Total for month	344

Returns Inwards

(31) Total for month	34

Returns Outwards

	(31) Total for month	9

Premises

(1) Balance	2,000

Motor Vans

(1) Balance	450
(14) Better Motors	300

Fixtures

(1) Balance	600

Stock

(1) Balance	1,289

Discounts Allowed

(31) Total for month	19

Discounts Received

	(31) Total for month	17

Better Motors

(31) Bank	300	(14) Motor Van	300

18.2 (a) Briefly: To keep detail out of cash book.
To reduce postings to expense accounts.
To enable petty cash to be kept by someone other than main cashier.

(b)

Petty Cash Book

Receipts		Total	Post and stationery	Travel expenses	Ledger accounts
1.13	(1) Balance b/d				
23.87	(2) Cash				
	(4) Postages	8.50	8.50		
	(9) Courtney Bishop	2.35			2.35
	(11) Bus fares	1.72		1.72	
	(17) Envelopes	0.70	0.70		
0.68	(23) Telephone reimbursed				
	(26)	10.00		10.00	
		23.27	9.20	11.72	2.35
	(30) Balance c/d	2.41			
25.68		25.68			
2.41	(1) Balance b/d				
22.59	(1) Cash				

(c)

Post and Stationery
(30) Petty cash 9.20

Travel Expenses
(30) Petty cash 11.72

Courtney Bishop
(9) Petty cash 2.35

Telephone
(23) Petty cash 0.68

19.1 (a) Style of invoice will vary.

Calculations:

	£
3 sets of Boy Michael Golf Clubs × £270	810
150 Watson golf balls at £8 per 10 balls	120
4 Faldo golf bags at £30	120
	1,050
Less trade discount 33⅓%	350
	700
Add VAT 10%	70
	770

(b)

D Wilson Ltd Ledger
G Christie & Son

	£
19X7	770
May 1 Sales	

G Christie & Son Ledger
D Wilson Ltd

	£
19X7	770
May 1 Purchases	

19.3

Sales Book

		Net	VAT
19X9			
Aug 1	M Sinclair & Co	150	15
„ 8	M Brown & Associates	260	26
„ 19	A Axton Ltd	80	8
„ 31	T Christie	30	3
		520	52

Sales Ledger

M Sinclair & Co
165 (1) Sales

M Brown & Associates
286 (8) Sales

A Axton Ltd
88 (19) Sales

T Christie
33 (31) Sales

General Ledger

Sales
(31) Credit sales for the month 520

Value Added Tax
(31) Sales book: VAT content 52

19.4

Sales Book

	Net	VAT
(1) B Davies & Co	150	15
(4) C Grant Ltd	220	22
(16) C Grant Ltd	140	14
(31) B Karloff	80	8
	590	59

Purchases Book

	Net	VAT
(10) G Cooper & Son	400	40
(10) J Wayne Ltd	190	19
(14) B Lugosi	50	5
(23) S Hayward	60	6
	700	70

19.6

(a)

Sales Day Book

Date Name and Details	List price less trade discount		VAT		Total	
	£	p	£	p	£	p
19X9						
Mar 9 Neville's Electrical	576	–	57	60	633	60
" 17 Maltby plc	3,000	–	300	–	3,300	–
" 29 Neville's Electrical	368	–	36	80	404	80
	3,944	–	394	40	4,338	40

Sales Ledger

B Davies & Co

(1) Sales 165

C Grant Ltd

(4) Sales 242
(16) Sales 154

B Karloff

88

Purchases Ledger

G Cooper & Son

(10) Purchases 440

J Wayne Ltd

(10) Purchases 209

B Lugosi

(14) Purchases 55

S Hayward

(23) Purchases 66

General Ledger

Sales

(31) Credit sales for month 590

Purchases

(31) Credit purchases for month 700

Value Added Tax

(31) VAT content in purchases book 70
(31) VAT content in sales book 59
(31) Balance c/d 11

70 | 70

(b)

Neville's Electrical

19X9
Mar 9 Sales 633.60
Mar 29 Sales 404.80

Maltby plc

19X9
Mar 17 Sales 3,300.00

Sales

19X9
Mar 31 Sales Day Book 3,944.00

Value Added Tax

19X9
Mar 31 Sales Day Book 394.40

(c)

Trial Balance as at 31 March 19X9

	Dr	Cr
Neville's Electrical	1,038.40	
Maltby plc	3,300.00	
Sales		3,944.00
Value Added Tax		394.40
	4,338.40	4,338.40

20.1

Columnar Sales Day Book

Inv No	Total	VAT	Hi Fi Dept	TV Dept	Sundries Dept
19X7					
Feb 1 P Small 586	2,860	260		2,600	
" 2 L Goode 587	1,980	180	1,800		
" 3 R Daye 588	1,760	160		1,600	
" 5 B May 589	320	–			320
" 7 L Goode 590	990	90		900	
" 7 P Small 591	3,740	340	3,400		
	11,650	1,030	5,200	5,100	320

General Ledger

Sales

	Hi Fi	TV	Sundries
19X7			
Feb 28 Total for month	5,200	5,100	320

Value Added Tax

19X7
Feb 28 Total for month 1,030

P Small

19X7
Feb 1 Sales 2,860
" 7 " 3,740

L Goode

Feb 2 Sales	1,980
" 7 " "	990

R Daye

Feb 3 Sales	1,760

B May

Feb 5 Sales	320

20.2

M Barber

Purchases Analysis Book

19X6		Total	Purchases	Light & Heat	Motor Exps	Stationery	Carriage Inwards
Jul 1	L Ogden	220	220				
" 3	E Evans	390	390				
" 4	North Electricity	88		88			
" 5	H Noone	110	110				
" 6	Kirk Motors	136			136		
" 8	Avon Enterprises	77				77	
" 10	Kirk Motors	55			55		
" 12	North Gas Board	134		134			
" 15	A Dodds	200	200				
" 17	O Aspinall	24		24			
" 18	J Kelly	310	310				
" 19	D Adams	85					85
" 21	J Moore	60				60	
" 23	H Noone	116	116				
" 27	D Flynn	62					62
" 31	Kirk Motors	185			185		
		2,252	1,346	246	376	137	147

20.3 General ledger : Purchases Dr 1,346; Lighting and heating Dr 246;
Motor expenses Dr 376; Stationery Dr 137;
Carriage inwards Dr 147.

Purchases ledger : Credits in Personal accounts should be obvious.

21.1

Gross pay		200
Less Income tax	27	
National insurance	16	
		43
Net pay		157

21.2

Gross pay 40 × 4		160	
5 × 6		30	
			190
Less Income tax*		25	
National insurance		17	
			42
Net pay			148

*190 − 80 = 110. First 50 × 20% = 10 + (60 × 25%) 15 = total 25

21.3

Salary		200
Commission		600
Gross pay		800
Less Income tax*	85	
National insurance	66	
		151
Net pay		649

*800 − 450 = 350. First 50 × 20% = 10 + (300 × 25%) 75 = total 85

21.4

Salary		2,000
Bonus		400
		2,400
Less		
Superannuation	120	
Income tax*	450	
National insurance	190	
		760
		1,640

*2,400 − 120 − 430 = 1,850. First 250×20% = 50+(1,600×25%) 400 = 450

22.1 See text section 22.10.

22.2 See text section 22.3–22.5.

22.3 See text section 22.8.

22.4 See text section 22.3.

23.1 (a) Per text.
(b) Capital: (i) (ii) Machine part of (v) (vi).
Revenue: (iii) (iv) Drinks part of (v).

23.3 Capital (a) (b) (e).

23.5 Capital (a) (c) (d) (f) (j) (l): Revenue (b) (e) (g) (h) (i) (k).

23.7

(a) Per text.

(b) Microcomputer – acquisition cost

Basic cost	4,000	
Installation and testing	340	
	4,340	
Less 5% discount	217	
	4,123	
Special wiring	110	
Modifications	199	
Staff training	990	
Total cost	5,422	

(c) 1. Revenue. 2. Capital. 3. Capital. 4. Revenue. 5. Revenue.
6. Revenue. 7. Capital. 8. Revenue. 9. Capital. 10. Capital.

23.8

(a) *Plant at Cost*

Balance 1 April 19X5	372,000
Add Acquisitions during year	96,000
	468,000
Less Disposals (36,000 + 4,000 + 4,400)	44,400
Balance 31 March 19X6	423,600

(b) *Provision for Depreciation of Plant*

Balance 1 April 19X5	205,400
Less Depreciation on disposals (W1)	25,200
	180,200
Add Provision for year 20% × (423,600 − 180,200)	48,680
Balance 31 March 19X6	228,880

Plant Sold

Cost: year to 31 March 19X2		40,000
Depreciation: year to 31 March 19X2	20%	8,000
		32,000
Depreciation: year to 31 March 19X3	20%	6,400
		25,600
Addition		4,400
		30,000
Depreciation: year to 31 March 19X4	20%	6,000
		24,000
Depreciation: year to 31 March 19X5	20%	4,800
		19,200

(W1) Depreciation accumulated: 8,000+6,400+6,000+4,800 = 25,200.

(c) *Sale of plant*

		13,700
Less Cost (40,000 + 4,400)	44,400	
Depreciation	25,200	
Book value at date of sale		19,200
Loss on disposal		5,500

24.1

Bad Debts

19X8			19X8		
Apl 30	H Gordon	110	Dec 31	Profit and loss	186
Aug 31	D Bellamy	64			
Oct 31	J Alderton	12			
		186			186

Provision for doubtful debts

19X8		
	Dec 31 Profit and loss	220

Profit and Loss (extracts)

Bad debts	186
Provision for doubtful debts	220

Balance Sheet as at 31 December 19X8 (extract)

Debtors		6,850
Less Provision for		
Bad debts	220	
		6,630

24.2

(a) *Bad debts*

19X7			19X7		
Dec 31	Various	540	Dec 31 Profit and loss		540

(b) *Provision for doubtful debts*

Dec 31 Balance c/d	310		Jan 1 Balance b/d	260
			Dec 31 Profit and loss	50
	310			310

(c) *Profit & Loss (extracts)*

Bad debts	540
Provision for doubtful debts	50

(d) *Balance Sheet (extract)*

Debtors		6,200
Less provision for doubtful debts		310
		5,890

24.3

(i)

Bad Debts

19X6			19X6	
Aug 31	W Beet	85	Dec 31 Profit and loss	225
Sep 30	S Avon	140		
		225		225
19X7			19X7	
Feb 28	L J Friend	180	Dec 31 Profit and loss	490
Aug 31	N Kelly	60		
Nov 30	A Oliver	250		
		490		490

Provision for Doubtful Debts

			19X6	
			Dec 31 Profit and loss	550
19X7			19X7	
Dec 31 Balance c/d		600	Dec 31 Profit and loss	50
		600		600

(ii)

Balance Sheet (extracts)

	19X6			19X7	
Debtors	40,500			47,300	
Less Provision for doubtful debts	550	39,950		600	46,700

24.6

Provision for Doubtful Debts

19X7			19X7	
May 31 Profit and loss (W1)	1,390		Jun 1 Balance b/d	2,300
,, 31 Balance c/d	910			
	2,300			2,300
			19X8	
			Jun 1 Balance b/d	910

Provision for Discounts Allowed

19X8	
May 31 Profit and loss (W2)	594

Workings

(W1) Provision 1.6.19X7   2,300

Less Provision 31.5.19X8

1% × 24,000	240
2% × 10,000	200
4% × 8,000	320
5% × 3,000	150
	910
	1,390

Reduction in Provision

(W2) Debtors liable for discounts   24,000

Less Provision for doubtful debts   240   23,760

Provision for discounts allowed 2½% × 23,760 = 594

24.8

(days and months omitted)

(a)

Bad Debts

19X7 Debtors	1,200	19X7 Profit and loss	1,200
19X8 Debtors	1,600	19X8 Profit and loss	1,600
19X9 Debtors	2,350	19X9 Profit and loss	2,350

(b)

Bad Debts Recovered

		19X8 Mrs P Iles	350
19X8 Profit and loss	350	19X9 Debtor	150
19X9 Profit and loss	150		

(c)

Provision for Bad Debts

		19X7 Profit and loss	2,000
19X8 Balance c/d	2,800	19X8 Profit and loss	800
	2,800		2,800
19X9 Profit and loss	700	19X9 Balance b/d	2,800
19X9 Balance c/d	2,100		
	2,800		2,800

(d)

Profit and Loss Account (extracts)

(19X7) Bad debts	1,200		
Provision for bad debts	2,000	(19X8) Bad debt recovered	350
(19X8) Bad debts	1,600		
Provision for bad debts	800	(19X9) Reduction in provision for bad debts	700
(19X9) Bad debts	2,350	Bad debt recovered	150

24.9

(A) *see Section 24.2*

(B) *see Section 24.5*

(C) (1) (i)

Provision for Doubtful Debts

19X7			19X7	
Dec 31 Profit and loss	33		Jan 1 Balance b/d	717**
,, ,, Balance c/d	750*			
	750			750

(ii)

Bad Debts

19X7				
? Debtors – A Stewart	900		Dec 31 Profit and loss	3,800
? Debtors	2,300			
Dec 31 Debtors – J Smith	600			
	3,800			3,800

(2) the net profit will increase by £33.

*3% 25,000 = 750; **3% 23,900

25.1

Straight Line

Cost	4,000
Yr 1 Depreciation	700
	3,300
Yr 2 Depreciation	700
	2,600
Yr 3 Depreciation	700
	1,900
Yr 4 Depreciation	700
	1,200
Yr 5 Depreciation	700
	500

4,000 − 500 = 3,500 ÷ 5 = 700

Reducing Balance

Cost	4,000
Yr 1 Depn 40% of 4,000	1,600
	2,400
Yr 2 Depn 40% of 2,400	960
	1,440
Yr 3 Depn 40% of 1,440	576
	864
Yr 4 Depn 40% of 864	346
	518
Yr 5 Depn 40% of 518	207
	311

25.2 *(a) Straight Line*

Cost	12,500
Yr 1 Depreciation	1,845
	10,655
Yr 2 Depreciation	1,845
	8,810
Yr 3 Depreciation	1,845
	6,965
Yr 4 Depreciation	1,845
	5,120

$$\frac{12{,}500 - 5{,}120}{4} = 1{,}845$$

(b) Reducing Balance

Cost	12,500
Yr 1 Depn 20% of 12,500	2,500
	10,000
Yr 2 Depn 20% of 10,000	2,000
	8,000
Yr 3 Depn 20% of 8,000	1,600
	6,400
Yr 4 Depn 20% of 6,400	1,280
	5,120

25.3 *(a) Reducing Balance*

Cost	6,400
Yr 1 Depn 50% of 6,400	3,200
	3,200
Yr 2 Depn 50% of 3,200	1,600
	1,600
Yr 3 Depn 50% of 1,600	800
	800
Yr 4 Depn 50% of 800	400
	400
Yr 5 Depn 50% of 400	200
	200

(b) Straight Line

Cost	6,400
Yr 1 Depreciation	1,240
	5,160
Yr 2 Depreciation	1,240
	3,920
Yr 3 Depreciation	1,240
	2,680
Yr 4 Depreciation	1,240
	1,440
Yr 5 Depreciation	1,240
	200

$$\frac{6{,}400 - 200}{5} = 1{,}240$$

25.7

		A	*Machines* *B*	*C*
Bought 1.1.19X7		3,000		
19X7 Depreciation	10% for 12 months	300		
		2,700		
Bought 1.4.19X8			2,000	
19X8 Depreciation	10% × 2,700	270		
"	10% for 9 months		150	
		2,430	1,850	
Bought 1.7.19X9				1,000
19X9 Depreciation	10% × 2,430	243		
"	10% × 1,850		185	
"	10% for 6 months			50
		2,187	1,665	950

19X9 Total Depreciation Provision 243 + 185 + 50 = 478

26.1

Motor Vans

19X1				
Jan 1	Bank	2,400	Dec 31 Balance c/d	3,800
Jul 1	Bank	1,400		
		3,800		3,800

Provision for Depreciation: Motor Vans

19X1			19X1	
Dec 31	Balance c/d	620	Dec 31 Profit and loss	620

26.2

Machinery

19X3			19X3	
Jan 1	Bank	800	Dec 31 Balance c/d	800
19X4			19X4	
Jan 1	Balance b/d	800	Dec 31 Balance c/d	2,400
Jul 1	Bank	1,000		
Oct 1	Bank	600		
		2,400		2,400
19X5			19X6	
Jan 1	Balance b/d	2,400	Dec 31 Balance c/d	2,600
19X6				
Apr 1	Bank	200		
		2,600		2,600

Provision for Depreciation: Machinery

19X3			19X3		
Dec 31	Balance c/d	80	Dec 31	Profit and loss	80
19X4			19X4		
Dec 31	Balance c/d	225	Jan 1	Balance b/d	80
			Dec 31	Profit and loss	145
		225			225
19X5			19X5		
Dec 31	Balance c/d	465	Jan 1	Balance b/d	225
			Dec 31	Profit and loss	240
		465			465
19X6			19X6		
Dec 31	Balance c/d	720	Jan 1	Balance b/d	465
			Dec 31	Profit and loss	255
		720			720

Balance Sheet Extracts

31 December 19X3			31 December 19X5		
Machinery at cost	800		Machinery at cost	2,400	
Less Depreciation	80	720	Less Depreciation to date	465	1,935
31 December 19X4			31 December 19X6		
Machinery at cost	2,400		Machinery at cost	2,600	
Less Depreciation to date	225	2,175	Less Depreciation to date	720	1,880

Provision for Depreciation: Plant

19X4			19X4		
Dec 31	Balance c/d	210	Dec 31	Profit and loss	210
19X5			19X5		
Dec 31	Balance c/d	510	Jan 1	Balance b/d	210
			Dec 31	Profit and loss	300
		510			510
19X6			19X6		
Dec 31	Balance c/d	865	Jan 1	Balance b/d	510
			Dec 31	Profit and loss	355
		865			865
19X7			19X7		
Sep 30	Disposals	675	Jan 1	Balance b/d	865
Dec 31	Balance c/d	555	Dec 31	Profit and loss	365
		1,230			1,230

26.4

Plant

19X4			19X4		
Jan 1	Bank	900	Dec 31	Balance c/d	1,500
Oct 1	Bank	600			
		1,500			1,500
19X6			19X6		
Jan 1	Balance b/d	1,500	Dec 31	Balance c/d	2,050
Jul 1	Bank	550			
		2,050			2,050
19X7			19X7		
Jan 1	Balance b/d	2,050	Sep 30	Disposals	900
			Dec 31	Balance c/d	1,150
		2,050			2,050

Plant Disposals

19X7			19X7		
Sep 30	Plant	900	Sep 30	Provn for depn	675
Dec 31	Profit and loss	50	,, 30	Bank	275
		950			950

Balance Sheets

Plant at cost	1,500	1,500		2,050
Less depn to date	210	510		865
	1,290	990		1,185

26.5

Machinery

19X9			19X9		
Jan 1	Balance b/d	52,590	Dec 31	Machinery disposals	2,800
Dec 31	Bank	2,480	,, 31	Balance c/d	52,270
		55,070			55,070

Office Furniture

19X9			19X9		
Jan 1	Balance b/d	2,860	Dec 31	Balance c/d	3,180
Dec 31	Bank	320			
		3,180			3,180

Provision for Depreciation: Machinery

19X9			19X9		
Dec 31	Machinery disposals	1,120	Jan 1	Balance b/d	25,670
" 31	Balance c/d	29,777	Dec 31	Profit and loss	5,227
		30,897			30,897

Provision for Depreciation: Office Furniture

19X9			19X9		
Dec 31	Balance c/d	1,649	Jan 1	Balance b/d	1,490
			Dec 31	Profit and loss	159
		1,649			1,649

Machinery Disposals

19X9			19X9		
Dec 31	Machinery	2,800	Dec 31	Provision for deprn	1,120
			" 31	Bank	800
			" 31	Profit and loss: Loss on sale	880
		2,800			2,800

Balance Sheet as at 31 December 19X9

Machinery at cost		52,270
Less Depreciation to date		29,777
		22,493
Office furniture at cost		3,180
Less Depreciation to date		1,649
		1,531

26.7 (a) (i) Time factor (ii) Economic factors (iii) Deterioration physically (iv) Depletion.

(b) (i) Depletion (ii) Physical deterioration (iii) Time (iv) Not usually subject to depletion, but depends on circumstances (v) Economic factors, obsolescence for example (vi) Time factor.

(c)

Equipment

Balance b/d		135,620	Asset disposals		36,000
Bank		47,800	Balance c/d		147,420
		183,420			183,420
Balance b/d		147,420			

Provision for Depreciation – Equipment

Asset disposals		28,224	Balance b/d		81,374
Balance c/d		90,858	Profit and loss		37,708
		119,082			119,082
			Balance b/d		90,858

Asset Disposals

Equipment	36,000	Provision for depreciation		28,224
		Bank		5,700
		Profit and loss		2,076
	36,000			36,000

26.9 (a) (i) Straight line depreciation method

Fixed Asset

Year 1 Bank	10,000	Year 3 Asset disposals		10,000

Provision for Depreciation

		Year 1 Profit and loss		2,000
		Year 2 Profit and loss		2,000
Year 2 Balance c/d	4,000			4,000
Year 3 Asset disposals	4,000	Year 3 Balance b/d		4,000

Asset Disposals

Year 3 Fixed asset	10,000	Year 3 Bank		5,000
		" 3 Provision for depn.		4,000
		" 3 Profit and loss		1,000
	10,000			10,000

(ii) Reducing balance method

Fixed Asset

Year 1 Bank	10,000	Year 3 Asset disposals		10,000

Provision for Depreciation

		Year 1 Profit and loss		4,000
		" 2 Profit and loss		2,400
Year 2 Balance c/d	6,400			6,400
Year 3 Asset disposals	6,400	Year 3 Balance b/d		6,400

Asset Disposals

Year 3 Fixed asset	10,000	Year 3 Bank		5,000
" 3 Profit and loss	1,400	" 3 Provision for depn.		6,400
	11,400			11,400

(b) (i) The purpose of depreciation provisions is to apportion the cost of a fixed asset over the useful years of its life to the organisation.

The matching concept concerns the matching of costs against the revenues which those costs generate. If the benefit to be gained is equal in each year then the straight line method is to be preferred. If the benefits are greatest in year 1 and then falling year by year, then the reducing balance method would be preferred. The impact of maintenance costs of the fixed asset, if heavier in later years, may also give credence to the reducing balance method.

(ii) The net figure at the end of year 2 is the amount of original cost not yet expensed against revenue.

(c) The charge in year 1 should be nil in this case. The matching concept concerns matching costs against revenues. There have been no revenues in year 1, therefore there should be no costs.

27.1

Motor Expenses

19X6			19X6	
Dec 31	Cash and bank	744	Dec 31	Profit and loss	772
" 31	Owing c/d	28			
		772			772

Insurance

19X6			19X6		
Dec 31	Cash and bank	420	Dec 31	Prepaid c/d	35
			" 31	Profit and loss	385
		420			420

Stationery

19X6			19X6		
Dec 31	Cash and bank	1,800	Jan 1	Owing b/d	250
" 31	Owing c/d	490	Dec 31	Profit and loss	2,040
		2,290			2,290

Rates

19X6			19X6		
Jan 1	Prepaid b/d	220	Dec 31	Prepaid c/d	290
Dec 31	Cash and bank	950	" 31	Profit and loss	880
		1,170			1,170

Rent Received

19X6			19X6		
Jan 1	Owing b/d	180	Dec 31	Cash and bank	550
Dec 31	Profit and loss	580	" 31	Owing c/d	210
		760			760

27.3

Rates

19X8			19X8		
Jan 1	Balance b/d	104	Dec 31	Profit and loss	1,229
Dec 31	Bank	1,500	" 31	Prepaid c/d	375
		1,604			1,604

27.5

Packing Materials

19X8			19X8		
Jan 1	Balance b/d	629	Dec 31	Profit and loss	5,499
Dec 31	Bank	5,283	" 31	Cash: Scrap	172
" 31	Owing c/d	357	" 31	Stock c/d	598
		6,269			6,269

(a)

Insurance

19X0			19X0		
Jan 1	Prepaid b/d	562	Dec 31	Profit and loss	1,236
Dec 31	Bank	1,019	" 31	Prepaid c/d	345
		1,581			1,581
19X1					
Jan 1	Prepaid b/d	345			

Wages

19X0			19X0		
Dec 31	Cash	15,000	Jan 1	Accrued b/d	306
" 31	Accrued c/d	419	Dec 31	Profit and loss	15,113
		15,419			15,419
			19X1		
			Jan 1	Accrued b/d	419

Rent Receivable

19X0			19X0		
Dec 31	Profit and loss	2,741	Jan 1	In advance b/d	36
			Dec 31	Bank	2,600
			" 31	Arrears c/d	105
		2,741			2,741
19X1					
Jan 1	Arrears b/d	105			

(b)

Profit and Loss (extract)

Insurance	1,236		Rent receivable	2,741
Wages	15,113			

(c) (i) Expenses accrued increase the amount charged as expense for that period. It reduces the recorded net profits. It shows as a current liability in the balance sheet.

(ii) Income received in advance reduces the revenue to be recorded for that period. It reduces the recorded net profit. It shows as a current liability in the balance sheet.

(d) (i) To match up expenses charged in the profit and loss account with the expense cost used up in the period.

(ii) To match up revenue credited to profit and loss with revenue earned for the period.

27.8

A Scholes
Trading and Profit and Loss Account for the year ended 28 February 19X7

Sales			19,740
Less Cost of goods sold:			
Opening stock		2,970	
Add Purchases		11,280	
		14,250	
Less Closing stock		3,510	10,740
Gross profit			9,000
Add Discounts received			360
			9,360
Less Expenses:			
Wages and salaries (2,580 + 90)		2,670	
Rent (1,020 – 140)		880	
Discounts allowed		690	
Van running costs (450 + 60)		510	
Bad debts (810 + 60)		870	
Depreciation:			
Office furniture	180		
Delivery van	480	660	6,280
Net profit			3,080

Balance Sheet as at 28 February 19X7

Fixed assets			
Office furniture		1,440	
Less Depreciation		180	
			1,260
Delivery van		2,400	
Less Depreciation		480	1,920
			3,180
Current assets			
Stock		3,510	
Debtors	4,920		
Less Provision for bad debts	330	4,590	
Prepaid expenses		140	
Cash at bank		1,140	
Cash in hand		210	
		9,590	
Less Current liabilities			
Creditors	2,490		
Expenses owing	150	2,640	
Working capital			6,950
			10,130

Financed by:		
Capital		
Balance at 1.3.19X6		9,900
Add Net profit		3,080
		12,980
Less Drawings		2,850
		10,130

27.10

John Brown
Trading and Profit and Loss Account for the year ended 31 December 19X7

Sales				400,000
Less Returns in				5,000
				395,000
Less Cost of goods sold				
Stock at 1.1.19X7				100,000
Add Purchases		350,000		
Less Returns out	6,200	343,800		
			443,800	
Less Stock at 31.12.19X7			120,000	323,800
Gross profit				71,200
Less Wages			35,000	
Rates			5,500	
Telephone			1,220	
Bad debts			200	
Provision for bad debts			180	
Depreciation: Shop fittings			4,000	
Van			6,000	52,100
Net profit				19,100

Balance Sheet as at 31 December 19X7

Fixed assets			
Shop fittings at cost		40,000	
Less Depreciation		4,000	36,000
Van at cost		30,000	
Less Depreciation		6,000	24,000
			60,000
Current assets			
Stock		120,000	
Debtors	9,800		
Less Provision	980	8,820	
Prepayments		500	
Bank		3,000	
		132,320	
Less Current liabilities			
Creditors	7,000		
Expenses accrued	5,220	12,220	
Working capital			120,100
			180,100

Financed by:
Capital

Balance as at 1.1.19X7		179,000
Add Net profit		19,100
		198,100
Less Drawings		18,000
		180,100

27.12

Mr Chai

Trading and Profit and Loss Account for the year ended 30 April 19X7

Sales (259,870 – 5,624)		254,246
Less Cost of goods sold		
Stock 1.5.19X6	15,654	
Purchases (135,680 – 13,407)	122,273	
Carriage inwards	11,830	
	149,757	
Less Stock 30.4.19X7	17,750	132,007
Gross profit		122,239
Discounts received		1,750
		123,989
Less Expenses		
Salaries and wages	38,521	
Rent, rates and insurances (25,973 – 1,120 – 5,435)	19,418	
Heating and lighting (11,010 + 1,360)	12,370	
Carriage out	4,562	
Advertising	5,980	
Postage, stationery and telephone	2,410	
Bad debts	2,008	
Provision for bad debts	223	
Discounts allowed	2,306	
Depreciation	12,074	99,872
Net profit		24,117

Balance Sheet as at 30 April 19X7

Fixed assets			
Fixtures and fittings at cost			120,740
Less Depreciation to date			63,020
			57,720
Current assets			
Stock			17,750
Debtors		24,500	
Less Provision for bad debts		735	23,765
Prepaid expenses			6,555
Bank			4,440
Cash			534
			53,044
Less Current liabilities			
Creditors		19,840	
Expenses accrued		1,360	
			21,200
Working capital			31,844
			89,564
Financed by:			
Capital: Balance as at 1.5.19X6			83,887
Add Net profit			24,117
			108,004
Less Drawings			18,440
			89,564

28.1

(i) FIFO Closing Stock 20 × £40 = £800

(ii)

LIFO	Received	Issued	Stock after each transaction	
Jan	10 × £30		10 × £30	300
Mar	10 × £34		10 × £30 300	
			10 × £34 340	640
April		8 × £34	10 × £30 300	
			2 × £34 68	368
Sept	20 × £40		10 × £30 300	
			2 × £34 68	
			20 × £40 800	1,168
Dec		12 × £40	10 × £30 300	
			2 × £34 68	
			8 × £40 320	688

(iii)

AVCO	Received	Issued	Average cost per unit stock held	No. of units in stock	Total value of stock
Jan	10 × £30		£30	10	£300
Mar	10 × £34		£32	20	£640
Apl		8	£32	12	£384
Sept	20 × £40		£37	32	£1,184
Dec		12	£37	20	£740

28.2

Trading Account for the year ended December 31 19X0
(All methods)

Sales	8 × £46	368	12 × £56	672	1,040

	FIFO	LIFO	AVCO
Purchases	1,440	1,440	1,440
Less Closing stock	800	688	740
Cost of goods sold	640	752	700
Gross profit	400	288	340
	1,040	1,040	1,040

28.5 (a) (*dates and calculations omitted*)

Cash

Loan: School fund	200.00	Purchases	53.50
Sales	51.36		

Purchases

		Cash	51.36

Sales

		Cash	53.50

(b) Stock valuation:

34	Break × 16p =	5.44
15	Brunch × 12p =	1.80
		7.24

Stock

Trading account	7.24

(c)

Broadway School

Trading Account for the month of December 19X9

Purchases	51.36	Sales	53.50
Less Closing stock	7.24		
	44.12		
Gross profit	9.38		
	53.50		53.50

(d)

	Break	Brunch
Purchases (units)	240	108
Less Sold	200	90
Stock should have been	40	18
Actual stock	34	15
Missing items	6	3

If there have been no arithmetical errors, one can only assume that someone has stolen 6 Breaks and 3 Brunch.

28.6 (This is a brief answer showing main points to be covered. In the examination the answer should be in report form and elaborated.)

1 For Charles Gray

(*i*) The concept of prudence says that stock should be valued at lower of cost or net realisable value. As 50% of the retail price £375 is lower than cost £560, then £375 will be taken as net realisable value and used for stock valuation.

(*ii*) The sale has not taken place by 30 April 19X9. The prudence concept does not anticipate profits and therefore the sale will not be assumed. The gun should therefore be included in stock, at cost price £560.

2 For Jean Kim

It appears that it is doubtful if the business can still be treated as a going concern.

If the final decision is that the business cannot continue, then the stock valuation should be £510 each, as this is less than cost, with a further overall deduction of auction fees and expenses £300.

3 For Peter Fox

Stock must be valued at the lower of cost or net realisable value in this case.

The cost to be used is the *cost* for Peter Fox. It is quite irrelevant what the cost may be for other distributors.

It would also be against the convention of consistency to adopt a different method. The consistency applies to Peter Fox, it is not a case of consistency with other businesses. Using selling prices as a basis is not acceptable to the vast majority of businesses.

28.8 (*a*) In one respect the consistency convention is not applied, as at one year end the stock may be shown at cost whereas the next year end may see stock valued at net realisable value.

On the other hand, as it is prudent to take the lower of cost or net realisable value, it can be said to be consistently prudent to consistently take the lower figure.

(*b*) Being prudent can be said to be an advantage. For instance, a shareholder can know that stocks are not overvalued and give him a false picture of his investment.

Someone to whom money is owed, such as a creditor, will know that the stocks in the balance sheet are realisable at least at that figure.

It is this knowledge that profits are not recorded because of excessive values placed on stocks that gives outside parties confidence to rely on reported profits.

29.1

Bank Reconciliation as on 31 December 19X6

Cash at bank as per cash book		678
Add Unpresented cheques	256	
Credit transfers	56	
		312
		990
Less Bank lodgements		115
Cash at bank as per bank statement		875

> **Note for students**
> Both in theory and in practice you can start with the cash book balance working to the bank statement balance, or you can reverse this method. Many teachers have their preferences, but this is a personal matter only. Examiners sometimes ask for them using one way, sometimes the other. Students should therefore be able to tackle them both ways.

29.3

(a)

Cash Book

19X9 (Totals so far)		2,328	19X9 (Totals so far)	497
Dec 31 J Walters		54	Dec 31 Bank Charges	22
			,, 31 Balance c/d	1,863
		2,382		2,382

Bank Reconciliation as on 31 December 19X9

Balance per cash book	1,863
Add Unpresented cheque	115
	1,978
Less Bankings not yet on bank statement (249 + 178)	427
Balance per bank statement	1,551

or

Bank Reconciliation Statement as on 31 December 19X9

Balance per bank statement	1,551
Add Bankings not yet on bank statement (249 + 178)	427
	1,978
Less Unpresented cheque	115
Balance per cash book	1,863

29.5

(a)

Cash Book (bank columns)

19X8			19X8	
Dec 31 Balance b/d		1,500	Dec 31 Bank charges	30
Dec 31 Dividends		240	Dec 31 RAC	70
Dec 31 Customs and Excise		260	Dec 31 Loan repayment	200
Dec 31 Deposit account		1,400	Dec 31 Balance c/d	3,100
		3,400		3,400

(b) *Bank Reconciliation Statement as on 31 December 19X8*

Balance per cash book	3,100
Add Unpresented cheques (250 + 290)	540
	3,640
Less Bankings not entered on statement	690
Balance per bank statement	2,950

29.7

Cash Book

19X6 (Totals so far)	737		19X6 (Totals so far)	6,017
Mar 31 M Turnbull	57		Mar 31 BKS	49
,, 31 Balance c/d	5,300		,, 31 Bank charges	28
	6,094			6,094

Bank Reconciliation Statement as at 31 March 19X6

Overdraft per cash book	5,300
Add Bankings not yet in bank statement	160
	5,460
Less Unpresented cheques	490
Overdraft per bank statement	4,970

30.1

Sales Ledger Control

Balances b/d	4,936		Returns inwards	1,139
Sales journal	49,916		Cheques and cash	46,490
			Discounts allowed	1,455
			Balances c/d	5,768
	54,852			54,852

30.3

Sales Ledger Control

19X5			19X5	
May 1 Balances b/d	6,420		May 31 Cash and bank	10,370
May 31 Sales	12,800		May 31 Discounts allowed	395
May 31 Balances c/d	50		May 31 Set-offs: purchases ledger	145
			May 31 Balances c/d	8,360
	19,270			19,270

30.5

Purchases Ledger Control

Returns outwards	2,648		Balances b/d	11,874
Bank	146,100		Purchases journal	154,562
Petty cash	78			
Discounts received	2,134			
Set-offs against sales ledger	1,036			
Balances c/d	14,530			
	*166,526			*166,436

*Difference between two sides 90

Sales Ledger Control

Balances b/d	19,744		Returns inwards	4,556
Sales journal	199,662		Bank and cash	185,960
			Discounts allowed	5,830
			Set-offs against purchase ledger	1,036
			Balances c/d	22,024
	219,406			219,406

30.7

Total Debtors Account

Balance b/d	26,555	Cash (600,570 – 344,890)	255,680
Credit sales	268,187	Discounts allowed	5,520
		Set-offs (Total debtors)	70
		Bad debts	780
		Returns inwards	4,140
		Balances c/d	28,552
	294,742		294,742
Balances b/d	28,552		

Total Creditors Account

Cash (503,970 – 14,440)	489,530	Balances b/d	43,450
Discounts received	3,510	Credit purchases	496,600
Set-offs (total creditors)	70		
Returns outwards	1,480		
Balances c/d	45,460		
	540,050		540,050
		Balances b/d	45,460

30.8

(a) To ensure an arithmetical check on the accounting records. The agreement of total of individual creditors balances with that of balance on control account provides that check.

If control account and ledger are kept by separate personnel, then a check on their work and honesty is provided.

(b) (i) Increase £198 (ii) Decrease £100 (iii) No effect (iv) Decrease £400 (v) Decrease £120.

(c) A computer will automatically enter two figures in different directions and will then confirm it in total fashion. As such there may seem at first sight for there to be no need for control accounts.

However, there is still the need to check on the accuracy of data input. It is important that both the skill and the honesty of the programmer are checked.

Accordingly there will still be a need for control accounts.

31.1 To economise on space, all narratives for journal entries are omitted.

(a)	J Harris	Dr	678	: L Hart	Cr	678
(b)	Machinery	Dr	4,390	: L Pyle	Cr	4,390
(c)	Motor van	Dr	3,800	: Motor expenses	Cr	3,800
(d)	E Fitzwilliam	Dr	9	: Sales	Cr	9
(e)	Sales	Dr	257	: Commissions rec'd	Cr	257
(f)	Cash needs double the amount.					
(f)		Dr	154	: T Heath	Cr	154
(g)	Purchases	Dr	189	: Drawings	Cr	189
(h)	Discounts allowed	Dr	366	: Discounts received	Cr	366

31.3

(a) 100 units × £1.39 = £139 not £1,390.

(b) (i) Stock overstated by £1,251 (i.e. 1,390 – 139).
(ii) Cost of goods sold understated by £1,251.
(iii) Net profit overstated by £1,251.
(iv) Current assets overstated by £1,251.
(v) Owner's capital overstated by £1,251.

31.4

(a)	Sales	Dr	10,000	: Capital	Cr	10,000
(b)	Drawings	Dr	700	: General expenses	Cr	700
(c)	Drawings	Dr	89	: Insurance	Cr	89
(d)	Purchases	Dr	270	: C Kelly	Cr	270
(e)	Bank	Dr	780	: Cash	Cr	780
(f)	Bank	Dr	400	: Cash	Cr	400
(g)	J Charlton	Dr	168	: M McCarthy	Cr	168
(h)	Motor expenses	Dr	1,000	: Motor disposals	Cr	1,000

32.1

(a) *The Journal (narratives omitted)*

	Dr	Cr
(i) Suspense	100	
Sales		100
(ii) J Cantrell	250	
J Cochrane		250
(iii) Rent	70	
Suspense		70
(iv) Suspense	300	
Discounts received		300
(v) Sales	360	
Motor disposals		360

(b)

Suspense Account

Sales	100	Balance b/d	330
Discounts received	300	Rent	70
	400		400

(c)

Net profit per accounts		7,900
Add (i) Sales undercast	100	
(iv) Discounts undercast	300	
	400	8,300
Less (iii) Rent undercast	70	
(v) Reduction in sales	360	
		430
Corrected net profit		7,870

32.3

Item	If no effect state 'No'	Debit side exceeds credit side by	Credit side exceeds debit side by
(i)	No		
(ii)			£3,400
(iii)	No		
(iv)		£1,500	
(v)			£610
(vi)			£170
(vii)	No		

(ii) Computation of Corrected Profit for year to 31 December 19X8

Profit as originally reported		47,240
Add Telephone expense overstated	100	
Sales understated	2,000	
Rent received omitted	1,500	3,600
		50,840
Less Machinery repairs understated	390	
Purchases omitted	765	1,155
Corrected profit figure		49,685

(b) (i) Per text (ii) Per text

32.4

Trial Balance as on 31 January 19X9

	Dr	Cr
Drawings	2,800	
Stock	2,597	
Debtors (2,130 − 6)	2,124	
Furniture (1,750 + 120)	1,870	
Cash	1,020	
Returns inwards	85	
Business expenses	950	
Purchases (4,380 − 120)	4,260	
Discounts allowed	38	
Capital		5,500
Creditors (2,735 − 75)		2,660
Sales (7,430 + 108)		7,538
Discounts received		46
	15,744	15,744

32.7

(a) *Difference on Trial Balance Suspense*

Per trial balance	2,513	J Winters	198
Discounts received	324	Wages	2,963
Discounts allowed	324		
	3,161		3,161

(b) *Computation of Corrected Net Profit for year to 30 April 19X7*

	−	+
Net profit per draft accounts		24,760
(i) Discounts		648
(ii) Wages	2,963	
(iv) Stationery stock		1,500
(vi) Remittance	3,000	
	5,963	2,148
Correct net profit	3,815	20,945

(iii) and (v) did not affect profit

(c) Per text

32.5

(a) (i) *The Journal*

	Dr	Cr
C Thomas	450	
Thomasson Manufacturing Ltd		450
Suspense	100	
Telephone		100
Suspense	2,000	
Sales account		2,000
Machine repairs	390	
Machinery		390
Suspense	1,500	
Rent received*		1,500
Purchases account	765	
P Brooks		765

* Assumed not invoiced to Atlas Ltd

33.1

R Stubbs

Trading Account for the year ended 31 December 19X9

Sales			60,000
Less Cost of goods sold:			
Stock 1.1.19X9		9,872	
Add Purchases	(D)	50,748	
	(C)	60,620	
Less Stock 31.12.19X9		12,620	
	(B)		48,000
Gross profit	(A)		12,000

Missing figures found in following order (A) to (D). Sales are 60,000 so
(A) Mark up is 25%. Therefore Margin is 20%.
Margin is 20% × 60,000 = 12,000 Gross Profit

(B) +(A) = 60,000. Therefore (B)+12,000=60,000 and accordingly is 48,000.
(C) − 12,620 = 48,000. Therefore (C) is 60,620.
(D) + 9,872 = 60,620. Therefore (D) is 50,748.

33.3

(a) We know that

$$\frac{\text{Cost of Goods Sold}}{\text{Average Stock}} = \text{Rate of Turnover}$$

Substituting $\dfrac{x}{12,600} = 7$

x = Cost of Goods Sold = 88,200.

(b) If margin is 33⅓% then mark-up will be 50%. Gross Profit is therefore 50% of 88,200 = 44,100.

(c) Turnover is (a) + (b) = 88,200 + 44,100 = 132,300.

(d) 66⅔% × 44,100 = 29,400.

(e) Gross Profit − Expenses = Net Profit = 14,700.

33.5

(a) Sales = 121,500 + 25% (30,375) = 151,875.

(b) 28,500 − (7% × 150,000) 10,500 = 18,000.

(c) $\dfrac{121,500}{(20,100 + 28,500) \div 2} = \dfrac{121,500}{24,300} = 5$

(d) Gross profit is 27½% × 140,000 = 38,500.
Sales are 140,000 + 38,500 = 178,500.
Expenses are 7% of sales = 12,495.
Net profit = 38,500 − 12,495 = 26,005.

34.1

B Arkwright
Statement of Affairs as at 31 December 19X5

Fixed assets		
Motor van at cost	2,800	
Less Depreciation	550	2,250
Current assets		
Stock	3,950	
Debtors	4,970	
Prepaid expenses	170	
Bank	2,564	
Cash	55	
	11,709	
Less Current liabilities		
Trade creditors	1,030	
Expenses owing	470	1,500
Working capital		10,209
Capital		12,459

Cash introduced (C) 10,000
Add Net profit (B)

Less Drawings (A)

5,673

Missing figures (A), (B) and (C) deducted in that order. (A) to balance is 12,459, thus (B) has to be 18,132 and (C) becomes 8,132.

34.3

Workings:

Purchases Bank	29,487
Cash	2,994
	32,481
− Creditors 31.12.19X6	5,624
	26,857
+ Creditors 31.12.19X7	7,389
Purchases for 19X7	34,246

Sales Banked	37,936
Cash	9,630
	47,566
− Debtors 31.12.19X6	9,031
	38,535
+ Debtors 31.12.19X7	8,624
Sales for 19X7	47,159

Opening Capital:

Bank	405	
Stock	13,862	
Debtors	9,031	
Rates prepaid	210	
Fixtures	2,500	
	26,008	
Less Creditors	5,624	
Rent owing	150	5,774
		20,234

Kelly
Trading and Profit and Loss Account for the year ended 31 December 19X7

Sales			47,159
Less Cost of goods sold:			
Opening stock		13,862	
Add Purchases		34,246	
		48,108	
Less Closing stock		15,144	32,964
Gross profit			14,195
Less Expenses:			
Wages		5,472	
Rent (1,650 − 150)		1,500	
Rates (890 + 210 − 225)		875	
Sundry expenses		375	
Depreciation: Fixtures		250	8,472
Net profit			5,723

Balance Sheet as at 31 December 19X7

Fixed assets			
Fixtures at valuation		2,500	
Less Depreciation		250	2,250
Current assets			
Stock		15,144	
Debtors		8,624	
Prepayments		225	
		23,993	
Less Current liabilities			
Trade creditors	7,389		
Bank overdraft	602	7,991	
Working capital			16,002
			18,252
Capital			
Balance at 1.1.19X7		20,234	
Add Net profit		5,723	
		25,957	
Less Drawings (1,164 + 6,541)		7,705	
			18,252

34.5

Jenny Barnes

Trading and Profit and Loss Account for the year ended 30 April 19X9

Opening stock		9,500	Sales *	102,908
Add Purchases				
(70,500 + 7,600)		78,100		
		87,600		
Less Closing stock		13,620		
Cost of goods sold		73,980		
Gross profit c/d		28,928		
		102,908		102,908
Sales assistants' wages		5,260	Gross profit b/d	28,928
Vehicle running expenses		1,020		
Bad debts		150		
Miscellaneous expenses **		1,370		
Light and heat		940		
Depreciation: Equipment		720		
Vehicles		1,000		
Net profit		18,468		
		28,928		28,928

*Sales 96,500 + takings in cash later spent 6,408
(drawings 6,000 + expenses 408)
**Bank 962 + cash 408 = 1,370

34.7

(a)

Creditors Control

Bank	101,500	Balances b/d	7,400
Cash	1,800	Drawings: Goods	600
Balances c/d	8,900	Purchases (difference)	104,200
	112,200		112,200

(b)

Janet Lambert

Trading and Profit and Loss Account for the year ended 31 August 19X9

Sales (deduced – as margin is 25% = 4 × gross profit)			128,000
Opening stock		8,600	
Add Purchases		104,200	
		112,800	
Less Closing stock		16,800	
Cost of goods sold			96,000
Gross profit (33⅓% of Cost of goods sold)			32,000
Less: Casual labour (1,200 + 6,620)		7,820	
Rent (5,040 + 300 – 420)		4,920	
Delivery costs		3,000	
Electricity (1,390 + 160 – 210)		1,340	
			17,080
Net profit			14,920

Balance Sheet as at 31 August 19X9

Current assets			
Stock		16,800	
Debtors		4,300	
Prepayments		420	
Bank		1,650	
Cash		330	23,500
Less Current liabilities			
Creditors		8,900	
Expenses owing		160	9,060
			14,440
Capital:			
Balance as at 1 September 19X8 (Workings 1)			7,850
Add Net profit			14,920
			22,770
Less Drawings (Workings 2)			8,330
			14,440

Workings:

(1) Capital as on 1.9.19X8. Stock 8,600 + Debtors 3,900 + Prepaid 300 + Bank 2,300 + Cash 360 = 15,460 – Creditors 7,400 – Accruals 210 = 7,850.

(2) Cash drawings. Step (A) find cash received from sales. Debtors b/d 3,900 + Sales 128,000 – Debtors c/d 4,300 = 127,600 cash received.

Step (B) find cash banked. Balance b/d 2,300 + cash received? – payments 117,550 = balance c/d 1,650. Therefore cash banked? = 116,900. Step (C) draw up cash account:

Balance b/d	360	Labour	1,200
Sales receipts	127,600	Purchases	1,800
		Banked	116,900
		Drawings (difference)	7,730
		Balance c/d	330
	127,960		127,960

(c) Per text.

34.9

David Denton

Profit and Loss Account for the year ended 31 December 19X0

Work done: Credit accounts		29,863	
For cash		3,418	33,281
Less Expenses:			
Materials (9,600 – 580)		9,020	
Secretarial salary		3,000	
Rent		225	
Rates (180 – 45)		135	
Insurance (800 – 200)		600	
Electricity (1,122 + 374 estimated)		1,496	
Motor expenses		912	
General expenses (1,349 + 295)		1,644	
Loan interest (4,000 × 10% × ¾)		300	
Provision for bad debts		425	
Accounting fee		250	
Amortisation of lease (650 × ¾)		487	
Depreciation: Equipment	960		
Van	900	1,860	20,354
Net profit			12,927

Balance Sheet as at 31 December 19X0

Fixed assets	Cost	Depreciation	
Lease	6,500	487	6,013
Equipment	4,800	960	3,840
Vehicle	3,600	900	2,700
	14,900	2,347	12,553

Current assets			
Stock			580
Debtors	4,250		
Less Provision for bad debts	425		3,825
Prepaid expenses (75 + 200)			275
Bank (see workings)			6,084
Cash			123
			10,887
Less Current liabilities			
Trade creditors		714	
Interest owing		300	
Accountancy fee owing		250	
Rates owing		135	
Electricity owing		374	1,773
Working capital			9,114
			21,667
Financed by:			
Capital			
Introduced (6,500 + 3,600)			10,100
Add Net profit			12,927
			23,027
Less Drawings (4,680 + 280 + 400)			5,360
			17,667
Loan			4,000
			21,667

Workings:

Bank 6,500 + 25,613 + 2,600 + 4,000 = 38,713 – 4,680 – 280 – 6,500 – 300 – 3,000 – 8,886 – 4,800 – 1,122 – 912 – 1,349 – 800 = 6,084

34.10 (a)

J Duncan

Capital Account on 1 January 19X8

Bank		8,000
Cash		300
Stock		4,100
Machinery		12,600
Rent Prepaid		200
Debtors		6,300
		31,500
Less: Creditors	2,400	
Loan	5,000	7,400
		24,100

(b)

J Duncan
Trading and Profit and Loss Account for the year ended 31 December 19X8

	£	£	£
Sales			40,450
Less: Sales returns			1,200
			39,250
Less: Cost of Sales			
Opening Stock at 1 January 19X8		4,100	
Add: Purchases		18,950	
		23,050	
Less: Withdrawn by the owner	300		
Less: Closing stock at 31 December 19X8	3,200	3,500	
			19,550
Gross profit			19,700
Add: Discount received			350
			20,050
Less: Expenses			
Rent		1,850	
Bad debts written off		400	
Wages		6,100	
Insurance		1,450	
Loan interest		400	
Depreciation		4,200	
Repairs		300	
Electricity		750	
			15,450
Net profit			4,600

Workings:
Sales 26,000 − 250 + 14,000 + 400 − 6,300 + 5,000 + 1,200 + 400 = 40,450
Purchases 18,500 − 2,400 + 2,500 + 350 = 18,950
Depreciation = balancing figure

34.11

J Duncan
Balance Sheet as at 31 December 19X8

	£	£	£	£
Fixed Assets				
Machinery at 1 January 19X8			12,600	
Add: Additions			7,500	
			20,100	
Less: Depreciation			4,200	15,900
Current assets				
Stock			3,200	
Debtors			5,000	
Bank			2,600	
Cash			50	
			10,850	
Current liabilities				
Creditors		2,500		
Accrued charges				
Loan interest	100			
Rent	250	350		
		2,850		
				8,000
				23,900
Capital Account				
Balance at 1 January 19X8			24,100	
Add: Net profit			4,600	
			28,700	
Less: Drawings			9,800	18,900
Long-term liabilities				
Bank loan 8%				5,000
				23,900

35.1

Uppertown Football Club
Income and Expenditure Account for the year ended 31 December 19X4

Income
Collections at matches		1,650
Profit on refreshments		315
		1,965

Less Expenditure
Rent for pitch (300 – 60)	240	
Printing and stationery (65 + 33)	98	
Secretary's expenses	144	
Repairs to equipment	46	
Groundsman's wages	520	
Miscellaneous expenses	66	
Depreciation of equipment	125	
		1,239
Surplus of income over expenditure		726

Balance Sheet as at 31 December 19X4

Fixed assets		
Equipment	625	
Less Depreciation	125	
		500
Current assets		
Prepayment	60	
Cash	879	
	939	
Less Current liabilities		
Expenses owing	33	
Working capital		906
		1,406

Financed by:
Accumulated fund		
Balance at 1.1.19X4 (500 + 180)		680
Add Surplus of income over expenditure		726
		1,406

35.3

The Happy Haddock Angling Club
Income and Expenditure Account for the year ended 31 December 19X8

Income:
Subscriptions		3,500
Visitors' fees		650
Competition fees		820
Snack bar profit (see workings)		1,750
		6,720

Less Expenditure:
Rent and rates	1,500	
Secretarial expenses	240	
Loan interest	260	
Depreciation on games equipment	400	
		2,400
Surplus of income over expenditure		4,320

Workings: Snack bar profit: 6,000 – (800 + 3,750 – 900) – 600 = 1,750

(b) *Balance Sheet as at 31 December 19X8*

Fixed assets		
Club house buildings		20,500
Games equipment	2,000	
Less Depreciation	400	
		1,600
		22,100
Current assets		
Snack bar stocks	900	
Bank	700	
	1,600	
Less Current liabilities		
Subscriptions received in advance	380	
		1,220
		23,320

Financed by:
Accumulated fund		
Balance 1.1.19X8 (see workings)	13,500	
Add surplus for year	4,320	
		17,820
Loan from bank		5,500
		23,320

Workings: 200 + 800 + 12,500 = 13,500

35.5

(a) *Accumulated fund 1 August 19X8*

Equipment		975
Stocks of prizes		38
Arrears of subscriptions		65
Cash and bank		210
		1,288
Less Subscriptions in advance	10	
Prizes suppliers	58	
		68
		1,220

(b) (i) Subscriptions

In arrears b/d	65	In advance b/d	10
In advance c/d	37	Cash	1,987
Income and expenditure	1,980	In arrears c/d	85
	2,082		2,082

(ii)

Competition prizes

Stocks b/d	38	Creditors b/d	58
Cash	270	Stock c/d	46
Creditors c/d	68	Cost of prizes given	272
	376		376

(c)

Miniville Rotary Club
Income and expenditure account for the year ended 31 July 19X9

Income

Subscriptions		1,980
Ticket sales	437	
Less Cost of prizes	272	165
Donations received		177
		2,322

Less Expenditure

Rent (1,402 – 500)	902	
Visiting speakers' expenses	1,275	
Secretarial expenses	163	
Stationery and printing	179	
Donations to charities	35	
Depreciation	195	2,749
Excess of expenditure over income		427

Balance sheet as at 31 July 19X9

Fixed assets

Equipment at cost		1,420	
Less Depreciation		640	780

Current assets

Stocks of prizes	46		
Arrears of subscriptions	85		
	131		
Less Current liabilities			
Creditors for prizes	68		
Advance subscriptions	37		
Bank overdraft	13	118	13
			793

Accumulated fund

Balance 1.8.19X8		1,220
Less Excess of expenditure over income		427
		793

35.7

(a) Café operations:

Takings		4,660
Less Cost of supplies:		
Opening stock	800	
Add purchases (1,900 + 80)	1,980	
	2,780	
Less Closing stock	850	1,930
		2,730
Wages		2,000
Profit		730
Sports equipment:		
Sales		900
Less Cost of goods sold:		
Opening stock	1,000	
Add Purchases (1,000 × 50%)	500	
	1,500	
Less Closing stock (*see note*)	900	600
Profit		300

Note: To find closing stock 900 is sales at 50% on cost profit so cost of sales is 600. By arithmetical deduction closing stock is found to be 900.

(b)

Subscriptions

Owing b/d	60	In advance b/d		120
		Cash: 19X7		40
Income and expenditure	1,280	19X8		1,100
		19X9		80
In advance c/d	80	Owing c/d		80
	1,420			1,420

Life Subscriptions

Income and expenditure	220	Balance b/d	1,400
(11 × 20)		Cash	200
Balance c/d	1,380		
	1,600		1,600

Used Sports Equipment

		Cash	14
Notes:		Income and expenditure a/c	486
1 Stock b/d	700	Stock c/d	700
Transferred from purchases	500		
	1,200		1,200

2 b/d 1,000 + bought (1,000 × ½) 500 = 1,500 – sold 600 = 900
3 b/d 1,210 + receipts 6,994 – paid 7,450 = 754

36.1

Loose Tools

19X4					**19X4**			
Jan	1	Stock	b/d	1,250	Dec	31	Manufacturing	994
Dec	31	Bank		2,000	,,	31	Stock c/d	2,700
,,	31	Wages		275				
,,	31	Materials		169				
				3,694				3,694
19X5					**19X5**			
Jan	1	Stock	b/d	2,700	Dec	31	Manufacturing	1,695
Dec	31	Bank		1,450	,,	31	Stock c/d	3,340
,,	31	Wages		495				
,,	31	Materials		390				
				5,035				5,035
19X6					**19X6**			
Jan	1	Stock	b/d	3,340	Dec	31	Bank: Refund	88
Dec	31	Bank		1,890	,,	31	Manufacturing	1,897
,,	31	Wages		145	,,	31	Stock c/d	3,680
,,	31	Materials		290				
				5,665				5,665

(c)
Happy Tickers & Social Club

Income and Expenditure Account for the year ended 31 December 19X8

Income:		
Subscriptions (1,280 + 220)		1,500
Profit on café operations		730
Profit on sports equipment		300
		2,530
Less Expenditure		
Rent	1,200	
Insurance	600	
Repairs to roller (½ × 450)	225	
Sports equipment depreciation (*see note 1*)	486	
Depreciation of roller (½ × 200)	100	
		2,611
Excess of expenditure over income		81

Balance Sheet as at 31 December 19X8

Fixed assets			
Share in motor roller at cost		1,000	
Less Depreciation to date		500	
			500
Used sports equipment at valuation			700
			1,200
Current assets			
Stock of new sports equipment (*see note 2*)		900	
Stock of café supplies		850	
Subscriptions owing		80	
Carefree Conveyancers: owing for expenses		225	
Prepaid expenses		350	
Cash and bank (note 3)		754	
		3,159	
Less Current liabilities			
Café suppliers	80		
Advance subscriptions	80		
		160	
			2,999
			4,199
Accumulated fund			
Balance at 1.1.19X8		2,900	
Less Excess of expenditure		81	
		2,819	
Life subscriptions		1,380	
			4,199

(d) To most people probably the best description of the item would be as deferred income, i.e. income paid in advance for future benefits.

It could, however, be described as a liability of the club. The club in future will have to provide and finance amenities for life members, but they do not have to pay any more money for it. This is therefore the liability of the future to provide these services without further payment.

36.2 (a) (i) Straight line

Cost £112,000 – trade in £12,000 = £100,000

Per month £100,000 ÷ 48 = 2,083.33

19X6	9 months	=		18,750
19X7	12 months	=		25,000
19X8	12 months	=		25,000
19X9	12 months	=		25,000
19X0	3 months	=		6,250
				100,000

(ii) Diminishing (Reducing) Balance:

Cost	112,000
Depreciation 19X6 (40%)	44,800
	67,200
Depreciation 19X7	26,880
	40,320
Depreciation 19X8	16,128
	24,192
Depreciation 19X9	9,677
	14,515
Depreciation 19X0	5,806
	8,709

(iii) Units of output (Total £100,000)

19X6	4,000/20,000	=	20,000
19X7	5,000/20,000	=	25,000
19X8	5,000/20,000	=	25,000
19X9	5,000/20,000	=	25,000
19X0	1,000/20,000	=	5,000

(b) (i)

Machine

19X7		19X7	
Jan 1 Balance b/d	112,000	Dec 31 Assets disposal	112,000

(ii)

Provision for Depreciation

19X7		19X7	
Dec 31 Assets disposal	31,250	Jan 1 Balance b/d	18,750
		Dec 31 Profit and loss	12,500
	31,250		31,250

(iii)

Assets Disposal

19X7		19X7	
Dec 31 Machine	112,000	Jun 30 Bank	80,000
		Dec 31 Depreciation	31,250
		,, 31 Profit and loss	750
	112,000		112,000

36.4

T Jackson

Manufacturing, Trading and Profit and Loss Accounts
for the year ended 31 December 19X7

Stock raw materials 1.1.19X7		18,450
Add Purchases		64,300
Add Carriage inwards		1,605
		84,355
Less Stock raw materials 31.12.19X7		20,210
Cost of raw materials consumed		64,145
Direct labour		65,810
Prime cost		129,955
Factory overhead expenses		
Rent ⅔	1,800	
Fuel and power	5,920	
Depreciation: Machinery	8,300	16,020
		145,975

Add Work in progress 1.1.19X7		23,600
		169,575
Less Work in progress 31.12.19X7		17,390
Production cost goods completed c/d		152,185
Sales		200,600
Less Cost of goods sold		
Stock finished goods 1.1.19X7	17,470	
Add Production cost goods completed b/d	152,185	
	169,655	
Less Stock finished goods 31.12.19X7	21,485	148,170
Gross profit		52,430
Less Expenses:		
Office salaries	16,920	
Rent ⅓	900	
Lighting and heating	5,760	
Depreciation: Office equipment	1,950	25,530
Net profit		26,900

36.6

D Saunders

Manufacturing Trading and Profit and Loss Account for the year ended
31 December 19X6

Stock of raw materials 1.1.19X6		8,565
Add Purchases		39,054
		47,619
Less Stock of raw materials 31.12.19X6		9,050
Cost of raw materials consumed		38,569
Manufacturing wages (45,470 + 305)		45,775
Prime cost		84,344
Factory overhead expenses:		
Factory lighting and heating	2,859	
General expenses: factory	5,640	
Rent of factory	4,800	
Depreciation: machinery	2,000	15,299
Production cost of goods completed c/d		99,643

Sales			136,500
Less Cost of goods sold:			
Stock finished goods 1.1.19X6		29,480	
Add Production cost of goods completed b/d		99,643	
		129,123	
Less stock finished goods 31.12.19X6		31,200	97,923
Gross profit			38,577
Less Expenses:			
Office salaries		6,285	
General expenses: office		3,816	
Office rent (2,200 – 108)		2,092	
Office heating and lighting		1,110	
Sales rep's commission		7,860	
Delivery van expenses		2,500	
Depreciation: Office equipment		1,500	
Premises		1,000	26,163
Net profit			12,414

Balance Sheet as at 31 December 19X6

	Cost	Depreciation	Net
Fixed assets			
Premises	50,000	11,000	39,000
Machinery	50,000	19,500	30,500
Office Equipment	15,000	5,500	9,500
	115,000	36,000	79,000
Current Assets			
Stocks: Finished goods		31,200	
Raw materials		9,050	
Debtors		28,370	
Prepaid expenses		108	
Bank		13,337	
		82,065	
Less current liabilities			
Creditors	19,450		
Expenses owing	305	19,755	
Working capital			62,310
			141,310
Capital			
Balance 1.1.19X6			137,456
Add Net profit			12,414
			149,870
Less Drawings			8,560
			141,310

36.8 (a)

Jane Seymour
Manufacturing, Trading and Profit and Loss Account for the year ended 31 July 19X6

Direct materials purchased	43,000	
Less Stock 31 July 19X6	7,000	
	36,000	
Direct factory wages	39,000	
Prime cost	75,000	
Factory overhead expenses:		
Indirect factory wages	8,000	
Machinery repairs	1,600	
Rent and insurance (11,600 – 800) × $\frac{2}{3}$	7,200	
Light and power (5,000 + 1,000) × $\frac{2}{3}$	4,000	
Loose tools (9,000 – 5,000)	4,000	
Motor vehicle running expenses (12,000 × $\frac{1}{2}$)	6,000	
Depreciation: Plant and machinery	6,000	
Motor vehicles (7,500 × $\frac{1}{2}$)	3,750	40,550
		115,550
Less Work in progress 31 July 19X6		12,300
		103,250
Transfer of goods manufactured to trading account		95,000
Loss on manufacturing		8,250
Sales		170,000
Less Goods manufactured transferred	95,000	
Stock at 31 July 19X6	10,000	85,000
Gross profit		85,000
Less Administrative staff salaries	31,000	
Administrative expenses	9,000	
Sales and distribution staff salaries	13,000	
Rent and insurance (11,600 – 800) × $\frac{1}{3}$	3,600	
Motor vehicle running expenses (12,000 × $\frac{1}{2}$)	6,000	
Light and power (5,000 + 1,000) × $\frac{1}{3}$	2,000	
Depreciation: Motors (7,500 × $\frac{1}{2}$)	3,750	68,350
Net profit in trading		16,650
Loss on manufacturing		8,250
Overall net profit		8,400

(b) *Conservatism.* The valuation of stock or work in progress does not include any element of expected future profit.
Matching. All of the prepayments and accruals adjusted for are examples of matching expenses against the time period, as also are the depreciation provisions.

Going Concern. When valuing stocks and work in progress, it has been assumed that the business is going to carry on indefinitely, and that they will be sold in the normal course of business rather than being sold because of cessation of activities.

37.1

Charnley's Department Store
Trading Account for the year ended 31 December 19X8

	Electrical		Furniture		Leisure Goods	
Sales		29,840		73,060		39,581
Less Cost of goods sold:						
Stock 1.1.19X8	6,080		17,298		14,370	
Add Purchases	18,195		54,632		27,388	
	24,275		71,930		41,758	
Less Stock 31.12.19X8	7,920	16,355	16,150	55,780	22,395	19,363
Gross profit		13,485		17,280		20,218

37.2

J Spratt
Trading and Profit and Loss Account for the year ended 31 March 19X9

	A		B	
Sales		15,000		10,000
Less Cost of goods sold:				
Stock 1.4.19X8	250		200	
Add Purchases	11,800		8,200	
	12,050		8,400	
Less Stock 31.3.19X9	300	11,750	150	8,250
Gross profit		3,250		1,750
Less Expenses:				
Wages	1,000		750	
Newspapers: delivery	150			
General office salaries	450		300	
Rates	26		104	
Fire insurance	10		40	
Lighting and air conditioning	24		96	
Repairs to premises	5		20	
Internal telephone	5		20	
Cleaning	6		24	
Accounting and audit	72		48	
General office expenses	36	1,784	24	1,426
Net profits		1,466		324

38.1

M Daly
Cash Flow Statement for the year ended 31 December 19X3

Net cash flow from operating activities (note 1)		2,850
Returns on investments and servicing of finance		
Payments to acquire tangible fixed assets		(1,000)
Financing		
Loan received	1,000	
Drawings	(1,500)	
		(500)
Increase in cash		1,350

Notes:

1 Reconciliation of net profit to net cash inflow:

Net profit		2,200
Depreciation	460	
Decrease in stock	30	
Decrease in creditors	(360)	
Decrease in debtors	520	
		650
Net cash flow from operating activities		2,850

2 Analysis of changes in cash during the year:

Balance at 1 January 19X3	(640)
Net cash inflow	1,350
Balance at 31 December 19X3	710

38.3

(a)

Malcolm Phillips
Cash Flow Statement for the year ended 30 April 19X9

Net cash flow from operating activities (note 1)		6,600
Returns on investments and servicing of finance		
Payments for fixed assets		(3,000)
Financing		
Capital introduced	2,000	
Drawings	(8,000)	
		(6,000)
Decrease in cash		(2,400)

Notes:

1 Reconciliation of net profit to net cash inflow:

Net profit		8,500
Depreciation		200
Increase in creditors		200
Increase in stock		(2,800)
Decrease in debtors		500
		(1,900)
		6,600

2 Analysis of changes in cash during the year:

Balance at 1.5.19X8	900
Net cash inflow	(2,400)
Balance at 30.4.19X9	1,500

(b) (i) $\dfrac{7,500}{30,000} \times \dfrac{100}{1} = 25\%$

(ii) $\dfrac{22,500}{(3,100 + 5,900) \div 2} = \dfrac{22,500}{4,500} = 5$

38.4

C Willis
Cash Flow Statement for the year ended 31 December 19X8

Net cash flow from operating activities (note 1)		11,747
Returns on investments and servicing of finance		
Receipts from sale of fixed assets		2,300
Financing		
Loan repaid to P Bond	(1,000)	
Drawings	(12,500)	
		(13,500)
Increase in cash		547

Notes:

1 Reconciliation of net profit to net cash inflow:

Net profit		16,122
Depreciation		1,090
Profit on sale of motor van		(570)
Increase in bad debt provision		120
Increase in stock		(6,855)
Decrease in debtors (5,490 – 3,800)		1,690
Increase in creditors		150
		(4,375)
		11,747

2 Analysis of changes in cash during the year:

Balance at 1 January 19X8	1,568
Net cash inflow	547
Balance at 31 December 19X8	2,115

39.1

Ollier's Books (dates ignored)
Joint Venture with Avon

Cars	60	Sales	900
Repairs and respraying	237		
Profit on venture	403		
Balance c/d	900		
	1,600		1,600
Cash to Avon	403	Balance b/d	403

Avon's Books
Joint Venture with Ollier

Garage rental	20	Balance c/d	403
Advertising	10		
Licence and insurance	36		
Car	100		
Profit on venture	237		
	403		403
Balance b/d	403	Cash from Ollier	403

Memorandum Joint Venture Account

Dr	£	Cr	£
Cars	1,000	Sales	1,600
Repairs and respraying	60		
Garage rental	20		
Advertising	10		
Licence and insurance	36		
Profit on venture:			
Ollier ½	237		
Avon ½	237		
	1,600		1,600

39.3

Plant, Hoe and Reap, Memorandum Joint Venture Account

Dr	£	Cr	£
Rent	156	Sales	987
Labour: Planting	105		
Labour: Fertilising	36		
Sundry expenses	18		
Lifting	73		
Fertiliser	29		
Motor expenses	17		
Seeds	48		
Sale expenses	39		
Sundries	10		
Profit shared: Plant 266			
Hoe 114			
Reap 76	456		
	987		987

Plant's Books

Joint Venture with Hoe and Reap

Dr	£	Cr	£
Rent	156	Balance c/d	620
Labour: Planting	105		
Labour: Fertilising	36		
Sundries	10		
Labour	18		
Fertiliser	29		
Share of profit	266		
	620		620
Balance b/d	620	Cash from Reap	620

Hoe's Books

Joint Venture with Plant and Reap

Dr	£	Cr	£
Seeds	48	Balance c/d	179
Motor expenses	17		
Share of profit	114		
	179		179
Balance b/d	179	Cash from Reap	179

Reap's Books

Joint Venture with Plant and Hoe

Dr	£	Cr	£
Lifting	73	Sales	987
Sale expenses	39		
Share of profit	76		
Balances c/d	799		
	987		987
Cash to Plant	620	Balance b/d	799
Cash to Hoe	179		
	799		799

40.1

(a) Gudgeon's books (years omitted)

R Johnson Ltd

Dr		£	Cr		£
Jul 1	Sales	2,460	Jul 1	Bills receivable	2,460

B Scarlet & Co Ltd

Dr		£	Cr		£
Jul 1	Sales	1,500	Jul 1	Bills receivable	1,500
Sep 4	Bills receivable (dishonour)	1,500			
" 4	Bank: Noting charge	6			

Bills Receivable

Dr		£	Cr		£
Jul 1	R Johnson Ltd	2,460	Jul 4	Bank	2,460
" 1	B Scarlet & Co Ltd	1,500	" 4	Bank	1,500

Bank

Dr		£	Cr		£
Jul 4	Bills receivable	2,460	Jul 4	Discounting charges	80
" 4	Bills receivable	1,500	" 4	Discounting charges	65
			Sep 4	B Scarlet (discounted bill)	1,500
			" 4	Noting charge (Scarlet)	6

Discounting Charges

Dr		£
Jul 4	Bank	80
" 4	Bank	65

(b) Johnson's books

N Gudgeon

Dr		£	Cr		£
Jul 1	Bills payable	2,460	Jul 1	Purchases	2,460

Bills Payable

Dr		£	Cr		£
Sep 1	Bank	2,460	Jul 1	N Gudgeon	2,460

(c) Scarlet's books

Bank

Sep 1 Bills payable	2,460	

N Gudgeon

Jul 1 Purchases	1,500	Jul 1 Bills payable	1,500
Sep 1 Bills payable	1,500		
,, 4 Noting charge	6		

Noting Charges

6

Bills Payable

		Jul 1 N Gudgeon	1,500

Sep 4 N Gudgeon	
Sep 1 N Gudgeon (discounted bill)	1,500

40.3

KC

Balance b/d	960	Bills receivable	960
Bank (dishonoured bill)	960	Bank	360
		Bad debts	600
	960		960

Bills Receivable

KC	960	Bank	960

Bank

Bills receivable	960	Discounting charges	12
KC	360	KC (dishonoured bill)	960

Bad Debts

KC	600

Discounting Charges

Bank	12

40.4

Sales Ledger Control (years omitted)

Aug 1	Balances b/d	12,370	Aug 1	Balances b/d	105
,, 31	Sales	16,904	,, 31	Returns in	407
,, 31	Bills receivable dishonoured	177	,, 31	Bank	15,970
,, 31	Balances c/d	88	,, 31	Bills receivable	1,230
			,, 31	Cash	306
			,, 31	Bad debts	129
			,, 31	Discounts allowed	604
			,, 31	Balances c/d*	10,788
		29,539			29,539

*difference

40.5

Purchases Ledger Control

Feb 1	Balances b/d	33	Feb 1	Balances b/d	8,570
,, 28	Returns outwards	568	,, 28	Purchases	11,375
,, 28	Bills payable	1,860	,, 28	Bills payable dishonoured	800
,, 28	Bank	9,464	,, 28	Noting charges	20
,, 28	Cash	177			
,, 28	Balances (difference c/d)	8,710	,, 28	Balances c/d	47
		20,812			20,812

41.1

Consignment to MB

Goods	3,000	Sales	3,500
Carriage	147		
Insurance	93	Stock c/d	
Freight	240	20/120 × 3,666	611
Port charges	186		
	3,666		
Commission	175		
Profit	270		
	4,111		4,111

MB

Sales	3,500	Freight	240
		Port charges	186
		Commission	175
		Bank	2,899
	3,500		3,500

41.3

Account Sales for Hughes of London
From Galvez of Madrid

Wooden case sales	250 × £20 =	5,000
	50 × £18 =	900
		5,900
Less Port and duty charges	720	
Storage and carriage	410	
Commission 6% of £5,900	354	
		1,484
		4,416

Consignment Inwards

Port and duty charges	720	Sales	250 × £20	5,000
Storage and carriage charges	410		50 × £18	900
Commission	354			
Cash	4,416			
	5,900			5,900

41.4

Consignment to Rock

			Rock: Sales		10,600
Goods sent		12,000	Value of stock c/d		
Expenses			Cost	12,000	
Freight and insurance	720		Add expenses	1,070	13,070
Rock: Expenses	350 → Rock	1,070			
Selling expenses – Rock		245	30% × 13,070		3,921
Commission: Rock					
5% of 10,600		530			
Bank charges provision c/d		12			
Profit to profit and loss		664			
		14,521			14,521

Rock					
Value of stock b/d		3,921	Bank charges		12
Bank charges		12	Provision b/d		
Selling expenses		200	Rock: Sales		4,800
Bad debts		120			
Commission 5% of £4,800		240			
Bank charges		9			
Profit and loss account		310			
		4,812			4,812

Consignment	10,600	Commission	530
		Expenses	350
		Selling expenses	245
		Cash – draft	7,475
		Balance c/d	2,000
	10,600		10,600

Balance b/d	2,000	Commission	240
Consignment	4,800	Selling expenses	200
		Bad debts	120
		Cash – draft	6,240
	6,800		6,800

42.1

Stephens, Owen and Jones

Appropriation Account for the year ended 31 December 19X6

Net profit			25,200
Less Salaries: Owen	3,000		
Jones	1,000	4,000	
Interest on capitals: Stephens	600		
Owen	400		
Jones	200	1,200	5,200
			20,000

Balance of profits shared:

Stephens 2/5	8,000	
Owen 2/5	8,000	
Jones 1/5	4,000	20,000

42.2

Roach & Salmon

(a) Profit and Loss Appropriation Account for the year ended 31 December 19X9

Net profit brought down			32,840
Less: Salaries: Roach	9,000		
Salmon	6,000	15,000	
Interest on capital:			
Roach	6,000		
Salmon	4,800	10,800	25,800
			7,040

Balance of profits shared:

Roach 1/2	3,520
Salmon 1/2	3,520
	7,040

Current Accounts (dates omitted)

	Roach	Salmon		Roach	Salmon
Drawings	12,860	13,400	Salaries	9,000	6,000
Balances c/d	5,660	920	Interest on capital	6,000	4,800
			Share of profits	3,520	3,520
	18,520	14,320		18,520	14,320

(b) Partnership Act 1890 (section 24).

42.3

Williams, Powell and Howe

Appropriation Account for the year ended 31 December 19X7

Net profit b/d			30,350
Add Interest on drawings: Williams		240	
Powell		180	
Howe		130	550
			30,900
Less Interest on Capitals: Williams	2,000		
Powell	1,500		
Howe	900	4,400	
Salaries: Powell	2,000		
Howe	3,500	5,500	9,900
			21,000

Balance of Profits Shared:

Williams	50%	10,500
Powell	30%	6,300
Howe	20%	4,200
		21,000

Because of this active involvement he will affect the profits made. It would seem appropriate to give him a salary commensurate with such work, plus a share of the profits.

(d) *Interest on capital*: Whatever is decided about profit-sharing, it would seem appropriate for each of the partners to be given interest on their capitals before sharing the balance of the profits.

42.6

Mendez & Marshall

Trading and Profit and Loss Account for the year ended 30 June 19X9

Sales			123,650
Less Cost of goods sold:			
Opening stock		41,979	
Add Purchases		85,416	
		127,395	
Less Closing stock		56,340	71,055
Gross profit			52,595
Add Reduction in provision for bad debts			80
			52,675
Less Salaries and wages (18,917 + 200)		19,117	
Office expenses (2,416 + 96)		2,512	
Carriage outwards		1,288	
Discounts allowed		115	
Bad debts		503	
Loan interest		4,000	
Depreciation: Fixtures	770		
Buildings	1,000	1,770	
			29,305
Net profit			23,370
Add Interest on drawings: Mendez		180	
Marshall		120	300
			23,670
Less Interest on capitals: Mendez	3,500		
Marshall	2,950	6,450	
Salary: Mendez		800	7,250
			16,420
Balance of profits shared: Mendez		8,210	
Marshall		8,210	16,420

42.5

Balance Sheet as at 31 December 19X7 (extracts)

Capitals: Williams		40,000	
Powell		30,000	
Howe		18,000	88,000

Current accounts:

	Williams	Powell	Howe	
Balances 1.1.19X7	1,860	946	717	
Add Share of profits	10,500	6,300	4,200	
Salaries		2,000	3,500	
Interest on capital	2,000	1,500	900	
	14,360	10,746	9,317	
Less Interest on drawings	240	180	130	
Drawings	9,200	7,100	6,900	
	4,920	3,466	2,287	10,673

Considerations

(a) *Legal position re Partnership Act 1890*: Partners can agree to anything. The main thing is that of mutual agreement. The agreement can either be very formal in a partnership deed drawn up by a lawyer or else it can be evidenced in other ways.

The Act lays down the provisions for profit sharing if agreement has not been reached, written or otherwise.

(b) As Bee is not taking active part in the running of the business he could be registered as a limited partner under the 1907 Limited Partnership Act. This has the advantage that his liability is limited to the amount of capital invested by him; he can lose that but his personal possessions cannot be taken to pay any debts of the firm.

As Bee is a 'sleeping partner' you will have to decide whether his reward should be in the form of a fixed amount, or should vary according to the profits made. In this context you should also bear in mind whether or not he would suffer a share of losses if they occurred.

If he were to have a fixed amount, irrespective as to whether profits had been made or not, then the question arises as to the amount required. This is obviously a more risky investment than, say, government securities. He therefore would naturally expect to get a higher return.

Bee would probably feel aggrieved if the profits rose sharply, but he was still limited to the amounts already described. There could be an arrangement for extra payments if the profits exceeded a given figure.

Cee is the expert conducting the operations of the business. He will consequently expect a major share of the profits.

One possibility would be to give him a salary, similar to his current salary, before dividing whatever profits then remain.

(c) Dee is making himself available, as well as bringing in some capital.

Balance Sheet as at 30 June 19X9

	Cost	Depn	
Fixed assets			
Buildings	75,000	26,000	49,000
Fixtures	11,000	4,070	6,930
	86,000	30,070	55,930
Current assets			
Stock		56,340	
Debtors	16,243		
Less Provision for bad debts	320	15,923	
Bank		677	
		72,940	
Less Current liabilities			
Creditors	11,150		
Expenses owing	296	11,446	
Working capital			61,494
			117,424
Financed by			
Capitals: Mendez		35,000	
Marshall		29,500	64,500

Current accounts	Mendez	Marshall	
Balance 1.7.19X8	1,306	298	
Add Interest on capital	3,500	2,950	
Add Salary	800		
Add Balance of profit	8,210	8,210	
	13,816	11,458	
Less Drawings	6,400	5,650	
Less Interest on drawings	180	120	
	7,236	5,688	12,924
			77,424
Loan from J King			40,000
			117,424

42.8 (a)

Brick & Stone

Trading and Profit and Loss Account for the year ended 30 September 19X9

Sales			322,100
Less Returns inwards			2,100
			320,000
Less Cost of goods sold			
Opening stock			23,000
Purchases (208,200 – 1,000)		207,200	
Carriage inwards		1,700	
		208,900	
Less Returns outwards		6,100	202,800
			225,800
Less Closing stock			32,000
Gross profit			193,800
			126,200
Less Establishment expenses:			
Rent and rates (10,300 – 600)		9,700	
Heat and light		8,700	
Depreciation: Fixtures		2,600	21,000
Administrative Expenses:			
Staff salaries		36,100	
Telephone (2,900 + 400)		3,300	
Printing, stationery and postages		3,500	42,900
Sales and distribution expenses:			
Motor expenses		5,620	
Carriage outwards		2,400	
Depreciation: Motors		9,200	17,220
Financial expenses:			
Discounts allowable	950		
Loan interest	250		
	1,200		
Less Discounts receivable	370		830
			81,950
Net profit			44,250
Less Salary: Stone			6,000
Balance of profits shared:			
Brick 3/5		22,950	
Stone 2/5		15,300	38,250
			44,250

Brick & Stone

Balance Sheet as at 30 September 19X9

	Cost	Depn	Net
Fixed assets			
Fixtures and fittings	26,000	13,800	12,200
Motor vehicles	46,000	34,200	11,800
	72,000	48,000	24,000
Current assets			
Stock		32,000	
Debtors (9,300 – 300)		9,000	
Prepayments		600	
Bank		7,700	
		49,300	
Less Current liabilities			
Creditors		8,400	
Accrued expenses		400	8,800
			40,500
			64,500

Financed by:

Capitals:			
Brick (33,000 – 10,000)		23,000	
Stone		17,000	40,000

Current accounts:	Brick	Stone
Balances 1.10.19X8	3,600	2,400
Salary		6,000
Loan interest	250	
Share of profits	22,950	15,300
	26,800	23,700
Less Drawings	24,000	11,000
Goods for own use	1,000	
	2,800	11,700

(current accounts total)	14,500
	54,500
Loan from Brick	10,000
	64,500

43.1

(a)

Balance Sheet as at 1 January 19X8

Goodwill	12,000
Other assets	14,000
	26,000
Capitals X (6,000 + 6,000)	12,000
Y (4,800 + 4,500)	9,300
Z (3,200 + 1,500)	4,700
	26,000

(b) *Goodwill Workings*

	Before		After		Loss or Gain		Action needed	
X	4/8	6,000	3/10	3,600	Loss	2,400	Credit X	2,400
Y	3/8	4,500	5/10	6,000	Gain	1,500	Debit Y	1,500
Z	1/8	1,500	2/10	2,400	Gain	900	Debit Z	900
		12,000		12,000				

Balance Sheet as at 1 January 19X8

Net assets	14,000
	14,000
Capitals X (6,000 + 2,400)	8,400
Y (4,800 – 1,500)	3,300
Z (3,200 – 900)	2,300
	14,000

43.3

(a)

	Dr	
Goodwill	6,000	
Capitals X		3,000
Y		3,000
Cash	7,000	
Capital Z		7,000

(b)

Balance Sheet

Goodwill		6,000
Fixed and current assets		15,000
Cash		9,000
		30,000
Capitals X	11,000	
Y	7,000	
Z	7,000	
		25,000
Current liabilities		5,000
		30,000

(c)

	Dr	
Capitals X	2,400	
Y	1,800	
Z	1,800	
Goodwill		6,000

43.5

(a)

Capital Accounts (000s)

	T	U	V	W		T	U	V	W
Bal c/d	26	33	8	20	Bal b/d	14	18	5	
					Cash				20
					Goodwill	12	15	3	
	26	33	8	20		26	33	8	20

(b) Goodwill 30,000; Other assets except cash 40,000; cash 26,000; Capitals as in (a); Creditors 9,000.

43.6

The senior partner's objection is a correct response. The money does not belong to the new partner once it has been paid.

This is because a new partner becomes an owner of part of the business, and this includes a part of the goodwill. This payment is specifically for that part of the goodwill. The goodwill was created by previous partners, and this is where the new partner buys his share from them. The £10,000 will be credited to the old partners in their old profit-sharing ratio.

If C, the new partner, has paid £10,000 for one-fifth of the goodwill, then total goodwill is £50,000. Should the business be sold at a future date, and the goodwill realise £50,000, then C would receive one-fifth of the proceeds, i.e. £10,000, thus getting his money back. This illustrates the fairness of the accounting treatment of his original payment for goodwill. If anything had been credited to his account from this original payment for goodwill then he would have received that in addition. Obviously this would be unfair.

43.7

(a) Stone, Pebble & Brick trading as Bigtime Building Supply Company
Profit and Loss Account for the year ended 31 March 19X9

		Apl–Dec	Jan–Mar
Net profit per accounts		27,225	9,075
Less Interest on Stone's Loan		—	385
		27,225	8,690
Interest on capitals:	Stone		250
	Pebble		200
	Brick		125
Salary: Brick			2,125
Balance of profits shared:			
	Stone	1/3 9,075	1/2 2,995
	Pebble	1/3 9,075	3/10 1,797
	Brick	1/3 9,075	2/10 1,198
		27,225	8,690

(b)
Capitals

	Stone	Pebble	Brick		Stone	Pebble	Brick
Goodwill adjustment		2,000	6,000	Balances b/d	26,000	18,000	16,000
Transfer to loan	14,000			Goodwill adjustment (see note)	8,000		
Balances c/d	20,000	16,000	10,000				
	34,000	18,000	16,000		34,000	18,000	16,000

Current Accounts

	Stone	Pebble	Brick		Stone	Pebble	Brick
Drawings	8,200	9,600	7,200	Interest on capital	250	200	125
Balances c/d	4,120	1,472	5,323	Salary			2,125
				Share of profits:			
				Apl–Dec	9,075	9,075	9,075
				Jan–Mar	2,995	1,797	1,198
	12,320	11,072	12,523		12,320	11,072	12,523

Note: Goodwill:

	Value of goodwill taken over	Elimination of goodwill	Net effect
Stone	30,000	22,000	8,000 Cr
Pebble	20,000	22,000	2,000 Dr
Brick	16,000	22,000	6,000 Dr
	66,000	66,000	—

44.1

Buildings

Balance b/d	8,000	Balance c/d	17,500
Revaluation: Increase	9,500		
	17,500		17,500

Motor Vehicles

Balance b/d	3,550	Revaluation: Reduction	950
		Balance c/d	2,600
	3,550		3,550

Stock

Balance b/d	2,040	Revaluation: Reduction	150
		Balance c/d	1,890
	2,040		2,040

Office Fittings

Balance b/d	1,310	Revaluation: Reduction	220
		Balance c/d	1,090
	1,310		1,310

Revaluation

Motor vehicles		950		Buildings	9,500
Stock		150			
Office fittings		220			
Profit on revaluation					
Hughes	4,090				
Allen	2,454				
Elliott	1,636	8,180			
		9,500			9,500

Capitals

	Hughes	Allen	Elliott		Hughes	Allen	Elliott
Balances c/d	13,650	8,874	6,476	Balances b/d	9,560	6,420	4,840
				Profit on revaluation	4,090	2,454	1,636
	13,650	8,874	6,476		13,650	8,874	6,476

Balance Sheet as at 1 January 19X9

Fixed assets

	£	£
Buildings at valuation		17,500
Motors at valuation		2,600
Office fittings at valuation		1,090
		21,190
Current assets		
Stock at valuation	1,890	
Debtors	4,530	
Bank	1,390	
		7,810
		29,000
Capitals:		
Hughes		13,650
Allen		8,874
Elliott		6,476
		29,000

44.3

(a)

Revaluation*

	£		£
Premises	90,000	Premises	120,000
Plant	37,000	Plant	35,000
Stock	62,379	Stock	54,179
Provision doubtful debts	3,000		
Profit on revaluation			
Alan 3/6	8,400		
Bob 2/6	5,600		
Charles 1/6	2,800		
	16,800		
	209,179		209,179

* Just the net increases/decreases could have been recorded. Either method acceptable.

Goodwill

	£		£
Capitals: Alan	21,000	Goodwill cancelled	
Bob	14,000	Capitals: Alan 3/7	18,000
Charles	7,000	Bob 2/7	12,000
		Don 2/7	12,000
	42,000		42,000

Capitals

	Alan	Bob	Charles	Don		Alan	Bob	Charles	Don
Goodwill	18,000	12,000	–	12,000	Balances b/d	85,000	65,000	35,000	–
Retirement			42,000		Goodwill	21,000	14,000	7,000	
Cash	21,000				Cash				79,000
Balances c/d	67,000	67,000		67,000					
	106,000	79,000	42,000	79,000		106,000	79,000	42,000	79,000
					Balances b/d	67,000	67,000	–	67,000

Current Accounts

	Alan	Bob	Charles	Don		Alan	Bob	Charles	Don
Balance b/d		2,509			Balance b/d	3,714		4,678	
Retirement			7,478		Profit on Revaluation	8,400	5,600	2,800	
Cash	9,023				Cash				3,091
Balances c/d	3,091	3,091		3,091					
	12,114	5,600	7,478	3,091		12,114	5,600	7,478	3,091

Charles: Retirement

	£		£
Car	3,900	Capital	42,000
Cash	53,578	Current	7,478
Balance c/d	20,000	Loan	28,000
	77,478		77,478

Bank

	£		£
Balance b/d	5,710	Retirement – Charles	53,578
Don: Capital	79,000	Repaid Alan – Capital	21,000
Don: Current	3,091	– Current	9,023
		Balance c/d	4,200
	87,801		87,801

(b) *Balance Sheet (summarised):*

Fixed assets total 168,100 + Current assets 86,919 – Current liabilities 24,746 = 230,273.

Capitals 67,000 each × 3 + Current accounts 3,091 × 3 = Total 230,273.

45.1

S, W and M

Appropriation Account for the year ended 31 December 19X9

	£	£		£
Salaries: W	3,000		Net profit b/d	25,200
M	1,000	4,000		
Interest on capital				
S	600			
W	400			
M	200	1,200		
Balance of profits				
S 2/5	8,000			
W 2/5	8,000			
M 1/5	4,000	20,000		
		25,200		25,200

45.3

Realisation

Buildings	800	Cash: Debtors		2,700
Tools and fixtures	850	Buildings		400
Debtors	2,800	Tools etc.		950
Cash: Expenses	100	Discounts		200
		Loss on realisation:	Moore	150
			Stephens	150
	4,550			4,550

Capital Accounts

	Moore	Stephens		Moore	Stephens
Loss on realisation	150	150	Balance b/d	2,000	1,500
Cash	1,850	1,350			
	2,000	1,500		2,000	1,500

Cash

Balance b/d	1,800	Expenses realisation	100
Debtors	2,700	Creditors	2,550
Buildings	400	Capitals: Moore	1,850
Tools	950	Stephens	1,350
	5,850		5,850

45.4

(a) Realisation

Fixed assets	14,000	Bank: Fixed assets		8,000
Stock	5,000	X: Fixed assets		7,000
Debtors	21,000	Bank: Stock		4,000
Bank: Dissolution costs	800	Bank: Debtors		3,000
		Discounts on creditors		500
		Loss: X ³⁄₆	9,150	
		Y ²⁄₆	6,100	
		Z ¹⁄₆	3,050	
	40,800			40,800

(b) Capital Accounts

	X	Y	Z		X	Y	Z
Fixed assets taken over	7,000			Balances b/d	4,000	4,000	2,000
Loss shared	9,150	6,100	3,050	Deficiency shared:			
Deficiency	525	525		X			525
				Y			525
				Bank to settle	12,675	2,625	
	16,675	6,625	3,050		16,675	6,625	3,050

Bank (as proof only)

Realisation: Fixed assets		8,000	Balance b/d	13,000
Stock		4,000	Creditors	16,500
Debtors		3,000	Realisation: Costs	800
Capital: X		12,675		
Y		2,625		
		30,300		30,300

45.7 Amis, Lodge & Pym

(a) (i)

Trading and Profit and Loss Account for the year ended 31 March 19X8

Sales				404,500
Less	Cost of goods sold:			
	Opening stock		30,000	
	Add Purchases		225,000	
	Add Carriage inwards		4,000	
			259,000	
Less	Closing stock		35,000	224,000
Gross profit				180,500
Add	Bank interest		750	
	Discounts received		4,530	5,280
				185,780
Less	Office expenses (30,400 + 405)		30,805	
	Rent, rates, light and heat (8,800 – 1,500)		7,300	
	Carriage outwards		12,000	
	Discounts allowed		10,000	
	Provision for bad debts		295	
	Depreciation:	Motor	15,000	
		Plant	20,000	95,400
Net profit				90,380
Add	Interest on current accounts and drawings:			
	Amis		1,000	
	Lodge		900	
	Pym		720	2,620
				93,000
Less	Salary – Pym			13,000
	Interest on capitals:	Amis	8,000	
		Lodge	1,500	
		Pym	500	10,000
				23,000
				70,000
Balance on profit shared:				
	Amis 50%		35,000	
	Lodge 30%		21,000	
	Pym 20%		14,000	70,000

45.9

(a) Lock, Stock and Barrel

Profit and Loss Account for the six months ended 1 February 19X7

Sales of completed houses			280,000
Less Costs of completing houses			
Houses in course of construction at start	115,000		
Materials used	35,750		
Land used (75,000 × ⅓)	25,000		
Wages and subcontractors	78,000	253,750	
Gross profit			26,250
Less Administration salaries	17,250		
General expenses	12,500		
Depreciation: Freehold land	300		
Plant and equipment (⁶⁄₁₂ × 10%)	7,500		
Vehicles (25% × ⁶⁄₁₂)	4,500	42,050	
Net loss			15,800
Shared: Lock 40%	6,320		
Stock 30%	4,740		
Barrel 30%	4,740		15,800

Capitals

	Lock	Stock	Barrel		Lock	Stock	Barrel
Drawings	6,000	5,000	4,000	Balances b/d	52,000	26,000	4,000
Loss shared	6,320	4,740	4,740	Balance c/d			4,740
Balances c/d	39,680	16,260					
	52,000	26,000	8,740		52,000	26,000	8,740

Lock, Stock and Barrel

Balance Sheet as at 1 February 19X7

	Cost	Depreciation	
Fixed tangible assets			
Freehold land and buildings	20,000	3,300	16,700
Plant and equipment	150,000	89,500	60,500
Motor vehicles	36,000	27,500	8,500
	206,000	120,300	85,700
Current assets			
Stock of land for building		50,000	
Stocks of materials		7,500	
Debtors for completed houses		35,000	
		92,500	
Less Current liabilities			
Trade creditors		52,250	
Bank overdraft		75,250	127,500
Working capital			(35,000)
Net assets			50,700

(a) (ii) *Current Accounts*

	Amis	Lodge	Pym		Amis	Lodge	Pym
Balances b/d	1,000	500	400	Salary			13,000
Drawings	25,000	22,000	15,000	Interest on capital	8,000	1,500	500
Interest on drawings	1,000	900	720	Balance on profits	35,000	21,000	14,000
Transfer to capital	16,000	—	11,380	Transfer to capital		900	
	43,000	23,400	27,500		43,000	23,400	27,500

(b)(i) *Realisation*

Motors (80,000 − 35,000)	45,000	Discount on creditors	500
Plant (100,000 − 56,600)	43,400	Amis: Motor	5,000
Debtors (14,300 − 715)	13,585	Bank: Debtors	12,985
Stock	35,000	Fowles Ltd (75,000 + 63,500)	138,500
Profit on realisation			
Amis 50%	10,000		
Lodge 30%	6,000		
Pym 20%	4,000	20,000	
	156,985		156,985

(ii) *Bank*

Balance b/d	4,900	Office expenses	405
		Creditors	16,000
		Capital: Amis	76,000
Realisation: Debtors	12,985		
Rent rebate	1,500		
Fowles Ltd	63,500		
Capitals: Lodge	4,900		
Pym	4,620		
	92,405		92,405

(iii) *Capital Accounts*

	Amis	Lodge	Pym		Amis	Lodge	Pym
Current a/c		900		Balances b/d	80,000	15,000	5,000
Fowles Ltd Shares	25,000	25,000	25,000	Current a/c	16,000		11,380
Realisation: Motor	5,000			Profit on realisation	10,000	6,000	4,000
Bank	76,000			Bank		4,900	4,620
	106,000	25,900	25,000		106,000	25,900	25,000

Financed by:
Capitals: Lock 39,680
Stock 16,260
Barrel (5,240)
50,700

(b) Amounts distributable to partners:
On 28 February there was only (6,200 + 7,000 + 72,500 – 75,250) 10,450 hence there was nowhere near enough to pay off the creditors, and so payment to partners could not be made.
On 30 April we treat it as though no more cash will be received.

(c) First distribution

	Lock	Stock	Barrel
Capital balances before dissolution	39,680	16,260	(5,240)
Loss if no further assets realised (85,700 + 92,500 – 6,000 – 6,200 – 7,000 – 72,500 – 35,000 – 50,000) = 1,500			
Loss shared in profit/loss ratios	(600)	(450)	(450)
Cars taken over	(2,000)	(2,000)	(2,000)
	37,080	13,810	(7,690)
Barrel's deficiency shared profit/loss ratio	4,394	3,296	7,690
Paid to partners	32,686	10,514	–

Second and final distribution

	Lock	Stock	Barrel
Capital balances before dissolution	39,680	16,260	(5,240)
Profit finally ascertained 100,000 – 1,500 = 98,500			
Shared	39,400	29,550	29,550
	79,080	45,810	24,310
Less Distribution and cars	34,686	12,514	2,000
Final distribution (100,000)	44,394	33,296	22,310

45.11 (a) **Dinho and Manueli**
Realisation Account

Property	290,000	Creditors	85,800
Equipment	65,000	Bank	56,700
Stock	143,500	Loan	160,000
Debtors	121,000	Bin Ltd	304,000
		Loss: Dinho	6,500
		Manueli	6,500
	619,500		619,500

(b) **Bin Ltd**

Goodwill [write downs (30,000+5,000) – realisation loss (13,000)]	22,000
Property	260,000
Equipment	65,000
Stocks	143,500
Debtors	116,000
Bank (120,000–56,700)	63,300
Creditors	(85,800)
	584,000

Ordinary Share Capital	300,000
10% Preference shares (D = 87,500; M = 16,500; P = 20,000)	124,000
Loan	160,000
	584,000

(c)(salary as before, therefore not relevant) earnings on savings were 120,000 @ 6% = 7,200; preference dividend will be 20,000 @ 10% = 2,000, therefore 5,200 needed from profit after preference dividend. Profit must be 3 × 5,200 = 15,600 + the total preference dividend of 12,400 = 28,000.

46.1 **GWR Ltd**
Profit and Loss Appropriation Accounts
(1) For the year ended 31 December 19X6

Profit for the year before taxation		42,005
Less Corporation tax		13,480
Profit for the year after taxation		28,525
Less Transfer to general reserve	6,000	
Preference dividend of 10%	5,000	
Ordinary dividend of 12%	12,000	
		23,000
Retained profits carried forward to next year		5,525

(2) For the year ended 31 December 19X7

Profit for the tax year before taxation		34,831
Less Corporation tax		11,114
Profit for the year after taxation		23,717
Add Retained profits from last year		5,525
		29,242
Less Transfer to general reserve	4,000	
Preference dividend of 10%	5,000	
Ordinary dividend of 9%	9,000	
		18,000
Retained profits carried forward to next year		11,242

46.2

LMS Ltd
Profit and Loss Appropriation accounts
(1) For the year ended 31 December 19X7

Profit for the year before taxation		27,929
Less Corporation tax		8,331
Profit for the year after taxation		19,598
Less: Transfer to general reserve	3,000	
Preference dividend 8%	3,200	
Ordinary dividend 8%	9,600	15,800
Retained profits carried forward to next year		3,798

(2) For the year ended 31 December 19X8

Profit for the year before taxation		32,440
Less Corporation tax		10,446
Profit for the year after taxation		21,994
Add Retained profits from last year		3,798
		25,792
Less: Transfer to general reserve	4,000	
Preference dividend 8%	3,200	
Ordinary dividend 10%	12,000	19,200
Retained profits carried forward to next year		6,592

(3) For the year ended 31 December 19X9

Profit for the year before taxation		36,891
Less Corporation tax		12,001
Profit for the year after taxation		24,890
Add Retained profits from last year		6,592
		31,482
Less: Transfer to foreign exchange reserve	2,000	
Preference dividend 8%	3,200	
Ordinary dividend 11%	13,200	18,400
Retained profits carried forward to next year		13,082

46.3

Balance Sheet as at 30 June 19X6

Fixed assets	Cost	Depn	
Buildings	105,000	22,000	83,000
Motors	62,500	15,350	47,150
Fixtures	11,500	3,750	7,750
	179,000	41,100	137,900

Current assets		
Stock	16,210	
Debtors	14,175	
Bank (difference)	4,998	
	35,383	
Less Current liabilities		
Creditors	9,120	
Proposed dividend	5,000	14,120
Net current assets		21,263
Total assets *less* current liabilities		159,163
Debentures: repayable in 19X9		40,000
		119,163
Capital and reserves		
Called-up share capital		100,000
Fixed assets replacement reserve		8,000
General reserve		6,000
Profit and loss account		5,163
		119,163

46.5

Chang Ltd
Trading and Profit and Loss Account for the year ended 31 December 19X8

Sales		316,810
Less Cost of goods sold		
Opening stock	25,689	
Add Purchases	201,698	
	227,387	
Less Closing stock	29,142	198,245
Gross profit		118,565
Less expenses		
Wages (54,207 + 581)	54,788	
Rent (4,300 – 300)	4,000	
Lighting	1,549	
Bad debts (748 + 77)	825	
General expenses	32,168	
Depreciation: Machinery	5,500	98,830
Net profit		19,735
Add Unappropriated profits from last year		34,280
		54,015
Less Proposed dividend		10,000
Unappropriated profits carried to next year		44,015

Balance Sheet as at 31 December 19X8

Fixed assets

Premises			65,000
Machinery		55,000	
Less Depreciation		21,300	33,700
			98,700

Current assets

Stock		29,142	
Debtors	21,784		
Less Provision	938	20,846	
Prepayments		300	
Bank		23,101	
		73,389	

Less Current liabilities

Proposed dividend	10,000		
Creditors	17,493		
Expenses owing	581	28,074	
Working capital			45,315
			144,015

Financed by:

Authorised and issued capital		100,000
Revenue reserves		
Profit and loss account		44,015
		144,015

46.7

T Howe Ltd

Trading and Profit and Loss Account for the year ended 31 December 19X8

Sales			135,486
Less Cost of goods sold			
Opening stock		40,360	
Add Purchases		72,360	
Add Carriage inwards		1,570	
		114,290	
Less Closing stock		52,360	61,930
Gross profit			73,556
Less Expenses			
Salaries		18,310	
Rates and occupancy		4,515	
Carriage outwards		1,390	
Office expenses		3,212	
Sundry expenses		1,896	
Depreciation: Buildings		5,000	
Equipment		9,000	
Directors' remuneration		9,500	52,823
Net profit			20,733

Add Unappropriated profits from last year		15,286
		36,019
Less Appropriations		
Proposed dividend	10,000	
General reserve	1,000	
Foreign exchange	800	11,800
Unappropriated profits carried to next year		24,219

Balance Sheet as at 31 December 19X8

	Cost	Depn	Net
Fixed assets			
Buildings	100,000	37,000	63,000
Equipment	45,000	25,000	20,000
	145,000	62,000	83,000

Current assets

Stock		52,360	
Debtors		18,910	
Bank		6,723	
		77,993	

Less Current liabilities

Creditors	12,304		
Expenses owing	470		
Proposed dividend	10,000	22,774	
Working capital			55,219
			138,219

Financed by:

Share capital: authorised and issued		100,000
Reserves		
Foreign exchange	5,000	
General reserve	9,000	
Profit and loss	24,219	38,219
		138,219

46.9 Burden plc: *Computation of corrected net profit*

1

Recorded net profit		58,070
Add Profit on sale of equipment		500
		58,570
Less Bad debt written off	300	
Stock reduced to net realisable value	700	1,000
Correct figure of net profit		57,570

2

Burden plc

Profit and Loss Appropriation Account for the year ended 31 May 19X9

Net profit for the year brought down		57,570
Add Retained profits from last year		36,200
		93,770
Less Transfer to general reserve	50,000	
Proposed dividend of 10%	20,000	70,000
Retained profits carried forward to next year		23,770

3 (i) *Current assets*

Stock	17,100	
Debtors	6,540	
Prepayments	760	
	24,400	
Less Current liabilities		
Trade creditors	8,500	
Accrued expenses	430	
Proposed dividend	20,000	
Bank overdraft	2,400	31,330
Working capital deficit		(6,930)

Note: Figures in brackets are negative.

(ii) *Capital and reserves*

Ordinary share capital: called up	200,000
Share premium	25,000
General reserve	70,000
Profit and loss account	23,770
Shareholders' funds	318,770

4 *Examples:*

Issue of shares: + Bank; + Share capital.

Sales of fixed assets: + Bank; – Fixed assets.

Debentures issued: + Bank; + Debentures.

46.11 (a) See text.

(b) The historical cost convention does not make the going concern unnecessary. Several instances illustrate this:

(i) Fixed assets are depreciated over the useful life of the assets. This presupposes that the business will continue to operate during the years of assumed useful life.

(ii) Prepayments also assume that the benefits available in the future will be able to be claimed, because the business is expected to continue.

(iii) Stocks are valued also on the basis that we will dispose of them during the future ordinary running of the business.

(iv) The accruals concept itself assumes that the business is to continue. All of this shows that the two concepts complement each other.

(c) A shareholder wants accounts so that he can decide what to do with his shareholding, whether he should sell his shares or hold on to them.

To enable him to decide upon his actions, he would really like to know what is going to happen in the future. To help him in this he also would like information which shows him what happened in the past. Ideally therefore he would like both types of report, those on the past and on the future.

If he had a choice, the logical choice would be to receive a report on the future providing that it could be relied on.

46.12 Extract 1

(a) The amount paid for goodwill.

(b) The excess represents share premium.

(c) Equity shares generally means ordinary shares.

(d) That although issued in 19X6 a dividend will not be paid in that year. The first year that dividends *could* be paid is 19X7.

Extract 2

(e) (i) A rate of 8% per annum interest will be paid on them, irrespective of whether profits are made or not.

(ii) These are the years within which the debentures could be redeemed, if the company so wished.

(f) (i) This is the rate per annum at which preference dividends will be paid, subject to there being sufficient distributable profits.

(ii) That the shares could be bought back by the company.

(g) Probably because there was currently a lower interest rate prevailing at the time of redemption and the company took advantage of it.

(h) Large amounts of both fixed interest and fixed dividend funds have resulted in a raising of the gearing.

(j) Debenture interest gets charged before arriving at net profit. Dividends are an appropriation of profits.

(k) Shareholders are owners and help decide appropriations. Debenture holders are external lenders and interest expense has to be paid.

46.13 (a) This is incorrect. The tax portion has to be counted as part of the total cost, which is made up of debenture interest paid plus tax. Holding back payment will merely see legal action taken by the Inland Revenue to collect the tax.

(b) This cannot be done. The repainting of the exterior does not improve or enhance the original value of the premises. It cannot therefore be treated as capital expenditure.

(c) This is not feasible. Only the profit on the sale of the old machinery, found by deducting net book value from sales proceeds, can be so credited to the profit and loss account. The remainder is a capital receipt and should be treated as such.

(d) This is an incorrect view. Although some of the general reserve could, if circumstances allowed it, be transferred back to the profit and loss account, it could not be shown as affecting the operating profit for 19X3. This is because the reserve was built up over the years before 19X3.

(e) This is not feasible. The share capital has to be maintained at nominal value as per the Companies Act. A share premium cannot be created in this fashion, and even if it could, it would still have to be credited to share premium account and not the profit and loss account.

(f) Incorrect. Although the premises could be revalued the credit for the increase has to be to a capital reserve account. This cannot then be transferred to the credit of the profit and loss account.

46.14 See Section 46.8. Points to be made include that there must be an expectation that sufficient profits will be made in future to meet the debenture interest payments when due; also, there may be cheaper sources of finance available; also, if secured debentures are to be issued, there must be sufficient assets available to act as security over the issue. Gearing is also an issue to be considered – see Sections 48.5–48.7.

47.1

Balance Sheet as at 31 December 19X8

	(a) S Walters		(b) R Jones	
Goodwill	8,200		9,300	
Premises	21,000		28,000	
Stock	9,600		9,200	
Debtors	6,300		6,300	
Bank	1,700		–	
	46,800		52,800	
Capital	40,000		46,000	
Creditors	6,800		6,800	
	46,800		52,800	

47.3

(a)
Spectrum Ltd
Balance Sheet as at 1 January 19X2

Fixed assets		
Goodwill (note 1)		94,000
Premises (75,000 + 80,000 + 90,000 + 60,000)		305,000
Delivery vans (7,000 + 10,000)		17,000
Furniture and fittings (12,000 + 13,000 + 13,000)		38,000
		454,000
Current assets		
Stock (8,000 + 7,000 + 12,000)	27,000	
Bank (note 2)	25,000	
	52,000	
Less Current liabilities		
Creditors (6,000 + 8,000 + 7,000)	21,000	
Working capital		31,000
		485,000
Financed by:		
Share capital		
Authorised 700,000 shares £1	700,000	
Issued 500,000 shares £1		500,000
Reserves		
Profit and loss (note 3)		(15,000)
		485,000

Notes:

1 Goodwill:

Red – paid		120,000	
Net assets taken over			
75,000 + 7,000 + 12,000 + 8,000 – 6,000 =	96,000		24,000
	130,000		
Yellow – paid		130,000	
Net assets taken over			
80,000 + 13,000 + 7,000 – 8,000 =		92,000	38,000
		150,000	
Blue – paid			
Net assets taken over			
90,000 + 10,000 + 13,000 + 12,000 – 7,000 =		118,000	32,000
			94,000

2 Bank:

Shares issued		500,000
Less: Preliminary expenses	15,000	
Warehouse	60,000	
Red	120,000	
Yellow	130,000	
Blue	150,000	
	475,000	25,000

3 Prior to the 1981 Companies Act this could have been shown as an asset. It must now be written off immediately to profit and loss.

(b) Spectrum Ltd can issue part or the remainder of the authorised capital, i.e. 700,000 – 500,000 = £200,000. £100,000 will buy the business but some extra working capital is also needed.

48.1

(a)

(i) Gross profit as % of sales $\dfrac{20{,}000}{80{,}000} \times \dfrac{100}{1} = 25\%$ $\qquad \dfrac{24{,}000}{120{,}000} \times \dfrac{100}{1} = 20\%$

(ii) Net profit as % of sales $\dfrac{10{,}000}{80{,}000} \times \dfrac{100}{1} = 12.5\%$ $\qquad \dfrac{15{,}000}{120{,}000} \times \dfrac{100}{1} = 12.5\%$

(iii) Expenses as % of sales $\dfrac{10{,}000}{80{,}000} \times \dfrac{100}{1} = 12.5\%$ $\qquad \dfrac{9{,}000}{120{,}000} \times \dfrac{100}{1} = 7.5\%$

(iv) Stockturn $\dfrac{60{,}000}{(25{,}000 + 15{,}000) \div 2} = 3\ \text{times}$ $\qquad \dfrac{96{,}000}{(22{,}500 + 17{,}500) \div 2} = 4.8\ \text{times}$

(v) Rate of return $\dfrac{10{,}000}{(38{,}000 + 42{,}000) \div 2} \times \dfrac{100}{1} = 25\%$ $\qquad \dfrac{15{,}000}{(36{,}000 + 44{,}000) \div 2} \times \dfrac{100}{1} = 37.5\%$

(vi) Current ratio $\dfrac{45{,}000}{5{,}000} = 9$ $\qquad \dfrac{40{,}000}{10{,}000} = 4$

(vii) Acid test ratio $\dfrac{30{,}000}{5{,}000} = 6$ $\qquad \dfrac{22{,}500}{10{,}000} = 2.25$

(viii) Debtor/sales ratio $\dfrac{25{,}000}{80{,}000} \times 12 = 3.75\ \text{months}$ $\qquad \dfrac{20{,}000}{120{,}000} \times 12 = 2\ \text{months}$

(ix) Creditor/purchases ratio $\dfrac{5{,}000}{50{,}000} \times 12 = 1.2\ \text{months}$ $\qquad \dfrac{10{,}000}{91{,}000} \times 12 = 1.3\ \text{months approx.}$

(b) Business B is the most profitable, both in terms of actual net profits £15,000 compared to £10,000, but also in terms of capital employed; B has managed to achieve a return of £37.50 for every £100 invested, i.e. 37.5%. A has managed a lower return of 25%. Reasons – possibly only – as not until you know more about the business could you give a definite answer:

(i) Possibly managed to sell far more merchandise because of lower prices, i.e. took only 20% margin as compared with A's 25% margin.

(ii) Maybe more efficient use of mechanised means in the business.

Note he has more equipment, and perhaps as a consequence kept other expenses down to 6,000 as compared with A's 9,000.

(iii) Did not have as much stock lying idle. Turned over stock 4.8 times in the year as compared with 3 for A.

(iv) A's current ratio of 9 far greater than normally needed. B kept it down to 4. A therefore had too much money lying idle and not doing anything.

(v) Following on from (iv) the Acid Test ratio for A also higher than necessary.

(vi) Part of the reasons for (iv) and (v) is that A waited (on average) 3.75 months to be paid by his customers. B managed to collect them on a 2 months' average. Money represented by debts is money lying idle.

(vii) A also paid his creditors quicker than did B, but not by much.

Put all these factors together, and it is obvious that B is running his business far more efficiently, and is more profitable as a consequence.

48.3

(a) **Durham Limited**

Profit and Loss Appropriation Account for the year ended 30.4.19X9

Net profit for the year b/d		16,500
Add Retained profits from last year		14,500
		31,000
Less Transfer to general reserve	5,000	
Preference dividend	4,000	
Proposed ordinary dividend	15,000	24,000
Retained profits carried forward to next year		7,000

(b) *Balance Sheet as at 30.4.19X9*

Fixed assets			
Premises at cost			86,000
Machinery and plant at cost	60,000		
Less Depreciation	40,000	20,000	106,000
Current assets			
Stock		60,000	
Debtors	20,000		
Less Provision	4,000	16,000	
Prepayments		900	
Bank		13,100	
		90,000	
Less Current liabilities			
Creditors	12,900		
Expenses owing	100		
Proposed dividends	17,000	30,000	
Working capital			60,000
			166,000

Capital and reserves
8% preference shares   50,000
Ordinary shares   100,000   150,000
General reserve   9,000
Profit and loss account   7,000
Shareholders' funds   166,000

(c) (i) *Return on Capital Employed (ROCE)*
This is the amount of profit earned compared with the amount of capital employed to earn it. Calculated:

$$\frac{\text{Net profit}}{\text{Average of shareholders' funds}} \times \frac{100}{1} = \frac{16,500}{(168,500 + 166,000) \div 2} \times \frac{100}{1}$$
$$= 9.83\%$$

(ii) *Current ratio*
This calculates how well the current assets can finance current liabilities. Calculated:

$$\frac{\text{Current assets}}{\text{Current liabilities}} = \frac{90,000}{30,000} = 3{:}1$$

Acid Test Ratio
This calculates whether the business has sufficient liquid resources to meet its current liabilities. Calculated:

$$\frac{\text{Current assets} - \text{Stock}}{\text{Current liabilities}} = \frac{30,000}{30,000} = 1{:}1$$

(d) ROCE. The return of 9.83% would appear to be adequate, but we cannot really comment further without more information.
Current Ratio. A figure of 2:1 is often reckoned as adequate. In this case a 3:1 figure is more than adequate.
Acid Test Ratio. All current liabilities can be met and the return is therefore adequate.

(e) 1 Previous years' figures.
2 We would need to know ratios for other similar businesses.

48.4 (a) (i) Gross profit: Sales

19X8
$$\frac{50}{200} \times \frac{100}{1} = 25\%$$

19X9
$$\frac{70}{280} = 25\%$$

(ii) Stock turnover

19X8
$$\frac{150}{(50 + 20) \div 2} = 4.28$$

19X9
$$\frac{210}{(20+30) \div 2} = 8.4$$

(iii) Net profit: Sales

19X8
$$\frac{12}{200} \times \frac{100}{1} = 6\%$$

19X9
$$\frac{20}{280} \times \frac{100}{1} = 7.14\%$$

(iv) Quick ratio

19X8
$$\frac{25}{25} = 1$$

19X9
$$\frac{33}{12} = 2.75$$

(v) Working capital (current ratio)

19X8
$$\frac{45}{25} = 1.8$$

19X9
$$\frac{63}{12} = 5.2$$

(vi) Net profit: Capital employed

19X8
$$\frac{12}{130} \times \frac{100}{1} = 9.23\%$$

19X9
$$\frac{20}{191} \times \frac{100}{1} = 10.47\%$$

(b) (Brief answer, but you should expand in an exam)
(i) No change.
(ii) Increase caused by lowering average stocks; also probably better sales management.
(iii) An increase in sales, without a larger increase in expenses, has led to a better return.
(iv) Issue of debentures has improved the cash situation and therefore a better quick ratio.
(v) Working capital has increased largely due to issue of debentures, although partly offset by fixed assets bought.
(vi) Increasing sales and better stockturn brought about better ROCE.

48.7

(a)

Joan Street

Trading and Profit and Loss Account for the year ended 31 March 19X8

Sales		(W3)	240,000
Cost of sales			
Opening stock		21,000	
Add Purchases	(W6)	174,000	
	(W7)	195,000	
Less Closing stock		15,000	
	(W1)	180,000	
Gross profit	(W2)	60,000	
Sundry expenses	(W5)	38,400	
Net profit	(W4)	21,600	

Balance Sheet as at 31 March 19X8

Fixed assets	(W9)		108,000
Current assets			
Stock	(W8)	15,000	
Debtors	(W15)	24,000	
Bank	(W14)	9,000	
	(W14)	48,000	
Less Current liabilities	(W14)	12,000	
Working capital	(W13)		36,000
	(W12)		144,000
Financed by:			
Capital:			
Balance at 1.4.19X7	(W11)		122,400
Add Net profit			21,600
	(W10)		144,000

Workings (could possibly find alternatives)

(W1) As average stock 21,000 + 15,000 ÷ 2 = 18,000 and stock turnover is 10, this means that cost of sales = 18,000 × 10 = 180,000

(W2) As gross profit is 25% of sales, it must therefore be $33\frac{1}{3}\%$ of cost of sales

(W3) As (W1) is 180,000 & (W2) is 60,000 therefore sales = (W1) + (W2) = 240,000

(W4) Net profit = 9% of sales = 21,600

(W5) Missing figure, found by arithmetical deduction

(W6) & (W7) Missing figures – found by arithmetical deduction

(W8)

$$\frac{\text{Debtors (?)} \times 365}{\text{Sales}} = 36\frac{1}{2}, \text{ i.e.}$$

$$\frac{? \times 365}{240,000} = 36\frac{1}{2}, \text{ by arithmetic}$$

$$\frac{24,000 \times 365}{240,000} = 36\frac{1}{2}$$

debtors = 24,000. Proof $\frac{24,000 \times 365}{240,000} = 36\frac{1}{2}$

(W9) 45% × 240,000 = 108,000

(W10) Knowing that net profit 21,600 is 15% of W10, so W10 = 21,600 × 100/15 = 144,000

(W11) Missing figure

(W12) & (W13) Put in after (W11)

(W14) If working capital ratio is 4, it means a factor of current assets 4, current liabilities 1 = working capital 3. As (W13) is 36,000, current assets therefore:

4/3 × 36,000 = 48,000

and current liabilities

1/3 × 36,000 = 12,000

(W15) Is new missing figure.

(b) Question limited to two favourable and two unfavourable aspects (four given here for reader's benefit)

Favourable: Stock turnover, liquidity, working capital, net profit on sales

Unfavourable: Gross profit to sales, debtors collection, return on capital employed, turnover to net capital employed.

(c) Drawbacks (more than two listed for reader's benefit)

(i) No access to trends over recent years.

(ii) No future plans etc. given.

(iii) Each business is often somewhat different.

(iv) Size of businesses not known.

48.9

(a)

(i) Current ratio: by dividing current assets by current liabilities.

(ii) Quick assets ratio: by dividing current assets less stock by current liabilities.

(iii) Return on capital employed (ROCE): can have more than one meaning. One in common use is net profit divided by capital plus long-term liabilities (e.g. loans), and shown as a percentage.

(iv) Return on owner's equity (ROOE): net profit divided by capital, shown as a percentage.

(v) Debtors turnover: Sales divided by average debtors, expressed in days or months.

(vi) Creditors turnover: Purchases divided by average creditors, expressed in days or months.

(vii) Gross profit percentage: Gross profit divided by sales, expressed as a percentage.

(viii) Net profit percentage: Net profit divided by sales.

(ix) Stock turnover: Cost of goods sold, divided by average stock, expressed in days.

(b) (This part of the question tests your ability to be able to deduce some conclusions from the information given. You have to use your imagination.)

First, an assumption, we do not know relative sizes of these two businesses. We will assume that they are approximately of the same size.

A has a higher current ratio, 2 to 1.5, but the quick assets ratio shows a much greater disparity, 1.7 to 0.7. As stock is not included in quick assets ratio, it can be deduced that B has relatively greater stocks. Expected also from these ratios is that A has high amounts of debtors, this being seen because debtors turnover is 3 times as great for A as for B.

The return on owner's equity (ROOE) is much greater for A than for B, 30% to 18%, but the ROCE for A is not that much different than for B, 20% to 17%. This shows that A has far more in long-term borrowings than B. The ROCE indicates that A is somewhat more efficient than B, but not by a considerable amount.

Gross profit percentage is far greater for A than B, but net profit percentage is the same. Obviously A has extremely high operating expenses per £100 of sales.

The last ratio shows that stock in A lies unsold for twice as long a period as for B.

A summary of the above shows that A has lower stocks, greater debtors, sells at a slower rate, and has high operating expenses. B has greater stocks, sells its goods much quicker but at lower prices as shown by the gross profit percentage.

All the evidence points to A being a firm which gives emphasis to personal service to its customers. B on the other hand emphasises cheap prices and high turnover, with not as much concentration on personal service.

48.11 (There is no set answer. In addition, as a large number of points could be mentioned, the examiner cannot expect every aspect to be covered.) The main points which could be covered are:

(i) The accounts are for last year, whereas in fact the bank is more interested in what might happen to the firm in the future.

(ii) The accounts are usually prepared on a historic cost basis. These therefore do not reflect current values.

(iii) The bank manager would want a cash budget to be drawn up for the ensuing periods. This would give the manager an indication as to whether or not the business will be able to meet its commitments as they fall due.

(iv) The bank manager wants to ensure that bank charges and interest can be paid promptly, also that a bank loan or overdraft will be able to be paid off. He will want to see that these commitments can still be met if the business has to cease operations. This means that the saleable value of assets on cessation, rather than the cost of them, is of much more interest to the bank manager.

To say that the accounts are 'not good enough' is misleading. What the manager is saying is that the accounts do not provide him with what he would really like to know. One could argue that there should be other types of final accounts drawn up in addition to those drawn up on a historic basis.

48.12 *(a)* The basis on which accounts are prepared is that of 'accruals'. By this it is meant that the recognition of revenue and expenditure takes place not at the point when cash is received or paid out, but instead is at the point when the revenue is earned or the expenditure is incurred.

To establish the point of recognition of a sale, several criteria are necessary:

(i) The product, or the service, must have been supplied to the customer.

(ii) The buyer must have indicated his willingness to pay for the product or services and has accepted liability.

(iii) A monetary value of the goods or services must have been agreed to by the buyer.

(iv) Ownership of the goods must have passed to the buyer.

(b) *(i)* This cannot be recognised as a sale. It does not comply with any of the four criteria above.

(ii) This also cannot be recognised as a sale. Neither criterion *(i)* nor *(iv)* has been covered.

(iii) If this was a cash sale, all of the above criteria would probably be achieved on delivery, and therefore it could be appropriate to recognise the sale.

If it was a credit sale, if the invoice was sent with the goods and a delivery note stating satisfaction by the customer is signed by him, then it would also probably be appropriate to recognise the sale.

(iv) Usually takes place after the four criteria have been satisfied. If so, the sales should be recognised.

(v) In the case of cash sales this would be the point of recognition.

In the case of credit sales it would depend on whether or not criteria *(a)* *(i)* and *(iv)* had also been satisfied.

(vi) This would only influence recognition of sales if there was serious doubt about the ability of the customer to pay his debts.

48.13 Obviously there is no set answer to this question. However, the following may well be typical:

(a) If the business is going to carry on operating, then the going concern concept comes into operation. Consequently, fixed assets are valued at cost, less depreciation to date. Stocks will be valued at lower of cost or net realisable value. The 'net realisable value' will be that based on the business realising stock through normal operations.

(b) Should the business be deemed as a case for cessation, then the going concern concept could not be used. The values on fixed assets and stocks will be their disposal values. This should be affected by whether or not the business could be sold as a whole or whether it would have to be broken up. Similarly, figures would be affected by whether or not assets had to be sold off very quickly at low prices, or sold only when reasonable prices could be achieved.

It is not only the balance sheet that would be affected, as the profit and loss account would reflect the changes in values.

48.14 (a) See text, Chapter 10.

(b) Various illustrations are possible, but the following are examples:

(i) Apportionment of expenses between one period and another. For instance, very rarely would very small stocks of stationery be valued at the year end. This means that the stationery gets charged against one year's profits whereas in fact it may not all have been used up in that year.

(ii) Items expensed instead of being capitalised. Small items which are, in theory, capital expenditure will often be charged up to an expense account.

(iii) The value of assets approximated, instead of being measured with absolute precision.

(c) (i) An illustration could be made under (b) (iii). A stock of oil could well be estimated; the true figure, if known, might be one or two litres out. The cost of precise measurement would probably not be worth the benefit of having such information.

(ii) What is material in one company may not be material in another.

48.15 No set answer. Question is of a general nature rather than being specific. A variety of answers is therefore acceptable.

The examiner might expect to see the following covered (this is not a model answer):

(a) Different reports needed by different outside parties, as they have to meet different requirements. Might find they therefore include:

(i) for bankers – accounts based on 'break-up' value of the assets if they have to be sold off to repay loans or overdrafts.

(ii) for investors – to include how business has fared against budgets set for that year to see how successful business is at meeting targets.

(iii) for employees – include details of number of employees, wages and salaries paid, effect on pension funds.

(iv) for local community – to include reports showing amounts spent on pollution control, etc.

And any similar instances.

(b) The characteristics of useful information have been stated in *The Corporate Report* 1975, and the accounting reports should be measured against this.

(c) Presentation (additional) in form of pie charts, bar charts, etc., as these are often more easily understood by readers.

48.16 (a) Accountants follow the realisation concept when deciding when to recognise revenue on any particular transaction. This states that profit is normally regarded as being earned at the time when the goods or services are passed to the customer and he incurs liability for them. For a service business it means when the services have been performed.

(b) The stage at which revenue is recognised could be either F or G. The normal rule is that the goods have been despatched, not delivered. For instance the goods may be shipped to Australia and take several weeks to get there.

Exactly where this fits in with F or G in the question cannot be stipulated without further information.

(c) If F is accepted as point of recognition, then £130 will be gross profit. If G is accepted as point of recognition the gross profit recognised will be £120.

(d) The argument that can be advanced is to take the prudence concept to its final conclusion, in that the debtor should pay for the goods before the profit can be recognised.

Until H is reached there is always the possibility that the goods will not be paid for, or might be returned because of faults in the goods.

(e) If the goods are almost certain to be sold, it could give a better picture of the progress of the firm up to a particular point in time, if profit could be recognised in successive amounts at stages B, C and D.

48.17 (a) A 'provision' is an amount written off or retained by way of providing for depreciation, renewals or diminution in value of assets, or retained by way of providing for any known liability of which the amount cannot be determined with 'substantial' accuracy. This therefore covers such items as provisions for depreciation. A 'liability' is an amount owing which can be determined with substantial accuracy.

Sometimes, therefore, the difference between a provision and a liability hinges around what is meant by 'substantial' accuracy. Rent owing at the end of the financial year would normally be known with precision; this would obviously be a liability. Legal charges for a court case which has been heard, but for which the lawyers have not yet submitted their bill, would be a provision.

Accrued expenses are those accruing from one day to another, but not paid at the year end. Such items as rates, electricity, telephone charges will come under this heading.

Creditors are persons to whom money is owed for goods and services.

Reserves consist of either undistributed profits, or else sums that have been allocated originally from such profits or have been created to comply with the law. An example of the first kind is a *general reserve*, whilst a *share premium account* comes under the second heading.

Provisions, accrued expenses and creditors would all be taken into account before calculating net profit. Reserves do not interfere with the calculation of net profit, as they are appropriations of profit or in the case of capital reserves do not pass through the profit and loss account.

(b) (i) Provision made for £21,000. Charge to profit and loss and show in balance sheet under current liabilities.

(ii) Accrued expenses, $\frac{2}{12} \times £6,000 = £1,000$. Charge against profit and loss account and show as current liability in balance sheet.

(iii) Creditor £2,500. Bring into purchases in trading account and show as current liability in balance sheet.

(iv) Reserve £5,000. Debit to profit and loss appropriation account as plant replacement reserve, and show in balance sheet under *reserves*.

48.18 (a) *The bank*
The bank will be interested in two main aspects. The first is the ability to repay the loan as and when it falls due. The second is the ability to pay interest on the due dates.

Mr Whitehall
He will be interested in the expected return on his investment. This means that recent performance of the company and its plans will be important to him. In addition the possible capital growth of his investment would be desirable.

(b) *Note:* More than four ratios for bank are given, but you should give four only as your answer.

Bank

Long-term ability to repay loan
(i) Members equity/Total assets
(ii) Loan capital/Members equity
(iii) Total liabilities/Members equity
(iv) Operating profit/Loan interest.

Short-term liquidity
(i) Liquid assets/Current liabilities.
(ii) Current assets/Current liabilities.

Mr Whitehall

Return on investment
(i) Price per share/Earnings per share
(ii) Trends of (i) for past few years.
(iii) Net profit – Preference dividend/Ordinary dividend.
(iv) Trends of (iii) for past few years.

48.19 See Section 48.5

Appendix V

Answers to multiple-choice questions

Set No 1

1	(C)	2	(D)	3	(B)	4	(C)	5	(A)
6	(C)	7	(C)	8	(A)	9	(C)	10	(A)
11	(B)	12	(D)	13	(B)	14	(D)	15	(B)
16	(C)	17	(C)	18	(A)	19	(D)	20	(C)

Set No 2

21	(A)	22	(B)	23	(A)	24	(D)	25	(C)
26	(A)	27	(D)	28	(A)	29	(C)	30	(A)
31	(C)	32	(D)	33	(C)	34	(C)	35	(D)
36	(B)	37	(A)	38	(B)	39	(C)	40	(C)

Set No 3

41	(A)	42	(C)	43	(A)	44	(D)	45	(A)
46	(A)	47	(B)	48	(C)	49	(D)	50	(C)
51	(A)	52	(D)	53	(C)	54	(C)	55	(D)
56	(C)	57	(A)	58	(A)	59	(B)	60	(C)

Set No 4

61	(B)	62	(A)	63	(D)	64	(A)	65	(C)
66	(A)	67	(D)	68	(D)	69	(B)	70	(A)
71	(D)	72	(C)	73	(D)	74	(B)	75	(B)
76	(C)	77	(D)	78	(A)	79	(B)	80	(C)

Set No 5

81	(B)	82	(B)	83	(C)	84	(D)	85	(A)
86	(B)	87	(A)	88	(C)	89	(C)	90	(A)
91	(C)	92	(B)	93	(B)	94	(D)	95	(C)
96	(B)	97	(C)	98	(B)	99	(D)	100	(B)

Index

Frank Wood's
Business Accounting 2
8th Edition

Frank Wood and **Alan Sangster**

Volume 2 of this popular textbook, extensively revised by Alan Sangster, completes the financial accounting coverage of syllabuses of the various examining bodies and in this eighth edition includes basic cost and management accounting in four new Parts: 6, 7, 8 and 9.

This edition maintains the traditional strengths of the book: comprehensiveness, clarity of expression, a large number of worked examples, questions and answers, and the structured build-up of knowledge in short, easily manageable chapters. A selection of recent questions from examining boards and professional bodies has been included.

Key features
- **now includes basic cost and management accounting**
- **gives comprehensive coverage of intermediate-level topics, including financial reporting and group accounting**
- **fully up to date with latest Financial Reporting Standards 1–13**
- **a large number of examples, questions and answers**
- **simple explanations in short chapters with logical progression**
- **a selection of questions from examining boards**

ISBN 0 273 63743 6

Frank Wood's Business Accounting
Multiple Choice Question Book
4th edition

Tommy Robinson, consultant lecturer in accounting, formerly at Dublin City University and now Director of One-to-One Accountancy Tuition

This book has been developed to test students' knowledge of basic bookkeeping and accounting. It is specifically linked to *Business Accounting 1*, but is general enough in content to be used alongside any text in basic accounting. It satisfies two needs. It can be used as a test bank to accompany a course in accounting used throughout the course, and for a source of exam-style revision material for last-minute examination preparation.

Key features
- **Dual function: can be used for practice and revision**
- **Comprehensive and wide-ranging – 400 questions and answers**

Approximately 400 questions are provided, with answers, explanations and workings given at the back of the book.

ISBN 0 273 62545 4

A time-saving **Solutions Manual**, including fully displayed answers to all questions with the suffix 'A' in the text, is available free of charge to lecturers who recommend **Business Accounting** Volumes 1 and 2 on their courses.

Please apply in writing on letterheaded paper of the institution where you teach, giving details of the course for which you are recommending **Business Accounting**, to:

Customer Service Department
Financial Times Management
12-14 Slaidburn Crescent
Southport
Merseyside
PR9 7BR
UK